Handbook of Software Quality Assurance

Fourth Edition

For a listing of recent related Artech House titles,
turn to the back of this book.

Handbook of Software Quality Assurance

Fourth Edition

G. Gordon Schulmeyer

Editor

ARTECH HOUSE

BOSTON | LONDON
artechhouse.com

Library of Congress Cataloging-in-Publication Data
A catalog record for this book is available from the U.S. Library of Congress.

British Library Cataloguing in Publication Data
A catalogue record for this book is available from the British Library.

ISBN-13: 978-1-59693-186-2

Cover design by Igor Valdman

© 2008 ARTECH HOUSE, INC.
685 Canton Street
Norwood, MA 02062

10 9 8 7 6 5 4 3 2 1

For my grandchildren,
Jimmy, Gabrielle, Chandler, Mallory, Neve, and Julian

In memory of James H. Heil,
prior contributor to former editions
of this handbook

Contents

CHAPTER 7

CHAPTER 8

CHAPTER 9

CHAPTER 10

CHAPTER 11

CMMI® PPQA Relationship to SQA   257

CHAPTER 12

SQA for Small Projects   291

CHAPTER 13

Development Quality Assurance

Preface

The software industry is witnessing a dramatic rise in the impact and effectiveness of software quality assurance (SQA). From its day of infancy, when a handful of software pioneers explored the first applications of quality assurance to the development of software, SQA has become integrated into all phases of software development. Most significant is the acceptance by software developers and managers of SQA personnel. There is a recognition that besides their primary function of auditing the software process and work products, the SQA personnel are real contributors to the success of the project. This is due to the closer integration and participation of SQA personnel in software-related project activities, including participation in team meetings, configuration control board meetings, peer reviews, and the like.

Another important transition taking place is that software quality assurance is being expanded to other aspects of development, such as systems and hardware development. Now, many organizations have expanded their software QA to include systems and hardware QA, implemented as development quality assurance (DQA). A significant force in bringing about this shift to DQA is the Capability Maturity Model Integration® for Development, version 1.2 (CMMI®-DEV, v1.2) provided by the Software Engineering Institute. This model flowed from the CMMI® for Systems Engineering and Software Engineering, version 1.1 that one can see from the title expanded beyond software to include systems engineering/development. Also with CMMI®-DEV, v1.2, hardware amplification was added to relevant practices to expand the practice coverage to include hardware engineering principles.

The practice of SQA/DQA is often thought of either as an auditing function or a "validation" (testing) function. (Validation is not to be confused here with verification and validation (V&V), which encompasses comprehensive technical activities to assure a product's conformance to requirements.) The SQA/DQA auditing function focuses on assuring that the processes are being followed and the work products are complete and consistent. The primary thrust of this book is on SQA/DQA as an auditing function, although I prefer the term "evaluation."

The SQA/DQA validation function focuses on testing—ensuring that you built the right thing. QA as a validation (testing) function has been the traditional function of the quality organization in software, but with the advent of the quality standards such as ISO and Capability Maturity Model® (CMM®)/CMMI®, the role of SQA (note the addition of the "S") assumed an auditing function.

Handbook of Software Quality Assurance, Fourth Edition, capitalizes on the talents and skills of the experts who deal with the implementation of software and development quality assurance on a daily basis. To have their accumulated knowledge at hand makes this book a valuable resource. Each author, because of his or her special skills, talents, foresight, and interests, has contributed to the maturing process occurring in the field of software and development quality today.

What this book brings to the reader, then, is a collection of experiences and expectations of some of the best people in the field of software and development quality assurance. Because of their early involvement in software and development quality and because of their continued pursuit to discover improved methods for achieving better on-the-job quality assurance, each author provides an insightful presentation of his personal involvement in quality assurance.

The structure of this book is relatively straightforward. There are 17 chapters covering many key areas of software and development quality assurance.

A brief summary of each chapter highlighting its main thrust is provided here for the reader to decide which topic is of immediate interest. If information is required from another chapter for additional insight, adequate cross-referencing has been provided within each chapter.

Chapter 1 presents a picture of how to organize for quality management. This chapter includes a discussion of the quality management framework and related quality program concepts. Then, organizational aspects of the quality program are discussed in terms of the organizational relationships for the quality program and the mapping of the quality program functions to project organizational entities, resulting in some example organizational implementations of a quality program. The role of assessing and measuring product quality during development and the controversy over the independence of QA versus being part of the development organization are discussed in this chapter.

Chapter 2 is an overview of the contributions made and the roles played by the dominant figures in the quality field. The individual contributions of the dominant quality experts—Kaoru Ishikawa, Joseph M. Juran, Yoji Akao, W. Edwards Deming, Genichi Taguchi, Shigeo Shingo, Philip Crosby, and Watts Humphrey—are related. The latest addition to this list of experts is Watts Humphrey, who provided so much to software development and quality assurance that he received the 2003 National Medal of Technology from the President of the United States.

Chapter 3 discusses the commercial standards and the impact that they have on quality assurance, with a special emphasis on software quality. This is a comprehensive chapter on SQA-related standards from ISO, IEEE, CobiT®, ITIL®, and others, and what they mean to you as a practitioner. This chapter concludes with some reminders about conformance and certification, as well as improtant future trends.

Chapter 4 discusses the personnel requirements for a good software quality engineer and how a software quality organization should deal with personnel issues such as training, roles for software quality engineers, paraprofessional possibilities, and career paths. The impact of the American Society for Quality (ASQ) software quality engineer certification program is covered.

Chapter 5 discusses the methods and techniques that will help one to determine how to train software and development quality engineers. The authors have extensive experience in performing this training and they provide much practical information on how to do it well.

Chapter 6 applies the well-known Pareto principle (80/20 rule) to the concerns and issues of software and development quality assurance. The impact and advantage of performing a Pareto analysis is supported by two classic examples: one deals with the World Wide Military Command and Control System (WWMCCS), and the other with the Federal Reserve Bank. How Pareto analysis is applied to defect prevention, its use in analysis of inspection data, and a unique aspect of how to compare Pareto charts are covered in this chapter.

Chapter 7 deals with the widely acclaimed use and application of inspections as a highly beneficial peer review method. The impact and benefits of conducting inspections during the software development cycle are covered in some detail. The inspection process is described and numerous results of inspections are provided to give the reader a firsthand picture of what to look for when evaluating inspection data. Emphasis is given to documentation inspections, inspection metrics, and even the national software quality experiment, which captures inspection results across the country.

Chapter 8 discusses the audit methods useful to software and development quality personnel. What makes up a comprehensive audit is covered, and there are many examples provided of each of those audit parts. Types of audits such as software piracy audits, security audit, information systems audit, ISO 9001:2000 software audit, CMMI®-DEV appraisal, internal project audits, and audit automation. The results of audits are discussed with concomitant ramifications to the audited organization being covered.

Chapter 9 deals with that aspect of quality assurance concerned with software safety. The various requirements related to software safety and hazard avoidance and mitigation techniques are covered. What it takes to develop a software safety assurance program is a key aspect of this important chapter.

Chapter 10 lays out the requirements for the software quality engineer certification program established by the ASQ. More specifically, the chapter deals with how one should prepare for the exam and what is in the body of software quality knowledge needed to pass the exam, and it includes a recommended bibliography that aides in preparation.

Chapter 11 provides an in-depth analysis of the relationship of process and product quality assurance (PPQA) to SQA. It focuses on the requirements for these process areas as they flow from the CMM® for software to the CMMI® for development (CMMI®-DEV). It provides an analysis of the PPQA process area in the CMMI®-DEV and provides various approaches to meeting the intent of PPQA.

Chapter 12 provides guidance on how to handle quality assurance on small projects. It starts with staff and training considerations, followed by tactical and strategic guidance for your projects. There are many recommendations provided on how to reduce cost and pressure for thorough quality assurance coverage on a small project.

Chapter 13 on development quality assurance shows the transition that quality assurance organizations/personnel need to make to be compliant with the latest standards, especially with the CMMI®-DEV. That transition addresses first the systems development process and then the hardware development process. Potential stumbling blocks and related suggestions on how to overcome them are provided.

Chapter 14 examines quality management in information technology (IT). The principles and concepts that apply to IT examined in this chapter include.

- Identifying key IT processes, their sequence, and interaction;
- Planning for defect prevention versus detection by applying IT best practices;
- Using and implementing standards to achieve internationally recognized registration or demonstrate appropriate levels of IT governance;
- Resolving the IT equivalent to software bugs, defects, and errors;
- Determining and documenting customer requirements;
- Monitoring and measuring service performance to assure customer requirements are met and continual improvement occurs;
- Assuring procurement quality when outsourcing key IT processes;
- Parallels in the bodies of knowledge between software and IT quality professionals.

Chapter 15 deals with the assessment of the total cost of software quality and examines what input is required, the value added, and the expected output. The chapter describes what a Cost of Software Quality (CoSQ) system is. How to implement that CoSQ system is covered as well, and the related difficulties in implementation are addressed. Also discussed are the *price of nonconformance* and the effect of budgetary constraints on the implementation of SQA. The chapter concludes with a recommended extended model for the cost of software quality.

Chapter 16 provides a survey of metrics proposed and currently used to determine the quality of the software development effort. Software quality metrics methodology, software quality indicators, and some practical software and systems measurements, CMMI® Measurement and Analysis, CMMI® Higher Maturity Measurements, and practical implementations are covered in this chapter.

Chapter 17 is an overview of software reliability. There is an outline of the software reliability engineering process to give you a feel for the practice, using a single consistent example throughout. The example provides information on preparation, execution, and guidance of testing from a software reliability engineering perspective. The chapter concludes with a list of some key resources.

Appendix A is a list of the acronyms used throughout the book.

I thank each and all of the contributors for their time, energy, and foresight for their contributions to this book.

I also appreciate the patience and help of Wayne Yuhasz, executive acquistions editor, Barbara Lovenvirth, developmental editor, and Rebecca Allendorf, senior production editor, at Artech House, without whose assistance and support this book would not have been accomplished.

G. Gordon Schulmeyer
Editor
Lothian, Maryland
September 2007

## CHAPTER 1

Organizing for Quality Management

Emanuel R. Baker and Matthew J. Fisher

The relationship between the quality of a product and the organization responsible for the development of that product is multidimensional. The relationship depends upon many factors such as the business strategy and business structure of the organization, available talent, and resources needed to produce the product. It also depends upon the combination of activities selected by the organization to achieve the desired product quality. The ultimate focus of this chapter is how organizations could be structured to implement a *Quality Program* and achieve the project's quality objectives. The Quality Program is a framework for building quality into a product, doing the evaluations necessary to determine if the framework is working, and evaluating the quality actually achieved in the product.

In Sections 1.1 and 1.2, we establish the context for the organizational discussions, and, in fact, for other chapters as well. We describe a *Quality Management Framework* first articulated in 1982 [1] to help clarify and place into context the multiple dimensions of this organizational relationship. The framework addresses the conceptual elements necessary for building quality into products, or any entity, and evaluating the quality actually achieved. This framework consists, in part, of a set of definitions and their attendant concepts that impact quality. These definitions constitute the structural members of the framework. Next we use these definitions to explore a Quality Program, which, in combination with the definitions, comprises the Quality Management Framework (QMF).

In Sections 1.3 through 1.6, we use the context of a Quality Program to examine various organizational aspects of implementing the tasks in the QMF. Two examples of organizations are described: one for a large organization and one for a small organization.

1.1 The Quality Management Framework

The original goal of the QMF that was developed in 1982 was to place quality in proper perspective in relation to the acquisition and development of products, including software products. Over time many of the concepts and principles articulated in the original framework have been implemented in various forms not only in venues such as the U.S. Department of Defense (DOD) standards, but also in process models of today, such as Capability Maturity Model Integration® (CMMI®). In such manifestations, the framework concepts have been applied to software and to other types of products and processes. Although the concept of relating process quality to product quality was first articulated in 1982, it was not until the development of the Process Maturity Model[1] in 1987 [2], and eventually the Capability Maturity Model® for Software (SW-CMM®) [3] and CMMI® [4], that these principles finally were codified in a concrete manner, making them easier to implement.

We describe here definitions and associated concepts that constitute the structural elements of the framework that will lead to the concept of a Quality Program.

The following terms and their definitions are provided to establish a basis for the definition of "quality" and to provide the foundation for the Quality Program:

- Object (entity);
- Process;
- Requirements;
- User;
- Evaluation;
- Measure and Measurement;
- Quality.

In presenting the definitions, we avoid any specific organizational connotations and relate only to activities and interrelationships.

1.1.1 Object (Entity)

The types of objects (entities) to which quality can be applied include:

- Product;
- Process;
- Service;
- Resource;
- Artifact;
- Activity;
- Measure or metric;
- Environment;
- Collection of entities or objects.

For conciseness, in this chapter we will focus on the quality associated with a product.

---

1.   The Process Maturity Model, developed by the Software Engineering Institute (SEI) in 1987, is the forerunner of the SW-CMM®.

1.1.2   Product

First, we define a *product* as any tangible output or service that is a result of a process [4, 5]. A product itself may include hardware, software, documentation, or a combination of these; also note that a service is included in the definition. Accordingly, even though the discussion focuses on products, it is important to remember that the same principles apply equally as well to a service, or to anything else included under our definition of object.

1.1.3   Process

Ultimately, what one is interested in is the quality of the delivered product or service. The quality of a product or service is dependent on the quality of the process used to create it [3]; consequently, we need to establish a definition of process, which will enable us to develop a definition of quality. As part of this development, we view *process* as a set of activities performed for a given purpose, for example, a software acquisition process [5].

1.1.4   Requirement

In defining the elements of a Quality Program, a definition of requirements is needed. There are various definitions of a requirement. We include here a general definition of requirements that we use for the remainder of this document. The references cited define a *requirement* as a needed capability, condition, or a property [attribute] that must be possessed by an entity to satisfy a contract, standard, specification, or other formally imposed documents [4, 5].

Simply put, a requirement is a way of characterizing a user's need in a way that allows a development team to implement that need in the product in a concrete way. Put another way, the achievement of the requirements are the yardstick by which we measure the quality of a product or a service. A user—for example, an airline—may need an aircraft that is capable of flying 600 passengers 10,000 miles nonstop with high fuel economy. To actually develop the aircraft, more specific characterizations of the need must be expressed. For instance, the aircraft must be supplied with four engines each with 110,000 pounds of thrust.

We must also be aware that as in the Software Acquisition Capability Maturity Model® (SA-CMM®) [5], there are several types of requirements such as technical, nontechnical, product, allocated, users development, and so on. As a caution, we must be cognizant of the type of requirements being discussed or specified. For example, fixed regulations may also be requirements and may be interpreted as a contract provision, an applicable standard or specification, or other contractual document. Thus, as defined in IEEE-STD-610, *IEEE Standard Glossary of Software Engineering Terminology*, a product requirement is a condition or capability that must be met or possessed by a product or product component in order to satisfy a condition or capability needed by the user to solve a problem. As noted earlier, these conditions may consist of a number of diverse types of attributes.

1.1.5 User

For our purposes, we define user as either the customer or the end user. Typically, three kinds of situations may be encountered in a development or maintenance effort. In the first situation, the customer (either internal or external) and the end user are one and the same (Figure 1.1). In the second situation, the end user is represented by a buyer, and all contact with the client organization is through the buyer (Figure 1.2). In this case, the buyer represents the user. The face presented by the buyer, therefore, is that of both buyer and user. The third situation is where both the buyer and the user community are accessible to the development or maintenance organization (Figure 1.3).

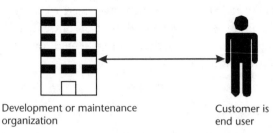

Development or maintenance   Customer is
organization   end user

Figure 1.1   Customer is end user.

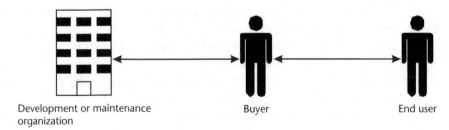

Development or maintenance   Buyer   End user
organization

Figure 1.2   Customer represents end user.

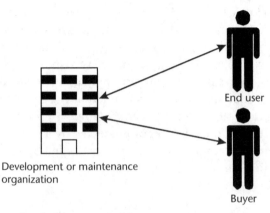

                                                                End user

Development or maintenance
organization

                                                                Buyer

Figure 1.3   Customer and end user are accessible.

For ease of reference, we will use the term "user" in this chapter to represent all three situations. The considerations for these three user situations become prominent when we discuss the first element of the Quality Program, *establish requirements*.

1.1.6 Evaluation

As part of a Quality Program, the concept and definition of evaluation is critical, particularly that of evaluation of product quality. As with requirements, the definitions of evaluation are varied. To place *evaluation* in the context of quality and a Quality Program, evaluation is defined as the process of determining satisfaction of requirements [5]. Kenett gives a more precise definition stemming from this basic definition: Evaluation is "a [process] to evaluate the quality of products and to evaluate associated documentation, processes, and activities that impact the quality of the products" [6].

According to both definitions, evaluations may include methods such as analyses, inspections, reviews, and tests. In this context, evaluation can be applied to acquisition, services, documentation, process, or any product or work product resulting from a process. In this technical note we are interested in evaluation of quality, specifically, determining process and product quality.

1.1.7 Measure and Measurement

As part of evaluation discussed above, we need to include in the QMF the ability to measure the quality of processes and products, and be able to assign actual quantitative values to the item's quality. Toward this end, the definitions and concepts of *measure* and *measurement* are as follows: Measure (v.) is to ascertain the characteristics or features (extent, dimension, quantity, capacity, and capability) of something, especially by comparing with a standard [5]; measurement (n.) is a dimension, capacity, quantity, or amount of something (e.g., 300 source lines of code or seven document pages of design) [5].

Other definitions for measure and measurement exist that convey similar meanings but reverse the definitions. That is, since the term "measure" can be used as a verb or a noun, and "measurement" can mean a process or an item of data, the community tends to use them interchangeably. For example, Fenton [7] describes measurement as the process by which numbers or symbols are assigned to attributes of entities in the real world in such a way as to characterize the attributes by clearly defined rules. This implies an action such as "to measure" in the above definitions.[2]

In addition, use of the terms "metric" and "measure" has become somewhat confused. In most cases they are used interchangeably, but be aware that in some cases various authors have made attempts to distinguish the two terms (and they have done so in different ways). For evidence of this, see [7, 8]. The *IEEE Standard*

---

2. There are numerous reference works on the subject of measurement: Krantz, D. H., et al., *Foundations of Measurement*, Volume 1, New York: Academic Press, 1971; and Ghiselli, E. E., J. P. Campbell, and S. Zedeck, *Measurement Theory for the Behavioral Sciences*, San Francisco: W. H. Freeman and Company, 1981. Some of these (Ghiselli, for example) provide excellent discussions of important issues such as measurement reliability and validity.

Glossary of Software Engineering Terms defines "metric" as follows: "A quantitative measure of the degree to which a system, component, or process possesses a given attribute." Note that the word "metric" is not used in ISO 15939, *Software Engineering—Software Measurement Process*. See Chapter 16 on further definitions of SQA measurements.

Measurement plays an important role in the QMF. As we will later see, an element of the QMF is quality evaluation. We are interested in evaluating the compliance of the product and processes with applicable standards and requirements. One means of achieving that is through measurement. Consequently, we are concerned with the act of measuring, as well as the measure itself (both the verb and noun forms of the word). Anyone familiar with the discipline of measurement and analysis knows the importance of operational definitions for the measures selected. Without them, there is ambiguity about what is being measured, and how it is being used. Likewise, an operational definition for measure and measurement is important in explicating the QMF in order to avoid ambiguity about what it is that the QMF is intending to accomplish.

1.1.8   Quality

A prime focus of the QMF is, of course, the definition of quality and its implication to a quality program. The definition discussed here has broad implications, especially in terms of implementations of a quality program. In the QMF, *quality* is defined as in this reference: Quality is the degree to which an object (entity) (e.g., process, product, or service) satisfies a specified set of attributes or requirements [5]. However, it is important to point out that a product possesses many quality attributes that are intrinsic to the product and that exist regardless of what is desired, specified, or measured, and only depend on the nature of the product [1].

Thus, the definition of quality includes two aspects:

- The concept of attributes;
- The satisfaction or degree of attainment of the attributes.

1.1.8.1   Attributes

An attribute is "a property or characteristic of an entity that can be distinguished quantitatively or qualitatively by human or automated means," from ISO 15939, *Software Engineering—Software Measurement Process*. The word "attributes" includes all specified requirements governing functional, performance, and other specified characteristics such as adaptability, maintainability, and correctness [1, 9]. The attributes (i.e., requirements and other specified characteristics) are considered the determinants of product or process quality.

1.1.8.2   Specifying Product Quality Using Attributes

The word "specified" implies that definitions of the needed quality attributes are documented. Without clear articulation of the quality attributes, it is impossible to develop a product or determine whether the finished product has the needed quality.

A specification is required to communicate to others which attributes constitute the product's quality. Contractually, this specification is critical [1].

In addressing product or process quality, it is therefore necessary that the specification or definition of the attributes is expressed quantitatively. This quantitative expression allows a determination of the degree to which a product or process satisfies or attains the specified attributes. For example, saying that a hardware product has high reliability does not tell us how reliable the hardware is. Stating that the reliability of a product is 0.9999999 mean time between failure (MTBF) expresses a characteristic that can be measured, which means there is a method used to determine if the specified attribute has been attained.

For implementation of a product, one selects those attributes most significant to the user community and evaluates, rates, or measures the product's quality on how well, or to what degree, the selected attributes meet those criteria for excellence. Often, these attributes address only functionality and performance and ignore the other attributes, often referred to as *-ilities*. The -ilities can be considered as attributes that address fitness for use. Conceivably, "if we look at the issue of the software meeting its requirements and if those requirements are solely functional and prescribe no -ilities, then clearly the software can meet the requirements but could be unable to fulfill any reasonable purpose" [10].

Thus, we recognize that just as beauty is in the eye of the beholder, so is quality [9].

Consequently, a set of attributes that one user community deems important as a measure of quality may not be deemed important by another user community. Rather, each user community is likely to have its own set of attributes with which to measure quality.

1.1.8.3   Considering User Needs

It is difficult to satisfy users if they cannot articulate what quality they are expecting. In many cases, users default to "give me something and I will tell you if I like it or not." Such a paradigm wastes time and resources in trying to satisfy the illusive user expectations. Clearly, vague notions such as "user needs," unless they are articulated, cannot be used to determine the quality actually achieved in a product. Something concrete, such as a user specification document, can be used. Obviously, the requirement to accurately capture the user needs in such a document is crucial. Typically, the documents are operational needs documents, which are then decomposed into system requirements documents and then further decomposed into software and hardware component requirements documents. All of these start from the documented user's needs. Codification of this set of activities, for example, is documented in the process area (PA) of Requirements Development in the CMMI®.

The fact that product quality requirements include the functionality and performance requirements and may include requirements for maintainability, portability, interoperability, and so on, leads us to the key point that product quality requirements stem from many sources, above all, from the stakeholders of the project, and this leads us to the idea that quality is everybody's business [11].

However, if we consider how product development projects are organized, the implication is quality is affected by many, but implemented by few [11].

What we will see in later sections (for example, Section 1.2.2) is that the actual activities of the Quality Program are distributed among a number of entities within an organization. No one organization has the capabilities to perform all the functions; consequently, the activities must be assigned to those entities most capable of performing them. As we shall also see later in Sections 1.3 through 1.6, it is necessary to have a central point of responsibility for coordinating all the elements of the Quality Program.

Finally, one must realize that the final quality of a product results from activities performed by the project developing the product. Everything that occurs within a project during development affects some attribute of the product and, therefore, the total product quality. However, all possible attributes may not be of equal relevance. Furthermore, all actions may not affect the specified attributes to the same extent and, therefore, the specified quality. In any event, quality is affected by activities such as requirements definition, design, coding, testing, and maintenance of the product, activities associated with the Quality Program for the product, and the interaction of these activities.

1.2 Quality Program Concepts

The foundation of the Quality Program stems from the definition of quality and the precept that many people supporting the project affect the quality of the product. The interaction of the Quality Program with the other parts of the project elements is necessarily complex. The involvement is at all levels of the project organization and takes place throughout the project's life. In some cases, the Quality Program directs the other activities; in other circumstances, it can only influence those activities. In any case, all the project activities, in some way, affect product quality. The Quality Program is defined as the overall approach to effect and determine the level of quality achieved in a product [9].

1.2.1 Elements of a Quality Program

The Quality Program incorporates three elements that cover the activities necessary to:

1. *Establish requirements and control changes:* Establish and specify requirements for the quality of an product.
2. *Establish and implement methods[3]:* Establish, implement, and put into practice methods, processes and procedures to develop, operate, deploy, and maintain the product.
3. *Evaluate process and product quality:* Establish and implement methods, processes, and procedures to evaluate the quality of the product, as well as to evaluate associated documentation, processes, and activities that have an impact on the quality of the product.

---

3. Methodology is a system of principles, procedures, and practices applied to a particular branch of knowledge. As used here, the organizations' processes and procedures in a development are instantiations of methodologies.

Figure 1.4 illustrates the interaction of these elements and the interaction of the Quality Program with a product's design and implementation activities to produce quality products. This interaction is continuous with the design and implementation activities affecting the Quality Program activities. The Quality Program addresses both technical and management activities. For instance, ensuring that quality is built into a product is a management activity, while specifying the methods used to build in the quality is considered a technical activity.

Given the precept that quality is everybody's business, it follows that a Quality Program covers both technical and management activities. For instance, if we look at the element of the Quality Program concerned with methodologies or product development, enforcing these methodologies (in order to build quality into the product) is a management activity, while the specification of the methodologies is a technical activity. The following discussion expands on the elements of the Quality Program.

One of the foundational aspects of the Quality Program is how well quality can be built into a product, not how well one can evaluate product quality. While evaluation activities are essential activities, they alone will not achieve the specified quality. That is, product quality cannot be evaluated (tested, audited, analyzed, measured, or inspected) into the product. Quality can only be "built in" during the development process [11].

Once the quality has been built in, the deployment, operation, and maintenance processes must not degrade it. Unfortunately, the very nature of maintenance and bug fixes for software often degrades the quality of the code. What was once structured code becomes messy "spaghetti" code with all the modifications resulting from bug fixes and enhancements.

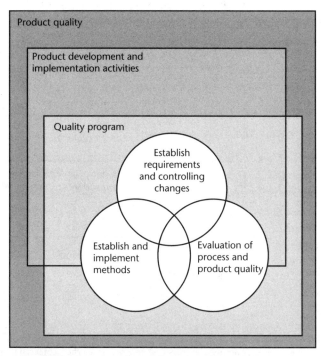

Figure 1.4   Interaction of the elements of a quality program.

For example, Figure 1.5 provides an indication of when the quality of the software likely has been compromised and qualification test procedures should be reexecuted or the software should be reengineered. A threshold level of 30% of the modules changed per software maintenance request was set as the point at which requalification of the software should take place.

Note that in Figure 1.5, the software is approaching the threshold level at which it should be reengineered (approximately 67% of the modules changed). Clearly, in this situation, there is a great potential for the quality of the software to be degraded as a result of maintenance activities. This quality degradation is shown in Figure 1.5 that is based on the following equation:

$$Volatility = \frac{\text{Number of modules changed due to a software maintenance request}}{\text{Total number of modules in a release over time}}$$

The Quality Program does not impose any organizational structure for performing the activities. Organizations are responsible for assigning resources to accomplish the Quality Program activities. We do suggest that organizations, especially at the corporate level, avoid assigning certain roles to carry out the Quality Program without clearly understanding the concept of product and process quality and how those are affected and implemented.

The idea of many people affecting the product quality should be obvious from the fact that so many disciplines are involved in accomplishing the array of quality requirements. Virtually everyone working on the project, from the project manager (PM)[4] to the most junior member of the staff, affects the quality of the product. However, only those actually producing the product (performing tasks such as

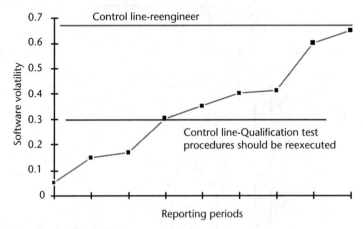

Figure 1.5   Software volatility indicator.

---

4.   A project manager is an individual assigned the management responsibility for acquiring, developing, or providing a product or service. The project manager has total business responsibility for an entire project and is the individual who directs, controls, administers, and regulates the project. The project manager is the individual ultimately responsible to the customer or end user (see [5]).

requirements analyses, design, and manufacturing/coding) build quality into the product. Even though, for example, code reviewers do affect the quality of the resultant product, like testers, they do not actually produce the code.

Thus, it is important to understand that the person ultimately responsible for the quality of the product is the PM. It is the project manager's responsibility to integrate the efforts of "the many" and "the few" to accomplish the project's quality objectives. The PM may, of course, delegate authority for any part of this function, but ultimately he or she is responsible. This is reflected in the often used phrase that, while authority may be delegated, responsibility cannot be.

1.2.1.1 Establish Requirements and Control Changes

The first element or set of activities of the Quality Program is to establish requirements. Product requirements must accurately reflect the product's desired overall quality, including functionality and performance, and must be documented and baselined (formalized). As noted previously, the requirements must accurately reflect the needs of the user community. The process for defining the requirements must ensure that the needs of all the stakeholders involved with the end product have been accurately captured. Thus, a process for establishing and controlling the requirements must be established. This indicates an interface with the second element of the Quality Program: *establish and implement methods*.

One problem associated with specifying a product's quality requirements is the inaccurate perception that the quality cannot be stated quantitatively or in a way that permits objective evaluation. As noted earlier, communicating the quality of an entity to others becomes difficult because people tend to interpret the quality of the same entity from their own perspective. The result is that verifying achievement of the desired quality can be quite subjective. Consequently, the methodology established must ensure that ambiguity is reduced and verifiable quality criteria are specified.

Simply defining and formalizing product requirements are insufficient. The baseline product requirements must be strictly adhered to and fully implemented. Failure to implement the requirements as specified can result in products that do not meet user needs and derived requirements. The resultant impact on product quality, such as functionality and performance, will range from negligible to severe. It follows that any changes to the product requirements must be controlled and documented, and the effects of those changes must be understood.

The activities of defining and establishing the requirements and controlling changes to them necessarily involve interfaces with the other two elements of the Quality Program: *establish and implement methods* and *evaluate process and product quality*.

To illustrate the interface between these two elements of the Quality Program, an organization may establish methods such as the use of data flow analysis, use cases, or object-oriented analysis for performing requirements analysis. Whatever method is selected and used must provide high confidence that the users' needs have been captured accurately; consequently, the evaluation of the requirements analysis process must demonstrate that it was followed and is effective in capturing the users' needs, and the evaluation of the requirements must indicate that the users' needs were captured correctly for the instances examined.

As another example, when establishing baseline requirements and controlling changes, a configuration management method must be selected and later implemented in order to:

- Establish a baseline as a reasonably firm point of departure from which to proceed into the other phases of project activity knowing that there is some reasonable degree of stability in at least the set or subset of requirements that were established.
- Prevent uncontrolled changes to the product baseline.
- Improve the likelihood that the development effort results in a quality product and that processes in subsequent life-cycle phases will not degrade it.

Again, the process evaluation must demonstrate that the process was followed and is effective, and the product evaluations must demonstrate the correctness of the outputs.

A second interface between elements of the Quality Program exists. It is between the *establish requirements and control changes* element and the *evaluate process and product quality* element. It is concerned with two things: the evaluation of the product against the requirements, and the determination that the process was adhered to for defining requirements. Total compliance with requirements does not guarantee a quality product if the requirements are not properly defined and errors exist in them. Then compliance with requirements produces a product that does not satisfy the intended end use. Clearly, evaluations/audits for compliance with the process for establishing requirements must be performed. Furthermore, the process and method by which the requirements are developed must be evaluated for adequacy in this regard during the development or maintenance process.

1.2.1.2   Establish and Implement Methods

The second element or set of activities of the Quality Program involves selecting, implementing, and putting into practice the appropriate processes, practices, and methods *to build quality into the product* and achieve the specified quality requirements. This is typically accomplished by codifying these processes, practices, and methods as standards and training the organization and project teams to use them. These standards may be tailored to meet the unique needs of the project in accordance with established tailoring guidelines (or as defined processes, in the context of the CMMI®).

Implementation of the methodologies may be facilitated by tools compatible with the methodologies and the standard practices and procedures.

The act of getting these standards into use is accomplished by corporate management, who can consistently and unequivocally require the application of the selected methods from project to project even under conditions of schedule pressure. The enforcement can be through various means, for example, assignment of appropriately trained personnel, or monitoring and controlling the project against a project plan, or both. The important point is that requiring compliance with standards is the responsibility of management and not some other organizational entity, like, for example, a quality assurance group.

Enforcing compliance does not preclude tailoring the methods to be consistent with the unique characteristics of the various projects. Tailoring should be permitted to account for the fact that there may be considerations that would militate against full compliance with the organization's standard process for some projects, or that perhaps might require additional, more stringent process steps. Guidelines should exist to cover those cases, and the resultant tailoring should be subject to review and approval. Reviews and audits of project activities for adherence with the established processes are performed to provide visibility or insight to management. Reviews or audits for adherence do not necessarily constitute enforcement; they can only determine if compliance has occurred. Management can use the result of audits to exercise its leadership responsibilities by active monitoring and control of project activities.

Typically, we believe there is a strong link between product quality and the processes used to develop (and maintain) it. If the processes used by the development organization are not well defined or organized, the quality of their products will not be predictable or repeatable from project to project. Based upon the maxim that the quality of a product is highly influenced by the quality of the processes used to produce it [3], the development community, in conjunction with the Software Engineering Institute (SEI) at Carnegie Mellon University, developed a process maturity model and associated appraisal methodology called Capability Maturity Model Integration® (CMMI®) and Standard CMMI® Appraisal Methodology for Process Improvement (SCAMPI^{SM}), respectively [12]. This process model and the appraisal methodology are used to characterize the maturity of the development processes and associated procedures and methodologies. Five levels of maturity are described by this model. The levels, their names, and the characteristics that describe when the organization has reached that level are shown in Figure 1.6.

Characterizing the process maturity in this way is an attempt to show one link between the quality of the product and the processes employed in its development. Note that process maturity is one way the development community describes the quality of the processes. While this quality attribute may not be the only link to

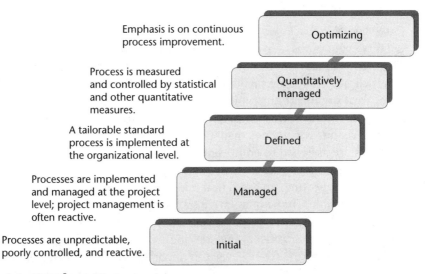

Figure 1.6   CMMI® maturity levels.

product quality, it does indicate the importance the community places on process (the establishment of methodologies) and why this is such an important element of the Quality Program.

Even with this attempt of linking product quality to process quality in terms of process maturity, at present, no formalized techniques exist for organizations to select and specify optimal methodologies necessary to achieve product quality; the selection is based on experience, intuition, literature search, common knowledge, and, to some extent, trial and error. In general, it is only the highest maturity level organizations that have the capability of quantitatively evaluating how effective their processes are, and this evaluation is typically made with reference to the processes already selected by the method described next.

Generally, the basis for determining which processes to implement when establishing standards is to look to past history. If a process produced "high-quality products" on some past projects, it is believed that properly implementing the process on an organizational basis will result in a high-quality product now. Establishing standards in this manner is somewhat misleading. The link between methods selected for product development and the resultant product quality has not been demonstrated quantitatively because establishing links is more heuristic or intuitive than analytical. For example, Ada was touted as promoting information hiding, which, in turn, should make the product more adaptable. However, to our knowledge, the actual quantitative cause and effect link has never been documented.

1.2.1.3 Evaluate Product and Process Quality

The third element or set of activities of the Quality Program involves both evaluating the implementation of processes and evaluating the quality of the resulting product(s). Evaluations are used to assess:

- The quality of the product;
- The adequacy of the processes and activities responsible for product quality;
- Compliance with established processes.

Evaluation of Product Quality

Quality evaluations help to define the "health" of the product and hence the project. Through evaluations, the project can determine whether its product satisfies the specified quality requirements within cost and schedule constraints. Because of the number of organizations typically involved in quality evaluation activities, coordinating the results of this process should be performed by the PM. Whatever assignment decisions are made, management must be sure that all quality evaluation activities are assigned to competent, unbiased reviewers.

Evaluation activities include reviews, assessments, tests, analyses, inspections, and so on. Depending on the action taken and the processes or products being evaluated, the results may be qualitative or quantitative in nature.

Any evaluation that requires reasoning or subjective judgment is referred to as an assessment. Assessments include analyses, audits, surveys, and both document and project performance reviews. On the other hand, measurement activities constitute quantitative evaluations such as tests, demonstrations, metrics, and, in some cases, inspections using checklists (although some checklists tend to be written only to allow a subjective evaluation). Accordingly, measurements can include tests for unit level, integration, and product or application level performance, as well as the output of a compare or a path analyzer program.

Evaluation activities will vary with each phase of the development cycle. Furthermore, they can be performed by individuals independent of the project, or one or several independent organizational units. Evaluation activities to be performed and responsibility for them are generally defined and documented in project management plans, product development plans, project-specific product quality procedures, and/or company quality plans and related product quality procedures.

Evaluation of Established Processes

Another form of process quality evaluation is doing reviews and audits for compliance to or adherence with the process. It is one thing to specify a process, but if that process is not being followed, the quality of the resultant product can be adversely affected. Periodic audits for compliance with the process need to be performed to ensure that the established process is being implemented. For example, external appraisals, such as a SCAMPI[SM] appraisal, are helpful in this regard.

It is also important to evaluate the processes used to determine if these processes are producing products that yield the required quality. Using a concept from the CMMI[®] to explain how processes are evaluated, low maturity organizations will do qualitative evaluations supported, in some cases, by rudimentary quantitative methods. High maturity organizations will use metrics and statistical analysis to determine how effective the processes have been. In the low maturity organization case, the evaluation will in most cases be experiential. For example, did the process performers experience making a number of mistakes and doing rework by following the process? In other cases, the organization might collect simple data, for example, defect data. If the number of defects appear to be large (a subjective determination at lower CMMI[®] maturity levels), then investigations will be performed to figure out where in the overall scheme of things the defects are being introduced. In the high maturity cases, process performance goals are established, processes will be quantitatively monitored (using statistical analysis for the most critical processes), and corrective action implemented when process performance goes off the track.

1.2.2   Considerations

1.2.2.1   Quality Evaluation Versus Quality Assurance

A point of confusion, especially related to organizational aspects of the Quality Program, is the role of quality assurance (QA) groups and the quality evaluation activities that group may perform. Part of this confusion stems from a misunderstanding by many project teams about the word quality and the belief that anything to do with quality is (or should not be!) the purview of a QA group. This belief flies in the face of the precept that quality is everybody's business, and that quality cannot be injected into a product, say, by a QA audit. Part of this confusion is also the blurred difference between QA functions and QA organizational entities. In fact, QA functions can be performed by many groups, not only groups designated as QA by corporate decree.

Thus, as far as an organizational perspective goes, if a QA entity exists in a corporate structure and the capability of this group is limited, let us say, to a checklist approach, a project manager may mistakenly conclude that the effort performed by this group is sufficient to satisfy all the quality evaluation needs of his or her project. This situation may preclude vital measurements (or tests) on critical parts of the product.

The Process and Product Quality Assurance (PPQA) process area of the CMMI® provides an excellent approach to QA functions. In doing so, the process area defines the QA function as providing insight into the implementation of the process and products against established standards. As noted above, this is part of the overall quality evaluation activities. In addition, this CMMI® process area does not relegate these functions to any specific group but allows the organization to assign these responsibilities. More detailed analysis and discussion of this is in Chapter 11.

What is crucial to any product development project is the definition and implementation of the activities necessary to assess and measure the quality of the products developed by that project and the processes used to develop them, in accordance with company and project requirements, such as quality goals, established for the project. When the quality evaluation activities have been defined, the assignment of these activities to specific organizations is a management prerogative. Where QA organizations have the capability to perform many or most of the quality evaluation activities, these can be assigned to the QA organizations.

1.2.2.2   The Concept of Independence

As part of quality evaluation activities, we discuss the concept of independence.

Relative to quality evaluation, independence implies performing product quality evaluations by an "outside" organization (or individuals).

In this case, *outside* means different from those that produced the product or those that executed the processes and activities being evaluated.

The concept of independence relates not only to performing the evaluation, but extends to establishing the evaluation criteria. The need for independence arises because the persons performing the process or creating the product may have a conscious or unconscious need to make the process or product look good. They might also have a biased expectation of what the result should be and consequently would fail to perform certain checks or could miss anomalies because of that expectation. Such evaluators can hardly be considered independent. By removing from them the responsibility for establishing the evaluation criteria and performing the evaluations, such problems will be substantially reduced.

Independence, as a concept, has two aspects:

1. Independence exercised within an organization, such as the use of a test team composed of individuals different from those who designed and developed the product;
2. Independence exercised by establishing a separate group outside the project, such as an independent verification and validation[5] agent from outside the

---

5.   Verification and validation can be characterized (based on the CMMI® [4]) as follows: verification determines if the product is being built right, and validation determines if the right product is being built.

organization that is producing the product. This form of independence is perhaps the most stringent.

Either way, the notion of independence is applied to reduce errors resulting from extensive familiarity with the product being evaluated. Decisions as to the application of independence, the degree of independence to apply, and the types of independent agencies to employ are a function of a number of variables, such as size and complexity of the product/project, corporate policy, available funds, and criticality of the product to its end use (human safety, destruction of equipment, severe financial loss, and so on).

1.3 Organizational Aspects of the Quality Program

Using the context for the Quality Program established in Sections 1.1 and 1.2, we address here organizational concepts in implementing the Quality Program.

Each of the elements of the Quality Program (QP) discussed above involves a number of organizations or functional entities within an organizational structure (e.g., a company or a department of the government). The discussion that follows describes the functions or activities these entities perform in the implementation of the QP. It also explores how these entities interact to implement the QP.

Sometimes the functions that will be described are not necessarily performed by separate organizations, but rather may sometimes be performed by different individuals within a single organization. In other words, when a company organizes to implement the QP, it is not a requirement that there be separate functional entities established to perform these activities. For instance, within an information technology (IT) department, the responsibility for some of the QP functions may be shared between a database administrator and a quality administrator.[6] Quality management in IT is further discussed in Chapter 14. For convenience in the following, the word "organization" will be used to refer to both actual organizations and to the situation where the functions are performed by separate individuals within an organizational entity, rather than separate organizations.

1.4 Quality Program Organizational Relationships

Many of the concepts that we discuss here have been addressed in previous editions of the *Handbook of Software Quality Assurance* [13]. These concepts have been codified in various process improvement and quality models, such as the CMMI® and ISO 9000. Since the CMMI® has become a process improvement model adopted by a large number of organizations worldwide, references will be made in what follows to the CMMI®, as appropriate and without additional references, to emphasize the importance of the concepts [4].

In what follows, we discuss the organizational aspects of the Quality Program in terms of:

---

6. The names for these roles are not standardized and will typically vary from organization to organization.

- Type of systems;
- Mapping quality program functions to project organizational entities;
- Example implementations.

The following discusses the organizational relationships for the Quality Program by using the Quality Program elements as the structure for the discussion; that is:

- Establish requirements and control changes;
- Establish and implement methods;
- Evaluate process and product quality.

1.4.1   Establish Requirements and Control Changes

A number of organizations participate in establishing, implementing, and controlling the product quality requirements (including, for example, the functional and performance requirements). The kinds of organizations that are involved will depend on the type of product under development. To illustrate, the kinds of organizations that will be involved in this effort for data-intensive systems, such as information management systems (IMS), will be very different from the kinds of organizations that will be involved for engineering applications, such as an avionics system for a commercial airliner. Nonetheless, the activities that occur in establishing and controlling the requirements, and the sequence in which they occur, will be essentially the same for all types of applications.

1.4.1.1   Information Management Systems

For IMS or similar applications, the development of the user requirements should be performed by the using organization and specified in a user specification, which defines the overall functionality of the product (and does not specify how it is to be implemented in the product). In many instances, the using organization should obtain assistance from the product development organization in order to ensure that the requirements are expressed correctly and unambiguously, in a manner that the users can concur with as being correctly representative of their needs and developers can understand and from which generate detailed processing requirements. This is an issue that is addressed in the CMMI® in the Requirements Management (REQM) process area under specific practice (SP) 1.1. The participation of the user is essential in order to ensure that the requirements are responsive to the user's needs. In parallel to this, as the user specification is being developed, preliminary processing and database design requirements should be developed by the development organization. Within IT organizations, this process typically involves product analysts, data analysts, and the database administrator. The user organization is also involved, insofar as they have a role to play in verifying that the (processing) requirements reflect the functionality they want in the product.

A formal review should occur after the product requirements have been defined and documented, to baseline the product requirements specification (in accordance with established configuration management procedures). For IMS systems, the review would involve project management and user personnel, the IT development organization (product analysts, data analysts, and database administrator), and IT configuration management and quality assurance administrators. After the formal review is successfully completed, the configuration management group is then charged with the responsibility for overseeing the control of the documented requirements to prevent unauthorized changes to them (also addressed in the CMMI® under the REQM PA in SP 1.3).

1.4.1.2   Engineering/Scientific Systems

In developing the requirements for a system,[7] there are also a number of organizations involved. For such systems, the product engineering organization should take the lead for developing the system requirements. In some cases, the starting point for that may be a customer or user statement of needs. The product engineering organization should be involved in the effort to ensure that the product requirements have been correctly captured, stated, and allocated to the product components and are being implemented, and to satisfy all concerned that the product requirements are traceable to the user or customer requirements. The using organization should also be involved in order to make sure that the product requirements reflect what is needed in the deliverable product. [Where the product is developed under contract, the using organization becomes the customer—or is represented by another agent acting on their behalf, for example, purchasing. In this case, such involvement in the requirements definition process may be difficult to achieve without affecting contract costs and/or schedule. To surmount these kinds of issues, creative innovations, such as integrated product teams (IPTs), have been implemented.]

As with IMS, a formal review for the product or system requirements should be held. It should occur after the product requirements have been defined and documented. The product requirements specification should then be baselined in accordance with procedures established by the configuration management group. For engineering/scientific systems, this review may involve the customer; project management and personnel from the product engineering, configuration management, product test, product engineering, and quality assurance groups; and various groups concerned with operating, fielding, and supporting the product. After the formal review is successfully completed, the configuration management group is then charged with the responsibility for overseeing the control of the documented requirements to prevent unauthorized changes to them.

The baselined system requirements become the point of departure for developing the requirements for all the major components (e.g., subsystems). The product engineering organization should take the lead for ensuring that the requirements stated at the component level (e.g., the software requirements) are compatible and consistent with the system level requirements.

1.4.1.3   All Systems

The manager and subordinate managers responsible for product engineering (or component development) are accountable for implementing the requirements as

---

7.   We define a system as a product comprised of two or more interacting components that can be separately developed and controlled. These components may be software, hardware, and/or personnel.

established and for assuring that they are not changed in an unauthorized manner. The quality assurance group may be responsible for monitoring the configuration management process to verify that no unauthorized changes have occurred. The quality assurance group may also be responsible for conducting audits to verify that the established requirements development process was followed [see Generic Practice (GP) 2.9 in the REQM and Requirements Development (RD) PAs in the CMMI®].

For this element of the Quality Program, then, we see that at least the following organizations are active in establishing and controlling the product quality requirements for engineering/scientific applications: user/customer organizations, product engineering, product test, configuration management, quality assurance, project management, and various support groups, such as a logistics group, field maintenance group, and the like. For IMS systems, it may involve the users, the IT development organization, quality assurance, and configuration management.

Within the structure of the CMMI®, there is a GP that exists within each process area, GP 2.7, "Identify and Involve Relevant Stakeholders." One of the roles of the quality manager (QM) clearly is to ensure that the relevant stakeholders, such as illustrated here, are properly identified and involved in the Requirements Definition and Requirements Management processes.

1.4.2 Establish and Implement Methods

Establishing and implementing methodologies to develop the product and maintain its quality include establishing the methodologies themselves and institutionalizing them in the form of standard practices, procedures, tools, and methodologies. These methodologies, practices, and procedures cover a wide number of areas. They include requirements analysis, documentation, design, coding, test, configuration management, installing and operating the product, and product maintenance.

In implementing this element of the QP, interactions occur with a number of organizations. Product engineering must be involved in the definition process since they will be the ultimate users of the methodologies, standards, procedures, and associated tools (if applicable). An interface with the quality evaluators exists. First, when the methodologies are initially developed, the points in the process where quality evaluation tasks must be performed need to be identified, along with the methodologies for performing the quality evaluations. Second, from time to time, changes are made to the specified methodologies and implementing documentation and tools. Consequently, it may be necessary to change the corresponding quality evaluation process. These changes may occur under two conditions: (1) the specified methodologies, documentation, or tools are not producing the required levels of quality; or (2) new methodologies have become available that will materially improve the quality of the product. Once the changes have been made to the processes, they must be monitored to determine if, in fact, improvements have been made. The determinations of methodology adequacy result from product and process evaluations. The personnel performing product quality evaluations typically provide the raw data for evaluating existing, new, or modified methodologies and tools, while product engineering personnel generally do the analyses of the data or of the methodologies. At the highest maturity levels on the CMMI®, such evaluations are typically performed on a quantitative basis. The project manager must be consulted regarding the adoption of new methodologies and/or tools to determine if such changes will negatively impact productivity, schedule, and/or cost for that project. Operations personnel, such as product librarians and database administrators for software or equipment operators for hardware, must be consulted to determine the effect on operations. Personnel must be assigned the task of producing standards and procedures for implementing the methodologies and using the tools in a manner compatible with the established standards. Clearly, company management must be involved in this element of the QP because of the investment in personnel to staff the function, as well as approval or disapproval for the acquisition of new methodologies, and tools to implement the methodologies.

Again, the multidisciplinary nature of the QP is evident. One can deduce from this that many organizations are involved in establishing and implementing the methodologies for development and maintenance and producing standard practices and procedures for these functions. In organizations that have adopted the CMMI® as the model for process improvement, the function of coordinating these activities is often assigned to a centralized function, sometimes referred to as an Engineering Process Group (EPG), Product Engineering Process Group (PEPG), or in organizations that are primarily software development organizations, a Software Engineering Process Group (SEPG). We will discuss this group in more detail later in this chapter. It should also be noted that the lower maturity level organizations tend to follow a more heuristic and qualitative approach to process change, whereas Maturity Level 5 organizations follow a structured and quantitative approach for implementing process change (see the description for the Organizational Innovation and Deployment process area [4]).

1.4.3 Evaluate Process and Product Quality

Finally, we come to the element of *evaluate process and product quality*, or Quality Evaluation (QE) activities. Activities involved here cover the establishment of standard processes and procedures for performing evaluations and also for implementing these evaluations in order to determine (1) the quality of product and (2) the quality of the processes and activities impacting the quality of the product.

The number of organizations involved in performing the QE activities can be large. Considering that QE includes analytical as well as measurement activities, it is easy to see that QE is a discipline that encompasses engineering as well as support groups. For example, analyses may be performed by systems engineering or a product engineering group. Tests may be performed by an integration test team or an independent product test group (or both), possibly with a quality assurance group monitoring. In some companies, a quality assurance group does testing as well.

Project reviews may include project management, and the system engineering, product engineering, configuration management, and quality assurance groups. Certainly a quality assurance entity would participate in and conduct audits. The configuration management and quality assurance groups would be involved in document reviews as would the system and product engineering groups.

In any event, it can be seen that the activities involved in QE requires the talents of almost all groups participating in the development process. See Chapter 13 on development quality assurance for an in-depth discussion of this point.

To complete this discussion of QE, it is imperative to introduce the concept of independence. As discussed earlier, relative to QE, independence implies performing product quality evaluations by an organization (or individuals) different from the organization (or individuals) that produced the products or documentation, or that execute the processes and activities being evaluated. Independence extends to establishing the evaluation criteria. The performer may have a conscious or unconscious need to make the process or product look good. Evaluators so inclined can hardly be considered independent. By removing from them the responsibility for establishing the evaluation criteria and performing the evaluations, such problems cannot arise. The criteria for the evaluations must be based on the requirements for the product, hence the importance of establishing good requirements, and ensuring that the user's or customer's needs are accurately reflected in the requirements documents.

Independent QE requires the collection of objective evidence that technical requirements have been established, products and processes conform to technical requirements, and that the products meet the specified quality requirements. This may mean that one organization does a specific evaluation, but another organization establishes the criteria for the evaluation, verifies that the evaluation has been performed, and impounds the data for eventual use in certifying the product or service. "Objective evidence" includes such items as measurement data, audit reports, certified test data sheets, verification and validation (V&V) reports, resolved product trouble reports, and the like.

1.5   Mapping Quality Program Functions to Project Organizational Entities

Numerous organizational structures can be applied to implement the Quality Program. The important point at the project level is allocating the related tasks to corporate organizations available to the project manager. This allocation of these tasks depends upon several interrelated factors. Obviously, one factor is the business structure and guidance established by the corporation or by the project manager to accomplish the project. The structure and guidance given to the project manager eventually reduces to authorized funding and permissible execution control within the corporate structure, both of which limit the flexibility the project manager has to conduct projects. Another factor is the extent and complexity of the tasks and the availability of personnel to perform them.

In many cases, the corporation has predetermined the responsibilities for these tasks, thereby predetermining the allocation of them. This a priori assignment of tasks may restrict the project manager in how he or she mobilizes a particular project and structures the Quality Program (which involves the coordination of so many disciplines). One way a project manager can help insure proper coordination is to appoint a quality manager to his or her staff. (But it must be remembered that even with the appointment of a QM, the project manager is still ultimately responsible for the Quality Program.)

If we assume that most, if not all, necessary resources and talent are usually available for the project manager's execution of the Quality Program, the project manager's task reduces to coordination of assigned activities. The project manager can choose to assign a QM to coordinate the Quality Program activities. If the necessary resources and talent are not available, the project manager must secure these through negotiation with company management and company subordinate entities from which the resources will be obtained.

The purpose of assigning a QM is to support the project manager in providing a quality framework for the project and, more important, making the Quality Program more visible to the rest of the project manager's organization. The quality manager does this by insuring that the Quality Program is planned as part of the overall product development process, by insuring that the Quality Program is implemented, and by keeping the project manager informed and on track with the overall product development. Based upon the definition of quality (i.e., product attributes including functionality, performance, and so forth), the quality manager has the tasks of planning and coordinating all the disciplines involved in the project. In this context the quality manager is the technical lead for the project. Again, based upon the definition and implications of product quality noted earlier in this chapter, the term quality manager does not imply that the individual is from the QA group, or that the individual is only managing the QA portion of the project. The quality manager has a much broader responsibility, especially in the coordination of all the activities that "build" quality into the product, not just simply testing for it. Note that there are some overlaps between the functions that a PEPG/EPG/SEPG and the QM would do. However, the PEPG/EPG/SEPG has responsibility for these activities across the entire organization, whereas the QM has responsibility for applying these activities to the project only. In the context of the CMMI®, there is a number of process areas that implement the various elements of the Quality Program described herein at the project level. The function of the project's quality manager is to ensure that these process areas are implemented as a cohesive whole, rather than as a set of unrelated, independent process areas.

Starting with the critical aspect of project planning, the following addresses organizational considerations in the mapping of Quality Program functions in terms of the Quality Program elements.

1.5.1 Planning

The quality manager must be an integral part of the project planning to insure that the Quality Program is addressed. He or she must play a very active role in this effort, setting up all the steps to follow in executing the Quality Program, including those in the evaluation effort.

Important in performing this role is the development of the Quality Program Plan. This can be either a major subset of the project management plan, or may be a separate document that is referenced within the project management plan. In any event, the vital task of the quality manager during the planning phase is to produce the Quality Program Plan.

The quality manager must work very closely with all participants in the project in order to generate the Quality Program Plan, specifically, to ensure that:

- The plan is produced.
- The plan is complete and the elements of the plan are integrated into the project management plan.
- The activities to be performed are integrated with each other to the extent that they should.
- The plan contains realistic schedules.
- The plan describes assignment of responsibilities and designates necessary authority to the appropriate performing organizations.
- Expected Quality Program outputs for the project are specified.
- Criteria for successful completion of tasks are stipulated.

During development, the quality manager uses the results of the evaluation efforts to track the progress of the Quality Program against the Quality Program Plan. A primary concern is not simply to determine compliance with the plan, but, more important, to determine if application of the planned activities of the Quality Program will achieve the desired quality, or, if the plan must be changed to effect the desired quality.

1.5.2 Establish Requirements and Control Changes

During the process of establishing the project and product quality requirements, the quality manager must have the authority to represent the project manager. Here, the quality manager ensures that the appropriate process is followed, and that the process is properly managed. As indicated earlier, a number of organizations (or functions within an organization) are typically involved in defining and establishing functional and performance requirements. These may include product engineering, user organizations, system engineering, and so on. Other groups, such as those representing human factors or maintenance, must have a chance to participate in the requirements definition process in order to ensure that their needs are also reflected in the requirements documentation. The kinds of groups involved will depend on the type of application under development. As the number of these groups increase, the job of establishing the requirements becomes more and more difficult. Having the quality manager coordinating and managing this process for the project manager and ensuring that the process is followed simplifies control and ensures that requirements are established and that they are quantitative, testable, and complete.

The quality manager can use several methods of accomplishing this process, orchestrating the various groups involved. For example, for software, he or she may depend totally upon the product engineering group or IT development group to both specify the processing requirements and perform checks (assessments) as to their adequacy. On the other hand, the quality manager may use some groups to define the requirements, and other groups to perform the evaluations. In some cases, the evaluations may be split between the developers and the evaluators. For instance, the assessment for traceability might be performed by the product developers, instead of other designated evaluators, utilizing the traceability capabilities embedded within the software engineering tools being used to develop the requirements.

Whoever is assigned to making these evaluations is designated in the Quality Program Plan.

As pointed out previously, there is an interface between the requirements definition element and the quality evaluation element of the Quality Program Plan. Requirements development involves a strong interplay between requirements analysis and QE. The requirements must be evaluated as they are being developed to make sure that the job is being performed completely and correctly. The quality manager utilizes those personnel designated in the Quality Program Plan to make such assessments (perform Quality Evaluation) and provide some independence. The quality manager uses the outputs of the assessments to:

- Ensure that the evolving requirements are modified where necessary.
- Ensure that requirements become baselined, when stable.
- Assist in revising the process of establishing requirements.
- Assist in changing methodologies used in this process.
- Enforce the procedures originally planned for this part of the Quality Program Plan.

Communication (see Figure 1.7) between the two elements can be conducted totally through the quality manager.

1.5.3   Establish and Implement Methods

As with the requirements portion, the second element of the Quality Program is easy to accomplish within the project structure by assigning responsibility for this function to the quality manager. There are really three parts to this job: (1) establishing the methodologies to be used for the project, (2) enforcing the methodologies, and (3) modifying the selected methodologies, when necessary.

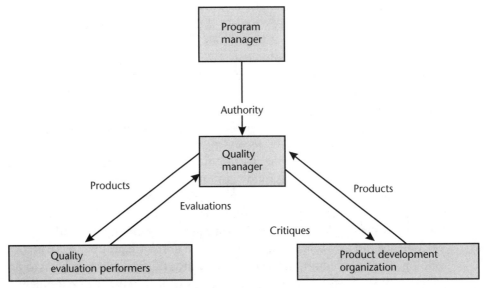

Figure 1.7   Quality manager communications.

One way in which the accomplishment of the first part of this element of the Quality Program can be facilitated is by establishing a Product Engineering Process Group (PEPG) [4] at the organizational level. A PEPG typically is a corporate asset that evaluates and selects methodologies for use by the organization and supports each project in selecting appropriate methodologies. It is the focal point for the methodology element of the Quality Program. Its main function is to serve as the initiator, sustainer, and evaluator of process change. In terms of the CMMI® model, this is the focus of the Organizational Process Focus (OPF) and Organizational Process Definition (OPD) process areas. The PEPG establishes a set of process assets and tailoring guidelines that are used by the project's quality manager to tailor or adapt the organizational process for use by the project. This is one of the intents of the Integrated Project Management (IPM) process area in the CMMI®.

At the very outset of a new project, the applicability of the established methodologies, techniques, and tools for the product to be developed is determined. If a PEPG exists within the company, the quality manager must consult with that function in order to adequately carry out this assignment. The methodologies, which are established by the PEPG, are established for use throughout the entire organization according to the different types of products produced by the organization. It may be necessary to modify these methodologies to suit the unique characteristics of the product to be produced on this project, utilizing the aforementioned tailoring guidelines. The QM, in conjunction with the PEPG, makes this determination and oversees the modifications, if required. These modifications will be reflected in the form of project-specific modifications to the standards and procedures. The tailoring of the standard processes for the unique characteristics of the project must go through an approval process, and the resultant modifications identified in the project plan.

When a PEPG does not exist, the QM then must assume much of the responsibility and coordination effort that the PEPG would have performed. In establishing methodologies to use in order to achieve the desired quality attributes for the product, the quality manager must bring to bear a wide range of disciplines, not just product engineering. The intent of this effort is to select those product engineering methodologies that offer the best promise of producing a product meeting all the specified requirements—an extremely difficult process due to varying maturity in available product engineering techniques. The quality manager must further assure that the interfacing disciplines (e.g., product engineering, testing, configuration management, and so on) are communicating with each other and coordinating on the methodologies to be employed on the project to assure that they are mutually compatible.

Once the project is started, the QM is responsible for enforcing the implementation of the methodologies (the second part of the job). This is accomplished by setting policy and monitoring the development, operation, and maintenance activities to verify that policy is being followed. Enforcement often depends upon an assessment or measurement of products and development, operation, maintenance activities, creating an interface between this element of the Quality Program and the QE element of the Quality Program. Products include preliminary and final versions of documents and preliminary hardware and/or software product releases. Since methodologies are procedural in nature, other kinds of products may be used to evaluate whether the processes are being properly implemented in the development activities.

These may be interim work products or work products resulting from other activities. For example, reports of peer reviews may be used to determine if the developers have followed the prescribed methodologies.

The methodologies established for the project must also be evaluated during the life of the project to determine if they are, in fact, achieving the desired results. They must be modified, and corrective action must be initiated if they are not. The basic information on which a decision to modify the methodologies is based depends on the CMMI® maturity level of the organization. At Maturity Level 3 and below, the decision is based primarily on the results of product quality evaluations, and process performer subjective perceptions of the processes, based on their own experience in using them. At Level 4 and above, the decision is based on quantitative process measurements. These adjustments (or corrective action of the processes) are initially at the project level; however, if it is determined that the corporate process is deficient, the corporate PEPG would take on the task of enterprise-wide corrective action or long-term improvement of the process.

Because of the interfaces that exist between this and the Quality Evaluation elements of the Quality Program, it becomes readily evident that the quality manager is the most logical individual to assign as the one responsible for ensuring that this job is properly coordinated and accomplished.

1.5.4   Evaluate Process and Product Quality

The QM is also responsible for the implementation of the Quality Evaluation program. The Quality Program Plan should have defined the totality of assessment and measurement activities and assigned these to the appropriate performing organizations. Clearly, the QA organization can be a major performer, and as indicated previously, a number of other organizations are likewise involved. Accordingly, it is essential that the QM completely and totally define the tasks and performers.

Quality Evaluation is the major instrument defining the health of the product and hence the project. Through the evaluations performed, the PM can determine if his or her product will satisfy the customers' or users' needs within cost and within schedule. Because of the number of organizations involved in the Quality Evaluation process, coordination of the results of this process is an essential role to be performed by the QM.

Whatever decision management makes, it must be sure that all Quality Evaluation activities have been assigned to an organization competent to perform that function and, where independence is specified, to an organization with the proper detachment as well.

1.6   Example Organizational Implementations of a Quality Program

A major determinant as to how the Quality Program is to be implemented is the size of the organization. A small organization, comprised of a number of small projects, cannot implement the Quality Program in the same way that a large organization can. The next section examines some approaches that organizations have used in implementing a Quality Program. We also describe the implementation of the PEPG concept.

1.6.1   Project Engineering Process Group

Many companies have adopted the PEPG concept. It is an important factor in successful implementation of the second element of the Quality Program, *establish and implement methods*. The PEPG is typically the focal point for methodology selection and evaluation. This has come about with the recognition that it is difficult to begin the process improvement journey without a centralized function responsible for it, regardless of the application domain in which the organization specializes.

Fowler [14] describes strategies for the implementation of PEPGs into the organizational structure. Organizational size is taken into account in the strategies discussed. We refer you to that technical report for a more comprehensive discussion of the organizational considerations in forming a PEPG.

1.6.2   Quality Program Structures in Large Projects

1.6.2.1   Large Development Project

The easiest organization structure to describe is that which exists for large organizations producing engineering or scientific applications. Figure 1.8 illustrates an organization chart from an actual project, although somewhat disguised to protect the identity of the actual organization. In the figure, the acronym APM means assistant project manager. In this structure, the quality manager, or, in this case, the project quality manager (PQM), as this person was called, was responsible for planning the performance of the Quality Program and documenting the output of the planning effort in the appropriate plans, coordinating the activities of the performers of the Quality Program activities, and monitoring their performance to verify that they were being performed properly.

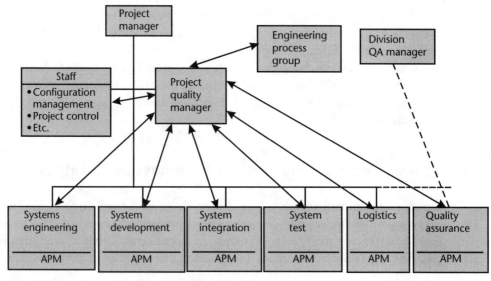

Figure 1.8   Example of a large project organization.

For the requirements element of the Quality Program, the organizations involved in the requirements definition effort included Systems Engineering, System Development, and Logistics. The Logistics organization participated in the definition of the maintainability and product supportability requirements for the operational product. In this structure, the PQM was responsible for coordinating and integrating the requirements definition activities of these areas of the project. The PQM, as can be seen from the figure, also coordinated with the configuration manager with regard to establishing the baseline for the requirements.

To establish and maintain the methodologies to be utilized on the project, the PQM coordinated with the EPG. The EPG was responsible for coordinating with the other organizations within the company with regard to establishing the methodologies in general usage and for determining their effectiveness. (Its position on the chart has no significance with respect to hierarchy or importance. Its position is only intended to show that, as an enterprise-wide resource, it was outside the organizational structure for the project.)

Product quality evaluation was performed by Quality Assurance, Product Test, System Integration and Test, and System Development. The PQM coordinated and monitored the performance of the product quality evaluation elements of the Quality Program. The functions that each organization performed in support of the quality evaluation element of the Quality Program were documented in the Product Quality Evaluation Plan (PQEP). Feedback of the evaluation results into the development, operations, and maintenance activities and products was provided for in the PQEP. The coordination and monitoring of the feedback process was another function performed by the PQM.

Because the PQM was a staff function to the project manager, he had a direct line of communication to him to ensure that all project staff members complied with the requirements of the Quality Program. In the event of a noncompliance that could not be resolved directly with the individual or organization involved, the PQM could call on the project manager to enforce compliance.

1.6.2.2   Integrated Product Team: A Special Case

Another organizational structure (shown in Figure 1.9) that has been effective is the integrated product team (IPT). This is sometimes used on large projects involving multiple contractors. Often, concurrent engineering is also involved. The intent of the IPT concept is to ensure effective communication of project-critical information between all members of the team, and all stakeholders involved in all aspects of the product life cycle. This is often accomplished through colocation of the team members. IPTs will often include customer representatives, prime contractors, and subcontractors to encourage rapid resolution of contractual issues, as well as speedy clarification of requirements-related questions.

IPTs may exist at various levels. For instance, in Figure 1.9, we see that IPTs exist at the system, segment, and subsystem level. Since a product exists at each of these levels, a PQM could exist at each level shown. For instance, one would exist at the space segment level, and one could likely exist for each one of the subsystems comprising the space segment. Furthermore, if the lower level subsystems were

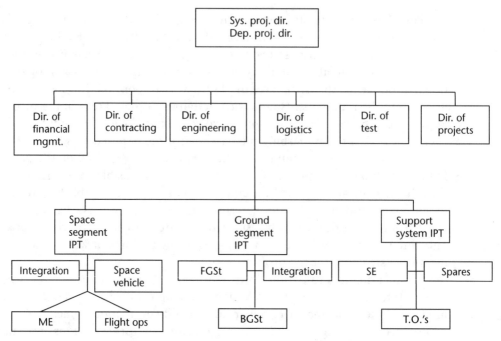

Figure 1.9 Example of a large project organization with IPTs.

sufficiently large and complex, IPTs could exist at lower levels. A PQM would be a member of each of these IPTs, as well, if each had a significant product component.

1.6.3   Quality Program Structures for Small Projects in Large Organizations

For small projects in large organizations, a PQM serves several small projects in a part-time capacity in each. For really small projects (three people or less), the project manager is undoubtedly performing some development roles, as well as the project management functions. In this case, the PM will be more dependent on a PQM to ensure that all the quality functions are being performed. Tailoring guidelines should exist to ensure that the Quality Program activities are commensurate with the size and criticality of the projects to avoid placing an onerous burden on the projects in complying with the Quality Program.

1.6.4   Quality Program Structures in Small Organizations with Small Projects

Small organizations face a totally different picture when it comes to implementing the elements of a Quality Program. In this situation, a number of conditions may exist. Two example situations are as follows: (1) the company is a one-project company, or (2) the company is working entirely on a number of small projects. Figure 1.10 is an example of how one IT department organized to implement the Quality Program. Again, the structure is somewhat disguised to protect the identity of the actual organization

Within the IT department, the IT standards committee fulfilled the function of the PEPG. It was comprised of key members of the department including the IT

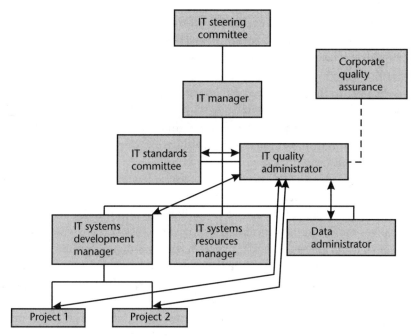

Figure 1.10   Example of a small IT organization.

quality administrator and representatives of the development, system resources, data administration, and configuration management areas of the department. Because of the size of the department, none of the members were assigned full time to the standards committee to do its work.

The IT quality administrator reported administratively to the IT manager, and was an employee of that department. By company policy, the IT quality administrator was deputized to act on behalf of corporate quality assurance to ensure that the provisions of the corporate Quality Program were carried out. The IT quality administrator had a responsibility to corporate quality assurance to provide periodic reports on the activities of the IT Quality Program. Note that in this case the quality administrator was not independent. The intent of independence was achieved, however, through a reporting channel to corporate quality assurance and periodic audits by corporate quality assurance to ensure that the provisions of the applicable policies and procedures were being correctly implemented.

In this structure, the IT quality administrator acted more as a coordinator and monitor with respect to the Quality Program functions. The responsibility for defining requirements was shared between the user community and the project. Requirements definition was performed in accordance with the procedures defined in the IT standards manual, and the individuals responsible for performing this task, the outputs they produced, the informal and formal reviews to be held, and the schedule for the entire activity were documented in the software development plan (SDP) for the project. The IT quality administrator monitored the activity to ensure that it was being performed as prescribed by the IT standards manual and the SDP. Any conflicts regarding implementation that could not be resolved directly with the development or user project leaders were raised to the IT systems development manager for resolution.

The responsibility for the methodology element of the Quality Program was vested in the IT standards committee. They performed the function of the PEPG. The IT quality administrator was a member of the IT standards committee and ensured that this function was being properly executed. The project-specific modifications, if applicable, to the standardized methodologies were documented in the SDP. Project-specific adaptations to the standards and procedures were also identified in the SDP. The IT quality administrator was a signatory party to the SDP, and consequently could coordinate and monitor the application of this aspect of the Quality Program for the project.

The QE element of the Quality Program was handled in a unique way by this company. The typical project size was approximately three to four developers. Because of the size of the entire organization, and the size of the projects, only two people—the IT quality administrator and one assistant—were dedicated full time to Quality Program tasks. Each project had their own part-time quality evaluator, and this person was also a part-time developer. He or she was responsible for performing the quality evaluations. Where necessary, the quality evaluators could call on other resources elsewhere within the IT department or within the affected user community to assist in the quality evaluations. For instance, in performing a quality evaluation of a requirements specification for a payroll program, the quality evaluator could call on personnel within the accounting department to assist in the review of a document.

The results of each evaluation were documented on a quality evaluation record. These were entered into a log and into a database. Both were available online. A major function performed by the IT quality administrator was auditing each individual project for compliance with the software quality evaluation plan (SQEP) and the standards and procedures specific to QE contained in the IT standards manual. Since the SQEP contained the definition of the QE tasks to be performed, the person responsible for performing it, and the schedule for its performance, the IT quality administrator could use it to determine when to perform the audits. The database was queried to determine if a record existed of a given evaluation's performance. The IT quality administrator had the authority to review the record and spot check the product itself to ensure that the review was performed in accordance with the approved procedures. The IT quality administrator could also participate in a review performed on an activity or product.

Another responsibility assigned to the IT quality administrator was the audit of the configuration management functions. The configuration management functions were distributed to various projects. The development baseline was under the control of the development project leader, which resulted in another interface with the project leader, and the production baseline was under the control of the IT software configuration control board, which was chaired by the IT manager. Changes to the applications product, corporate and project data dictionaries, and databases were handled by the librarian, data administrator, and database administrator, respectively, and their functions were audited by the IT quality administrator.

Audits performed on the IT area by corporate quality assurance determined if these functions were being properly performed by the IT quality administrator. Other related methods for small projects are covered in Chapter 12.

1.7   Summary

In organizing to implement a Quality Program, several concepts must be kept in mind.

First, it must be emphasized that the foundation for the organization is tied to achieving the requisite product quality. One must understand what product quality is and the technical aspects of specifying, developing, and evaluating it. Product quality is achieved with proper product design and implementing appropriate processes and methodologies. Quality cannot be achieved by "assuring" and "testing" the product.

Second, the ideas associated with product quality lead to the Quality Program. General principles of such a program have been discussed. Three elements of the Quality Program were described in some detail; these elements interact not only with each other but also with all other project activities. This interaction is extremely complex, occurring at many levels within the development project and throughout a project's life.

From the perspective of the Quality Program, an organization can be derived based upon corporate structure (controlling policies) and available talent. It is recommended that the project manager be allowed to structure his or her own project organization without the restriction caused by a priori corporate organizations. The project manager needs to recognize and understand the Quality Program. Given this understanding, the project manager allocates tasks of the Quality Program to those with appropriate talent. Because of its broad nature, the Quality Program requires a range of disciplines including product engineering as well as evaluation expertise. It is recommended that a quality manager be appointed who is steeped in this expertise and in the methodologies needed to achieve product quality.

References

[1]   Baker, E. R., and M. J. Fisher, "A Software Quality Framework," *Concepts—The Journal of Defense Systems Acquisition Management*, Vol. 5, No. 4, Autumn 1982.

[2]   Humphrey, W. S., "A Software Process Maturity Model," *IEEE Software*, Vol. 10, No. 4, July 1987.

[3]   Paulk, M. C., et al., *The Capability Maturity Model: Guidelines for Improving the Software Process*, Reading, MA: Addison-Wesley, 1995.

[4]   Chrissis, M. B., M. Konrad, and S. Shrum, *CMMI®: Guidelines for Process Integration and Product Improvement*, 2nd ed., Reading, MA: Addison-Wesley, 2006.

[5]   Cooper, J., and M. Fisher, (eds.), Software Acquisition Capability Maturity Model (SA-CMM®) Version 1.03 (CMU/SEI-2002-TR-010, ADA399794), Pittsburgh: Software Engineering Institute, Carnegie Mellon University, 2002, available at http://www.sei.cmu.edu/publications/documents/02.reports/02tr010.html.

[6]   Kenett, R. S., and E. R. Baker, *Software Process Quality: Management and Control*, New York: Marcel Dekker, 1999.

[7]   Fenton, N. E., and R. Whitty, "Introduction," in *Software Quality Assurance and Measurement, A Worldwide Perspective*, N. Fenton, R. Whitty, and Y. Iizuka, (eds.), London, U.K.: International Thomson Computer Press, 1995.

[8]   Melton, A., *Software Measurement*, New York: International Thomson Computer Press, 1996.

[9]   Baker, E. R., and M. J. Fisher, "A Software Quality Framework," *Fourth International Conference of the Israel Society for Quality Assurance*, Herzliyah, Israel, October 18–20, 1982.

[10] Voas, J., "Software's Secret Sauce: The –ilities," *IEEE Software*, November/December 2004.

[11] Baker, E. R., and M. J. Fisher, "Organizational Aspects of the Software Quality Program," in *The Handbook of Software Quality Assurance*, 3rd ed., G. G. Schulmeyer and J. I. McManus, (eds.), Upper Saddle River, NJ: Prentice-Hall, 1999.

[12] Members of the Assessment Method Integrated Team, Standard CMMI® Appraisal Method for Process Improvement (SCAMPI^{SM}), Version 1.1: Method Definition Document (CMU/SEI-2001-HB-001, ADA3399204), Pittsburgh, PA: Software Engineering Institute, Carnegie Mellon University, 2001, available at http://www.sei.cmu.edu/publications/documents/01.reports/01hb001.html.

[13] Schulmeyer, G. G., "Software Quality Lessons from the Quality Experts," in *The Handbook of Software Quality Assurance*, 3rd ed., G. G. Schulmeyer and J. I. McManus, (eds.), Upper Saddle River, NJ: Prentice-Hall, 1999.

[14] Fowler, P., and S. Rifkin, "Software Engineering Process Group Guide," Pittsburgh, PA: Software Engineering Institute, CMU/SEI-90-TR-24, September 1990.

## CHAPTER 2

Software Quality Lessons Learned from the Quality Experts

G. Gordon Schulmeyer

Quality is never an accident; it is always the result of intelligent effort.
—John Ruskin

2.1 Introduction

Those personnel performing development quality assurance need to apply the teachings of the quality experts. What important lessons learned in the recent past are the eminent quality experts telling us? The results achieved worldwide by following the lead of significant quality thinkers mandate that we in product development should follow that lead.

The principles of the quality experts have generally been applied to manufacturing, and less frequently to product development. The issue of applying another person's approach (i.e., the experts) to a different problem (i.e., product development) should be addressed. The generic nature of "quality" production is applicable whether the product is automobiles, stereos, computer software, or entire systems development.

Although production lines (that are machine intensive, repetitive, and result in many units) and computer software (that are people intensive, intellectual, and result in one software system) do differ; the transference of the quality principles described below from one to the other is reasonable. A fundamental principle is learning from other people's experience, and so the product development and development quality assurance (including software) personnel may learn from the quality principles covered in this chapter.

This chapter looks to the works of Kaoru Ishikawa, Joseph M. Juran, Yoji Akao, W. Edwards Deming, Genichi Taguchi, Shigeo Shingo, Philip Crosby, and Watts Humphrey. Certainly, in the United States the trio of Deming, Juran, and Crosby are the real leaders [1]. This trio of gurus seems to agree on certain basic points. They believe that until top management gets permanently involved in quality, nothing will work. They set little store in robots, automation, and other gadgetry. They have little use for quality circles except as an adjunct to other methods [2]. The fundamental message of all three gurus is basically the same: Commit to quality improvement throughout your entire organization. Attack the system rather than the employee. Strip down the work process—whether it be the manufacturing of a product or customer service—to find and eliminate problems that prevent quality. Identify your customer, internal or external, and satisfy that customer's requirements in the work process and the finished product. Eliminate waste, instill pride and teamwork, and create an atmosphere of innovation for continued and permanent quality improvement [3].

The impact of Watts Humphrey on software quality, development quality, and the Capability Maturity Model® has been great. His influence in the United States initially, and ultimately worldwide, for quality product development has been immense. This chapter highlights some major points from these U.S. quality experts and their Japanese counterparts with conclusions applicable to product development.

The work of these contributors each contain important quality messages, which have been applied to product development. Typically, quality applications to product development have been supplied by product (i.e., software) specialists. However, the concepts available that address quality production must now be used for the production of quality products containing software. The definition of "quality," more narrow than "fitness for use," is that supplied by Philip Crosby, which is "conformance to requirements" [4]. The logical extension of that definition to software quality is "to conform to software requirements and to provide useful services" [5] ("the fitness for use of the software product").

First, we look to Japan with the six major features of quality as seen by Kaoru Ishikawa. Second we discuss Joseph M. Juran's three ways to meet the quality challenge. This is followed by a look at Quality Function Deployment (QFD), commonly called the *House of Quality*, of Dr. Yoji Akao, as applied to software by Dr. Tadashi Yoshizawa.

Then, we review the statistical methods to achieve quality control provided by W. Edwards Deming, along with an application of his 14 points to software development. The goal of reduced variability in production, as described by Genichi Taguchi, through online quality control and off-line quality control is covered. The zero quality control methods of Shigeo Shingo with source inspections and the *poka-yoke* system are applied to software development. The implementation concepts successfully incorporated at International Telephone & Telegraph (ITT) by Philip Crosby are discussed. Finally, specific extensions from Crosby made by Watts S. Humphrey to software development with a Capability Maturity Model® (CMM®) are covered.

A lesson learned from the Japanese devotion to quality is that Toyota has become the largest automobile seller in the United States, overtaking General Motors. This point illustrates the impact of quality taught by the experts. Japanese companies, originally behind Western companies in quality, took heed of the quality concepts and principles proposed by the quality experts. Western companies were previously the quality leader, but they have ignored the quality concepts and have fallen behind.

For software in the twenty-first century, Western companies (led by those in the United States) have a relative superior position in software quality, similar to that which existed in the 1960s for overall product quality. But, it is relevant to note that

India today has about 35% of the world's CMMI®. The point of this chapter is that as costs and the importance of product development (including software) increases through the years, the Western world does not want to experience a duplication of the relative product quality loss in software quality. Therefore, to remain competitive, the product development (including software) community must heed the warnings from the past and follow the advice of the quality experts.

2.2   Kaoru Ishikawa

To explain the quality "miracle" in Japan, Kaoru Ishikawa offers six features of quality work there [6]:

- Company-wide quality control;
- Top management quality control audit;
- Industrial education and training;
- Quality Circles activities;
- Application of statistical methods;
- Nationwide quality control promotion activities.

Company-wide quality control means that all departments and all levels of personnel are engaged in systematic work guided by written quality policies from upper management. The consequences of this point to software quality are that the software developers are committed to producing a quality product and are guided by software development management (upper management) trying to achieve the same objective. This is how to build quality into the software product.

Ishikawa recommends that a quality control audit team of executives visits each department to uncover and eliminate any obstacles to the productivity and quality goals. This recommendation comes from the belief that the executives are in a position to make corrective action happen quickly and thoroughly. Normally this auditing of software is placed in the hands of the software quality experts, but with the backing of executives, such as happens with a sponsor to a CMMI®-based SCAMPI^SM appraisal. Such appraisals report findings to executives (especially the sponsor) that result in executive attention to the matter of correcting the findings, as necessary.

Education and training in quality control must be given to everybody in all departments at each level, because company-wide quality control requires participation by everyone involved. The initial training has to take place within the development quality assurance organization so that development quality personnel, per Kaoru Ishikawa's advice, will "train ourselves before we are fit to train others." Then, the quality organization can provide a concentrated, intensive development quality training program to be attended by product developers and their managers. This is a necessary, but not sufficient, way to develop quality products that include software. Education about how to develop "quality" products solidifies the awareness and discipline necessary for meeting that objective. The teachers in this arena should be the development quality personnel who also carry out the evaluation functions on a daily basis. Having development quality personnel as the teachers brings uniformity to the effort by providing knowledge common to all quality development.

A Quality Circle (QC) is "a small group [which met] voluntarily to perform quality control within the workshop to which they belonged" [7]. QCs originated in Japan in the early 1960s as part of a drive for quality and a critical economic need to overcome a reputation for cheap, poorly made goods. W. Edwards Deming and J. M. Juran introduced the concepts of statistical quality control and quality management to the Japanese. Dr. Ishikawa, merging these two disciplines, created a system called *quality control circles*. In 1961, a series of exploratory meetings were sponsored by the Union of Japanese Scientists and Engineers (JUSE) under the leadership of Dr. Ishikawa, an engineering professor at the University of Tokyo. The objective was to develop a way for hands-on workers to contribute to the company. In 1962, the first circle was registered with JUSE, and a total of 20 circles were registered and operating by the end of the year. Since that time, QC techniques have been taught to and applied by the entire Japanese work force. Today, there are an estimated 1 million Quality Circles in Japan with more than 10 million members [8].

The QC has traditionally been applied to the manufacturing process, and has recently been used to enhance some management and professional (engineering) quality. The product developers could use the QC as another tool to guide the production of quality product. The QC provides a forum to discuss product production problems.

The QC frequently uses Ishikawa diagrams to highlight influential factors. Ishikawa diagrams are usually drawn to identify control points; the ingredients include people, materials, machines, organization, and processes [9]. Using Ishikawa's "fishbone" cause-and-effect diagram provides a useful tool to find the specific cause(s) of the software production problem(s) and the resolution(s) to it (them).

A sample Ishikawa diagram is shown (Figure 2.1) that explores the possible causes of a slipped software development schedule. Each of the probable causes is written onto the fishbone in relation to the major control points of Manpower, Machines, Methods, and Materials (the 4 Ms). The group then reviews all the possible causes in detail to determine the most likely ones. Those that are most likely are circled and receive the appropriate attention. In the sample, "insufficient development computers" is the most likely cause of software development being behind schedule.

Statistical methods for quality control include the Pareto analysis, cause-and-effect diagram, stratification, check sheet, histogram, scatter diagram, and the Shewhart control chart. Thomas McCabe has advocated the use of Pareto analysis to software quality techniques that are further explored in Chapter 6. Suffice it to say that these various statistical concepts were so influential in Japan through the guidance of W. Edwards Deming that they brought about Japan's "quality revolution." Each of these statistical methods may provide help to the product developer, and a few are explored in Section 2.5, on W. E. Deming. Since the details of these methods are sufficiently covered in various textbooks, they are not covered here.

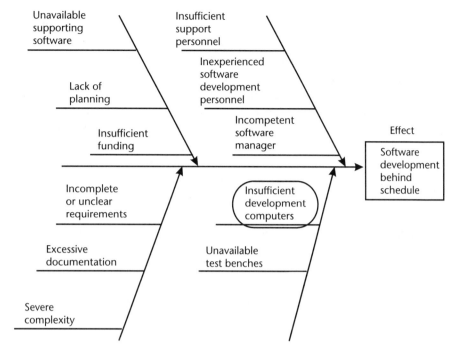

Figure 2.1   Sample Ishikawa diagram.

Nationwide quality promotion activities reach their peak in Japan in November (Quality Month) when the Deming Prize is awarded. The Deming Prize is used to advertise the company's products because it instills such a high degree of customer confidence that the consumer can be sure of a quality product. In the United States, quality interest in product development is stimulated with the IEEE Computer Society/SEI Software Process Achievement Award. It is an annual award given by the IEEE Computer Society and the SEI to recognize outstanding achievement in improving an organization's ability to create and evolve software-dependent systems. In addition to rewarding excellence, the purpose of this award is to foster continuous advancement in the practice of software engineering and to disseminate insights, experiences, and proven practices throughout the relevant research and practitioner communities. Why not also stimulate quality interest more locally by providing incentives in contracts for measurable product development that involves software quality achievements? These types of awareness continually reinforce the quality concepts for product and software developers.

2.3   Joseph M. Juran

To meet the challenges of solid quality achievement, Joseph M. Juran prescribes the following [10]:

- Structured annual improvements in quality;
- A massive quality-oriented training program;
- Upper management leadership of the company's approach to product quality.

In the early 1950s the Japanese faced a grim reality; no alarm signal is as insistent to industrial managers as the inability to sell the product. Since their major limitation was quality, not price, they directed their revolution at improving quality. They learned how to improve quality and became proficient at it, and they are now reaping the rewards of their efforts. Their managers are equally at home in meeting current goals and in making improvements for the future [10]. The story of the Japanese electronics industry, with transistor radios, for example, illustrates the dedication to annual improvements in quality that exists in Japan.

There is a grim reality in product development involving software that quality needs immediate attention and can stand improvement yearly. Too many software-intensive systems never meet their requirements, either because development overruns financial or time budgets, or because the user is unsatisfied. Product management must plan for and make this same total commitment to quality product improvements from within. Now, software managers of software-intensive product developments must not only be technically aware, but they also need to be committed to annual improvements in quality.

To accomplish these annual quality improvements, Joseph M. Juran advises that a team [10]:

1. Study the symptoms of the defects and failures;
2. Develop a theory on the causes of these symptoms;
3. Test the theory until the cause(s) is known;
4. Stimulate remedial action by the appropriate department(s).

Defects can be separated into those that are worker-controllable and those that are management-controllable. The latter are defects that cannot possibly be avoided by workers. Whether a certain defect should be regarded as a worker-controllable defect or a management-controllable defect depends on the extent to which the following conditions are met:

1. The worker knows what he or she is to do.
2. The worker knows the result of his own work.
3. The worker has the means of controlling the result.

If all three conditions are met and the work is still defective, the worker is responsible. However, if one or more of the conditions have not been met, this is a management-controllable defect [11].

W. Edwards Deming makes two relevant points on the responsibility for defects that apply to product development (substitute "product developer" for "worker") [12]:

To call to the attention of a worker a careless act, in a climate of general carelessness, is a waste of time and can only generate hard feelings, because the condition of general carelessness belongs to everybody and is the fault of management, not of any one worker, nor of all workers.

Many managers assume they have solved all the problems once they have brought worker-controllable defects under control, when, in fact, they are just ready to tackle the most important problems of variation, namely, the management-controllable causes [13].

During software-intensive product development many worker-controllable defects can be controlled by software developers. However, there is a wide class of defects in software because the developer does not know what he/she is supposed to do. This occurs because of the inevitable intertwining of specification and implementation. In other words, the problems are that during the software development (the implementation), the requirements (the specification) are continually being changed. Many times the software developer is continually "engineering" something new, without the benefit of "frozen" requirements.

Contrary to claims that the specification should be completed before implementation begins (the idea that "the worker knows what he is supposed to do"), there are two observations that the two processes must be intertwined. First, limitations of available implementation technology may force a specification change. That is, the hardware hosting the computer software may require software workarounds because of hardware limitations. Second, implementation choices may suggest augmentations to the original specification. That is, as more is accomplished, more is learned, making it reasonable to augment with a better approach than what was originally specified.

Only because the already-fixed and yet-to-be-done portions of this multistep system development process have occurred unobserved and unrecorded, the multistep nature of this process has not been more apparent [14]. This is especially true of the large software development for prototype (unprecedented) systems where the entire system is pushing hardware and software technology. In most of these systems the hardware does not even exist to test the software, but is under concurrent development with the software.

In software development, that "the worker (software developer) knows the result of his own work" is very immediate, and sometimes humbling for the worker who made a stupid mistake, for he or she receives results immediately from the computer *exactly* as he or she commanded, whether correctly or incorrectly. On the other hand, there are the subtle errors that are not found for years. This is a worker-controllable defect, but one where "the worker does not know the result of his/her own work." Quality software development must continually resolve to remove this type of error.

In software development "the worker has the means of influencing the result." Assuming a reasonable task assignment, the worker is directly involved in the production of the result (computer program) and is the first to see that result. Consider as one example a situation where the worker looses that influence, say, when the computer is unavailable. It is usually not worker-controllable to make the computer available.

To summarize this discussion of the annual quality improvements suggested by Joseph M. Juran, it is clear that software developers must first know where they stand before setting up the program for improvement. In this specialty area of product development, to know where one stands from a quality viewpoint is essential. The only way to know where one stands from a quality viewpoint is that the defects (errors) must be identified and the causes determined. Only when this is accomplished is movement toward quality improvement possible.

Most recently, selective training in quality sciences in Western companies has been largely confined to members of the specialized quality departments, which constitute only about 5% of the managerial and specialists forces in various companies. In contrast, the Japanese have trained close to 100% of their managers and specialists in the quality sciences.

This massive quality-oriented training program carries the education and training nostrum of Kaoru Ishikawa to its logical conclusion. Joseph M. Juran points out that common quality training needs to include [10]:

1. The universal sequence of events for improving quality and reducing quality-related costs (creation of beneficial change);
2. The universal feedback loop for control (prevention of adverse change);
3. Fundamentals of data collection and analysis.

Particular training for software developers in quality disciplines should include design reviews, reliability analysis, maintainability analysis, failure modes and effects analysis, life-cycle costing, quality cost analysis, and concepts of inspection for design and code.

An example of Japanese upper management commitment to quality is the observation made by Lennart Sandholm to the International Quality Control Conference held in Tokyo. Almost half of the Japanese participants at the conference were from upper management—presidents, general managers, division heads, and directors. At conferences held in Europe or the United States, almost all participants are from the quality profession—quality assurance engineers, reliability engineers, and quality managers—and there are only a few upper managers in attendance [15].

W. Edwards Deming also observed that in Japan top people in the companies took charge of the problems of production and quality. All the reports showing successful implementation of quality principles quoted in his paper were written by men with the position of president of the company, managing director, or chairman of the board [16].

Dr. Deming said, "All of top management came, not only to listen, but to work. They had already seen evidence from their own engineers that what you've got is this chain reaction. As you improve the quality, costs go down. You can lower the price. You capture the market with quality and price. Americans do not understand it. Americans think that as you improve quality, you increase your costs" [17].

The need for upper management leadership stems from the need to create major changes, two of which include annual improvements in quality and a massive quality oriented training program already discussed above. The recommended step for upper management in Western companies is to perform a comprehensive company-wide quality audit to understand what needs to be done.

An organizational weakness in Western companies is the large, central quality department with numerous functions of quality planning, engineering, coordination, auditing, inspection, and testing. In Japan, most of these quality-oriented functions are carried out by line personnel (who have the necessary training to carry out such functions). The Japanese do have quality departments, but they are small in terms of personnel and they perform a limited array of functions: broad planning, audit, and consulting services. Upper management quality audits evaluate the effectiveness of the organization and only upper management has the authority to institute the necessary changes. This principle of Dr. Juran's, again, is being performed when a sponsor (senior executive) commits to having a SCAMPI[SM] appraisal of the development processes.

For product development involving software, senior product development management is the upper management. The commitment, then, of senior product development management to producing quality products containing software is necessary to accomplish that objective. Also, taking this a step further, putting responsibility for software quality in the software development department is a correct posture for senior software management to enforce. The most obvious benefit of this posture is the close awareness of development quality brought to the various development organizations.

2.4   Yoji Akao

In the early 1970s, Dr. Yoji Akao performed the first applications of Quality Function Deployment (QFD) in Japan to address the issue of meeting all customer requirements—that is, making the customer happy. To accomplish this he devised a matrix of customer requirements versus technical product specifications; when portrayed, this matrix had a roof-like appearance, hence the popular name of "House of Quality." Shortly after Dr. Akao's development of the tools and techniques of QFD, Dr. Tadashi Yoshizawa applied QFD to software [18]. Software QFD is a front-end requirements solicitation technique, adaptable to any software engineering methodology, which quantifiably solicits and defines critical customer requirements [19].

With QFD, Dr. Yoji Akao provides a voice to the user. QFD should then provide views from three user, or customer, perspectives (known as Kano) [20]:

1. What the users can verbally express (normal requirements);
2. What they silently take for granted that they will get (expected requirements);
3. What the developers can anticipate will truly excite the users (exciting requirements).

QFD has the following benefits [20]:

• Increases user communication;
• Identifies critical success factors;
• Prioritizes user influence;
• Requirements traceability;
• Prioritizes features and functions;
• Reinforces front-end emphasis;
• Identifies release candidates;
• Provides basis for schedule reduction.

QFD is quite different from traditional quality systems, which aim at minimizing negative quality (such as defects). With these systems the best you can get is zero defects—which is not good enough. The absence of a negative does not make a positive. In addition to minimizing defects, we must also maximize positive quality—that is, value. Just because there is nothing wrong with the software does not mean there is anything right with it from the customer's perspective. It does not necessarily mean that it has any value to the customer [21].

Stephen Haag et al. [22] state that most of the problems in the software development process are associated with the specification of user requirements. When these user requirements are incorrect, incomplete, or inconsistent, this leads to significant budget overruns through increased programming and testing costs and product rework. Techniques must be implemented to facilitate correct specification of user requirements. QFD applied to software significantly helps with this. Implementing QFD will allow productivity increases to be realized, resulting in shorter systems development cycles. The findings for the use of QFD applied to software are summarized as follows [22]:

- Improves user involvement;
- Improves management support and involvement;
- Shortens the life cycle;
- Improves project development;
- Is a structured methodology;
- Supports team involvement;
- Structures communication processes;
- Provides a preventive tool for improving quality;
- Avoids loss of information.

It is significant that all of the organizations that utilize software QFD also use quality policies based on Total Quality Management (TQM) in other areas of the organization [23]. Although TQM seems passé to many today, it provided a basis for the original Capability Maturity Model® for Software from the Software Engineering Institute.

2.5   W. Edwards Deming

W. Edwards Deming is the guiding consultant for the application of statistical methods to quality control as laid out by Walter A. Shewhart. The Japanese Union of Scientists and Engineers (JUSE)'s Board of Directors established the Deming Prize to repay Deming for his friendship and kindness [24]. The namesake of the coveted annual Deming Prize in Japan has declared:

> [The] economic and social revolution, which took hold in Japan, upset in fifteen years the economy of the world, and shows what can be accomplished by serious study and adoption of statistical methods and statistical logic in industry, at all levels from the top downward.

The statistical control of quality is the application of statistical principles and techniques in all stages of production, maintenance, and service, directed toward the economic satisfaction of demand [25].

Statistics have been proven to have wide application in many different aspects of business, which would lead one to believe that there are many different statistical theories. However, Dr. Deming cleared up this point [13]:

> Rather than a separate and distinct theory for probability for process-control, another theory for acceptance sampling, another for reliability, another for problems of estimation, another for design of experiment, another for testing materials, another for design of studies for statistics, another for engineering, there is instead one statistical theory.

This statistical theory may be applied in many ways to software development. Some proven statistical methods for software are covered next.

This body of statistical knowledge has a variety of applications to the production of quality software. *An Introduction to Software Quality Control* by Chin-Kuei Cho [26] compares a statistical sampling method for testing of software to a statistical sampling method for manufactured products. It is usually impossible to test every input to a computer program. But by using Dr. Cho's sampling method, a broad range of input values previously never considered can be evaluated. This technique results in having a confidence value for when it is acceptable to complete testing of the software system.

The analysis of errors either for type of error or cause of error will help control errors. An accepted method of error analysis in software quality assurance is the use of the *inspection technique*. Both design and code error types are categorized in a post inspection analysis, which leads to a determination of the cause of the error. Don O'Neill covers the direction and details of this method in Chapter 7 of this book.

Observations made by W. Edwards Deming include the idea that you must build in quality. You must make the product so that it has quality in it, if you want quality. Quality is not built by making a great number of articles, hoping that some of them will be good, and then sorting out the bad ones. "Even 100 percent inspection using automatic testing machines doesn't guarantee quality. It's too late—the quality is already there" [27].

These remarks apply directly to the production of quality products involving software. The test and evaluation phase of product development is too late to retrofit quality into the product. The product has to be built with quality foremost from the beginning.

In addition to the statistical knowledge, W. Edwards Deming professes that everyone should learn a common method of attacking and describing problems. This commonality of method is essential if people from different parts of the company are to work together on quality improvement. The method is referred to as the P-D-C-A approach (Plan-Do-Check-Analyze and Act), and is usually represented as the Deming Circle (see Figure 2.2).

When the company president visits the various operations of the company to discuss their respective performance, he or she comes prepared to discuss intelligently how well each operation is doing and what can be done to improve the

"Plan-Do-Check-Analysis/Act"

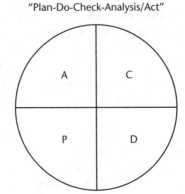

Figure 2.2   The Deming Circle.

system by reading the P-D-C-A information ahead of time. This approach should be contrasted with the usual "management by exception" approach, under which, when things go wrong, the manager then tries to figure out what is wrong and what to do about it [6].

A significant step can be taken when senior management use the Deming Circle in conjunction with the product development cycle so that each development phase is subject to the P-D-C-A approach. This method focuses attention as the development proceeds and so allows time to "Act" when required.

This Deming Circle has been used by the SEI as a model for a method for continuous process improvement. This model is called IDEAL[SM] and it provides a usable, understandable approach to continuous improvement by outlining the steps necessary to establish a successful improvement program. Following the phases, activities, and principles of the IDEAL[SM] model has proven beneficial in many improvement efforts. The model provides a disciplined engineering approach for improvement, focuses on managing the improvement program, and establishes the foundation for a long-term improvement strategy. The model consists of five phases [28][1]:

1. *I—Initiating:* Laying the groundwork for a successful improvement effort;
2. *D—Diagnosing:* Determining where you are relative to where you want to be;
3. *E—Establishing:* Planning the specifics of how you will reach your destination;
4. *A—Acting:* Doing the work according to the plan;
5. *L—Learning:* Learning from the experience and improving your ability to adopt new technologies in the future.

The quality approach of Deming is a management approach for continuous improvement of quality. Richard Zultner has adapted Deming's 14 points for management, seven deadly diseases, and obstacles to quality to software development. Table 2.1 contains the Fourteen Points for Software Development; Table 2.2

---

1.   Special permission to reproduce "The IDEAL[SM] Model: A Practical Guide for Improvement," © 1997 by Carnegie Mellon University, is granted by the Software Engineering Institute.

Table 2.1   The Fourteen Points for Software Managers

1. Create constancy of purpose for the *improvement* of systems and service, with the aim to become excellent, satisfy users, and provide jobs.

2. Adopt the new philosophy. We are in a new age of software engineering and project management. Software managers must awaken to the challenge, learn their responsibilities, and take on leadership for change.

3. Cease dependence on mass inspection (especially testing) to achieve quality. Reduce the need for inspection on a mass basis by building quality into the system in the first place. Inspection is not the answer. It is too late and unreliable—it does not produce quality.

4. End the practice of awarding business on price alone. *Minimize total cost.* Move toward a single supplier for any one item or service, making them a partner in a long-term relationship of loyalty and trust.

5. Constantly and forever improve the system development process, to improve quality and productivity, and thus constantly decrease the time and cost of systems. Improving quality is not a one time effort.

6. Institute training on the job. Everyone must be well trained, as knowledge is essential for improvement.

7. Institute leadership. It is a manger's job to help their people and their systems do a better job. Supervision of software managers is in need of an overhaul, as is supervision of professional staff.

8. Drive out fear, so that everyone may work effectively. Management should be held responsible for faults of the organization and environment.

9. Break down barriers between areas. *People must work as a team.* They must foresee and prevent problems during systems development and use.

10. Eliminate slogans, exhortations, and targets that ask for zero defects, and new levels of productivity. Slogans do not build quality systems.

11. Eliminate numerical quotas and goals. *Substitute leadership.* Quotas and goals (such as schedules) address numbers—not quality and methods.

12. Remove barriers to pride of workmanship. The responsibility of project managers must be changed from schedules to quality.

13. Institute a vigorous program of education and self-improvement *for everyone.* There must be a continuing training and education commitment to software managers and professional staff.

14. Put everyone to work to accomplish the transformation. The transformation is everyone's job. Every activity, job, and task is part of a process. Everyone has a part to play in improvement.

Source: [29].

Table 2.2   The Seven "Deadly Diseases" for Software Quality

1. Lack of constancy of purpose to plan systems that will satisfy users, keep software developers in demand, and provide jobs.

2. Emphasis on short-term schedules—short-term thinking (just the opposite of constancy of purpose toward improvement), fed by fear of cancellations and layoffs, kills quality.

3. Evaluation of performance, merit rating, and annual reviews—the effects of which are devastating on individuals, and therefore, quality.

4. Mobility of software professionals and managers. Job hopping makes constancy of purpose, and building organizational knowledge, very difficult.

5. Managing by "visible figures" alone—with little consideration of the figures that are unknown and unknowable.

6. Excessive personnel costs. Due to inefficient development procedures, stressful environment, and high turnover, software development person-hours are too high.

7. Excessive maintenance costs. Due to bad design, error ridden development, and poor maintenance practices, the total lifetime cost of software is enormous.

Source: [29].

contains the Seven "Deadly Diseases" for Software Managers; and Table 2.3 contains the Obstacles to Software Quality.

The following common principles drawn from Deming's 14 points are being applied in some excellent companies [30][2]:

1. Recognize the entire work force as thinking people, not just management, but everyone.

2. Encourage product developers to identify errors, propose solutions, and solve problems in the workplace. In other words, follow Dr. Deming's advice and *drive out fear*.

3. Promote teamwork by eliminating the us-versus-them attitude, such as, between developers and testers. In a typical organization, management and the employees are divided into two camps—stop that.

4. Make everyone a shareholder in the future of the company.

Table 2.3   The Obstacles to Software Quality

1. Hope for instant solutions. The only solution that works is knowledge, solidly applied, with determination and hard work.

2. The belief that new hardware or packages will transform software development. Quality (and productivity) comes from people, *not* fancy equipment and programs.

3. "Our problems are different." Software *quality* problems aren't unique—or uncommon.

4. Obsolescence in schools. Most universities don't teach software quality—just appraisal techniques.

5. Poor teaching of statistical methods. Many software groups don't have good statistical-oriented training in quality or project management.

6. "That's good enough—we don't have time to do better"—but time *will* be spent later to fix the errors. Doing the right things right the first time (and every time) is fastest.

7. "Our quality control people take care of all quality problems." Quality is management's responsibility, and cannot be delegated. Either management does it, or it does not happen.

8. "Our troubles lie entirely with the programmers." Who hired the programmers? Trained them (or not)? Manages them? Only management can do what must be done to improve.

9. False starts with quality (or productivity). Impatient managers who don't understand that quality is a long term proposition quickly lose interest.

10. "We installed quality control." Quality is a never-ending *daily* task of management. Achieve consistency (statistical control), then continuously improve.

11. The unmanned computer, such as a CASE package used without solid knowledge of software engineering.

12. The belief is only necessary to meet specifications. Just meeting specifications is not sufficient. Continue to improve consistency and reduce development time.

13. The fallacy of zero defects. Constant improvement doesn't end with zero defects (all specs met). The mere absence of defects is no guarantee of user satisfaction.

14. Inadequate testing of prototypes. The primary purpose of testing prototypes is to learn and then apply that knowledge to a robust production system.

15. "Anyone that comes to help us must understand all about our systems." Software managers may know all there is to know about their systems and software engineering, except how to improve.

Source: [29].

5. Establish "pride" in workmanship and products.

6. Concentrate on prevention.

Deming's fourth point states, "End the practice of awarding business on price tag alone." When awarding business based solely on the price tag, other important rules of nature, such as quality and schedule, are ignored. If consumers made every purchase based on the lowest price, they might soon go broke repairing and replacing piles of cheap, shoddy merchandise. As consumers, people consciously or subconsciously base their buying decisions on a trade-off between quality and price. Shouldn't the products containing software purchased by businesses and governments also be purchased based on such a trade-off [31]?

Dr. Deming says that it is a bad supposition that it is only necessary to meet specifications. For example, Zultner relates that a programmer learns, after she finishes the job, that she programmed very well the specifications as delivered to her, but that they were deficient. If she had only known the purpose of the program, she could have done it right for the purpose, even though the specifications were deficient [32].

2.6   Genichi Taguchi

Dr. Taguchi has been using and teaching methods to reduce variability at Bell Labs and throughout Japan, Taiwan, and India from 1955 through 1980. The Taguchi Method shows techniques for reducing variability in products and processes at the design stage, thus enhancing their ability to overcome the many uncontrollable changing conditions in production. In the United States these methods are taught by the American Supplier Institute, Inc., [33], which has given permission to use the material in this section.

Off-line quality control (Figure 2.3) attempts to reduce product or process variability by controlling noise factors and control factors. Noise factors are items categorized as outer noise (environmental conditions such as thermal, mechanical, electrical, customer misuse), and inner noise (deterioration such as wear and embrittlement, and piece to piece variation). Control factors are items categorized as follows:

• Increase robustness: change location and robustness;

• Adjust location: change location;

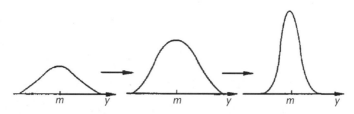

Figure 2.3 Off-line quality control. (*From:* [33]. © 1988 American Supplier Institute, Inc. Reprinted with permission.)

- Increase robustness: change robustness;
- Reduce cost: change neither.

The application of off-line quality control to product development involving software would place development variables under control factors. This applies the analogy to the software development process for the production of software units. The key control factors for software development are personnel, software tools, methodologies (i.e., object oriented design, structured analysis, structured programming), workstations, languages, database management systems, work areas, and desk layout. The measurement of these factors would be elements in the matrices resulting in signal to noise (S/N) ratios that would provide indications of what controls need to be applied.

Even after optimal production conditions have been determined, Dr. Taguchi says that the following remain:

- Variability in materials and purchased components;
- Process drift, tool wear, machine failure, and so on;
- Variability in execution;
- Measurement error;
- Human error.

These sources of variability are dealt with by quality control during normal production by online (real-time) quality control (Figure 2.4), which is truly feedback control. There are three online quality control techniques: (1) measurement and disposition, (2) prediction and correction, and (3) diagnosis and adjustment. *Measurement* is made on every product (100% is Taguchi's philosophy) and a *disposition* of deliver, scrap, or repair is made. To control variable quality characteristics in a production line, measurement is made every nth unit. From the measurement, the average quality of the next n units is *predicted*. If the predicted value deviates from a target value by more than specified limits, *corrective action* is taken by adjusting a controllable variable. A manufacturing process is *diagnosed* at a constant interval. When normal, production continues; otherwise, the cause of the abnormality is investigated, and *adjustment* to the abnormality is made.

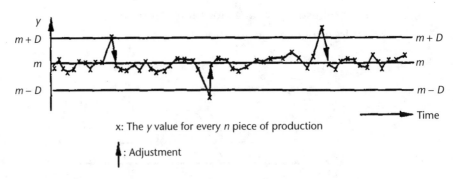

x: The y value for every n piece of production

: Adjustment

Figure 2.4 Online quality control. (*From:* [33]. © 1988 American Supplier Institute, Inc. Reprinted with permission.)

Online quality control applies to software development when a company has a defined, repeatable process. Such a process is subject to measurement, prediction and diagnosis. In fact, online quality control methods are exactly right to provide insight into how to constantly improve the process, as described for a Level 5 organization in the CMMI® for Development.

2.7 Shigeo Shingo

Much of the information in this section is from Dr. Shigeo Shingo's book, *Zero Quality Control: Source Inspections and the Poka-yoke System* [34], the English translation of which is copyrighted by Productivity, Inc., and is provided with the publisher's permission [35]:

> The title of this book refers to three critical and interrelated aspects of quality control. As taught by Shigeo Shingo, Zero Quality Control (Zero QC) is the ideal production system—one that does not manufacture any defects. To achieve this ideal, two things are necessary:
> *Poka-yoke* (in English, "mistake-proofing") looks at a defect, stops the production system, and gives immediate feedback so that we can get to the root cause of the problem and prevent it from happening again. *Source Inspections* looks at errors before they become defects and either stops the system for correction or automatically adjusts the error condition to prevent it from becoming a defect. Using *poka-yoke* devices and source inspection systems has enabled companies like Toyota Motors to virtually eliminate the need for statistical quality control (SQC), which has been the very heart of quality control in this country for years.

The author, in his book *Zero Defect Software* [36], has followed many of Shigeo Shingo's ideas as applied to software development. The primary elements of the zero defect software method are the software development process chart and its associated activities checklist, inspections and zero defects software checklists, *poka-yoke* (software tools) methods, and the importance of the concept of an internal and external customer.

Error prevention and detection techniques at predefined checkpoints are basic to the zero defect software method. In defining a zero defect software program, a distinction must be made between an "error" and a "defect."

An *error* is an unwanted condition or occurrence that arises during a software process and deviates from its specified requirement. A *defect* is that specific kind of unwanted condition or occurrence that has defied all attempts (inspections, reviews, walkthroughs, tests, and corrective action measures) to be eliminated during development and so is delivered to the customer.

Inspection methods are based on discovering errors in conditions that give rise to defects and performing feedback and action at the error stage so as to keep those errors from turning into defects, rather than stimulating feedback and action in response to defects. Every product, whether it be a document or work product of software development, has an informal review to check its integrity, which is the self-checking by the worker who produced it. This also takes place whenever a work product is updated, which happens frequently during software development. This is called source inspection.

If this work product is to be handed off to another, this is the time to get that other person—the internal customer—into the process. The receiver has a vested interest in what he or she is going to have to work with and so will be critically sure that this is a good product. This is called a successive inspection.

Jim McCarthy, while at Microsoft, described an inspection method inherent in the software development at Microsoft as follows [37]:

> The ratio is usually something like six developers, two or three QA people, one program manager, and two documentation people. The ratio varies all over Microsoft and will probably be slightly different for your team, too. But you are not going to get away with many more than two developers for every one QA person. The QA group is in charge of shipping the software. The first place we look when a product is late is QA. Are there enough of them? Are they adequately empowered? Did they get a vote on the design? Are they caught up with development, or are they lagging substantially? Do they raise red flags promptly and efficiently? Are their expectations being met? Are there dozens of small "contracts" or handshake dates between development and QA?

How is *poka-yoke* (mistake-proofing) applied to the zero defects software program? Throughout the process, software tools need to be incorporated to automate the process and the inspection thereof. These software tools will make the process more "mistake proof."

Inherent in the zero defect software program is the need for consistency. Checklists, as applied to products and processes, will reveal where consistency can be or (more importantly) needs to be stressed. When such consistency is desirable, new tools can be integrated into the process to reinforce the "expected" level of achievement [38].

2.8 Philip Crosby

The five maturing stages of uncertainty, awakening, enlightenment, wisdom, and certainty, through which quality management evolves, are shown in the Quality Management Maturity Grid (Table 2.4) developed by Philip Crosby in his book, *Quality is Free*. The measurement categories in the grid include management understanding and attitude, quality organization status, problem handling, cost of quality as a percent of sales, quality improvement actions, and a summation of company quality posture. Drawing upon the Quality Management Maturity Grid as a guide, the Software Quality Assurance Measurement Category is shown in Table 2.5. The quality maturity stages established by Philip Crosby are examined below in relation to the production of quality software.

In the stage of uncertainty there are a number of deeply rooted "facts" that "everybody knows" about software quality [4]:

1. Quality means goodness; it cannot be defined.
2. Because it cannot be defined, quality cannot be measured.

Table 2.4 Quality Management

Measurement Categories	Stage 1: Uncertainty	Stage 2: Awakening	Stage 3: Enlightenment	Stage 4: Wisdom	Stage 5: Certainty
Management understanding and attitude	No comprehension of quality as a managment tool. Tend to blame quality departments for "quality problems."	Recognizing that quality management may be of value but not willing to provide money or time to make it all happen.	While going through quality improvement program, learn more about quality management; becoming supportive and helpful.	Participating. Understand absolutes of quality management. Recognize their personal role in continuing emphasis.	Consider quality management an essential part of company system.
Quality organization status	Quality in hidden in manufacturing or engineering departments. Inspection probably not part of organization. Emphasis on appraisal or sorting.	A stronger quality leader is appointed but main emphasis is still on appraisal and moving the product. Still part of manufacturing or other.	Quality department reports to top management, all appraisal is incorporated and manager has role in management of company.	Quality manager is an officer of company; effective status reporting directors and preventive action. Involved with consumer affairs and special assignments.	Quality manager on board of prevention is main concern. Quality is a thought leader.
Problem handling	Problems are fought as they occur; no resolution; inadequate definition; lots of yelling and accusations.	Teams are set up to attack major problems. Long-range solutions are not solicited.	Corrective action communication established. Problems are faced openly and resolved in an orderly way.	Problems are identified earlier in their development. All functions are open to suggestion and improvement.	Except in the most unusual cases, problems are prevented.
Cost of quality as % of sales	Reported: unknown Actual: 20%	Reported: 3% Actual: 18%	Reported: 8% Actual: 12%	Reported: 6.5% Actual: 8%	Reported: 2.5% Actual: 2.5%
Quality improvement actions	No organized activities. No understanding of such activities.	Trying obvious "motivational" sort-range efforts.	Implementation of the 14-step program with thorough understanding and establishment of each step.	Continuing the 14-step* program and starting Make Certain* program.	Quality improvement program is a normal and continued activity.
Summation of company quality posture	"We don't know why we have problems with quality."	"Is it absolutely necessary to always have problems with quality?"	"Through management commitment and quality improvement we are identifying and resolving our problems."	"Defect prevention is a routine part of our operation."	"We know why we do not have problems with quality."

* Names of specific programs used to make a quality improvement.
Source: [4].

Table 2.5   Software Quality Management Maturity Grid

Measurement Category	Stage 1: Uncertainty	Stage 2: Awakening	Stage 3: Enlightenment	Stage 4: Wisdom	Stage 5: Certainty
Software quality assurance (SQA)	There are five quality "facts" that software development believes.	SQA is called upon in crisis situations.	The SQA Plan is written first as the "driver" to the software development effort.	SQA management and software development management are working together to produce quality software.	Quality software is produced on time within cost every time.

Source: [4].

3. The trouble with quality is that American workers don't give a damn.
4. Quality is fine, but we cannot afford it.
5. Data processing is different—error is inevitable.

Among software developers there will usually be agreement about these quality "facts," especially the inevitability of errors in software. Education is required to dispel these erroneous "facts," better identified as mind-sets.

When education is completed, there is usually lip service given to quality where people will say "yes" from their minds while they feel "no" in the pits of their stomachs. They will pay lip service to quality without really realizing it [39]. They will say they want quality but will continue to judge performance solely by schedule and budget.

There seems to be an implied assumption that the three goals of quality, cost, and schedule are all conflicting; all mutually exclusive. It is not true. Significant improvements in both cost and schedule can be achieved *as a result of focusing on quality* [40]. Fundamental to W. Edwards Deming teachings is that the only way to increase productivity and lower cost is to increase quality [9].

Often, it is company policy to supply exactly what a customer orders every time. This may seem too elementary to be important, but it *is* important. Remember that software quality is "to conform to requirements and to provide useful services" to the customer. Too often, companies place the emphasis on making the shipment, whether it's right or just close to right [41].

Some cost is incurred from the massive educational and procedural reworking effort that will be required. Each project will have to relearn what it really takes to achieve quality software production. To effectively increase quality, the SQA person has to get into the "barrel" with software development to see that the relearning takes place on every project.

In the *awakening stage* of software quality, the only times that SQA personnel are looked toward are times of crisis for the software development activity. One crisis during the awakening stage is customer assaults on the integrity of the software development activities. SQA personnel can contribute by acting as a buffer to absorb these assaults. Usually this takes the form of special intensive quality investigations into the software development resulting in a report to the customer. There is value to be gained by highlighting the quality perspective of the software development.

Another crises in software development is the software documentation trap. Software documentation is usually a deliverable item along with the computer programs, but due prior to the computer programs. Often the format and content requirements are so stringent that the computer programs are neglected to meet these documentation requirements. The SQA person is ultimately requested to perform a detailed software documentation audit, which leads to the establishment of a checklist that may quickly be fulfilled. The checklist makes it much easier for the software development team to meet the format requirements.

Philosophically, the *enlightenment stage* occurs when it is understood that SQA contributes in a meaningful way to the role of software development management. Quality goals and objectives must be established first as a matter of corporate policy and then must be enforced through management involvement, procedural policy, and universal commitment. In essence the quality role becomes a management role in which software quality principles and objectives are upheld at the start of the contract by software management, and development practices are driven by the quality objectives of those developing the software.

In the typical case of a product development project involving software, the requirements are imposed on the contractor to produce plans for product development and management, software development, software configuration management, and SQA. The usual organizational alignments are such that each of these plans is developed independently by project management, software development, configuration management, and SQA.

Because of this planning process, each organization has its job to do and goes on to do it. When organizational interactions are required to implement the plans, each of the organizational elements tolerates the activities of the others. Seemingly, the quality of the software under development is being assured by SQA personnel through their use of planned tools, techniques, and methodologies.

Contrary to the usual practice of writing the Software Development Plan before or concurrent with the SQA Plan, there is a strong case for requiring the SQA Plan to be written first. For software development to "build quality in," the Software Development Plan, written by and subscribed to by the software development team, must follow the concepts included in the SQA Plan.

The SQA Plan should be the first document written in a software development project. The SQA Plan has to tell more than the usual implementation auditing techniques. It must set the tone for those developing the software and espouse the quality principles inherent in producing quality software. These software quality principles may vary on different software development projects, so the particular software quality principles for this project are written into the SQA Plan.

With the "guidance system" in place for quality software, then software development can write the software development plan following the principles in the SQA Plan. Only in this manner can software development write a software development plan that has quality inherent in the product.

The *wisdom stage* occurs when it is realized that software quality can only be built-in. It must be the management objective of the software development management and software quality assurance management teams! Since software development management is responsible for making the decisions for planning the project, software quality assurance management must contribute to this up-front decision-making process. Software quality assurance personnel must be active participants in the entire software development effort.

Throughout the software development cycle the software development management can produce quality software and the software quality assurance management can ensure the quality of that product. As a result of putting increased emphasis on the *quality* of everything we do, we are beginning to realize some very significant gains—*as a result of*, not in place of or instead of other performance measures [19]. In software, often there is a subcontractor producing software that must integrate with the overall software system. By emphasizing the quality of that subcontractor provided software, the quality of the overall software system gains.

In the *certainty stage* the objective of development management and development quality management of producing quality products that include software on time within cost every time is possible. The guidance given by the quality experts as applied to the development of quality software in this chapter should help lead to this objective.

2.9 Watts S. Humphrey

Watts S. Humphrey, founder of the SEI Software Process Program and a fellow of the SEI, has been awarded the prestigious 2003 National Medal of Technology for his contributions to the software engineering community. The National Medal of Technology is the highest honor awarded by the President of the United States to America's leading innovators. A formal ceremony took place March 14, 2005, at the White House. Speaking as a recognized authority on software development and software quality, Watts Humphrey made these comments about software quality [42][3]:

> Software suppliers do not generally take responsibility for the defect content of their products. They often even ship products that contain known defects, and they commonly charge customers for a significant part of the costs of fixing these defective products. The public is increasingly aware of and unhappy with these practices. Software is routinely blamed for common problems in almost any industry that serves the public, and the public has come to expect software to perform badly.
>
> While today it may seem rational for the software industry to disclaim all responsibility for the quality of their products, this is tantamount to insisting that the market change before the industry will. This stance guarantees that when the market changes, as it must, the public must first be damaged. This will cause avoidable harm and discredit the present suppliers. Continuing with this strategy will mean that software quality will inevitably become a hot political issue.

At the start of his book, *Managing the Software Process*, Watts Humphrey states: "The framework used here ... roughly parallels the quality maturity structure defined by Crosby" [43]. (See Section 2.8.) This framework, of course, are the maturity levels in the CMM® for Software. The five maturing stages through which systems and software development evolve are as follows:

• Initial;
• Managed;

---

3.   Special permission to reproduce is granted by the Software Engineering Institute.

- Defined;
- Quantitatively managed;
- Optimizing.

Table 2.6 updates these maturity levels from the *CMMI® for Development* (CMMI®-DEV, v1.2), which was based upon the Capability Maturity Model® (CMM®) for Software that Watts Humphrey provided conceptual leadership for while at the SEI. For each of the process areas listed, such as Requirements Management, there are required goal(s) and associated specific and generic practices. The practices describe the activities that are expected to result in achievement of the goals of a process area. CMM® for Software became the generally accepted standard for assessing and improving software processes worldwide. Now, the CMMI®-DEV, v1.2 is becoming the standard for product development.

The CMM® for Software and its successors (e.g., CMMI®-DEV) have become the industry accepted standard for understanding the maturity of software development in many parts of the world. It is this incisive concept of Watts Humphrey that motivated his receiving the 2003 National Medal of Technology. The measured improvements in software development have arisen from the CMM® for Software and its successors (e.g., CMMI®-DEV) over the past few years.

Table 2.6   CMMI® for Development (v 1.2) Maturity Levels

[Category for that Process Area in the Continuous Representation] *{LEVEL 1—Initial}*
Ad hoc *{LEVEL 2—Managed}*
Requirements Management (REQM) [Engineering] Project Planning (PP) [Project Mgmt.] Project Monitoring and Control (PMC) [Project Mgmt.] Supplier Agreement Management (SAM) [Project Mgmt.] Measurement and Analysis (MA) [Support] Configuration Management (CM) [Support] Process and Product Quality Assurance (PPQA) [Support] *{LEVEL 3—Defined}*
Requirements Development (RD) [Engineering] Technical Solution (TS) [Engineering] Product Integration (PI) [Engineering] Verification (VER) [Engineering] Validation (VAL) [Engineering] Organizational Process Focus (OPF) [Process Mgmt.] Organizational Process Definition (OPD) + IPPD [Process Mgmt.] Organizational Training (OT) [Process Mgmt] Integrated Project Management (IPM) + IPPD [Project Mgmt.] Risk Management (RSKM) [Project Mgmt.] Decision Analysis and Resolution (DAR) [Support] *{LEVEL 4—Quantitatively Managed}*
Organizational Process Performance (OPP) [Process Mgmt.] Quantitative Project Management (QPM) [Project Mgmt.] *{LEVEL 5—Optimizing}*
Causal Analysis and Resolution (CAR) [Support] Organizational Innovation and Deployment (OID) [Process Mgmt.]

Source: [44].

Recognizing the benefits of the CMM® for Software, during the 1990s Watts Humphrey decided a method was needed to have those benefits accrue to individual and teams of software developer(s). So he defined the Personal Software Process (PSP^{SM}) and the Team Software Process (TSP^{SM}). The PSP^{SM} project was aimed at demonstrating that a CMM® process could be used by an individual to develop high-quality software without excessive process overhead. PSP^{SM} proved quite successful and TSP^{SM} was developed to provide a framework for applying PSP^{SM} in a team setting to develop high quality software (Figure 2.5). The two processes are licensed SEI technologies. They are almost always used together in a project setting [45]:

> The PSP^{SM} is an SEI technology that brings discipline to the practices of individual software engineers, dramatically improving product quality, increasing cost and schedule predictability, and reducing development cycle time for software.
>
> The TSP^{SM} is a complementary SEI technology that enables teams to develop software-intensive products more effectively. TSP^{SM} shows a team of engineers how to produce quality products for planned costs and on aggressive schedules.
>
> PSP^{SM} is a lightweight CMM® process designed for cost effective individual use. It

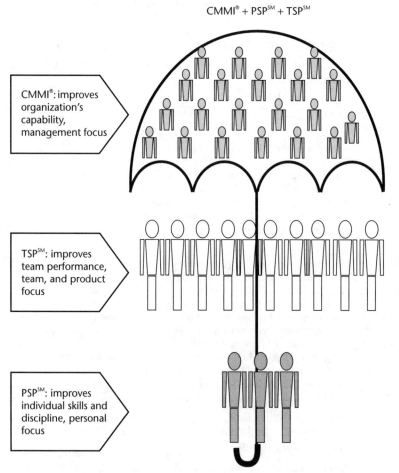

Figure 2.5 CMMI®, TSP^{SM} and PSP^{SM} relationships. (*From:* [46]. © 2000 Software Engineering Institute. Reprinted with permission.)

applies to most structured software development tasks including requirements definition, architecture design, module development, and documentation production. It
is capable of efficiently producing very high quality software products. There is no
cost overhead involved in achieving these high software quality levels. In fact, PSP^{SM}
projects are generally faster and cheaper than more conventional approaches to
software development.

   TSP^{SM} adds a project management layer to the PSP^{SM}. It helps engineers to produce
quality products for planned costs and on aggressive schedules. It addresses the
CMM® levels 2 and 3 management processes using high performance interdisciplin-
ary work teams. Engineers manage their own work and take ownership of their
plans and processes. TSP^{SM} helps the engineers to build a gelled, self-directed team
and to perform as effective team members. It shows management how to guide and
support these teams and how to maintain an environment that fosters high team
performance.

   PSP^{SM} augmented by TSP^{SM} can support the development of large-scale software
systems. It can be used to accelerate an organization from CMM® level 2 to level 5.
It provides an excellent foundation for application of six sigma statistical tools. It
does not require a high level of process maturity for introduction. CMM® level 1
organizations have used it very successfully.

   The SEI has provided a representation of the relationships among the CMMI®,
TSP^{SM}, and PSP^{SM} to highlight the goals and improvements provided by each.

   The SEI produced a technical report for those interested in both CMMI® and
the TSP^{SM} and in how these two technologies might be used together to accelerate
their process improvement efforts. Key to the report is Figure 2.6; it shows TSP^{SM}
practice coverage by process category in the CMMI®. This type of overview provides support to how well the technologies thought of by Watts Humphrey become
useful and complimentary within an organization.

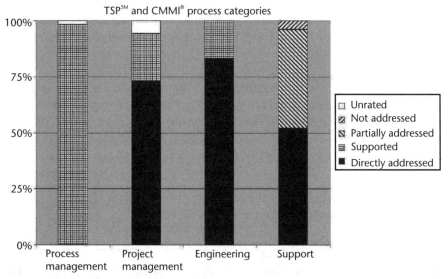

Figure 2.6   Summary of TSP^{SM} project practice coverage by process category. (*From:* [47]. © 2005
Software Engineering Institute. Reprinted with permission.)

2.10   Conclusion

This chapter applies the overall quality principles of leaders in the quality revolution to the specialty area of software and development quality. These principles lead to a philosophy about the application of what may appear to be remote principles to the reality of producing quality products involving software.

Kaoru Ishikawa has laid a quality framework of six features, each of which have applicability to development of quality software-intensive products. Joseph M. Juran's three methods for meeting the Japanese quality challenge all have applicability to the production of quality software-intensive products. The QFD concepts of Dr. Yoji Akao because of their focus on customer satisfaction also show applicability to software quality. Statistical methods and the Deming Circle taught by W. Edwards Deming have very specific application to software reliability and quality. Also, Dr. Deming's 14 Points are shown to be applicable to development of software-intensive products. The Taguchi Method of reduction in variability of production is applied to the production of software. Shigeo Shingo's zero quality control applies source inspection for the zero defect software methodology. Software quality can be shown as progressing through the five maturing stages of Philip Crosby's Quality Management Maturity Grid. Through the influence of Watts Humphrey, Crosby's Quality Management Maturity Grid morphed into the Capability Maturity Model® for Software.

These experts have been responsible for a revolution in world economics brought about by attention to quality. The state of computer software will improve significantly by applying these revolutionary quality principles to software-intensive product development. The groundwork has been surveyed in this chapter, but there is so much to learn and apply from each expert that it is hoped others will expand the scope of their work and apply their teachings to the quality of software-intensive product development. The key message from Juran, Deming, and others in the quality movement is that long-term improvement only comes about from systematic study and action, not from slogans or arbitrary objectives [48].

This chapter started with a quotation: "Quality is never an accident; it is always the result of intelligent effort," and so it concludes with a philosophical quotation from Robert Persig about the need to understanding quality in order to use it [49]:

> A real understanding of quality doesn't just serve the System, or even beat it or even escape it. A real understanding of quality *captures* the System, tames it and puts it to work for one's own personal use, while leaving one completely free to fulfill his inner destiny.

References

[1]   Oberle, J., "Quality Gurus: The Men and Their Message," *Training*, January 1990, p. 47.

[2]   Main, J., "Under the Spell of the Quality Gurus," *Fortune*, August 18, 1986, p. 30.

[3]   Oberle, J., "Quality Gurus: The Men and Their Message," *Training*, January 1990, p.48.

[4]   Crosby, P., *Quality Is Free*, New York: New American Library, reproduced with permission of The McGraw-Hill Company, 1979, pp. 32, 33.

[5] Tice, Jr., G. D. "Management Policy & Practices for Quality Software," *ASQC Quality Congress Transactions*, Boston, MA: Copyright American Society for Quality Control, Inc., 1983.

[6] Ishikawa, K., "Quality Control in Japan," *13th IAQ Meeting*, Kyoto, Japan, 1978.

[7] QC Circle Koryo, "General Principles of the QC Circles," Tokyo: Union of Japanese Scientists and Engineers (JUSE), 1980.

[8] Aubrey, II, C. A., and P. K. Felkins, *Teamwork: Involving People in Quality and Productivity Improvement*, New York: American Society for Quality Control, 1988, p. 5.

[9] Tribus, M., "Prize-Winning Japanese Firms' Quality Management Programs Pass Inspection," *AMA Forum, Management Review*, February 1984.

[10] Juran, J. M., "Product Quality—A Prescription for the West, Part I: Training and Improvement Programs," *Management Review*, June 1981; and "Product Quality—A Prescription for the West, Part II: Upper-Management Leadership and Employee Relations," *Management Review*, July 1981.

[11] Juran, J. M. "Quality Problems, Remedies and Nostrums," *Industrial Quality Control*, Vol. 22, No. 12, June 1966, pp. 647–653.

[12] Deming, W. E., "On Some Statistical Aids Toward Economic Production," *Interfaces*, Vol. 5, No. 4, August 1975, p. 8.

[13] Deming, W. E., "What Happened in Japan?" *Industrial Quality Control*, Vol. 24, No. 2, August 1967, p. 91.

[14] Swartout, W., and R. Balzer, "On the Inevitable Intertwining of Specification and Implementation," *Communications of the ACM*, Vol. 25, No. 7, July 1982, pp. 438–440.

[15] Sandholm, L., "Japanese Quality Circles—A Remedy for the West's Quality Problems?" *Quality Progress*, February 1983, pp. 20–23, Copyright American Society for Quality Control, Inc., Reprinted by permission.

[16] Deming, W. E., "My View of Quality Control in Japan," *Reports of Statistical Application Research, JUSE*, Vol. 22, No. 2, June 1975, p. 77.

[17] Gottlieb, D., "The Outlook Interview: W. Edwards Deming, U.S. Guru to Japanese Industry, Talks to Daniel Gottlieb," *The Washington Post*, January 15, 1984, p. D3.

[18] Zultner, R. E., *Quality Function Deployment (QFD) for Software*, Princeton: Zultner & Company, 1992, p. 1.

[19] Haag, S., M. K. Raja, and L. L. Schkade, "Quality Function Deployment: Usage in Software Development," *Communications of the ACM*, Vol. 39, No. 1, January 1996, p. 42.

[20] Zells, L., *Applying Japanese Total Quality Management to U.S. Software Engineering*, Washington D.C.: ACM Lecture Notes, 1991, pp. 51, 52.

[21] Zultner, R. E., *Quality Function Deployment (QFD) for Software*, Princeton, NJ: Zultner & Company, 1992, p. 2.

[22] Haag, S., M. Raja, and L. Schkade, "Quality Function Deployment (QFD) Usage in Software Development," *Communications of the ACM*, Vol. 39, No. 1, January 1996, p. 41.

[23] Haag, S., M. K. Raja, and L. L. Schkade, "Quality Function Deployment (QFD) Usage in Software Development," *Communications of the ACM*, Vol. 39, No. 1, January 1996, p. 45.

[24] Noguchi, J., "The Legacy of W. Edwards Deming," *Quality Progress*, December 1995, p. 37.

[25] Deming, W. E., "My View of Quality Control in Japan," *Reports of Statistical Application Research, JUSE*, Vol. 22, No. 2, June 1975, p. 73.

[26] Cho, C.-K., *An Introduction to Software Quality Control*, New York: John Wiley & Sons, 1980.

[27] Deming, W. E., "It Does Work," Reprinted with permission from *Quality*, August 1980, A Hitchcock publication, p. Q31.

[28] Gremba, J., and C. Myers, "The IDEAL℠ Model: A Practical Guide for Improvement," *Bridge*, Pittsburgh, PA: Software Engineering Institute, Issue 3, 1997, p. 8. Special permission to reproduce "The IDEAL℠ Model: A Practical Guide for Improvement," © 1997 by Carnegie Mellon University, is granted by the Software Engineering Institute.

[29] Zultner, R., "The Deming Way—A Guide to Software Quality," adapted by Richard Zultner, brochure from Zultner & Co., Princeton, NJ: Zultner & Co., 1988.

[30] Hansen, R. L., "An Overview to the Application of Total Quality Management," Aeronautical System's Division, U.S. Air Force, 1990, © 1990 IEEE, pp. 1465, 1466.

[31] Windham, J., "Implementing Deming's Fourth Point," *Quality Progress*, December 1995.

[32] Zultner, R., CQE, "SPC for Software Quality," *NSIA Software Quality Conference*, Alexandria, VA, 1989.

[33] *Taguchi Method One Day Seminar*, August 10, 1988, Dearborn, MI: American Supplier Institute, Inc., 38705 Seven Mile Road, Suite 345, Livonia, MI 48152, Tel: (734) 464-1395, (800) 462-4500, Fax: (734) 464-1399, all rights reserved, 1988.

[34] Shingo, S., *Zero Quality Control: Source Inspections and the Poka-yoke System*, Tokyo: Japan Management Association, 1985; English translation: Cambridge, MA: Productivity, Inc., 1986.

[35] Shingo, S., *Zero Quality Control: Source Inspections and the Poka-yoke System*, Tokyo: Japan Management Association, 1985; English translation: Cambridge, MA: Productivity, Inc., 1986, pp. v, vi.

[36] Schulmeyer, G. G., *Zero Defect Software*, New York: McGraw-Hill, 1990, p. 33.

[37] McCarthy, J., *Dynamics of Software Development*, Redmond, WA: Microsoft Press, 2006, p. 35. All rights reserved.

[38] Schulmeyer, G. G., *Zero Defect Software*, New York: McGraw-Hill, 1990, p. 38. Reproduced with permission.

[39] Burrill, C. W., and L. W. Ellsworth, *Quality Data Processing, The Profit Potential for the 80's*, Tenafly, NJ: Burrill-Ellsworth Associates, 1982, p. 176.

[40] Walter, C., "Management Commitment to Quality: Hewlett-Packard Company," *Quality Progress*, August 1983, p. 22.

[41] Turnbull, D., "The Manual—Why?" *Quality*, August 1980, p. Q5.

[42] Humphrey, W. S., "Comments on Software Quality," Pittsburgh, PA: Software Engineering Institute, Carnegie Mellon University, http://www.cs.queensu.ca/~cisc853/readings/papers/humphreyOnSW.pdf#search=%22watts%20s%20humphrey%22, December 2006. Special permission to reproduce is granted by the Software Engineering Institute.

[43] Humphrey, W., *Managing the Software Process*, Reading, MA: Addison-Wesley, 1989, p. 4.

[44] *Capability Maturity Model Integration® for Development*, version 1.2 (CMMI®-DEV, v1.2), CMU-SEI-2006-TR-008, Pittsburgh, PA: Carnegie Mellon University, August 2001.

[45] PS&J Software Six Sigma, "Personal Software Process & Team Software Process," http://www.softwaresixsigma.com/Tsp_Main_PspTsp.htm, December 2006.

[46] Humphrey, W., *The Team Software Process℠ (TSP℠)*, Technical Report CMU/SEI-2000-TR-023, Pittsburgh, PA: Software Engineering Institute, November 2000, p. 8. Special permission to use portions is granted by the Software Engineering Institute.

[47] McHale, J., and D. Wall, *Mapping TSP℠ to CMMI®*, CMU/SEI-2004-TR-014, Pittsburgh, PA: Software Engineering Institute, April 2005, p. 7. Special permission to use portions is granted by the Software Engineering Institute.

[48] Fowler, P., and S. Rifkin, *Software Engineering Process Group Guide*, Software Engineering Institute Technical Report CMU/SEI-90-TR-24, Pittsburgh, PA: Software Engineering Institute, September 1990, p. 95.

[49] Persig, R. M., *Zen and the Art of Motorcycle Maintenance*, New York: Bantam Books, 1974, p. 200.

## CHAPTER 3

Commercial and Governmental Standards for Use in Software Quality Assurance

Lewis Gray

Among all the software-related standards in the world, there are a few that every person who practices software quality assurance (SQA) should encounter at least once. Every SQA practitioner should know at least a little something about ISO standards, IEEE standards, and United States military standards. Those topics, and much more, are covered in this chapter.

Some important standards have SQA as their topic, but others do not. A standard that is mentioned in this chapter either describes something that an SQA person might have to do, or something that someone else would do that an SQA person might have to audit (and some standards do both). So, in addition to providing a list of important standards, this chapter also summarizes the content of each standard that it mentions.

The other thing that this chapter does is to explain what it takes to conform to each of the described standards (except for some military standards that are mentioned only for historical reasons). The most common SQA task is an audit of a product or a process against a standard, a contract, or a plan. An audit is useless, or worse, unless it is based on an understanding of what conformance to (or "compliance with") the standard, the contract, or the plan means.

The information in this chapter was accurate at the time it was written. But, when using this chapter with a particular standard on the job, it is a good idea to keep in mind that the standard may have evolved since this chapter was written.

3.1 SQA in ISO Standards

The International Organization for Standardization (ISO) is a nongovernmental organization that consists of the national standards institutes of more than 150 countries. Its Central Secretariat is located in Geneva, Switzerland. For more information about ISO, see its Web site [1].

ISO standards deserve first mention in this chapter because they have established an influential vocabulary and a conceptual framework for quality. They can be purchased online at http://webstore.ansi.org/ansidocstore/ and at http://www.iso.org/iso/en/prods-services/ISOstore/store.html.

3.1.1   ISO 9000:2005 and ISO 9001:2000

Although there are several standards within the ISO 9000 collection, two of them, ISO 9000:2005 [2] and ISO 9001:2000 [3], establish the vocabulary and the conceptual framework for the others. In this conceptual framework, quality assurance is accomplished as part of quality management.

ISO 9000:2005 defines the common vocabulary for the ISO 9000 family of documents.

ISO 9001:2000 puts the vocabulary in ISO 9000 to use in defining the conceptual framework and requirements for a quality management system. In clause 4, the standard defines general requirements, and the same clause includes requirements to prepare and control key quality management system documents, such as a quality manual.

In clause 5, ISO 9001:2000 defines management requirements, such as commitment, customer focus, a quality policy, planning, communication, and review responsibilities. Clause 6 of the standard defines requirements related to personnel competence and infrastructure.

In clause 7, the standard defines requirements related to developing and delivering the product. There are planning requirements, and requirements related to determining the customer's needs. There are requirements for design and development activities, and requirements related to acquisition—when components of the product are purchased. There are requirements related to delivering/providing the product. And there are requirements related to the control of monitoring and measuring devices.

Clause 8 of the standard defines requirements for measurement, analysis, and improvement processes. These include requirements for internal audit and for other monitoring and measurement. They also include requirements related to controlling nonconforming product.

In general, "conformity to ISO-9001" means conformity to all its requirements. However, requirements in clause 7 may be excluded in certain situations that the standard defines. A requirement of ISO:9001:2000 is expressed with the verb form "shall."

3.1.2   ISO/IEC 90003

To audit a quality management system for software products or services, ISO 9001 requirements must be mapped to software development management and technical practices. ISO/IEC 90003:2004 is the result of one approach to doing that [4].

ISO/IEC 90003:2004 is a product of a joint technical committee (JTC 1) that ISO and the International Electrotechnical Commission (IEC) have established in the field of information technology. For more information about IEC, see its Web site [5].

The body of ISO/IEC 90003:2004 follows that of ISO 9001:2000 from clause 1 through clause 8. In each clause, ISO/IEC 90003:2004 repeats the text in ISO 9001:2000 and adds clarifying content that is derived from other ISO standards. The clarifications of clause 7 (Product realization) and clause 8 (Measurement, analysis and improvement) are derived mostly from material in ISO/IEC12207 [6–8] and ISO/IEC 9126 [9–12], and they are detailed and very useful.

Conformance to ISO/IEC 90003:2004 is not defined, because there are no requirements in the standard.

3.1.3   ISO/IEC 2500n—ISO/IEC 2504n (SQuaRE)

SQuaRE means the collection of 14 ISO/IEC standards and technical reports that will carry the common name Software engineering–Software product Quality Requirements and Evaluation. SQuaRE documents fall into five divisions: Quality Management, Quality Model, Quality Measurement, Quality Requirements, and Quality Evaluation.

SQuaRE replaces the ISO/IEC 9126 series [9–12] and the ISO/IEC 14598 series [13–18]. However, at the time this chapter was written, only two SQuaRE standards had been released, in the Quality Management Division. The standards are ISO/IEC 25000:2005 [19] and ISO/IEC 25001:2007 [20].

ISO/IEC 25000:2005 is called the "Guide to SQuaRE." Clause 4 provides definitions for 64 terms, which will appear throughout the SQuaRE series of documents. In clause 5, the standard describes each document that is planned for the SQuaRE series. Clause 5 also defines a structure and a life cycle of software product quality, which will be common to all the SQuaRE documents. In Annex C, the standard provides guidance for users of the ISO/IEC 9126 series or the ISO/IEC 14598 series who must make a gradual transition to SQuaRE standards as they become available.

Conformance to SQuaRE as a whole is not defined; and conformance to ISO/IEC 25000:2005 is also not defined, because it does not contain requirements.

ISO/IEC 25001:2007 is a planning and management standard that may be used both at the project level and at a higher department or corporate level to create the management context for project-level product evaluation. In clause 4, the standard defines "evaluation activity," "evaluation group," and "evaluation technology." In clause 5, it explains the role of the evaluation group.

Clause 6 of the standard contains "requirements and recommendations for software quality requirements specification and quality evaluation." There are general requirements, and there are requirements of seven different kinds related to management at the organizational level. There are also requirements to plan an evaluation project, as well as requirements to collect and analyze the results of each evaluation project.

An organization can conform to ISO/IEC 25001:2007 either by satisfying the requirements in clause 6 and explaining any exclusion, or by providing its own recommendations for planning and managing software product quality requirements and evaluation, and mapping those recommendations to the requirements in clause 6.

3.1.4   ISO/IEC 14598 and ISO/IEC 15504

3.1.4.1   ISO/IEC 14598 [13–18]

ISO/IEC 14598 is a series of standards that jointly "give methods for measurement, assessment and evaluation of software product quality" [13].

ISO/IEC 14598-1 provides a foundation for the series by defining the basic vocabulary, and by explaining where the quality characteristics and metrics that are defined in ISO/IEC 9126 [9–12] will be used. It presents a generic, mandatory evaluation process that is elaborated in [15–17].

Conformance to the ISO/IEC 14598 series as a whole is defined to be "conformance to all applicable published parts" of the series [13]. Each of the standards in the series has its own conformance clause. Conformance to the ISO/IEC 14598-1 standard can be achieved by using the mandatory evaluation process that it defines and a quality model that meets the requirements in its clause 8.3.

ISO/IEC 14598-2 has been replaced by ISO/IEC 25001:2007.

ISO/IEC 14598-3 and ISO/IEC 14598-4 are written for use at the project level. ISO/IEC 14598-3 elaborates the generic evaluation process into a collection of requirements that developers fulfill by evaluating products as they are developed. In ISO/IEC 14598-4, the generic process is expanded into requirements for acquirers, for evaluating commercial off-the-shelf products, and requirements for evaluating custom software and modifications to software.

An organization can conform to ISO/IEC 14598-3 simply by reviewing all requirements in its clause 6 and then stating which of them (if any) the organization has not implemented. However, conformance to ISO/IEC 14598-4 is defined in terms of "compliance," and it is more complicated, because an acquirer organization that imposes the standard is required to specify an evaluation process publicly that, when it is followed, achieves compliance with the standard.

ISO/IEC 14598-5 is intended for use at the project level also. It is written for, "software suppliers, when planning evaluation of their products," "software acquirers, when requesting evaluation information from a supplier or testing service," "testing laboratory evaluators, when providing software product evaluation services," "software users...," and "certification bodies..." [17]. Conformance to ISO/IEC 14598-5 is like conformance to ISO/IEC 14598-4. An organization that imposes the standard is required to specify an evaluation process publicly that, when it is followed, achieves compliance with the standard.

ISO/IEC 14598-6 defines requirements for documenting an evaluation module. An evaluation module specifies the method and the data that will be used to evaluate a specific quality characteristic of a specific product. Conformance to ISO/IEC 14598-6 is achieved when an evaluation module meets the requirements of its clause 6.

3.1.4.2   ISO/IEC 15504 [21–25]

The ISO/IEC 15504 series is a complement to the ISO/IEC 14598 series. The topic of ISO/IEC 14598 is software product evaluation, and ISO/IEC 15504 "provides a structured approach for the assessment of processes..." [21]. ISO/IEC 15504 is a replacement for the older series of technical reports ISO/IEC TR 15504-1:1998 through ISO/IEC TR 15504-9:1998. The technical reports focused on software processes. However, in the standards that replace them, the focus has broadened to include all processes of any kind.

This series of standards is written for assessors, developers of process assessment models or methods, tool developers, assessment sponsors, sponsors of internal process improvements, and sponsors of initiatives to determine the capability of one or more supplier processes.

ISO/IEC 15504-1 introduces the vocabulary for the series, and explains the concepts that coordinate the requirements in ISO/IEC 15504-2. Two terms that are critical to understanding this series are "process reference model," which means a model that links life-cycle processes, each with its purpose and its outcomes described, together into an architecture of relations; and "process assessment model," which means a model that is based on one or more process reference models, that also incorporates capability levels, process attributes, and a rating scale that make it possible to assess the capability of a process.

ISO/IEC 15504-2, clause 4, states the requirements for performing an assessment. A specific process assessment is said to be in conformity to ISO/IEC 15504-2 if there is objective evidence that it conforms to all these requirements.

ISO/IEC 15504-2 also states the requirements that a process reference model must satisfy, and the requirements that a process assessment model must satisfy. A process reference model can be said to be in conformity to this standard if there is objective evidence that the model fulfills the requirements in clause 6.2. A process assessment model can be said be in conformity to ISO/IEC 15504-2 if there is objective evidence that it fulfills the requirements in clause 6.3.

Because this is the only standard in the ISO/IEC 15504 series that states requirements, conformity is defined only here.

The purpose of ISO/IEC 15504-3, aside from its short discussions about the competency of assessors and about selecting assessment tools, is to restate and explain the content of ISO/IEC 15504-2.

ISO/IEC 15504-4 reviews how a process assessment, as defined by ISO/IEC 15504-2, might be used in process improvement or to determine the capability of a potential supplier's processes before hiring the supplier as a contractor.

ISO/IEC 15504-5 provides a sample process assessment model that is based on ISO/IEC 12207.

3.1.5   ISO/IEC 9126

ISO/IEC 9126 [9–12] is a four-part series that defines a model of software product quality, and related metrics. ISO/IEC 9126 and ISO/IEC 14598 were written for joint use (and both of them will be replaced by SQuaRE). Within the software product evaluation process that ISO/IEC 14598 defines, there is a step to specify a quality model and another step to select metrics. ISO/IEC 9126 provides a suitable quality model, and an SQA auditor who chooses that model for an ISO/IEC 14598 assessment benefits immediately from the pool of related metrics in ISO/IEC 9126 from which the metrics for the assessment may be selected.

The model of software product quality in ISO/IEC 9126 rests on three concepts: internal quality (attributes of the product itself); external quality (attributes of the product when the product is executed in a system); and quality in use (the extent to which the product meets users' needs in specified situations).

ISO/IEC 9126-1 organizes the attributes of internal quality and external quality into six categories that it calls "characteristics." For each characteristic, the standard defines subgroups of attributes that it calls "subcharacteristics." In the same standard, the product attributes associated with quality in use are organized into four characteristics.

A software product quality requirement, specification, or evaluation can be said to conform to ISO/IEC 9126-1 if it uses the product characteristics and subcharacteristics that are in the standard (with an explanation of exclusions), or its own characteristics that are mapped to those in the standard.

Three parts of the ISO/IEC 9126 series are technical reports. ISO/IEC TR 9126-2 defines metrics for quantitative measurement of the subcharacteristics in ISO/IEC 9126-1 based on the behavior of the system in which the software product is a part. ISO/IEC TR 9126-3 defines metrics for measuring the subcharacteristics by measuring the product itself. ISO/IEC TR 9126-4 defines metrics for measuring the characteristics of quality in use.

The technical reports in the ISO/IEC 9126 series only provide guidance, not requirements; so conformity to these parts of the series is not defined.

3.1.6   The Special Role of ISO/IEC 12207

ISO/IEC 12207 [6–8] defines a vocabulary and an architecture of 17 software life-cycle processes, plus a tailoring process. It is intended for use in situations where a two-party binding agreement to acquire software products or services applies. The binding agreement might be in the form of a legal contract between two different organizations (e.g., between a government organization and a contractor), or it could be a simple informal agreement, even an informal agreement between different parts of the same organization.

One of the ways that ISO/IEC 12207 is special within ISO standards is that it serves as the normative description of the software life cycle for many other ISO standards that are SQA-related, for example, ISO/IEC 90003 and ISO/IEC 15504.

ISO/IEC 12207 models a quality management system as a collection of cooperating processes. The processes are Management, Improvement, and Development (e.g., the internal evaluations, by developers, of development work products), together with the supporting processes configuration management, quality assurance, verification, validation, joint review, audit, and problem resolution. A project implements these processes in its own particular way. The standard suggests that ISO-9001 should be used, when appropriate, to assure the implementation.

The collection of life-cycle processes in ISO/IEC 12207 is comprehensive in the sense that the 17 processes include activities that span the entire software life cycle. The ISO/IEC 12207 authors anticipated that an organization might want to use only a subset of the processes, for a particular situation and a particular purpose. So, the standard incorporates a tailoring process that adapts it by ignoring life cycle processes in the standard that are not applicable (e.g., to the situation or the purpose), and by adding processes and activities that are applicable that are outside the standard. The tailoring process can be difficult, because there are many decisions to make. However, main utility of this standard, in every situation, is the benefit from the tailoring process itself.

Its emphasis on tailoring is a second way that ISO/IEC 12207 is special within ISO standards.

Compliance with the standard is achieved when all the processes, activities, and tasks in the standard that were selected by the tailoring process are performed. In the special case where an organization imposes the standard "as a condition of trade" [6, clause 1.4], the organization is responsible for making clear which processes, activities, and tasks in the standard suppliers must perform to achieve compliance.

3.2   SQA in IEEE Standards

The IEEE[1] was formed in 1963 when the American Institute of Electrical Engineers (AIEE) merged with the Institute of Radio Engineers (IRE). Its corporate headquarters is in New York City. Usually, an IEEE standard that is related to SQA is conceived and sponsored by the IEEE Computer Society and developed by the IEEE Standards Association (IEEE-SA). For more information about the standards process at IEEE, see the IEEE-SA Web site [26]. For more information about the Computer Society, see its Web site [27].

Second only to ISO standards, IEEE software engineering standards provide the most significant pool of requirements and guidance on software quality assurance. They can be purchased online at http://shop.ieee.org/ieeestore/ and http://webstore. ansi.org/ansidocstore/.

3.2.1   IEEE Std 730-2002

IEEE Std 730-2002 [28] provides "uniform, minimum acceptable requirements for preparation and content of software quality assurance plans." It is written for use during a period when software is developed or maintained.

In clause 4, IEEE Std 730-2002 describes the minimum content of an SQA plan. Within the descriptions, the standard implicitly identifies core elements of the SQA process, because any activity that must be described in an SQA plan is a core software quality assurance activity that must at least be considered whenever SQA is implemented. An SQA plan might apply or cite requirements and guidance on software quality assurance in many other IEEE standards.

Using the standard as a guide, core SQA activities would include management, documentation, measurement, reviews, testing, problem reporting and corrective action, media control, supplier control, records management, training, and risk management. Indirectly, in its descriptions of related parts of the SQA plan, IEEE Std 730-2002 gives useful guidance about each of these activities. And additional, detailed guidance about many of the activities, for example documentation, software reviews, and SQA methods can be found in the IEEE software and systems engineering standards collection.

---

1.   IEEE was formerly called The Institute of Electrical and Electronics Engineers, Inc., which is still its legal name at the time of this writing.

It is possible to make two different claims of conformance to this standard. A particular SQA plan can be said to be in conformance to the content of IEEE Std 730-2002 if the plan carries out all the requirements in the standard. They are all in clause 4. A requirement is indicated by the verb form "shall." The plan can be said to be in conformance to the format of the standard if it has the format specified in clause 4 of the standard.

3.2.2   IEEE Std 829-1998

In clauses 4 through 11, IEEE Std 829-1998 [29] describes eight different documents that are associated with software testing. The documents are: test plan, test design specification, test case specification, test procedure specification, test item transmittal report, test log, test incident report, and test summary report. Each description explains the purpose of the document, and it outlines the structure of the document and clarifies the content of each section.

The eight document descriptions are written as requirements. The standard allows the content of each section of a document to be tailored "to the particular application and the particular testing phase" [29], by adding content, or reorganizing sections, or adding other documents. But, the language in the standard suggests that tailoring may not delete (ignore) any of the required content.

Annex A of the standard gives useful examples of several testing documents.

A reasonable person can interpret the language in the standard to require that every software item[2] that is tested must be accompanied by documents that jointly contain all of the eight different types of content that clauses 4 through 11 require. Although the standard does not define conformance, interpreting the standard in this way would mean that conformance to IEEE Std 829-1998 would be achieved when the required content is contained in one or more documents like the ones that clauses 4 through 11 describe, or in other documents that they reference.

Conformance to this standard could be a hidden, heavy burden for a project. So, binding agreements should invoke the standard with care. (Also, see Section 3.7.)

3.2.3   IEEE Std 1028-1997

IEEE Std 1028-1997 [30] models five different types of reviews: management reviews, technical reviews, inspections, walk-throughs, and audits. For each type, the standard specifies six different kinds of requirements: related to responsibilities, input, entry criteria, procedures, exit criteria, and output.

Annex B of the standard compares the different types of reviews to one another in very useful ways. And Annex A contains a very helpful table that maps review types in the standard to elements of ISO/IEC 12207:1995 [6].

A claim of conformance to IEEE Std 1028-1997 will be relative, always, only to a specific type of review. Conformance to the standard for a type of review, for example an inspection, is achieved when all the mandatory actions for the review type are carried out as the standard defines (mandatory actions are identified in

---

2.   In this standard, "'software item" means "source code, object code, job control code, control data, or a collection of these items."

the standard by the use of "shall"). See Chapter 7 for a further elaboration on inspections.

3.2.4 The Special Role of IEEE/EIA 12207

IEEE/EIA 12207 [31–33] is a three-volume series that incorporates and extends ISO/IEC 12207:1995 [6]. This joint series by IEEE and EIA (see more about EIA below) provides the common terminology and framework of life-cycle processes that organize and relate the standards in the IEEE software and systems engineering standards collection. This is one of the ways that IEEE/EIA 12207 is special within IEEE standards.

3.2.4.1 IEEE/EIA 12207.0-1996 [31]

This standard contains the text of ISO/IEC 12207:1995,[3] but not the later amendments to the ISO standard. The major differences between IEEE/EIA 12207.0-1996 and ISO/IEC 12207:1995 include two additional, normative annexes that describe objectives to consider when interpreting what the standard says about software life-cycle processes and life-cycle data, and a different approach to compliance.

The standard contains a comprehensive set of processes that must be tailored for a particular situation and a particular purpose. The tailoring process in IEEE/EIA 12207.0-1996 is the same as the one in ISO/IEC 12207:1995. Its emphasis on tailoring is a second way that the IEEE/EIA 12207 series is special within IEEE standards.[4]

Conformity to this standard is not defined. However, Annex F defines compliance. In F.1, compliance with IEEE/EIA 12207.0-1996 is "defined similarly" to the definition of compliance in ISO/IEC 12207:1995. Clause F.2 adds compliance conditions related to the situation—whether compliance is claimed for an organization, a project, a multisupplier program, or to comply with regulatory decisions. Clause F.3 defines two different levels of compliance, tailored and absolute. Clause F.4 adds two different sets of criteria for performing a life-cycle process in the standard that was selected by the tailoring process: accomplishment "as specified," and accomplishment by an "alternative method." A claim of compliance with IEEE/EIA 12207.0-1996 must contain all three elements: the situation (clause F.2), the selected level (clause F.3), and the chosen criteria (clause F.4).

3.2.4.2 IEEE/EIA 12207.1-1997 [32]

This volume is the guide to the information items (the life-cycle data) that IEEE/EIA 12207.0-1996 (the base standard) mentions. Altogether, more than 100 different information items are either required or recommended by the base standard.

---

3. The IEEE working group for the standard made only 12 minor corrections or changes to the text of the ISO standard. These are reported in Annex J.

4. IEEE/EIA 12207.2-1997 contains guidance about the tailoring process and about Annex F that would severely restrict the use of the tailoring process, for example, to the period after a contract is in place, or merely to interpreting language in the standard that refers to "the contract" (for an example, see task 5.2.5.6 in the standard). However, this guidance is not part of the conditions for compliance with IEEE/EIA 12207.0-1996.

Information items are listed alphabetically in Table 1 (in clause 4), which is the heart of this guide. For each item, Table 1 states where the item is mentioned in the base standard, and which kind, of seven different kinds of items—description, plan, procedure, record, report, request, or specification—it is.

For some items, Table 1 points to additional guidance such as a detailed outline within the guide or to additional sources of information outside the guide, such as to other IEEE standards. This suggests a third way in which the IEEE/EIA 12207 series is special within the collection of IEEE standards. Eventually, data described by the standards in the IEEE software and systems engineering standards collection will be harmonized with the IEEE/EIA 12207 series, in part by the mapping in Table 1 to the other IEEE standards, and, in part, by harmonization language (e.g., annexes) in the other standards.

Conformance to IEEE/EIA 12207.1-1997 is not defined. However, the volume contains a compliance clause that allows it to be used as a standard. When it is used as a standard, rather than merely as a guide, there are two different claims of compliance that can be made. First, one or more documents can be claimed to comply with one or more of the information items in Table 1 when they satisfy the characteristics that the related rows of the tables summarize. Second, an organizational process can be claimed to comply with IEEE/EIA 12207.1-1997 when each of the documents that it produces can be claimed to comply with one or more of the information items in Table 1.

3.2.4.3   IEEE/EIA 12207.2-1997 [33]

This volume is the guide to implementing the software life-cycle processes that IEEE/EIA 12207.0-1996 defines. In IEEE/EIA 12207.2, the normative text from the base standard has been updated by incorporating changes that are identified in Annex J (Errata) of IEEE/EIA 12207.0-1996.

Clause 5, clause 6, clause 7, and Annexes A through E repeat normative text in the base standard and add implementation guidance about selected topics. Annex A provides guidance about the tailoring process. Annex B provides guidance about compliance with IEEE/EIA 12207.0-1996. Other annexes provide additional guidance.

Conformance is not defined, and compliance is not defined, with respect to this guide.

3.3   SQA in COBIT®

Control Objectives for Information and related Technology (COBIT®) is a collection of guidance and tools for managing and controlling information technology (IT). The collection consists of COBIT® 4.0 [34], the *Board Briefing on IT Governance, Second Edition* [35], *IT Control Objectives for Sarbanes-Oxley, Second Edition* [36], and five other products that were still being revised or developed when this chapter was written (*Control Practices, IT Assurance Guide, IT Governance Implementation Guide, COBIT® Quickstart,* and *COBIT® Security Baseline*). Guidance on obtaining COBIT® products can found at http://www.itgi.org/ (click on "Recent Publications").

COBIT® 4.0 is the latest edition of a document whose first edition was published in 1996. It describes best practices for IT governance, in a way that is intended to be helpful to "chief information officers, senior management, IT management and control professionals" [34].

COBIT® 4.0 is published by the IT Governance Institute (ITGI) and the Information Systems Audit and Control Association (ISACA). ISACA is an international professional association with headquarters in Rolling Meadows, Illinois. ISACA has become the principal standards development organization for "the information system audit and assurance profession." ISACA members are individual IT professionals. For more information about ISACA, see its Web site [37].

In 1976, ISACA created a foundation to carry out research on IT governance and control. That research mission was passed to ITGI when ITGI was established in 1998. ITGI is colocated with ISACA in Rolling Meadows, Illinois. See the ITGI Web site [38] for more information.

Within COBIT®, "IT governance" means an extension of enterprise and corporate governance to IT. COBIT® identifies five IT governance focus areas: strategic alignment, value delivery, resource management, risk management, and performance management. An organization's IT products and services in these five areas must be controlled to ensure that they will support the organization's strategies and objectives.

Within COBIT®, IT activities are collected into four domains of responsibility: Plan and Organize (PO); Acquire and Implement (AI); Deliver and Support (DS); and Monitor and Evaluate (ME).

In Appendix I, COBIT® 4.0 identifies 20 generic business goals that reflect four different perspectives of an organization: the financial perspective, the customer perspective, the internal perspective, and a learning and growth perspective. For each business goal, the same appendix identifies one or more generic IT goals that support it; in total there are 28 of these.

For each of its four domains of responsibility, COBIT® 4.0 defines controls for from 4 to 13 processes that accomplish the activities of the domain. PO has 10, AI has 7, DS has 13, and ME has 4—in total, controls for 34 IT processes are defined. Each IT process tackles one or more of the generic business goals in Appendix I by focusing on one or more of the IT goals in the appendix.

Within COBIT® 4.0, the 34 processes (each with its own controls) are organized into chapters by their domain. So, there is a chapter for Plan and Organize, and another for Acquire and Implement, and so on. The Executive Overview chapter in COBIT® 4.0, and the COBIT® Framework chapter, jointly summarize this approach.

Each of the 34 COBIT® processes contains multiple detailed control objectives. These detailed objectives are requirements. In addition, six generic process control requirements apply, PC1 through PC6, which are defined on pages 14 and 15 of the COBIT® Framework. These include, for example, "assign an owner for each COBIT® process such that responsibility is clear," and "measure the performance of each COBIT® process against its goals."

Each COBIT® process also contains informative examples of generic inputs and outputs, process activities (and their assignment among various functional roles), additional goals (e.g., activity goals), and metrics. These are not requirements. For example, the activities could be implemented, or replaced, by ITIL® practices that achieved the required objectives. (For more information about ITIL®, see Section 3.4.)

In addition, each process contains its own maturity model. Using the COBIT® maturity models, management can identify how well IT is being managed in their organization and compare that to what they know about their competitors and about the industry as a whole.

Several COBIT® processes contain control objectives or activities related to SQA. For example, the detailed control objectives of PO8 Manage Quality include, PO8.1 to "establish and maintain a QMS that provides a standard, formal and continuous approach regarding quality management that is aligned with the business requirements...," PO8.6 to "define, plan and implement measurements to monitor continuing compliance to the QMS, as well as the value the QMS provides...," and PO8.5 that requires that "an overall quality plan that promotes continuous improvement is maintained and communicated regularly."

Conformance, or compliance, to COBIT® 4.0 is not defined within the document itself. However, based on language in the document, and in related documents, it is reasonable to believe that conformance to COBIT® 4.0 is achieved by an IT process that satisfies the detailed control objectives of one or more COBIT® processes, and the six generic process control requirements. Probably, the *IT Assurance Guide* will clarify conformance (or compliance) when it is released.

3.4   SQA in ITIL®

The IT Infrastructure Library (ITIL®) is a library of products that presents best practices for IT service management (ITSM). ITSM is what an organization does to provide and support IT services "of a quality corresponding to the objectives of the business, and which meet the requirements and expectations of the customer" [39]. Each organization that follows an ITIL® publication is expected to implement the ITIL® processes in its own way.

ITIL® organizes ITSM best practices into generic processes. In most cases, a core ITIL® publication is a collection of topically related processes. Historically, two topics, service support and service delivery, have been the focal points around which ITIL® has been organized.

When this chapter was written, there were eight core ITIL® publications [40–47], *Service Support, Service Delivery, Planning to Implement Service Management, Security Management, ICT Infrastructure Management, Application Management, Business Perspective Volume 1*, and *Business Perspective Volume 2*, and several complementary products (for example, *Introduction to ITIL®* [39], *Software Asset Management* [48], and *ITIL® Small-Scale Implementation* [49]). However, the material in the core publications was being rewritten, and repackaged in version 3 of ITIL®, as *Service Strategy, Service Design, Service Transition, Service Operation*, and *Continual Service Improvement*, and released in June 2007.

ITIL® is a responsibility of the Office of Government Commerce (OGC) within the U.K. Treasury. For more information, see the ITIL® page at the OGC Web site [50]. ITIL® products are published by The Stationery Office (TSO) in London [51]. To learn more about ITIL® publications, or to purchase them directly, see [52].

The publication *Service Support* [40] presents processes for incident management, problem management, configuration management, change management, and release management. It also describes a service desk, but not as a process, rather as a part of an organization. Within ITIL® publications, a service desk is a group of people who carry out some or all activities of the ITIL® service support processes, particularly incident management, release management, change management, and configuration management.

The ITIL® publication *Service Delivery* [41] describes processes for service level management, financial management, capacity management, IT service continuity management, and availability management.

Security management is still emerging as a profession of its own, so software-market-wide consensus about what it is, exactly, may not exist yet. However, within ITIL®, security management activities aim to provide an acceptable level of information confidentiality, integrity, and availability. Security management activities are described in the publication *Security Management* [43].

Within ITIL® publications, the word "infrastructure" (sometimes replaced by "technical infrastructure") means the collection of hardware and software components and services that underlie applications. Within ITIL®, "application" has a meaning that is very similar to the meaning of "information system." The publication *ICT Infrastructure Management* [44] describes four infrastructure management processes: design and planning, deployment, operations, and technical support.

The publication *Planning to Implement Service Management* [42] tackles the problems that organizations face when introducing IT service management practices for the first time, or when improving service management practices that are already in place. It suggests a six-stage continuous service improvement program.

The ITIL® publication *Application Management* [45] presents a set of practices that integrate application development with service delivery and service support processes. The goal is to identify activities that increase the likelihood that, when application elements of the IT infrastructure are developed, application products that result will be well matched to the activities in the other ITIL® processes.

Many ITIL® processes in these publications have activities that SQA might support or do, in some implementations, for example:

- Monitoring the effectiveness of the incident cycle (during incident management);
- Carrying out a configuration audit (during configuration management);
- Evaluating implemented changes (during change management);
- Testing or accepting releases (during release management);
- Assessing ITSM processes (as described in [42]).

The two remaining core ITIL® publications, *Business Perspective, Volume 1* [46], and *Business Perspective, Volume 2* [47], aim to explain IT service customers to IT service providers, with the goal of clarifying how the IT service providers can improve what they do.

"Conformance to ITIL®" is not defined within ITIL® itself, in the sense that the ITIL® publications do not define the conditions that would justify a claim of conformance to the library of core publications, or even a claim of conformance to the collection of all the processes that they define.

Some ITIL® processes, for example Change Management, include individual guidance on evaluating compliance with the practices that they document. But, most do not. And, OGC does not provide or accredit assessments of conformity, either to ITIL® as a whole or to individual ITIL® documents.

There are commercial firms who perform assessments of service management processes against the ITIL® model. Also, self-assessment tools for the same purpose can be downloaded (e.g., from itSMF). However, it is probably best to think of ITIL® simply as a collection of best practices that are intended for use with reasonable care, even with the help of professional advice in some situations.

Organizations that wish to demonstrate conformity to ITIL® processes can opt for certification against ISO/IEC 20000 instead. As the next section of this chapter explains, ISO/IEC 20000 is aligned with ITIL®.

ITIL® publications are sometimes used with the COBIT® standard. To compare ITIL® to COBIT®, ITIL® focuses on processes, while COBIT® focuses on control objectives. Implementing ITIL® processes can support the achievement of COBIT® objectives.

3.4.1 ISO/IEC 20000

ISO/IEC 20000 [53, 54] is a two-part standard for ITSM. It maps easily to ITIL®, because, in its original form, it was BS 15000, which was aligned with ITIL® by agreement between OGC [50], BSI [55], and itSMF [56].

ISO/IEC 20000-1:2005 [53] defines requirements. Clause 3 defines general management requirements, including responsibility requirements, documentation requirements, and requirements related to staff training and competence. Clause 4 adds requirements for a Plan (planning)-Do (implementation)-Check (monitoring and measuring)-Act (continuous improvement) cycle. See Chapter 2 for further elaboration on a Plan-Do-Check-Act cycle. Clause 5 presents requirements for planning and implementing new or changed services.

Clause 6 of the standard specifies requirements for service-level management, service reporting, service continuity and availability management, budgeting and accounting for IT services, capacity management, and information security management.

Clauses 8, 9, and 10 present requirements for incident management, problem management, configuration management, change management, and release management.

In clauses 6, 8, 9, and 10, the alignment between ITIL® and ISO/IEC 20000: 2005 is clear. It is planned that version 3 of ITIL® will continue the alignment. The intended relationship between the two standards is that ISO/IEC 20000:2005 will define requirements for ITSM, and ITIL® will present generic practices for achieving conformance to them.

Conformance to ISO/IEC 20000-1:2005 is not defined explicitly by the standard. However, many provisions of the standard are expressed using "shall." And according to ISO/IEC rules for writing an international standard, the verb form "shall" indicates requirements that must be followed (and that may not be violated) if conformance to the standard is to be achieved. So, conformance to the standard could be said to be achieved when these requirements are satisfied.

ISO/IEC 20000-2:2005 [54] does not contain requirements (so, conformance to this part of the standard is not defined). The clauses in ISO/IEC 20000-2:2005 track exactly with those in ISO/IEC 20000-1:2005. Each clause recommends or suggests several things that, while they are not required, would help to satisfy the related requirements in ISO/IEC 2000-1. More information on this collection of IT standards is provided in Chapter 14.

3.5   SQA and Other Standards

3.5.1   ANSI/EIA-748-A-1998

The Electronics Industries Alliance (EIA)—formerly the Electronic Industries Association (until 1997) and before that the Radio Manufacturers Association (RMA)—is an alliance of several high-tech associations and companies. The EIA headquarters is in Arlington, Virginia. For more information about the EIA, see the organization's Web site [57].

The EIA standards of most interest to SQA people are developed by the Government Electronics & Information Technology Association (GEIA). For more information about GEIA, see its Web site [58]. Recently, GEIA has collaborated with several other associations in publishing a very influential standard on earned value management systems (EVMS).

ANSI/EIA-748-A-1998 [59] (which was reaffirmed in 2002) presents common terminology and guidelines for establishing and applying an EVMS.

The standard was prepared under the guidance of the Program Management Systems Committee (PMSC) of the National Defense Industrial Association (NDIA). For more information about the NDIA PMSC, see its page on the NDIA Web site [60]. Currently, the U.S. Office of Management and Budget requires that U.S. Federal agencies "…must use a performance-based acquisition management or earned value management system, based on the ANSI/EIA Standard 748, to obtain timely information regarding the progress of capital investments" [61].

Clause 1 of the standard, the Introduction, states seven EVMS principles, and it makes a useful distinction between these principles and the EVMS guidelines that follow in clause 2. The distinction is this: Every program management system should make use of an EVMS application that is "compliant" with the principles. However, the EVMS guidelines in clause 2 are only applicable to "large complex and/or high-risk programs…."

Clause 2 contains the guidelines, 32 of them, for establishing and applying an integrated EVMS. The guidelines are collected into five categories:

- Organization;
- Planning, Scheduling, and Budgeting;

- Accounting Considerations;
- Analysis and Management Reports;
- Revisions and Data Maintenance.

The guidelines depend upon common terms that are defined in clause 2.6.

The guidelines are described at a high level. The intent of the standard is to state them in a way that does not mandate implementation details. Here is a sample of the guidelines:

- "Define the authorized work elements for the program. A work breakdown structure (WBS), tailored for effective internal management control, is commonly used in this process." (Organization)
- "Identify physical products, milestones, technical performance goals, or other indicators that will be used to measure progress." (Planning, Scheduling, and Budgeting)
- "Record all indirect costs, which will be allocated to the contract." (Accounting Considerations)

As the sample shows, the guidelines in clause 2 are written in a way that the manual for writing GEIA standards calls a "direct instruction." They are not written as requirements, which must be followed to conform to the standard. They do not depend on "shall."

Clause 3 contains supplementary information that clarifies some of the terms and instructions in the guidelines in clause 2. For example, in clarifying what a program organization is, clause 3.3 discusses control accounts, control account managers, subcontract management, and intercompany work transfers.

Clause 4 explains that the form of EVMS documentation should be whatever is standard for documenting systems and policies and procedures within the company where the EVMS is used.

Clause 5 discusses how a company might go about assuring that its EVMS achieves "conformity" to the guidelines in clause 2 (and the language in this clause suggests that "conformity" and "compliance" are used interchangeably here). This is the only claim of conformance that the standard offers, because the standard is written without requirements. If a company has an EVMS that has achieved earlier acceptance against C/SCSC (U.S. Department of Defense Cost/Schedule Control Systems Criteria) for a government contract, clause 5 suggests that the company might benefit more from citing the C/SCSC acceptance than from documenting conformity to the guidelines in this standard. However, in other cases, the basic process for assuring conformity to the EVMS guidelines in clause 2 is to document that the company's program management system "meets the full intentions of the guidelines" [59]. The clause makes it clear that the company is responsible for the evaluation of its system, and for preparing the documentation.

Demonstrating conformity to the guidelines in clause 2 depends upon an understanding of their "full intentions." However, there is no explicit explanation of those intentions within the standard itself. The content of clause 3 does provide some clarification, but it does not explain the intentions to a degree that is adequate to demonstrate conformity.

The best explanation of conformity to ANSI/EIA-748-A-1998 appears in a publication by the NDIA PMSC—the same group that guided the development of the standard. The publication is the *Earned Value Management Systems Intent Guide* [62]. For each guideline in clause 2 of the standard, the publication provides:

- An explanation of its intent;
- A list of typical attributes that business processes and system documentation would have if they complied with the guideline;
- A list of typical outputs that provide objective evidence that the business processes and system documentation do comply with the guideline.

To document that business processes and system documentation comply with (are in conformity to) the guidelines in the standard, the NDIA PMSC publication recommends that the processes and documentation be mapped to the intent, the typical attributes, and the typical outputs, and that this mapping be verified by an "independent" party. The publication provides mapping templates for all the guidelines in the standard, and also it provides an example of how to use them.

3.5.2   RTCA/DO-178B

RTCA/DO-178B [63] provides guidelines for producing software that will be used in airborne systems. The intent is that software developed according to the guidelines in the standard will not compromise the safety of a system in which it is embedded or the system's compliance with airworthiness requirements.

The standard was developed by RTCA, Inc. (formerly the Radio Technical Commission for Aeronautics), which has headquarters in Washington, D.C. RTCA is a not-for-profit corporation whose mission is to develop "consensus-based recommendations regarding communications, navigation, surveillance, and air-traffic management (CNS/ATM) system issues." Its members are government, industry, and academic organizations. For more information about the RTCA, see its Web site [64].

Sections 1, 2, and 10 of this standard describe the context in which the standard will be used. The airworthiness of aircraft systems and their engines must be certified, and software that is part of an aircraft or an engine is considered during the certification process. Sections 1 and 2 explain key relations between the software and an aircraft or engine system that contains it. Section 2 also defines six levels of failure that software might cause or allow.

Section 3 discusses the software life cycle. Also, it introduces the concept of transition criteria between processes.

Sections 4 through 9 of the standard describe a software planning process, and four software development processes (software requirements, software design, software coding, and integration). They also define four integral processes (software verification, software configuration management, software quality assurance, and certification liaison) that provide assistance to the software development processes and to each other. For each process that it describes, the standard states objectives, and it provides guidance on how to achieve the objectives. Most of the objectives in these sections are associated with the software verification process, in section 6, which includes software testing.

Section 11 provides a topical outline for each of the major software life-cycle data items that is mentioned in one or more of the nine processes in sections 4 through 9.

Section 12 of the standard contains discussions of considerations that, for various reasons, do not fit neatly into other sections of the standard. These considerations include, for example, use of previously developed software (and the quality assurance considerations associated with that), criteria for qualifying tools, and alternative methods for achieving the objectives.

In Annex A, which is normative, the standard presents an important collection of tables. For each process in sections 4 through 9, other than verification, there is one table in the collection. For the verification process, there are five tables because the verification process verifies each of the four development processes and it performs testing. Each table maps objectives of the process to the levels of failure to indicate which objectives should be satisfied for which levels, and to indicate whether or not the objective should be satisfied "with independence." The table also indicates for each level and each objective how rigorous the process should be for controlling changes to related outputs.

Conformance or compliance is not defined explicitly by RTCA/DO-178B. However, language in the standard indicates that a software practice (e.g., use of robustness test cases), or software method (e.g., an alternative method), or a life-cycle process, can be said to comply with the standard if it satisfies the related objectives in the standard.

3.6 Whatever Happened to U.S. Department of Defense Standards?

In the 1970s, 1980s, and 1990s, the standards of most interest to SQA people were publications of the U.S. Department of Defense (DoD). Today, people who do SQA pay attention mostly to nongovernment standards (NGSs), such as the standards that have been discussed already in this chapter.

The main reason for the change is that, beginning in the mid-1990s, the federal government has directed its agencies, including the DoD, to use voluntary consensus standards in the place of government-unique standards, "except where inconsistent with law or otherwise impractical" [65]. However, DoD adoption does not mean that an adopted, software-related standard is mandatory for use in all software-related contracts. Adoption simply is "an expression of acceptance of a NGS for repetitive use by the DoD." Adoption helps DoD "to provide for document visibility, ensure document availability to DoD personnel, and identify a DoD technical focal point" [66].

All DoD standardization efforts—including compliance with the related DoD policy—are coordinated and managed by the Defense Standardization Program (DSP). For more information about the DSP, see its Web site [67].

3.6.1 Influential Past Standards

Here is a quick review of some of the most influential DoD standards of the past 20 to 30 years.

3.6.1.1   Software Development Standards Before MIL-STD-498

DOD-STD-1679A, *Software Development* (1983) [68], superseded MIL-STD-1679, *Weapon System Software Development* (1978). This series was an early, influential, standalone, description of what has come to be known as the development process for software. It included requirements for core development activities such as management, requirements definition, design, coding and testing, and also what are now called support activities, such as configuration management and quality assurance. Associated with it, there were (data item) descriptions of 17 different kinds of data. The standard was superseded in 1985 by DOD-STD-2167. However, DOD-STD-1679A had become an active DoD standard again at the time this chapter was written.

DOD-STD-2167, *Defense System Software Development* (1985), was a different look at the same part of the software life cycle (development) that DOD-STD-1679A had described. DOD-STD-2167 was different from the earlier standard in several ways. It incorporated parts of seven other standards by reference. It described configuration management and software quality assurance. Also, it packaged elements of both together with the engineering processes that they supported, in a phase-like relation. Associated with it, there were (data item) descriptions of 27 different kinds of data (counting engineering change proposals and specification change notices). This standard was an influence on early capability maturity models for software. It was superseded by DOD-STD-2167A in 1988.

DOD-STD-2167A, *Defense System Software Development* (1988), was a refinement and reduction of DOD-STD-2167. It reduced the number of other standards that were incorporated by reference. It dropped separate requirements for configuration management and software quality evaluation. It repackaged the phase-like relations of engineering and supporting processes, and added a table of evaluation criteria for each. It added an explicit connection between software development and the surrounding context of system development. Associated with it, there were (data item) descriptions of 18 different kinds of data (counting engineering change proposals and specification change notices). It was superseded by MIL-STD-498 in 1994.

DOD-STD-2168, *Defense System Software Quality Program* (1988), became a companion standard to DOD-STD-2167A. The standard was a description of a software quality program for the acquisition, development, and support of software systems. It interpreted applicable requirements of MIL-Q-9858 for software, and it incorporated the applicable requirements of MIL-STD-1535. Software quality evaluation requirements in DOD-STD-2167 that had not carried over to DOD-STD-2167A were elaborated here. Associated with the standard, there was a single description of data, for a software quality program plan. The standard was cancelled in 1995.

DOD-STD-7935A, *DOD Automated Information Systems (AIS) Documentation Standards* (1988), described requirements for 11 different kinds of documents for what are now called IT systems, or applications. In contrast, DOD-STD-2167A was used for software in weapons (and intelligence) systems. DOD-STD-7935A was superseded by MIL-STD-498 in 1994.

3.6.1.2 MIL-STD-498

MIL-STD-498, *Software Development and Documentation* (1994), harmonized and superseded two earlier standards, DOD-STD-2167A and DOD-STD-7935A, and thereby brought the development of all DoD software under a single standard. It interpreted all applicable clauses in MIL-Q-9858A for software, thereby providing an alternative to DOD-STD-2168. It also interpreted all applicable clauses in ISO 9001 for software, and it implemented the development process and the documentation process in ISO/IEC 12207 (the Draft International Standard version), thereby harmonizing the U.S. military standard for software development with key international standards for quality and for software life-cycle processes.

MIL-STD-498 was different from earlier standards in several other ways also. It was standalone once again (as DOD-STD-1679A is)—that is, it depended on no other standards. It removed the phase-like groupings of engineering activities and supporting activities that DOD-STD-2167 had created. The groupings in the DOD-STD-2167 series had suggested a "waterfall" life cycle. But MIL-STD-498 was clear in its requirements, and in a technical appendix, that alternative life-cycle models were encouraged also, so long as they were appropriate for the development situation.

Consistent with its increased breadth of scope and the increased flexibility in its requirements, MIL-STD-498 placed increased responsibility on users to adapt the standard to their development situation by tailoring it.

Associated with MIL-STD-498, there were (data item) descriptions of 22 different kinds of data. These blended many of the data descriptions associated with DOD-STD-2167A and DOD-STD-7935A.

As DOD-STD-2167 and DOD-STD-2167A had before it, MIL-STD-498 influenced the content of the Capability Maturity Model® for software, and ISO/IEC 12207:1995 [6], which appeared in their first versions during the same period in the 1990s when the standard was under development. Later, ideas and large amounts of text from MIL-STD-498 were embedded within IEEE/EIA 12207.2 [33] (some without any change).

MIL-STD-498 was cancelled in 1998, when the DoD adopted IEEE/EIA 12207 [31–33].

3.6.2 SQA in Active DoD Standards

At the time this chapter was written, there were still dozens of active military data item descriptions, for documents such as the following, to name just a few:

- Quality Program Plan (DI-QCIC-81722);
- Software Test Plan (STP) (DI-IPSC-81438A);
- Configuration Audit Plan (DI-SESS-81646);
- Acceptance Test Plan (DI-QCIC-80553A).

Apart from the active data item descriptions, a few active military standards still contain useful guidance for SQA, in some contexts. DOD-STD-1679A [68] contains important requirements for software quality assurance, and also for software acceptance. MIL-STD-961E [69] contains useful guidance for preparing and auditing (software) requirements specifications.

Military data item descriptions, standards, and handbooks can be downloaded from ASSIST [70] for no charge.

In general, a requirement in a military data item description or military standard is expressed with the verb form "shall." Conformity to a data item description or standard is achieved when all its requirements are satisfied.

3.7   Reminders About Conformance and Certification

3.7.1   Conformance

If a person or an organization is a party to a binding agreement that requires their products or their services to conform to a standard, then that person or that organization is responsible for satisfying the requirements in the standard.

However, a person or an organization that has made no commitment with respect to conformance to a particular standard is free to follow, or ignore, the guidance in the standard, including requirements, in any way they choose. (Of course, a person might still be compelled to conform to the standard by a supervisor, for example. And an organization might be compelled by a parent organization or by regulations, to conform to the standard.)

3.7.2   Conformance to an Inactive Standard

In principle, there are no constraints on the standards that a binding agreement might invoke. An agreement could incorporate an inactive standard, such as MIL-STD-498, *Software Development and Documentation*. However, whether the standard was active or not, conformance to the standard would be decided in the same way, according to the terms of the agreement and the language in the standard.

3.7.3   Certification

It is possible to obtain independent certification of conformance to some standards. In the context of software-related standards, "certify" is usually synonymous with "register."[5] In this sense of the word, "certification" means a process in which an independent, accredited individual or organization (1) performs an audit against the requirements of the standard, (2) issues a certificate stating that conformance to the standard has been achieved, (3) arranges for an accredited organization to register the certificate thereby creating a permanent record of it, and (4) thereafter revisits the organization to which the certificate was issued, periodically, to confirm that conformance to the standard has continued. So, certification/registration depends upon proof of conformance, but not vice versa.

---

5.   "Certify" has a related but different meaning with respect to personal credentials. See the discussion of personal credentials in Section 3.8. To understand how accreditation and certification are different in the context of conformance to a standard, the "Introduction" at http://www.iso.org/iso/en/info/ISODirectory/intro.html# is a excellent place to start.

To compare conformance to certification, a particular contract might require conformance to one or more of the software-related standards that are discussed in this chapter. Although an audit might prove conformance to a standard (which would be adequate to satisfy the contract), it is not possible to "certify" conformance to a standard that is discussed in this chapter, with the exceptions of ISO-9001:2000 and ISO/IEC 20000, because the necessary combination of accredited auditors and accredited certification/registration organizations does not exist.

For more information about accreditation and certification, see the "Introduction" at http://www.iso.org/iso/en/info/ISODirectory/intro.html#.

3.8   Future Trends

Here are two trends that will affect how standards are used in SQA. In some cases, there is data to show that a trend has started already. But, in a few cases, a trend can be predicted on the basis of difficulties that are well known and the (maybe questionable) assumption that at least some organizations that acquire software will act rationally and start a trend by taking influential steps to overcome them.

3.8.1   Demand for Personal Credentials Will Increase

Résumés and college transcripts are no longer adequate indicators of skills that employers and their customers seek. Résumés are notoriously difficult to compare, for example, and skills shown in transcripts can go out-of-date very quickly.

The best personal credentials are based on an exam that is standardized nationally, sometimes worldwide. Different people can be compared objectively on the basis of their exam results. Further, personal certification can be an adequate demonstration of competence in areas that were not taught, or had not even emerged, during a person's college and earlier work years.

Some of the credentials likely to become important for SQA people are achieved (at least in part) by passing an exam that demonstrates knowledge of a standard (e.g., ISO 9001, CobiT®, or the content of the IEEE standards).

As the worldwide market for software products and services evolves in the future, two different kinds of personal credentials will become more important for demonstrating software quality assurance competence. First are certifications that demonstrate adequate assurance skills. These could range in credibility from a training certificate from a one-day class, on the low end, to something on the high end that is registered by a certification organization, like a certificate from the American Society of Quality (ASQ) [71] as discussed in Chapter 10, or Certified Information Systems Auditor (CISA) [72] certification from ISACA.

Second there are certifications that demonstrate adequate competence in areas that SQA will audit. The idea here is that people who have some technical understanding of what they audit will be better auditors. Once again, these credentials could range in credibility from a training certificate to something more impressive like a certificate from CompTIA [73], or the IEEE Computer Society [74].

3.8.2 Systems Engineering and Software Engineering Standards Will Converge

Already, there are several indications of this. ISO is exploring the convergence of its system life-cycle processes standard [75] and its software life-cycle processes standard [6–8]. Also, the SQuaRE standards from ISO, which focus only on software product quality, already use system life-cycle processes, rather than software life-cycle processes and activities, as the basis for developing software quality requirements.

IEEE is exploring the convergence of its system life-cycle processes standard and its software life-cycle processes standard. Also, the Software Engineering Standards Committee (SESC) has become the Software and Systems Engineering Standards Committee (S2ESC).

Capability maturity models for software engineering and systems engineering have converged (e.g., [76]). Also, the annual Software Technology Conference by the U.S. Department of Defense has morphed into a Systems and Software Technology Conference [77].

These indicators, and others, give evidence of an increasing desire within the international market to blend models of software life-cycle activities into broader models of a system's life cycle.

References

[1] "Overview of the ISO System," http://www.iso.org/iso/en/aboutiso/introduction/index.html, December 2006.

[2] ISO 9000:2005, *Quality Management Systems—Fundamentals and Vocabulary*, Geneva, Switzerland: International Organization for Standardization, 2005.

[3] ISO 9001:2000, *Quality Management Systems—Requirements*, Geneva, Switzerland: International Organization for Standardization, 2000.

[4] ISO/IEC 90003:2004, *Software engineering—Guidelines for the Application of ISO 9001:2000 to computer software*, Geneva, Switzerland: ISO/IEC, 2004.

[5] "About the IEC," http://www.iec.ch/helpline/sitetree/about/, December 2006.

[6] ISO/IEC 12207:1995, *Information Technology—Software Life Cycle Processes*, Geneva, Switzerland: ISO/IEC, 1995.

[7] ISO/IEC 12207:1995/Amd.1:2002, *Information Technology—Software Life Cycle Processes—Amendment 1*, Geneva, Switzerland: ISO/IEC, 2002.

[8] ISO/IEC 12207:1995/Amd.2:2004, *Information Technology—Software Life Cycle Processes—Amendment 2*, Geneva, Switzerland: ISO/IEC, 2004.

[9] ISO/IEC 9126-1:2001, *Software Engineering—Product Quality—Part 1: Quality Model*, Geneva, Switzerland: ISO/IEC, 2001.

[10] ISO/IEC TR 9126-2:2003, *Software Engineering—Product Quality—Part 2: External Metrics*, Geneva, Switzerland: ISO/IEC, 2003.

[11] ISO/IEC TR 9126-3:2003, *Software Engineering—Product Quality—Part 3: Internal Metrics*, Geneva, Switzerland: ISO/IEC, 2003.

[12] ISO/IEC TR 9126-4:2004, *Software Engineering—Product Quality – Part 4: Quality in Use Metrics*, Geneva, Switzerland: ISO/IEC, 2004.

[13] ISO/IEC 14598-1:1999, *Information Technology—Software Product Evaluation—Part 1: General Overview*, Geneva, Switzerland: ISO/IEC, 1999.

[14] ISO/IEC 14598-2:2000, *Information Technology—Software Product Evaluation—Part 2: Planning and Management*, Geneva, Switzerland: ISO/IEC, 2000.

[15] ISO/IEC 14598-3:2000, *Information Technology—Software Product Evaluation—Part 3: Process for Developers*, Geneva, Switzerland: ISO/IEC, 2000.

[16] ISO/IEC 14598-4:1999, *Information Technology—Software Product Evaluation—Part 4: Process for Acquirers*, Geneva, Switzerland: ISO/IEC, 1999.

[17] ISO/IEC 14598-5:1998, *Information Technology—Software Product Evaluation—Part 5: Process for Evaluators*, Geneva, Switzerland: ISO/IEC, 1998.

[18] ISO/IEC 14598-6:2001, *Information Technology—Software Product Evaluation—Part 6: Documentation of Evaluation Modules*, Geneva, Switzerland: ISO/IEC, 2001.

[19] ISO/IEC 25000:2005, *Software Engineering—Software Product Quality Requirements and Evaluation (SQuaRE) – Guide to SQuaRE*, Geneva, Switzerland: ISO/IEC, 2005.

[20] ISO/IEC 25001:2007, *Software Engineering—Software Product Quality Requirements and Evaluation (SQuaRE) – Planning and Management*, Geneva, Switzerland: ISO/IEC, 2007.

[21] ISO/IEC 15504-1:2004, *Information Technology—Process Assessment—Part 1: Concepts and Vocabulary*, Geneva, Switzerland: ISO/IEC, 2004.

[22] ISO/IEC 15504-2:2003, *Information Technology—Process Assessment—Part 2: Performing an Assessment*, Geneva, Switzerland: ISO/IEC, 2003.

[23] ISO/IEC 15504-3:2004, *Information Technology—Process Assessment—Part 3: Guidance on Performing an Assessment*, Geneva, Switzerland: ISO/IEC, 2004.

[24] ISO/IEC 15504-4:2004, *Information Technology—Process Assessment—Part 4: Guidance on Use for Process Improvement and Process Capability Determination*, Geneva, Switzerland: ISO/IEC, 2004.

[25] ISO/IEC 15504-5:2006, *Information Technology—Process Assessment—Part 5: An Exemplar Process Assessment Model*, Geneva, Switzerland: ISO/IEC, 2006.

[26] "Backgrounder: Standards Development at the IEEE Standards Association," http://standards.ieee.org/announcements/bkgnd_stdsprocess.html, December 2006.

[27] "IEEE Computer Society," http://www.computer.org/portal/site/ieeecs/index.jsp, December 2006.

[28] IEEE Std 730-2002, *IEEE Standard for Software Quality Assurance Plans*, New York: IEEE, 2002.

[29] IEEE Std 829-1998, *IEEE Standard for Software Test Documentation*, New York: IEEE, 1998.

[30] IEEE Std 1028-1997, *IEEE Standard for Software Reviews*, New York: IEEE, 1998.

[31] IEEE/EIA 12207.0-1996, *Industry Implementation of International Standard ISO/IEC 12207: 1995, (ISO/IEC 12207) Standard for Information Technology—Software Life Cycle Processes*, New York: IEEE, 1998.

[32] IEEE/EIA 12207.1-1997, *IEEE/EIA Guide for Information Technology—Software Life Cycle Processes—Life Cycle Data*, New York: IEEE, 1998.

[33] IEEE/EIA 12207.2-1997, *IEEE/EIA Guide—Software Life Cycle Processes—Implementation Considerations*, New York: IEEE, 1998.

[34] COBIT® 4.0, *Control Objectives for Information and Related Technology (COBIT®): Control Objectives, Management Guidelines, Maturity Models*, Rolling Meadows, IL: ITGI, 2005.

[35] *Board Briefing on IT Governance*, 2nd ed., Rolling Meadows, IL: ITGI, 2003.

[36] *IT Control Objectives for Sarbanes-Oxley: The Role of IT in the Design and Implementation of Internal Control over Financial Reporting*, 2nd ed., Rolling Meadows, IL: ITGI, 2006.

[37] "ISACA® – Serving IT Governance Professionals," http://www.isaca.org/, December 2006.

[38] "ITGI," http://www.itgi.org/, December 2006.

[39] Office of Government Commerce (OGC), *Introduction to ITIL®*, London, U.K: TSO (The Stationery Office), 2005.

[40] Office of Government Commerce (OGC), *Service Support*, London, U.K: TSO (The Stationery Office), 2000.

[41] Office of Government Commerce (OGC), *Service Delivery*, London, U.K: TSO (The Stationery Office), 2001.

[42] Office of Government Commerce (OGC), *Planning to Implement Service Management*, London, U.K: TSO (The Stationery Office), 2002.

[43] Office of Government Commerce (OGC), *Security Management*, London, U.K.: TSO (The Stationery Office), 1999.

[44] Office of Government Commerce (OGC), *ICT Infrastructure Management*, London, U.K: TSO (The Stationery Office), 2002.

[45] Office of Government Commerce (OGC), *Application Management*, London, U.K: TSO (The Stationery Office), 2002.

[46] Office of Government Commerce (OGC), *Business Perspective Volume 1*, London, U.K: TSO (The Stationery Office), 2004.

[47] Office of Government Commerce (OGC), *Business Perspective Volume 2*, London, U.K: TSO (The Stationery Office), 2006.

[48] Office of Government Commerce (OGC), *Software Asset Management*, London, U.K: TSO (The Stationery Office), 2003.

[49] Office of Government Commerce (OGC), *ITIL® Small-Scale Implementation*, London, U.K: TSO (The Stationery Office), 2006.

[50] "ITIL®," http://www.ogc.gov.uk/guidance_itil.asp, December 2006.

[51] "Who Are We?" http://www.tso.co.uk/about/whoAreWe/, December 2006.

[52] "ITIL®," http://www.tsoshop.co.uk/bookstore.asp?FO=1162745, December 2006.

[53] ISO/IEC 20000-1:2005, *Information Technology—Service Management—Part 1: Specification*, Geneva, Switzerland: ISO/IEC, 2005.

[54] ISO/IEC 20000-2:2005, *Information Technology—Service Management—Part 2: Code of practice*, Geneva, Switzerland: ISO/IEC, 2005.

[55] "BS 15000 Past, Present, and Future," http://www.bsi-global.com/ICT/Service/BS15000 articles.xalte, January 2007.

[56] "What Is itSMF?" http://www.itsmf.org/about/itsmf, January 2007.

[57] Electronic Industries Alliance, http://www.eia.org/, January 2007.

[58] GEIA, http://www.geia.org/, January 2007.

[59] ANSI/EIA-748-A-1998 (Reaffirmed: 2002), *Earned Value Management Systems*, Arlington, VA: GEIA, 1998.

[60] "NDIA: Program Management Systems Committee," http://www.ndia.org/Template.cfm?Section=Procurement&Template=/ContentManagement/ContentDisplay.cfm&ContentID=2310, January 2007.

[61] Circular No. A-11, Part 7, *Planning, Budgeting, Acquisition, and Management of Capital Assets*, Washington, D.C.: Office of Management and Budget (OMB), June 2006.

[62] NDIA PMSC ANSI/EIA-748-A Intent Guide, *National Defense Industrial Association (NDIA) Program Management Systems Committee (PMSC) Earned Value Management Systems Intent Guide, November 2006 Edition*, Arlington, VA: NDIA PMSC, 2006.

[63] RTCA/DO-178B, *Software Considerations in Airborne Systems and Equipment Certification*, Washington, D.C.: RTCA, 1992.

[64] RTCA, Inc., http://www.rtca.org/aboutrtca.asp, January 2007.

[65] Circular No. A-119, Revised, *Federal Participation in the Development and Use of Voluntary Consensus Standards and in Conformity Assessment Activities*, Washington, D.C.: Office of Management and Budget (OMB), February 1998.

[66] DoD 4120.24-M, *DSP Policies & Procedures*, Washington, D.C.: Department of Defense, OUSD (Acquisition, Technology and Logistics), March 2000.

[67] "Welcome to the DSP Home Page," http://www.dsp.dla.mil/, January 2007.

[68] DOD-STD-1679A, *Military Standard—Software Development*, Washington, DC: Department of Defense, October 22, 1983.

[69] MIL-STD-961E, *Department of Defense Standard Practice—Defense and Program-Unique Specifications Format and Content*, Washington, D.C.: Department of Defense, August 1, 2003.

[70] assistdocs.com, http://www.assistdocs.com/search/search_basic.cfm, January 2007.

[71] "Find the ASQ Certification That's Right for You," http://www.asq.org/services/training/certification-right-for-you.html, January 2007.

[72] "CISA Certification," http://www.isaca.org/Template.cfm?Section=CISA_Certification&Template=/TaggedPage/TaggedPageDisplay.cfm&TPLID=16&ContentID=4526, January 2007.

[73] "CompTIA Certifications," http://certification.comptia.org/, January 2007.

[74] "CSDP: Is Certification for You?" http://www.computer.org/portal/site/ieeecs/menuitem.c5efb9b8ade9096b8a9ca0108bcd45f3/index.jsp?&pName=ieeecs_level1&path=ieeecs/education/certification&file=cert_for_you.xml&xsl=generic.xsl&, January 2007.

[75] ISO/IEC 15288:2002, *Systems Engineering—System Life Cycle Processes*, Geneva, Switzerland: ISO/IEC, 2002.

[76] *CMMI® for Development, Version 1.2*, CMU/SEI-2006-TR-008, Pittsburgh, PA: Carnegie Mellon University, August 2006.

[77] "Systems & Software Technology Conference," http://www.sstc-online.org/, January 2007.

## CHAPTER 4

Personnel Requirements to Make Software Quality Assurance Work

Kenneth S. Mendis

4.1 Introduction

This chapter has a primary focus of software quality assurance (SQA) personnel who perform as evaluators/auditors of the software development and management processes and work products. There is recognition of the validation/testing activities many SQA personnel perform, but this is not the primary focus in the chapter. Obtaining qualified engineers and keeping them motivated in what they are doing is a problem most of the engineering disciplines have been facing for some time. The problem is compounded when we focus on the software engineering discipline. At the level of SQA, we find ourselves battling with the software developers for the few software engineers who are available.

To be effective and contribute to a project's success in a manner that is professionally acceptable, the SQA organization must be staffed with qualified software engineers. In addition, these individuals must also possess the credentials that make them good quality assurance representatives. Achieving any of the promised benefits of SQA is directly related to an organization's ability to staff the operation. Some of the issues that the manager will be confronted with are engineer motivation, career training, and recruiting techniques.

The commercially available *Software Life Cycle Process* standard, ISO/IEC 12207, is a well-known standard containing sections on software quality as well as auditing techniques. Additionally, ISO 9001:2000 and the ISO 90003 *Guidelines for the application of ISO 9001:2000 process requirements to the development, supply and maintenance of software* are also influencing the software development and quality decisions of many organizations. Also along these lines is the Code of Federal Regulations that direct the Food and Drug Administration (FDA), as it monitors food production, the development of medical devices, the medicines we take, and other FDA relevant consumer products and services. Each standard defines a structured approach for developing software, and with that approach comes the need to staff positions within the organization to enforce the plans that have been set in motion. Unfortunately, the glamour and challenges provided by a developing environment attracts the interest of the majority of software engineers.

This leaves SQA with a limited number of qualified personnel from which to choose.

The Capability Maturity Model Integration® for Development (CMMI®-DEV) has had a significant impact on SQA through its Process and Product Quality Assurance process area. Personnel working in a CMMI®-DEV environment must be knowledgeable to perform the practices in the Model. Particularly essential is how to perform, record, and promulgate process and work product evaluations/audits.

At a high level, the personnel requirements that make SQA work are as follows:

- Approximately 3 to 5 years developing software;
- Experienced software engineer who has seen it all and has survived the software battles;
- Individual seeking to advance to management or a program manager's position;
- Good communication skills;
- Computer science academic background;
- Willingness to meet and accept new challenges.

There will be further discussion later of these important attributes.

The Defense Logistic Agency has developed an approach to software quality assurance. The procedure, known as the Single Process Initiative for In-Plant Quality Assurance makes use of continuous improvement tools and problem solving techniques to examine the adequacy of a contractor's process to continuously produce conforming products and to identify opportunities for product improvements.

The concept of Single Process Initiative includes management commitment, people development, quality excellence, and user satisfaction. Implementation of Single Process Initiative embraces techniques that use process and product quality to evaluate the quality of an organization's software products. Single Process Initiative focuses on working with the software developers, working with the software users, and working with contracting agencies to produce a product that meets the users' needs. It means working as a team to measure and continuously improve the process.

4.2   Facing the Challenge

Why consider software quality assurance? A review of warning letters issued by the U.S. FDA to firms in the United States, Europe, and Asia, as a result of formal inspections, highlighted the weakness of firms to adequately institute a SQA program that contributes to a more complete and consistent software design, development, testing, documentation, and change control. In most cases reviewed, FDA actions usually had a negative impact on the validation status of the computer system and on a firm's bottom line.

Imagine the impact on a war if the United States Army had to wait to validate the performance of its missiles after installation in a war zone. What if the computer control and guidance system had not been validated to do what it was supposed to do every single time—that is, intercept and destroy incoming enemy missiles? Or in another instance, picture yourself several hundred feet below sea level sitting in front of a computer terminal in the submarine command and control center ready to fire a missile. What if the installed guidance software used to deliver the missile had not been validated? Think of the destruction it would cause if it ended up somewhere hundreds of miles from its intended target! SQA plays an important part in the outcome of recent wars, where software-intensive systems are used.

If the SQA process helps to assure systems that land men on the moon and bring them back safely, defend a country against external attack, help pilots land safely at our busiest airports during a blinding snow storm, then why not apply such a trustworthy methodology to all software development efforts?

Our academic institutions today still do not provide the required training for SQA engineers. An SQA engineer is a software engineer trained in the disciplines of software quality assurance. Today, little or no training is provided in the techniques of software design review, good software documentation, and software reliability and maintainability. Training is also inadequate for software attributes such as the use of program design languages, top-down development, object oriented methods, and structured programming techniques, which are used to assess and measure the progress of software development. About the only way an individual becomes knowledgeable of SQA principles and disciplines is by hands-on work-related experience, which only makes the SQA staffing problem even more difficult.

Individuals involved in developing, staffing, and maintaining an SQA organization within their company are familiar with the daily battles of SQA staffing. It is not uncommon to search through countless résumés and interview many applicants in an effort to find those individuals who would make good SQA engineers. In many instances, if an applicant is technically acceptable, then he or she still lacks those special attributes that turn a software engineer into an SQA engineer. Therefore, recruiting and hiring qualified personnel to staff SQA positions is expensive and time consuming.

Thus, before the organization proceeds on a recruiting campaign, it is necessary to define and set priorities for those issues and positions that are critical to the success of the SQA function, The organization must consider the following factors:

- Is it possible to promote from within and train individuals to fill the openings?
- Can contract employees help fill the organization's needs, and if so, in what capacity should these employees be utilized?
- Should the recruiting effort be national, regional, or local?
- What does it take to attract qualified trained individuals to your company?
- What does an organization do to retain its qualified staff?

Another problem that one has to face is how to hold the qualified individuals' interest and motivation in job assignments. Developing and outlining career paths is another important factor in the problems facing SQA staffing. Indeed, in my opinion, the most serious problem a manager faces is to prevent his or her department from becoming a stepping stone to other opportunities within the organization. The SQA department, if it is to develop into an effective organization dedicated to assuring a product's software quality, must consist of professionals both seasoned in software and dedicated to quality, and capable of providing guidance, training, and quality-consciousness within the organization.

Lastly, top management support is of prime concern. The lack of top management support or lack of a clear understanding of SQA's needs is perhaps the major issue confronting most SQA organizations today. To properly staff the organization, management must clearly understand the problems of personnel and assurance goals and be willing to address them. Support and understanding must go hand in hand; one without the other is ineffective.

4.3   Organization Structure

In April 1979 the Software Management Subgroup of the Joint Coordinating Group on Computer Resource Management (JCG, CRM) sponsored a Joint Logistics Commanders software workshop. One of the key findings of the workshop stressed the difficulties facing the implementation of SQA, such as the lack of a well-defined and consistent set of requirements, differences in SQA approaches across the various branches of the services and industry, and the unavailability of a good source of experienced personnel. Nearly three decades later, this requirement continues to be a concern within organizations.

Experience has shown that independence is the key to success in implementing SQA programs. The SQA organization should be situated in the overall organization so that it always reports to the same level that the department which it must evaluate and audit reports to. The quality organization must have the organizational status and access to top management as do the other functions. Figure 4.1 shows how this concept may be instituted within an organization and how the assurance function can use its position within an organization to achieve its goals and objectives.

An industry survey conducted by the National Security Industrial Association in 1983 and a 1995 assessment by the American Society for Quality (ASQ) reveal that the typical profile of most SQA organizations possesses the following attributes:

- The SQA organization is located within the quality assurance organization.

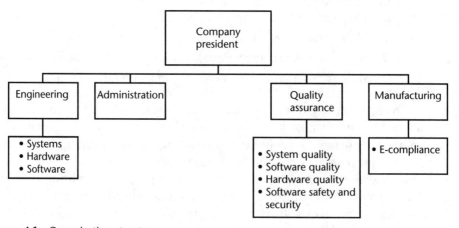

Figure 4.1   Organization structure.

- SQA is staffed with people who possess approximately 1 to 5 years of software engineering experience.
- The person in charge of the SQA organization has more than 5 years of software experience and is a middle manager within the organization.
- The career path for these individuals is into development and management.

Johanna Rothman advises the following [1]:

Product development organizations focused on developing quality products that their customers will buy need to consider the organizational structure that works best for them. It is not an organizational requirement to separate the tasks and people into functional groups. The product may require a project-focused group, focused on the product, not the organizational hierarchy.

When product development groups consider their organizational needs, they need to consider their staff, quality requirements, the process requirements, and the kinds of projects they have. In many cases, integrating the product developers and product verifiers onto a project team will have multiple positive effects in terms of project schedule, product quality, and increase in team knowledge. As the team increases its knowledge, management can trust the team more to meet schedules and deliver the promised product.

The SQA function, established to evaluate the software development effort, must possess the objective and authoritative controls required. An SQA function that reports to the development organization lacks the independence needed to get the job done properly. Moreover, the members of the development organization are by first love software designer/programmers, therefore making their quality tasks secondary in nature. An organizational structure of the type shown in Figure 4.1 allows itself to develop the SQA engineers into a position of responsibility, leadership, and independent management reporting. It is from here that the SQA engineer derives a perceived responsibility that allows him or her to translate that into getting the job done right.

A common problem of many organizations arises from appointing project-related software engineers as SQA personnel. These individuals function as senior staff members within the project organization, directing and managing the SQA effort of the project, while reporting to project management. A shortcoming of this approach is that, if SQA is relatively new and not completely defined, its implementation varies sharply from individual to individual trying to enforce it—particularly those with a loyalty divided between the project and assurance.

Experience has shown that to establish any new discipline within an organization, a central motivating force is needed. Fragmented efforts are diluted and end up being ineffective. In my own experience, project-related SQA activity generally lacks depth and maturity. All too often, the SQA activity functions as a workhorse of the developer performing tasks for the developer.

SQA will work effectively only if all project SQA personnel report to a single SQA manager. This organizational posture allows for specialization—that is, all personnel meeting the needs of the project as well as uniformity, and all projects meeting the same minimum acceptance criteria. Members of the SQA staff should have relatively high technical expertise and a thorough knowledge of good software and quality assurance practices. The manner in which the staff is organized depends largely on staff size, estimated workload, and personnel skills.

4.4   Identifying Software Quality Assurance Personnel Needs

A 10-step process to identify SQA personnel needs is shown graphically in Figure 4.2. The process is presented sequentially with each step using the results of the previous step to build upon the next. What is particularly important about this pro-

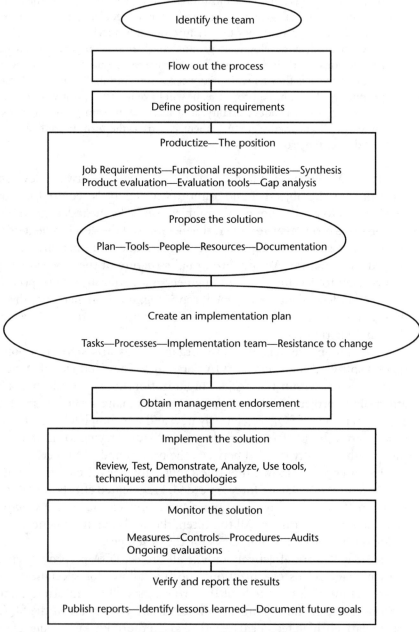

Figure 4.2   Ten-step process to identify SQA personnel based on Deming's Circle.

cess is that it is established on a Total Quality Management (TQM) foundation. Using a team from within the organization, together with continuous improvement techniques, and buy-in by the organization and those involved in developing the system, personnel requirements to make software quality assurance work is treated as an integral part of the organizations staffing activity.

The 10-step process will assure the organization that the individuals selected will require minimal effort to train and integrate into the organization. The process is based on W. Edward Deming's circle (Plan-Do-Check-Act) and on the fact that a successful computer system is achieved only if QA is built into the design, development, and release process.

Step 1: Identify the Team

When formulating this approach, first consider how you intend to answer the following questions. What is the person suppose to do in SQA? What are the required qualifications for the position? How will you know if the solution will meet the needs of the organization and the project? Who is the responsible individual(s) for monitoring progress? How will you know if the results were a success or a failure? To get the answers to these and other questions, use the team approach to develop solutions. Do this by convening past and present software development process owners. The team leader should be someone who has prior experience in computer system development combined with a strong background in software quality assurance and software/system engineering and expertise in post-development software support. This person must understand today's computer software development, testing, quality assurance, and change management methodologies. He or she must possess skills that foster teamwork, and he or she must understand the requirements for computer systems development. The technique of team dynamics depends on a working relationship that each team member brings a specialized expertise during the selection process and that these team members are capable of critiquing and providing the needed expertise to develop the solution.

Step 2: Flow Out the Process

Before beginning the selection process tasks, it is helpful to first flow out the computer system development process and the quality assurance tasks associated with the process, if not already done so. Interview developers and process owners to determine which processes and functions are under computer control and monitoring and which are not. Prioritize each task, assigning a high priority to those tasks which are critical to product quality and personnel safety. Using the process, develop a plan that outlines those processes that need to be implemented in order to assure a quality software product.

Step 3: Define Position Requirements

The next task that will be handled by the team is to develop the position requirements—that is, job descriptions. As a minimum, address the following topics. Identify and define qualifications and position tasks. Evaluate the design process and determine current results, compare current results to requirements and expectations, and identify problems to solve and opportunities for improvement. Process capability requirements and problem identification and management are the build-ing blocks that help define if the position requirements can be met.

Step 4: Productization
This task is associated with determining what engineering documentation will be required to support the position. Productization can be grouped into four steps, requirements analysis, functional analysis, synthesis, and solution. Although repre-sented sequentially, these steps are interacting and interdependent. Each step not only feeds the next step but also provides new considerations for the previous step. The outcome of this step will be a job description and the tasks associated with the requirements of SQA.

Step 5: Propose the Solution
This step requires that the plans, tools, people, and resources be documented. Pro-posing the solution also means determining the cost and benefits associated with implementation. In proposing the solution, also consider the following:

- Describe the proposed solution;
- Create the new process flowchart;
- Identify appropriate in-process and outcome measures;
- Identify change in techniques, resources, information;
- Determine people aspects, roles, training, interactions;
- Cost and benefits;
- Estimate the costs;
- Estimate the savings;
- Identify performance improvements;
- Identify customer benefits.

Step 6: Create an Implementation Plan
In addition to those items discussed in step 5, the team should develop an implemen-tation plan that also addresses the following:

- The SQA process to be implemented;
- Identify and plan for resistance to changes;
- Establish implementation team.

Step 7: Obtain Management Endorsement
For the solution to be successful, management buy-in is crucial. In order to secure this approval, consider the following tasks during this step:

- Prepare a presentation for management;
- Present the solution to management;
- Present the solution to those affected after obtaining management approval.

Step 8: Implement the Solution

The implementation phase begins with a briefing that explains the goals and objectives of the SQA solution. Implementation is the responsibility of the team (quality, development, and manufacturing) responsible of producing and using quality software. A team approach is recommended because SQA should be viewed as a task that involves both developer and user.

Step 9: Monitor the Solution

The responsibility of the team during this step is to assure that the solutions that have been developed are consistent throughout all phases of the development effort and that in process product and process audits, evaluations, controls, and procedures are being used to assure adherence to the plan. The solution monitoring process may consist of three activities: a capability audit, a product compliance audit of documentation, and problem identification and management.

Step 10: Verify and Report the Results

At the conclusion of predefined intervals, management should be briefed on the findings and should be given an opportunity to offer evidence or to refute any finding. Following the completion of each validation task, an exit interview shall be conducted with process owners to debrief them of the validation team's findings. The findings and recommendations should be published in a validation report and made available to process owners and cognizant personnel affected by the validation findings. Follow-up investigations of validation findings should be conducted by the validation team or their representatives to verify that corrective actions have been implemented.

4.5   Characteristics of a Good SQA Engineer

As mentioned earlier, the shortage of software professionals makes recruiting software engineers into the quality assurance profession a difficult task. Two factors appear to work against SQA:

- Developing software is far more attractive to the software engineer.
- The career path for someone in the development environment is clearly more attractive.

A salary survey from 2000 shows average full-time salaries by various IT related technical skills. According to this survey, SQA personnel received a very competitive salary [2]. The subtler prestige and glamour aspects can be addressed, so long as salary is not a major issue in the IT industry. If an organization is willing to take the time, it can probably find suitable candidates within its wage and salary guidelines. But time is money, and the longer it takes to hire the talent required, the longer it takes to bring the SQA function up to the engineering level now required to produce quality software products.

More recently the new incentive by companies to have SQA engineers certified by the ASQ as Certified Software Quality Engineers (CSQE) makes selecting qualified SQA engineers easier. Built on topics that constitute the "Body of Knowledge for Software Quality Engineers," CSQEs are certified on their knowledge in software quality management; software process; software metrics; measurement; and analytical methods; software inspection; testing, verification, and validation; software audits; and software configuration management. Refer to Chapter 10 in this book for more details about the certification process.

What makes a good software quality assurance engineer? Consider the following characteristics:

- The individual who seems to work the best appears to have spent approximately 3 to 5 years developing software. This individual recognizes the limited involvement he or she has had in the total developmental effort, and now wants a bigger piece of the pie. SQA clearly will provide this opportunity. This is an opportunity to get system and managerial exposure in a relatively short period of time. It is to the SQA manager's advantage to point this out to a prospective new hire. However, finding such an individual with the necessary qualities, as listed below, can be difficult and may require a national recruiting policy.

- The experienced software engineer who has seen it all and has survived the software battles is a good candidate. This individual can truly contribute to improving software development methodologies, being inherently familiar with the existing developing techniques and capable of assuming a position of leadership in a very short time. The reader is cautioned to be aware that a lack of motivation on the part of these individuals may sometimes be a problem.

- The individual seeking to advance to management or a program manager's position clearly is a good candidate. It is within the SQA organization that one learns how to deal with people, learns about design and development approaches and techniques, and learns how to manage and report on software development projects, which are some of the attributes one would look for when recruiting for a management position.

- A good SQA engineer must possess good communication skills. This is especially true if he or she is to be effective in performing SQA duties. As we are well aware, software engineers at times can be an unfriendly breed of professionals, very possessive of their work, and often protective of what they have designed as confidential. An SQA engineer has to be able to deal with this and win the trust and respect of software design engineers. Communication skills play a vital role in this regard; the individual should be skillful in expressing ideas both orally and in writing.

- An academic background in computer science is essential. Over the years many individuals who possess a degree in education or the liberal arts have made the switch to software. They were hired as programmers and function in this capacity. I have found that for the most part their ability in the software engineering field is limited to that of being programmers rather than being effective in design. These individuals work well under the supervision of a good software designer, but they make poor SQA engineers.

- The individual who will succeed as an SQA engineer must be willing to meet and accept new challenges and be able to carry out independent research and analysis assignments that deal with analysis of the techniques used to develop software. Such an individual must be capable of evaluating software development methodologies with an eye to improving software productivity and performance.
- The introduction of the SQA person into the CMMI®-DEV appraisals and ISO 9001:2000 audits provides a position of great importance and influence to the organization. For the first time SQA engineers are now being called upon to help establish and manage the cultural environment and monitor performance improvement goals set by management, therefore requiring the SQA engineer to sharpen the needed people development skills.

4.6   Training the Hardware QA Engineer

Training the hardware QA engineer is one method of obtaining and retaining good SQA engineers. Some hardware QA engineers of yester-year now may be in a very unmotivated position because of obsolescence in hardware engineering. Selecting those individuals willing to be retrained in software engineering is the first step. Such individuals will tend to stay within the SQA field the longest. Furthermore, they bring to the function the needed expertise to deal with designers and managers, a quality that is learned over years of on-the-job training.

A hardware QA engineer requires a number of years of training to become an effective SQA engineer. However, the return on this type of investment is, in my opinion, the surest method of developing a staff of highly qualified engineers in software quality. This approach to SQA staffing allows for a permanent core within the function, which is essential if the SQA activity is to survive as a long-range objective of the company.

The training of hardware QA engineers in software should follow one of two paths. The engineer should be encouraged to pursue a degree in computer science. Also, in-house training and learning by example should be pursued, with job assignments utilizing newly learned skills. Today's highly technological advances in the computer engineering field mandates that these individuals obtain the required academic training before releasing them to perform SQA work.

4.7   Training the Software Engineer

The optimal approach—the one the author has found to work the best with software engineers—is the mentor approach to training in the SQA discipline. A mentoring SQA is a teacher or an advisor, someone who has worked in SQA for a number of years. This individual is charged with teaching the software engineer the principles of SQA engineering. This technique to training works well with recent college graduates. Selective training is needed if this approach is to be applied to the more experienced software engineer.

The basic principle under the mentor approach to staffing is to hire software engineers into the SQA organization and to assign them to an experienced SQA engineer. The mentor's responsibility will be to outline a program of task training and to closely monitor the new hire's work output. This mentor–new hire relationship gives the new hire access to someone who will provide guidance and leadership during the learning phase. For this approach to training to work, it is imperative that a training plan exist. An example of such a plan is outlined next.

The following steps will be taken to indoctrinate new personnel into the SQA team:

- Describe the organization surrounding the project to which the new hire is to be assigned, and explain what each department does and how it interacts with the other departments. As a minimum, the departments to be discussed should include the following:
  - System engineering;
  - Software engineering;
  - Software configuration management;
  - Data management;
  - Software integration;
  - Software quality assurance;
  - Software test.
- Indoctrinate the new hire in the use and availability of existing tools and how to utilize tools to their full potential.
- Assign as reading assignments project-related software development plans, software quality assurance plans, and software configuration management plans. The objective in these assignments is to orient the new hire in the company's software development and quality assurance process.
- Define SQA's involvement in the development process and monitor compliance by the establishment of entry and exit criteria associated with the respective development phases as outlined in Figure 4.3. The reviews of the program technical approach with SQA personnel involvement include (1) a requirements review, (2) design reviews that include preliminary and critical reviews, and (3) documentation reviews. Also, SQA personnel involvement is beneficial during the build and test phase reviews that include test readiness and test exit reviews, and prior to release and use, the conduct of physical and functional reviews.

The benefits to be derived from such a program are twofold. The new hire has easy access to someone who is capable of guiding him or her in the performance of work assignments. Most important, the new hire is able to learn first-hand from someone who has been through the process and knows all of its ups and downs. The organization must be willing to devote a minimum of one calendar year to such a training program before the individual can be utilized effectively as a junior contributor within the organization.

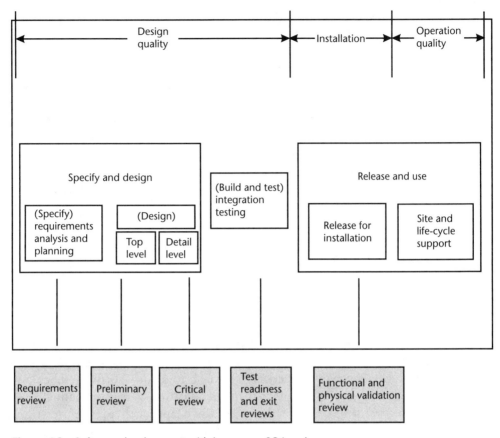

Figure 4.3 Software development with in-process SQA reviews.

4.8 Rotating Software Engineers

Rotating software engineers through the SQA function is an approach that brings to the software QA function bright and capable software professionals. They should be expected to serve a minimum of at least one year within the SQA function. But the following problems will have to be worked out before such an approach to SQA engineering will benefit the organization:

- There exists a shortage of qualified software professionals within the software development environment. A software manager would be hard pressed to release a good software engineer to SQA, if he or she is facing a manpower problem that could impact schedule completion of a project. In many instances the tendency is to release those individuals who are poor performers.
- A rotating SQA policy requires support from upper management to become effective and not to end up as a dumping ground for the bad programmer or software engineer. The choice of who makes the rotation into the SQA section should be mutually agreed to by all concerned. Motivating the software engineer to participate willingly in such a program is necessary, and the only sure means of accomplishing this is to institute a promotional policy that gives special consideration to individuals who have already served as SQA engineers.

The same policy should also hold true for one being considered for a manager's position in software engineering.

The author knows of three organizations that have tried such a program: IBM, Raytheon, and ITT. The benefits these organizations have derived from such a program have been limited to how successful they have been in retaining the services of the individuals that participated in the rotation program. Because the majority of those participating in the program were recent college graduates, all companies reported that many participants had left for assignments in other companies. For a rotation policy of this type to succeed as a means of increasing the awareness of SQA within an organization, what is needed is a core of resident SQA experts to learn from so as to continue the smooth operation of the SQA function. Furthermore, individuals selected to participate in the program should have between 3 and 5 years of industry experience, therefore reducing the possibility of their departure after the rotation assignment.

4.9 New College Graduates

The recent college graduate is ideal for certain specialized tasks within the SQA organization. Many SQA organizations are evolving from a labor-intensive approach to a more computerized approach to quality software. Such a transition requires developing SQA tools to perform tasks that were once manually performed, hence the transition from a labor-intensive approach to QA to an automated approach. Based on the author's experience, the recent college graduate is an excellent source of expertise to perform some of the tasks needed to orchestrate such a transition.

It is a well-known fact that the interest and professional development of recent college graduates in computer science tends to follow these broad guidelines. First, the graduate seeks out programming tasks and appears to find satisfaction in the activities associated with such a task. After a short period, from 3 to 6 months, his or her interest focuses on the challenges provided with being involved in software design. Some time later in terms of career growth, task assignments in software architecture become appealing. Employing a recent college graduate to perform SQA tasks at the onset has been proved to be a poor management decision, and the organization runs the risk of losing that employee because of a lack of interest in the work assigned.

The procedure that appears to work best is to combine programming tasks with SQA tasks. Obviously the mixture of programming and SQA tasks must be tailored to the needs of both the organization and the individual. During the first 6 months of a college graduate's employment, a 60/40 ratio of programming tasks to SQA tasks seems to work well. The benefits to be derived from such a mixture are many, but most of all the recent college hire's perception is that of performing a constructive task. He or she is also able to observe the benefits of these efforts, while the benefits to be derived from purely SQA tasks are more subjective and therefore a demotivator.

Orienting the new hire to the SQA methodology employed by the organization is an important training procedure that must not be ignored. Typically the SQA training process takes somewhere between 1 and 2 years before such an individual should be allowed to make independent SQA decisions without supervision. This orientation should involve exposure to overall company policies and procedures as well as the specific software tools and techniques employed by the organization to develop software.

4.10   SQA Employment Requisitions

Recruiting, hiring, and training software engineers in quality assurance can be very expensive and time-consuming. It would be wise for the SQA organization to define and set priorities for key positions in the form of job descriptions and responsibilities (see Appendix 4A). Before proceeding, the organization should consider these issues:

- Is the organization located in an area that can provide a local pool of software quality people? Should recruiting policy be national, regional, or local, considering that the degree of staff turn-around is directly related to where the new hire comes from? Can contract employees help and how best can they be utilized? Can the company promote from within and train individuals to fill SQA openings?
- What tasks should be assigned to a new SQA organization?

Whether SQA personnel are acquired from within or from outside of the company, care must be given to distinguishing between software professionals and paraprofessionals. Job descriptions for these individuals should be documented to inform the placement office of the specific tasks they will be called on to perform and the backgrounds needed to sustain these tasks. Furthermore, the careful allocation of tasks between professionals and paraprofessionals will determine the attrition rate the organization will experience. Typical professional job titles within the SQA function are:

- Software quality assurance manager;
- Engineer software quality assurance;
- Software reliability engineer;
- Software configuration management specialist;
- Software safety engineer.

The SQA manager is typically responsible for supervising the operation of the SQA section through planning and directing the utilization of personnel. This position in the organization also requires that counseling and guidance be given to company management in matters pertaining to the quality and reliability of software products developed or purchased. From a global viewpoint, the SQA manager must set the framework that will dictate the use of a software development methodology that lends itself to quality software. The engineering reliability and configuration staff supporting this effort will provide the technical expertise necessary to assure that the objectives of the QA effort are achieved and maintained. Specific duties of the SQA function should include, but not be limited to, the following:

- Provide SQA support and improve upon the existing SQA system;
- Develop SQA tools that sense software problems during the design, development, and life-cycle phases;
- Keep management aware of the quality status of software development projects during the design, development, and life-cycle phases;
- Monitor the continuing needs and requirements of the SQA program and implement them;
- Participate in software design reviews, testing, configuration control, problem reporting and resolution, and change control;
- Provide inputs to technical and cost proposals relative to the company's participation in computer software quality;
- Audit, monitor, evaluate, and report on subcontractor software development efforts.

Many of the tasks within the SQA function can be performed by individuals who are paraprofessionals. It would be to the benefit of the organization to use these individuals to perform those tasks. This category may include the following positions:

- Software librarian aide;
- Senior software librarian;
- Software quality assurance engineering assistant;
- Software quality engineering assistant;
- Software quality assurance aide.

The role of these paraprofessionals can be viewed as assisting the professionals in achieving the SQA objectives defined by management. Work assignments are, in many instances, related to performing tasks that have been defined in detail by the professionals assigned to the SQA function. The manager employing the services of such paraprofessionals should realize that these individuals, properly trained and with formal education, could in the future make excellent SQA professionals.

4.11   What to Expect from Your SQA Engineering Staff

Members of the QA staff should have a relatively high level of technical expertise and a thorough knowledge of good software quality assurance policies. The manner in which the staff is organized depends largely on staff size, estimated workload, and personnel skills. Several alternatives are suggested:

- Each SQA staff member could be specialized to perform one task for all software products.

- Each SQA staff member could perform all software QA tasks associated with a particular product.
- The SQA organization could act as a team in which all members would cooperate in performing the QA tasks.

If it is properly staffed and organized, you can expect from your SQA organization, the staff to have the ability to work independently.

If your staff and organization are to grow and meet the demands placed upon them, the individuals assigned to perform SQA tasks must possess an understanding and involvement in their assigned projects. This understanding and involvement is achieved if the system requires their independent involvement and participation. The part-time SQA engineer is ineffective and does little to improve the quality and reliability of the software product. Productivity with minimum supervision is achieved only if the policies and procedures in place lend themselves to a team approach to quality assurance. Productivity with supervision does not permit individuals the freedom to develop into professionals who function independently.

Other qualities that one could expect from an SQA engineering staff include the following:

- *Ability to devise new and improved methods to perform SQA tasks.* The discipline of SQA is relatively new, and the whole process is being transformed from an approach that is labor-intensive to one that can be automated. The SQA engineer must be expected to develop the necessary tools, techniques, and methodologies to accomplish tasks that have been assigned.
- *Good judgment and objectivity in approaching problems.* It is imperative that the SQA engineer be able to apply good judgment and objectivity when dealing with other members of the software development team. These attributes are important, because the SQA engineer must have the support of the software development team to function effectively. If an SQA engineer alienates himself or herself from the development team, the SQA function is no longer contributing to the team's effort.
- *Communication skills for a better understanding.* The SQA engineer must possess good communication skills. Skill in expressing ideas both orally and in writing are crucial, for example, when communicating SQA review and audit findings to the software development team, or making presentations to upper management. Since most findings are of a negative nature, challenge provided by the developing environment to these findings will require considerable skill to get the message across. Furthermore, SQA is frequently called upon to present its needs and requirements to the developers. Good communication can make this job easier.
- *Technical competence and knowledge of the project are imperative.* An SQA staff (or member or portion of the staff) not knowledgeable about software development cannot support the objectives of the SQA organization. Moreover, these individuals cannot provide the expertise needed to perform the software QA tasks that the position will demand. Such individuals will therefore not be able to complete assignments rapidly or at all without compromising standards of quality.

4.12 Developing Career Paths

A software quality assurance organization without engineering-defined career paths will not survive the tests of time and effectiveness. It is essential that SQA engineers have the opportunity to ascend the corporate ladder. One of the disadvantages of some corporate organizational structures is that many of the SQA organizations exist within a hardware matrix organization, which limits the career paths for the software professionals within the product assurance organization. It is imperative that the organization recognize this critical shortfall and take steps to remedy it in order to permit the SQA function to develop into an essential and capable factor in software development.

What should be done? Obviously, if the organization is to survive, career paths from SQA to other disciplines within the organization must exist, such as SQA engineers becoming lead software engineers or SQA management moving into software development management. Specifically, a dual ladder system must exist: this allows highly competent technical employees to continue their career growth without assuming management responsibilities. It also allows management-oriented engineers to climb organizational ladders and assume management responsibilities. (In fact, the editor of this book moved from manager of software quality engineering to manager of software development engineering. Another example, at the same firm, occurred when an experienced software quality engineer transferred into software systems engineering.) This parallel structure bridges the gap between engineering and management. The organization's main goal, however, for such an approach to staff development, must be to allow engineers to progress up the ladder without becoming managers, if they desire not to.

4.13 Recommendations

Remember that the personnel requirements that make SQA work, discussed earlier, are:

- Approximately 3 to 5 years developing software;
- Experienced software engineer who has seen it all and has survived the software battles;
- Individual seeking to advance to management or a program manager's position;
- Good communication skills;
- Computer science academic background;
- Willingness to meet and accept new challenges.

The organizational environment plays a decisive role in how successful the software QA function will be. Success can be measured only in terms of a team of dedicated individuals contributing in a supportive posture to a project. To give this success its best chance, the following recommendations are offered:

- The salaries of the SQA engineers should be generally competitive and specifically in line with those of software development engineers.
- Project-related SQA functions are dysfunctional and present too many problems. A central, independent SQA function driving all projects is a more effective method to achieve SQA goals.
- A rotating SQA policy should be used as a long-range plan and only after a core of experienced SQA individuals already exists. The rotation program is not a recommended approach to starting up an SQA function.
- Responsibilities of SQA must be clearly defined and firmly supported by corporate management.
- The best approach to starting an SQA function is to first create a position within the corporate organization for an SQA manager, then promote or hire an individual to fill that position.
- The SQA organization should be situated in the corporate organization so that it always reports to the same level as the department, which it must evaluate and audit.

References

[1]   Rothman, J., "Software Quality Assurance: Should It Remain a Separate Organization?" http://www.jrothman.com/Papers/SQAseparate.html, May 1996, accessed December 2006.

[2]   computerjob.com, "Average Income by Skill," http://www.computerjobs.com/salary2000/index.asp?display=skills&emptype=perm, December 2006.

Selected Bibliography

Arthur, L. J., *Measuring Programmer Productivity and Software Quality*, New York: John Wiley & Sons, 1984, pp. 12–35.

Mendis, K. S., "A Software Quality Assurance Program for the 80s," *ASQC Technical Conference Transactions*, 1980, pp. 379–388.

Mendis, K. S., "Software Quality Assurance Staffing Problems," *ASQC Technical Conference Transactions*, 1983, pp. 108–112.

Ryan, J. R., "Software Product Quality Assurance," *Proceedings of the National Computer Conference*, 1981, pp. 393–398.

Appendix 4A   Typical Software Quality–Related Job Descriptions

Software Quality Assurance Manager

Experience required: 8 years of software related experience, 3 years in SQA, 1 year management experience.

Education required: B.S., computer science, information technology, or related technical discipline; M.B.A or M.S. in software engineering highly desirable.

Duties: Manage the SQA organization. Provide personnel to support the projects that require SQA activities. Do strategic planning for the SQA organization. Interview and hire SQA personnel. Inform upper management of the status of SQA and its activities across the projects supported. Monitor the SQA portion of proposals and estimates. Provide management interface with software engineering and software process organizations. (Refer to Sections 4.5 and 4.10.)

Engineer Software Quality Assurance

Experience required: 4 years of software related experience, 1 year in SQA.

Education required: B.S., computer science, information technology, or related technical discipline.

Duties: Perform SQA activities on the projects. Participate in software design reviews, testing, configuration control, problem reporting and resolution, and change control. Audit, monitor, evaluate and report on the software subcontractor activities. Assist in the Interviewing of SQA personnel. Produce write-ups and estimates for the SQA portion of proposals. Interface with software engineering, software configuration management and the software process organizations. (Refer to Sections 4.5 and 4.10.)

Software Reliability Engineer

Experience required: 4 years of software related experience, 1 year in SQA or reliability engineering.

Education required: B.S., computer science, statistics, or related technical discipline.

Duties: Perform the reliability calculations for the software projects that require them. Utilize the software reliability tools available on the PC to perform the calculations. Advise the other software quality engineers on what the meaning of and results of the software reliability calculations are for the project.

Software Configuration Management Specialist

Experience required: 4 years of software related experience, 1 year in SQA or software configuration management.

Education required: B.S., computer science, software engineering, or related technical discipline.

Duties: Perform the software configuration management functions for the project. This includes software identification, configuration control, and configuration status accounting and configuration audits. Coordinate these activities with software development and SQA. Review subcontractor's software configuration management activities. Orient the software related personnel on projects as to the software configuration management requirements. Evaluate and support software configuration management tools for the project.

Software Safety Engineer

Experience required: 4 years of software related experience, 1 year in SQA, software safety, or human factors.

Education required: B.S., computer science, software engineering, or related technical discipline.

Duties: Perform the software safety functions for the project. This includes the evaluation of human factor, human-machine interface, and life critical functions of the software. Coordinate these activities with software development and SQA. Review subcontractor's software safety activities. Evaluate and support software safety tools for the project.

Software Librarian Aide

Experience required: None.

Education required: AA degree in computer related field, or computer technical school diploma, or high school diploma with proven competency in PC software.

Duties: Assist the software configuration management person on the project in performing the software library duties. These duties include both the hard copy library management and the electronic library control. Handling the releases and baselines of the software and documents are an integral part of these function. Keeping access control is a critical function to be performed.

Senior Software Librarian

Experience required: 2 years as a software librarian aide.

Education required: AA degree in computer related field, or computer technical school diploma, or high school diploma with proven competency in PC software.

Duties: Handle for the project the software library duties. These duties include both the hard copy library management and the electronic library control. Handling the releases and baselines of the software and documents are an integral part of this function. Keeping access control is a critical function to be performed.

Software Quality Assurance Engineering Assistant

Experience required: 1 year as a software quality engineering assistant.

Education required: AA degree in computer related field, or computer technical school diploma, or high school diploma with proven competency in PC software.

Duties: Handle administrative activities for the SQA engineer on the project. Place information into the SQA tool used for the project to report deficiencies. Be the interface to the SQA tools in use on the project. Where necessary keep the SQA hard copy Project Book on SQA findings. Assist in test witnessing. Fill out SQA evaluation reports where appropriate. Interface with software configuration management as necessary.

Software Quality Engineering Assistant

Experience required: 1 year as an SQA aide.

Education required: AA degree in computer related field, or computer technical school diploma, or high school diploma with proven competency in PC software.

Duties: Handle administrative activities for the SQA engineer on the project. Place information into the SQA tool used for the project to report deficiencies. Be the interface to the SQA tools in use on the project. Where necessary keep the SQA hard copy Project Book on SQA findings. Assist in test witnessing. Fill out SQA evaluation reports where appropriate. Interface with software configuration management as necessary.

Software Quality Assurance Aide

Experience required: None.

Education required: AA degree in computer related field, or computer technical school diploma, or high school diploma with proven competency in PC software.

Duties: Handle administrative activities for the SQA engineer on the project. Place information into the SQA tool used for the project to report deficiencies. Be the interface to the SQA tools in use on the project. Where necessary keep the SQA hard copy Project Book on SQA findings.

## CHAPTER 5

Training for Quality Management

Emanuel R. Baker and Matthew J. Fisher

5.1 Introduction

In Chapter 1 we discussed the Quality Program: its concepts, structure, and organizational considerations. In this chapter, we discuss the Quality Program from the perspective of training, in particular, training for that Quality Program element called Evaluate Process and Product Quality, often referred to as *quality evaluation*. Here, we focus on training aspects for those individuals or groups carrying out such evaluations for projects or an organization. In this chapter, we are proffering our own formulation for an effective quality evaluation training program.

5.2 Context for a Quality Evaluation Training Program

5.2.1 Quality Evaluation to Quality Assurance

As stated in Chapter 1, the Quality Program incorporates three elements covering the activities necessary to:

- *Establish Requirements and Control Changes:* Establish and specify requirements for the quality of an product;
- *Establish and Implement Methods:*[1] Establish, implement, and put into practice methods, processes, and procedures to develop, operate, deploy, and maintain the product;
- *Evaluate Process and Product Quality:* Establish and implement methods, processes, and procedures to evaluate the quality of the product, as well as to evaluate associated documentation, processes, and activities that have an impact on the quality of the product.

In this chapter, we discuss the last element, Evaluate Process and Product Quality. There is a difference between this element of the Quality Program and what is often considered to be the purview of quality assurance (QA). Although there are standard *definitions* of QA, there is really no standard definition of what QA

---

1. Methodology is a system of principles, procedures and practices applied to a particular branch of knowledge. As used here, the organizations' processes and procedures in a development are instantiations of methodologies.

organizations do. QA functions often depend on what the organization chooses to assign to the QA organization, ranging from examining adherence to organizational standards [1] to performing overall verification and validation activities. Furthermore, this range of functions can be implemented in a variety of ways. Therefore, QA training depends upon the organization's assignment of quality evaluation functions to QA; that is, what functions constitute the QA organization's charter. Mistakenly assuming that the role of the QA organization completely satisfies the purpose of the quality effort will often result in a project manager failing to assign key quality evaluation roles to qualified personnel or entities on the project. Thus, the quality evaluation effort will suffer. Consequently, we will focus the training discussion on quality evaluation.

5.2.2 Audience for Quality Evaluation Training

Training to implement any program, process, methodology, tool, software application, and the like, must be geared to those people interacting with it. For example, people who interact with a configuration management system only with respect to the processing of change requests or problem reports do not need to know the specifics of how the library management tool works. The operative words here are "interact with."

As a consequence, the primary audiences for training in quality evaluation are those that implement the evaluation and interact with the following:

- Requirements development;
- Requirements management;
- Process developers and evaluators;
- Process and product quality evaluators.

From the discussion in Chapter 1 on the Quality Program, it can be seen that the program can involve personnel from a fair number of disciplines, and can involve a large number of people. Consequently, to emphasize again, we are limiting the scope of this discussion to training for implementing the quality evaluation aspect of the Quality Program.

5.2.3 Organizational Training Program

Training for quality evaluation must be set in the overall context of the organization's mission, structure, and training program. The objective of any organizational training program is to develop the skills and knowledge of people so they can perform their roles effectively and efficiently [1]. Accordingly, the training needs for each organization varies widely but should have the following aspects:

- Strategic training geared to the organization's mission and business goals;
- Training that is common across projects;
- Training that meets needs specific to individual projects.

Exactly where the responsibility for training that covers these aspects resides depends on the operations of the organization and interface with the projects.

In general, any training program involves [1]:

- Identifying the training needed;
- Obtaining and providing training to address the needs;
- Establishing and maintaining the training capability;
- Establishing and maintaining training records;
- Assessing training effectiveness.

There are a variety of ways to accomplish these tasks.

5.2.4   Needed Skills and Knowledge

The needed skills and knowledge of an individual performing the quality evaluation role depends on his or her assignment—meaning the quality evaluation functions or responsibility assigned to that individual to implement. We believe that the following components are essential to the training program.

5.2.4.1   Organizations Goals and Objectives

Individuals performing these roles need to know the context in which they are performing their roles. They need to know why what they are doing is important. Such training is best provided by the organization—that is, it should not be contracted out to external trainers.

5.2.4.2   Specific Project Goals, Objectives

Organizational goals and objectives are often supplemented by the goals and objectives unique to the project. Any additional goals and objectives specific to the project should be the subject of training offered by the project.

5.2.4.3   Domain Knowledge

Domain knowledge is essential. For example, if a quality evaluator is assigned to an avionics project, any meaningful role performed by a quality evaluator relies on knowledge of and experience in the avionics domain. It is doubtful that a quality evaluator can competently determine the adequacy of any avionics work product without such knowledge, nor could the quality evaluator properly assess a developer's compliance with the organization's development process. The necessity for domain knowledge is even more apparent when we look at the evaluation for adequacy of an element of the avionics development process. Such knowledge is necessary if we want to be able to insert measures into the process to see how effective it is.

Without domain knowledge, the quality evaluation role effectively becomes a checklist function. For example, in checking a document for compliance with standards, the evaluator can at best only determine if the format has been followed, and that all the sections are there. That provides little insight into whether the right information has been inserted into the sections. We would not expect that the quality evaluator should be a domain expert, but we would expect that the quality evaluator would know enough about the domain to determine that on the face of things, the information appears to be the right information. As a further example, where domain knowledge is lacking, evaluations for compliance with the process reduce to merely asking the performer questions to determine if the performer has followed the process. Without domain knowledge, the evaluator has no basis for evaluating answers to questions or to assess interim work products for compliance, or to know (as the worst case) if the performer is being less than truthful about what he or she is doing. A checklist function without domain knowledge adds very little value to the project or to the organization.

We would not expect the organization's training program in the applicable domains to make source material experts of the quality evaluators. We would expect, however, that the training program would provide enough of an overview to make the quality evaluator sufficiently cognizant of the subject material to understand what is going on. A quality evaluator would then know the type of questions to ask. The quality evaluator may not be able to perform a detailed analysis of the work, but he or she would be able to make some judgments about the reasonableness of what he or she is evaluating. Such domain training should be provided by the organization if the domain for the project to which the evaluator is assigned is one that is part of the enterprise's product line. If the domain is specific to a project, and not part of the enterprise's product line, the project should provide the training.

5.2.4.5   Quality Evaluation Requirements

It is important for the quality evaluator to know how requirements should be written, for example, the requirements for verification and validation.

Here is an example of the difference between quality evaluation and quality assurance, leading to a brief discussion of requirements for quality evaluation. The CMMI® [1] defines the function of quality assurance in its formulation of the Process and Product Quality Assurance process area as evaluating the performance of processes for compliance with their governing process description and evaluating work products for compliance with their governing standards. Our formulation of the Quality Program takes a broader view and defines the function of quality evaluation, not only quality assurance. Given the CMMI® definition of quality assurance, evaluating a process, product, or service for technical adequacy (and potentially other quality attributes except for compliance) is outside the scope of the quality assurance function (no organizational connotation is intended here). Evaluations for technical adequacy must nevertheless be performed, and this, too, is a quality evaluation function.

One of the technical adequacy evaluations that must be performed is the evaluation of requirements. Knowledge of what constitutes a properly written requirement is essential for performing this role. There are a number of different types of requirements, including:

- Functional requirements;
- Performance requirements;

- Interface requirements;
- Data requirements;
- Security and privacy requirements;
- Data integrity requirements;
- The "ilities" (e.g., reliability, maintainability, and so on).

Each of these categories has a unique set of characteristics. Training should be provided for those who participate in requirements reviews (e.g., requirements peer reviews, requirements document reviews) so that the various types of requirements can be adequately evaluated for completeness, necessity, feasibility, correctness, and testability. Clearly, requirements that are included in a requirements specification should be there only if they are necessary for the product to work as the user intended. Requirements statements should be complete and should have the attributes associated with the type of requirement that it is (e.g., functional, performance, and so on). Correctness of a requirement as written should be self-evident: there should not be any errors in the statement of the requirement. Testability of a requirement has a major influence on the ability to perform verification and validation against the requirements.

5.2.4.6   How to Generate Criteria to Be Used in Judging Process and Product Quality

Ultimately, those that perform quality evaluations need criteria by which to objectively judge the acceptability of the product or process under evaluation. Training should be provided in the techniques for specifying the criteria for judging process and product quality. Different types of products require different quality criteria, just as different processes will have different criteria. A measurement and analysis process will require different criteria for judging its quality than a requirements elicitation process. Here again the need for domain-specific training is important.

5.2.4.7   Limitations and Constraints on Performing and Implementing Quality Evaluation Functions

Limitations and constraints on executing functions will always exist. Some may relax the standard way of doing business, while others may require stricter controls. Quality evaluators who work in the medical device industry will have very rigid constraints imposed by the FDA, just as quality evaluators working on commercial aircraft with consideration of safety of flight components will as well. On the other hand, quality evaluators who work on the software for commercial aircraft entertainment systems may have a more relaxed set of requirements. Just as appraisal teams who perform CMMI® SCAMPI^SM appraisals must be trained in the intricacies of the appraisal methodology (which is one form of quality evaluation), quality evaluators in all industries and application domains must be trained in the constraints, requirements, and limitations imposed by the policies, standards, and regulations applicable to them.

5.2.4.8   How to Write Plans and Procedures for Their Assignments

A quality evaluation plan or, more than likely, a set of quality evaluation plans, should exist for all projects. In virtually all cases, there will be a set; for example, one for document evaluation, one for peer reviews, another for test, and so on. It is important to know the appropriate type of content to include for each type of plan that must be written. Here again, domain knowledge comes into play. A plan written about a quality evaluation to be performed where the author is not knowledgeable in the domain will often be less than useful. Furthermore, the plans must accurately reflect what needs to be done to implement the necessary evaluation. Training should cover how to write such plans. Considering the variety of evaluations that will be done during the course of a project, it will take more than one training course to accomplish this. One size does not fit all in this case.

A similar argument can be made for procedures. But an additional consideration enters the picture here, and that is the level of detail. A procedure that is too detailed may be ignored, whereas a procedure that does not have enough detail may fail to adequately accomplish the required evaluation. The training program should focus on establishing the right balance between too little and too much detail. In some cases, this balance could be a function of the organization's preferences. Some organizations prefer their procedures to be quite detailed, whereas others prefer high level procedures, with the details embedded in the training materials. Consequently, this training should be the organization's responsibility.

5.2.4.9   How to Do the Evaluation

One cannot pick up a procedure and immediately become a productive quality evaluator. Training in how to do evaluations is necessary. This should include helping the evaluator understand what the individual steps are, but also should include sample problems for the evaluator to exercise his or her newly acquired skills on. This training should be a part of a formal training program. While mentoring may be helpful in accomplishing this training, too often the mentor's own biases get passed to the trainee. Training in how to perform the various evaluations should be structured to accomplish a uniform application of the procedures. Relying totally on mentoring typically will not accomplish that.

5.3   Two Examples

The most difficult training aspect for quality management is how best to approach the training for quality evaluations. Because the scope, audience, and functions of quality evaluation cover a considerable range of activities, we offer two examples at the ends of this range.

5.3.1   Evaluation of Adherence to Process (PPQA)

An example of quality evaluation comes from the Process and Product Quality Assurance (PPQA) process area from the CMMI® [1]. This process area focuses on evaluating work products for adherence to standards, and evaluations of the performance of the various process areas within the model for compliance with their process descriptions. The requirement to evaluate a process area for compliance with its process descriptions is specified in Generic Practice (GP) 2.9 for each process area. For purposes of this discussion, suffice it to say that the PPQA process area is the umbrella set of requirements for performing quality evaluations, and what evaluations to perform are defined in GP 2.9 for each process area. See Chapter 11 for a further discussion of the PPQA process area. (For those who are interested in a more detailed discussion of the CMMI® structure, a discussion of the structure of the model in terms of process areas, specific and generic practices, and the like, can be found in [1].)

Within the PPQA process area, there is another generic practice, GP 2.2, which calls for a plan for performing the process and product quality evaluations. In our discussion of the needed skills and knowledge, we pointed out the necessity for training in writing plans. We also noted the importance for training in the appropriate application domains. Both are important for producing a good plan for the PPQA process. The process areas of the CMMI® are diverse, running the gamut from project management activities, to engineering, to process management, and various support functions such as configuration management, measurement and analysis, and so on. Knowing how to write a plan that adequately addresses the ability to perform process and product quality evaluations for such a diverse set of activities can only be accomplished by training the lead evaluators in writing plans of this nature.

Training in domain knowledge comes into play here in that establishing the procedures for determining compliance with the process descriptions for the process areas in question require at least a high level knowledge of the domain to determine if the process execution is in compliance. For example, for the Technical Solution process area, if agile methods are the process being implemented, the quality evaluator must have some knowledge of these methods; otherwise, the quality evaluation becomes a checklist activity reliant on asking the process performers if they are following the process. As one can imagine, the ability to be fooled is quite high and the value added from such an evaluation is quite low. Obviously, training in how to write both plans and procedures for quality evaluation is necessary, along with the need for domain-specific training. Any constraints or limitations imposed on the process in question to be evaluated must be known as well, otherwise the evaluations will yield incorrect results.

Training in how to do the process evaluations is also important. It is one thing to be trained in writing quality evaluation plans and procedures, but if one does not know how to implement the procedures, then the value of the training in writing plans and procedures is diminished. How to do process evaluations will be a function of the kind of process evaluated. The evaluation of a peer review process for compliance is different from the evaluation of a testing process. This, in turn, is different from the evaluation of a design process that will clearly depend on the design methodology being implemented. In software, evaluations of a design process being implemented using agile methods will require different knowledge than evaluation of a design process using object-oriented techniques. Clearly, there is an interaction with domain knowledge and basic engineering methodology skills. One might easily (and correctly) assume that certain evaluations should be performed by personnel trained in the skills necessary to perform the processes in question.

Superimposed on these training needs is the need to be trained in goals and objectives of the project and the organization. These provide a context for the evaluations to be performed. In addition to the constraints and limitations imposed by client and industry standards and regulations, the organization's and project's business needs provide an additional set of constraints and limitations.

Finally, the ability to specify quality evaluation criteria also comes into play. If these are incorrectly specified, processes that do not comply with governing process descriptions may be evaluated as adequate when they are not. One can clearly see the importance of training in this area.

5.3.2 Evaluation of Product Quality

As noted earlier, if we use the CMMI® as a reference point, the PPQA process area addresses both process and product quality evaluations. In the previous example, we discussed the need for training in writing plans and procedures, and the need for training in the domains of interest. We also discussed the need to be trained in the constraints and limitations applicable to the domain of interest. These needs apply as well for training in product evaluation.

In the CMMI® PPQA process area, evaluations of product quality are defined as evaluations for compliance with governing standards. One can easily conclude from this that the focus is on compliance with specified templates and formats. In the defense industry, this conceivably could be considered compliance with Data Item Descriptions (DID) imposed by contract. In performing such evaluations, the evaluator looks to see if all the specified content has been provided and if the format of the document is correct. Knowing if the proper content has been provided requires at least some domain-specific training. On the other hand, knowing if the work product is in the appropriate format requires very little training if the product is a document. A template, or a DID, along with a bona fide sample from a project in the Process Asset Library, provides sufficient information for performing a format compliance evaluation.

On the other hand, if the work product is an item of software, and format requirements (e.g., coding standards) have been specified, the quality evaluator must know how to read source code in the specified coding language, requiring either that such training be provided or that an evaluator familiar with that coding language be used for performing the evaluation. While this can often be accomplished by software tools, there are times when organizations specify unique coding standards. The quality evaluator should at least be able to determine if the output of the software tool (if one is used) will adequately determination violations of the coding standards.

There are some training needs that are unique to the evaluation of products. Previously, we discussed the need for training in writing requirements. If a quality evaluator is responsible for evaluating the content of a requirements specification, clearly, that person must know how to write requirements for the various types of requirements that are to be included in the specification, the subject of training we have previously discussed. In the case of evaluations of requirements specifications, two separate evaluations may take place: one for the proper statement of the requirements and another for format and content of the requirements specification. These requirements become the requirements for performing validation of the product. Being able to assess if the requirements are testable, as written, requires training in writing requirements, as we previously discussed. Training in the ability to write test plans, test cases, and test procedures follows from this.

5.4 Summary

In setting the context for quality assurance training we considered the entire quality evaluation aspect of a Quality Program. The rationale is that quality evaluation is broader in scope and typically covers more functions than what have been perceived as the "traditional" quality assurance functions, depending on the organizations concept of quality assurance. A further analysis of this idea is covered in Chapter 13.

Too frequently, the role of quality evaluation has been perceived as not requiring much in the way of training. Mentoring has often been used as a method of training. Mentoring, in many cases, has meant pairing a new quality evaluator with an experienced one. In many cases, mentoring may be an adequate method of training; in other cases, not. All too often, the so-called experienced quality evaluator is lacking in the knowledge to perform the role properly, and he or she passes down information that is inadequate to the new quality evaluator. In other cases, the mentor may have biases that should not be passed on to the new evaluator.

Other mistaken approaches have often been applied. Training in how to do peer reviews has sometimes relied on an implicit requirement for the participants to read the procedures and then know how to perform their roles in peer reviews on the basis of their reading. In addition, many companies do not provide training in how to do testing or how to construct a test program. While information on how to conduct various aspects of a testing program can be found from public seminars, instruction on how to construct a total, comprehensive test program, say, beginning with bench testing and ending in a full-blown qualification or acceptance test, is lacking.

In many cases, the situation existing in quality evaluation has resulted from a lack of understanding or appreciation for the importance of the quality evaluation role. In this chapter, we have provided some context to the requirements for and scope of an effective quality evaluation program.

Reference

[1] Chrissis, M. B., M. Konrad, and S. Shrum, *CMMI®: Guidelines for Process Integration and Product Improvement*, 2nd ed., Reading, MA: Addison-Wesley, 2006.

## CHAPTER 6

The Pareto Principle Applied to Software Quality Assurance

Thomas J. McCabe and G. Gordon Schulmeyer

6.1 Introduction

Concentrate on the vital few, not the trivial many. This admonition borrowed from J. M. Juran (see Chapter 2), the quality consultant, epitomizes the Pareto Principle as he applied it to quality management. Thomas J. McCabe has extended this Pareto Principle to software quality activities.

The Natural Law of Software Quality says that Pareto's rule holds true, especially in software systems: 20% of the code has 80% of the defects—Find them! Fix them! Remember from Fred Brooks' analysis of the development of OS/360 for IBM Corporation: 4% of OS/360 had more than 60% of the errors. Similarly, on a reusable software library, two of the first 11 modules (20%) had *all of the errors*. Also, 20% of the code requires 80% of the enhancements—find them by looking into enhancement logs to find out where most changes occur [1].

Barry Boehm has provided information that software phenomena follow a Pareto distribution [2]:

- 20% of the modules consume 80% of the resources;
- 20% of the modules contribute 80% of the errors;
- 20% of the errors consume 80% of repair costs;
- 20% of the enhancements consume 80% of the adaptive maintenance costs;
- 20% of the modules consume 80% of the execution time;
- 20% of the tools experience 80% of the tool usage.

This chapter explores the Pareto Principle as related to software. It is during the software development cycle that the application of the Pareto Principle pays off. Software quality assurance (SQA) and software development personnel should know how to apply the Pareto Principle during the software development cycle, which is what this chapter is all about. Depending on the structure and environment in your organization, the use of the Pareto analysis may be done by developers, managers, or the SQA personnel. SQA personnel should note that use of the Pareto Principle promotes a win-win situation for SQA, for the project, and for the company.

Briefly, the 80/20 rule states that 20% of an activity contains the significant 80% of what is important to the activity, resulting in the Pareto Principle that postulates for many phenomena, 80% of the consequences stem from 20% of the causes. So a Pareto analysis statistically examines distributions of items and ranks them according to their frequency of occurrence. Often, this analysis results in a representation called a Pareto diagram (Figure 6.1) pictured to show Module 1 causing most of the problems to the system.

First, two specific examples undertaken by McCabe & Associates, Inc., for the World Wide Military Command & Control System (WWMCCS) and the Federal Reserve Bank are covered in some detail, which are considered classic examples of the use of Pareto analysis to software development. The various ways that the Pareto Principle can apply to software and the results of those applications are discussed.

Some extensions of the Pareto Principle to other fertile areas previously exposed by J. M. Juran are defect identification, inspections, and statistical techniques. Each of these areas is discussed in relation to software and its probable payoff in better quality.

For defect identification in software, some of the common symptoms of defects in software are uncovered, and suggestions as to the basic causes of defects in software are provided.

Inspections have been a mainstay in the factory to ensure the quality of the product. That inspections have been applied to software is well known, but tying inspections to the Pareto Principle is not well understood. So, the explanation of that phenomenon is also covered in this chapter.

A unique application of Pareto analysis in comparing Pareto charts, discussed by Ron Kennett, is also covered.

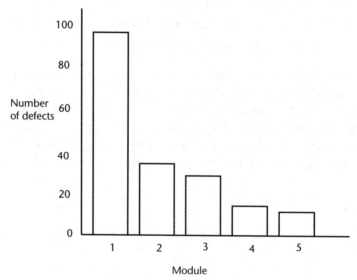

Figure 6.1 Pareto diagram example.

6.2 WWMCCS—Classic Example 1

The example cited is from an actual study of quality assurance conducted by Thomas McCabe in 1977 for the World Wide Military Command and Control System (WWMCCS) [3]. At that time, WWMCCS was a large network of 35 Honeywell H6000's with a specialized operating system and hundreds of user application programs. The WWMCCS ADP Directorate is the organization responsible for WWMCCS software acquisition, integration, and testing. The quality assurance program was for the WWMCCS ADP Directorate organization, and the following are examples of ways in which the Pareto Principle was applied to that organization.

6.2.1 Manpower

This heading represents internal WWMCCS ADP Directorate personnel expenditures. The first task was to identify the different functions performed in the WWMCCS ADP Directorate (e.g., planning, scheduling, task preparation, demonstration test, integration, stability testing, regression testing, and so on) and then analyze the WWMCCS ADP Directorate personnel expenditure on each task. The few functions that Pareto analysis determined as consuming 80% of the manpower were identified as strong candidates to be placed under the microscope to determine the reasons for this consumption. The goal was to reduce personnel expenditures by reducing the number of people required to complete the task—that is, without diminishing the quality of the complete job. In doing this, one could distinguish between technical and managerial manpower. This yielded two initial distributions for quality assurance, which resulted in identifying two distinct classes of internal WWMCCS ADP Directorate functions.

A chart similar to the one in Table 6.1 aids in the analysis. The statistics assume a 3-month time frame.

For managerial personnel, note that scheduling and "crisis reaction" required more than half of the expended time; and for technical personnel, note that software purchase analysis and planning utilized just under half of the expended time. A particular interesting WWMCCS ADP Directorate function in the table is "crisis reaction." It is informative to determine how much of the personnel resources this category actually consumed and then see which types of crisis were most frequently repeated and most costly. The crisis reaction function for managerial personnel turned out indeed to be significantly expensive. So, a key point is that a program should be directed at more careful planning and coordination.

For a simpler representation, in graph form, for the data shown in Table 6.1, see Figure 6.2.

6.2.2 Cost of Contracts

This category of examination is concerned with the internal software quality of a WWMCCS release. There are two steps in applying the Pareto Principle to the quality of the product. First, the WWMCCS ADP Directorate decides how to define quality—this could be done by prioritizing the software quality factors (metrics) listed in Table 6.2, and selecting a subset of the factors as an operational definition

Table 6.1   Hours Expended on Personnel Tasks

Personnel Tasks	Hours Expanded	% of Hours Expanded	Cumulative Hours Expanded	Cumulative % of Hours Expanded
*Managerial Personnel**				
Scheduling	600	43	600	43
"Crisis reaction"	300	21	900	64
Planning	200	14	1,100	78
Decision making	150	11	1,250	89
Contract administration	100	7	1,350	96
Controlling	30	3	1,380	99
"Task preparation"	20	1	1,400	100
*Technical Personnel**				
Software purchase analysis	2,500	25	2,500	25
Planning	2,000	20	4,500	45
Contract administration	1,500	15	6,000	60
Integration	1,200	12	7,200	72
Stability testing	1,000	10	8,200	82
Regression testing	1,000	10	9,200	92
Demonstration tests	500	5	9,700	97
"Crisis reaction"	300	3	10,000	100

*Assumes 3 management and 22 technical.

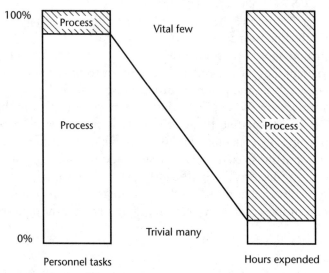

Figure 6.2   Pareto Principle simplified. (*After:* [4].)

of quality as shown in Table 6.3. The hurdle rates shown in Table 6.3 are the values set up-front that must be achieved during the measurement of these factors in the development phases when the evaluation (count) is made.

Table 6.2 List of Software Quality Factors

Correctness	Reliability	Efficiency
Integrity	Usability	Maintainability
Testability	Flexability	Portability
Reusability	Interoperability	

Table 6.3 Example Hurdle Rates for Selected Software Quality Factors

Software Quality Factor	Hurdle Rate*
Correctness	97%
Reliability	95%
Maintainability	95%
Usability	90%
Testability	85%

*Hurdle rate is the values set up-front that must be achieved during the measurement of these factors in the development cycle phases when the evaluation (count) is made.

Once the definition of quality is agreed upon, the second step is to apply it to the different modules, software documentation, and software development notebooks, which are components or packages in a WWMCCS release. That is, the quality of each of the components of the WWMCCS release is analyzed. This results in a "quality distribution" through which Pareto analysis can identify the critical components.

6.2.3 By Release

Analyze the various historical releases processed by the WWMCCS ADP Directorate and rank their quality. By identifying and analyzing the releases with the poorest quality, some pitfalls can be avoided, and the beginning of a corrective program formed. Analyzing the best quality releases will likely result in positive principles to follow that would become part of a standards program.

The "moving mountain" phenomenon occurs with the issuance of new releases. This phenomenon refers to a graphical representation of the number of defects in a software system plus new defects, which are uncovered in a new release. The basic graph, Figure 6.3, shows defects being removed over time with a software system.

The "moving mountain" occurs when the basic graph is drawn for each *new release* of the software system on the same graph, as shown in Figure 6.4.

With a graph such as Figure 6.4 it becomes easy to recognize that release 4 is rather good in comparison to releases 1, 2, and 3. It even seems likely that one is better off by remaining with release 1, but, of course, release 1 lacks the enhancements incorporated in releases 2, 3, and 4.

6.2.4 By Function

Analyze the "quality" of various WWMCCS ADP Directorate functions. The first step is to list the various WWMCCS ADP Directorate functions as under

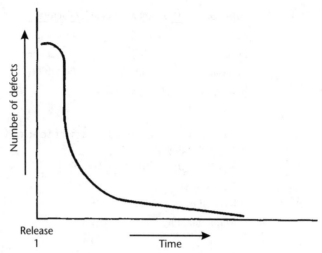

Figure 6.3   Software release defects.

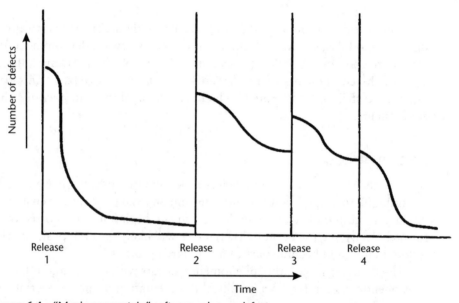

Figure 6.4   "Moving mountain" software releases defects.

"manpower" discussed above. Second, determine which of the functions lead to the most problems and direct the corrective program at these troublesome functions.

A chart similar to Table 6.4 aids in the "by function" analysis of problems. The statistics assume 3 months' time. Implicit in this approach is that Pareto analysis is applied recursively within individual functions to determine which of the substeps have the most problems. A chart such as Table 6.5 aids in the "by subfunction" analysis of problems.

Also resulting from this approach is the formulation of internal "quality criterion" to be applied to each of the internal WWMCCS ADP Directorate functions.

Table 6.4 Problems Encountered by Personnel Functions

Personnel Task	Problems Encountered	% of Problems Encountered	Cumulative Problems Encountered	Cuulative % of Problems Encountered
Managerial Personnel				
Contract administration	10	48	10	48
"Crisis reaction"	8	38	18	86
Scheduling	2	9	20	95
Decision making	1	5	21	100
Planning	0	0	21	100
Controlling	0	0	21	100
"Task preparation"	0	0	21	100
Technical Personnel				
Software purchase analysis	110	42	110	42
Contact administration	58	22	168	64
Integration	40	15	208	79
"Crisis reaction"	25	9	233	88
Planning	15	6	248	94
Stability testing	7	3	255	97
Regression testing	5	2	260	99
Demonstration tests	4	1	264	100

It should be noted that the functions of the various vendors can be analyzed in a similar manner. In this case, the program would monitor the quality of the functions performed by the various vendors.

6.3 Federal Reserve Bank—Classic Example 2

The example cited is from another actual study of quality assurance conducted by McCabe & Associates, in 1982 for the Federal Reserve Bank [5]. As part of a functional management program to improve the operations of the General Purpose Computer Department of the Federal Reserve Bank of New York, and to establish a departmental quality assurance program, McCabe & Associates was asked to conduct a software quality assurance study. The scope of the study, the analysis process, and the conclusions are stated below.

The scope of this effort was restricted to the ongoing operations and related interfaces of the General Purpose Computer Department of the Federal Reserve Bank of New York and how the quality of those operations might be improved. Specifically related to the project development cycle, the nature and extent of General Purpose Computer Department involvement in the following phases were investigated:

- Project Proposal (Stage I):
  - Development schedule;
  - Resource requirements for:

Table 6.5   Problems Encountered by Personnel Subfunctions

Personal Tasks	Problems Encountered	% of Problems Encountered	Cumulative Problems Encountered	Cumulative % of Problems Encountered
Managerial Personnel				
Contract Administration:				
Monitor contract fullfillment	5	50	5	50
Receive contract	2	20	7	70
Resolve contractual conflict	2	20	9	90
Discover contractual conflict	1	10	10	100
Close out contract	0	0	10	100
Send out contract	0	0	10	100
"Crisis reaction":				
System crashes	5	56	5	56
Loss of best analysis	2	22	7	78
Previously unplanned customer	1	11	8	89
Presentation tomorrow				
System late for delivery	1	11	9	100
Boss needs report by tomorrow	0	0	9	100
Technical Personnel				
Software Purchase Analysis:				
Program to aid in vendor analysis	50	45	50	45
Package history check	45	41	95	86
Vendor history check	10	9	105	95
Benchmark conduct	4	4	109	99
"Perfect" package cost too much	1	1	110	100
Contact Administration:				
Contractor disputes	30	52	30	52
Contractor inadequate	20	34	50	86
Contractor delivers late	7	12	57	98
Monitor contract fulfillment	1	2	58	100
Letter recommending cancellation	0	0	58	1,003

- Acceptance testing;
- Production operations.
- Design Phase (Stage II):
  - Data conversion plan;
  - Acceptance test planning;
  - User's guide review.
- Implementation Phase (Stage III):
  - Completion criteria for "runbooks";
  - Completion criteria for operator/user training.
- Postimplementation (Stage IV):

- Postimplementation review;
- Postimplementation evaluation.

Further, the effort was limited to those software quality factors directly affecting the General Purpose Computer Department as then chartered. The primary factor for this project was *usability.*

Attributes, or criteria, as developed by McCabe & Associates and others [6] associated with the usability factor are as follows:

- *Operability:* Those attributes of the software that determine operation and procedures concerned with the operation of the software;
- *Training:* Those attributes of the software that provide transition from the current operation or initial familiarization;
- *Communicativeness:* Those attributes of the software that provide useful input and output which can be assimilated.

Of these criteria, operability and training were considered to have impact on the General Purpose Computer Department, with communicativeness impacting mainly the user.

The metric for stating requirements and measuring the accomplishments of the above criteria is the number of occurrences of program failures (ABENDS in the General Purpose Computer Department environment) attributable to operator error.

Other, or secondary, software quality factors, that have a high positive relationship with usability are *correctness* and *reliability.* These features were not analyzed in as much depth as the primary factor, usability.

The process used to conduct the analysis consisted of three major components:

- An analysis of the process used by the General Purpose Computer Department in accepting new or modified applications and placing them in production;
- An investigation of the classes of errors occurring;
- An investigation of the causes of the errors.

The analysis of the General Purpose Computer Department acceptance and production process was divided into two parts: (1) the introduction and acceptance of new or modified applications, including documentation, training, testing activities, as well as General Purpose Computer Department participation in the development process; and (2) running the applications in production including acceptance of user inputs, job setup and scheduling, and delivery of output. In both cases, the analysis included studying input, procedures, output, supporting documentation, and error reporting and correction procedures.

The investigation of the classes of error occurrence dealt with objective errors (i.e., those causing reruns of a portion or all of the application), and also subjective errors (i.e., those which, while not causing reruns, contributed to inefficiency and lack of management control). In this investigation, formal error (ABEND) reports were analyzed using the Pareto technique to determine which classes of errors occurred most frequently and had the most severe impact on operations and/or the user.

The final and most detailed, analysis was aimed at determining potential causes for the various types of errors. Specifically, an attempt was made to attribute the cause of failure to one of the following areas:

• System design;
• Operating procedure;
• Training;
• Documentation.

Part of the document review consisted of a review of a typical set of application operations documents called "runbooks." The payroll system was chosen as an example of a large system that was frequently run and considered to be of below-average quality. The payroll system is normally run 90 times a year, sometimes as often as three times in a single week. The system consists of 23 jobs (and hence 23 runbooks) in three major categories: prepayroll processing, payroll processing, and postpayroll processing. Each runbook contains about 20 pages of information (460 pages total), and an average of eight control cards in a plastic pouch (177 cards total). These 23 jobs are set up, including reading in the control cards and mounting at least one tape for each job, each time payroll is run. The setup is done manually and the payroll system ABENDs approximately every other time it is run. In addition, sometimes the attempted rerun also ABENDs. The ABENDs are almost always caused by human error in setup or processing. The conclusion reached was that the runbook procedure is largely a manual process. Thus, it is excessively error prone.

The most detailed step in the analysis process was to review the file of General Purpose Computer Department Incident (ABEND) Reports of the past year. This file consisted of a stack of completed ABEND forms. The origin of the form is as follows.

When a job or job step is unable to complete normally, for whatever reason, the job is suspended by the system and the operator is notified with a diagnostic code. This event is called an ABEND and the codes provided are ABEND codes. Upon the occurrence of such an event, the operator fills out the top portion of a General Purpose Computer Incident Report and notifies the shift production support analyst. The analyst is provided the report and any supporting documentation, such as printouts. The analyst then takes action to diagnose and correct the error and initiate a rerun of the job, if appropriate. The analyst then completes the ABEND form as to corrective action and disposition.

The review of the ABEND file was performed using Pareto-type analysis to identify which of the potentially many error types were most frequent and thus impacted most severely on productivity and quality. The analysis yielded a relatively small number of error types, and an even smaller number of classes of errors, which occurred with dominating frequency. A disturbing aspect of the analysis was that, of the 1,536 forms reviewed, 21% of the forms had no information entered as to cause of error and another 21% were unclear as to cause although job disposition was given; there remained only 58% of the file for meaningful analysis. The results of this analysis are provided in Table 6.6.

What can be inferred from the analysis is that a relatively small number of error types (nine) have occurred during the last year. Six of these types, comprising 78%

Table 6.6   ABEND Analysis

Corrective Action	Number	% of Total	% of Sample
Changed JCL card	195	11.6	22
System error	154	10	17
(Hardware/tape/system)	—	—	—
Return to user	127	8.3	14
Changed procedure	115	7.4	13
Override file catalog	115	7.4	13
Incorrect job setup	97	6.3	11
File not found (late mount)	41	2.6	5
Contact programmer	23	1.5	3
Restored and rerun	14	0.9	2
(error not found)	—	—	—
Sample Total	882	58.0	100
No information	324	21	
Insufficient information	330	21	
Total	1,536	100	

of the total, can be classified as human errors on the part of either the operator or the user, as shown in Table 6.7.

The other significant error class was hardware or system errors. These are primarily tape read errors, which are corrected by varying the drive off line or switching drives. The large proportion of human error could be attributable to one or more of the following:

• Poor human factors design of the application;
• Inadequate training of operators and users;
• Inadequate performance aids for the operators and users; that is, runbooks, checklists, and automated tools.

These human errors relate directly to the usability factor discussed earlier. In fact, these errors are the metric measurement for the operability and training criteria.

With regard to the software quality factors and their criteria, as discussed above, the following conclusions may be drawn:

Table 6.7   Rate of Human Errors Inferred from Analysis

JCL card in error	22%
User input in error	14%
Procedure JCL in error	13%
File catalog/designation in error	13%
Job improperly set up	11%
Tape not mounted on time	5%
Total	78%

- The usability of the software application being run in production by General Purpose Computer Department must be considered low. The per-shift rate of 1.6 ABENDS represents a high resource cost and an unpredictable and disruptive environment.

- The operability criteria in particular are not being adequately met by systems development, as evidenced by the high error rate (i.e., every other run for payroll). Nor are operability requirements being fed to system development during the project development cycle.

- The involvement of General Purpose Computer Department in the project development cycle is minimal. No requirements for the usability of systems are fed in on a formal basis and review of development documentation is informal and inadequate.

- There exists an opportunity to reduce the number of error-prone human procedures through the use of installed packages such as APOLLO and ABENDAID and SCHEDULER. Other, related quality factors such as correctness and reliability appear to be satisfactory. This judgment is based on the lack of user complaints and the relatively infrequent need to call for programmer assistance. However, it should be noted that no evidence could be found that these factors were formally and rigorously tested prior to entering production.

The impact of the above findings and conclusions upon the operation of General Purpose Computer Department can be characterized as follows.

The 1,536 ABENDS, plus an estimated additional 384 (25%) errors not causing ABENDS, create an extremely disruptive environment. As has been stated, this is approximately two ABENDS per shift, with at least one application ABENDing every other time it is run. Some recoveries and reruns require more than a day to accomplish.

In financial terms, the recovery and rerun procedures require an estimated 65% of the production support personnel resources of the Central Support Division. The dollar value of these services is approximately $150,000 annually or 20% of the Division's budget. This cost can also be stated as 6% of the General Purpose Computer Department salary budget. If this 6% were extended to the entire General Purpose Computer Department budget, the dollar value would be $390,000 annually. If the useful life of an average application is 5 years, this would amount to almost $2 million merely to deal with operational errors over a 5-year period. Probably most important is the consideration that as applications become more complex and database oriented, the ability of the production support team to maintain processing may be exceeded.

6.4 Defect Identification

Defect identification is a fertile area for Pareto analysis in the software field. Some software data on frequency of occurrence of errors is available from Rubey, TRW, and Xerox.

6.4.1 Rubey's Defect Data

First, Rubey's "Quantitative Aspects of Software Validation" [7] data is presented. Table 6.8 shows the basic cause error categories. Then, for the major causes the common symptoms are shown in Tables 6.9 through 6.12.

Several inferences can be drawn from the data in Table 6.8 by SQA personnel. First, there is no single reason for unreliable software, and no single validation tool

Table 6.8 Basic Causes Error Categories for Software

Error Category	Total		Serious		Moderate		Minor	
	No.	%	No.	%	No.	%	No.	%
Incomplete or erroneous specification	340	28	19	11	82	17	239	43
Intentional devaiation from specification	145	12	9	5	61	13	75	14
Violation of programming standards	118	10	2	1	22	5	94	17
Erroneous data accessing	120	10	36	21	72	15	12	2
Erroneous decision logic or sequencing	139	12	41	24	83	17	15	3
Erroneous arithmetic computations	113	9	22	13	73	15	18	3
Invalid testing	44	4	14	8	25	5	5	1
Improper handling of interrupts	46	4	14	8	31	6	1	0
Wrong constants and data values	41	3	14	8	19	4	7	1
Inaccurate documentation	96	8	0	0	10	2	86	16
Total	1,202	100	171	14	478	40	553	46

Table 6.9 Common Symptoms for Software Defects: Incomplete or Erroneous Specifications

Error Category	Total		Serious		Moderate		Minor	
	No.	%	No.	%	No.	%	No.	%
Dimensional error	41	12	7	37	17	21	17	7
Insufficient precision specified	15	4	0	0	11	13	4	2
Missing symbols or lables	4	1	0	0	0	0	4	2
Typographical error	51	15	0	0	0	0	51	21
Incorrect hardware description	7	2	3	16	3	4	1	0
Design consideration	177	52	8	42	47	57	122	51
Incomplete or incorrect ambiguity in specification or design	45	13	1	5	4	5	40	17

Table 6.10 Common Symptoms for Software Defects: Erroneous Data Accessing

Error Category	Total		Serious		Moderate		Minor	
	No.	%	No.	%	No.	%	No.	%
Fetch or store wrong data word	79	66	17	47	52	72	10	83
Fetch or store wrong portion of data word	10	8	10	28	0	0	0	0
Variable equated to wrong location	10	8	4	11	6	0	0	0
Overwrite of data word	10	8	4	11	4	2	2	17
Register loaded with wrong data	11	9	1	3	10	0	0	0
Total	120	100	36	30	72	60	12	10

Table 6.11 Common Symptoms for Software Defects: Erroneous Decision Logic or Sequencing

Error Category	Total		Serious		Moderate		Minor	
	No.	%	No.	%	No.	%	No.	%
Label place on wrong instruction/statement	2	1	2	5	0	0	0	0
Branch test incorrect	28	20	10	24	15	18	3	20
Branch test setup incorrect	2	2	1	2	1	1	0	0
Computations performed in wrong sequence	9	6	1	2	2	2	6	40
Logic sequence incorrect	98	71	27	66	65	78	6	40
Total	139	100	41	29	83	60	15	11

or technique is likely to detect all types of errors. Many possibilities are discussed in Chapter 2 for improving software reliability. Second, the ability to demonstrate a program's correspondence to its specification does not justify complete confidence in the program's correctness, since a significant number of errors due to an incomplete or erroneous specification, and the documentation of the program cannot always be trusted. Third, intentional deviation from specification and the violation of established programming standards more often leads to minor errors than to serious errors. On the other hand, invalid timing or improper handling of interrupts almost always results in a significant error.

The data presented in Table 6.8 summarizes the errors found in independent validations. In practice, however, the organization responsible for independent validation does not wait until the developer has completed program debugging. Instead, the independent validation organization often becomes involved at each program

Table 6.12 Common Symptoms for Software Defects: Erroneous
Arithmetic Computation

Error Category	Total		Serious		Moderate		Minor	
	No.	%	No.	%	No.	%	No.	%
Wrong arithmetic operations performed	69	61	12	55	47	64	10	56
Loss of precision	9	8	1	5	6	8	2	11
Overflow	8	7	3	14	3	4	2	11
Poor scaling of intermediate results	22	20	4	18	15	21	3	17
Incompatible scaling	5	4	2	9	2	3	1	5
Total	113	100	22	19	73	65	18	16

development phase to check that intermediate products (such as the program specification and program design) are correct.

The errors occurring in the categorization of Table 6.9, incomplete or erroneous specifications, indicate either deficiencies in, or the absence of, the verification
of the program specification or program design, since there should be no errors in
the final programs attributable to program specification if the preceding verification efforts were perfect. As shown in Table 6.9, 19 serious and 82 moderate errors
have escaped the verification efforts and have been found only during the checking
of the actual coding. In 239 additional cases, an error due to incomplete or erroneous specification is considered of minor consequence; this is largely because the coding had been implemented correctly even though the program specification is itself
in error.

If all of the 239 minor erroneous or incomplete specification errors were faith-
fully translated into coding, the total number of serious errors in the resultant coding would be 84 and the total number of moderate errors would be 162. Only 94 of
the 239 minor errors would remain minor errors, even if the coding implemented
the erroneous specification. This would make the incomplete or erroneous specification error category in Table 6.8 the largest error source by a factor of 2, and
would increase the total number of serious errors by 38% and the total number of
moderate errors by 12%. Obviously, verification of the program specification and
design in advance of coding and debugging is a very beneficial activity, and indeed is
probably essential if reliable software is desired [8].

6.4.2   TRW Defect Data

Another source of data for a cost by type analysis is provided in *SoftwareReliability*
[9]. This book presents an extensive collection of analysis of error data performed at
TRW. Project TRW1 is broken down into four subprojects. Each is a project unto
itself because of the differing management, languages, development personnel,
requirements, and so on.

Table 6.13 presents an analysis that is similar to the breakdown of the Rubey
data. Although the definition of error types does not completely agree for the two

Table 6.13   Percentage Breakdown of Code Change Errors into Major Error Categories

Project TRW1

Project TRW₁ Major Error Categories	Proj. TRW₂ (%)	Proj. TRW₃ (%)	Applications Software (%)	Simulator Software (%)	Operating System (%)	PA Tools (%)
Computational (A)	9.0	1.7	13.5	19.6	2.5	0
Logic (B)	26.0	34.5	17.1	20.9	34.6	43.5
Data input (C)	16.4	8.9	7.3	9.3	8.6	5.5
Data output (E)						
Data handling (D)	18.2	27.2	10.9	8.4	21.0	9.3
Interface (F)	17.0	22.5	9.8	6.7	7.4	
Data definition (G)	0.8	3.0	7.3	13.8	7.4	3.7
Data base (H)	4.1	2.2	24.7	16.4	4.9	2.8
Other (J)	8.5	0	9.4	4.9	13.6	35.2

studies, there is a striking similarity in the two sets of data: logic errors and data-handling errors rank first and second in the serious error category in the Rubey data, and they likewise rank first and second in the TRW data (in fact, their respective percentages are similar) [10].

The TRW study further analyzes various subtypes of errors. For example, logic errors are divided into the following types:

- Incorrect operand in logical expression;
- Logic activities out of sequence;
- Wrong variable being checked;
- Missing logic on condition test.

It is very important as well as interesting to examine this more detailed analysis of the two most costly errors: logic and data handling. The results are shown for Project TRW1. Table 6.14 shows the results for logic errors and Table 6.15 shows the detailed data handling errors. This data indicates that the most frequent error subtype (according to TRW's data) and the most serious subtype (according to Rubey's data) is *missing logic or condition tests*. The second most frequent and serious error subtype is *data initialization done improperly*.

Another interesting study performed by TRW was to analyze error types according to major error categories. A particular error will have its source in one of the fol-

Table 6.14   Project TRW1 Detailed Error Category Breakdown

Detailed Error Categories	Percent of Major Category			
	Applications Software	Simulator Software	Operating System S/W	PA Tools
B000 LOGIC ERRORS	2.1	8.3	0	4.3
B100 Incorrect operand in logical expression	21.3	6.2	7.1	4.3
B200 Logic activities out of sequence	17.0	29.2	10.7	10.6
B300 Wrong variable being checked	4.3	8.3	14.3	2.1
B400 Missing logic or condition test	46.8	39.6	60.7	76.6

Table 6.15   Project TRW1 Detailed Error Category Breakdown

Detailed Error Categories	Percent of Major Category			
	Applications Software	Simulator Software	Operating System S/W	PA Tools
D000 DATA HANDLING ERRORS	10.0	21.1	11.8	70.0
D100 Data initialization not done	6.7	10.5	17.6	0
D200 Data initialization done improperly	20.0	10.5	41.2	10.0
D300 Variable used as a flag or index not set properly	20.0	5.3	23.5	10.0
D400 Variable referred to by wrong name	6.7	21.1	0	0
D500 Bit manipulation done incorrectly	10.0	0	0	0
D600 Incorrect variable type	3.3	10.5	0	0
D700 Data packing/unpacking error	10.0	5.3	0	10.0
D900 Subscripting error	13.3	15.7	5.9	10.0

lowing stages of development: requirements, specifications, design, or coding. TRW performed this detailed analysis for 23 major error categories during the design and coding stages of development for Project TRW2. The results are shown in Table 6.16.

Table 6.16   Project TRW2 Error Sources

Major Error Categories		% of Total Code Change Errors	Probable Sources	
			% Design	% Code
Computational	(AA)	9.0	90	10
Logic	(BB)	26.0	88	12
I/O	(CC)	16.4	24	76
Data handling	(DD)	18.2	25	75
Operating system/ system support software	(EE)	0.1	(1)	
Configuration	(FF)	3.1	24	76
Routine/routine interface	(GG)	8.2	93	7
Routine/system software interface	(HH)	1.1	73	27
Tape processing interface	(II)	0.3	90	10
User requested change	(JJ)	6.6	83	17
Data base interface	(KK)	0.8	10	90
User requested change	(LL)	0	(2)	
Preset data base	(MM)	4.1	79	21
Global variable/ compool definition	(NN)	0.8	62	38
Recurrent	(PP)	1.3	(1)	
Documentation	(QQ)	0.8	(1)	
Requirements compliance	(RR)	0.4	89	11
Unidentified	(SS)	1.0	(1)	
Operator	(TT)	0.7	(1)	
Questions	(UU)	1.1	(1)	
Averages			62%	38%

Notes: (1) Although errors in these categories required changes to the code, their source breakdown of design versus code is not attempted here. Those categories considered in all other categories encompass 95% of all code change errors. (2) For Project TRW2 product enhancements or changes to the design baseline were considered "out-of-scope" and therefore are not present here.

The following observations are offered about the data in Table 6.16. The overall result shown—62% of all errors being design errors and 38% coding errors—is very representative of what other studies of similar data have shown. A rule-of-thumb used in the industry is that about 65% of all the errors will be design errors and 35% coding errors. The fact that 65% of all errors are design errors suggests why the average cost of an error is so high. Another important point illustrated by Table 6.16 is the high cost of logic errors. Indeed, logic errors are the most frequent, and, considering that 88% of logic errors are design errors, they contribute enormously to the cost of a given development. This data and observation reinforce the point made by Rubey's data: logic errors are the most serious error type. One of the implications of this result is that work done by SQA personnel with specifications should be heavily concentrated in the areas of logic and data handling.

A further area to investigate is the identification of internal modules within a system that can result in high cost. That is, is there a way to identify the modules whose errors will have a large impact on the cost of the system? Specifically, a module's error becomes costly if that module has many affects on the rest of the modules in a system. A given module could be highly "coupled" with the rest of a system as a result of the parameters it passes, the global data it affects, the interrupts it can cause, or the modules it involves. If such a highly coupled module has errors, it can be very costly since erroneous assumptions made in the module can be spread throughout the rest of the system. The SQA personnel should look at module coupling to assure that it is minimized. It should be noted that the term *module* can be applied to any internal unit of a system.

6.4.3   Xerox Defect Data

The main references for this section are "Module Connection Analysis" [11] and *Applied Software Engineering Techniques* [12].

Assume that a system is decomposed into N modules. These are $N2$ pairwise relationships of the form

Pij = probability that a change in module i necessitates a change in module j

Let P be the $N \times N$ matrix with elements Pij.

Let A be a vector with N elements that corresponds to a set of "zero-order" changes to a system. That is, A is the set of immediate changes that are contemplated for a system without considering intramodule side effects. The total number of changes T will be much greater than A because of the coupling and dependency of the modules. An approximation of the total amount of changes T is given by

$$T = A(I - P)^{-1}$$

where I is the identity matrix.

An example from a Xerox System will be used to illustrate. The probability connection matrix P for the Xerox System is shown in Table 6.17.

Let us look at P_{48}; $P48 = 0.1$, indicating a 10% probability that if module 4 is changed then module 8 will also have to be modified.

Table 6.17   Probability Connection Matrix **P**

	1	2	3	4	5	6	7	8	9	10	11	12	13	14	15	16	17	18
1	.2	.1	0	0	0	.1	0	.1	0	.1	.1	.1	0	0	0	.1	0	0
2	0	.2	0	0	.1	.1	.1	0	0	0	0	0	.1	.1	.1	0	.1	0
3	0	0	.1	0	0	0	0	0	0	0	0	0	0	0	0	0	0	0
4	0	.1	0	.2	0	.1	.1	.1	0	0	0	0	0	0	.1	0	.1	0
5	.1	0	0	0	.4	.1	.1	.1	0	0	0	0	0	0	0	0	.1	0
6	.1	0	0	0	0	.3	.1	0	0	.1	0	0	0	.1	0	0	.1	0
7	.1	0	0	.1	.2	.1	.3	.1	0	.1	0	0	0	.1	0	.1	.1	0
8	.1	.1	0	.1	.2	0	.1	.4	0	.1	0	0	0	.1	0	0	0	.1
9	0	0	0	0	0	0	0	0	.1	0	0	0	0	0	0	0	0	0
10	.1	0	0	0	0	.1	.1	.1	0	.4	.2	.1	.2	.1	.1	.1	.1	.1
11	.1	0	0	.1	0	0	0	0	0	.2	.3	.1	0	0	0	0	0	0
12	.2	0	0	0	0	.1	0	0	0	0	.2	.3	0	0	.1	.1	0	0
13	.1	.1	0	0	0	.1	.1	.1	0	.2	.1	0	.3	0	0	0	0	0
14	0	0	0	0	0	0	0	0	0	0	0	0	0	.2	0	0	0	0
15	0	0	0	0	0	0	0	0	0	0	0	0	0	0	.2	0	0	0
16	0	0	0	0	0	0	0	0	0	0	0	0	0	0	0	.2	0	0
17	0	0	0	0	0	0	0	0	0	0	0	0	0	0	0	0	.2	0
18	0	0	0	0	1	0	1	0	0	.1	0	0	0	0	0	0	0	.3

Let us assume that a global change to the system is to be made that will result in modification to many of the modules. This global set of zero-order changes can be represented as a vector A (Table 6.18). (These are actual changes per module that were applied to the Xerox System during a specified period.)

Given A, one can now compute the approximation T of the total number of changes that will be required. This is done by computing the following:

$$T = A(I - P)^{-1}$$

where I is the 18×18 identity matrix.

The results are shown in Table 6.19.

Table 6.18   Changes per Module

A(1)	2	A(2)	8
A(3)	4	A(4)	6
A(5)	28	A(6)	12
A(7)	8	A(8)	28
A(9)	4	A(10)	8
A(11)	40	A(12)	12
A(13)	16	A(14)	12
A(15)	12	A(16)	28
A(17)	28	A(18)	40

Table 6.19   Module Changes Required

Module	Initial Changes (A)	Total Changes $T = A(I - P)^{-1}$
1	2	241.817
2	8	100.716
3	4	4.4444
4	6	98.1284
5	28	248.835
6	12	230.376
7	8	228.951
8	28	257.467
9	4	4.4444
10	8	318.754
11	40	238.609
12	12	131.311
13	16	128.318
14	12	157.108
15	12	96.1138
16	28	150.104
17	28	188.295
18	40	139.460
Totals	296	2,963.85

Notice the factor of 10 increase of total work over the initial set of changes; this is caused by the ripple effect of a change through highly coupled modules. The approximation of 2,963.85 is within 4% of what Xerox actually experienced [11].

The results in Table 6.19 clearly indicate that modules 10, 1, and 7 are highly coupled with the rest of the system. Module 10, for example, initially has eight changes and ends up with 318 spill-over cumulative changes in all modules. On the other hand, module 3 initially has four changes and ends with only four changes.

The point is that by identifying the modules with the highest coupling (modules with maximum rows of probabilities in P) one can anticipate which modules are most dangerous to modify. Similarly, errors in these same modules will have an enormous impact on the rest of the system since the errors have to be removed not only from these modules but also from all the coupled modules. The errors made in these highly coupled modules will be the most costly [13]. It is clear from this that Pareto analysis helps by identifying focus areas that cause most of the problems, which normally means you get the best return on investment when you fix them [14].

6.5 Inspection

This section uses the principles discussed in Michael E. Fagan's "Design and Code Inspections to Reduce Errors in Program Development" [15] to guide the use of the

Pareto Principle in the programming process (detailed analysis is made by Don O'Neill in Chapter 7). For design inspection, participants, using the design documentation, literally do their homework to try to understand the design, its intent, and logic. To increase their error detection in the inspection, the inspection team should first study the ranked distributions of error types found by recent design and code inspections such as shown in Tables 6.20 and 6.21. This study will prompt them to concentrate on the most fruitful areas (what we are calling the vital few). It should be noted that the design and code inspections defect distributions shown in Tables 6.20 and 6.21 are adapted from Fagan by arranging the data according to the Pareto analysis. Tables 6.22 and 6.23 show how they originally appeared in the article.

Tables 6.20 and 6.21 show the common symptoms for defects in the design and code, respectively. From the defect identification section above, it is a logical extension to the basic causes for these defects. The basic causes are shown in Tables 6.24 and 6.25.

One of the most significant benefits of inspections is the detailed feedback of results on a relatively real-time basis. Because there is early indication from the first few units of work inspected, the individual is able to show improvement, and usually does, on later work even during the same project [17].

Table 6.20 Summary of Design Inspections by Error Type (Order by Error Frequency)

Inspection File

VP Individual Name	Missing	Wrong	Extra	Errors	Error %
LO logic	126	57	24	207	39.8
PR prologue/prose	44	38	7	89	17.1
CD CB definition	16	2	—	18	3.5 } 10.4
CU CB usage	18	17	1	36	6.9
OT other	15	10	10	35	6.7
MD more detail	24	6	2	32	6.2
IC interconnect calls	18	9	—	27	5.2
TB test & branch	12	7	2	21	4.0
MN maintainability	8	5	3	16	3.1
RM return code/msg.	5	7	2	14	2.7
IR interconnect reqts.	4	5	2	11	2.1
PE performance	1	2	3	6	1.2
RU register usage	1	2	—	3	.6
L3 higher lvl. docu.	1	—	—	2	.4
PD pass data areas	—	1	—	1	.2
FS FPFS	1	—	—	1	.2
MA mod. attributes	1	—	—	1	.2
ST standards	—	—	—	—	—
	295	168	57	520	100.0
	57%	32%	11%		

Source: [16].

Table 6.21 Summary of Code Inspections by Error Type (Order by Error Frequency)

VP Individual Name	Inspection File				
	Missing	Wrong	Extra	Errors	Error %
LO logic	33	49	10	92	26.4
DE design error	31	32	14	77	22.1
PR prologue/prose	25	24	3	52	14.9
CU CB usage	3	21	1	25	7.2
CC code comments	5	17	1	23	6.6
IC interconnect calls	7	9	3	19	5.5
MN maintainability	5	7	2	14	4.0
PU PL/S or BAL use	4	9	1	14	4.0
PE performance	3	2	5	10	2.9
FI	—	8	—	8	2.3
TB test & branch	2	5	—	7	2.0
RU register usage	4	2	—	6	1.7
SU storage usage	1	—	—	1	.3
OT other					
	123	185	40	348	100.0

Source: [15].

Table 6.22 Summary of Design Inspections by Error Type

VP Individual Name	Inspection File				
	Missing	Wrong	Extra	Errors	Error %
CD CB definition	16	2	18	3.5	10.4
CU CB usage	18	17	1	36	6.9
FS FPFS	1	—	—	1	.2
IC interconnect calls	18	9	—	27	5.2
IR interconnect reqts.	4	5	2	11	2.1
LO logic	126	57	24	207	39.8
L3 higher lvl. docu.	1	—	—	2	.4
MA mod. attributes	24	6	2	32	6.2
MN maintainability	8	5	3	16	3.1
OT other	15	10	10	35	6.7
PD pass data areas	—	1	—	1	.2
PE performance	1	2	3	6	1.2
PR prologue/prose	44	38	7	89	17.1
RM return code/msg.	5	7	2	14	2.7
RU register usage	1	2	—	3	.6
ST standards					
TB test & branch	12	7	2	21	4.0
	295	168	57	520	100.0
	57%	32%	11%		

Source: [15].

Table 6.23 Summary of Code Inspections by Error Type

| VP Individual Name | Inspection File | | | | |
	Missing	Wrong	Extra	Errors	Error %
CC Code comments	5	17	1	23	6.6
CU CB Usage	3	21	1	25	7.2
DE Design Error	31	32	14	77	22.1
FI	—	8	—	8	2.3
IC Interconnect Calls	7	9	3	19	5.5
LO Logic	33	49	10	92	26.4
MN Maintainability	5	7	2	14	4.0
OT Other	—	—	—	—	—
PE Performance	3	2	5	10	2.9
PR Prologue / Prose	25	24	3	52	14.9
PU PL/S or BAL Use	4	9	1	14	4.0
RU Register Usage	4	2	—	6	1.7
SU Storage Usage	1	—	—	1	0.3
TB Test & Branch	2	5	—	7	2.0
	123	185	40	348	100.0

Source: [16].

Table 6.24 Basic Causes for Design Defects

	Errors	%	Cumulative %
Unclear requirements	17	3	100
Missing requirements	34	7	97
Design	307	59	59
Poor standards	125	24	83
Miscellaneous	37	7	90

Table 6.25 Basic Causes for Code Defects

	Errors	%	Cumulative %
Unclear design	84	24	91
Missing design	117	34	34
Coder	115	33	67
Poor standards	24	7	98
Miscellaneous	8	2	100

6.6 Pareto Charts Comparison

Quality improvement teams use the Pareto chart extensively to focus on the important causes of trouble. But what happens when a team needs to compare one Pareto chart against another? The answer provided by Ron Kennett in "Making Sense Out of Two Pareto Charts" [18] is the M-test, which signals significant differences in the distribution of errors. The M-test indicates whether differences between two Pareto charts can be attributed to random variation or to special causes. Such a signal is crucial if one wants to determine the impact of changes in working procedures or of new engineering tools and techniques.

Without such a statistical tool, random differences can be mistakenly interpreted as improvements (or deteriorations) and real improvements ignored as just noise. For concreteness, the technique is explained based upon data from an article by D. E. Knuth on changes made in development of TEX, a software system for typesetting, during a period of 10 years.

Knuth's logbook contains 516 items for the 1978 version, labeled TEX78, and 346 items for the 1982 version, labeled TEX82. These entries are classified into 15 categories ($K = 15$):

A = Algorithm;

B = Blunder;

C = Cleanup;

D = Data;

E = Efficiency;

F = Forgotten;

G = Generalization;

I = Interaction;

L = Language;

M = Mismatch;

P = Portability;

Q = Quality;

R = Robustness;

S = Surprise;

T = Typo.

The A, B, D, F, L, M, R, S, and T classifications represent development errors. The C, E, G, I, P, and Q classifications represent "enhancements" consisting of unanticipated features that had to be added in later development phases. These enhancements indicate that the developers did not adequately understand customer requirements and, as such, can be considered failures of the requirements analysis process.

Taking the 516 reported errors in TEX78 as a standard against which the 346 errors in TEX82 are measured provides another opportunity to use the M-test. In this example, the categories are in alphabetical order to facilitate the comparison between TEX78 and TEX82. For Knuth's data $K = 15$ and for a significance level of 1%, one derives by interpolation in the M-test table that $C = 3.2$. Table 6.26 presents the various data and computations necessary to perform the M-test. An asterisk indicates a significant difference at the 1% level. TEX82 contains significantly more errors in the cleanup (C), efficiency (E), and robustness (R) categories than TEX78. Significantly fewer errors are found in blunder (B), forgotten (F), language (L), mismatch (M), and quality (Q).

Table 6.26   Data and Computations Needed to Perform M-test

Category	TEX78	Pi	TEX82	Ei	Si	Zi
A	23	0.04	14	15.42	3.84	−0.37
B*	42	0.08	7	28.16	5.09	−4.16*
C*	37	0.07	85	24.81	4.80	12.54*
D	36	0.07	19	24.14	4.74	−1.08
E*	17	0.03	23	11.40	3.32	3.49*
F*	50	0.10	13	33.53	5.50	−3.73*
G	60	0.12	48	40.23	5.96	1.30
I	74	0.14	59	49.62	6.52	1.44
L*	30	0.06	2	20.12	4.35	−4.16*
M*	25	0.05	0	16.76	3.99	−4.20*
P	10	0.02	12	6.71	2.56	2.06
Q*	54	0.10	14	36.21	5.69	−3.90*
R*	23	0.04	30	15.42	3.84	3.80*
S	24	0.05	20	16.09	3.92	1.00
T	11	0.02	0	7.38	2.69	−2.75

Source: [19].
*Indicates differences significant at least at the 1% level.

The Pareto chart is an essential ingredient in any quality improvement effort. Most report packages on software error data include such charts. The M-test helps to compare different Pareto charts by pointing out what differences are indeed significant and therefore deserve further attention.

6.7 Conclusions

In summary, the steps for the application of the Pareto are given by Juran [20] as follows:

1. Make a *written* list of all that stands "between us and making this change."
2. Arrange this list *in order of importance*.
3. Identify the *vital few* as projects to be dealt with individually.
4. Identify the *trivial many* as things to be dealt with as a class.

In software, as well as in general, the list of the vital few (through use of the Pareto Principle) does *not* come as a complete surprise to all concerned: some of the problems on the list have long been notorious. But, to be sure, some of the problems will come as a genuine surprise. Indeed, that is the big accomplishment of the Pareto analysis! From Pareto analysis, it should be clear:

1. Some notorious projects are confirmed as belonging among the vital few.
2. Some projects, previously not notorious, are identified as belonging among the vital few.

3. The trivial many are identified. This is not new, but the extent is usually shocking.
4. The magnitudes of both the vital few and the trivial many are, to the extent practicable, quantified. Ordinarily, this has never before been done.
5. There is established a *meeting of the minds as to priority* of needs for breakthrough. This is the biggest contribution of all since the Pareto analysis sets the stage for action.

The Pareto analysis also provides an early check on the attitude toward break-through. If either the vital few or the trivial many look like good candidates for change, then the original hunch is confirmed, so far. If, on the other hand, the Pareto analysis shows that none of these is economically worth tackling, that conclusion is likely the end of the matter [21].

Much has already been done in the application of the Pareto Principle to soft-ware, but there is much more to work on. Emphasis on the vital few has produced a payoff, but there are always ways to improve the take. In fact, with the availability of the PC and its related software packages on the desk of every manager or analyst to perform Pareto analysis, there is more reason for greater payoff. Some available examples follow:

*   Quality assurance departments in today's companies tend to rely heavily upon personal computers as tools to aid in preventing, detecting, and solving prob-lems before or as they occur. PCs with a basic Microsoft Excel package could create Pareto charts [22].
*   Another package is Pareto Analysis from Mind Tools. This tool helps decision makers improve profitability or customer satisfaction or code generation, as examples [23].
*   There is a Pareto Creator from Grant Wood Area Education Agency that "instantly" creates Pareto charts [24].

Even in the latest implementation at the personal level, Watts Humphrey (see Chapter 2) has included Pareto analysis as an integral aspect of the process: "With PSP [Personal Software Process^{SM}] quality management and engineers track their own defects, find defect removal yields, and calculate cost-of-quality measures. Pareto defect analysis is used to derive personal design and code review checklists, which the engineers update with defect data from each new project" [25].

References

[1]   Arthur, L. J., "Quantum Improvements in Software System Quality," *Communications of the ACM*, Vol. 40, No. 6, June 1887, p. 51.
[2]   Boehm, B., "Industrial Software Metrics Top 10 List," *IEEE Software*, © IEEE September 1987, pp. 84–85.
[3]   McCabe, T. J., *SQA—A Survey*, Columbia, OH: McCabe Press, 1980, pp. 154–156.
[4]   Juran, J. M., *Managerial Breakthrough*, New York: McGraw-Hill, 1964, p. 47.
[5]   McCabe & Associates, Inc., *Phase I Report of Software Quality Assurance Project for the Federal Reserve Bank of New York*, General Purpose Computer Dept., July 29, 1982.

[6]   Perry, W. E., *Effective Methods of EDP Quality Assurance*, Wellesley, MA: Q.E.D. Information Sciences, Inc., 1981.

[7]   Rubey, R., J. Dana, and Biche "Quantitative Aspects of Software Validation," *IEEE Transactions on Software Engineering*, © IEEE June 1975.

[8]   McCabe, T. J., "Cost of Error Analysis and Software Contract Investigation," *PRC Technical Note PRC 819-5*, February 20, 1979, Contract No. DCA 100-77-C-0067, pp. 7, 8.

[9]   Thayer, R., et al., *Software Reliability*, New York: North-Holland Publishing Co., 1978.

[10] McCabe, T. J., "Cost of Error Analysis and Software Contract Investigation," *PRC Technical Note PRC 819-5*, February 20, 1979, Contract No. DCA 100-77-C-0067, p. 8.

[11] Haney, F. A., "Module Connection Analysis," *AFIPS Conference Proceedings*, Vol. 4, 1972 Fall Joint Computer Conference, AFIPS Press, 1972.

[12] McCabe, T. J., *Applied Software Engineering Technique,* Baltimore, MD: Control Data Corp., 1975.

[13] McCabe, T. J., "Cost of Error Analysis and Software Contract Investigation," *PRC Technical Note PRC 819-5*, February 20, 1979, Contract No. DCA 100-77-C-0067, pp. 17–21.

[14] Kan, S. H., *Metrics and Models in Software Quality Engineering*, Reading, MA: Addison-Wesley Publishing Company, 1995, p. 133.

[15] Fagan, M. E., "Design and Code Inspections to Reduce Errors in Program Development," *IBM System Journal*, Vol. 15, No. 3, 1976, pp. 182–211.

[16] Fagan, M. E., "Design and Code Inspections to Reduce Errors in Program Development," *IBM System Journal*, Vol. 15, No. 3, 1976, p. 192.

[17] Fagan, M. E., "Design and Code Inspections to Reduce Errors in Program Development," *IBM System Journal*, Vol. 15, No. 3, 1976, p. 197.

[18] Kennett, Ron S., "Making Sense Out of Two Pareto Charts," *Quality Progress*, May 1994, pp. 71–73.

[19] Kennett, Ron S., "Making Sense Out of Two Pareto Charts," *Quality Progress*, May 1994, p. 72.

[20] Juran, J. M., *Managerial Breakthrough,* New York: McGraw-Hill, 1964, p. 44.

[21] Juran, J. M., *Managerial Breakthrough,* New York: McGraw-Hill, 1964, pp. 51, 52.

[22] Six Sigma Pareto Analysis, http://www.isixsigma.com/tt/pareto/, December 2006.

[23] Pareto Analysis—Decision Making Techniques from Mind Tools, http://www.mindtools.com/pages/article/newTED_01.htm, December 2006.

[24] Grant Wood Area Education Agency—Data Collection and Analysis Tools, http://www.aea10.k12.ia.us/leadership/consortiums/datacollection/datacollectionindex.html, December 2006.

[25] Humphrey, W., "Making Software Manageable," *CrossTalk*, Vol. 9, No. 12, December 1996, pp. 3–6.

## CHAPTER 7

Inspection as an Up-Front Quality Technique

Don O'Neill

7.1 Origin and Evolution

Software inspections are considered a best industry practice for detecting software defects early and learning about software artifacts. Software inspections and software walkthroughs are peer reviews and are integral to software product engineering activities. A collection of coordinated knowledge, skills, and behaviors facilitates the best possible practice of peer reviews. Software inspections are the most rigorous form of peer reviews and fully utilize the elements of practice in detecting defects. These elements include the structured review process, standard of excellence product checklists, defined roles of participants, and the forms and reports. Software walkthroughs draw selectively upon the elements in assisting the producer to obtain the deepest understanding of an artifact and reaching a consensus among participants. Measured results reveal that software inspections produce an attractive return on investment obtained through accelerated learning and early defect detection. For best results, they are rolled out within an organization through a defined program of policy and procedure preparation, practitioners and managers training, measurement definition and collection within a database structure, and roll out of a sustaining infrastructure.

Software inspections provide value by improving reliability, availability, and maintainability [1]. IBM Corporation originated and adopted software inspections in the early 1970s and recognized Michael Fagan with an Outstanding Contribution Award for his pioneering work [2, 3]. Software inspections are known to add economic value in detecting and correcting defects early at greatly reduced cost [4]. IBM reported an 83% defect detection rate resulting from software inspections practice; AT&T Corp., 92% [5].

Gerald Weinberg and Daniel Freedman gave real thought to the dynamics of the software inspection role players providing deep and interesting insights useful to practitioners [6]. Robert Ebenau provided leadership in the roll out of software inspections at AT&T Corp. and documented his knowledge [7], as did Tom Gilb and Dorothy Graham [8].

The Software Engineering Institute (SEI) identified software inspections as an industry practice essential to managing the software process [9] and offered practitioner training [5, 10]. Peer reviews are included in the SEI Capability Maturity Model® (CMM®) for Software as a level 3 key process area [11]. The ongoing Capability Maturity Model Integration® (CMMI®) project spanning software, systems engineering, and integrated product development includes peer reviews in its product verification process area.

7.2   Context of Use

Software inspections are considered a best industry practice for use on software projects. Senior managers consistently ranked peer reviews as the significant enabler of software product quality among all key process areas [12]. These are integral to the software product engineering life-cycle activities associated with software requirements and specifications, designs and code, and test plans and procedures [11]. The best practices for software management and engineering on the project and the context of use for peer reviews are shown in Figure 7.1.

7.3   Scope

Peer reviews are composed of software inspections and software walkthroughs [13, 14]. Software inspections are the most rigorous form of peer reviews. Both software inspections and software walkthroughs are composed of a collection of coordinated knowledge, skills, and behaviors associated with process, standards, roles,

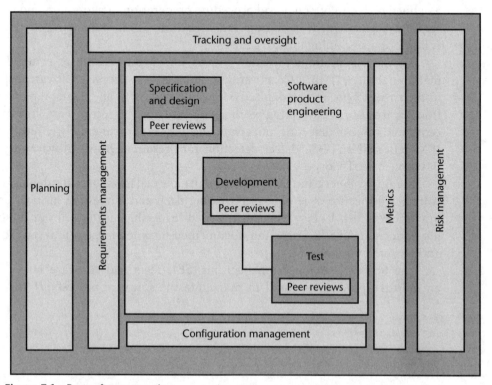

Figure 7.1   Best software practices.

and measurement. Peer reviews are conducted as an integral part of each life-cycle activity. See Figure 7.2.

7.3.1   Software Inspections and Walkthroughs Distinguished

Peer reviews are a group activity organized to systematically reason about a software artifact. There are two types of peer reviews: software walkthroughs and software inspections. Each of these serves different purposes. Software walkthroughs are an informal review used to confirm the understanding of the producer and validate the approach being taken. Software inspections are a formal review used to verify that the artifact complies with the standard of excellence. In a life-cycle activity, the software inspection is the exit criteria or gate that concludes the activity. See Table 7.1.

7.3.1.1   Software Walkthrough

The software walkthrough is organized to serve the needs of the producer or author of the software artifact in acquiring superior knowledge of all aspects of the software artifact. It is a learning experience. A desirable side effect of the software walkthrough is the forging of a shared vision among the reviewers and consensus among participants on the approaches taken, product and engineering practices applied, completeness and correctness of capabilities and features, and rules of construction for the domain product. Since the software walkthrough caters to the needs of the author, it is the author who initiates the session. Consequently, there may be several walkthroughs in each life-cycle activity. Software walkthroughs yield open issues and action items. While these issues and action items may be tracked to closure, the only measurement taken is a count of the software walkthroughs held.

7.3.1.2   Software Inspection

The software inspection is structured to serve the needs of quality management in verifying that the software artifact complies with the standard of excellence for software

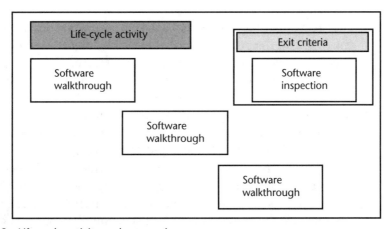

Figure 7.2   Life-cycle activity and peer reviews.

Table 7.1   Peer Reviews Scope

Focus	*Software Inspection*	*Software Walkthrough*
Purpose	Do the job right	Do the right job
	Detect defects	Learning
	Conformance	Consensus
Initiation	Exit criteria for life-cycle activity	Author request
Measurement	Product and process measurements	Instances

engineering artifacts. The focus is one of verification, on doing the job right. The software inspection is a formal review held at the conclusion of a life-cycle activity and serves as a quality gate with an exit criteria for moving on to subsequent activities.

The software inspection utilizes a structured review process of planning, preparation, entry criteria, conduct, exit criteria, report out, and follow-up. It ensures that a close and strict examination of the product artifact is conducted according to the standard of excellence criteria, which spans completeness, correctness, style, rules of construction, and multiple views and may also include technology and metrics. This close and strict examination results in the early detection of defects. The software inspection is led by a moderator and assisted by other role players including recorder, reviewer, reader, and producer. The software inspection is initiated as an exit criteria for each activity in the life cycle. Product and process measurements are recorded during the software inspection session and recorded on specially formatted forms and reports. These issues and defects are tracked to closure.

7.4   Elements

The software inspections process is made up of several elements: the structured review process, standard of excellence, system of checklists, defined roles of participants, and forms and reports. See Tables 7.2 and 7.3.

1. A structured review process is a systematic procedure integrated with the activities of the life-cycle model. The process is composed of planning, preparation, entry criteria, conduct, exit criteria, reporting, and follow-up [2, 15].
2. A system of checklists governs each step in the structured review process and the review of the product itself, objective by objective. Process checklists are used as a guide for each activity of the structured review process. Product checklists house the strongly preferred indicators that set the standard of excellence for the organization's software products [16].
3. The role of each participant in the structured review process is defined. The roles include the moderator, producer, reader, reviewer, recorder, manager, and consumer. Each role is characterized by particular skills and behaviors [6].
4. Forms and reports provide uniformity in recording issues at all software inspections, reporting the results to management, and building a database useful in process management. Data collection utilizes three recording instruments: Inspection Record, Inspection Reporting Form, and Report

Table 7.2 Peer Reviews: Entry, Task, Verification, Exit

Entry Criteria	Task	Exit Criteria
Product artifact	Structured review process	Forms and reports
Participants in defined roles		
Standard of excellence		
	Verification	
	Product checklists	
	Process checklists	

Table 7.3 Elements of Peer Reviews

Elements	Software Inspection	Software Walkthrough
Structured review process	Planning	Planning: optional
	Preparation	
	Conduct	Conduct
	Report out	
	Follow up	Follow up
Standard of excellence	Completeness	Completeness
	Correctness	Correctness
	Style	
	Rules of construction	Rules of construction
	Multiple views	
		Product and engineering practice
Defined roles of participants	Moderator	Moderator: optional
	Recorder	
	Producer	Producer
	Reviewer	Reviewer
	Reader	
Forms and reports	Inspection record	
	Inspection reporting form	
	Report summary form	
		Open issues
		Action items

Summary Form. The results of software walkthroughs are recorded as open issues and action items [7].

7.4.1 Structured Review Process

The activities of the structured review process are organized for software inspections. Software walkthroughs may employ variations for planning, conduct, and follow-up.

7.4.1.1 Planning

The structured review process begins early in the project when the manager plans for software inspections of requirements, specifications, designs, code, and test procedures. The schedule for each software inspection is recorded in the project's software development plan (SDP) or project plan. A trained moderator is assigned to each software inspection, and moderator training is scheduled as necessary. The Software Quality Assurance (SQA) Plan also discusses the use of software walkthroughs and software inspections in terms of their contribution to product verification and validation.

7.4.1.2   Preparation

Preparation is initiated by the moderator a week before the inspection session. The readiness of the product for inspection is assessed by the moderator and the producer. The moderator obtains the reviewers, recorder, and reader and briefs them on their roles along with the key principles of software inspections.

In assessing product volatility, the moderator ascertains the status of the baseline change activity and the completion of the preceding life-cycle activity. The producer conducts a brief overview of the product to be inspected to assist the inspection team in their preparation for the inspection session.

The inspection materials are distributed to team members, the time and place for the inspection session are announced, and reviewers are encouraged to prepare individually for the inspection session. Individual preparation is the mother's milk of the software inspections process.

7.4.1.3   Entry Criteria

Entry criteria are checked by the moderator at the start of the inspection session. Before the conduct activity begins, the moderator determines that the software product is ready to be inspected and the inspection team is prepared to inspect it. The moderator again assesses the product volatility indicators. Inspection team members are asked for their preparation effort, and the recorder notes this information. Where the entry criteria are not satisfactorily met, the moderator may reschedule the inspection session.

The moderator script for directing the entry criteria includes:

1. Has the preceding life-cycle activity been concluded?
2. Are there any changes to the baseline?
3. Are review participants in place and briefed?
4. Have all participants received all the review materials and checklists?
5. How many minutes of preparation did each participant perform?

7.4.1.4   Conduct

The inspection session including entry, conduct, and exit is directed by the moderator and attended by the producer, reviewers, recorder, and reader. The manager does not attend. Some key principles govern the inspection session:

1. The inspection is limited to periods of peak concentration (1 to 2 hours).
2. The product is reviewed, not the producer.
3. Issues are identified, not proposed solutions.

Each product component is inspected using the strongly preferred indicators found in the appropriate software product checklists. Each inspection team member in turn is asked if there is an issue to be raised for the product component and product checklist now before the group. If so, the issue is stated, discussed, and recorded. The producer may wish to obtain clarification of the issue at the time it is raised, but there is no need for the producer to defend or even explain the approach taken. The producer will have the opportunity to resolve the issue during the follow-up activity.

The moderator script for directing the conduct activity includes:

1. Are there any issues in completeness?
2. Are there any issues in correctness?
3. Are there any issues in style?
4. Are there any issues in rules of construction?
5. Are there any issues in multiple views?

7.4.1.5   Exit Criteria

Exit criteria are checked by the moderator at the close of the inspection session. The moderator verifies that all product components have been inspected and that the intended product checklists have been utilized. The recorder verifies that all the metrics have been recorded including preparation effort of each team member, the duration of the inspection session, and the size of the product being inspected as well as the defect type, defect category, defect severity, and defect origin for each issue raised. Finally, the moderator asks the producer for any closing comments, permitting the producer to have the last word.

The moderator script for directing the exit criteria includes:

1. Have all product elements been inspected?
2. Have all checklists been processed?
3. Have the inspection results been recorded?
4. Have metrics been collected?
5. Would the recorder read back the issues?
6. What should be the disposition of the inspection?
7. Would the producer like an opportunity to comment?

7.4.1.6   Reporting

The moderator, with the help of the recorder, reports the findings of the inspection session to the manager within a week. This report provides a review summary, the preparation effort and conduct time expended, the types of defects detected, and follow-up recommendations.

7.4.1.7   Follow-Up

The follow-up rework on the product is performed by the producer. The follow-up actions are prepared jointly by the manager and the producer and entered in the project action log. As these follow-up actions are completed, the action log reflects the closure. Tracking issues to closure is an important indicator of software process maturity.

7.4.2 System of Checklists

Checklists are at the heart of software inspections. They fuel the structured review process and form the standard of excellence expected for the software product. Checklists provide the criteria for evaluating the quality of the product as well as progress within the process. Process and product checklists promote uniformity in the use of software inspections throughout a project and across an organization. Process checklists are used as a guide for each activity of the structured review process to ensure that the software inspections process runs smoothly. Product checklists provide reviewers with the thorough technical focus needed to guide the review of each product component from all viewpoints [10]. The system of checklists helps to overcome human limitations on information processing by focusing on just one consistent perspective at a time. See Tables 7.4 through 7.8 for examples of Requirements, Specification, Architecture, Design and Code, and Test Procedure Checklists [10].

Table 7.4   Requirements Checklist

Completeness

1. Do the requirements specified carry out the mission in a consistent fashion?
2. Do the requirements include the essential needs of the user, operational, and maintenance communities?
3. Does each requirement stand alone or have clearly stated dependencies?
4. Is the requirements document complete with all TBDs eliminated?
5. Are any requirements missing?
6. Are necessary requirements distinguished from those that are simply nice to have?

Correctness

1. Does each requirement not conflict with any other requirement?
2. Does the organization of the requirements facilitate traceability to design and code?
3. Is each specific requirement identified by unique paragraph number?

Style

1. Are the requirements clearly understandable?
2. Are changes clearly distinguished between editorial and functional?
3. Is the nomenclature of terms and their definition complete?

Rules of Construction

1. Are requirements that are likely to change and evolve distinguished from those that are likely to be stable?
2. Has all available tool assistance been applied it the production, analysis, and review the requirements?
3. Does the requirements document follow the documentation standard?
4. Is each requirement testable?

Multiple Views

1. Have users participated in the production, analysis, and review of these requirements?
2. Have operational personnel participated in the production, analysis, and review of these requirements?
3. Have maintenance personnel participated in the production, analysis, and review of these requirements?
4. Have software engineering designers participated in the production, analysis, and review of these requirements?
5. Has the software development team participated in the production, analysis, and review of these requirements?
6. Have test engineers participated in the production, analysis, and review of these requirements?
7. Has the test team participated in the production, analysis, and review?

Table 7.5 Architecture Checklist

Completeness

1. Is the commonality of functions and components identified?
2. Is permissible variability of inputs and parameters defined?

Correctness

1. Are responses derivable from stimuli?
2. Are responses and stimuli identified for all permissible states and modes?
3. Are adaptation parameters governing permissible variability properly defined?

Style

1. Are architecture artifacts recorded in accordance with project selected templates?

Rules of Construction

1. Does the architecture utilize the underlying algorithms and data stores intrinsic to any existing domain specific reference architecture?
2. Are guidelines for commonality followed to facilitate alignment of interfaces and components and preserve open system possibilities?
3. Does the architecture provide for explicit identification of reusable components and commercial off-the-shelf products choices?
4. Does the architecture support reasoning about scalability and capacities?

Multiple Views

1. Does the architecture support reasoning about performance?
1.1 For each stimulus mode, source and frequency are identified.
1.2 For architectural adaptations computer resources, their arbitration (queuing policy), and loading are identified.
1.3 For each response latency, throughput, and precedence are identified.
2. Does the architecture support reasoning about modifiability?
2.1 Anticipated or likely additions, modifications, and deletions are appropriately encapsulated and separated.
3. Does the architecture support reasoning about availability and ensuring continuous operation including hardware and software faults and failures, hardware and software redundancy, service levels, and fail soft backup?

Technology

1. Have appropriate logical structures been specified?
2. Are the principles of good software engineering applied including: abstraction, information hiding, and separation of concerns?
3. Have the appropriate mechanisms been used to present information including text, tables, lists, matrices, equations, logical diagrams, diagrams, and pictures?

7.4.2.1 Completeness

Completeness is based on traceability among software product artifacts of various types including requirements, specifications, designs, code, and test procedures. Completeness analysis may be assisted by tools that trace the components of a product artifact of one type to the components of another type. Completeness analysis of predecessor and successor artifacts reveals what sections are missing and what fragments may be extra. A by-product of the completeness analysis is a clear view of the relationship of requirements to the code product: straightforward (one to one), simple analysis (many to one), and complex (one to many).

The moderator script for inquiring about completeness includes:

Table 7.6   Specification Checklist

Completeness

1. Scope and Traceability
    1.1 Is each operational capability fully described in terms of its purpose and function?
    1.2 Are all identified functions and data traceable to the higher level specification?
2. Completeness of Detail
    2.1 Is the decomposition of each identified function sufficiently fine-grained and uniquely allocated to a physical component?
    2.2 Have all TBS and TBD indicators been replaced with the required information?
    2.3 Are all logical operations specified completely?
    2.4 Are all exception conditions explicitly identified and all necessary error processing defined?
3. Data and Interface
    3.1 Has the necessary and sufficient set of input data been specified for each function?
    3.2 For each function specified, are the required output data derived from the input data and accessible retained data?
    3.3 Is the boundary of each identified function described in terms of all required input data and all required output data?
    3.4 Is all the data identified that must be retained within the system for reference?
    3.5 Is each interfunction data flow or signal accounted for by both senders and receivers?
    3.6 Are the semantics for each interfunction data flow or signal the same for all senders and all receivers?
    3.7 Does each data item have appropriately specified initialization values and required range of permissible values?
4. Testability
    4.1 Does each requirement have a corresponding test requirement that identified how it is to be verified and the required testing limits? (Verification methods include: by test and review of data, by inspection or observation, by data collection and analysis, or not required.)
    4.2 Has the appropriate level of test been identified for verifying each requirement? (Levels of test include: unit, computer program, element, or system test level.)
    4.3 Have the stress test and regression test requirements for each test requirement been described?

Correctness

1. Have the higher level requirements been allocated correctly and appropriately to the specification?
2. Does each function specification and its inputs correctly produce the required outputs?
3. Is each equation correctly specified for performing the needed computations?
4. Is each logical operation correctly defined?
5. Is each interface signal identified in the interface design specification properly reflected in the specification?
6. Is each external interface signal in the specification properly reflected in the respective interface design specification?

Style

1. Does the format of the specification follow the documentation style guide?
2. For each mnemonic used, is it defined when first used and entered in the glossary with the page number of this definition?

Rules of Construction

1. Is interprocessor communication properly addressed?
2. Are interfunction notifications properly addressed?
3. Are alternate modes considerations included?
4. Are data representation considerations property accounted for?
5. Are design constraints properly accounted for?
6. Are control requirements properly accounted for?

Multiple Views

1. Have initialization considerations been considered?
2. Has computer resource loading been assessed including memory, timing, and I/O?
3. Have alternate mode considerations been properly addressed?
4. Are the requirements sufficiently complete to support high level design?
5. Have user interface and display impacts been properly accounted for?

Table 7.6 (continued)

Technology

1. Have appropriate logical design structures been specified?
   1.1 Are the principles of good design applied including: abstraction, information hiding, and separation of concerns?
2. Have the appropriate mechanisms been used to present information including text, tables, lists, matrices, equations, logical diagrams, diagrams, and pictures?

1. Has traceability been assessed?

2. Have all predecessor requirements been accounted for?

3. Were any product fragments revealed not to have traceability to the predecessor requirements?

4. Was traceability found to be straightforward, simple, or complex?

7.4.2.2 Correctness

Correctness is based on reasoning about programs through the use of informal verification and correctness questions derived from the prime constructs of structured programming and their composite use in proper programs [17, 18]. Input domain and output range are analyzed for all legal values and all possible values. State data is similarly analyzed. Adherence to project-specified disciplined data structures is analyzed. Asynchronous processes and their interaction and communication are analyzed [19].

The moderator script for inquiring about correctness includes:

1. Is the function commentary satisfied?
2. Are programs limited to single entry and single exit?
3. Is the loop initialized and terminated properly?
4. Does the input domain span all legal values?
5. Is there systematic exception handling for illegal values?
6. Are disciplined data structures used?

7.4.2.3 Style

Style is based on project-specified style guidance. This guidance is expected to call for block-structured templates. Naming conventions and commentary are checked for consistency of use along with alignment, highlighting, and case. More advanced style guidance may call for templates for repeating patterns and semantic correspondence among software product artifacts of various types.

The moderator script for inquiring about style includes:

1. Are style conventions for block structuring followed?
2. Are naming conventions followed?
3. Are style conventions for commentary followed?
4. Are the semantics of the product component traceable to the requirements?
5. Are templates used for repeating patterns?

Table 7.7   Design and Code Checklist

Completeness

1. Has traceability been assessed?
2. Has available tool assistance been applied in assessing traceability?
3. Have all predecessor requirements been accounted for?
4. Were any product fragments revealed not to have traceability to the predecessor requirements?
5. What is the relationship of requirements to product component:
    5.1 One to one <straightforward>?
    5.2 Many to one <simple analysis>?
    5.3 One to many <complex>?

Correctness

1. Are structured programming prime constructs used correctly:
    1.1 Sequence: Is the function commentary satisfied for the sequence?
    1.2 If-then: If the test is true, is the function commentary satisfied?
    1.3 If-then-else: If the test is true, is the function commentary satisfied?
    1.4 While-loop: If the condition is true, is the function commentary satisfied? Does the loop terminate?
    1.5 Loop-until: If the condition is false, is the function commentary satisfied? Does the loop terminate? Is a one time loop acceptable?
    1.6 For-do: Is the function commentary satisfied? Are there discrete steps through the loop? Is the control variable not modified in the loop? Is the loop initialized and terminated properly?
    1.7 Case: For each leg, is the function commentary satisfied? Is the domain partitioned exclusively and exhaustively?
2. Are proper programs composed of multiple prime programs limited to single entry and single exit?
3. Are disciplined data structures used to manipulate and transform data?
4. Does the input domain span all legal values?
5. Does the input domain span all possible values, with systematic exception handling for illegal values?
6. Does the output range span all legal values?
7. For modules, does the state data span all legal values?

Style

1. Are style conventions for block structuring defined and followed?
2. Are naming conventions defined and followed?
3. Are the semantics of the product component traceable to the requirements?
4. Are style conventions for commentary defined and followed?
5. Are style conventions for alignment, upper/lower case, and highlighting defined and followed?
6. Are templates used for repeating patterns?

Rules of Construction

1. Are guidelines for program unit construction followed?
2. Is the interprocess communication protocol followed?
3. Are data representation conventions followed?
4. Is the system standard time defined and followed?
5. Are encapsulation, localization, and layering used to achieve object orientation?
6. Is logical independence achieved through event driven and process driven paradigms, late binding, and implicit binding?
7. Is scalability achieved through uniformity, parameterization, and portability?
8. Are fault tolerance, high availability, and security achieved?

Multiple Views

1. Has the logical view of user interface and object orientation considerations been assessed?
2. Has the static view of packaging considerations been assessed including program unit construction, program generation process, and target machine operations?
3. Has the dynamic view of operational considerations been assessed including communications, concurrency, synchronization, and failure recovery?
4. Has the physical view of execution considerations been assessed including timing, memory use, input and output, initialization, and finite word effects?
5. Has the product component been assessed for safety considerations?
6. Has the product component been assessed for open systems considerations?
7. Has the product component been assessed for security considerations?
8. Has the product component been assessed for innovation considerations?

Table 7.8 Test Procedure Checklist

Completeness

1. Have objectives been established for each test case?
2. Have all predecessor requirements been accounted for?
3. Has available tool assistance been applied in assessing traceability?
4. Were any test cases revealed not to have traceability to the predecessor requirements?
5. Have test prerequisite conditions been established?
6. Have test input conditions been established?
7. Have expected test results been established?

Correctness

1. Is the test case testable within the test category (Review, Lab, Field)?
2. Does the test case objective reflect requirements?
3. Are the test prerequisite conditions necessary and complete?
4. Are the input conditions correct and obtainable?
5. Do the test results reflect the requirements?
6. Do the test procedures satisfy the test case objectives?
7. Are the test procedure steps correct and in logical order?

Style

1. Are style conventions for test procedure structuring defined and followed?
2. Are procedures written in "Device/Action/Observation/Comment" format?
3. Are style conventions for alignment, upper/lower case, and highlighting defined and followed?
4. Has a version number been assigned?
5. Are templates used for repeating patterns?

Multiple Views

1. Have test cases been assessed for integration considerations, such as input and output, integration of multiple components, and test efficiency?
2. Have the test procedures been assessed for packaging considerations?

Metrics

1. Have the total pages inspected been recorded?
2. Have the total minutes of inspection preparation effort been recorded?
3. Have the total minutes of inspection conduct time been recorded?
4. For each defect, have defect category, severity, type, and origin been recorded?

7.4.3 Rules of Construction

Rules of construction are based on the software application architecture and the specific protocols, templates, and conventions used to carry it out. For example, these include interprocess communication protocols, tasking and concurrent operations, program unit construction, and data representation.

The moderator script for inquiring about rules of construction includes:

1. Are guidelines for program unit construction followed?
2. Is the interprocess communication protocol followed?
3. Are data representation conventions followed?
4. Is the system standard time defined and followed?
5. Are encapsulation, localization, and layering used to achieve object orientation?
6. Is logical independence achieved through event driven and process driven paradigms, late binding, and implicit binding?
7. Is scalability achieved through uniformity, parameterization, and portability?
8. Are fault tolerance, high availability, and security achieved?

7.4.4 Multiple Views

Multiple views are based on the various perspectives and view points required to be reflected in the software product. During execution many factors must operate harmoniously as intended including initialization, timing of processes, memory management, input and output, and finite word effects. In building the software product, packaging considerations must be coordinated including program unit construction, program generation process, and target machine operations. Product construction disciplines of systematic design and structured programming must be followed as well as interactions with the user, operating system, and physical hardware.

The moderator script for inquiring about multiple views includes:

1. Has the logical view of user interface and object orientation considerations been assessed?
2. Has the static view of packaging considerations been assessed including program unit construction, program generation process, and target machine operations?
3. Has the dynamic view of operational considerations been assessed including communications, concurrency, synchronization, and failure recovery?
4. Has the physical view of execution considerations been assessed including timing, memory use, input and output, initialization, and finite word effects?

7.4.5 Defined Roles of Participants

Software inspections are a reasoning activity performed by practitioners playing the defined roles of moderator, recorder, reviewer, reader, and producer. Some may name these roles facilitator, scribe, inspector, and author. Each role carries with it the specific behaviors, skills, and knowledge needed to achieve the expert practice of software inspections [6].

Individuals attending the inspection session may take on more than one role. For example, the producer may also be a reviewer. The moderator and recorder roles are demanding ones, and the individual assigned is usually dedicated to the single role. The reader role is not always utilized in software inspections. When the reader is used, one of the reviewers, not the producer, is assigned this role. In software walkthroughs, the producer serves as reader.

7.4.5.1 Manager

The manager is active in the planning, preparation, reporting, and follow-up activities. In planning, the manager identifies and schedules all software inspections in the project plan. The manager identifies personnel resource needs in terms of labor hours and allocates them to each inspection. The moderator is assigned by the manager, who ensures that only trained moderators are appointed.

The manager generally does not attend the inspection session. Practitioners are wary that managers attending an inspection session might use the results in the personnel performance appraisal of the producer. In addition, reviewers are reluctant to identify defects in the artifacts of their peers in the presence of managers. However, if the manager is an expert in the application and must be present to make a technical contribution, the manager must first convincingly check management and organizational behaviors at the door and attend the inspection as a technical peer.

After the software inspection is conducted, the manager receives the moderator's report, meets with the producer to plan the follow-up, and administers the follow-up oversight.

7.4.5.2   Moderator

The moderator is the keystone of the software inspections process and is active in the preparation, entry criteria, conduct, exit criteria, and reporting activities. The moderator directs the activities of the software inspection. During the preparation activity, the moderator briefs the inspection team members on their roles in the structured review process, asks the producer to overview the software product to be inspected, distributes the inspection materials, and announces the time and place for the inspection session.

During the inspection session, the moderator directs the entry criteria, conduct, and exit criteria activities and facilitates the interaction among the inspection team members. The moderator intervenes as little as possible and as much as necessary to ensure that an effective and efficient software inspection session takes place.

A skillful moderator recognizes the role specific needs of inspection team members. For example, a producer with a "good catch" on his own product is called upon first. A talkative reviewer with little preparation effort is controlled. Where the moderator has issues to bring up, it is good form to insert these after the other team members have spoken. The moderator collaborates with the recorder in preparing the report for the manager on the findings of the inspection session.

7.4.5.3   Producer

The producer is active during the preparation, entry criteria, conduct, exit criteria, and follow-up activities. The producer is responsible for creating the materials to be inspected. The producer attends the inspection as reviewer and is expected to raise issues. From time to time the producer may offer a technical explanation of the product as necessary.

The producer expects criticism of the product and need not offer any defense as issues are raised. It is understood that the producer may be in a protective state of mind with respect to the product being inspected. What is asked of the producer is that the protective state not be exhibited as defensive behavior. Where an issue is surfaced that is not understood by the producer, a dialogue may be needed to obtain clarification.

At the conclusion of the conduct activity, the producer is afforded the opportunity to comment on the inspection session and to acknowledge the value of the issues raised. The producer meets with the manager to plan the rework and performs the follow-up actions resulting from the inspection.

7.4.5.4   Recorder

The recorder is active in the preparation, entry criteria, conduct, exit criteria, and reporting activities. The recorder completes the Inspection Record, the Inspection

Reporting Form, and the Report Summary Form. The practice of the recorder is "to leave no bits on the floor." In other words, the recorder is expected to record every issue without exception.

During the entry criteria, the recorder notes the preparation effort of each inspection team member, the start and stop time of the meeting, the project and product name and size, and the life-cycle activity for which the inspection is an exit criteria. As issues are raised, the recorder describes each issue and notes defect category, defect severity, defect type, and defect origin. The recorder uses the key word "investigate" in recording issues that may be defects but require additional research following the meeting. At the conclusion, the recorder tabulates the issues by defect type, severity, and category.

The role of the recorder is to be transparent to the inspection session and to record all issues completely and accurately. This requires a high degree of concentration, judgment, and technical knowledge.

7.4.5.5   Reviewer

Reviewers are active in the preparation, entry criteria, conduct, and exit criteria activities. A reviewer is expected to spend sufficient time preparing and to raise issues and concerns about the software product. Reviewers are asked to refrain from proposing solutions and to direct their comments at the product not the producer. Reviewers accept the discipline imposed by the round robin, checklist structure of the inspection session. In return for accepting these responsibilities and disciplines, each reviewer is assured of an uninterrupted opportunity to raise issues.

7.4.5.6   Reader

The reader is active in the preparation, entry criteria, conduct, and exit criteria activities. Where necessary, the moderator may ask the reader to read parts of the product aloud so as to focus attention on a particular trouble spot. The reader does this by paraphrasing not by reading line by line. Using the reader for this task helps promote the egoless behavior of the producer. The reader is responsible for bringing to the inspection session and being prepared to navigate any background materials, such as, baseline documentation and style guide.

7.4.6   Forms and Reports

All data collected and reported during the software inspections process is recorded by the recorder. This includes data about the product being inspected and about the inspection process itself. The requirements for data collection are defined and focus on three recording instruments: Inspection Record, Inspections Reporting Form, and Report Summary Form.

7.4.6.1   Inspection Record

The Inspection Record is initiated during the entry criteria activity when the recorder gathers the preparation effort from each inspection team member. The name of the project and the product component are recorded along with the size of the product to be inspected. The life-cycle activity for which this inspection serves as the exit criteria is recorded. The start time for the inspection session is entered at the beginning of the meeting, and the stop time is recorded at the close. Also at the close of the session, the disposition is recorded in terms of acceptance, re-inspection, or conditional. See Figure 7.3.

7.4.6.2   Inspection Reporting Form

During the conduct activity as issues are raised, the recorder documents a description of each issue and assigns attributes that characterize the issue. Each issue is assigned a sequence number, and the page and line number are pinpointed. Similar issues that occur a few times are recorded as separate issues. An issue type that occurs an unaccountably large number of times is recorded once.

A defect category is assigned as missing, wrong, or extra. A defect severity is assigned as major or minor. The defect origin is noted as the life-cycle activity during which this defect was inserted. The defect type is entered [7]. See Figure 7.4.

A major defect affects execution; a minor defect does not. In practice, some prefer to extend defect severity to include the extremes of critical and trivial. Other severity gradations used to classify defects, faults, and failures detected in testing and field operations are not used in software inspections. These test and operational execution-based severities often revolve around the criticality of the defect and its impact on sustaining testing or operations. Another dimension of defect severity is related to the effort needed to correct the defect.

The appropriate defect type is assigned as follows:

Inspection Record			
Project Name: Product Component: Start Time: _____ Stop Time: _____		Date: Size:_____ lines _____pages Elapsed Time: _____	
Role	Name	Preparation Minutes	Additional Comments
Moderator			
Recorder			
Producer			
Reviewer			
Reviewer			
Reviewer			
Reader			
Total Prep Effort			
Checklists Used		Disposition	Life-Cycle Activity
Completeness Correctness Style Rules of Construction Multiple Views Technology Metrics		Accept ____ Conditional ____ Reinspect ____	Planning Requirements Specification Design Code Test

Figure 7.3   Inspection Record.

Inspection Reporting Form							
Issue Number	Page/ Line	Checklist	Defect Category	Defect Severity	Defect Type	Defect Origin	Defect Description

Defect Category: Missing, Wrong, Extra
Defect Severity: Major, Minor

Defect Type: Interface, Data, Logic, UO, Performance, Functionality, Human Factors, Standards, Documentation, Syntax, Maintainability, Other

Figure 7.4   Inspection Reporting Form.

1. Interface: error in parameter list;
2. Data: error in data definition, initial value setting, or use of disciplined data structures;
3. Logic: error revealed through informal correctness questions spanning prime constructs of structured programming;
4. I/O: error in formatting, commanding, or controlling I/O operations;
5. Performance: error in managing or meeting constraints in computer resource allocations and capacities for CPU, memory, or I/O;
6. Functionality: error in stating intended function or in satisfying intended function through refinement or elaboration;
7. Human Factors: error in externally visible user or enterprise interface or interaction;
8. Standards: error in compliance with product standards for construction or integration including programming style guidelines, open systems interfaces, or guidelines for the application domain architecture;
9. Documentation: error in guidance documentation;
10. Syntax: error in language defined syntax;
11. Maintainability: error in uniformity and consistency;
12. Other: any other error.

7.4.6.3   Report Summary Form

During the exit criteria, the recorder completes the meeting stop time, verifies the completeness of all recorded results, and completes the Report Summary Form. This form is a frequency count of issues presented as a matrix of defect types by defect severity and defect category. This form serves several purposes. Since it cannot be constructed unless the recorder has completed the Inspection Reporting Form, it serves as an on–the-spot check of the recorded results. Once completed, weaknesses are highlighted and some opportunities for defect prevention suggest themselves. When the results of numerous inspection sessions are overlaid on the Report Summary Form, these frequency counts divided by the total defects serve as the probability of occurrence for each defect type, defect severity, and defect category. See Figure 7.5.

7.5   Preparation for Expert Use

A collection of coordinated knowledge, skills, and behaviors facilitates the best possible practice of peer reviews. As Deming reminded us, there is no substitute for superior knowledge. In conducting peer reviews, superior knowledge is sought in the application domain, the computing platform both hardware and operating system, and programming language. In addition, participants must be knowledgeable in the peer review process and the standard of excellence expected in the product artifact.

For best results, participants filling certain defined roles must possess particular skills. The moderator needs facilitation, conflict identification, and conflict resolution skills. The recorder needs listening, synthesizing, and recording skills. The reviewer needs code reading skills.

Participants in peer reviews are expected to adopt certain behaviors known to contribute to effective and harmonious review sessions. First, the rules of civility apply. For example, one person speaks at a time, and personal attacks are not permitted. Second, since people make mistakes sometimes, it is necessary to

Report Summary Form						
Defect Types	Major Defects			Minor Defects		
	Missing	Wrong	Extra	Missing	Wrong	Extra
Interface						
Data						
Logic						
I/O						
Performance						
Functionality						
Human Factors						
Standards						
Documentation						
Syntax						
Maintainability						
Other						

Figure 7.5   Report Summary Form.

decriminalize defects so that they do not remain hidden. Recognizing that, assigning blame for defects is discouraged. Third, participants are encouraged to direct their comments towards the product not the person who authored the artifact being reviewed. Finally, everyone is encouraged to give way to the individual who possesses superior knowledge.

7.6 Measurements

While many organizations have adopted software inspections, few have published their results. Those that have published results typically have done so following early successes in the new practice adoption cycle. Organizations with published results have included the Jet Propulsion Laboratory [20], Litton Data Systems [21], Bull HN Information Systems, Inc. [22], AT&T Corp. [23], and Lockheed Martin Corporation [24]. While they all used software inspections and have documented measured results, the particular adaptations are not well aligned, and the results do not lend themselves to systematic comparison.

7.6.1 National Software Quality Experiment

In 1992 the DOD Software Technology Strategy set the objective to reduce software problem rates by a factor of 10 by 2000. The National Software Quality Experiment is being conducted to benchmark the state of software product quality. The experiment has measured progress towards the national objective [16, 25, 26] and continues with the measurements. Industry problem rates ranged from 1 to 10 defects per thousand lines of source code. Meeting the objective shifts the range to 0.1 to 1 defect per thousand lines of source code.

The centerpiece of the experiment is the Software Inspection Lab where data collection procedures, product checklists, and participant behaviors are packaged for operational project use. The uniform application of the experiment and the collection of consistent measurements are guaranteed through rigorous training of each participant.

Approximately 3,000 participants from nearly 60 organizations have populated the experiment database with nearly 15,000 defects of all types along with pertinent information needed to pinpoint their root causes. These results are highlighted below in the discussion of the common problems, Inspection Lab operations, defect type ranking, and return on investment.

7.6.2 Common Problems Revealed

Analysis of the issues raised in the experiment has revealed common problems that reoccur from session to session. Typical organizations that desire to reduce their software problem rates should focus on preventing the following types of defects:

1. Software product source code components are not traced to requirements. As a result, the software product is not under intellectual control, verification procedures are imprecise, and changes cannot be managed.

2. Software engineering practices for systematic design and structured programming are applied without sufficient rigor and discipline. As a result, high defect rates are experienced in logic, data, interfaces, and functionality.

3. Software product designs and source code are recorded in an ad hoc style. As a result, the understandability, adaptability, and maintainability of the software product are directly impacted.

4. The rules of construction for the application domain are not clearly stated, understood, and applied. As a result, common patterns and templates are not exploited in preparation for later reuse.

5. The code and upload development paradigm is becoming predominant in emerging e-commerce applications.

As a result, the enterprise code base services only the short term planning horizon where code rules and heroes flourish, but it mortgages the future where traceable baseline requirements, specification, and design artifacts are necessary foundations.

7.6.3   Inspection Lab Operations

The Inspection Lab is the consistent operation of software inspection sessions as part of the National Software Quality Experiment. These sessions apply the elements of software inspections including the entry, conduct, and exit processes; defined roles of participants; product checklists; and forms and reports. Through 2002, 3,040 participants conducted inspection sessions. A total of 1,020,229 source lines of code have received strict and close examination in the Software Inspection Lab. There have been 181,471 minutes of preparation effort and 71,283 minutes of conduct time expended to detect 14,903 defects. See Figure 7.6. For each metric, control panels are derived by ordering all values for the metric and selecting the data points at the 20th percentile, 50th percentile, and 80th percentile. With these values the Software Inspections Control Panel in Figure 7.7 is produced.

Of these 14,903 defects, 2,512 were classified as major, and 12,391 as minor. A major defect effects execution; a minor defect does not. It required 12.18 minutes of preparation effort on the average to detect a defect. To detect a major defect required 72.24 minutes of preparation effort on the average. On the average, 0.858 thousand source lines of code were examined each inspection conduct hour. There were 2.46 major defects detected in each thousand lines, and 12.15 minor defects. There were 4.90 defects detected in inspecting 335.60 lines per session. The preparation effort was 0.64 of conduct effort. The Software Inspection Labs produced a return on investment of 4.50.

7.6.4   Defect Type Ranking

The foremost defect types that accounted for more than 90% of all defects detected include the following (see Figure 7.8):

- *Documentation*: 40.51% error in guidance documentation;
- *Standards*: 23.20% error in compliance with product standards;

Sessions	Prep Effort	Conduct Time	Major Defects	Minor Defects	Size in Lines
3,040	181,471	71,283	2,512	12,391	1,020,229

Metrics:

1.	12.18	Minutes of preparation effect per defect
2.	72.24	Minutes of preparation effort per major defect
3.	2.46	Major defects per thousand lines
4.	12.15	Minor defects per thousand lines
5.	858.74	Lines per conduct hour
6.	4.90	Defects per session
7.	0.64	Preparation/conduct effort
8.	335.60	Lines per session
9.	4.50	Return on investment

Figure 7.6 Inspection Lab operations.

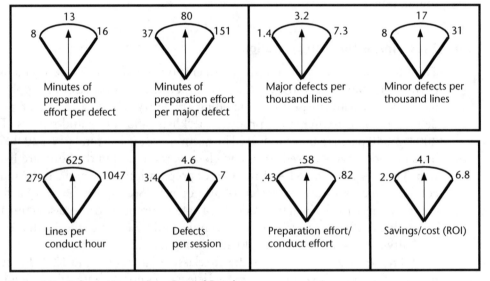

Figure 7.7 Software Inspections Control Panel.

- *Logic:* 7.22% error revealed through informal correctness questions function;
- *Functionality:* 6.57% error in stating or meeting intended;
- *Syntax:* 4.79% error in language defined syntax compliance;
- *Data:* 4.62% error in data definition, initial value setting, or use;
- *Maintainability:* 4.09% error in good practice impacting the supportability and evolution of the software product.

7.6.5 Return on Investment

Managers are interested in knowing the return on investment to be derived from software process improvement actions. The software inspections process gathers the data needed to determine this [4].

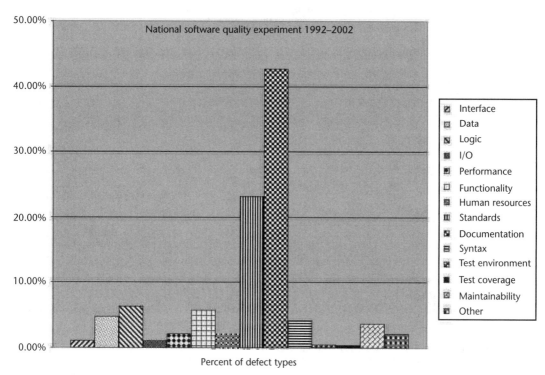

Figure 7.8   Defect type distribution.

The return on investment for software inspections is defined as net savings divided by detection cost, where net savings is cost avoidance less cost to repair and detection cost is the cost of preparation effort and the cost of conduct effort. The defined measurements collected in the Software Inspections Lab may be combined in complex ways to form this derived metric.

The model for return on investment bases the savings on the cost avoidance associated with detecting and correcting defects earlier rather than later in the product evolution cycle. A major defect that leaks from development to test may cost as much as 10 times to detect and correct. Some defects, undetected in test, continue to leak from test to customer use and may cost an additional 10 times to detect and correct. A minor defect may cost two to three times to correct later.

Figure 7.9 is a graph showing the return on investment measurements for each organization participating in the National Software Quality Experiment. This graph suggests that the return on investment for software inspections ranges from 4:1 to 8:1. For every dollar spent on software inspections, the organization can expect to avoid $4 to $8 on higher rework cost. Table 7.9 provides the return on investment expressions needed to perform the calculation [27].

7.7   Transition from Cost to Quality

In using software inspections, the goals vary with the maturity of the software product engineering method used, transitioning from cost to quality. Three levels of achievement of software product engineering are identified:

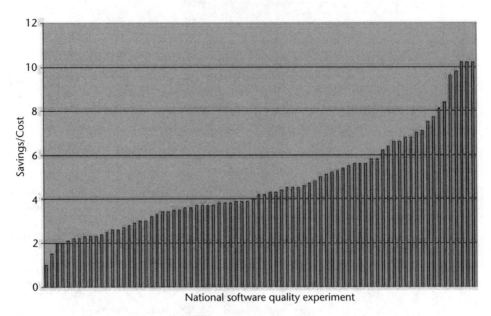

Figure 7.9   Return on investment measurements.

Table 7.9   Return on Investment Expressions

Return on Investment

Return on Investment is Net Savings divided by Detection Cost, or
ROI = Net Savings/Detection Cost

Net Savings

Net Savings is Cost Avoidance minus Cost to Repair Now, or
Net Savings = Cost Avoidance – Cost to Repair Now

Cost Avoidance

Cost Avoidance = Major Defects*{(M1*DD)+(M1*DD)*(M2*TL)*C1}+Minor Defects*M3

Net Savings

Net Savings = Major Defects*{(M1*DD)+(M1*DD)*(M2*TL)*C1-C1}+Minor Defects*(M3-C2)
   where:
   • M1: (2–10) Additional Cost to Repair Multiplier for Development to Test Major Deflect Leakage
   • M2: (2–10) Additional Cost to Repair Multiplier for Test to Customer Use Major Defect Leakage
   • M3: (2–4) Additional Cost to Repair for Minor Defect Leakage
   • DL: (0.5–0.95) Defect Detection Rate for Development to Test
   • TL: (0.05–0.5) Test Leakage Rate for Test to Customer Use
   • C1: Average Cost to Repair Major Defect
   • C2: Average Cost to Repair Minor Defect

   1. Ad hoc programming is characterized by a code and upload life cycle and a
      hacker coding style. This is common in low software process maturity
      organizations especially those facing time-to-market demands.

2. Structured software engineering employs structured programming, modular design, and defined programming style and pays close attention to establishing and maintaining traceability among requirements, specification, architecture, design, code, and test artifacts.

3. Disciplined software engineering is more formal and might be patterned after Clean Room software engineering, Personal and Team Software Process, and Extreme Programming techniques [14, 19].

By necessity, the focus of ad hoc programming practitioners is on reducing cost by detecting as many defects as possible. With 40 to 60 defects inserted, a defect detection rate of 0.50–0.65, and an additional cost multiplier of 8 to 10, the result is a net savings of 234.80 to 285 labor hours and a defect leakage expectation of 8.75 to 12.50 per thousand lines of code, numbers that promote a focus on cost. For this group, finding defects is like finding free money, and there are always more defects to find; however, managers struggle to meet cost and schedule commitments.

Structured software engineering focus is split between reducing cost and improving quality. With 20 to 30 defects inserted, a defect detection rate of 0.70–0.80, and an additional cost multiplier of 5 to 7, the result is a net savings of 65.00 to 85.23 labor hours and a defect leakage expectation of 2.5 to 3.75 per thousand lines of code, numbers that promote an attraction to both goals. For this group, there is constant dithering between cost and schedule.

Without question, the focus of disciplined software engineering practitioners is on eliminating every possible defect even if defect detection costs exceed net savings and the return on investment falls below the break even point. With 10 to 15 defects inserted, a defect detection rate of 0.85 to 0.95, and an additional cost multiplier of 2 to 4, the result is a net savings of 12.49 to 18.55 labor hours and a defect leakage expectation of 0.3125 to 0.9375 per thousand lines of code, numbers that promote a focus on quality. For this group, every practitioner is riveted on achieving perfection.

7.8 Software Inspections Roll Out

Software inspections have application throughout the software organization. Consequently a systematic approach is needed to introduce it to all participants. The steps in the defined program for rolling out software inspections within the organization include [28, 29]:

1. Assess software inspections practice.
2. Obtain management commitment.
3. Conduct software inspections training for practitioners, managers, and executives.
4. Prepare and disseminate software inspections policy and procedure documents.
5. Establish a coordination infrastructure, assign personnel, and formulate a program agenda.
6. Establish an inspection-based measurement program and database.

7. Set management objectives for planning, training, conducting, and using software inspections and measurements.

8. Continue to evolve the organization's process and product checklists.

The initial step in the roll out is to conduct an assessment of the software inspections practice. This will identify the strengths and weaknesses in planning, training, conduct, and reporting and use of results. Armed with this assessment, the change agent seeks management commitment and sponsorship for the improvements needed to offset the weaknesses. The following key practice indicators are assessed at regular intervals for each project in terms of approach, deployment, and results:

1. The project follows a documented organization policy for performing software inspections.

2. Adequate resources and funding are provided for performing software inspections on each software work product to be reviewed.

3. Moderators and reviewers receive required training in how to lead software inspections, as well as in objectives, principles, and methods of software inspections.

4. Software inspections are planned and documented.

5. Software inspections are performed according to a documented procedure.

6. Data on the conduct of the software inspections is recorded.

7. Measurements are made and used to determine the status of the software inspections activities.

8. The software quality assurance group reviews and/or audits the activities and work products for inspections and reports the results.

A clear management commitment is needed to approve and fund the training program including the cost of the instructor, training site, labor and burden for student attendance, and scheduling and administration of student enrollment and attendance.

With training underway and inspections being initiated by projects, peer reviews policy and procedure documents provide the guidelines for the well-defined process being deployed. The policy applies to all software development projects and states that each project involved in software development shall prepare, plan, conduct, and utilize software inspections. The purpose of the procedure is to provide the step-by-step instructions needed to carry out consistent examinations of work products on the project.

To fully stimulate the software inspections roll out program among project personnel, an infrastructure of coordinators drawn from active projects is convened. These project coordinators meet periodically to share experiences, compare results, and discuss common problems.

As inspection results and measurements are accumulated, a measurement database and the operations for analyzing, reporting, and acting upon these measurements are established. The measurements are recorded in the Software Inspection Lab. These measurements include preparation effort, conduct time, and the artifact size in lines of code or pages inspected and for each defect detected the defect severity, defect category, defect type, and defect origin. Using the measurements, metrics are derived to continually assess the efficiency and effectiveness of the process and its operation. These metrics include:

1. Minutes of preparation effort per defect;
2. Minutes of preparation effort per major defect;
3. Major defects per thousand lines;
4. Minor defects per thousand lines;
5. Lines per conduct hour;
6. Defects per session;
7. Preparation/conduct effort;
8. Lines per session;
9. Return on Investment.

7.9   Future Directions

In reasoning about future trends of peer reviews, the topics considered include increasing rate of software problems, improving the practice of defect prevention and prediction, extending the practice of peer reviews to systems engineering, understanding the process of experimentation in software development, exploiting technology in automating the peer reviews, and adapting to changes in business environment.

Software problem rates are not decreasing. The results of the National Software Quality Experiment 1999 show no systematic improvement towards fulfilling the national goal of a 10 times reduction in software problems set in 1992. The defect rates continue to range from 1 to 10 defects per thousand lines of source code.

The factors that may be contributing to defect rates include:

1. The emphasis on quicker, better, and cheaper;
2. The trend towards code and upload practice as the life-cycle model;
3. The preoccupation on improving software process maturity and mastering the management track practices of the Software Engineering Institute's CMMI® for Development, Maturity Level 2, an obstacle to many;
4. The downsizing of middle management and senior technical staff known to hold the line on product quality.

While software inspections have been in use for more than 25 years, defect prevention remains an immature practice. Causal analysis and resolution are a CMMI® for Development Maturity level 5 process area whose purpose is to identify causes of defects and take action to prevent them, and some organizations have achieved level 5. As more organizations seek to adopt the practice of defect prevention, its benefits and methods may become better understood, stimulating others to adopt the practice.

Similarly, defect prediction remains an underdeveloped practice. If software defects, faults, and failures can be predicted, perhaps they can be detected, controlled, and prevented. Model-based techniques calibrated with defect detection early in the life cycle to predict defect rates in later life-cycle activities have been demonstrated [30]. More modest efforts utilizing software inspections data to estimate the number of defects remaining to be found in testing are being applied on the project [31]. However, there is insufficient defect, fault, and failure data available from the nation's factory floor [26]. In addition there is insufficient process, method, and tooling to combine defect data obtained through software inspections practice, software fault data obtained through software product test and use, and software failure data obtained through software system operation into predictions of trustworthy software system operation [32].

While the benefits and usage of software inspections on code artifacts is well known, there is increasing interest in extending software inspections to all phases of the life cycle including requirements, specifications, design, code, and test artifacts. The CMMI® model with the inclusion of peer reviews in the product verification process area extends peer reviews to both systems engineering and software artifacts.

To achieve the best possible practice of software inspections, both managers and technical practitioners are encouraged to decriminalize defects. People make mistakes sometimes, yet software must be bit perfect. When managers and technical participants view with alarm the defects detected in software inspections, it produces a negative impact. On the other hand, when managers genuinely decriminalize defects and use their detection as a means to prevent their recurrence, it produces a positive result. During a software inspection session, the litmus test for decriminalization lies in the reaction of participants when a major defect is detected. Does the group say "good catch" or "bummer"?

With the growing recognition that fielding software involves a process of experimentation and with the increasing pressures of competition and demand for innovation, software walkthroughs may experience increasing usage. Software walkthroughs encourage and support the learning essential to experimentation. In favoring the group interaction needed to achieve consensus, software walkthroughs may contribute to increased innovation in software products.

There is interest in automating software inspections. The value of programming languages with strong typing, robust compilers, static analyzers and traceability tools, and complexity metrics [18] is recognized. However, software inspections practice is a reasoning activity and will remain essentially a human activity. The use of information technology innovations to support the logistics of preparation, scheduling, conduct, and results repository operations are sources for improved industry practice.

Software inspections are being conducted effectively using groupware tools. However, where global software development teams conducting geographically dispersed inspection sessions are using "follow the sun" software development tactics, software inspection participants may be separated by both geography and time zones, complicating the logistics of their application [33].

Software inspections usage is increasing in e-commerce applications where code and upload is the typical life-cycle practice. In an environment of rapid change and frequent releases, there is an absence of robust testing and sometimes even regression testing.

7.10 Conclusion

Software inspections deliver value to the organization through the close and strict examinations on life-cycle product artifacts that detect defects early and promote the deepest possible understanding of the artifact. The organization that sets the standard of excellence for its software engineered products in terms of completion, correctness, style, rules of construction, and multiple views and disciplines its practitioners to meet the standard set is able to reap an attractive return on investment while earning higher customer satisfaction. The measurements taken during software inspections promote an understanding of common problems and reveal opportunities for product and process improvement.

References

[1] O'Neill, D., "Software Inspections," *Software Technology Guide*, Software Engineering Institute, January 10, 1997.

[2] Fagan, M., "Design and Code Inspections to Reduce Errors in Program Development," *IBM Systems Journal*, Vol. 15, No. 3, 1976, pp. 182–211.

[3] Fagan, M., "Advances in Software Inspections," *IEEE Transactions on Software Engineering*, Vol. 12, No. 7, 1987.

[4] McGibbon, T., "A Business Case for Software Process Improvement," *Rome Laboratory DACS Report*, September 30, 1996.

[5] O'Neill, D., "Software Inspections Course and Lab," Software Engineering Institute, 1989.

[6] Freedman, D. P., and G. M. Weinberg, *Handbook of Walkthroughs, Inspections, and Technical Reviews*, New York: Dorset House, 1990, pp. 89–161.

[7] Ebenau, R. G., and S. H. Strauss, *Software Inspection Process*, New York: McGraw-Hill, 1994, pp. 236–240.

[8] Gilb, T., and D. Graham, *Software Inspection*, Reading, MA: Addison-Wesley, 1993.

[9] Humphrey, W. S., *Managing the Software Process*, Reading, MA: Addison-Wesley, 1989, pp. 171–190.

[10] Special permission to reproduce O'Neill, D., and A. L. Ingram, "Software Inspections Tutorial," as contained in the *Software Engineering Institute Technical Review*, 1988, pp. 92–120, by Carnegie Mellon University, is granted by the Software Engineering Institute.

[11] Paulk, M. C., et al., *The Capability Maturity Model: Guidelines for Improving the Software Process*, Reading, MA: Addison-Wesley, 1995, pp. 270–276.

[12] Johnson, D. L., and J. G. Broadman, "Realities and Rewards of Software Process Improvement," *IEEE Software*, Vol. 13, No. 6, © IEEE, November 1996.

[13] Humphrey, W. S., *Managing the Software Process*, Reading, MA: Addison-Wesley, 1989, pp. 463–486.

[14] Humphrey, W. S., *A Discipline for Software Engineering*, Addison-Wesley, 1995, page 233.

[15] Gilb, T., and D. Graham, *Software Inspection*, Reading, MA: Addison-Wesley, 1993, pp. 40–136.

[16] O'Neill, D., "National Software Quality Experiment: A Lesson in Measurement 1992–1997," *CrossTalk*, Vol. 11, No. 12, Web Addition, December 1998.

[17] Linger, R. C., H. D. Mills, and B. I. Witt, *Structured Programming: Theory and Practice*, Reading, MA: Addison-Wesley, 1979, pp. 147–212.

[18] McCabe, T. J. and A. H. Watson, "Software Complexity," *CrossTalk*, Vol. 7, No. 12, December 1994, pp. 5–9.

[19] Prowell, S. J., et al., *Cleanroom Software Engineering: Technology and Process*, Reading, MA: Addison-Wesley, 1999, pp. 17, 33–90.

[20] Kelly, J., and J. Sherif, "An Analysis of Defect Densities Found During Software Inspections," *Proceedings of the Fifteenth Annual Software Engineering Workshop*, Goddard Space Flight Center, Greenbelt, MD, December 1990.

[21] Madachy, R., L. Little, and S. Fan, "Analysis of a Successful Inspection Program," *Proceedings of the Eighteenth Annual Software Engineering Workshop*, Goddard Space Flight Center, Greenbelt, MD, December 1993, pp. 176–188.

[22] Weller, E. F., "Lessons from Three Years of Inspection Data," *IEEE Software*, September 1993, pp. 38–45.

[23] Ebenau, R. G., "Predictive Quality Control with Software Inspections," *CrossTalk*, Vol.7, No. 6, June 1994, pp. 9–16.

[24] Bourgeois, K. V., "Process Insights from a Large-Scale Software Inspections Data Analysis," *CrossTalk*, Vol. 9, No. 10, October 1996, pp. 17–23.

[25] O'Neill, D., "National Software Quality Experiment: A Lesson in Measurement 1992–1996," *Quality Week Conference*, San Francisco, CA, May 1997, and *Quality Week Europe Conference*, Brussels, November 1997, pp. 1–25.

[26] O'Neill, D., "National Software Quality Experiment: A Lesson in Measurement 1992–1997," *First Annual International Software Assurance Certification Conference*, Chantilly, Virginia, March 1, 1999, pp. 1–14.

[27] O'Neill, D., "Determining Return on Investment Using Software Inspections," *CrossTalk*, March 2003, pp. 16–21, http://members.aol.com/ONeillDon/roi-essay.html.

[28] O'Neill, D., "Issues in Software Inspection," *IEEE Software*, Vol. 14, No 1, January 1997, pp. 18–19.

[29] O'Neill, D., "Setting Up a Software Inspections Program," *CrossTalk*, Vol. 10, No. 2, February 1997, pp. 11–13.

[30] Gaffney, J. E., "Software Defect Estimation, Prediction, and the CMM®," *Metrics '97 Conference*, 1997.

[31] Harding, J. T., "Using Inspection Data to Forecast Test Defects," *CrossTalk*, Vol. 11, No. 5, May 1998, pp. 19–24.

[32] Wallace, D. R., L. M. Ippolito, and H. Hecht, "Error, Fault, and Failure Data Collection and Analysis," *Quality Week*, San Francisco, CA, May 1997.

[33] Carmel, E., *Global Software Teams: Collaborating Across Borders and Time Zones*, Englewood Cliffs, NJ: Prentice-Hall, 1999, pp. 27–33.

## CHAPTER 8

Software Audit Methods

G. Gordon Schulmeyer

"Quebec auditor says millions squandered"
—*The Globe and Mail* newspaper headline, December 2006 [1]

8.1 Introduction

Although horseracing is the subject for the headline quoted above, there are other just-as-relevant headlines from the area of software and software quality that demonstrate the importance of this audit area. This chapter on audit methods addresses what areas related to software should be audited, but also the accepted manner to execute those preferred audits. The author has performed many software-related audits and provides examples of what and how to audit. The goal is to provide a guide to those responsible for software-related auditing and how best to achieve the final outcome of a fair, objective, and useful software-related audit that improves the situation as found.

On the one hand, *IEEE Standard Glossary of Software Engineering Terminology* defines a software audit as "An independent examination of a work product or set of work products to assess compliance with specifications, standards, contractual agreements, or other criteria" [2]. Then, on the other hand, *IEEE Standard for Software Reviews* defines the purpose of a software audit "to provide an independent evaluation of conformance of software products and processes to applicable regulations, standards, guidelines, plans, and procedures" [3]. Key to understanding the thrust of this chapter is the words "and processes" in the purpose because my audit experience has included processes as a key element to the audits performed. Following on that theme, a Software Quality Assurance Subcommittee of the United States Department of Energy stated that the goal of a software audit is to provide an independent determination as to whether the software, its documentation, and/or the development and maintenance *processes* meet stated requirements.

A software-related audit is not much different than any other type of audit. Configuration items of software may sometimes be a little harder to put your finger on, but they are still auditable. An audit is usually conducted for one of the following reasons [4]:

- A specific project milestone has been reached and an audit is initiated as planned or as required by the auditing organization's charter.
- External parties or customers request an audit of a specific item, at a specific date, or at a project milestone. This could be part of a contract agreement.
- An internal organization has requested the audit, establishing a clear and specific need.

It is appropriate to introduce some of the roles and related responsibilities for software-related audits at this early stage of the chapter in order to set some expectations. A software-related audit involves:

- The client, person, or organization that requests the audit;
- The auditor or team who performs the audit;
- The auditee whose work is being examined.

The client (i.e., person or organization) is responsible for authorizing the audit and for defining the scope and identifying the requirements of the audit. The management of the auditing organization assumes responsibility for the audit and allocates the necessary resources to perform the audit.

When the auditor(s) and the auditee agree on respective roles and responsibilities, they can improve communication, agree on findings, use the audit time more efficiently, and make the overall audit more effective. The audit team performs the audit. The audit team is composed of one or more people. Normally, one individual is designated the lead auditor. It is the lead auditor's responsibility to organize and direct the audit and to coordinate the preparation and issuance of the audit report. *IEEE Software Reviews* says, "The lead auditor shall be free from bias and influence that could reduce his ability to make independent, objective evaluations" [5]. The lead auditor is also responsible for:

- Determining the team size;
- Briefing team members on the audit scope and areas to be audited;
- Providing background about the organization being audited;
- Assigning the workload of who will audit what areas;
- Determining the audit schedule;
- Notifying and briefing the audited organization on the scope of the audit and materials that need to be provided;
- Ensuring that the audit team is prepared to conduct the audit;
- Ensuring that the audit plan or procedures are performed;
- Issuing reports in accordance with the audit plan or procedures.

The audit team should have auditor training and technical expertise in the area being audited. The audit team assists the lead auditor by helping prepare and review checklists, doing background work, conducting research, fulfilling their assigned part of the audit, and creating the report.

The auditee is the party being audited and is responsible for [6]:

- Establishing a professional, positive attitude about the audit among the members of the audited organization;
- Participating in the audit;
- Providing all relevant materials and resources to the audit team;
- Understanding the concerns of the auditors and verifying their factual accuracy;
- Providing a response to the audit report;
- Correcting or resolving deficiencies cited by the audit team.

8.2   Types of Software Audits

The word "audit" according to ISO 9001:2000 includes auditing for all types of standards, whether quality, environmental, software, or other. Consequently, many audit methods are common no matter what type of system or market sector is being audited. The differences are in some auditing techniques, objectives, and performance standards [7]. The types of software audits addressed in this section include an eclectic variety:

- Software piracy audit;
- Security audit;
- Information systems audit;
- ISO 9001:2000 software audit;
- CMMI®-DEV appraisal;
- Personal audit experiences;
- Automated audits.

The reason for this diverse coverage is to introduce the reader to many types of software-related audits and what they are trying to uncover. This should establish a basis for the reader to understand the auditing field and how it affects software quality personnel.

For each of the audit types covered in this section an initial clarification table is provided (Table 8.1 is a sample clarification table and Table 8.2 is for software piracy audits).

8.2.1   Software Piracy Audit

The Business Software Alliance (BSA) is interested in helping all software users ensure that they use only fully licensed software and are educated about the ethical and digital security risks associated with unlicensed software use. The BSA Web site wonders when was the last time you conducted an audit of your company's computers to check for unlicensed software? Similarly, the Software & Information Industry Association's (SIIA) Anti-Piracy Division conducts a comprehensive, industry-wide campaign to fight software and content piracy. The proactive campaign is premised on the notion that one must balance enforcement with education in order to be effective. The Anti-Piracy Division even recommends a list of audit software to aid in this task [8].

Table 8.1   Sample Clarification Table

Audit Type = _____	Clarification
Purpose of the audit	Provided below
Identification of the auditing organization	Provided below
Formal audit process	Provided below
Identification of the client	Provided below
Identification of the auditor	Provided below
Identification of the auditee	Provided below
What is audited by the organization to prepare for the audit	Provided below
What is audited by the auditor	Provided below

Table 8.2   Software Piracy Audit

Audit Type = Software Piracy Audit	Clarification
Purpose of the audit	To determine if the software on the organization's computers is legal
Identification of the auditing organization	Business Software Alliance (BSA); Software & Information Association (SIIA); or directly from a software vendor
Formal audit process	Run a software program provided by auditing organization(s) listed in this section
Identification of the client	Organization requiring a review of software piracy status
Identification of the auditor	Self or organization's information systems person
Identification of the auditee	Personnel assigned computer systems
What is audited by the organization to prepare for the audit	Nothing
What is audited by the auditor	Computer system(s) that may contain illegal software

John Tomeny, International Business Software Managers Association (IBSMA) 2007 Software Asset Management Practitioner of the Year, provides the following guidance [9]:

1. Collect Proofs of Ownership
   - Purchase Orders
   - Paid Invoices
   - Receipts for Purchase
   - Original License Certificates

The "proofs of ownership" list is arranged in order of the potentially easiest items to locate and in reverse order of the most acceptable proof. That is not to say that purchase orders are not acceptable. They are often the most reliable, and most accurate, proof you will be able to locate. Auditors generally will prefer original license certificates over all other forms, but will usually accept anything on the list.

The most important thing to keep in mind in step one is that the list can be divided into two types of "ownership proof" and only one or the other is acceptable in a compliance audit.

The first three items represent different types of "receipts" while the fourth is a "certificate of ownership." You may mix the first three receipts as long as you can demonstrate that there is no overlap. But you may not mix receipts with license certificates.

2. Audit Installed Software
   - Systematically Inspect Every
     - Desktop
     - Portable
     - Server
     - Home computer (optional)

Steps one and two can be reversed or done simultaneously. Both must be completed prior to reconciling and proving license ownership in step three. You will need an exhaustive list of all copies of software and their version numbers installed on all computers in your organization. ... Once you have completed steps one and two you are ready to discover how much of your organization's installed software is legally licensed.

3. Reconcile Audit & Proof of Ownership
   - Product Names
   - Version Numbers
   - Types of Licenses (Single-user, Concurrent use, other restrictions)
   - Serial Numbers

Compare the details in list three from your audit list and ownership proofs list for matches.

The goal of step three is to discover any software in use on your site that cannot be traced back to its license. With each such discovery you then make the decision of whether to buy a license or delete the software. That's it in a nutshell—easy to describe, extremely difficult to accomplish—unless you have automated auditing and usage management tools in place.

The heart of compliance assurance is the auditing of the installed software aided by the use of the auditing tool provided the BSA or SIIA organization for your use.

8.2.2   Security Audit

The following issues presented for a security audit (see Table 8.3) are not a comprehensive audit of the security requirements of a specific organization. They are a checklist that give an indication of the kinds of steps that an organization should take in securing its computer and information systems. It should always be kept in mind that security of information systems is not a static solution that can be fixed once. Constant attention has to be paid to the issues, as the risks, the threats, and the things that have to be protected are always changing.

Each of the following issues should be considered, and appropriate action taken to protect your information:

1. *Backups* (addressed here rather than under information systems audit because a method to restore the system is an integral aspect of security, if it is breached). Factors to consider in arranging your backups are:
   • What information or data do I have that has to be backed up?
   • How often should I back my information up?
   • What is an efficient and cost effective medium for backing up onto?

Table 8.3   Security Audit

Audit Type = Security Audit	Clarification
Purpose of the audit	Verify the correct functioning of a software product from a security standpoint in terms of its relationship to the system's other components
	Attempt to penetrate a computer system's security measures
	Test for evading measures to obtain greater privileges
Identification of the auditing organization	Company accredited by National Accreditation Body
Formal audit process	Quality Standard, ISO/IEC 27001:2005 (formerly BS 7799-2:2002)
Identification of the client	Company wanting to start or continue a program designed to maintain their information systems security
Identification of the auditor	ISO/IEC 270001:2005 certified auditor
Identification of the auditee	Information systems organization and equipment within company
What is audited by the organization to prepare for the audit	Preaudit of items listed below audited by the auditor
What is audited by the auditor	Business continuity planning Systems access control System development and maintenance Physical and environmental security Compliance Personnel security Security organization Computer and operations management Asset classification and control Security policy

- Have I got the ability to restore my information in the event of a loss of the computer(s), the backup machine, and the backup software?
- Have you tried to restore data to ensure that your backup processes are working?
- Where will I store my backups?

2. *Antivirus.* There are numerous software vendors who sell antivirus software. There are two important things to bear in mind:
   - Ensure that your antivirus software has the most recent updates.
   - Ensure that your antivirus software is configured to identify viruses by all means that they can come into your computer (e-mail, Web browsing, floppy disks, CDs, archives, and so on).

3. *Firewall.* Specific information on the configuration of whatever firewall you use should be available from the manufacturer of your particular firewall. If you have an always-on connection, you should realize that instant messaging and chat facilities offer an excellent opportunity for a hacker to gain access to your systems, and are also a route by which spam can be propagated.

4. *Access control.* If you are not the only person who has access to a PC, it may be worth while considering implementing a log-on system. This can be achieved through specialized user authentication systems; however, simple use of the user name and password facilities in Windows products

is effective. For larger networks and companies many additional considerations must be taken into account in order to maintain information security.

Business decisions have to be taken in implementing IT security to ensure that there is an appropriate balance between freedom of access to increase business activity and security to prevent loss of data and resources. If you are serious about the security of your business' information and computer systems, then it is advisable to consider the implementation of the Quality Standard, ISO 17799 (BS 7799). ISO 17799 is a standard that is a code of practice for information security management. It is organized into 10 sections [10]:

- Business continuity planning;
- Systems access control;
- System development and maintenance;
- Physical and environmental security;
- Compliance;
- Personnel security;
- Security organization;
- Computer and operations management;
- Asset classification and control;
- Security policy.

Possibly the best method to validate one's attempt to provide an effective information security management is to first benchmark with ISO 27001 standard using the guidance in the 10 sections and then certify the same through an external vendor. ISO/IEC 17799:2005 is the standard code of practice, which can be regarded as a comprehensive catalog of "the best things to do in Information Security." ISO/IEC 27001:2005 is a standard specification for information security management systems, which is the means by which senior management can control their security, minimizing the residual business risk and ensuring that security continues to fulfill corporate, customer, and legal requirements.

In order to be awarded a certificate, an ISO27001 assessor will audit the information security management systems. The certification body will award you the certificate. The certificate will document the scope of your information security management systems and other relevant details, such as the statement of applicability. Only certification bodies that have been duly accredited by a national accreditation body can issue certificates. The assessor will return periodically to check that your information security management system is working as intended [11].

8.2.3 Information Systems Audit

Ron Weber, the author of the classic book *Information Systems Control and Audit*, says that information systems auditing (see Table 8.4) evaluates whether computer-based information systems safeguard assets, maintain data integrity, achieve organizational objectives effectively, and consume resources efficiently.

Table 8.4   Information Systems Audit

Audit Type = Information Systems Audit	Clarification
Purpose of the audit	Evaluate whether computer-based information systems: • Safeguard assets • Maintain data integrity • Achieve organizational objectives effectively • Consume resources efficiently
Identification of the auditing organization	Various companies provide these services (some have certifications to perform these audits; others do not, but are audit software specialists)
Formal audit process	Often based on published checklists; Embedded in the audit software: ITIL®; CobIT® (see Chapters 3 and 14)
Identification of the client	Organization requesting certification of their information systems
Identification of the auditor	Sometimes certified auditors; sometimes software audit program specialists
Identification of the auditee	Information support organization
What is audited by the organization to prepare for the audit	Usually preaudit information systems to be audited
What is audited by the auditor	Information systems in the organization

Auditing is a responsible task as it may involve accessing live systems, and assurances need to be made that there is minimum interference to the business. The scope of the audit should be very clearly defined, and the entire audit process should be closely monitored and documented. The audit may involve tools, which bypass the normal authentication mechanisms or software controls. Care has to be taken that no data is altered or in any way compromised.

Access and use of the system audit tools should be properly controlled and these should not be available to normal users. One may use a password-cracking tool to check and report the strength of passwords. Availability of this tool to general users may not be a good idea. In fact, possession of these tools should be strictly forbidden as per the security policy.

The information systems lead auditor must be sensitive to the following [12]:

- All audits should be conducted only with prior approval of the management.
- Consult an advocate for all the applicable legislation—that is, if you do not want to be caught by surprise later.
- Ensure that one does not violate the software copyright in any form.
- Ask the accounts department how long they retain financial records.
- Ensure that there is no misuse of the information processing facilities by any person, insider as well as outsider.
- If you are traveling with your notebook PC where you have stored encrypted files, you may be breaking a few laws of the land.

- Ensure that the evidence is admissible in court. The quality and completeness of evidence is beyond doubt, and you are really able to nail the cyber criminal.
- Apart from adherence to procedural aspects of security, also ensure that periodic technical compliance checks are done.
- Access and use of the system audit tools should be properly controlled and these should not be available to users.

8.2.4   ISO 9001:2000 Software Audit

ISO 9001:2000 requires that an organization conduct internal audits at planned intervals to determine compliance to the standard and effective implementation (see Table 8.5). The organization must also ensure that the processes in place achieve planned results. This is accomplished through monitoring and, as applicable, measuring process performance through internal audits and measuring programs. Concluding section 8.2 of ISO 9001:2000, the organization is required to monitor the characteristics of the product to verify product requirements have been met [13].

ISO/IEC 90003:2004 explains how ISO 9001:2000 can be applied to software-related services. In Table 8.6 are some samples of how ISO/IEC 90003:2004 interprets ISO 9001:2000 for software-related services. With a complete checklist expanded from the samples in Table 8.6, one could perform an audit of software-related services based upon ISO 9001:2000.

Table 8.5   ISO 9001:2000 Software Audit

Audit Type = ISO 9001:2000 Software Audit	Clarification
Purpose of the audit	To demonstrate that the acquisition, supply, development, operation, and maintenance of computer software complies with ISO 9001:2000.
Identification of the auditing organization	Third-party auditing organizations that are referred to as registrars. These organizations are accredited by a national accreditation body such as ANSI-ANAB (ASQ National Accreditation Board).
Formal audit process	ISO 9001:2000 (using ISO/IEC 90003:2004 or TickIT as a guide).
Identification of the client	Organization interested in obtaining or maintaining their ISO 9001 certification.
Identification of the auditor	ISO QMS lead auditor certified by organizations such as the RABSQA (Registrar Accreditation Board and the Quality Society of Australasia International) or IRCA (International Register of Certified Auditors) or similar organization.
Identification of the auditee	The audit covers the entire organization that is within the scope of the organization's Quality Management System (QMS).
What is audited by the organization to prepare for the audit	ISO 9001:2000 requires periodic internal audits of the implementation of the QMS and compliance to the standard. Evidence of internal audits are shown to the ISO auditor during the registration audit or surveillance.
What is audited by the auditor	Organization's Quality Manual as applied to the acquisition, supply, development, operation, and maintenance of computer software by projects and the organization.

Table 8.6   Sample Checklist Based Upon ISO/IEC 90003:2004

6.3 Provide quality infrastructure

Identify infrastructure needs.

Identify the infrastructure you need in order to develop software.
Identify the hardware you need in order to develop software.
Identify the software you need in order to develop software.
Identify the facilities you need in order to develop software.
Identify the tools you need in order to manage software.
Identify the tools you need in order to develop software.
Identify the tools you need in order to support software.
Identify the tools you need in order to protect software.
Identify the tools you need in order to control software.

Provide needed infrastructure.

Provide the infrastructure you need in order to develop software.
Provide the hardware you need in order to develop software.
Provide the software you need in order to develop software.
Provide the facilities you need in order to develop software.
Provide the tools you need in order to manage software.
Provide the tools you need in order to develop software.
Provide the tools you need in order to support software.
Provide the tools you need in order to protect software.
Provide the tools you need in order to control software.

Maintain your infrastructure.

Maintain the infrastructure you need in order to develop software.
Maintain the hardware you need in order to develop software.
Maintain the software you need in order to develop software.
Maintain the facilities you need in order to develop software.
Maintain the tools you need in order to develop software.
Maintain the tools you need in order to support software.

Maintain the tools you need in order to manage software.

Maintain the tools you need in order to protect software.
Maintain the tools you need in order to control software.

7.3 Control software design and development

7.3.1.1 Plan software design and development

Define your software product design and development stages.
Establish procedures to control software design and development.
Clarify design and development responsibilities and authorities.
Manage interactions between design and development groups.
Update your design and development plans as changes occur.
Document your planning outputs as changes occur.

7.3.1.1 Plan software design and development.

Identify the activities that must be performed.

Identify the inputs that each activity requires.
Identify the outputs generated by each activity.
Identify the management activities that will be needed.
Identify the support services that will be required.
Identify the team training that will be necessary.
Identify the resources that your project will need.
Identify verification and validation activities.
Identify design and development rules and conventions.
Identify software development tools and techniques.

Source: [14].

Notice in Table 8.6 that there appears to be extreme repetition of the requirements. But upon sufficient reflection it becomes clear that that repetition provides a checklist of adequate coverage for the various aspects of what needs to be audited. Take the one example of [14]:

Identify the tools you need in order to manage software.
Identify the tools you need in order to develop software.
Identify the tools you need in order to support software.
Identify the tools you need in order to protect software.
Identify the tools you need in order to control software.

Clearly there are multiple tools involved in a development project and this repetition helps the auditor recognize that he or she needs to find tools to manage, develop, support, protect, and control software.

ISO 19011 is *The Auditing Standard & How to Conduct Your Own Audits* for ISO-related audits. This subsection is from Dr. Terry Russell's Web page on ISO auditing [15]. ISO 10011 (the former ISO auditing standard) was replaced by ISO 19011 in 2003. However, at present the 2000 Version of ISO 9001:2000 still refers to ISO 10011. ISO 19011 describes the controls of:

- *Requirements of auditors:* That is, their previous qualification and experience and the training that they must undergo before conducting audits. Also, their independence and ability must be considered.
- *Requirements of auditing:* That is, how they must be planned, conducted and recorded. Also, what proofs must be gathered during the audits and what records must be kept of the audits.

In order to perform your own internal quality ISO 9001:2000 audits, you need a number of things.

First, a trained, experienced auditor is needed. Although not essential to the requirements of ISO 9001:2000, it is strongly recommended that your Internal Quality Auditor has passed an internal auditor's course, which should be accredited by a reputable organization, such as RABSQA or IRCA. Although it is possible to perform audits without such training, your assessment body will be entitled to place less reliance upon such audits, which may well result in more assessment visits, which will be expensive.

In addition to the training, your auditor should perform a regular amount of auditing—at least 2 days or more per month—in order to ensure that the training is developed by ongoing practice. A common mistake is for a member of an organization to attend a training course, then not perform enough audits to keep in practice. This is an almost certain route to failure.

Second, a written standard against which to audit is necessary. All auditors must have a documented standard against which the audit must be performed. In the case of ISO 9001:2000, this would be ISO 9001:2000 and your own written procedures, instructions, and Quality Manual.

Third, something to audit is needed. Another common failing is for auditors to begin audits before there are sufficient records to enable a meaningful audit to take place. This does not mean that your organization must wait for 6 months before conducting audits. It may be sufficient to conduct audits after only a few weeks, provided that there are adequate records for the auditor to check the entire process.

8.2.5 CMMI®-DEV Appraisal

"An audit is not a software assessment," says the Software Quality Assurance Subcommittee of a branch of the United States Department of Energy. They continue, "A software assessment appraises software processes and identifies potential areas for improvement" [4]. I have included assessments in this section on types of audits because the audit definition I adhere to includes examining products as well as processes. See Table 8.7.

Under the CMM® for Software the assessment methods were termed: CMM®-Based Assessment for Internal Process Improvement (CBA-IPI) and Software Capability Evaluation (SCE). With the CMMI® these methods were combined under the SCAMPI^SM method. The Standard CMMI® Appraisal Method for Process Improvement (SCAMPI^SM) A is designed to provide benchmark quality ratings relative to CMMI® models [16]. The term "appraisal" is a generic term used throughout the CMMI® Product Suite to describe applications in these contexts, traditionally known as assessments and evaluations. An appraisal is an examination of one or more processes by a trained team of professionals using an appraisal reference model as the basis for determining strengths and weaknesses. An appraisal is typically conducted in the context of process improvement or capability evaluation.

The basic difference between an assessment and an evaluation is that an assessment is an appraisal that an organization does to and for itself for the purposes of process improvement. Assessments provide internal motivation for organizations to initiate or continue process improvement programs. An evaluation is an appraisal in which an external group comes into an organization and examines its processes as input to a decision regarding future business or for monitoring current business.

Table 8.7   CMMI®-DEV Appraisal

Audit Type = CMMI®-DEV Appraisal	Clarification
Purpose of the audit	Determine the maturity of a development organization
Identification of the auditing organization	Software Engineering Institute (SEI) Partner or the SEI
Formal audit process	Standard CMMI® Appraisal Method for Process Improvement (SCAMPI^SM)
Identification of the client	Sponsor from the development organization
Identification of the auditor	Authorized lead appraiser
Identification of the auditee	Multiple projects and the process organization within the development organization
What is audited by the organization to prepare for the audit	Objective evidence matrix is established containing the project's and process organization's artifacts; lower level Class C and/or Class B appraisals
What is audited by the auditor	Objective evidence artifacts from the projects and the process organization along with relevant interviews

Evaluations are typically externally imposed motivation for organizations to undertake process improvement [17].

The remainder of this section on CMMI®-DEV appraisals is from the *SCAMPI^{SM} Method Definition Document, version 1.2* [18].

SCAMPI^{SM} A consists of three phases and several essential processes, as shown in Table 8.8. Each phase is described in detail next.

Phase 1: Plan and Prepare for Appraisal   The sponsor's objectives for performing SCAMPI^{SM} A are determined in phase 1, process 1.1, Analyze Requirements. All other planning, preparation, execution, and reporting of results proceed from this initial activity according to the phase and processes outlined. Because of the significant investment and logistical planning involved, considerable iteration and refinement of planning activities should be expected in phase 1. With each subsequent phase, the amount of iteration will decrease as data are collected, analyzed, refined, and translated into findings of significance relative to the model.

A team of experienced and trained personnel performs a SCAMPI^{SM} A over a period of time negotiated by the sponsor and the appraisal team leader. The scope of the organization to be appraised, as well as the scope of the CMMI® model (process areas), must be defined and agreed to. The scope of the organization and model provides the basis on which to estimate personnel time commitments, logistical costs (e.g., travel), and overall costs to the appraised organization and to the sponsoring organization.

Table 8.8   Phases of a SCAMPI^{SM} Appraisal

Phase	Process
1	Plan and Prepare for Appraisal
1.1	Analyze Requirements
1.2	Develop Appraisal Plan
1.3	Select and Prepare Team
1.4	Obtain and Inventory Initial Objective Evidence
1.5	Prepare for Appraisal Conduct
2	Conduct Appraisal
2.1	Prepare Participants
2.2	Examine Objective Evidence
2.3	Document Objective Evidence
2.4	Verify Objective Evidence
2.5	Validate Preliminary Findings
2.6	Generate Appraisal Results
3	Report Results
3.1	Deliver Appraisal Results
3.2	Package and Archive Appraisal Assets

During the appraisal, the appraisal team verifies and validates the objective evidence provided by the appraised organization to identify strengths and weaknesses relative to the CMMI® model. Objective evidence consists of documents or interview results used as indicators for implementation and institutionalization of model practices. Before the Conduct Appraisal phase begins, members of the appraised organization typically collect and organize documented objective evidence. The information-processing "engine" of the appraisal is thus fueled by the objective evidence already available, saving the appraisal team the time and effort of a discovery process.

While it is not absolutely required for performance of a SCAMPI^{SM} A appraisal, this advance preparation by the appraised organization is key to the most efficient execution of the method. Analysis of preliminary documented objective evidence provided by the appraised organization plays an important role in setting the stage for appraisal execution. If substantial data are missing at this point, subsequent appraisal activities can be delayed or even cancelled if the judgment is made that continuing appraisal activities will not be sufficient to make up for the deficiency.

The collection of documented objective evidence by the appraised organization in advance of the appraisal not only improves appraisal team efficiency, but also offers several other benefits to the organization:

- Improved accuracy in appraisal results delivered by external appraisal teams (i.e., clear understanding of implemented processes, strengths, and weaknesses);
- Detailed understanding of how each project or support group has implemented CMMI® model practices, and the degree of compliance and tailoring of organizational standard processes;
- Assets and resources for monitoring process compliance and process improvement progress;
- Residual appraisal assets that can be reused on subsequent appraisals, minimizing the effort necessary for preparation.

Phase 2: Conduct Appraisal   In phase 2, the appraisal team focuses on collecting data from the appraised organization to judge the extent to which the model is implemented. Integral to this approach is the concept of coverage, which implies (a) the collection of sufficient data for each model component within the CMMI® model scope selected by the sponsor, and (b) obtaining a representative sample of ongoing processes (spanning the lifecycle phases consistent with the model scope of the appraisal). For a benchmarking appraisal methodology, this means collecting data and information on all the CMMI® model practices for each process instantiation being appraised within the organizational unit. The data-collection plan developed in phase 1 undergoes continuous iteration and refinement until sufficient coverage is achieved.

Upon determining that sufficient coverage of the CMMI® model and organizational unit has been obtained, appraisal findings and ratings may be generated. Goal ratings are determined within each process area, which collectively can be used to determine a capability level rating for the individual process areas, as well as a process maturity rating for the organizational unit.

Phase 3: Report Results   In phase 3, the appraisal team provides the findings and ratings to the appraisal sponsor and the organization. These artifacts become part of the appraisal record, which becomes protected data in accordance with the Appraisal Disclosure Statement. The level of protection and the plan for the disposition of appraisal materials and data is determined in phase 1 in collaboration with the sponsor. A completed appraisal data package, which includes a subset of the contents of the appraisal record, is forwarded to the CMMI® Steward. The Steward adds it to a confidential database for summarization into overall community maturity and capability level profiles, which are made available to the community on a semiannual basis.

8.2.6   Project Audits (Internal CMMI®-DEV/ISO 9001:2000 Audits)

As just discussed, an official appraisal for the CMMI®-DEV includes processes and work products as highlighted in Figure 8.1. Project audits from an organizational perspective are those that internal SQA personnel (often I sat in for SQA as an auditor) usually perform, but if appropriate, the organization process group or other organizational entities may be audited. Typical project audits are carried out by the local SQA person assigned to the project, whereas this project audit from an organizational perspective reviews the SQA's work on the project and other random processes and artifacts. This is often done to comply with ISO 9001:2000 requirement for periodic internal audits (see Table 8.9). The work products are covered during the review of all the objective evidence for each project. The processes are covered by reviewing objective evidence of the existence of the process documents and through interviews of involved personnel performing them. Also, presentations may provide the "affirmation" required to assure that the processes are being followed.

When SQA is performing an internal audit the focus is often the projects, and less frequently the organizational elements. When examining the projects, SQA

Table 8.9   Project Audits (Internal CMMI®-DEV/ISO 9001:2000 Audits)

Audit Type = Project Audits	*Clarification*
Purpose of the audit	Ensure project's or organization's processes are followed and work products are consistent and correct
Identification of the auditing organization	SQA organization in a company, but usually not the SQA person assigned to the project
Formal audit process	ISO 9001:2000 requirement for internal audits
Identification of the client	Company maintaining ISO 9001:2000 compliance
Identification of the auditor	Experienced auditing person representing the internal SQA organization
Identification of the auditee	Project designated, or organization element (e.g., process group)
What is audited by the organization to prepare for the audit	Standard SQA process and work product audits carried on during the usual project life cycle
What is audited by the auditor	Project's processes and work products; project's SQA person's artifacts

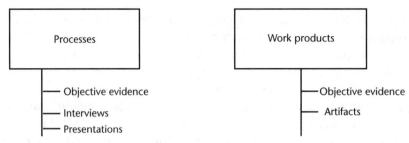

Figure 8.1   Appraisal structure.

looks at the processes and work products, similar to the methods discussed in Chapter 5. The criteria used for the processes include:

- Usually the project plan(s) describes the project's processes.
- Are there project directives detailing the project's processes?
- Then SQA determines if the project is following the plan/directive.
- Often the plan(s) refers to or defaults to the organization's standard process for a particular section of the plan.

Similarly the criteria for the work products on the project(s) are:

- Is there a template that should be followed?
- Is the document consistent?
- Is the work product satisfactory from an editorial perspective?

If the work product is code then SQA would look to the coding standards on the project as the criteria to be used to evaluate the code.

Many organizations are not familiar with project directives. It is worthwhile introducing the concept here for future use by organizations not familiar with them. Project directives levy the same requirement on the project as does the project plan(s), but are often added later in the life of the project. Writing a project directive reduces the requirement to have to update the project plan(s) and then have to have it reapproved. It is an expansion of an area of the project plan(s) where the detail usually is inappropriate for the project plan(s)—that is, too much detail. However, that amount of detail is often needed for the project personnel to understand what they should do for a particular aspect of the project. For example, if the requirement management area of the project is using a tool to manage requirements there are specific ways the project will want to implement the use of the tool on that project. The details of how the project is implementing use of the requirement management tool is inappropriate for the project plan—requirements section, but needs to be made available for the project personnel who have to interface with the requirements management tool. That detail of how this project wants to interface with their requirements management tool may be described in the project directive for requirements management tool use.

When auditing an organization functional group, it often is the organizational process group responsible for process improvement (the organization's standard process). Other organization areas SQA should audit include quality assurance, systems engineering, contracts, purchasing, and so on. For the quality assurance area there needs to be an independent (objective) SQA person. When examining the organization, the criteria are:

- What do the procedures require the organizational unit to do?
- Is the organization doing what the procedures require?

If the auditor prefers, then the criteria used (procedures) may be made into a checklist. Many auditors find having a checklist enhances their focus on the main points of the audit.

Even prior to an internal individual audit, it is a responsibility of the auditor to ensure that the standard process documents (policy, procedures, processes, work instructions) comply with the companies requirements for their process (Quality Management System in ISO terms). So, if ISO 9001:2000 is the organizational requirement, then an initial understanding must exist that the company's process complies with ISO 9001:2000. Similarly, if CMMI®-DEV is required to be complied with, then an initial understanding must exist that the company's process complies with CMMI®-DEV.

8.2.7   Automated Audits

There are an overwhelming number of software tools available to help auditors prepare, perform, and report audits (see Table 8.10). Of particular interest, because of the enormous effort they put forth to provide access to many audit programs, is the AuditNet Audit Program Web site (at http://www.auditnet.org). Just a tiny subset from AuditNet Audit Programs is provided in Table 8.11 to show the wide scope of these software tools. After appropriate registration on AuditNet, there are two options available: (1) a free option to gain access to the free audit programs, and (2) access to the premium content requires payment.

Table 8.10   Automated Audits

Audit Type = Automated Audits	Clarification
Purpose of the audit	Perform the audit with automated tool(s)
Identification of the auditing organization	Too numerous
Formal audit process	Rule-based programmed into the auditbot
Identification of the client	Often financial institutions
Identification of the auditor	auditbot
Identification of the auditee	Information system residing on a computer
What is audited by the organization to prepare for the audit	Continuous automated auditing (or is it monitoring?)
What is audited by the auditor	Continuous automated auditing (often computerized financial systems)

Table 8.11   Audit Software Available

Web site contains 7 categories with about 1,500 entries. Small example list below:

Information Systems Technology Audit Programs (371 listed on Web site)

1. Access Controls
2. Application Security Review
3. Application Systems IT Audit Program
4. Call Center Audit Program
5. Computer Room—Physical Security Audit Checklist
6. Cisco Router Audit Program
7. E-Mail Policy Compliance
8. Internet Banking Audit Program
9. Oracle Audit Program
10. PeopleSoft Audit Program
11. SAP Audit Program
12. Windows NT Audit Program Risks/Controls
13. Wireless Networking

Mainframe and Technical Audit Programs (71 listed on Web site)

1. Access Control Facility Review
2. DB2 Audit Program
3. System Implementation Audit

Source: [19].

When I perform SCAMPI[SM] A appraisals, I use an internal company-provided tool to step through that process with the appraisal team. It captures the team's analysis of all the objective evidence and interview results and simplifies our ability to perform the audit in an expeditious manner.

Knowing the availability of such audit tools is helpful to an audit team to perform an audit. What about the situation when you remove the audit team and just let the tool do the auditing? Such a discussion follows from "The Never-Ending Audit" [20]. The basic idea behind continuous-auditing software, sometimes known as "auditbot" technology, is fairly simple: a piece of software runs in concert with standard financial-application suites such as those offered by SAP, Oracle, and PeopleSoft, monitoring each transaction conducted by the suite and watching for violations of the company's rules and practices. (These rules are programmed in beforehand by the company's internal audit group or an outside auditor.) If and when the software detects a violation, it issues a warning report or an alert to top management.

Such auditbots are built around a kind of software known as a rule-based system. In contrast to most software, which represents information in a relatively static way, a rule-based system constantly compares one data type with others, using the programmer's classic "if-then" formulation. For example, a standard computer system for determining the day of the week would simply store calendar information, in effect saying, "Today is Monday and tomorrow is Tuesday." But for the same task, a rule-based system would compare days, saying, in effect, "If today is Monday, then tomorrow is Tuesday." In an accounting situation, a rule-based system could formulate: "If an invoice is paid in full, then book the payment as revenue."

Much of the early work on continuous-auditing software was done in the telecom industry, which, not coincidentally, was one of the first to have real-time electronic records of all its transactions—in this case, telephone calls—on hand. One of these early projects was undertaken at Bell Labs in the mid-1980s and led by a pioneer in the field, Miklos Vasarhelyi. The system, called Continuous Process Auditing System (CPAS), was tested over a 4-year period but was never implemented. A reason provided for not using the auditbot was that some felt that it is not auditing, but it is monitoring.

Still, that debate has not prevented other companies from testing auditbots. They include those that conduct large numbers of real-time transactions, mainly financial-services companies such as Citibank, Schwab, and PayPal. However, it is unlikely that auditbots could stop the next Enron or WorldCom.

8.3   Preparation for a Software Audit

"The first rule of auditing is restraint. Just because you can audit something doesn't mean you should," is wise advice from Brien Posey in "Creating an Audit Policy" [21]. The caveat, then, is not to prepare for something that should not have been done in the first place. Make sure your audit is going to provide value to the organization before planning it.

The *IEEE Standard for Software Reviews* states that an audit shall be conducted only when all of the following conditions have been met: (1) the audit has been authorized by the appropriate authority, (2) a statement of objectives of the audit is established, and (3) the required audit inputs are available [22].

I was recently asked to perform an audit of a large project that is supported by multiple organizations. The *IEEE Standard for Software Reviews* came to mind and I immediately asked that not only the project manager authorize the audit in writing, but also that senior executives from all the supporting organizations also provide written evidence that they support this audit.

Some pertinent questions that require responses to establish the objectives of an audit should include [23]:

- What is the audit's scope?
- What should the audit achieve?
- Does the audit cover the entire project? Does it cover the total system or part of the system?
- What is the authority for the audit?
- What background information is needed?

What the required audit inputs that need to be available are should be asked during this preparation phase for an audit. Inputs to the audit shall be listed in the audit plan and shall include the following [24]:

- Purpose and scope of the audit;
- Background information about the audited organization;
- Software products or processes to be audited;
- Evaluation criteria, including applicable regulations, standards, guidelines, plans, and procedures to be used for evaluation;
- Evaluation criteria, for example, "acceptable," "needs improvement," "unacceptable," "not rated";
- Records of previous similar audits.

A basic flow of the preparation for an audit is:

1. Client makes the decision to conduct an audit;
2. Request is made to an auditing organization;
3. Auditing organization then assigns a lead auditor;
4. Lead auditor working with the client decides:
   - Purpose of the audit;
   - Audit's scope;
   - Standards or documents to be used;
   - Schedule and time frame for the audit;
   - Commitment of resources necessary to meet the audit's scope and depth.

After a preliminary review is conducted, if no major problems are found, the lead auditor provides the auditee with a formal notification of the audit. The lead auditor provides:

- Notification with the objective and scope of the audit;
- Preliminary schedule;
- Request for the names of the people responsible for each task or area to be audited;
- An audit team.

Based upon the fact that the audit inputs are established, the lead auditor is responsible for producing an audit plan. According to ISO 19001:2002, the audit plan should contain the following:

- Audit objective and scope;
- Identification of the individuals having significant direct responsibilities regarding the objectives and scope;
- Identification of reference documents (such as the applicable quality system standard and the auditee's quality manual);
- Identification of audit team members;
- Language of the audit;
- Date and place where the audit is to be conducted;
- Identification of the organizational units to be audited;

- Expected time and duration for each major audit activity;
- Schedule of meetings to be held with auditee management;
- Confidentiality requirements;
- Audit report distribution and the expected date of issue.

The audit plan should be approved by both the client and the auditee, and any issues should be resolved before the audit's performance phase begins.

The lead auditor, together with the audit team, should prepare the checklists that will be used to evaluate each audit task or area. Additionally, they should prepare any forms for recording and collecting the necessary information to document their observations throughout the audit [25].

When conducting an audit for software piracy, as described above in Section 8.2, there is an excellent preparatory step that most other audit types do not require. Using survey forms prior to on-site activities can save much time for a software piracy audit. The auditors should use the Software Audit Form (or a similar form) (Figure 8.2) to record all software in use on all organization PCs. The form will help identify:

1. Number of employees at each organization;
2. Number of PCs owned or used by each organization;
3. Identity of all software programs installed on each PC.

The auditor should also use the Software Usage Survey (or a similar survey) (Figure 8.3) to examine the existing policies and procedures in place by the organization regarding software use and management [26].

Date:
To: All Employees
From: IT Department
Subject: Audit of Computer Software

During the month of _____, the Information Technologies Department will conduct an audit of software used by (Organization). Your department is scheduled to be visited on _____ (day)_____, _____ (date) _____. The purpose of the audit is to:

- Determine what software is in use at each workstation and whether the original CDs, diskettes, manuals, licenses and other documentation exist for each program
- Remove unauthorized copies of software
- Determine whether there is software you may need to do your job that you do not currently have
- Scan each system for viruses
- Confirm the serial numbers for each piece of hardware (modems, printer, monitors, etc.)

In order to make the audit less disruptive to your workday, we will try to accomplish these tasks quickly. Please locate the appropriate original CDs, diskettes and documentation if they were issued to you. Also, please make a note of any personal software you have installed on your workstation and have available for us copies of the CDs, diskettes and documentation for these programs.

The result of the audit will be better utilization of software in (Organization) and the ability to better provide you with the software you need.
Your cooperation is greatly appreciated.

Figure 8.2   Software Audit Form. (*Source:* [27].)

The following is a short survey intended to help us determine how you are using
software on your PC and how we can assist you by providing the best tools for your job.
Your input and participation are appreciated.

1. List the software programs you use most often in your work and how often you use them:
_____ _____ hours per day
_____ _____ hours per day
_____ _____ hours per day
_____ _____ hours per day
_____ _____ hours per day
_____ _____ hours per day
_____ _____ hours per day

2. What software do you need that you do not currently have?
_____

3. What software do you want that you do not currently have?
_____

4. Are you currently using any work software on your home computer? ___Yes ___ No

5. Are you currently using any personal software on your office computer? ___Yes ___ No

6. We appreciate your comments about buying or using software.

Figure 8.3   Software Usage Survey. (*Source:* [28].)

For most auditees, the audit process is one of uncertainty, unpredictability, and
uneasiness. The process preparation is tiring, frantic and sometimes grueling. For
many auditors, the audit process involves extensive planning and performance with
attention to details because the audit report may have major impact on a company.
For many companies, the failure of any audit may be not only become very costly,
but also very concerning.

The following suggestions provide preparation guidance for an organization to
enhance chances of a successful resolution [29]:

- Ensure that critical procedural documentation is available for review during
  the course of the audit.
- Request an "Audit Agenda" from the auditor. This document will be used to
  determine the level of preparation required for the audit.
- Prior to the date of the audit, challenge the agenda to ensure that all of the
  requirements are met.
- Conduct an internal audit using a predefined audit checklist prior to entertain-
  ing an outside audit.
- Prepare an internal audit report and resolution documentation to present to
  the auditor.
- Control the course of the audit by ensuring that all of the auditor's requests are
  fully addressed in a predefined timeline.
- Develop and submit to the auditor, prior to the audit, an on-site agenda by the
  auditee, which includes documentation that verifies appropriate challenges to
  the auditee's agenda.

8.4   Performing the Audit

The performance phase of an audit consists of auditors interviewing, reviewing records, observing operations, and collecting information. There are usually daily meetings by the audit team, as well as briefings to the auditee by the auditors to discuss observations. These are informal sessions usually held at the end of each day. Their purpose is to share information such as facts, tentative conclusion, problems, and so on. This allows everyone involved in the audit to understand where the audit is headed before the final report. During the performance phase, the auditee gives the audit top priority. Questions should be answered promptly, accurately and honestly. The auditee can challenge the auditor if the auditor makes a dubious conclusion. More evidence may be presented or requirements reviewed to substantiate the challenge. If problems are discovered, the auditee should correct them immediately, if possible, and inform the auditors.

The performance phase has three main activities:

- Opening meeting;
- Performance of the audit;
- Closing meeting.

The first day of the on-site part of an audit starts with an opening meeting in which the scope of the audit is reviewed, schedules are determined, auditor and auditee personnel are introduced, and logistics and the time for the closing meeting are determined. The auditor communicates to the auditee the audit's objectives, areas of concentration as seen by the auditor, and a preliminary assessment of the organization. The lead auditor establishes the audit's tone and sense of cooperation, and acts as a seeker of information and facts. The audit team describes the audit process, clarifies any administrative matters, and solicits the auditee's input.

Guided by their audit criteria (which may be in the form of checklists), the auditors check compliance with requirements by reviewing written instructions and procedures, conducting interviews, checking records, and observing work activities. They follow up on questions that arise during these checks and observations, and assemble factual evidence of the auditee's compliance with requirements and effectiveness in achieving the goals of their organization. The audit records include auditors' notes from interviews and observations, and examples from the record reviews. The facts noted in the audit are reviewed by the lead auditor and conclusions are drawn as to the existence and extent of deficiencies or good practices. The performance phase of an audit ends with the closing meeting or exit interview where the lead auditor reports the audit team's conclusion [30].

With the audit flow in mind, the audit team needs to be in tune with the level of this audit. The following are the levels of review that may be performed [31]:

- *Level 1:* Verify the existence of the work product or deliverable. Review to assure the work product or deliverable exists and is complete.
- *Level 2:* Verify minimum content exists. Review to ensure the minimum level of information has been provided. Verify the existence of content by checking sections/headings.

- *Level 3:* Verify content is logical and rational. Review to make judgments as to the quality and validity of the deliverable.

Every audit that I have been involved in includes all three levels.

The next subsection describing the audit conduct is primarily from the Software Quality Subcommittee of the United States Department of Energy [30]. During the conduct of an audit, the audit team should maintain a professional manner and a positive and friendly attitude at all times during the audit. During the opening audit meeting each audit team member should be introduced with a short description of their expertise as well as their role and responsibility during the audit. The lead auditor should clearly and concisely state the scope (levels investigated during this audit), objectives, requirements, and ground rules of the audit. The audit schedule should be discussed, and the audited organization should be given the opportunity to request revision to accommodate their schedules.

The audit in-briefing is usually held on the first day of the audit. Participants in this in-briefing normally include the audit team members and representatives from within the audited organization. The purpose of this in-briefing is to familiarize the audit team with physical layouts, organizational structures, topical material breakdowns, and so forth. This in-briefing should carry a high priority in the audited organization.

Since the briefing can set the tone for the entire audit period, the auditee and the auditor should strive to project a helpful, professional image during the briefing. While not providing any unnecessary gratuitous information, the leader of the audited organization team should attempt to control the in-briefing and provide as much useful information to the audit team as possible.

Basic ground rules of the audit should be established during this briefing. These ground rules should include such things as where the office space for the audit team will be located, what material the audit team will need to perform the audit, and in what form. The audited organization should attempt to establish a daily routine with audit team members including a firm schedule for the following day, daily validation meetings, management briefings, and rapid notification of audit team findings or significant deficiencies.

The audit is then conducted through interviews with personnel in the audited organization and through documents and records review. Here are several useful techniques auditors should use when conducting interviews:

- Listen. It is difficult to gather information if you are talking.
- Listen ACTIVELY. Do not formulate new questions while interviewees are responding to previous ones.
- Observe the interviewee's body language and monitor your own body language to reflect listening, understanding, and empathy.
- Take notes and explain why you are taking them.
- Question. Start with open-ended questions; for example, why, when, how, who, what, where, to what extent. Keep questions short and to the point. Move to close-ended questions, answered by yes or no, to start the clarification process.

- Clarify details to make sure the information received is clear and complete. Use follow-up questions for more information. Use paraphrasing and repeating to ensure that you heard correctly, and summarize to validate information

To ensure the success of an audit it is important for each auditor to:

- Establish a rapport with the interviewee.
- Avoid nit-picking or judgmental comments about individuals.
- Avoid placing blame or fault for problems.
- Always operate ethically.

Remember, you are taking up the valuable time of the auditee, so minimize intrusions and avoid wasting time. Here is a list of tips in conducting a successful audit:

- Rely upon objective evidence and maintain objectivity.
- Use random sampling to get representative results.
- Obtain confirmation or explanation of apparent problems or concerns.
- Revisit if needed.
- Document results and retain notes.
- Get a positive identification of persons contacted.
- Report known problems and avoid opinions.
- Avoid surprises: keep your contacts informed.

During the audit, the audited organization personnel must maintain a professional image while interacting with the audit team. Audit team members should not be allowed to wander freely and unescorted through the audited organization. Although there will ordinarily be fairly stringent rules limiting the help an employee may be given in answering questions, a knowledgeable person, or supervisor, should accompany auditors at all times. Questions will arise concerning specific terminology and semantic differences between the audited organization and the audit team. A knowledgeable person needs to be present to "interpret" in these instances.

The closing meeting is the time for the auditors to explicitly state the results of the audit. There should be no surprises. The lead auditor should control the meeting. He or she should define the terms used and clearly state each result. It is important to report excellence as well as problems and major deficiencies. The audited organization should be told when to expect the audit report and when and how they are expected to reply. Always close the meeting by thanking the individuals for their time and cooperation.

By final closing meeting time, the audited organization should clearly understand the issues that have been identified as findings, deviations, exemplary practices, and observations. If there will be a lapse between the time of the closing meeting and the submission of the final audit report, the audited organization should make every attempt to obtain at least a draft of this report. This is to avoid any potential surprises or miscommunications. The audited organization should obtain clarification of what "credit" they will receive for corrective actions taken during the audit to eliminate or mitigate deficiencies observed during the closing meeting. The audit team should be urged to comment on positive, as well as negative, observations.

Similarly, the performance of a CMMI®-DEV Appraisal is described in Section 8.2. It is clear from the list:

2.1 Prepare Participants;

2.2 Examine Objective Evidence;

2.3 Document Objective Evidence;

2.4 Verify Objective Evidence;

2.5 Validate Preliminary Findings;

2.6 Generate Appraisal Results;

that the appraisal performance bears striking similarity to that already described for the various audits. I believe a key step that the other audits do not perform is to validate preliminary findings. My experience has shown that often, after the preliminary findings presentation to the audited organization, the auditees present objective evidence that had been previously missed. This opportunity provides a more accurate and complete audit for the appraised organization.

8.5   Results and Ramifications

Most of this section on results and ramifications of audits is abstracted from the Software Quality Assurance Subcommittee of the United States Department of Energy [32]. The lead auditor is responsible for generating the audit report that is the product of the audit. Team meeting discussions and the facts collected will help guide the report. At the closing meeting, the lead auditor will provide a summary of the written report. The summary allows for factual corrections and explanations.

Let us focus on how the lead auditor should handle audit results. Although many times audit reports have addressed only negative points, experience clearly shows that the credibility and acceptance of audit reports are substantially improved if they include an assessment of over-all performance. "How well are we doing?" is a fair question, and some statement of the audit team's opinion will go a long way in getting the auditee's management attention. Auditing organizations should identify three types of results (Table 8.12) during the course of an audit.

Typically observations and exemplary practices do not require a response from the audited organization. The term "exemplary practice" should be reserved for those very few instances where the auditee:

- Has established an elegant, effective system;
- Has developed an unusually high degree of awareness and cooperation internally;
- Has adopted a practice that is clearly superior to anything you have seen elsewhere.

Table 8.12   Auditing Results

Audit Results	Description
Exemplary practice	A practice, procedure, or instruction that is well above the expected norm of performance
Deviation or finding	Any nonconformance or inadequacy that results in a product nonconformance to a specified requirement
	Lack of a system or controls to satisfy a customer or system requirement
	Any nonconformance to a procedural requirement or inadequate procedure that causes the conformance of product, practices, or activities to be unknown
Observation	An opinion regarding a condition not covered by a specific requirement; or a procedure, practice, or instruction whose effectiveness could be improved

Deviation or findings are the main output of the audit and so require special attention by the audit team, as shown in Table 8.13.

The lead auditor usually conducts the closing meeting. The following items are a portion of the closing meeting:

- Verbally report audit findings to the audited organization's representatives.
- Call upon individual auditors for additional input.
- Explain that the deviations are "draft" until the audit report is issued and may not appear on the audit report if found unwarranted. (The Corrective Action Requests are intended to give the audited organization an opportunity to begin corrective action on any deviations issued at the conclusion of the audit, instead of waiting until the audit report is received.)
- A copy of each Corrective Action Request is left with the audited organization(s) upon conclusion of the close out meeting.
- Usually a Corrective Action Request is not required when a deficiency noted during the audit has been corrected and verified prior to the close out meeting.

Table 8.13   Deviation Handling

Deviation(s) are normally recorded on a form such as a Corrective Action Request by the auditor who identified the deficiency:

Corrective Action Requests are completed and numbered consecutively in correlation with each finding by the lead auditor.

Each Corrective Action Request has the identity of the auditor who issued the finding.

The lead auditor has the responsibility to:

Review each deviation noted on the Corrective Action Requests and discuss any ambiguous or conflicting observations with the auditor(s).

Verify that the deviation is a "condition adverse to quality," or a "statement regarding noncompliance with established policy, procedures, and so forth."

Remain aware that one objective of auditing is to induce performance improvement. This requires that deviations, in particular, be stated in terms that will arouse management interest, and as a minimum, convince them that there are significant problems which need to be investigated.

Ensure that each final deviation is a clear, concise statement of a problem.

Resolve any possible differences or discrepancies among the audit team.

(This will be reported as a deviation, which will indicate correction and verification prior to completion of the audit.)

The lead auditor usually prepares an audit report within 10 working days of the close out meeting. The audit report includes the following:

- Audit report cover sheet;
- Audit number;
- Audited organization or activity;
- Date of audit;
- Scope of audit;
- Audit team with lead auditor identified;
- Executive summary of audit results;
- Exemplary practices, if applicable;
- Requirements or deviations, if applicable;
- Observations, if applicable;
- Key personnel contacted;
- Documents reviewed;
- Applicable signatures.

Unresolved deviations require corrective actions or plans from the audited organization. Deviations not corrected within the 30-day response period require a Corrective Action Plan including a milestone schedule for each deviation. Information should include:

- Corrective action to correct the unresolved deviations identified in the written audit report;
- Cause identification;
- Actions to prevent recurrence;
- Lessons learned;
- Actions to be taken for improvement.

The auditing organization should:

- Provide guidance for unacceptable corrective action;
- Request review by appropriate management for unacceptable corrective action;
- Provide notification of inability to verify or validate completion of acceptable corrective action, with a copy to their client;
- Determine acceptability of corrective action;
- Evaluate overdue response or corrective action correspondence;
- Approve corrective action, and see it through: evaluation, verification, and closure of corrective action(s).

Now, let us focus on how the auditee should handle audit results. If the audit report identifies problems, the auditee proposes corrective actions, which may be reviewed by the client or auditor. The resolution of a problem requires three steps that should be outlined in a corrective action plan:

1. Correction of the specific deficiency found;
2. Resolution of the root cause of the problem;
3. Setting a date when corrective action will be in place to prevent a recurrence.

The audited organization should attempt to maximize its benefit from the audit. Where exemplary practices were noted by the auditors, those practices may be publicized and their use reinforced where applicable. Observations, conveying an auditor's opinion that best management practices were not followed, should be evaluated and may serve to improve beyond simple compliance and help to achieve excellence. Exemplary practices and observations do not require a response to the auditing organization.

Deficiencies normally require response from the auditee to the auditing organization. Maximizing the benefit from deficiencies requires several steps to be taken by the auditee. Site procedures must be followed, and these generally include the steps shown in Table 8.14.

A follow-up audit may be required or requested to verify that each finding is resolved by a proposed corrective action, the corrective action has been implemented, and the problem has been resolved. The follow-up activities include: evaluation of the response, reaudit, closing, and documentation. The lead auditor is responsible for requesting a timely response from the auditee. The authority for evaluating the adequacy of the response is the responsibility of the lead auditor who performed the particular audit. When all the findings have been resolved, the auditee is notified that the audit is closed.

The closing activity is the final acknowledgment that the audit is formally and officially at an end. The documentation activity includes the collection and filing of all the documentation related to the audit. Normally the lead auditor receives all the information for storage.

8.6 Conclusions

The main conclusions here are that there are many types of software-related audits, just a few of which are examined in this chapter. The emphases in this chapter are on the CMMI®-DEV and ISO 9001:2000 audit methodologies. They are rather similar and focus on preparation, execution, and feedback. The feedback results in actions by the audited organization.

For auditing principles, ISO 9001:2000 uses the ISO 19011—*The Auditing Standard & How to Conduct Your Own Audits for Auditing Rules.* For auditing principles, the CMMI®-DEV uses the *Standard CMMI® Appraisal Method for Process Improvement (SCAMPI^SM) A, Version 1.2: Method Definition Document.* Each of these has some coverage in Section 8.2.

Table 8.14   Auditee Steps When Responding to Deficiencies

1. Verify the factual accuracy of each deviation statement. This may require checking with the persons interviewed by the auditor, reading the documents that the auditor read, or observing an activity that was observed by the auditor. Finally, verify that the requirement cited is applicable to the activity and was correctly interpreted by the auditor.

2. Identify the scope of the deficiency. While the auditors may have found one or two instances, there could be more that were not observed by the auditors due to their limited time and resources. Corrective actions are needed for all instances, whether found by the audit or not.

3. Identify the person(s) responsible for corrective actions. Generally, site procedures and organizational charters will guide this step. Deficiencies covering more than one parallel organizational unit are normally addressed by the next higher level of management.

4. Once responsibility has been assigned and accepted, a corrective action plan is made for each deficiency. This plan, with brief action statements and stated or clearly defined deliverables and due dates, can become part of the response to the auditing organization.

5. Each deficiency should be graded for significance. High-risk, safety-related deficiencies are normally given priority for correction. Some deficiencies have so little consequence that they are noted and no corrective action is taken, where this is agreed to by clients and regulatory authorities.

6. Root cause analysis should be considered for the more significant deficiencies. This may lead to an improved corrective action plan that prevents recurrence.

7. Where corrective actions cannot be completed for a long time, mitigating actions for the short term should be included in the plan as needed.

8. Tracking the corrective actions in a management commitment system is done to ensure an orderly completion and to provide a means for changing dates, responsible persons, and details of the action.

9. Verification of completed actions by assembling evidence files, reaudit, or other means allows closure in the tracking system.

10. Lessons learned from the audit, root cause analysis, and corrective actions should be written and disseminated to those who can apply them in their activities. Sometimes exemplary practices noted in the audit report are the basis for a positive lesson.

The American Society for Quality (ASQ) offers a Certified Quality Auditor (CQA) program. To become an ASQ CQA, one takes a 4-hour exam to meet the requirements. This program is similar to programs like Certified Public Accountant or Professional Engineer. It is well designed, professionally maintained, and highly respected [33].

The Software Engineering Institute (SEI) has a similar program for the authorization of lead appraisers who may lead SCAMPI[SM] A appraisals. To become an authorized Lead Appraiser, one must fulfill multiple requirements including: (1) participation in SCAMPI[SM] appraisals, (2) completion of various CMMI[®] and SCAMPI[SM]-related courses, and (3) leading a SCAMPI[SM] appraisal while being observed by an SEI-provided observer. It is well designed, professionally maintained, and highly respected.

References

[1]   Seguin, R., *The Globe and Mail*, Canadian Newspaper, December 13, 2006, p. A4.

[2]   *IEEE Standard Glossary of Software Engineering Terminology*, IEEE Std 610.12-1990, New York: IEEE, p. 11.

[3]   *IEEE Standard for Software Reviews*, IEEE Std 1028-1997, New York: IEEE, p. 25.

[4]   Software Quality Assurance Subcommittee of the Nuclear Weapons Complex Quality Manager, *Preparation for a Software Quality Audit*, Albuquerque Operations Office: United States Department of Energy, June 1996, p. 12.

[5]   *IEEE Standard for Software Reviews*, IEEE Std 1028-1997, New York: IEEE, p. 26.

[6]   Software Quality Assurance Subcommittee of the Nuclear Weapons Complex Quality Manager, *Preparation for a Software Quality Audit*, Albuquerque Operations Office: United States Department of Energy, June 1996, pp. 13, 14.

[7]   Russell, J. P., "All About Auditing," *Quality Progress*, May 2000, p. 98.

[8]   Business Software Alliance (BSA) Web site, http://www.bsa.org/usa/about/ and http://www.bsa.org/usa/antipiracy/Tools-Resources.cfm; and Software & Information Industry Association (SIIA) Web site, http://www.siia.net/piracy/ and http://www.siia.net/piracy/audit.asp; both accessed May 2007.

[9]   Tomeny, J., (IBSMA 2007 SAM Practitioner of the Year), *How to Survive a Software Audit through Effective Software Management*, http://www.sassafras.com/whitepaper.html, Sassafras Software Inc., May 2007.

[10] Rose, C., *Computer Security Audit Checklist*, http://www.itsecurity.com/papers/iomart2.htm, April 8, 2002, accessed November 2006.

[11] *Part 3: BS 7799 Certification*, http://www.iso17799software.com/7799part3.htm, November 2006.

[12] *Secured View: Audit Compliance: Preparing for the Audit*, http://www.networkmagazineindia.com/200309/security02.shtml, *Network Magazine*, September 2003, accessed October 2006.

[13] International Standard ISO 9001, *Quality Management Systems—Requirements*, 3rd ed., 2000-12-15, Reference number ISO 9001:2000(E), © ISO 2000.

[14] ISO IEC 90003 2004 Software Standard in Plain English, Alberta: Praxiom Research Group Limited, http://www.praxiom.com/iso-90003.htm, December 2006.

[15] "Related Standards ISO 19011—The Auditing Standard & How to Conduct Your Own Audits," (c) Dr. Terry Russell, http://www.iso-9000.co.uk/faqs_01.html, updated January 2007, accessed April 2007.

[16] SCAMPI^SM Upgrade Team, *Standard CMMI® Appraisal Method for Process Improvement (SCAMPI^SM) A, Version 1.2: Method Definition Document*, Handbook CMU/SEI-2006-HB-002, August 2006, pp. i–xi.

[17] SCAMPI^SM Upgrade Team, *Standard CMMI® Appraisal Method for Process Improvement (SCAMPI^SM) A, Version 1.2: Method Definition Document*, Handbook CMU/SEI-2006-HB-002, August 2006, pp. I-16, I-17.

[18] SCAMPI^SM Upgrade Team, *Standard CMMI® Appraisal Method for Process Improvement (SCAMPI^SM) A, Version 1.2: Method Definition Document*, Handbook CMU/SEI-2006-HB-002, August 2006, pp. I-10–I-12.

[19] *AuditNet Audit Programs*, http://www.auditnet.org/subscribers/login.asp, http://www.auditnet.org/freeaccess.asp, January 2007.

[20] Leibs, S., and P. Krass, "The Never-Ending Audit," *CFO Magazine*, October 1, 2002.

[21] Posey, B., *Creating an Audit Policy*, http://networking.earthweb.com/netos/article.php/10951_624801_3, November 2000, accessed December 2006.

[22] *IEEE Standard for Software Reviews*, IEEE Std 1028-1997, copyright 1997 by IEEE, all rights reserved, New York: IEEE, p. 28.

[23] Software Quality Assurance Subcommittee of the Nuclear Weapons Complex Quality Manager, *Preparation for a Software Quality Audit*, Albuquerque Operations Office: United States Department of Energy, June 1996, p. 14.

[24] *IEEE Standard for Software Reviews*, IEEE Std 1028-1997, New York: IEEE, p. 27.

[25] Software Quality Assurance Subcommittee of the Nuclear Weapons Complex Quality Manager, *Preparation for a Software Quality Audit*, Albuquerque Operations Office: United States Department of Energy, June 1996, pp. 16, 17.

[26]   UAE Business Software Alliance, http://www.bsa.org, December 2006, p. 4.

[27]   UAE Business Software Alliance, http://www.bsa.org, December 2006, p. 6.

[28]   UAE Business Software Alliance, http://www.bsa.org, December 2006, p. 7.

[29]   *Preparing for a Computer Systems & 21 CFR Part 11 Audit*, http://www.auditing.com/PreparingfortheAudit.htm, November 2006.

[30]   Software Quality Assurance Subcommittee of the Nuclear Weapons Complex Quality Manager, *Preparation for a Software Quality Audit*, Albuquerque Operations Office: United States Department of Energy, June 1996, p. 16.

[31]   U.S. Department of Energy, Office of Chief Information Officer, *DOE Systems Engineering Methodology: In-Stage Assessment Process Guide*, Version 3, September 2002, p. 6.

[32]   Software Quality Assurance Subcommittee of the Nuclear Weapons Complex Quality Manager, *Preparation for a Software Quality Audit*, Albuquerque Operations Office: United States Department of Energy, June 1996, pp. 16–23.

[33]   Russell, J. P., "All About Auditing," *Quality Progress*, May 2000, p. 99.

## CHAPTER 9

Software Safety and Its Relation to Software Quality Assurance

Kenneth S. Mendis

9.1   Introduction

Software safety is an issue that has gained some prominence in the software community today. On the positive side, software managers and developers are becoming more aware of the need to consider safety as a design factor. On the negative side, the news media occasionally carries stories reflecting the impact of not adequately designing for safety. In either case, safety issues are not yet treated with the desired level of competence and consistency that one would expect of a mature organization. One probable cause for this is the way safety requirements are presented to the designer—that is, in too general a fashion and in too standalone a manner. In order to assure that software safety issues receive adequate consideration up front in the life cycle, support must come from within. This is where software quality comes in.

For all practical purposes, safety is a quality concern. Consider the following: whenever delivered software products cause bodily harm or system damage, either directly or indirectly, we have not delivered a quality product. Consequently, there is ever increasing need to examine the function or discipline of Software Safety Assurance.

Software Safety Assurance is comprised of activities performed on safety critical systems during the software development life cycle. The objective of this effort should be to eliminate and/or reduce potential safety risks that are associated with software critical systems. Software Safety Assurance includes activities such as Software Security Assurance, Software Integrity Assurance, and Software Hazard-Free Assurance. Of particular importance in a Software Safety Assurance program is the fact that the requirements for Software Safety Assurance can be effectively addressed only as an integrated activity of the software development process. Software Safety Assurance, therefore, should be concerned with reducing the potential risks associated with software and computers in safety-critical software systems applications. This effort is best performed by individuals who are trained in software safety measures and who have the organizational support to assure their proper implementation.

The standards for safety-related software systems are defined by Underwriters Laboratory, Inc., the National Aeronautics and Space Administration (NASA), the

Institute of Electrical and Electronics Engineers (IEEE), the Organization of International Standardization (ISO), and the Department of Defense (DoD), as well as numerous European bodies described herein. All stipulate safety-related requirements for system software in terms of hazard avoidance. How these are interpreted and implemented is discussed in this chapter.

9.2 Software-Caused Accidents

The number of accidents relating to poor software safety practices, having resulted in death and/or serious injury to people and damage to other systems and the environment, is constantly increasing as our control systems become more and more software intensive. Robert Sibley, a staff writer for *The Citizen,* a Texas newspaper, reported that software errors in a linear particle accelerator-based cancer radiation therapy machine caused the machine to deliver lethal overdoses of radiation to several patients, five of whom died. Another article in *World News* reported that a nuclear power fuel-handling machine, containing a software error that was introduced into the computer system approximately 4 years earlier, caused a radioactive heavy water spill at the Ontario Hydro's Nuclear Power facility in Ontario, Canada. An error in the design of a blood data bank program allowed over 1,000 pints of blood that may have been contaminated with Acquired Immune Deficiency Syndrome (AIDS), to be distributed. Instrument failure, which caused the crash of the SAAB JAS39 Gripen fighter plane, was traced to a safety-related software issue. A Patriot missile system shutdown during the Gulf War, which left unprotected the U.S. barracks that were hit by a SCUD missile killing 27 and wounding 97 others, was caused by a software error. Finally, it is interesting to note that many of the incidents, both publicly and privately known, involving critical software, did not take place immediately following the release of the new software. All too often, the problem within the software had existed for some time before it resulted in an accident. Typically, software-caused accidents are time independent. Many software errors have gone undetected because they were not found using standard validation and verification techniques.

Lawsuits are commonplace as a result of death or injury caused by unsafe software. Most of these cases are settled out of court, often on the condition that the injured person keep silent about the accident, the lawsuit, and the settlement. An emerging legal theory, which deals with software engineering malpractice and imposes new legal liability on software engineers and software developers for errors in software, has companies scrambling to implement preventive measures.

9.3 The Confusing World of Software Safety

The confusion between *reliability* and *safety* can best be answered by providing some key definitions.

Safety is defined as freedom from those conditions that can cause death, injury, illness, damage to or loss of equipment or property, or environmental harm. Safety attempts to assure no accidents; whereas reliability attempts to ensure no failures will exist within the software. The expectation is that a system is safe when it does not, under defined conditions, lead to a state in which human life, health, property, or the environment is endangered.

Reliability—it is appropriate to restate the definition of *software reliability* from Chapter 18—is the ability of the software to perform its required function under stated conditions for a stated period of time. Using these definitions, reliability and safety are not similar. A reliable system can be unsafe and a safe system can be unreliable.

Hazard analysis is an interactive process composed of identification and evaluation of hazards to enable them to be eliminated or, if that is not practical, to assist in the reduction of the associated hazard to an acceptable level. The term has often been associated with Failure Modes and Effects Analysis (FMEA) and with Fault Tree Analysis. It also, at times, applies to various forms of analysis stipulated by standards such as MIL-STD-882.

Critical analysis is a procedure by which each potential failure mode is ranked according to the combined influence of severity and probability.

Fail Safe is safety-critical software that remains in or moves to a safe state after a failure.

Fail Soft is a methodology applied to a safety failure in which the system continues operation either with reduced performance and/or functionality.

Safe System is a system that prevents unsafe states from producing safety failures. In other words, the system never produces an output that will transform the state into an unsafe state.

Safety Critical Software is software whose use in a system can result in unacceptable risk. Safety critical software includes software whose operation or failure to operate can lead to a hazardous state, software intended to recover from hazardous states, and software intended to mitigate the severity of an accident (IEEE).

9.4 Standards, Guidelines, and Certifications

Are there too many standards, guidelines, and/or regulations? Do they help reduce the number of deaths? Are the regulatory bodies necessary? The argument that software is different from hardware in that its only failure modes are through design faults rather than from physical mechanisms, such as aging, makes applying safety standards difficult. Many potential software-caused accidents remain dormant, while others can be very difficult to diagnosis. Another reason why we have not seen more software-caused accidents is because we normally use the systems in accordance with how they are tested and how they are supposed to be used. We can attribute our success in avoiding software-caused accidents to the manner of our training to use these systems. Software-caused accidents are awaiting the unusual and uncommon caused inputs. Therefore, we must address this when developing a software safety program.

The standards most frequently referenced are:

- *IEEE Standard for Software Safety Plans*, IEEE STD 1228-1994.
- *ISO15026 Information Technology—System and Software Integrity Levels*, November 15, 1998.

- National Aeronautics and Space Administration, *Software Safety Standard*, NASA-STD-8719.13A, September 15, 1997.

- Underwriters Laboratory, *Standard for Software in Programmable Components*, UL 1998. (This UL standard is especially interesting because of the different tack UL has taken. Most software safety-related standards concentrate on the software development process, but the UL has developed a software standard that is very product oriented. This is probably worth examining at least to find some potential practical measures for reducing software risks, even if your product does not need to conform to this standard.)

- MIL-STD-882D, *Standard Practice for System Safety*, February 10, 2000.

- Place, P. R. H., and K. C. Kang, *Safety-Critical Software: Status Report and Annotated Bibliography*, Technical Report CMU/SEI-92-TR-5, June 1993, p. 45 (an entire chapter is on safety standards and some reasons why safety standards are not always the most beneficial to a software safety program).

Certification is the "procedure by which a third party gives written assurance that a product, process, or service conforms to specified requirements." Certification, then, should assure conformance with the applicable requirements for a given purpose, within specific operations scenarios [1].

There are several European initiatives addressing dependability and other issues of safety-critical software-intensive systems [2]:

- FAA-SSAC: address concerns about time and expense associated with software aspects of certification;

- ISO JTC1/SC7: ISO standards for software engineering that lead to a safer system;

- IEC Technical Committee 56: Includes (1) TC 56/WEG 10—Dependability assessment of software, (2) SC 65A/WG 9—Safe software, and (3) SC 65A/WG 10—Functional safety of Programmable Electronic Devices;

- Squale (Security, Safety, and Quality Evaluation for Dependable Systems): Esprit Project examines existing standards and practices in the safety and security areas;

- Esprit Project 22187: Safety and Risk Evaluation Using Bayesian Nets;

- Information Society Standardization System: Ensure that the approval, certification, and evaluation process for safety-critical systems in which a software failure could be a safety hazard is handled within the European Union;

- RTCA/EUROCAE SC-190/WG-52: Improving RTCA DO-1788 standard for the certification of software in airborne systems;

- IEEE Safety Study Group: Study compatibility of IEEE standards with IEC standards.

All of these standards have one theme in common: they make a convincing case for the fact that most of the safety-critical errors found in software systems are design-related errors. These errors arise from a variety of sources that include a lack of understanding of how a system is to be used, errors in assumptions of how the software and hardware work together, and unclear design requirements. Therefore, a significant part of the software system safety effort should be focused on eliminating design errors and testing the system with the understanding that the system should be capable of operating in environments that are not traditional "what if" conditions. It is also important to consider that the development of the system with specific accident avoidance requirements should be taken into account.

9.5   What Does It Take to Develop a Software Safety Assurance Program?

The goal of an MIT Safety Project is to develop a theoretical foundation for safety and a methodology for building safety-critical systems built upon that foundation. The methodology includes special management structures and procedures, system hazard analysis, software hazard analysis, requirements modeling and analysis for completeness and safety, design for safety, design of human-machine interaction, verification (both testing and code analysis), operational feedback, and change analysis.

The problem with software is that "safe" software is a difficult concept to design for. It is an attribute that seemingly can only be tested. The goal then is to ensure that software can execute within a potentially hazardous system without causing or contributing to unacceptable risk or loss such as death.

Items to consider when implementing such a program are the following:

- Software safety system requirements are established and specified as part of the organization's design policy.
- Software system safety requirements are consistent with contract-specific requirements and are designed into the system.
- Human computer interface requirements are consistent with contract-specific requirements and are designed into the system.
- Software system safety is quantifiable to a defined risk level using standard measurement tools.
- Software system safety is addressed as a team effort involving management, engineering, and quality assurance.
- Hazards associated with the software system are identified, tracked, evaluated, and eliminated as required.
- Changes in design, configuration, or mission requirements are accomplished in a manner that maintains an acceptable risk level.
- Historical software safety data, including lessons learned from other systems, are considered and used in future software development efforts.

Organizations concerned with safety assurance must be able to determine what needs to be done in order that the software system safety program will satisfy applicable contractual standards. The implementation of these requirements in a Software Safety Assurance Plan makes the process go smoothly. The IEEE 1228-1994 *Standard for Software Safety Plans* defines the minimum acceptable requirements for the contents of a software safety plan [3]. Such a plan must address the following:

1.0 Purpose

2.0 Definitions, Acronyms, and References

3.0 Software Safety Management

3.1 Organization and Responsibilities

3.2 Resources

3.3 Staff Qualification and Training

3.4 Software Life Cycle

3.5 Documentation Requirements

3.6 Software Safety Program Records

3.7 Software Safety Configuration Management Activities

3.8 Software Quality Assurance Activities

3.9 Software Verification and Validation Activities

3.10 Tool Support and Approval

3.11 Previously Developed or Purchased Software

3.12 Subcontractor Management

3.13 Process Certification

4.0 Software Safety Analysis

4.1 Software Safety Analyses Preparation

4.2 Software Safety Requirements Analyses

4.3 Software Safety Design Analyses

4.4 Software Safety Testing Analyses

4.5 Software Safety Change Analyses

5.0 Postdevelopment

5.1 Training

5.2 Release and Use

5.3 Monitoring

5.4 Maintenance

5.5 Retirement and Notification

The minimum acceptable requirement for such an assurance plan must be defined, and it must apply to the software safety assurance requirements associated with development, procurement, maintenance, and the retirement of safety-critical software. In essence, the software safety assurance program must:

- Assure that safety is designed into the system in a timely and cost-effective manner;
- Assure that hazards associated with each system are identified, evaluated, and eliminated or reduced to an acceptable level;

- Capture historical safety data and lessons learned from other systems for continuous improvement;
- Seek minimum risk when accepting and using new designs, materials, and production and test techniques;
- Minimize retrofit actions required to improve safety through the timely inclusion of safety features during R&D;
- Accomplish changes in design configuration or user requirements in a manner that maintains an acceptable risk level;
- Document significant safety data as lessons learned, and submit as proposed changes to applicable designs.

9.6   Requirements Drive Safety

This section is derived from Donald Firesmith's Engineering Safety-Rrelated Requirements for Software-Intensive Systems [4]. Safety engineering is the engineering discipline within systems engineering that lowers the risk of accidental harm to valuable assets to an acceptable level to legitimate stakeholders. It is through systems engineering analysis (Figure 9.1) that an organization arrives at the needed safety-related requirements to achieve software safety. Notice the flow from safety engineering to safety analysis to its substructure to safety-related requirements.

Remember, safety is the quality factor capturing the degree to which:

- Accidental harm to valuable assets is eliminated or mitigated;
- Safety events (accidents, incidents, and hazardous events) are eliminated or their negative consequences mitigated;
- Hazards are eliminated or mitigated;
- Safety risks are kept acceptably low;
- The preceding problems are prevented, detected, reacted to, and possibly adapted to.

Figure 9.2 provides an example of these terms in a possible real-life situation.

Further reviewing these items of safety as a quality factor, let us start with "harm." Harm is any significant negative consequence to a valuable asset. Accidental harm is any unauthorized, unintentional (i.e., nonmalicious) harm (e.g., due to an accident).

Harm severity is an appropriate categorization of the amount of harm. These need to be clearly identified and appropriately and unambiguously defined.

The following is an example from the commercial aviation standard, Software Considerations in Airborne Systems and Equipment Certification (RTCA/DO 178B: 1992):

Catastrophic:

- Failure condition, which prevents the continued safe flight and landing of the aircraft.

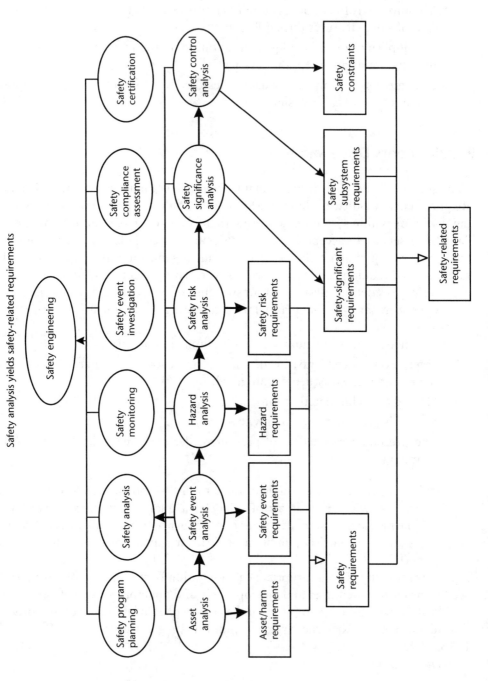

Figure 9.1   Safety engineering analysis. (*From:* [5]. © 2006 Software Engineering Institute. Reprinted with permission.)

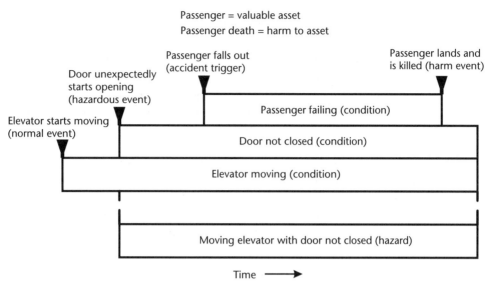

Figure 9.2 Hazard and harm events illustrated. (*From:* [6]. © 2006 Software Engineering Institute. Reprinted with permission.)

[Critical] Severe:

• Failure conditions, which reduce the capability of the aircraft or the ability of the crew to cope with adverse operation conditions;
• Serious or potentially fatal injuries to some passengers.

Major:

• Failure conditions, which reduce the capability of the aircraft or the ability of the crew to cope with adverse operating conditions;
• Discomfort and possible injury to the passengers.

Minor:

• Failure conditions, which do not cause a significant reduction in aircraft safety.

[Negligible] No effect:

• Failure conditions, which do not affect the operational capability of the aircraft or increase the crew's workload.

Now, let us examine safety-related events.
A safety event is any event with significant safety ramifications; for example:

• An accident trigger is a safety-related event that directly causes an accident.
• A harm event is a safety-related event that causes significant harm.
• A hazardous event is a safety-related event that causes the existence of a hazard (i.e., hazardous conditions).

A network of safety events is any cohesive set of safety events; for example:

- An accident is a *series* of one or more related *safety events* causing actual, nonmalicious (i.e., accidental) harm to valuable assets.
- A safety incident (also known as, close call, near miss) is a *series* of one or more related *hazardous events* that only by luck did not cause nonmalicious actual harm.

Safety event likelihood categorization is an appropriate categorization of the probability that a safety event occurs. Safety event likelihood categories can be standardized (ISO, military, industry-wide) or be endeavor specific; these need to be identified and defined.

Example safety event likelihood categories (further discussed later in this chapter) include:

- Frequent;
- Probable;
- Occasional;
- Remote;
- Implausible;

Now, what is a safety hazard? A safety hazard is a danger[1] that can cause or contribute to the occurrence of a *safety event*. A threat (security and survivability) is a danger that can cause or contribute to the occurrence of a *security or survivability event* (e.g., a security vulnerability combined with an attacker with means, motive, and opportunity).

Finally, how are safety risks identified and kept acceptably low? The safety integrity levels (SILs) are examined to attempt to force them to the "acceptable" level:

- *Intolerable:* The risk associated with the requirement(s) is totally unacceptable to the major stakeholders. The requirement(s) *must* therefore be deleted or modified to lower the associated risk.
- *Undesirable:* The risk associated with the requirement(s) is so high that major (e.g., architecture, design, implementation, and testing) steps should be taken to lower the risk (e.g., risk mitigation and risk transfer) to lower the risk.
- *As low as reasonably practical (ALARP):* Reasonable practical steps should be taken to lower the risk associated with the requirement(s).
- *Acceptable:* The risk associated with the requirement(s) is acceptable to the major stakeholders and no additional effort must be taken to lower it.

Then a safety risk matrix (Table 9.1) is produced that defines safety risk (and SIL) as a function of: harm severity, and accident/hazard frequency of occurrence.

---

1.   Danger (defensibility) is one or more conditions, situations, or states of a system that in conjunction with condition(s) in the environment of the system can cause or contribute to the occurrence of a *defense-related event.*

Table 9.1   Safety Risks Integrity levels

	Frequency of Accident / Hazard Occurrence				
Harm Severity	Frequent	Probable	Occasional	Remote	Implausible
Catastrophic	Intolerable	Intolerable	Intolerable	Undesirable	ALARP
Critical	Intolerable	Intolerable	Undesirable	ALARP	ALARP
Major	Undesirable	Undesirable	ALARP	ALARP	Acceptable
Minor	Undesirable	ALARP	ALARP	Acceptable	Acceptable
Negligible	ALARP	ALARP	ALARP	Acceptable	Acceptable

Source: [7].

9.7   Design of a System Safety Program

Figure 9.3 shows the design of a system safety program. Such a process is highly iterative and includes continual updating of what has been done previously as new information is gained through the system development process. The center column of Figure 9.3 shows the standard systems engineering tasks, while the right-hand column shows special safety tasks and how they interact. There also is operations research modeling and analysis performed to demonstrate how information might be obtained and used to assist in making trade-offs between alternative system designs [8].

Tor Stålhane notes that the goal of safety analysis is to identify problems that can occur in the future, when the system is put into use in its real environment. We need to identify problems as early as possible so that we can insert barriers in the code or change the functionality so that we remove or reduce the probability of future dangers. The methods used—called HazOp and Preliminary Hazard Analysis (PHA)—are really just methods used to add structure to a brain-storming session and to help people with a rather disparate background to communicate effectively. The important information comes from the participants, who are experts in system development and experts in the application domain who reuse their accumulated experience.

In order to perform a HazOp on a process, we need a detailed process description: what are the activities, what is their purpose, how are they related, and what are the results and a flow such as related in the safety program of Figure 9.3. The process description provides what the HazOp method calls the study nodes. The guidewords come next.

Guidewords are words used to initiate and focus the discussions and exchange of ideas among the HazOp participants. There exist a generic set of guidewords: "none," "less," "more," "part of," "opposite," and "as well as." These were designed, however, for analysis of chemical processes and need an SPI interpretation in order to become useful. In addition, it is customary to add timing guidewords—for instance "too late," "too early," and "never."

In order to trigger a discussion, we combine a guideword and a study node. If our study node is "inspection activity" and the guideword is "less," this could trigger the discussion on how the inspection process could fail so that it identifies too few errors—also called a deviation. The discussion will identify problem items, causes, and proposed solutions. The results are documented in the HazOp table. A simple example is shown in Table 9.2 [9].

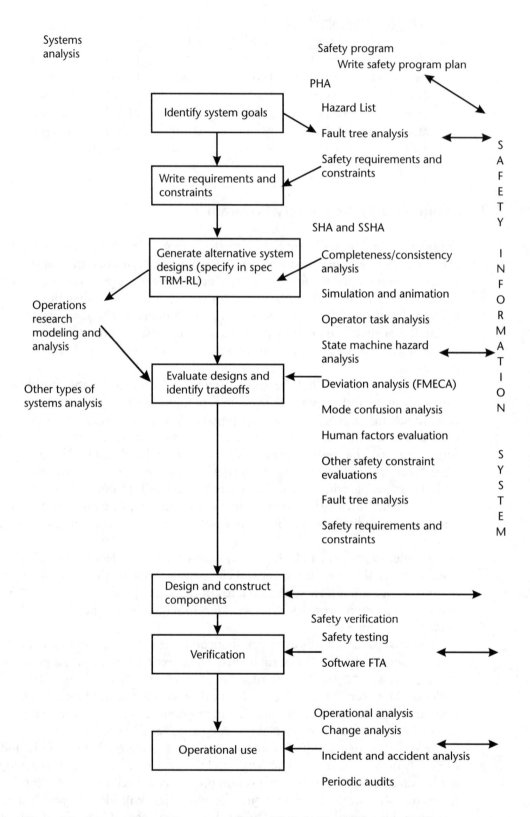

Figure 9.3 System safety program design. (*From:* [8]. © 1997 Goddard Space Flight Center Software Symposium. Reprinted with permission.)

Table 9.2 Inspection Activity

Guideword Used	Deviation	Consequences	Cause	Solution
Less	Too few errors found	Errors in input to next activity	Too little preparation time used	Check that all participants have used their time quota for inspection preparation
More	False positives—not an error	Unnecessary work for the author	Lack of experience with language or application domain	Use only personnel with the right knowledge

Source: [9].

9.8 Hazard Avoidance and Mitigation Technique

To avoid hazards, the system design must be analyzed in order to identify potential hazards that affect system safety. This can be accomplished by employing a technique known as hazard analysis. From this, safety risks can be defined and used to establish a risk mitigation plan. The best method to evaluate potential safety hazards is by using either fault tree analysis or failure modes and effects analysis and by documenting the resulting hazards in an event probability and occurrence matrix similar to the one shown in Table 9.3.

In order to develop an approach to reduce the probability of event occurrence, the concept of risk must be used. The risk from a system is the condition of the event probability and its consequence. The risk assessment is developed from the event probability and occurrence matrix. See Table 9.4 for risk classification interpretation.

The safety risk is the combination of the probability of occurrence and the severity of the incident, which results in the hazard risk assessment index as shown in Table 9.5.

The aim is to eliminate all category I safety-critical exposures and to minimize category II exposures. Each hazard can be assigned a numerical rating that dictates the level of action required to satisfy the user requirements. This hazard analysis results from the foundation of documentation known as a risk assessment report [10, 11].

9.9 Recommendations

Because the consequences of failure of a safety-critical system are so extreme (including death or injury), it is essential to have an ethic surrounding such systems.

Table 9.3 Event Probability and Occurrence Matrix

Event Occurrence	Event Probability
(A) Frequent	Likely to be continually experienced
(B) Probable	Likely to occur often
(C) Occasional	Likely to occur several times
(D) Remote	Likely to occur sometime
(E) Improbable	Unlikely, may occur under exceptional conditions

Table 9.4   Risk Classification

Risk Class	Interpretation
Category I—Catastrophic	Intolerable. Will cause death or severe injury to personnel and could result in system damage and loss.
Category II—Critical	Undesirable. Will cause personnel injury or major system damage.
Category III—Marginal	Tolerable. Can be countered or controlled without resulting in personnel injury or major system damage.
Category IV—Negligible	Acceptable. Will not result in personnel injury or system damage.

Table 9.5   Risk Index

	Risk Class			
Event Occurrence	I	II	III	IV
(A) Frequent	1	1	4	3
(B) Probable	1	1	3	4
(C) Occasional	1	2	3	4
(D) Remote	2	3	4	5
(E) Improbable	3	4	5	5

Where:

Hazard Risk Index		Acceptance Criteria
1–2	=	Intolerable
3	=	Undesirable, decision
4	=	Tolerable with review and approval
5	=	Tolerable without review

Jonathan Bowen has provided this ethic of software safety-critical systems. Any scientifically based activity requires a level of responsibility and understanding of associated moral questions. Science has developed nuclear technology that may cause great harm or good. Safety is not an attribute that can be added to software after the event; it must be designed into the software from the start, and it must be checked to ensure that unsafe functions have not been added or necessary functions have not been removed. Successful development of safety-critical software depends on appropriate system requirements engineering, system hazards identification, and system design and software requirements engineering, design and development [12].

System engineering is particularly important because we still have an imperfect understanding of the ways in which software failures can affect the system. It is important, wherever possible, to offer alternative backups to the safety-critical software that allow the system operators to perform degraded, yet safe, operation of the system.

There is no substitute for high-quality developers, particularly when determining the ways in which the system may fail and thus lead to potential mishaps [13].

References

[1] Rodriguez-Dapena, P., "Software Safety Certification: A Multinational Problem," *IEEE Software*, July/August 1999, p. 31, © 1999 IEEE.

[2] Rodriguez-Dapena, P., "Software Safety Certification: A Multinational Problem," *IEEE Software*, July/August 1999, p. 35, © 1999 IEEE.

[3] Raytheon Company, *Cobra Dane System Modernization ADP Security Plan Rev 3*, CRTL 0131, Contract No. F19628-90-0070, © January 1994, IEEE.

[4] Firesmith, D., "Engineering Safety-Related Requirements for Software-Intensive Systems," *SEPG Conference*, Software Engineering Institute, March 2006, pp. 22–45. Special permission to use portions of "Engineering Safety-Related Requirements for Software-Intensive Systems," © 2006 Carnegie Mellon University, is granted by the Software Engineering Institute.

[5] Firesmith, D., "Engineering Safety-Related Requirements for Software-Intensive Systems," *SEPG Conference*, Software Engineering Institute, March 2006, p. 74. Special permission to use portions of "Engineering Safety-Related Requirements for Software-Intensive Systems," © 2006 Carnegie Mellon University, is granted by the Software Engineering Institute.

[6] Firesmith, D., "Engineering Safety-Related Requirements for Software-Intensive Systems," *SEPG Conference*, Software Engineering Institute, March 2006, p. 38. Special permission to use portions of "Engineering Safety-Related Requirements for Software-Intensive Systems," © 2006 Carnegie Mellon University, is granted by the Software Engineering Institute.

[7] Firesmith, D., "Engineering Safety-Related Requirements for Software-Intensive Systems," *SEPG Conference*, Software Engineering Institute, March 2006, p. 45. Special permission to use portions of "Engineering Safety-Related Requirements for Software-Intensive Systems," ©2006 Carnegie Mellon University, is granted by the Software Engineering Institute.

[8] Leveson, N., et al., "Demonstration of a Safety Analysis on a Complex System," *Goddard Space Flight Center Software Symposium*, December 1997.

[9] Stålhane, T., "SPI and Safety," *Improve Software Process Improvement Newsletter* 1-2005, http://www.sintef.no/improve, pp. 4, 5, based on "SPI and Safety," by Tor Stålhane, which appeared in *Improve* 1-2005. Tor Stålhane may be contacted at NTNU (The Norwegian University of Science and Technology) in Trondheim.

[10] Keene, S. J., Jr. "Assuring Software Safety," *Proceedings IEEE Annual Reliability and Maintainability Symposium*, © 1992 IEEE.

[11] Voas, J., L. Morell, K. Miller, "Predicting Where Faults Can Hide from Testing," *IEEE Software*, © March 1991, IEEE.

[12] Bowen, J., "The Ethics of Safety-Critical Systems," *Communications of the ACM*, Vol. 43, No. 4, April 2000, pp. 91–97, pp. 93, 94, © 2000 ACM, Inc., Included by permission.

[13] Place, P. R. H., and K. C. Kang, "Safety-Critical Software: Status Report and Annotated Bibliography," *Technical Report CMU/SEI-92-TR-5*, June 1993, p. 45. Special permission to use portions of "Safety-Critical Software: Status Report and Annotated Bibliography," *Technical Report CMU/SEI-93-TR-5*, © 1993 Carnegie Mellon University, is granted by the Software Engineering Institute.

## CHAPTER 10

American Society for Quality's Software Quality Engineer Certification Program

Katharine B. Harris

10.1 ASQ Background

The American Society for Quality (ASQ), formerly the American Society for Quality Control (ASQC), is an international society of individual and organizational members dedicated to the ongoing development, advancement, and promotion of quality concepts, principles, and techniques. ASQ's vision is "By making quality a global priority, an organizational imperative, and a personal ethic, the American Society for Quality becomes the community for everyone who seeks quality concepts, technology, and tools to improve themselves and their world" [1].

In 1946, 17 local quality control societies formed the American Society for Quality Control, as manufacturers sought ways to continue the improvements in quality that had occurred during World War II. For many years, the focus of ASQC remained on improving quality practices in manufacturing. In the past 25 years, though, the quality profession has changed, as professionals began to see how quality concepts could be applied in areas beyond manufacturing. Today, ASQ continues to uphold quality standards while promoting innovation in quality practices and application in a variety of industries and settings. ASQ has more than 100,000 individual and organizational members, and membership is open to anyone interested in quality.

ASQ members belong to one of 252 local sections, which are organized geographically to serve members and community needs on the local level. Located throughout the United States and in Canada and Mexico, sections provide ASQ members with the opportunity to meet others interested in quality to discuss common issues and concerns and to share ideas. The sections have regular activities that include meetings and plant tours; they may also offer workshops or seminars on quality topics of particular interest to the section membership. Most sections use a Web site to publicize their activities, and some also provide members with a printed newsletter that includes articles about quality-related issues and information about certification, conferences, and training courses. Sections may provide outreach to their community and may be involved with local businesses, schools, and government agencies to promote quality concepts. Sections are run by volunteer leaders who donate several hours of time each month to ensure that the quality interests of the local members are identified and appropriate resources are made available for them.

Additionally, ASQ members worldwide may join a division or a forum that serves the needs of members who are involved with specific industries and applications. For example, the Software Division provides specialized training, information, and professional programs for those interested in applying quality principles to the field of software development. The Software Division has responsibility for the following activities and services:

- Developing the software quality engineer certification program;
- Sponsoring the International Conference on Software Quality;
- Publishing a quarterly newsletter;
- Publishing the *Software Quality Professional,* a professional journal;
- Maintaining liaison with national and international standards bodies such as ANSI and ISO;
- Interacting with other professional software organizations such as IEEE and the Association for Computing Machinery (ACM);
- Cooperating with academia to make available educational resources to the software quality profession;
- Reviewing tools and techniques for improving the quality of software products.

10.2   ASQ Certification Program

The ASQ certification program was developed to recognize individuals who have demonstrated proficiency within a specific area, called a *Body of Knowledge* (see Section 10.5 for details of the current CSQE Body of Knowledge). In the more than 35 years of the certification program, more than 152,000 professionals have become certified in one or more of the 14 certification areas. These areas include highly technical certifications as well as certifications for people who have limited experience in quality practices. Table 10.1 provides a brief summary of each of the current exams, explaining the intended audience for each; there are specific employment and educational requirements for each certification as well. New certifications are developed on a regular basis, and for the most current information on the certifications available, visit the ASQ Web site at http://www.asq.org.

The ASQ membership identifies the certification program as one of the most important activities of the society and the program has become a marketplace requirement for quality professionals.

10.2.1   What Is Certification?

Certification is a formal recognition that an individual has demonstrated proficiency in a subject at a point in time. ASQ certification requires education and/or work experience in a specific field and demonstrated knowledge through the successful completion of a written examination. Certification is *not* a license or registration. It

Table 10.1   ASQ Certification Areas

Certification	Intended Audience
Quality Auditor (CQA)	Designed for the professional who understands the standards and principles of auditing and auditing techniques.
Biomedical Auditor (CBA)	Designed for the professional who conducts audits of biomedical systems.
HAACP Auditor (CHA)	Designed for the professional who understands the standards and principles of auditing a hazard analysis and critical control point (HACCP)-based (or process-safety) system.
Calibration Technician (CCT)	Designed for the individual who tests, calibrates, maintains, and repairs electrical, mechanical, electromechanical, analytical, and electronic measuring, recording, and indicating instruments and equipment for conformance to established standards.
Manager of Quality/Organizational Excellence Certification (CMQ/OE)	Designed for the professional who manages and motivates people and who leads and champions process-improvement initiatives—everywhere from small businesses to multinational corporations, in multiple departments or functions—that can have regional or global focus in a variety of service and industrial settings.
Quality Engineer (CQE)	Designed for the professional who understands the principles of product and service quality evaluation and control, such as the development and operation of quality control systems, application and analysis of testing and inspection procedures, the ability to use metrology and statistical methods to diagnose and correct improper quality control practices, and facility with quality cost concepts and techniques.
Quality Inspector (CQI)	Designed for an individual who, in support of and under the direction of quality engineers, supervisors, or technicians, can evaluate hardware documentation, perform laboratory procedures, inspect products, measure process performance, record data, and prepare formal reports.
Quality Technician (CQT)	Designed for a paraprofessional who, in support of and under the direction of quality engineers or supervisors, analyzes and solves quality problems, prepares inspection plans and instructions, selects sampling plan applications, prepares procedures, trains inspectors, performs audits, analyzes quality costs and other quality data, and applies fundamental statistical methods for process control.
Quality Improvement Associate (CQIA)	Designed for an individual who has a basic knowledge of quality tools and their uses and is involved in quality improvement projects, but who does not necessarily come from a traditional quality area.
Quality Process Analyst (CQPA)	Designed for a paraprofessional who, in support of and under the direction of quality engineers or supervisors, analyzes, and solves quality problems and is involved in quality improvement projects.
Reliability Engineer (CRE)	Designed for the professional who understands the principles of performance evaluation and prediction to improve product/systems safety, reliability, and maintainability.
Six Sigma Black Belt (CSSBB)	Designed for the professional who can explain and apply Six Sigma philosophies and principles, including supporting systems and tools, and who has conducted successful Six Sigma projects to completion.
Six Sigma Green Belt (SSGB)	Designed for an individual who operates in support of or under the supervision of a Six Sigma Black Belt to analyze and solve quality problems through quality improvement projects.
Software Quality Engineer (CSQE)	Designed for an individual who understands software quality development and implementation, software inspection, testing, verification, and validation; and who implements software development and maintenance processes and methods.

Source: [1].

is peer recognition of competence because the certified individual has passed an examination developed by industry subject matter experts covering the most important aspects of a specific professional area.

10.2.2 Why Become Certified?

For an individual, certification can be an important step in career advancement. Certification helps to ensure that professional skills are kept current, provides credibility in a job interview, and can lead to higher pay and faster career growth. Leonard Turi, owner of TMS Consulting Services, Inc., states, "Certified candidates are requested for more interviews and placed on consulting jobs sooner and for longer duration" [2]. This is not to say that individuals without certification cannot get a job, but companies are increasingly looking for highly qualified candidates, and possession of one or more certifications can be a differentiator in a hiring decision.

For many organizations, the global business environment requires the maximum utilization of technology to remain competitive. Companies need a tool to accurately assess and choose information technology (IT) professionals who can best help an organization reach its goals and objectives. Many organizations are turning to certification as a way to help make hiring and promotion decisions. More than 125 companies have formally recognized ASQ certification as a way to ensure their workforce is proficient in the principles and practices of quality. Supporting certification also demonstrates a commitment to quality and an investment in the future of these highly skilled employees.

An International Data Corp. survey of more than 250 IT managers found definite advantages to having certified personnel. Although it is difficult to quantify the benefits of certification, most IT managers surveyed believe that certified personnel are worth higher salaries—almost $10,000 per year over noncertified personnel [3]. A recent salary survey of ASQ members shows the same correlation, with individuals holding one or more certifications reporting higher salaries than noncertified individuals in nearly all cases [4]. Certification provides a professional badge of competence and a mark of excellence.

10.2.3 What Is a Certified Software Quality Engineer (CSQE)?

The ASQ definition of a Certified Software Quality Engineer is an individual "who understands software quality development and implementation, software inspection, testing, verification, and validation; and implements software development and maintenance processes and methods" [1].

Those subject-matter experts who developed the current Body of Knowledge expect that a CSQE will be able to demonstrate understanding and expertise in the following areas [1]:

- Quality philosophies, principles, methods, tools, standards, organizational and team dynamics, interpersonal relationships, and professional ethics;
- Software quality management principles, and developing and implementing software quality programs;

- Software development and maintenance processes and methods, quantifying the fundamental problems and risks associated with implementing software development support processes, and assessing, supporting, and implementing process and technology changes;
- Project management principles and techniques as they relate to software project planning, implementation, and tracking;
- Selecting, defining, and applying software measurement, metrics, and analytical techniques, and communicating results;
- Software inspection, testing, verification, and validation;
- How and when to perform software audits;
- Configuration management processes to include planning, configuration identification, configuration control, change management, status accounting, and reporting.

10.2.4 What Qualifications Are Necessary to Become a CSQE?

The requirements for a CSQE fall into three categories:

1. *Education and experience:* The candidate for certification must have 8 years of on-the-job experience in one or more of the Body of Knowledge topics (see Section 10.5). At least 3 of those years must have been in a decision-making, technical, professional, or management position. Up to 5 years of the 8-year experience requirement will be waived if the candidate has completed a degree from a college, university, or technical school with accreditation recognized by ASQ.

2. *Proof of professionalism:* Proof of professionalism may be demonstrated by membership in ASQ or registration as a Professional Engineer.

3. *Examination:* The successful candidate must pass a 4-hour written examination. Each examination consists of 160 multiple-choice questions that cover all topics in the Certified Software Quality Engineer Body of Knowledge.

10.2.5 How Many People Have Earned Their CSQE? And Who Are They?

In the 10 years since the CSQE examination was first administered, more than 4,000 people have passed the examination. Since 1999, more than 600 people have taken the examination each year, and the pass rate has been just over 60% for nearly every administration.

CSQEs can be found in a wide range of industries that rely on software. Jobs held by certified individuals run the gamut of quality and software development positions and include such titles as software quality engineer, quality manager, test engineer, quality assurance analyst, program and project manager, software engineer, director of quality, and Six Sigma black belt, as well as president and owner.

10.2.6   Is There Value in the CSQE Certification?

In the 2006 salary survey conducted by ASQ, professionals holding the CSQE certification reported average salaries that were more than $13,000 higher than their peers without the certification [4]. In response to a Value of Certification survey conducted in 2004, certified individuals offered the following comments:

- "I am very sure that the CSQE has given me an edge in qualifying for and acquiring employment positions."
- "Both in being hired by my company and when I am presented to external clients, the CSQE has helped me to stand out amongst other candidates."
- "We are now making CSQE a requirement versus a nice to have. This is based on a few of us getting certified last year. Now my company has detailed required skills, put a core training program in place and is making the certification a requirement for managers and aligning other certifications for key quality positions."
- "In preparing for the certification exam I learned a great deal more about the process of developing software properly than I ever did in taking my college classes. Since becoming certified, my opinion has become much more respected in the various process teams I serve on within my company. They now recognize me as a process expert because of [my certification]."
- "Preparing for the CSQE exam was a very fruitful process as the exam required that I have a working knowledge in a broad range of software quality related topics. This has made me one of the most knowledgeable individuals at our company concerning software quality."
- "The 'Certified Quality Manager' designation testifies to the breadth of my knowledge and interest, and the CSQE to the depth—both together increase my credibility as quality manager in a software company."

10.3   How Is a Certification Exam Developed?

The process for establishing a new ASQ certification or updating an existing certification is a multistep process that may span several years. The chart in Figure 10.1 depicts the steps necessary for developing or updating an ASQ certification examination. This chart is followed by an explanation of each step.

10.3.1   Proposal for New Certification

Initiation of a new ASQ certification requires a sponsoring group. Usually a division or forum within ASQ is that sponsoring group.

The sponsoring group must document how the proposed certification meets each of the following seven criteria:

1. The discipline shall be in a sufficiently unique body of knowledge relative to existing certifications and aligned with ASQ policies, procedures, and strategic plan.

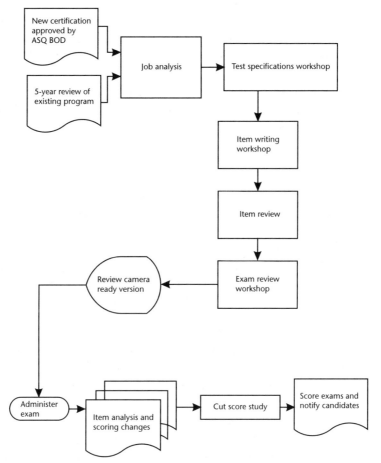

Figure 10.1 Steps in the development of an examination. (*From:* [5]. © 2006 ASQ. Reprinted with permission.)

2. All examinations will be generic without specific application to any industry, location, service, or product, unless the examination is targeted to a specific group.

3. The discipline shall have a substantial and authoritative body of knowledge in the public domain describing proven principles and practices of the technology.

4. Training in the principles and practices of the technology shall be readily available to the potential candidates

5. The area of technology shall have the commitment and active support of a sponsoring organization capable of providing adequate testing criteria for proficiency in the discipline. The sponsoring organizations can be one or more ASQ committees, divisions, or interest groups, or external sponsoring group.

6. There must be a sufficient, definable, continuing market as evidenced by a suitable market analysis and plan for certification.

7. The degree to which the body of knowledge of the proposed new certification overlaps with current certifications, and the effect the proposed new certification might have on the value of current certifications.

The ASQ Certification Board may give tentative approval for the division or forum to proceed with the next step, or they may request additional information before approval is given.

10.3.2   Job Analysis

The Job Analysis defines the major tasks that a certified individual would be expected to be able to perform and the associated knowledge and skill set. Conducting the initial Job Analysis is the responsibility of the division or forum proposing the new certification.

Several different committees and groups meet to complete the Job Analysis, which is developed as a survey and is used to identify the skills and knowledge areas currently being used in the subject to be tested. The committees include:

- *Job Analysis Advisory Committee:* This committee consists of 10 to 12 experienced practitioners in the discipline of the certification; the committee meets for 2 days to review and revise a draft of the Job Analysis Survey. In the final survey, respondents are asked to rate each item in terms of criticality (How important is this task or knowledge?) and frequency (How often is this task performed or the knowledge used?).
- *Survey Group:* The survey is sent to a randomly selected group of 1,000 to 2,000 practitioners in the discipline of the new certification. These practitioners include members of the ASQ division or forum, attendees at related conferences, or members of other related professional societies. Their responsibility is to provide professional opinion on the level of importance of each item as a necessary part of the certification discipline.

The responses received from the surveys are summarized in a report that indicates whether each item in the questionnaire should be included in the Body of Knowledge for the certification, should be excluded from the Body of Knowledge, or is marginal. Members of the Job Analysis Advisory Committee and the Executive Committee of the division or forum review these results and make a recommendation for inclusion or exclusion of each item in the certification Body of Knowledge.

A final report describing the Job Analysis process, the method of data analysis, and a summary of the results including inclusion/exclusion recommendations for the Body of Knowledge is presented to the ASQ Certification Board. The board reviews this report and then determines the final content of the Body of Knowledge. It should be noted that while the sponsoring division and Certification Board *approve* the results of the Job Analysis activity, it is really the ASQ members who answer the survey who truly determine what should be in the Body of Knowledge and, by extension, what material will be covered in the exam itself.

10.3.3 Certification Approval

Upon completion of the Job Analysis, the division or forum updates their proposal on how the certification meets the seven criteria for a new certification, and the proposal is taken through a series of approval meetings. Once final approval is given, the certification becomes an official ASQ Certification, and ASQ's Certification Department assumes future responsibility for the certification.

10.3.4 Creating the Examination

Creating the Examination involves several steps. Participants in the committees for these steps are volunteers from the ASQ membership; all are experienced practitioners in the subject matter and practices of the examination under development.

Test Specification.   This committee consists of 10 to 12 participants. This group takes the results of the Job Analysis and creates the Body of Knowledge for the certification. They also define the framework for administering the examination. This includes specifying the number of questions that will be included in the examination, the distribution of these questions over the Body of Knowledge, and the format of the examination (e.g., multiple-choice questions, short-answer questions, or a combination). The completed Test Specification is used for all examinations that occur until the Job Analysis is updated and a revised Body of Knowledge is developed.

Item Writing.   This committee involves 16 individuals who are responsible for writing the actual examination questions. Each question must test a specific area of the Body of Knowledge and have not only a correct answer (key) but also three viable incorrect answers (distracters) that someone without the specific knowledge could possibly select as a correct answer. For each question, a written justification must explain why the key is the correct answer as well as why the distracters are incorrect. In addition, specific references in relevant literature must be cited to show that this information is publicly available in the literature to a person taking the examination.

   The volunteers who attend this meeting must have diverse skills in order to provide coverage for each of the areas in the Body of Knowledge. During the meeting, the large committee is divided up into smaller groups, each concentrating on a specific area of the Body of Knowledge. It is not unusual for a question to take several hours to write, review with other experts in the group, rewrite, and obtain sign-off by each person in the small group. For a new exam, Item Writing sessions are typically held annually to ensure that there are enough questions to create different versions of the examination and to ensure that the questions in the database are kept current. For more mature exams, Item Writing Committee sessions may be scheduled only occasionally.

Item Review.   This committee consists of 12 participants. This group reviews each new or revised examination question for wording, accuracy, and validity. Approved questions are added to the pool of available examination questions. Unapproved items may be discarded or flagged to be returned to the next Item Writing Committee for rework. Item Review meetings are held after each Item Writing session.

Examination Review.   Prior to the administration of each examination, the ASQ test developer for the exam selects questions for the examination. The mix of questions on the exam is based on the distribution of questions over the Body of Knowledge, as defined in the Test Specification. After the examination is selected, an Examination Review committee is convened. This committee consists of 10 to 12 people who review the examination's accuracy, consistency, and validity. Each member of the committee must take the exam and answer each question and note any concerns and comments. In the committee meeting, committee members go through the examination question by question. The group can change the wording of the question, change the wording of the answers, or replace the question with another one from the pool that tests the same area of knowledge. Once the contents of the examination are approved, a few members of the committee review the exam when it has been prepared for printing, to ensure that the appearance of the final exam is correct.

It should be noted that this preparation process ensures that each item included on the final examination has been reviewed by dozens of qualified professionals prior to its being used.

10.3.5 Cut Score Study

Following the first administration of a new or revised examination, a Cut Score Study committee is convened. This committee consists of 10 to 12 professionals who meet to recommend a written standard of minimum competency for the certification based on the Body of Knowledge and a recommended minimum passing score for the examination.

10.3.6 Examination Administration

Typically, certification examinations are administered twice a year. The ASQ certification staff members are responsible for the administration of the examination. They screen potential candidates based on the certification requirements. Local ASQ Sections provide sites and proctors for the examination.

Determine Passing Score.   Completed examinations are sent to ASQ, where they are scored. The certification staff runs statistical validation checks on each examination question. Statistically questionable items are reviewed. Just as great care is taken in developing an exam, ASQ goes to great lengths to ensure that the grading process provides an accurate assessment of a candidate's proficiency. ASQ uses procedures that meet the *Standards for Educational and Psychological Testing*, which were developed jointly by the American Educational Research Association, the American Psychological Association, and the National Council on Measurement in Education [6]. Based on the established passing score, individuals who passed the examination are awarded certification. Individuals who do not meet the minimum passing score are given a report that indicates areas of the examination where they did well and areas where they need improvement.

10.3.7   Sustaining the Examination

The ASQ Certified Software Quality Engineer reference list (see Section 10.6) is updated occasionally to reflect new publications that provide information about topics in the Body of Knowledge.

   The Job Analysis process is repeated approximately every 5 years to ensure that the certification continues to reflect the state of the practice in the discipline. As a result, the content of the Body of Knowledge could change.

   The next update to the CSQE Body of Knowledge was scheduled to be completed in 2007–2008. Information on the updates to the Body of Knowledge and any changes to the format of the exam was scheduled to be available on the ASQ Certification Web site (http://www.asq.org/certification/) in 2008.

10.4   How Should You Prepare for the Exam?

Preparing to take an exam is highly dependent on an individual's learning style. For some people, carefully reading reference texts is very helpful, while others may find value in reviewing study guides, taking an ASQ section refresher course, or forming a study group with other quality professionals. All certification candidates must be responsible for their own preparation for the examination.

   Successful candidates have stated that they study a wide variety of materials from the reference list, in addition to relying on their experiences in the workplace. It is important to understand that the CSQE Body of Knowledge is very comprehensive and that *no single source of information* should be relied upon in order to prepare for the examination [6].

   To identify focus areas for your studies, the best approach to prepare for the examination is to review the Body of Knowledge. Then review the reference list and identify key references that should be used for study in those focus areas. Begin preparation well in advance of the exam date; waiting until the last minute will only bring on frustration and confusion. As the examination date gets closer, make sure your reference materials are organized so you can locate information quickly. No single reference should be relied on as a sole resource for the exam.

   Refresher courses may also be available to help you prepare for the examination. These courses are neither sponsored nor endorsed by ASQ. Attending a refresher course does not ensure that you will pass the examination. Also, be aware that a refresher course may not cover the exact topics on the examination. Anyone offering a refresher course cannot participate in the question writing or in the examination review, so they do not have any "inside" information as to the specific content. The majority of each examination is new, so past questions do not reflect future questions on any given version of the examination. Refresher courses may be helpful to motivate early study and review, but be aware that they do not replace individual preparation.

Historically, there are no areas of the Body of Knowledge that all or most certification candidates have found to be most difficult. Individuals need to determine which areas are weak points for them and spend their study time reviewing material that will help them in those areas.

10.4.1 Apply for the Examination Early

The Certification Exam Application, available on the ASQ Web site (http://www.asq.org) must be submitted approximately 2 months before the date of the examination. Current fees for taking the exam are: $210 for ASQ members, and $360 for nonmembers.

10.4.2 What Reference Materials Can Be Used During the Exam?

The CSQE examination is open book, and your personal notes from preparation and materials from refresher courses are allowed. However, materials containing sample questions and answers are not allowed. Any reference materials taken into the examination room must be made available to the proctor for review. Reference materials *cannot* replace having an understanding of the material. The average time to answer each question is 1.5 minutes (4 hours for 160 questions); therefore, there will not be time to dig through reference material for many answers.

Calculators may be used during the examination, but laptop computers are not allowed.

10.4.3 In What Languages Is the Exam Offered?

Historically, ASQ certification exams have been offered in English only, worldwide. Recently, however, the Certification department has begun translating some of the exams into other languages for examination in those countries where that language is the primary language. The translations of particular exams are developed when they are requested by ASQ's global partners. International candidates who are interested in updated information on the availability of examinations in languages other than English should contact the Certification department directly.

10.5 What Is in the Body of Knowledge?

The following is a high-level outline of the topics that constitute the current Body of Knowledge for Software Quality Engineering [7]. Note: the number in parentheses following the title of each major topic (see I–VII) represents the number of questions for that section for the exam. This Body of Knowledge contains subtext under each topic to provide additional information about the topic. The descriptor in parentheses following the subtext indicates the highest cognitive level at which questions will be written for that topic area. An explanation of the cognitive levels, which are based on Bloom's taxonomy (1956), follows the Body of Knowledge.

I. GENERAL, KNOWLEDGE, CONDUCT, and ETHICS (16 Questions)

A. Quality philosophy and principles

1. Benefits of software quality
   Describe how software quality engineering can benefit an organization. (Comprehension)

2. Prevention vs. detection
   Describe how quality engineering methodologies can reduce the length of time for testing and can influence other defect detection methods. (Comprehension)

3. Organizational and process benchmarking
   Identify, analyze, and model best practices at the macro (organizational) and micro (process and project) levels. Identify and develop business objectives, use metrics to monitor their achievement, and provide feedback to close the process improvement loop. (Analysis)

B. Standards, specifications, and models
   Identify and use software process and assessment models, including ISO 9001, ISO 15504, IEEE software standards, IEEE/EIA 12207, SEI Capability Maturity Model Integration® (CMMI®), etc., in a variety of situations. (Application)

C. Leadership tools and skills

1. Organizational leadership
   Define, describe, and apply leadership tools and techniques, including analyzing current situations, proposing, justifying, implementing, and managing change (using change-agent tools), developing and implementing quality initiatives, obtaining cross-functional commitment and collaboration, ensuring knowledge transfer, motivating personnel, etc. (Application)

2. Team management
   Define and use various team management techniques, including identifying and assigning roles and responsibilities (e.g., champion, sponsor, facilitator, leader, coach), identifying and assessing team member skills, interpreting team dynamics and stages of team development, handling dominant or disruptive team members, recognizing how diversity in teams strengthens the creative process, etc. (Application)

3. Team tools
   Define, describe, and use tools such as brainstorming, nominal group technique (NGT), joint application development (JAD), rapid application development (RAD), etc. (Application)

4. Facilitation skills
   Use various tools to manage and resolve conflict. Use negotiation techniques to produce win-win outcomes. Identify and use time and meeting management tools to maximize performance. (Application)

5. Communication skills
Define, describe, and apply various communication elements used in verbal, written, and presentation formats, including interviewing and listening skills. Apply communication elements to create effective process and procedural documents, including identifying roles and responsibilities. (Application)

D. Ethical conduct and professional development

1. ASQ Code of Ethics
Determine appropriate behavior in situations requiring ethical decisions, including identifying conflicts of interest and recognizing/resolving ethical issues related to software licensing and use. (Evaluation)
2. Software liability and safety issues
Identify legal issues related to software product liability and safety, including negligence, customer notification requirements, and other legal or regulatory issues. (Application)
[NOTE: Other aspects of product safety and hazard analysis are covered in IV.C.4.]
3. Professional training and development
Define, describe, and apply training needs analysis methods for software quality professionals, and manage training resources and materials. (Application)

II. SOFTWARE QUALITY MANAGEMENT (30 Questions)

A. Goals and objectives

1. Quality goals and objectives
Describe, analyze, and evaluate quality goals and objectives for programs, projects, and products. (Evaluation)
2. Outsourced services
Define, analyze, and evaluate the impact of acquisitions, subcontractor services, and other external resources on the organization's goals and objectives. (Evaluation)
3. Planning
Identify, apply, and evaluate scheduling and resource requirements necessary to achieve quality goals and objectives. (Evaluation)
4. Software quality management (SQM) systems documentation
Identify and describe various elements related to SQM system documentation. (Comprehension)
5. Customer requirements
Analyze and evaluate customer requirements and their effect on programs, projects, and products. (Evaluation)
[NOTE: Changes in requirements are covered in III.B.3. The focus in this section is to ensure that customer requirements are evaluated properly.]

B. Methodologies

1. Review, inspection, and testing
   Define, describe, evaluate, and differentiate between these defect detection methods. (Evaluation)

2. Change management methods
   Identify and apply various methods appropriate for responding to changes in technology, organizations, environment, human performance, etc. (Evaluation)
   [NOTE: Change-agent tools are covered in I.C.1.]

3. Cost of quality (COQ)
   Define, differentiate, and analyze COQ categories (prevention, appraisal, internal failure, external failure) and their impact on products and processes. (Analysis)
   [NOTE: Interpreting and reporting COQ data are covered in IV.B.2.]

4. Quality data tracking
   Define, describe, select, and implement information systems and models used to track quality data in various situations. (Evaluation)

5. Problem reporting and corrective action procedures
   Define, describe, analyze, and distinguish between these procedures for software defects, process nonconformances, and other quality system deficiencies. (Evaluation)

6. Quality improvement processes
   Define, describe, analyze and distinguish between various defect prevention, detection, and removal processes, and evaluate process improvement opportunities in relation to these tools. (Evaluation)

C. Audits

1. Program development and administration
   Identify roles and responsibilities for various audit participants, including team leader, team members, auditee, auditor, etc. (Comprehension)

2. Audit preparation and execution
   Define and distinguish between various audit types, including process, compliance, supplier, system, etc. Define and describe various steps in the audit process, from scheduling the audit through the closing meeting and subsequent follow-up activities. Define and identify various tools and procedures used in conducting audits. (Comprehension)

3. Audit reporting and follow up
   Identify, describe, and apply the steps of audit reporting and follow up, including the need for and verification of corrective action. (Application)

III. SOFTWARE ENGINEERING PROCESSES (26 Questions)

A. Environmental conditions

1. Life cycles
   Compare and evaluate the characteristics of spiral, waterfall, incremental,

rapid prototyping, V-model, etc. Differentiate these life cycles, describe what they are designed to do, what their benefits are, and in what situations they should be used. (Evaluation)

2. Systems architecture
   Identify, describe, evaluate, and distinguish between system architectures, including client server, n tier, B to B, B to C, and B to E, web (internet/intranet/extranet) and wireless development, messaging and collaboration software, etc. (Analysis)

B. Requirements management

1. Requirements prioritization and evaluation
   Describe, assess, prioritize, and evaluate the requirements for verifying software correctness, consistency, completeness, and testability. Determine what should be covered in a requirements statement, how to specify a requirement, etc. (Evaluation)

2. Requirements change management
   Define, describe, and evaluate various elements of managing requirements change, including what processes should be followed, when requirements need to change, what review processes to use, etc. Define the effect of changing requirements at various stages of the project life cycle. (Evaluation)

3. Bi-directional requirements traceability
   Describe, select, and evaluate various traceability elements, including requirements to design, design to code, and requirements to test. Describe and apply traceability tools and mechanisms, such as system verification diagrams, traceability matrices, etc. (Evaluation)
   [NOTE: Traceability of configuration items is covered in VII.C.5.]

C. Requirements engineering

1. Requirement types
   Define, describe, and analyze various requirement types such as security, regulatory, quality, feature and product functionality, etc., and the significant elements of each. (Analysis)

2. Requirements elicitation
   Define and describe various elicitation methods, including using tools such as quality function deployment (QFD), joint application development (JAD), customer needs analysis, etc. Describe the key steps necessary for gathering product requirement details, and identify common causes of failure to comply with requirements. (Comprehension)

3. Requirements analysis and modeling
   Describe, select, and analyze tools such as data flow diagrams (DFDs), entity relationship diagrams (ERDs), use cases, etc. Describe how they are used at different phases of development and requirements specifications. (Analysis)

4. System and software requirements specifications
   Define and distinguish between these two types of specifications and their purpose, and describe their relationship to each other. (Analysis)

D. Analysis, design, and development methods and tools

1. Software design methods
   Define and use various design methods, including object-oriented analysis and design (OOAD), structured analysis and design (SAD), unified modeling language (UML), etc. Identify the steps used in program design and explain their uses. (Application)
2. Types of software reuse
   Define, describe, and differentiate the use of various reuse methods including reengineering, reverse engineering, plug-and-play, etc., and describe the design paradigms that address these concepts. (Application)
3. Clean room and other formal methods
   Define and describe these methods and their benefits. (Comprehension)
4. Software development tools
   Identify, describe, use, and distinguish between various tools used for modeling, code analysis, documentation, relational databases, etc. (Application)

E. Maintenance management

1. Maintenance types
   Describe the characteristics of corrective, adaptive, and perfective maintenance types and their benefits and risks. (Comprehension)
2. Operational maintenance
   Describe the various categories of and activities involved in providing operational services to the customer, managing application portfolios, and providing basic software maintenance. (Comprehension)

IV. PROGRAM AND PROJECT MANAGEMENT (24 Questions)

A. Planning

1. Project planning elements
   Describe and use factors such as forecasts, resources, schedules, etc., to develop, initiate, and accomplish project goals. (Application)
2. Goal-setting and deployment
   Identify and use milestones, objectives achieved, task duration, and other goal-setting and deployment methods. (Application)
3. Project planning tools
   Define, apply, and analyze various methods of managing risk, estimating costs, scheduling resources, etc., using tools such as PERT charts, critical path method (CPM), work breakdown structure (WBS), etc. (Analysis) [NOTE: Gantt charts are covered in IV.B.1.]
4. Cost and value data
   Identify and use various methods for calculating project-related data such as earned value, development investment costs, etc. (Application)

B. Tracking and controlling

1. Phase transition control techniques
Develop and use various control techniques for tracking projects, including entry/exit criteria, phase gate reviews, Gantt charts, etc. (Analysis)

2. Interpreting and reporting cost of quality (COQ) data
Review, interpret, and report COQ data and evaluate how each category is affected by continuous improvement strategies. (Evaluation)
[NOTE: The definitions and distinctions between these categories are covered in II.B.3.]

3. Tracking elements and methods
Describe, assess, and apply different tracking methods, including establishing metrics for costs, deliverables, productivity, etc., creating and evaluating status reports and life-cycle phase reports, measuring changes in earned value, evaluating changes in business conditions, etc. (Evaluation)
[NOTE: Calculating earned value is covered in IV. A. 4.]

4. Project reviews
Define, use, and differentiate various types of reviews, including post-project, senior management, team, etc., and use closed-loop methodologies to improve projects as a result of lessons learned. (Analysis)

C. Risk management

1. Risk management planning methods
Define, integrate, and analyze various risk management methods, including assessing, preventing, and mitigating risk with respect to critical aspects of a project and its supporting strategies. (Synthesis)

2. Risk probability
Describe and evaluate various risk warning signs, assess risk probability and impact, and develop contingency plans. (Evaluation)

3. Product release decisions
Identify situations and factors that require trade-offs on product release decisions. Develop and analyze various ways of bringing a project back on track when problems occur that affect quality, scheduling, customer requirements, product functionality, etc. (Evaluation)

4. Software security, safety, and hazard analysis issues
Identify, review, and evaluate various factors related to software security, safety-critical software, and hazard analyses. Identify and describe rationales for developing safety plans and for implementing hazard analyses. (Analysis)
[NOTE: The legal aspects of product safety are covered in I.D.2.]

V. SOFTWARE METRICS, MEASUREMENT, AND ANALYTICAL METHODS (24 Questions)

A. Metrics and measurement theory

1. Definitions
Define, describe, and explain various terms related to metrics and

measurement, including error, reliability, internal vs. external validity, explicit vs. derived measures, etc. (Comprehension)

2. Basic measurement theory and techniques
Define, describe, and use basic measurement scales (nominal, ordinal, ratio, interval), the central limit theorem and related terms, including mean, median, mode, standard deviation, variance, etc. (Application)

3. Psychology of metrics
Define and describe various uses of metrics. Compare and contrast how metrics affect people and how people affect metrics. (Comprehension)

B. Process and product measurement

1. Process, product, and resource metrics
Describe and use various metrics to assess processes, products, and resources. (Application)

2. Commonly used metrics
Define and use metrics to measure various aspects of software, including software complexity, lines of code (LOC), non-commented lines of code (NCLOC), design defects, requirements volatility, system performance, etc. (Application)
[NOTE: Code coverage metrics are covered in VI.D.4.]

3. Software quality attributes
Identify and describe various criteria for measuring attributes such as maintainability, verifiability, reliability, usability, reusability, testability, expandability, etc. (Comprehension)

4. Defect detection effectiveness measures
Define, describe, and use defect detection measures such as cost, yield, customer impact, etc., and track their effectiveness. (Application)

5. Program performance and process effectiveness
Identify and use various methods of examining performance and effectiveness. (Analysis)

C. Analytical techniques

1. Data integrity
Define, use, and interpret various techniques to ensure the quality of metrics data, its accuracy, completeness, timeliness, etc. (Synthesis)

2. Quality tools
Define, select, and use quality analysis and problem-solving tools such as flow charts, Pareto charts, cause and effect diagrams, check sheets, scatter diagrams, control (run) charts, histograms, root cause analysis, affinity diagrams, tree diagrams, process decision program charts (PDPCs), matrix diagrams, interrelationship digraphs, prioritization matrices, activity network diagrams. (Analysis)

3. Sampling theory and techniques
Describe, differentiate, and analyze various sampling techniques for use in auditing, testing, product acceptance, etc. (Analysis)

VI. SOFTWARE VERIFICATION AND VALIDATION (V&V) (24 Questions)

A. Theory

1. V&V planning procedures and tasks
   Identify and select various methods for verification and validation, including static analysis, structural analysis, mathematical proof, simulation, etc. Identify and analyze which tasks should be iterated as a result of proposed or completed modifications. (Synthesis)

2. V&V program
   Describe and analyze methods for managing and reviewing a V&V program, including technical accomplishments, resource utilization, program status, etc. (Analysis)

3. Evaluating software products and processes
   Analyze and select various ways of evaluating documentation, source code, test and audit results, etc., to determine whether user needs and project objectives have been satisfied. (Synthesis)

4. Interfaces
   Identify various interfaces used with hardware, user, operator, and software applications. (Comprehension)

B. Reviews and inspections

1. Types
   Define, describe, and use various types of reviews and inspections, including desk-checking, walk-throughs, Fagan and Gilb inspections, technical accomplishments, resource utilization, future planning, etc. (Application)

2. Items
   Identify, describe, and use various review and inspection items, including proposals, project charters, specifications, code, tests, etc. (Application)

3. Processes
   Define, describe, and use various review and inspection processes to examine objectives, criteria, techniques, methods, etc. (Application)

4. Data collection, reports, and summaries
   Define, describe, and use terms related to data collection, including preparation rates, defect density yield, phase containment, etc. (Application)

C. Test planning and design

1. Types of tests [6B1]
   Select, apply, and develop various types of test, including functional, performance, regression, certification, environmental load, stress, worst case, perfective, exploratory, etc. (Synthesis)

2. Test tools
   Define and describe the application and capabilities of commonly used test tools such as acceptance test suites, utilities (for memory, screen capture, string-finding, file viewer, file comparison, etc.), and diagnostics (for hardware, software, configuration, etc.). (Comprehension)

3. Test strategies
    Identify, analyze, and apply various test strategies, including top-down, bottom-up, black-box, white-box, simulation, automation, etc. (Synthesis)

4. Test design
    Identify, describe, and apply various types of test design including fault insertion, fault-error handling, equivalence class partitioning, boundary value, etc. (Application)

5. Test coverage of specifications
    Identify, apply, and develop various test coverage specifications, including functions, states, data and time domains, etc. (Synthesis)

6. Test environments
    Identify various environments and use tools such as test libraries, drivers, stubs, harnesses, etc., in those environments, and describe how simulations can be used in test environments. (Synthesis)

7. Supplier components and products
    Identify the common risks and benefits of incorporating purchased software into other software products. Use various methods to test supplier components and products in the larger system. (Application)

8. Test plans
    Identify, describe, and apply methods for creating and evaluating test plans including system, acceptance, validation, etc., to determine whether project objectives are being met. (Application)

D. Test execution and evaluation

1. Test implementation
    Define, describe, and use various implementation elements, including scheduling, freezing, dependencies, V-model, error repair models, acceptance testing, etc. (Application)

2. Test documentation
    Define, describe, and use various documentation procedures, including defect recording and tracking, test report completion metrics, trouble reports, input/output specifications, etc. (Application)

3. Test Reviews
    Describe, develop, and analyze various methods of reviewing test efforts, including technical accomplishments, future planning, risk management, etc. (Synthesis)

4. Code coverage metrics
    Define and apply various metrics including branch-to-branch, condition, domain, McCabe's cyclomatic complexity, boundary, etc. (Application)
    [NOTE: Other types of metrics are covered in V.B.2.]

5. Customer deliverables
    Identify and select various methods for testing the accuracy of customer deliverables, including packaged or downloaded products, license keys, user documentation, marketing and training materials, etc. (Synthesis)

6. Severity of anomalies
   Identify and select various methods for evaluating severity of anomalies in software operations. (Evaluation)

VII. SOFTWARE CONFIGURATION MANAGEMENT (16 Questions)

A. Configuration infrastructure

1. Configuration management
   Describe the roles and responsibilities of the configuration management group. (Comprehension)
2. Library/repository processes
   Define and identify processes used in a library system including dynamic, static, controlled, etc., and their related procedures. (Comprehension)
3. Defect tracking and library tools
   Define and describe configuration management tools used for defect tracking, library management tools, etc. (Comprehension)

B. Configuration identification

1. Configuration items
   Define, select, and use various items, including documentation, code interfaces, training materials, customer-supplied equipment, etc. (Application)
2. Baselines
   Define and identify when configuration baselines are created and used. (Comprehension)
3. Configuration identification methods
   Define and describe how these methods relate to schemes, naming conventions, versions, serializations, etc. (Comprehension)
4. Software builds
   Define and describe the primary purpose of software builds and their relation to configuration management functions. Describe and use various methods for controlling builds, including automation, new-version builds, etc. (Synthesis)

C. Configuration control

1. Item and baseline control
   Define, describe, and apply various control processes, including version control, traceability requirements, specifications, concurrent development, verifying milestones, etc. (Application)
2. Proposed modifications
   Describe how to assess proposed modifications, enhancements, or additions in terms of their impact on an existing or planned system. (Comprehension)
3. Review and configuration control boards (CCBs)
   Define, describe, and differentiate the roles and responsibilities of and procedures used by these boards. (Application)

4. Concurrent development
   Describe how configuration management control principles can be used in concurrent development processes. (Application)

5. Traceability
   Identify and apply various tools and methods for establishing and maintaining traceability design, including backward and forward traceability, naming conventions, etc., and explain how they are related to configuration management objectives. (Application)
   [NOTE: Traceability through product development is covered in III.B.3. The focus for this area is on traceability and evolution of configuration items in code archives and other configuration management elements.]

6. Version control
   Define, describe, and use version control methods such as source code version management and others, and how such methods can be used effectively by both small and large development teams. (Application)

7. Configuration item interfaces
   Define, describe, and apply management control processes for configuration item interfaces. (Application)

D. Configuration status accounting

1. Status reporting
   Describe various processes for establishing, maintaining, and reporting the status of configuration items. (Comprehension)

2. Changes to configuration items and baselines
   Describe the processes that should be used when changes are proposed to configuration items and baselines. (Comprehension)

3. Documentation control
   Define and describe related procedures for document distribution, approval, storage, retrieval, revision, etc. (Comprehension)

E. Configuration audits

1. Functional configuration audit
   Describe the primary purpose of these types of audits in relation to product specifications and in contrast to physical configuration audits. (Comprehension)

2. Physical configuration audit
   Describe the primary purpose of these types of audits in relation to product specifications and in contrast to functional configuration audits. (Comprehension)

F. Release and distribution issues

1. Product release process issues
   Identify and describe product release issues such as planning, scheduling, hardware and software dependencies, etc. (Comprehension)

2. Packaging, production, and distribution
   Define and describe these components in relation to product release
   requirements and related issues. (Knowledge)

10.5.1   Six Levels of Cognition Based on Bloom's Taxonomy (1956)

The cognition levels used in the CSQE Body of Knowledge are based on "Levels of Cognition" (from *Bloom's Taxonomy,* 1956) and are presented in rank order, from least complex to most complex:

- *Knowledge Level:* (Also commonly referred to as recognition, recall, or rote knowledge.) Being able to remember or recognize terminology, definitions, facts, ideas, materials, patterns, sequences, methodologies, principles, and so on.
- *Comprehension Level:* Being able to read and understand descriptions, communications, reports, tables, diagrams, directions, regulations, and so on.
- *Application Level:* Being able to apply ideas, procedures, methods, formulas, principles, theories, and so on, in job-related situations.
- *Analysis:* Being able to break down information into its constituent parts and recognize the parts' relationship to one another and how they are organized; and identify sublevel factors or salient data from a complex scenario.
- *Synthesis:* Being able to put parts or elements together in such a way as to show a pattern or structure not clearly there before; and identify which data or information from a complex set is appropriate to examine further or from which supported conclusions can be drawn.
- *Evaluation:* Being able to make judgments regarding the value of proposed ideas, solutions, methodologies, and so on, by using appropriate criteria or standards to estimate accuracy, effectiveness, and economic benefits.

10.5.2   Sample Questions

The following examples are intended to provide a general overview of question types that appear on the CSQE certification examination. These questions are examples only; they are not included in the CSQE database and will not appear on any examination.

1. Which of the following reviews are required in order to ensure proper tracking of software between phases of a project?
   I. Product feasibility
   II. Software requirements
   III. Software design
   IV. Acceptance test
   a. I and II only
   b. II and III only
   c. I, II, and III only
   d. II, III, and IV only

Answer: d

2. What happens to the relative cost of fixing software errors from the requirements phase through the test phase?
    a. It decreases linearly.
    b. It remains fairly constant.
    c. It increases linearly.
    d. It increases exponentially.

Answer: d

3. When an audit team concludes that a finding demonstrates a breakdown of the quality management system, the finding should be documented as
    a. a minor nonconformance
    b. a major nonconformance
    c. a deficiency
    d. an observation

Answer: b

4. According to Crosby, it is less costly to
    a. let the customer find the defects
    b. detect defects than to prevent them
    c. prevent defects than to detect them
    d. ignore minor defects

Answer: c

5. Which of the following is LEAST likely to be used during software maintenance?
    a. Software project management plan
    b. Customer support hot line
    c. Software problem reports
    d. Change control board

Answer: a

6. An effective software development environment consists of tools that
    a. are freestanding and free from access by other tools
    b. have different user interfaces for each tool depending on the development phase supported by each tool
    c. allow maximum flexibility while maintaining security and traceability
    d. are integrated, linked to other tools, and have common user interfaces

Answer: d

7. A software firm has just signed a contract to deliver an inventory tracking/online transaction system for use by 500 entry clerks. The client has demanded a schedule of rigorous checkpoints but the requirements for the project are poorly defined. Which of the following would be most suitable as a development model?
    a. Spiral
    b. Top-Down

     c. Rapid Prototyping

     d. Waterfall

Answer: c

8. Which of the following is NOT an accepted code inspection technique?

     a. Domain analysis

     b. Item-by-item paraphrasing

     c. Mental code execution

     d. Consistency analysis

Answer: a

9. The defect density for a computer program is best defined as the

     a. ratio of failure reports received per unit of time

     b. ratio of discovered errors per size of code

     c. number of modifications made per size of code

     d. number of failures reported against the code

Answer: b

10. When a company evaluates its own performance, it is conducting what type of audit?

     a. First-party

     b. Second-party

     c. Third-party

     d. Extrinsic

Answer: a

11. The primary task of the Change Control Board (CCB) is to

     a. define change procedures

     b. approve and/or disapprove changes to software products

     c. evaluate cost and schedule impact of changes

     d. authorize personnel to implement change

Answer: b

12. A module includes a control flow loop that can be executed 0 or more times. The test most likely to reveal loop initialization defects executes the loop body

     a. 0 times

     b. 1 time

     c. 2 times

     d. 3 times

Answer: b

10.6 Recertification

For many certifications, including the CSQE, ASQ has a maintenance of certification program that requires recertification every 3 years, beginning from the date you were originally certified. It is necessary to accumulate 18 recertification units during the 3-year period. Recertification units are earned by participating in activities relevant to the field in which you are certified that maintain or increase your expertise. These activities include professional employment, continuing education, attending conferences and workshops, teaching, or publishing articles or papers.

ASQ provides a recertification journal that explains the types of activities and how recertification credit is earned for these activities. The journal also provides examples of the documentation necessary to claim recertification credit for your activities. Recertifying is much more easily accomplished if you collect the needed documentation throughout the recertification period. If you are unable to accumulate 18 recertification units, it will be necessary to pass the examination again in order to be a Certified Software Quality Engineer.

If you are retired from your profession, you may want to retire your certification as well. Retiring your certification means that you no longer have to recertify every 3 years, and your certification will remain in good standing. If your employment situation changes and you need to return to work, you can reactivate your certification. When your certification is reinstated, your recertification period begins again, and you have a 3-year period to accumulate 18 recertification units.

Since the Body of Knowledge and bibliography for Software Quality Engineering change over time, always contact ASQ for the latest information. The ASQ certification Web site (http://www.asq.org/certification/index.html) is regularly updated and provides current information.

For questions about the ASQ Certification program, check the Web site or call the Certification Department at ASQ headquarters, 800-248-1946 (United States, Canada, and Mexico) or 414-272-8575.

Acknowledgments

Special thanks to Mary Rehm, Senior Test Developer, ASQ Certification department, for contributing certification exam development information contained in this chapter.

References

[1]   ASQ Web site, http://www.asq.org.

[2]   Kleiman, C., "'Certified' Is the Magic Word in Qualifying Computer Specialists," *Chicago Tribune*, February 9, 1997.

[3]   King, J., "Are There Big Benefits in Certification?" *Info Canada*, June 1996.

[4]   Bemowski, K., "More Than 10,000 Reasons to Review QP's 2006 Salary Survey Results," *Quality Progress*, December 2006, pp. 40–48.

[5]   ASQ Certification Department, *Steps in Test Development*.

[6]   ASQ Certification Department, *Score Report Handbook*.

[7]   ASQ Certified Software Quality Engineer Certification brochure, Item B0110.

Selected Bibliography

ANSI/ISO/ASQ Q9001-2000: *Quality Management Systems: Requirements.*

ANSI/ISO/IEETICKIT Guidelines.

Arter, D., *Quality Audits for Improved Performance*, 3rd ed., Milwaukee, WI: ASQC Quality Press, 2003.

Beizer, B., *Black-Box Testing: Techniques for Functional Testing of Software and Systems*, New York: John Wiley & Sons, 1995.

Booch, G., J. Rumbaugh, and I. Jacobson, *The Unified Modeling Language User Guide*, Reading, MA: Addison-Wesley, 1999.

Booch, G., *Objected-Oriented Analysis and Design with Applications*, 2nd ed., Reading, MA: Addison-Wesley, 1994.

Brassard, M., and D. Ritter, *The Memory Jogger II: A Pocket Guide of Tools for Continuous Improvement and Effective Planning*, Goal/QPC, 1994.

Brooks, F. P., Jr., *The Mythical Man-Month: Essays on Software Engineering, Anniversary Edition*, Reading, MA: Addison-Wesley, 1995.

Capability Maturity Model Integration® (CMMI®), Version 1.1. CMMI® for Systems Engineering, *Software Engineering, Integrated Product and Process Development, and Supplier Sourcing*, March 2002.

Daughtrey, T., *Fundamental Concepts for the Software Quality Engineer*, Milwaukee, WI: ASQ Quality Press, 2002.

Dunn, R. H., and R. S. Ullman, *TQM for Computer Software (System Design and Implementation)*, 2nd ed., New York: McGraw-Hill, 1994.

Fewster, M., and D. Graham, *Software Test Automation: Effective Use of Test Execution Tools*, Reading, MA: Addison-Wesley, 1999.

Freedman, D., and G. M Weinberg, *Handbook of Walkthroughs, Inspections, and Technical Reviews: Evaluating Programs, Projects, and Products*, Third Edition, New York: Dorset House, 1990.

Futrell, R. T., D. F. Shafer, and L. I. Shafer, *Quality Software Project Management*, Upper Saddle River, NJ: Prentice-Hall, 2002.

Gilb, T., and D. Graham, *Software Inspection*, Reading, MA: Addison-Wesley, 1993.

Grady, R. B, *Practical Software Metrics for Project Management and Process Improvement*, Englewood Cliffs, NJ: Prentice-Hall, 1992.

Gryna, F. M., *Quality Planning and Analysis: From Product Development through Use*, Fourth Edition, New York: McGraw-Hill, 2001.

Hetzel, B., *Complete Guide to Software Testing*, 2nd ed., Wellesley, MA: QED Information Sciences, 1988.

Hetzel, B., *Making Software Measurement Work*, Boston, MA: QED Publishing Group, 1993.

Humphrey, W., *A Discipline for Software Engineering*, Reading, MA: Addison-Wesley, 1995.

Humphrey, W., *Managing the Software Process*, Reading, MA: Addison-Wesley, 1989.

IEEE Standard 12207.0-1996: *IEEE Standard for Industry Implementation of ISO/IEC 12207:1995.*

ISO/IEC TR 15504-1998: Parts 1-9 *Information Technology—Software Process Assessment.*

Juran, J. M., *Juran's Quality Handbook*, 5th ed., New York: McGraw-Hill, 1999.

Kan, S. H., *Metrics and Models in Software Quality Engineering*, 2nd ed., Reading, MA: Addison-Wesley, 2003.

Kaner, C., J. Falk, and H. Q. Nguyen, *Testing Computer Software*, New York: Wiley Computer Publishing, 1999.

Kerzner, H., *Project Management: A Systems Approach to Planning, Scheduling, and Controlling*, 8th ed., New York: John Wiley & Sons, 2003.

Kit, E., *Software Testing in the Real World: Improving the Process,* Reading, MA: Addison-Wesley, 1995.

Lyu, M. R., *Handbook of Software Reliability Engineering,* Los Alamitos, CA: IEEE Computer Society Press, New York: McGraw-Hill, 1996. Complete book available online at http://www.cse.cuhk.edu.hk/%7Elyu/book/reliability/index.html.

McConnell, S., *Rapid Development: Taming Wild Software Schedules,* Redmond, WA: Microsoft Press, 1996.

Myers, G. J., *The Art of Software Testing,* New York: John Wiley & Sons, 1979.

Nguyen, H., *Testing Applications on the Web: Test Planning for Internet-Based Systems,* New York: John Wiley & Sons, 2001.

Paulk, M. C., et al., *The Capability Maturity Model—Guidelines for Improving the Software Process,* Reading, MA: Addison-Wesley, 1995.

Pressman, R. S., *Software Engineering: A Practitioner's Approach,* 5th ed., New York: McGraw-Hill, 2000.

Rakitin, S. R., *Software Verification and Validation for Practitioners and Managers,* 2nd ed., Norwood, MA: Artech House, 2001.

Russell, J. P., (ed.), ASQ Quality Audit Division, *The Quality Audit Handbook,* 2nd ed., Milwaukee, WI: ASQ Quality Press, 2000.

Scholtes, P. R., B. L. Joiner, and B. J. Streibel, *The Team Handbook,* 3rd ed., Madison, WI: Oreil Inc., 2003.

Schulmeyer, G. G., and J. I. McManus, *Handbook of Software Quality Assurance,* 3rd ed., Upper Saddle River, NJ: Prentice-Hall, 1999.

## CHAPTER 11

CMMI® PPQA Relationship to SQA

Tim Kasse

11.1 Software Quality Engineering/Management

In order to set proper expectations regarding implementing software quality assurance (SQA) based on the guidance provided by the Software Engineering Institute's (SEI), Capability Maturity Model Integration® for Development version 1.2 (CMMI®-DEV v1.2), it is important to first present a set of software quality engineering/management functions and establish who is responsible for implementing them throughout the project life cycle. Software quality engineering/management can be thought of as the larger scope offered by software quality engineering over software quality assurance. It also implies that SQA engineers, managers, representatives, or other persons responsible for SQA be capable engineers before they enter the world of software quality assurance. For the remainder of the chapter, the term SQA representative will be used to refer to a person who is supporting one or more projects in the SQA role.

11.1.1 Software Quality Engineering/Management Functions

Software quality engineering (SQE) includes all technical and management functions that determine the quality policy, objectives, and responsibility for software life-cycle work products whether they are part of the product to be delivered or not.

These quality functions include, but are not limited to:

- Setting quality goals for the project that support the organization's business objectives;
- Establishing and enforcing a quality policy;
- Planning for quality (normally in the form of a Project Quality Plan);
- Developing processes at the project and organizational level;
- Establishing the use of standards and procedures;
- Performing multiple levels of testing such as unit testing, integration testing, systems testing, acceptance testing, and regression testing;
- Conducting peer reviews throughout the product life cycle;

- Designing in quality factors such as maintainability, expandability, and reliability;
- Conducting quality audits or objective evaluations with respect to product quality;
- Conducting quality audits or objective evaluations with respect to process quality;
- Providing visibility into the process and product quality for management and practitioners through quality reporting;
- Ensuring noncompliance issues are resolved before the product is delivered to the customer;
- Conducting objective evaluations of customer and maintenance documentation;
- Implementing complementary configuration management functions;
- Identifying measurements that support the information needs of the project and organization and can be used to improve both product and process quality;
- Conducting performance evaluations to ensure the system converges to established performance constraints;
- Conducting appropriate verification functions to show that the product meets the requirements;
- Conducting appropriate validation functions to show that the product will work in the operational environment by the intended users.

It should be noted that while the project manager is the person ultimately responsible for the quality produced by the project team, these quality functions may be performed by:

- Project leaders together with product and product component developers;
- Quality managers or quality representatives;
- Organizational level quality assurance group;
- Configuration management group;
- Systems engineering;
- Integration and systems test;
- Documentation;
- Database;
- Others.

Figure 11.1 shows a number of the quality functions mentioned above, which revolve around a software product development effort. The intent is that the project manager must choose and contract for each of these quality functions to correspond with the size, complexity, and criticality of the product components and eventually the delivered product.

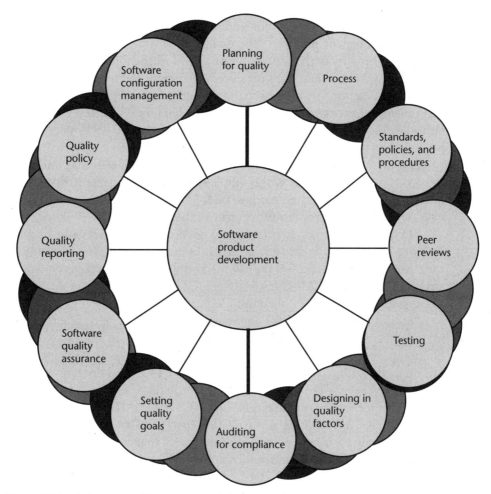

Figure 11.1   Software quality management function.

11.2   Software Engineering Institute's CMMI®

In the current marketplace, there are many maturity models, standards, methodologies, and guidelines that can help guide an organization to improve its processes, the quality of its products and services, and ultimately its business.

Most of these other models focus on a specific part of the business and do not take a systematic approach to the overall business problems that organizations face. The CMMI® goes beyond the specific needs of each engineering discipline to show how an organization can take "good" practices from the projects and build them into organizational "best" practices that address both development and maintenance activities that are applied to its products and services.

In the 1930s, Walter Shewhart began work in process improvement with his principles of statistical quality control. These principles were refined by individuals such as W. Edwards Deming, Homer M. Sarasohn, Charles W. Protman, Phillip Crosby, and Joseph Juran. Watts Humphrey, Ron Radice, and others extended these principles and began to apply them to software, in their work at IBM and the SEI. See further elaboration about quality experts in Chapter 2.

Based on the work of Deming and others mentioned above, the SEI adopted the process management premise, "the quality of a system or product is highly influenced by the quality of the process used to develop and maintain it" and embedded it in all of the CMM®s that it has produced. Deming's 14 Points for Management provides the source for this process management premise. Deming's third point states, "Cease Dependence on Inspection to Achieve Quality." Routine 100% inspection to improve quality is equivalent to planning for defects and acknowledgment that the process does not have the capability required for the specifications.

End-item inspection to improve quality is too late, ineffective, and costly. When the product leaves the door of the supplier, it is clearly too late to do anything about quality. As Dr. Deming frequently stated, "You cannot inspect quality into a product." Quality comes from improvement of the process!

Many people, the world over, have wondered how the SEI came up with its original five-level Maturity Model. It turns out that "having five fingers and/or five toes" was not the motivation that Watts Humphrey had utilized for establishing its structure. The initial CMM® for Software (CMM®) was based on the work of Phillip Crosby, as documented in his book *Quality Is Free* [1].

Phillip Crosby worked for International Telephone and Telegraph (IT&T) in manufacturing. He developed a method that would focus both managers and production personnel alike on a common path to increase measurable product quality. His maturity grid, partially completed in Figure 11.2, had different names from the CMM®'s five levels. However, the "Cost of Quality as a percentage" is still one of the driving forces for organization's to achieve CMMI® Maturity Level 5 today. Crosby's focus, like Deming's, was *quality first*. October 6, 1986, Watts Humphrey started to apply software engineering concepts to that five-level model concept. This resulted in the first SEI Maturity Framework (Figure 11.3).

The ideas that went into the CMM® were summarized from "Characterizing the Software Process: A Maturity Framework" by Watts Humphrey [2]. Instead of

Measurement categories	Stage I: Uncertainty	Stage II: Awakening	Stage III: Enlightenment	Stage IV: Wisdom	Stage V: Certainty
Management understanding and attitude					
Quality organization status					
Problem handling					
Cost of quality as % of sales	20	18	12	8	2.5
Quality improvement actions					
Summation of company quality posture	We don't know why we have problems with quality				We know why we do not have problems with quality

Figure 11.2 Quality management maturity grid. (*From:* [1]. © 1999 McGraw-Hill Book Company, Inc. Reprinted with permission.

Maturity level	Key actions required to advance to the next level
Optimized	
Managed	Automate process data collection, turn management focus from product to process
Defined	Process measures, process database, measurement support, product quality targets and assessment
Repeatable	Process group, process architecture, software engineering methods and technologies
Initial	Project management, management oversight, product assurance, change control

Figure 11.3   A maturity framework. (*From:* [2]. © 1988 IEEE. Reprinted with permission.)

characterizing the Maturity Levels, Mr. Humphrey provided the motivation to move to the "next" maturity level. So, if your organization was at the Initial level, it was suggested that the organization focus its work on project management, management oversight, product assurance, and change control.

The CMMI® has evolved from these roots into the CMMI®-DEV v1.2 constellation for development and maintenance today, as shown in Figure 11.4.

It is important to observe that while Crosby's model was always focused on quality management, the CMM® for Software indicated that for an organization to

Level	Process Characteristics	Process Areas	
Optimizing 5	Focus is on quantitative continuous process improvement	Causal analysis and resolution Organizational innovation and deployment	
Quantitatively managed 4	Process is measured and controlled	Quantitative project management Organizational process performance	
Defined 3	Process is characterized for the organization and is proactive	Requirements development Technical solution Product integration Verification Validation Decision analysis and resolution	Organizational process focus Organization process definition Organizational training Integrated project management Risk management
Managed 2	Process is characterized for projects and is often reactive	Requirements management Project planning Project monitoring and control Supplier agreement management	Product and process Quality assurance Configuration management Measurement and analysis
Initial 1	Process is unpredictable, poorly controlled, and reactive		

Figure 11.4   CMMI® overview.

achieve a Maturity Level higher than Initial or ML 1, a strong focus on software quality was needed. Today, for the CMMI®, the process area is called Process and Product Quality Assurance, and the focus has been expanded to include quality for all engineering disciplines and to include product quality as well as process quality.

11.3 PPQA in the CMMI®

There are two types of representations in CMMI® models:

- Staged;
- Continuous.

A representation in CMMI® is analogous to a view into a data set provided by a database. Both representations provide ways of implementing process improvement to achieve business goals. Levels are used in CMMI® to describe an evolutionary path for an organization that wants to improve the processes it uses to develop and maintain its products and services. Within the continuous representation, capability levels are used to determine an organization's process improvement achievement in individual process areas such as requirements development or configuration management. Within the staged representation, maturity levels are used to determine an organization's process improvement achievement across multiple process areas that are predefined at for each of the five Maturity Levels. Process and Product Quality Assurance (PPQA) appears in the special category identified as Maturity Level 2 that makes up the Staged Representation of the CMMI®-DEV v1.2. See Figure 11.4. From the continuous representation point of view, PPQA is part of the category called Support. See Figure 11.5.

From a process improvement point of view, one can view PPQA as either a project management function or as a quality management function depending on the

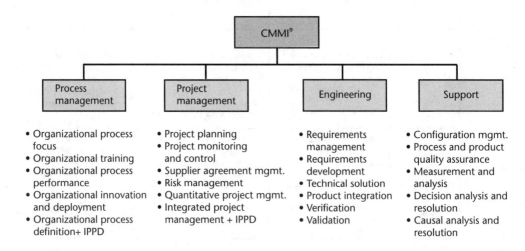

Figure 11.5 CMMI®-DEV continuous representation.

organization's culture and orientation to project management or quality management and still make it work.

11.3.1   Process and Product Quality Assurance Purpose Statement

The purpose of PPQA is to provide staff and management with objective insight into both processes and associated work products. Objective insight will be expanded in the description of Specific Practice 1.1 Objectively Evaluate Processes. It is important to point out now, however, that objective insight is to be provided to all levels of management including project management, middle management, and senior management to ensure that they understand both how the processes are being implemented on the projects and whether they are helping the project members to produce the desired product quality or not.

The CMMI® presents the significant PPQA activities as:

- Objectively evaluating performed processes, work products, and services against the applicable process descriptions, standards, and procedures;
- Identifying and documenting noncompliance issues;
- Ensuring that noncompliance issues are addressed and followed up;
- Providing feedback to project staff and managers on the result of quality assurance activities.

Quality assurance activities and involvement should begin in the early phases of a project to facilitate the effective establishment of plans, processes, standards, and procedures that will:

- Add value to the project;
- Satisfy the requirements of the project and organizational policies.

Quality assurance representatives should participate in the establishment of those plans, processes, standards, and procedures to ensure they will fit or can be tailored to fit the project's needs. It is also important that the project's documents can be audited or objectively evaluated.

11.3.2   Quality Control

PPQA is often misunderstood or purposefully equated to testing. It is important to distinguish between "quality control" and "quality assurance." Quality control evaluates or checks the quality of the products and life-cycle work products. Quality control functions or activities help to determine if the product or work product is within defined tolerances and of acceptable quality. Early U.S. Department of Defense quality standards included Mil-I-45208—Inspection System Requirements, and Mil-Q-9858A—Quality Program Requirements.

Tools and techniques used for quality control include peer reviews such as inspections or structured walkthroughs and the different levels of testing. Peer reviews and most testing techniques are described in the CMMI® process areas of verification and validation. In CMMI® V1.2, the introductory material makes clearer the relationship between quality assurance and verification:

> The practices in the Process and Product Quality Assurance process area ensure that planned processes are implemented, while the practices in the Verification process area ensure that the specified requirements are satisfied. These two process areas may on occasion address the same work product but from different perspectives. Projects should take advantage of the overlap in order to minimize duplication of effort while taking care to maintain the separate perspectives.

11.3.3 Quality Assurance

Quality assurance, in contrast, evaluates or checks to see if the process is working. Is the process being followed? Are the quality control checks being applied with the proper rigor? Are the quality control checks efficient and effective? Is the process causing quality problems? Is the process working for the organization? Tools and techniques used by QA representatives include objective evaluations such as process audits and product audits:

- Process audits, sometimes also known as process reviews, are performed in order to verify both the logical flow and usability of a particular documented process, and also to verify whether it is, in fact, being "used" in the organization or project.
- Product audits are performed in order to verify whether the products and work products that were created have been "developed in accordance with the requisite internal standards," such as forms, templates, coding guidelines, and so on.

It is important that these process audits and product audits be performed at the time in the project life-cycle when they can actually provide the most useful feedback to the project. Quite often the performance of these audits take place at points much later in the project life cycle. Because timing is very important, the QA representative should plan the timing of these audits with the project manager, in order to maximize the benefit received.

In addition, Engineering Process Groups (EPG) as they are referred to in the CMMI®, also may perform or procure internal assessments or appraisals such as a gap analysis, or even a SCAMPI^SM appraisal, in order to verify that the organization and its projects have achieved an overall compliance to CMMI® guidelines.

11.3.4 Project Quality Plan

Given that a project development plan exists, it is expected that the project also produce a Project Quality Plan that lists all of the quality functions that are expected to be conducted throughout the project life cycle to support the project in achieving its required quality goals. The Project Quality Plan must describe:

- What quality functions will be performed?
- Who will perform them?

- During what phase of the product life cycle will they be performed?
- Who has approval authority?
- How will conflicts over nonconformance be resolved?

The following questions should be asked and answered in the Project Quality Plan:

- What peer reviews will take place and when?
- How will the data from the peer reviews be utilized?
- Which tests will be conducted and by whom?
- Which tests will a QA representative either witness or monitor?
- What objective evaluations will a QA representative conduct?
- What metrics will be used for the capture and analysis of identified defects?
- How will the correction of the discrepancies be assured?
- What are the criteria for the acceptance of the product from a quality point of view?

As the project leader or project manager is ultimately responsible for the product quality produced by his/her project members, it is important that the project leader work with the QA representative supporting his/her project to develop and manage this Project Quality Plan.

It is important to note that the Project Quality Plan *is not the same* as the Quality Assurance Plan that may be developed by the Quality Assurance Group documenting how QA representatives will support the project with their advice and quality evaluations.

11.3.5   PPQA as Defined by the CMMI® Specific Goals and Specific Practices

The CMMI® is composed of many different components. Of course, this book and this chapter are not focused on describing the CMMI®, but a few words on goals and practices may be of value. Each process area, such as PPQA, is defined by required, expected, and informative components. *Required components* describe what an organization must achieve to satisfy a process area. The required components in the CMMI® are the specific goals and generic goals. *Expected components* describe what an organization may implement to achieve a required component. Expected components guide those who implement improvements or perform appraisals. Expected components include the specific practices and generic practices. *Informative components* provide details that help organizations get started in thinking about how to approach the required and expected components. Figure 11.6 illustrates the CMMI® components and their relationships.

Other CMMI® component definitions relevant for this section include:

- *Specific goal:* A specific goal describes the unique characteristics that must be present to satisfy a process area.
- *Generic goal:* A generic goal describes the characteristics that must be present to institutionalize the processes that implement a process area.

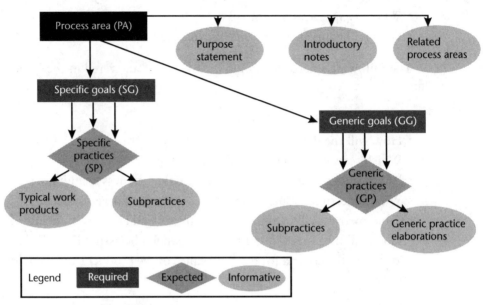

Figure 11.6 CMMI® model components.

- *Specific practice:* A specific practice is the description of an activity that is considered important in achieving the associated specific goal. The specific practices describe the activities that are expected to result in the achievement of the specific goals of a process area.
- *Generic practice:* A generic practice is the description of an activity that is considered important in achieving the associated generic goal.
- *Subpractice:* Subpractices are detailed descriptions that provide guidance for interpreting and implementing a specific or generic practice. While the CMMI® places subpractices in the category of informative components, it cannot be stressed enough that a significant number of subpractices must be considered as significant subpractices. Without these subpractices, the meaning of the practice they support would be weakened and possibly completely misunderstood and misinterpreted.

The specific goals and associated specific practices for PPQA are as follows:

- SG1—Objectively Evaluate Processes and Work Products:
  - Objectively Evaluate Processes;
  - Objectively Evaluate Work Products and Services.
- SG2—Provide Objective Insight:
  - Communicate and Ensure Resolution of Noncompliance Issues;
  - Establish Records.

Let us examine these specific goals and specific practices in detail.

SG1—Objectively Evaluate Processes and Work Products
Adherence of the performed process and associated work products and services to applicable process description, standards and procedures is objectively evaluated.

SP 1.1—Objectively Evaluate Processes
Objectively evaluate the designated performed processes against the applicable process descriptions, standards, and procedures. These quality audits for process compliance are not meant to replace inspections or walkthroughs or status review activities. They do not get rid of the need for quality assurance. They are not a substitute for testing. They should not be used to accept or reject products. They should absolutely not be used to assign blame. These objective evaluations are normally designated for one of more of the following purposes:

- To determine the conformity or nonconformity of the quality system elements with specified requirements;
- To determine the effectiveness of the implemented quality system in meeting specified quality objectives;
- To provide process owners with insights into possible ways to improve their own performance;
- To meet regulatory requirements.

For decades, most quality standards insisted on "independence" for the Quality Assurance Group. Independence meant being independent from the projects that were being developed and normally was implemented by having an organization chart that showed the quality manager for the business unit or division reporting up to the senior manager of that business unit. But it became clear after a short time that independence by itself was not sufficient.

The QA representatives who were performing the quality assurance activities also needed to have the appropriate knowledge and skills, including some development experience, some management experience, and some knowledge of configuration management, testing, standard and procedures, and quality assurance itself. In SP 1.1—Objectively Evaluate Processes, the emphasis is on objective evaluation. Objectivity in process evaluations is critical to the success of the project. It provides the QA representatives with the organizational freedom to examine documents and talk to individuals without restraint. It protects the QA representatives from adverse personnel actions by the managers of the project. It provides management with the *confidence* that the information about the processes and work products of the project being reported is indeed objective. Objectivity may be provided by an independent quality assurance group to the project. Regardless of how quality assurance is implemented, these issues must be adhered to:

- Everyone performing quality assurance activities should be trained in quality assurance.
- Those designated to perform the QA activities *should be separate* from those directly involved in developing or maintaining the work products.

- An independent reporting channel should exist to the appropriate level of organizational management to *allow noncompliance issues to be escalated* as necessary.

A significant subpractice for SP 1.1 is subpractice 2.

Subpractice 2   Establish and Maintain Clearly Stated Criteria for the Evaluations. The intent of this subpractice is to provide criteria, based on business needs, such as the following:

- What will be evaluated?
- When or how often a process will be evaluated?
- How the evaluation will be conducted?
- Who must be involved in the evaluation?

SP 1.2—Objectively Evaluate Work Products and Services

Objectively evaluate the designated work products and services against the applicable process descriptions, standards, and procedures. In the CMMI® Product Suite, a work product is defined as a useful result of a process. This useful result may take the form off a file, document, product, product component, service, process description, specification, or invoice, to offer only a few examples. According to the glossary in the CMMI®-DEV v1.2 technical report, the key distinction between a work product and a product component is that a work product is not necessarily part of the product. The project's work products and services, as defined in the project plan, must be objectively evaluated for compliance against the applicable process descriptions, standards, and procedures using defined criteria during those evaluations.

SG 2—Provide Objective Insight

Non-compliance issues are objectively tracked and communicated, and resolution is ensured.

SP 2.1—Communicate and Ensure Resolution of Noncompliance Issues

Noncompliance issues are problems identified in evaluations that reflect a lack of adherence to applicable standards, process descriptions, or procedures. Quality issues include noncompliance issues and results of trend analysis

Quality reports in the form of evaluation reports, corrective action reports, and quality trends should be tracked, openly communicated to all relevant stakeholders in a timely manner, and resolved. Noncompliance issues must be resolved at a level as close as possible to the source of the issue. Quality assurance credibility is damaged if the QA representatives immediately report their noncompliance findings to higher level management without giving the project members or project leader a chance to respond to the issues. Noncompliance issues should be analyzed to determine if there are any quality trends that should be discussed with the project leader that might motivate preventative actions being put in place.

SP 2.2—Establish Records
Records of the quality assurance activities must be established and maintained. To be complete, trends discovered from analysis of quality reports and documentation of the PPQA activities should be recorded in sufficient detail so that the results can be available and understood by all relevant stakeholders that are concerned with product quality.

11.3.6   Institutionalization

As stated in the definitions above, generic goals and generic practices describe the characteristics that must be present to institutionalize the processes that implement a process area together with its significant activities that help an organization achieve those goals. To complete the definition of PPQA within the context of the CMMI®-DEV v1.2, it is appropriate to examine a sampling of the generic practices from Generic Goal 2–Institutionalized a Managed Process. Institutionalization means that the process is ingrained in the way the work is performed; that is, "That's the way we do things around here."

Now let us examine selected generic practices from Generic Goal 2.

GP 2.1—Establish an Organizational Policy
Establish an organizational policy for planning and performing the activities described in the PPQA process area. This quality policy should establish organizational expectations for:

- Objectively evaluating that processes and associated work products adhere to the applicable process descriptions, standards, and procedures;
- Addressing and resolving all noncompliance issues;
- Ensuring the PPQA functions are in place on all projects;
- Ensuring sufficient independence from project management exists to provide objectivity in identifying and reporting noncompliance issues.

GP 2.2—Plan the Process
Establish and maintain the plan for performing the process and product quality assurance process. The main question that must be answered is: What is necessary to successfully implement the process and product quality processes on my project? Is training in quality management concepts necessary? Is consulting necessary? Are there adequate quality resources in the form of people, tools, funding, schedule, and so on, to carry out the process and product quality assurance functions? Has a Project Quality Plan been defined? Has a supporting Quality Assurance Plan been defined? Have quality measures been defined to help determine if the quality goals for the project have been achieved? Is it possible to carry out all required process and product quality assurance practices on my project?

GP 2.3—Provide Resources
Provide adequate resources for performing the PPQA process, developing the work products, and providing the services of the process. The most important point to be made here focuses on the words "adequate resources." Adequate is a reserved word

in the CMMI® and does not necessarily mean "the minimum." Having two highly qualified QA representatives to serve 500 developers is not adequate. Having 50 QA representatives to serve 500 developers who do not have the necessary knowledge and skills to do the quality assurance job is not adequate. In the discussion of how to approach a successful implementation of PPQA in an organization, alternatives will be provided that have solved this problem in the past.

GP 2.4—Assign Responsibility

Assign responsibility and authority for performing the process, developing the work products, and providing the services of the PPQA process. The assignment of responsibility and authority from senior management will ensure clear accountability for planning the quality process and achieving measurable quality results over the life of the process. The "and authority" portion of the generic practice is also acknowledged and enforced from GP 2.1 on quality policy.

11.3.7 Quality Assurance Representatives

The QA representatives should be providing consultation and objective evaluation of the project's plans, processes, standards, procedures, guidelines, templates, and checklists with regard to:

- Compliance with the organizational policies;
- Compliance with externally imposed requirements, standards, and procedures required by the customers;
- Processes, standards, and procedures that are appropriate for use by the project;
- Required knowledge and skills of the staff;
- Training needs;
- Historical data.

Project leaders should be able to expect the following support from QA representatives to help them manage and control their project better:

- Knowledge of the processes;
- Input as to the efficiency of the process being used by project members;
- Assistance in creating an executable and successful project plan;
- Assistance in creating the project's quality plan;
- Assistance in choosing the right standards for the project's needs;
- Assistance in tailoring the standards and processes for practical use by the project;
- Assistance in setting up peer reviews for the life-cycle work products;
- Assistance in putting together the right quality plan to match the criticality of the life-cycle work products;
- Performing objective evaluations and traceability audits to ensure that the quality goals are being met and the system's integrity is maintained.

GP 2.5—Train People

Train the people performing or supporting the PPQA process as needed. All QA representatives and quality managers in the PPQA reporting chain to the senior manager should be knowledgeable in their roles and responsibilities along with the appropriate authority, as follows:

- A senior manager knowledgeable in the PPQA function with the authority to take managerial actions on behalf of the organization should be designated to receive and act on noncompliance issues.
- Organizations must establish the appropriate organizational structure that will support activities that require independence such as quality assurance. This must take into consideration the business objectives and business environment

All people who will perform or support the Process and Product Quality Assurance process should receive appropriate training, including:

- Project related skills and practices;
- Interpersonal communications;
- Customer relations;
- Application domain of the project;
- Process descriptions, standards, procedures, guidelines, and templates for the project;
- Quality assurance objectives, process descriptions, standards, procedures, methods, and tools, such as:
  - IEEE standards;
  - ISO 9001:2000 and ISO 90003;
  - ISO 12207 for software life-cycle processes;
  - ISO 15288 for systems life-cycle processes.

GP 2.6—Manage Configurations

Place designated work products of the PPQA process under appropriate levels of control. This generic practice basically gives the directive to establish and maintain the integrity of the work products of the PPQA process throughout the life cycle of the process including:

- PPQA plan;
- Quality audit reports;
- Noncompliance reports;
- Quality trends.

GP 2.7—Identify and Involve Relevant Stakeholders

Identify and involve the relevant stakeholders of the process and product quality assurance process as planned. Questions such as these must be answered: Which subset of all of the relevant stakeholders identified for the entire project life cycle must be involved in each of the PPQA activities? Who will carry out the objective evaluations for process and product compliance? Who is responsible for resolving the noncompliances? Who is responsible for tracking the noncompliances to closure?

GP 2.8—Monitor and Control the Process

Monitor and control the PPQA process against the Project Quality Plan for performing the process and take appropriate action. Examples of process measures used in monitoring and controlling the activities of the PPQA process are:

- Number of noncompliances found and resolved within a given time period;
- Number of processes improved because of the monitoring in a given time period;
- Changes in the number of defects in the delivered system per release, compared with the last release;
- Amount of time/effort spent in all rework activities compared with the total product time/effort.

GP 2.9—Objectively Evaluate Adherence

Objectively evaluate adherence of the PPQA process against its process description, standards, and procedures and address noncompliance. This generic practice can be seen to be a subset of the entire PPQA process area. Another point of view is that the PPQA process area enables or supports the implementation of GP 2.9. Examples of activities that are objectively evaluated for adherence to applicable requirements and standards include:

- Participating in the preparation of the project's plans, processes, standards, and procedures;
- Evaluating the performed processes, work products, and services;
- Documenting, reporting, and tracking noncompliance issues;
- Conducting reviews with the customer's quality assurance personnel.

GP 2.9 for quality assurance is one of the major inputs to GP 2.10 to enable higher level management to have objective insight into process and product quality.

It is important to note that GP 2.9 applied to PPQA means that an independent group to the organization's Quality Group must be involved with objectively evaluating the Quality Group's processes.

GP 2.10—Review Status with Higher-Level Management

Review the activities, status, and results of the PPQA process with higher level management and resolve issues. Higher-level management must be able to answer the following questions regarding quality to take appropriate action:

- What processes are being followed on the projects?
- Are those processes efficient?
- Are those processes effective?

- Are those processes helping the project members to achieve the necessary product quality that is being demanded of the project?

Without this quality assurance input along with any trend analysis, higher level management cannot properly react to provide more resources, training, equipment, or personnel, or even assign the process group to improve process descriptions.

11.3.8   What Is the Relationship Between PPQA as Defined in the CMMI® and SQA?

The CMM® for Software focused only on software, while the CMMI®-DEV v1.2 focuses on quality assurance for all disciplines and support activities that contribute towards the quality of the products and services produced and offered by the organization. SQA must provide and support all of the specific goals and specific practices plus show adherence to the generic goals and practices as discussed in the previous section with a focus on software. This has special meaning when one examines a project that is starting at the beginning of the project/product life cycle. SQA representatives are expected to be objectively involved with the evaluation process, work products, and services in the very early phases of the life cycle until product delivery. This means that SQA should begin its involvement from requirements elicitation, through the establishment of plans, processes, standards, and procedures for the project, to the development of the architecture, detailed design, coding, unit testing, integration testing, and to systems testing. SQA must ensure that the software requirements of the project are being satisfied according to the requirements of the project and the organizational policies. It is expected that SQA adds value to the project and does not merely act as a response to a box on a checklist.

SQA is also expected to work closely with other representatives who are providing quality support for other required disciplines such as electrical engineering, mechanical engineering, optical engineering, hydraulics, electro-optics, and electro-mechanics. It is supposed to provide support to manufacturing, as is required for integration and systems testing.

When an organization is seeking to achieve the requirements for CMMI® v1.2 Maturity Level 3, it is expected that the SQA Plan be tightly integrated with all of the other related software engineering plans such as Risk Management Plan, Configuration Management Plan, Systems and Integration Plan, Stakeholder Plan, and so on. It is also expected that SQA be integrated with the other engineering discipline quality plans so that a seamless quality assurance effort can be seen throughout the project as the system moves from its architectural components to subsystems and finally systems to be delivered. This SQA effort must be based on the set of standard processes put in place for the organization together with the appropriate approved tailoring guidelines.

Along with the other engineering disciplines, SQA is expected to support the overall project quality effort by performing objective evaluations on support functions such as configuration management, data management, technical writing, and development of maintenance and operational documentation. It includes ensuring that the quality control functions such as design reviews, peer reviews, and testing are performed according to their processes, plans, procedures, guidelines, templates, and checklists.

11.4   Approach to Meeting PPQA Requirements

In the following sections we will provide an approach to meeting the PPQA requirements in the CMMI® v1.2 by briefly examining the topics listed here:

- Quality management and quality assurance infrastructure;
- Using criticality and configuration management status accounting to govern quality control activities;
- Quality auditing;
- Quality reporting;
- Proactive support of projects;
- SQA support levels;
- Quality factors, quality criterion, and quality metrics.

11.5   Quality Management and Quality Assurance Infrastructure

There are many possibilities for setting up a quality assurance or quality management organization. One in particular that has proven popular for many different types of organizations and in many different countries is described in Figure 11.7.

A centralized quality management group is established at the organizational level and is headed up by a middle-senior manager. The quality engineers (QE), or QA representatives as we have been referring to them, that serve in this organizational quality management group are individuals that have between 10 and 20 years of experience including development and project management experience. A normal

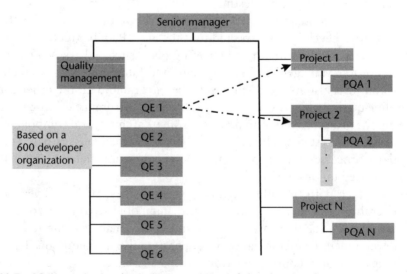

Figure 11.7   SQA organizational structures: organizational and project focus.

ratio is about 1.5% to 2% of highly qualified QEs compared to the total development staff. One financial organization in the Netherlands had approximately six senior QEs compared to 600 software developers, which is only 1% of the total. Each project of medium to large size is required to nominate at least one project quality assurance (PQA) coordinator. This person does, in fact, report to the project manager but is only responsible for ensuring that the necessary quality functions for the project are carried out. The PQA coordinator is normally assigned to support the project for its quality needs for 9 months to 1 year.

The QEs mentor and coach the PQA coordinators on a regular basis, usually monthly.

The QEs support the quality directives of the organization by representing the independent and objective point of view on process and product quality. When necessary, the QEs will confront the project manager and escalate any serious noncompliances up to the highest management level in the organization.

Once per month the QEs meet with all of the PQA coordinators to discuss quality processes and procedures. Presentations are made on a selected quality topic. Approaches to dealing with difficult project situations regarding quality are discussed. Expert consulting is brought in periodically to address this forum and provide CMMI® interpretation and quality management guidance. Once per month, the QEs meet with the project managers to discuss what quality support they need and the responsiveness of the PQA coordinators, as well as their own responsiveness and process improvements that could be made to assist the project in producing higher quality products and services.

It is this author's experience that a Chinese CIO put this infrastructure into place but insisted that the PQA chosen for Project 1 would serve as the SQA coordinator for Project 2 and the PQA for Project 2 would serve as the SQA coordinator for another project, and so on. In this way, each project had two independent and more objective QA representatives supporting that project's quality needs.

Of course, an organization could have a number of small projects. In this instance, the senior QE would support many of those projects and they would not have any PQAs because of their small size.

11.6   Using Criticality and Configuration Management Status Accounting to Govern Quality

In the ideal world all standards and procedures would be strictly adhered to, all plans would be complete, testing would be exhaustive, all software life-cycle work products would be reviewed, all modules would be independently tested, and regression testing would cover the entire system each time a change is made. In the practical, everyday world, such completeness is too costly. But if we are not going to perform 100% of the peer reviews on all life-cycle work products, or if we are not going to conduct 100% testing in all phases of testing, including regression testing, we need to define when it is critical to perform peer reviews or tests. One input that is not mentioned clearly in the CMMI® but is a strong feature of the IEEE standards is that of criticality. Software parts may be classified as "critical" because a failure would be costly and may result in a:

- Negative impact on safety;
- Large financial loss;
- Loss of market share;
- Loss of customer confidence;
- Loss of business.

All product building blocks (subsystems) should be assigned criticality levels based on established risk criteria, such as:

- Desired quality factors and criteria;
- Corporate or local strategy;
- Market strategy;
- Customer requirements;
- Regulatory standards;
- Product complexity;
- Multicompany or multisite developed;
- Mission constraints;
- Safety criticality;
- Base for future use.

Criticality levels may be labeled as high, medium, or low; A, B, or C; or red, yellow, or green.

A simple criticality identification scheme could be:

- Red: quality activity is critical.
- Yellow: quality activity is essential.
- Green: quality activity is nonessential, "nice to have."

Each organization/product line/project needs to define the implications of the criticality levels up front so that the projects can use the definitions to tailor their Project Quality Plan. For example, for organization XYZ, the following criticality levels were defined along with their corresponding verification activities:

- Criticality level Red:
    - All code modules are software inspected to detect major defects.
    - Module testing is conducted by an independent test team.

- Criticality level Yellow:
    - Walkthroughs are conducted for 70% of the code modules.
    - Unit testing done by developers.

- Criticality level Green:
    - Peer reviews are conducted on 25% of the code modules.
    - Unit testing done by developers.

Configuration management status accounting can also contribute towards the selection of the appropriate level of verification activity. Criticality combined with status accounting information make a very powerful rationale for conducting or not conducting verification activities throughout the project life cycle. For example, if a project had 50 code modules and the project manager was trying to decide which of the code modules upon which to conduct software inspections and thorough unit testing, he/she could examine the criticality guidance for the parts of the system for which the code modules were designed. In addition, imagine that 5 of the 50 modules were changing perhaps 10 times each month but the other 45 modules were only changing once every 6 months.

Combining the criticality information and the status accounting input, the decision might be to conduct formal software inspections for the five modules that were changing 10 times in a month and the code modules in the subsystem that had been identified as critical. Five to ten modules is only 10% to 20% of the total amount of modules, yet with this data behind the decision, it would satisfy even the peer review requirements of CMMI® Maturity Level 3.

11.7   Quality Auditing

A quality audit is an independent evaluation of products and processes to certify adherence to approved standards, guidelines, specifications, and procedures. Internal quality audits may correspond to the objective evaluations described in PPQA and in GP 2.9.

Audits are not meant to be a replacement for software review activities. Conducting audits does not mean that the entire SQA function is satisfied. Quality audits are not a substitute for testing. Quality audits should not be used to accept or reject products, and quality audits should never be used to assign blame. A full discussion on quality audits is available in Chapter 8.

Quality audits are generally conducted for one or more of the following reasons:

- To evaluate a supplier where there is a desire to establish a contractual relationship.
- To verify that a supplier's quality system continues to meet requirements and is being implemented. This might entail looking closely at your own organization's requirements as well as regulatory requirements. It might also entail determining how effective the supplier's quality system is in meeting your organization's quality needs.
- To verify that an organization's own quality system continues to meet requirements and is being implemented. These may be corporate requirements, business unit requirements, project requirements and regulatory requirements.
- To evaluate an organization's own quality management system against a quality standard. This helps to determine the effectiveness and efficiency of the quality system and looks at the resulting product quality. It also provides the process owners with insights into possible ways to improve their own performance.

As Figure 11.8 illustrates, the quality audit looks at various organizational components and compares them against policies, standards, and contractual agreements. The Quality Management System along with the way the organization is structured, its resources and its procedures, should be captured in the organization's Quality Manual and associated documentation. This Quality Manual must be in line with the organization's Quality Policy. The activities that are described in the Quality Management System and carried out must satisfy the contract with the customer. Finally, the records that are kept must show that all processes being implemented correctly, and that the resulting life-cycle work products and resulting system products are compliant with all quality system standards. This, then, gives focus to quality audit teams.

During an audit, the audit team examines documentation and conducts interviews with select personnel to answer the following three questions:

1. What does the Quality Management Systems manual say you should be doing?
2. What are you saying that you are doing?
3. What do the records say is actually happening?

Figure 11.9 indicates the steps for a generic audit. It should be noticed that all information that comes from the evaluation of the existing documentation and from the interviews must be corroborated from multiple sources and must be verified by those who are actually doing the work.

At the end of the audit, it is important that the audit team hold a final meeting with the management of the organization, product line, or project that was audited to describe the quality system capabilities that were observed, to describe the findings and provide recommendations, and to ensure the findings and recommendations are clearly linked to quality objectives and business objectives where possible.

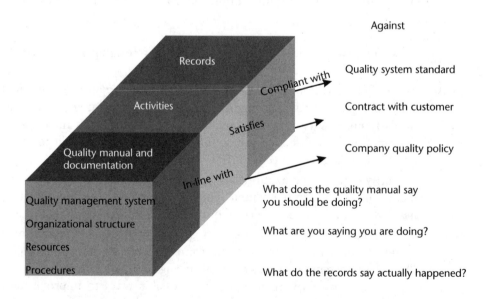

Figure 11.8 The audit process.

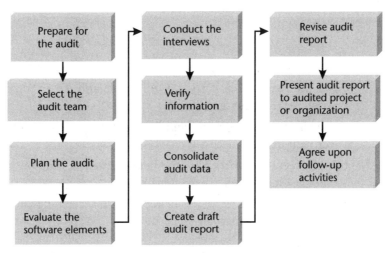

Figure 11.9 Audit flow.

Agreement on when and how the follow-up activities will be conducted by the organization must be discussed.

11.8 Quality Reporting

Quality reports should provide basic information that supports the project manager and project members resulting in improved project control, project processes, and product quality. Quality reporting from the project point of view should not focus on how many quality audits were conducted in a particular reporting period. Those numbers are meaningless unless the information that came out of them is of use to the projects themselves. The following questions can provide a starter kit of ideas that supports software quality management at the project and organizational levels.

- Process and Product Audits:
  - Are the project's documented processes being followed?
  - Are they efficient?
  - What improvements could be made to the process to help the project keep to the schedule, work within the budget and resource constraints, produce high quality products, and reduce rework?
  - Is the training timely and helping the software developers to gain necessary skills to perform the tasks they have been given?
  - Are the software life-cycle work products of the desired quality?
  - Does the resulting system quality match the project's quality goals?

- Requirements:
  - Are the necessary quality requirements being designed into the product from the point of view of the customer, organization, and project?
  - Are the requirements traceable?

- Project Management:
  - Is the project plan realistic?
  - Are all affected groups informed and synchronous with the project plan?
  - Are the supporting plans (SQA, SCM, and Test) harmonized with the Software Development Plan?
  - Are all of the corresponding plans updated whenever changes to the Project Plan become necessary?
  - Are project members able to spend sufficient time on the primary tasks that they have been given?
  - Are the actuals to estimates being tracked accurately and being acted upon in a responsible manner?

- Peer Reviews:
  - Are peer reviews being conducted? Are they being conducted according to the Project Plan and according to the defined procedure based on organizational and/or industry standards?
  - Are qualified, trained people attending these reviews?
  - Are they efficient (uncovering enough errors for the time spent)?
  - Are they effective (reducing the downstream testing time)?
  - What can be predicted from their outcome?

- Testing:
  - Are the test plans adequate?
  - Will the test data exercise the modules according to the test plans?
  - Is the test methodology being followed?
  - Are test results being recorded and acted upon?

- Configuration Management:
  - Are the identified software life-cycle work products being placed under configuration control at the appropriate time?
  - Is developmental configuration management effective?
  - Are software life-cycle work products kept consistent after each change request is processed?

- Documentation:
  - Technical documentation:
    - Does it match the standards?
    - Is it complete?
    - Is it accurate?
    - Is it kept consistent with the other documents?
    - Will it help to maintain the system after it is delivered?
  - User Documentation:
    - Does it match the system that is being delivered?

• Is it clear and understandable?
• Is it easy to use?
• Is it accurate?

11.9   Proactive Support of Projects

Proactive support from SQA for projects means that the SQA representatives do not just show up at the project manager's door and ask if his or her project members have conducted their peer reviews this past month or if they have conducted unit testing. Proactive support implies that the SQA representatives are actively studying the processes required by the organization, proactively providing feedback to the project to let them know if the processes they are following are efficient and effective and what might be done at the project level to improve them, providing feedback to the Process Group on the organizational processes so they can be improved at the organizational level, and providing visibility into those processes and the resulting product quality to the senior management team so they can take the appropriate business decisions. See Figure 11.10. If the Process Group is the keeper of the software processes, SQA is the defender of the software processes!

Another form of proactive SQA support is what I call *hand-holding* support. Some years before I became deeply involved with Quality Management, I moved to Arizona and bought my first house. It had wood accents and needed painting. I had never painted a house before but reasoned that all that one needed was a bucket of paint, a ladder, and a paint brush. A neighbor who was a professional painter observed my first attempts at painting my house and eventually brought his ladder over and put it against the house next to mine. But he did not help me paint my house. Instead, he literally took my hand and showed my how to properly use the

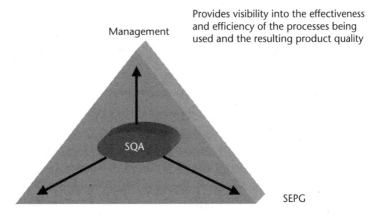

Figure 11.10   Agent for process improvement.

paint brush in order to produce a quality job that would protect the wood from the elements and look attractive in the neighborhood. That event taught me the value of hand-holding as a highly effective training and mentoring technique.

One example was the support the SQA representatives provided for an emulator project. The project was significantly behind on schedule and the project manager asked me, the software quality management manager if I would be willing to use some of my resources to help his project with unit testing. I must admit that, then and now, such a request sends me into a spin. But I agreed to help if we could support the project "with them" and not "for them." The project manager was puzzled, but agreed. My SQA representatives were moved into the project area and given desks so they sat side-by-side with developers to perform the unit testing. The SQA representatives talked to developers and developed unit test plans according to organizational standard processes and then proceeded to conduct the unit tests. The project was successful. The vice president of engineering complimented the development team. The project manager came to me and thanked me and asked if I would be willing to perform that service again. I smiled and responded with a polite "No; but we will help you understand the process we followed and support you in a collaborative way."

To achieve success in software quality assurance, hand-holding support is the only way that I know how personal results focused on quality can be transferred to those who are working on the projects. To be proactive, SQA representatives must preach the gospel of software quality and work together with the projects, with sleeves rolled up, to show them the proper process and help them to achieve the measurable results that all in the organization want.

11.10 SQA Support Levels

It is not uncommon to conduct an initial appraisal on an organization and find out that the number of SQA staff that are qualified and truly able to support the different project needs throughout the organization is not adequate for the demands being put on them. One approach that was developed in the 1980s at Motorola Microsystems and now has been implemented in many different types of organizations in the United States, Europe, and Asia, is to borrow the concept of criticality and apply it to what I call *SQA support levels*. At Motorola Microsystems, the Quality Management Group was required to support more than 90 different products with a very small qualified staff. Rather than try to spread the quality assurance resources very thin and have them become only auditors with a checklist mentality, we reviewed each project and assigned each one of them an SQA support level. This level of support from SQA was then discussed with the top VP of engineering and the project managers and a decision made. At times our input was accepted immediately. At other times, the VP of engineering was asked by the project manager for more SQA support, and a trade-off discussion on SQA resources happened. The SQA resources were distributed to the projects to match as completely as possible the business needs and quality demands for the project and for the organization. The SQA support levels were defined according to criteria that included:

- Demands on the project;
- Skill level of the project members;
- Experience with similar projects;
- Experience with quality management activities;
- Attitude of the individuals and the project leader towards quality;
- Success in meeting quality goals on past projects.

The following are SQA support level definitions:

- SQA Support Level 0:
  - Products that do not contain software or interface directly with software/firmware.
- SQA Support Level 1:
  - Products that contain software, firmware, or interface directly with software or firmware;
  - Either the quality of the software is considered low risk and/or the project team has extensive software experience and a proven reputation for producing quality software products.
- SQA Support Level 2:
  - Products that contain software, firmware, or interface directly with software/firmware;
  - Either the quality of the software is considered only medium risk and/or the project team is determined to have adequate software experience that has resulted in software products with reasonable quality.
- SQA Support Level 3:
  - Products that contain software, firmware, or interface directly with software/firmware;
  - Either the quality of the software is considered medium to high risk and/or the project team has fair software experience that has resulted in software products with acceptable quality.
- SQA Support Level 4:
  - Products that contain software, firmware, or interface directly with software/firmware;
  - Either the quality of the software is considered high risk and/or the project team has little software experience.

Subsequent to defining levels of criticality and then determining what verification activities would be assigned to each level, the SQA support activities were assigned to the various SQA support levels so that each project could know exactly what type of SQA support they would get. One example appears in Table 11.1.

Table 11.1   SQA Support Activities

SQA Levels					SQA Activities
SQA-L0	SQA-L1	SQA-L2	SQA-L3	SQA-L4	
X	—	—	—	—	SQA manager signs release form
—	X	—	—	—	Review SQA plan
—	X	X	X	X	Advise, monitor, and audit development testing
—	X	—	—	X	Witness demo of functionality system testing
—	X	X	X	X	Generate SQA report /observed quality levels
—	—	X	—	X	Review functional specification
—	—	X	—	X	Review software development plan
—	—	X	X	X	Help develop SQA plan
—	—	X	X	X	Assist choosing development and coding standards
—	—	X	—	X	Witness performance evaluation
—	—	—	X	X	Review and approve functional specification
—	—	—	X	X	Develop product evaluation plan
—	—	—	—	X	Prepare and review S/W development plan
—	—	—	X	X	Review and approve S/W life-cycle work products
—	—	—	X	X	Review specifications for performance requirements
—	—	—	X	X	Design and code reviews, code walkthroughs, inspections
—	—	—	X	X	Review test suite/kernel for all testing
—	—	—	X	X	Witness performance evaluation
—	—	—	X	X	Evaluate user documentation
—	—	—	X	X	Approve for beta site release
—	—	—	—	X	Audit process and product
—	—	—	—	X	Submit quality reports to senior management team
—	—	—	—	X	Review specifications for performance and functional specifications
—	—	—	—	X	Witness performance and functional evaluations

11.11   Software Configuration Management

A discussion on SQA without software configuration management is similar to having a fish tank but with no water for the fish to swim and breathe in—it is ridiculous. Configuration management is focused on the rigorous control of the managerial and technical aspects of the work products, including the delivered system. The purpose of configuration management is to establish and maintain the integrity of the work products using configuration identification, configuration control, configuration status accounting, and configuration audits throughout the product life cycle.

The most frustrating software problems are often caused by poor configuration management; for example:

- The latest version of source code cannot be found.
- A difficult bug that was fixed at great expense suddenly reappears.
- A developed and tested feature is mysteriously missing.
- A fully tested program suddenly does not work.
- The wrong version of the code was tested.
- There is no traceability between the software requirements, documentation, and code.
- Programmers are working on the wrong version of the code.
- The wrong version of the configuration items is being baselined.
- No one knows which modules comprise the software system delivered to the customer.

All of these very classic configuration management problems can and often do result in product releases infected with problems, clearly indicating to the customer the poor quality of the product.

Software configuration management may be one of the most valuable process improvement mechanisms a project leader could have. A strong understanding and implementation of software configuration management helps the project leader to control changes to the software requirements. It also allows the project members to develop at a fast pace without interference during the early stages of development.

Software configuration management helps the project managers control developers from tweaking the code when it is at the infamous 90% complete stage.

Software configuration management provides status reports to the project manager indicating what modules are undergoing the most change in terms of number of changes and frequency of changes. This, in turn, allows the project manager to find out what is going wrong: Is the module too complex? Was the design a good design? Do the developers have the appropriate skill set? Were appropriate peer reviews conducted? Was the module properly unit tested?

Software configuration management also provides the project manager with a level of confidence that what the software developers are developing is what is demanded by the requirements and nothing more. It ensures the integrity and consistency of the evolving system so that the code and associated documentation and specifications are synchronized. In short, software configuration management assists the project leader to develop in an incremental approach thereby reducing complexity and risk.

Software configuration management consists of the following components:

- *Configuration identification:* Identifying the systems architectures and the software life-cycle work products.
- *Baselining:* Placing the identified configuration items under configuration control at appropriate points in the software life cycle.
- *Configuration control:* Establishing a change control process that specifies:
  - Who can initiate the change request;

- The individuals, group, or groups who are responsible for evaluating, accepting, and tracking the change proposals for the various baselined products;
- The "change impact" analysis expected for each requested change;
- How the change history should be kept.

- *Establishing a software configuration control board:* A board having the authority for establishing and managing the project's baselines to ensure that every change request is properly considered and coordinated and that every software release is built from baselined components according to approved component build lists.
- *Establishing a software library or configuration management system:* The software library stores the configuration items created during the software life cycle and prevents unauthorized changes to the baselined items.
- *Software configuration status accounting:* Maintaining a continuous record of the status and history of all baselined items and proposed changes to them;
- *Configuration auditing:* Configuration auditing verifies that the software product is built according to the requirements, standards, or contractual agreements.
- *Interface control:* Describes which interfaces must be defined and controlled by the project including organizational interfaces and the more well known technical interfaces.
- *Supplier control:* Ensures that the subcontractor is able to maintain the integrity of the subsystem it has contracted for.

If we do not have control over the life-cycle work products and related configuration items that lead the organization to deliver a product that both satisfies its requirements and is delivered with all of its components and up-to-date documentation, it is hard to imagine or state that we deliver quality products and services.

11.12   Traps in SQA Implementation of PPQA

There are many traps or mistakes that organizations make when it comes to implementing SQA while satisfying the CMMI® requirements. The more common ones are listed here:

- Establishing an SQA group at the organizational level that has an independent reporting chain to the top management but has either inadequate resources or unskilled resources or both. Independence certainly assists the SQA representatives to objectively evaluate the processes deployed by the projects, but it is not sufficient to cover both the number of resources nor the required skill level.
- Believing that having a division or corporate ISO quality audit once per year is sufficient to satisfy GP 2.9—Objectively Evaluate Adherence of the Process Against its Process Description, Standards, and Procedures and Address

Noncompliance. GP 2.9 must be successfully applied against all of the process areas including PPQA and their practices for the life of the project.

- Issuing policies and statements like "quality is everybody's job" and expecting that will make up for implementing the goals and practices for PPQA and for Generic Goal 2 and Generic Practice 2.9.

- Staffing the SQA group with individuals that neither have any engineering background nor any project management nor supplier management experience. Too often, organizations staff the SQA function with individuals that have little to no technical background, nor any management experience. The explanation offered is that the organization cannot afford to place their "best" people in software quality assurance. The SQA staff, without the proper knowledge and skills, quickly takes on the characteristic of having a checklist mentality as they depend more on the checklist they are given to conduct their quality assurance activities rather than draw upon sound engineering and management experience. Without credibility that only comes from experience, these SQA representatives are not able to stand up to any seasoned project manager. They become disappointed with themselves, and the projects become disappointed with them.

- Trying to perform the SQA function without having a thorough understanding of the processes that are defined for the software engineering activities. The SQA representatives should have as detailed understanding of the organization's set of standard processes as the Process Group members do. Without that understanding, SQA cannot be proactive, anticipate project behavior, or provide added-value quality services.

- Having a lack of visible senior management support for quality, especially software quality, because senior management feels it must focus its attention on critical engineering projects. Lack of support for quality is never so obvious when senior management routinely gives waivers to projects to ship their products that have poor quality.

- Not providing adequate training in quality functions and principles. Senior managers often are willing to appoint individuals who seem to have an interest in fulfilling the SQA role but do not believe they need any special training. The concept that is promoted is that if the individuals do have some engineering experience they can pick up the tasks that an SQA representative must handle without any special training.

- Believing that the SQA function can be accomplished with a predominance of part-time people. Some full-time SQA staff must be engaged in the SQA activities. If part-time staff are to be used to augment the full-time staff, they should be allocated at least 50% of the time. Allocating a person 20% or less, which many organizations do, normally results in that person not being able to devote any useful time to the needed SQA functions. The project demands always seem to take priority over quality. In addition, if a person is assigned to the SQA function part-time, this must be part of their job description and their performance evaluation must include the 50% of the time they served as an SQA responsible as well as the 50% of the time they served as a developer.

Any organization that wishes to successfully implement the SQA function needs a quality policy backed by visible senior management support, adequate and skilled resources, and an uncompromising attitude towards quality.

11.13 Summary

SQA is more than a group of SQA representatives or a need to improve software quality. SQA is most effective if it fits within a larger focus on software quality management. Software quality management is management philosophy, an attitude toward doing business. Software quality management is a set of techniques for guiding software development projects so that they produce high-quality software products, a tool for assuring product success, and a program of planned and systematic activities to determine, achieve, and maintain software quality requirements.

Software quality management gets us back closer to total quality thinking. It embodies the following:

- Setting quality goals that support business objectives;
- Quality policy;
- Planning for quality;
- Process;
- Standards and procedures;
- Reviews;
- Testing;
- Designing in quality factors;
- Quality auditing;
- Software quality assurance;
- Quality reporting;
- Software configuration management.

Supporting proactive SQA activities within the umbrella of software quality management enables most organizations to not only satisfy the total quality management needs of their organization for software quality but the many standards such as ISO 9001:2000 and models like CMMI®-DEV v1.2 as well.

References

[1]   Crosby, P., *Quality Is Free*, New York: New American Library, 1979.
[2]   Humphry, W., "Characterizing the Software Process: A Maturity Framework, *IEEE Software*, Vol. 5, No. 2, March 1988.

Selected Bibliography

Babich, W., *Software Configuration Management*, Reading, MA: Addison-Wesley, 1986.
Belse, J.-Y., *Software Quality Management Guidelines*, Alcatel Alsthom, 1994.

Benn, C., et al., *TickIT, Guide to Software Quality Management System Construction and Certification Using EN29001*, TickIT Project Office, 1992.

CMMI® Product Development Team, *CMMI® for Development*, Version 1.2, (CMMI®-DEV v1.2) (CMU/SEI-2006-TR-008, ESC-TR-2006-008).

CMMI® Product Development Team, *CMMI® for Systems Engineering/Software Engineering/Integrated Product and Process Development/Supplier Sourcing*, Version 1.1 Staged Representation (CMU/SEI-2002-TR-012, ESC-TR-2002-012), Pittsburgh, PA: Software Engineering Institute, Carnegie Mellon University, March 2002.

Deming, W. E., *Out of the Crisis*, Cambridge, MA: MIT Press, 1982.

Deutsch, M., and R. Willis, *Software Quality Engineering: A Total Technical and Management Approach*, Englewood Cliffs, NJ: Prentice-Hall, 1988.

Dunn, R., *Software Quality Concepts and Plans*, Englewood Cliffs, NJ: Prentice-Hall, 1990.

Dunn, R., and R. Ullman, *Quality Assurance for Computer Software*, New York: McGraw-Hill, 1982.

Evans, M. and J. Marciniak, *Software Quality Assurance & Management*, Hoboken, NJ: Wiley Interscience, 1987.

Hetzel, W., *The Complete Guide to Software Testing*, Emerville, CA: QED Information Sciences, 1988.

Humphrey, W., *Managing the Software Process*, Reading, MA: Addison-Wesley, 1990.

IEEE, *IEEE Software Engineering Standards Collection*, Piscataway, NJ: IEEE Press, 1994.

Juran, J. M., *Juran on Planning for Quality*, New York: Free Press, 1988.

Kasse, T., "Software Quality Engineering Workshop," Plano, TX: Kasse Initiatives, 2006.

Kasse, T., "Software Configuration Management Workshop," Plano, TX: Kasse Initiatives, 2006.

Kasse, T., *Software Quality Management Manual*, Plano, TX: Kasse Initiatives, Revised 2001.

Kasse, T., *Practical Insight into CMMI®*, Norwood, MA: Artech House, 2004.

McDermid, J., *Software Engineer's Reference Book*, Boca Raton, FL: CRC Press, 1994.

Paulk, M., M. B. Chrissis, and C. Weber, *Capability Maturity Model for Software*, Version 1.1, Pittsburgh, PA: Software Engineering Institute, CMU/SEI-93-TR-24, February 1993.

Schulmeyer, G., and J. McManus, *Handbook of Software Quality Assurance*, 2nd ed., New York: Van Nostrand Reinhold, 1992.

Shewhart, W. A., *Economic Control of Quality of Manufactured Product*, New York: Van Nostrand, 1931.

## CHAPTER 12

SQA for Small Projects

Jean Swank, Jeanne Balsam, and Mark Pellegrini

12.1   Introduction

> How does an organization with limited resources implement a software quality
> assurance program that is effective?

The purpose of this chapter is to share lessons learned from implementing software
quality assurance (SQA) in an organizational unit of 150 people. The organization
creates and updates a broad variety of products, developed by small project teams
addressing multiple technology areas. The authors led their organization to a successful Maturity Level 3 appraisal under the Software Engineering Institute's (SEI's)
Capability Maturity Model® for Software in June 2003, and are leading its transition to the SEI's Capability Maturity Model Integration for Development
(CMMI®-DEV). Performing effective SQA is challenging in any work environment,
but performing SQA on small projects and/or within small organizations brings its
own unique set of problems and opportunities. In this chapter we discuss practicing
SQA in these environments with an eye towards avoiding (or at least mitigating) the
problems, and taking advantage of the opportunities. Much of the information provided in this chapter applies equally well to the area of development quality assurance (DQA), as described in Chapter 13.

In order to effectively assure quality, an organization must have defined processes, procedures, and standards. These process assets must be communicated to
the organization in multiple ways, improved over time, and institutionalized. How
can a small organization accomplish this? This chapter provides guidance and suggestions based on real-world implementation efforts and explains why these actions
are beneficial:

1. Hire and/or recruit quality engineers with enough experience to ensure the
   managers and technical staff respect their recommendations, as
   recommended in Chapter 4. These people can supplement technical and
   managerial expertise of the project team, which visibly adds value to the
   development effort.
2. Develop a generic SQA plan and schedule that can be easily tailored for
   specific project/product needs.
3. Encourage quality engineers to act as mentors to the project team.

4. Analyze project and product risks to determine the most cost-effective SQA strategy:
   - Take advantage of established, ongoing projects that have project-team process maturity. These projects require less quality engineering resources than projects with teams that are inexperienced or have already demonstrated process-compliance problems.
   - Concentrate quality engineering resources on projects or product development efforts that have high risks or are important to the organization out of proportion to their size.

5. Collect objective evidence for external evaluations without breaking the bank.

6. Develop compliance with ISO 9001:2000 and Capability Maturity Model® Integration (CMMI®) requirements as a natural output of a value-added process.

In our organization, responsibility for project outcome rests on the project director's shoulders and those of senior management. Quality engineers do not directly enforce process compliance, but rather are responsible for bringing concerns to the attention of the project director and, if necessary, senior management, for their disposition. The quality engineers act as the conscience of the organization, not the police. For them to be effective, senior management must support them with a concrete stance on processes and policies. In order for senior management to give that support, they must respect the decisions of the quality engineers. Tailoring of processes should be allowed when it makes sense. Variance should be approved when necessary. Quality of the product should always be the guiding value, not who is in charge. Thus, quality engineers should mentor project team members and listen to their concerns to ensure that the best quality processes are utilized and best quality products are built. Make sure that there is a two-way street for communications.

This chapter describes a method to implement effective SQA in small organizations, or for small projects, in order to produce best-in-class products with limited resources. The discussion in this chapter is aimed at projects that are small in size, hosted within small companies, or both. However, even if your situation does not appear to fall into these categories, this material may still apply. Since most organizations want to implement their processes in the most efficient way possible, many of the lessons we have learned are valuable for large organizations and projects as well.

12.2 Definitions

Who is the audience for this chapter and what do we mean by small project and small organization?

The processes described in this chapter were developed by a small quality engineering group (of one to five people) over a 7-year period. The definition of small organization and small project vary greatly from organization to organization. Therefore, we shall provide explicit definitions of each.

12.2.1   Small Organization

A small organization in the context of this chapter is an organization with 150 or fewer employees, doing a wide variety of product development, and with no functional silos. Employees typically have multiple functions through all phases of the product development life cycle. We recognize that an organization that has fewer than 150 employees and develops only a single product may not face the same challenges that the authors did while implementing SQA in their organization. Conversely, a much larger but equally diverse organization may have similar difficulties. Therefore, in addition to size, we also use an operational definition of small organizations based on their characteristics:

- They have difficulty leveraging economy-of-scale with regard to developing processes, procedures, materials, and training assets.
- They cannot afford to subsidize SQA activities on projects that are too small to reasonably support SQA.

12.2.2   Small Project

A small project in the context of this chapter is a project with 25 or fewer people. In the authors' organization, projects usually average five or fewer people, and are of durations of less than one calendar-year. These projects may be new development, maintenance, update, or prototype efforts. Additionally, these projects have the following characteristics:

- The project does not normally have a full-time quality engineer assigned to it.
- The team members fulfill multiple roles on the project.

12.3   Staff Considerations

Are there special staffing considerations for small organizations when hiring quality engineers?

Staffing considerations for recruiting and hiring qualified quality engineers (see Chapter 4) in our organization are consistent with those for hiring any other type of research scientist or engineer, with the additional requirements that the individual be not only technically qualified but also managerially qualified, and the individual must have excellent judgment, communication, and people skills. This skill set allows the quality engineers to provide objective oversight for each project to which they are assigned. According to the Software Engineering Institute, "The purpose of Process and Product Quality Assurance is to provide staff and management with objective insight into processes and associated work products" [1]. For small projects there is one key word in this phrase unique to those projects: "objective." Generally, everyone on a very small project has fairly good insight into what is happening on the project; what is missing is an objective set of eyes. On large projects there is inherently some oversight from other team members. Regardless of whether the project is large or small, management external to the project should be kept objectively informed of the technical and process status of the project.

Note that the role of the quality engineer is not to check the output of a product as it rolls off the assembly line. Ideally, the quality engineer continuously monitors the development of a product from requirements gathering to final delivery, verifying that the product is developed in accordance with the project's tailored processes. Although embedded within the project team, the quality engineer is organizationally independent of the team, generally acting in the role of an observer. The quality engineer verifies compliance with a specified process. Quality products are created by competent developers who not only follow the defined processes but also are empowered to improve those processes through established improvement activities.

12.3.1   Qualifications

To add the greatest value, it is essential that quality engineers be well qualified in both managerial and technical areas. They should have technical degrees in either computer science or engineering, with practical experience in product development, including project management, in the same type of development they are monitoring. In addition to being familiar with the organization's defined engineering processes, they also need to understand project planning and risk management. They should be capable of performing the technical and managerial work on the programs they monitor, although they are assigned to the project strictly as an organizationally independent monitor.

12.3.1.1   Technical Competence

Technical competence in the discipline of the assigned project makes it more likely that the quality engineer will quickly detect risks and/or defects. Highly qualified quality engineers bolster the capabilities of the project team because they add technical and managerial experience as well as an independent set of eyes to the project team. They attend meetings, review project documentation, and are aware of what the team is doing. Not only can they help spot problems, they can provide valuable suggestions and advice when their experience and knowledge is respected.

12.3.1.2   Management Competence

In process models such a CMMI®, more process areas are aimed at management activities than development. This reflects the fact that projects more often go astray from management failures than technology problems. Having experience in actually managing product development makes the quality engineer much more valuable in detecting problems on a project early enough to allow management to act to solve them efficiently. Quality engineers must, of course, be knowledgeable of the organization's defined processes, but having actual experience developing products gives them a qualitative understanding of what they are monitoring that is not gained simply by knowing a step-by-step process. They also carry an advantage that the project director does not have—they are observers, and they are not directly responsible for the outcome of the project. This gives the quality engineer the ability to realistically assess the state of a project; whereas the project director, as well as the project team, will usually suffer from the natural human optimism of assuming the best-case scenarios rather than the most likely ones. Small organizations frequently do not have easily accessible measurement systems, which will allow quantitative analysis of project status; therefore, they must depend on qualitative assessments of risk and status. This is where the experienced quality engineer adds value with his objective assessment of the available evidence.

12.4   Training Considerations

What are the training considerations for both quality engineers and project team members when implementing SQA following the methods described in this chapter?

Training is important to the success of any organization (see Chapter 5). The training budget in a small organization or on a small project is generally limited; therefore, training plans must be as efficient and frugal as possible.

Classroom training alone is seldom enough to provide a practice capability. In small organizations typically it is expected that employees will learn through self-study and informal mentoring from other project team members. Training is further constrained in small organizations by the number of people needing training at any one time. When the goal is to standardize and improve the organization, employees generally benefit more from training in internal processes, procedures, and standards than in generic training. This section describes recommended methods for implementing an effective training plan in a small organization.

12.4.1   Quality Engineers

As described in previous sections, hiring well-qualified quality engineers to perform quality assurance functions is critical, but it is not sufficient to enable them to perform their duties effectively and productively. Effective training and tools must also be provided. We have found that "work instructions" in the form of a Quality Engineer's Guide and mentoring from senior quality engineers brings the most value; that value being consistent reviews and audits of work products and processes, shorter learning curve, and the ability to work effectively as a team member. Quality engineers also receive the same tool-specific training and process orientations as required for other engineers. Thus, training of the quality engineer includes self-study, classroom training and orientations, and mentoring from senior quality engineers.

12.4.2   Mentoring the Project Personnel

The quality engineer is in a good position to identify project team members who are in need of mentoring to develop a practice capability with the organization's standards and processes. The organization's process, procedures, and standards can be considered the training materials that a project team and the quality engineer can use to guide them in their every day activities. The defined engineering process for an organization may be rather extensive, but at the same time it does not always go down to the level of work instructions. Therefore, these processes allow flexibility to the project team to define work-level processes that meet the needs of their development effort. It is not uncommon for project team members to need guidance on how to perform some process activities, especially newly hired personnel, or ones who are acting in a role that they have not previously performed. The quality engineer should not only make him or herself available to provide instruction and guidance, but should plan time for this in his or her SQA schedule. More time should be planned for projects with many inexperienced people than for projects where everyone has performed his role before.

12.5   What Makes Sense for Your Organization/Project(s)?

How do you make the best use of resources when planning SQA both tactically and strategically?

Here is the problem: your organization currently needs X amount of quality engineering resources to do a decent job of covering all of the projects currently in progress, but there is only 0.5X available. You obviously cannot do everything you would like to do. Flipping a coin to allocate your resources might be one solution, but it is certainly not a good one. So what do you do?

When planning for SQA within the organization and determining how to allocate the quality engineers among all the organization's projects, there are several considerations that must be examined. These include project risks associated with the personnel on the project team, the amount of quality engineering time that can be allocated during each development phase, cost of project failure, and the project team familiarity with the subject area. In order to properly apply scarce quality engineering resources to projects, it is first necessary to identify and analyze risks both for the project and the organization. A number of factors need to be considered. Some are tactical and relate directly to the project, while others are strategic.

12.5.1   Tactical

12.5.1.1   Personnel

Knowledge of the capabilities and work habits of the people on a project team can be valuable in deciding where to allocate resources. If the team members are known to generally conform to the organization's defined processes—with everything else being equal—it would be more effective to allocate quality engineers to other project teams that are known to be less process compliant or technically challenged. Quite simply, it makes sense to spend time looking for process violations among people who have a history of violating the organization's processes. Another personnel factor is the level of technical experience of the team. Inexperienced developers would ordinarily warrant closer inspection than those who are veterans. If the quality engineers are well trained and capable of doing technical work, as the authors contend they should be, they can periodically sample the work and sound a warning if there appears to be a problem. In any case, sufficient and appropriate peer reviews (see

Chapter 7) of an inexperienced developer's work should be conducted; proper SQA verifies that these reviews are being scheduled and completed.

12.5.1.2 Development Phases

Ideally, a defined process would be followed throughout the entire life cycle of every product, including a continuous verification by a quality engineer that the product is being built correctly. However, in the absence of enough resources to verify continuously, there are certain key phases of development where the quality of the output needs to be verified; for example, the requirements, design, development, and testing phases. Unquestionably it would be better to have requirements written correctly from the start, but if there is a problem with them, it is better to detect and correct the problem before they are used as the foundation for design, rather than afterwards. Likewise, a poor design should be identified and corrected before it is implemented. If the SQA budget only permits limited involvement of a quality engineer in the product's development, it is better to schedule the time at the critical phases, rather than concentrating in a single phase. A set of rock-solid requirements is a good start, but if the entire SQA budget was spent on their development and the project goes astray during design, this is not a good trade-off.

12.5.1.3 Familiarity with the Subject Area

If the product being developed uses new technologies, is planned for deployment in unfamiliar environments, or has problems that the organization has never faced before (i.e., unprecedented system), it is probably a good candidate for more quality engineering resources than one without these challenges. If it is a new product that is very similar in function and scope to an earlier product, it will pose less risk than an unfamiliar one. However, the experience of the project team needs to be considered. Even if the product is very similar to other ones that the organization has created, if the project team has no direct experience with those similar products, the risk to the new project may still be high.

12.5.2 Strategic

12.5.2.1 Cost of Failure

Sometimes if a product fails, the cost of failure can exceed the money spent on developing it. For example, it could be a key component of some other much larger product or system whose success is dependent upon the smaller one. Loss of reputation or team morale is also an important consideration. But sometimes a small product is just a small product, and if it fails it does not have dire consequences for the organization. If two projects have an equal chance of having problems, but one has far greater consequences to the organization if it fails, it makes sense to put more quality engineering resources on the one that is more important.

12.5.2.2   Adapt to Changes

Do not be afraid to replan quality engineering activities just as you would any other project activities. Despite the best attempts to get the right amount of quality engineers allocated to the various projects, resources will not always be optimally applied. Sometimes the risks of a project are not assessed accurately at the beginning, and it becomes obvious as the project progresses that it needs more scrutiny by quality engineers than was originally planned. Conditions such as staff turnovers or major requirements modifications may change the project risks during its development. If it becomes clear that there is a greater need for quality engineers on a project than is in the current plan, a judgment must be made as to whether that need is great enough to justify pulling resources from another project.

12.6   Success Without Stress and Undue Expense

> How do you implement a successful SQA program without undue stress and expense?

We have addressed what to consider when assigning scarce quality engineering resources by looking at the project risks. Now let us look at some practical ideas that can make the implementation of SQA more efficient.

12.6.1   Use a Generic SQA Plan and Schedule

Through years of experience, the authors have determined that having a generic SQA plan for the organization is most effective, both in cost and functionality. Additionally, a generic schedule that includes all tasks required by the organization's standard process is used as the starting point for each project. When an organization has a generic SQA plan and a template for the SQA schedule, then the quality engineer can jump start the quality engineering activities, and this will save time and money. A database can be used to track these schedules and any other supplemental material that is project or product specific. Over time, the organization should develop a library of generic schedules for each product development life cycle. In the authors' organization, the generic SQA plan serves approximately 70% of the projects without revision. The generic plan may be supplemented to address specific tailored processes, risks, and mitigation strategies.

The generic schedule is a superset of all typical quality engineering tasks. When tailoring the generic schedule for a specific project, the nonrelevant tasks are deleted from the schedule. Then the remaining tasks are scaled appropriately or eliminated based upon the recommendations given elsewhere in this chapter. Starting with a schedule that includes all of the common tasks (e.g. "Audit Software Requirements Specification" or "Moderate Peer Review of Software Design Description") already included makes it less likely to accidentally omit a necessary task, as the planner must actively eliminate unneeded tasks rather than add needed ones. Some projects may have special aspects that require special tasking. Any unusual, or nonstandard, tasks are added to the schedule as necessary for the particular project being planned.

The guidelines shown in Table 12.1 are provided as an example for developing a generic SQA plan for the organization. In general the SQA plan needs to be consistent with plans developed for other purposes. It should include the introductory sections including: identification, scope, document overview, referenced documents, and organizational structure. Additionally, it should have standard tasks that parallel those of the organization's standard process.

12.6.2   Efficiently Audit Work Products

Auditing work products requires the quality engineer's time to conduct the audit as well as the author's time to respond to it. Minimizing the author's burden to respond to a quality engineering audit results in greater efficiency and also encourages a more cooperative audit process. There are three major components to any audit (see Chapter 8 for further elaboration):

1. Performing the audit;
2. Communicating the findings to the author;
3. Closing the audit.

12.6.2.1   Performing the Audit

To efficiently perform an audit, the quality engineer should have a checklist based on the standard to which the work product is being audited. This checklist makes it easier to reference sections of the audited work product and to key comments to those sections. We have found that incorporating these checklists into audit reports enhances the audit process significantly. Additionally, it provides an artifact for the audit that can be produced for external auditors to demonstrate compliance to the current process and corrective actions for noncompliance. There are multiple methods for indicating required or suggested modifications to a work product. One method of documenting findings is to key each comment to the section of the checklist that corresponds to the work-product section that it describes. The comment must describe in detail the deficiency and/or suggest a method of correction. An alternate method is for the quality engineer to enter changes and comments directly into the work product with change tracking turned on. A formal report would still be required, including the checklist, but without the need for recommended changes to be specified in the report. This method requires the use of document version control and a word processing tool (e.g., MS Word) that allows tracked-changes to be accepted or rejected, and findings to be entered explicitly as comments.

12.6.2.2   Communicating the Findings

In the authors' organization, audit reports contain a list of defects as determined by the quality engineer, and a proposed solution to correcting each defect. Authors are presented with three options with regard to responding to findings:

1. Agree with the finding and proposed correction;
2. Agree with the finding, but propose an alternate solution;
3. Disagree with the finding.

Table 12.1 SQA Plan Guidelines

Section Name	Description
Tasks	This section provides an outline with detailed expectations for each type of audit and review that QA will provide oversight and support
Perform Start-Up Tasks Attend Project Initiation Meeting Generate QA Plans and Schedules Prepare for and Attend the Plan Review Meeting Prepare Orientation for and Attend Project Kick-off Meeting Attend Customer Meetings	These tasks are normally executed a single time, but may be repeated for major contractual changes or for incremental developments where this level of coordination/replanning is necessary
Conduct Periodic Reviews of QA Activities QA Manager CEO Senior Management Project Director Project Team	Explicitly define what reviews of QA activities are required; define what type of data is shared at each level and the minimum frequency of communication
Mentor Project Team in Organizational Process Activities	Define general mentoring activities that quality engineers will conduct during the life of the project, including the value of those activities
Support Customer Quality Management System	Define minimum types of support that will be provided by the quality engineer to the customer
Resolving Disputes	Define methods for resolving disputes between the quality engineer and the project team
Documentation	Define where additional documentation associated with QA activities will be stored (may be by reference)
Standards, Practices, and Conventions	Define where the official organizational standards, practices, policies, guidelines, and conventions are located
Tailoring of Standard Process	Reference tailoring practices for the organization's standard process
Monitoring Compliance	Define how compliance will be monitored and how deviations will be processed
Reviews and Audits	Define who will conduct reviews and audits and how the respective processes and standards will be used in these reviews
Technical Reviews Conduct Periodic Reviews of Project Activities Configuration Management Software Product Engineering Process Peer Reviews Technical Audits Collect Measurement Data and Document Deviations Analyze Data and Report Results Managerial Reviews	Reference applicable procedures and standards for conduct of technical reviews.; include the level of detail necessary for each type of review and audit to be conducted; define how data collected during the reviews will be analyzed and reported

Table 12.1   (continued)

Section Name	Description
Configuration Management	Detail specific processes for configuration management audits
Problem reporting and corrective actions	Define how problems are reported and corrective actions are tracked to closure
QA Document Identification Conventions	Define document identification conventions for QA artifacts

A standard cover e-mail that goes along with every audit report makes it clear to the author that the quality engineer does not want them to spend a lot of time documenting their responses to the audit report. Their reply can consist of simply cutting-and-pasting a copy of the findings into an e-mail and annotating each finding with a response. When they agree with a finding, they can simply state "Agreed" or "Done." When they disagree with a finding or a quality engineer's proposed solution, they are encouraged to limit their response to a sentence or two, or else contact the quality engineer by phone or in person to discuss the disagreement. It is not necessary for the authors to spend an hour crafting a detailed refutation of the finding when a 5-minute conversation will accomplish the same goal. It is also worth noting that authors are encouraged to disagree with any findings (particularly in a technical area) they believe are in error. The quality engineer must create an environment where authors, regardless of their level of experience, feel empowered to dispute findings. Quality engineers are not infallible. When a quality engineer performs SQA on a number of projects, they may not have the depth of knowledge that the team members do, and will, from time-to-time, make an honest mistake in their assessments of technical issues.

12.6.2.3   Closing the Audit

After all findings have been resolved by the author and the quality engineer, a final e-mail is sent by the quality engineer indicating the version of the work product that is approved. All e-mails between the author and the quality engineer are archived together with the audit report to provide future audit trail for external assessments and process improvements.

12.6.3   Efficiently Review Processes

Just like an audit of a work product, a process review requires the quality engineer's time to conduct the review as well as the project team members' time to participate in the review. To minimize the burden on project team members, we converted procedures into checklists by adding a box next to each step that did not directly produce an artifact for proof of completion. The project team member(s) responsible for performance of a particular process checks off these boxes as the process is completed. These completed procedure-checklists allow the quality engineer to perform significant portions of the process review without having to directly interact with project team members. Additionally, we have SQA checklists for each phase of development (planning, requirements definition, design, and so on) that lists activities that should be performed; these SQA checklists guide the quality engineer through process reviews. After the procedure-checklists for the process under review have been examined along with the relevant work product audits and meeting minutes, the quality engineer completes the SQA checklist for the phase or process area being assessed. The quality engineer discusses findings with the project team members to ensure that the process has been completed correctly. The completed SQA checklist becomes part of the process review report that is distributed to stakeholders. Additionally, these process checklists contribute to the periodic (e.g., monthly) review of the project, which is part of the project status report to senior management. Completion of a procedure checklist may be waived for processes that are repeated multiple times during a product development life cycle when the project team has demonstrated consistent compliance with the procedure. The process review report documents the findings of the review, and these findings are tracked to closure, either through verification of compliance, generating a waiver, or documenting a deviation.

12.6.4   Develop a Quality Engineer's Guide

Development of a Quality Engineer's Guide allows the organization to share best practices across the SQA organization. Additionally, this guide can be used by developers to better understand SQA functions. The Quality Engineer's Guide may be developed over time, with the sections that provide the greatest value being developed first.

The Quality Engineer's Guide supports and references the relevant organizational process and procedures manuals including the Quality Assurance Manual and Policy. These top-level documents should include information about a quality engineer's responsibilities, processes, procedures, standards, and checklists for each phase of product development. The checklists assist the quality engineer in process reviews of a project team, including project planning, configuration management, requirements definition, design, implementation, integration, and test planning. The Quality Engineer's Guide provides the detailed implementation instructions for work product audits, process reviews, and peer review oversight. Additionally, specific information about how to handle deviations and their resolution, and the importance of independent reporting of project/product strengths and weaknesses to the project director, the project team, and senior management are described. Additionally, the Quality Engineer's Guide should reference quality engineer support tools like audit templates, the generic SQA plan, and the SQA schedule template. Providing examples of audits, process reviews, and deviations will help bring a new quality engineer up to speed.

12.6.5   Provide Senior Management Insight into the Project

On larger projects, even the project director may not have good insight into what is happening "in the trenches," and the quality engineer may be able to give him a better assessment of the product's status than he would get on his own. On smaller projects of only two or three people, where the project director is one of the developers, the project director is normally well aware of what is going on. In these cases the quality engineer usually is not going to provide insight into the project to the project director; it is senior management that needs to know what is happening. Although there are standard process mechanisms for projects to report status to senior management, these are done through the normal chain-of-command, may not be timely, and are potentially subject to some distortion due to unfounded optimism, or other means. The quality engineer, although considered a project team member, should be funded independently of the project director and report administratively to senior management outside the project chain-of-command. This gives the quality engineer an independence that is more conducive to providing an accurate assessment of the current status of the project. One of the most valuable things a quality engineer can do is provide early warning to the project director and senior management of possible problems before they work their way into the project's other reporting channels.

12.6.6   Act as a "Gatekeeper" for Deliverables

The quality engineer will normally audit all deliverable documents (including drafts) and products that are released to the customer. On a small project, this may put the quality engineer in a similar situation to that of the project director in the sense that he is one of only two project team members through whom all deliverables must pass. This is another situation in which a technically qualified person may add value, and this sometimes helps to avoid a costly or embarrassing mistake.

12.6.7   Add Engineering Experience

The quality engineer has an engineering or computer science background and experience as a product developer; therefore, it is not only appropriate, but expected, for him to contribute technically to the product. Because the quality engineer is involved in all stages of the product's development, he has many opportunities to make technical suggestions for things that are not process issues, but specific product issues. The quality engineer should not assert himself technically if it is not necessary, but neither should he hesitate to do so if his training and experience lead him to believe that his input will lead to a better product.

12.6.8   Keep an Eye on Configuration Management

Good configuration management practices are important to any project or organization. But for small projects, where the loss of a team member or the crash of a development system could cause catastrophic damage to product development, good configuration management is essential. Quality engineers for a small project must devote sufficient resources to monitoring the project's compliance with the organization's defined configuration management practices, as well as the project's own configuration management plan. Compliance needs to be verified not only at delivery-critical times, but also at phase-independent intervals as described below.

12.6.8.1 Baseline Audits

Controlling the components used to build the product is essential if the organization intends to continue development of the product in the future. If some components cannot be located, the project team must spend time and money trying to locate them or recreate them. A baseline audit verifies that the product being delivered is reproducible from its controlled constituent parts. This means that not only can the product be redelivered, but it can be rebuilt from all of the pieces that were used to originally build it. In the case of software, this means that all of the source files can be located, the development environment can be reconstructed, and the code recompiled into the same product that was originally delivered to the customer.

In some organizations, the group that is responsible for preparing products for release is separate and independent of the development team, and therefore acts as an independent auditing function. On a small software project where the developers build their own releases, the lack of independent verification creates a danger of releasing a product that is not reproducible. It is therefore essential that a project-independent person verify that a product can be built from the configuration management system, using documentation provided by the project team. This role can be fulfilled by the project's quality engineer, or it can be delegated to a specialist within the SQA organization. Regardless of how it is done, the project quality engineer needs to assure that it is done.

12.6.8.2 Configuration Management Plan Compliance

As has been discussed elsewhere in this chapter, smaller projects tend to have less self-detection-and-correction mechanisms built into them than larger ones. The most extreme example is a single-person project: that person is going to do things in a certain manner and is unlikely to examine his own process and products and criticize himself for not doing things the correct way. Larger projects have more people within the project team who see each other's work and can provide some degree of correction when things go astray.

Very small teams can go off into the weeds in terms of configuration management, unaware (or not caring) that they are making horrible mistakes, with the issues remaining undetected until they cause expensive problems. The authors' organization manages this concern by making periodic assessments of the project team's compliance with its own configuration management plan and the organizational configuration management policies. This is normally done at a minimum of once every 3 months, in addition to inspection at certain phase-driven events (such as a product release). If problems are detected, they are documented in an audit report and corrective action is taken. Unless the nature and severity of the problems is minor, the project is inspected on a monthly basis until it is clear that the problems have been corrected and the defined process is being followed. In some cases, corrective action includes training of personnel in configuration management tools or processes. The importance of configuration management to quality assurance is stressed in Chapter 11.

12.6.9   Walk the Halls

Good quality engineering consists of more than attending meetings, conducting interviews, or sitting in an office auditing documents and filling out checklists. Just as the police officer who walks the beat understands the neighborhood better than one who never leaves his patrol car, quality engineers should try to find time to leave their offices and walk the halls, see what the developers (including those outside their own projects) are up to, and chat with other employees at the coffee pot. In addition to making themselves more accessible and a part of the team, interesting and useful information can be learned. Sometimes a quality engineer will discover what another project team is doing that might benefit one of his projects. Knowing the skills and interests of other members of the organization is helpful when a project the quality engineer is working on has a technical challenge and needs help from outside the project team. And sometimes, even though the quality engineer should be notified of all meetings, customer visits, project-wide correspondence, and other important events, he is sometimes "accidentally" excluded. Keeping in touch with the project team equates to keeping in touch with the team's status. When a quality engineer's time is split between so many projects that he must leave them unmonitored for extended periods of time, important asynchronous events or status changes can occur during these intervals. It is helpful when the project team members feel comfortable and even compelled to inform the quality engineer of such changes, which he might not otherwise detect until his next periodic review.

12.6.10   Colocate Quality Engineers

Our experience has been that keeping the quality engineers colocated, in a set of adjacent offices, is beneficial. It facilitates easy communication with each other. This is helpful when mentoring a new quality engineer, when a quality engineer has a question or wants advice from other quality engineers, or someone wishes to share a lesson-learned. It also helps to foster an esprit-de-corps among the quality engineers.

12.6.11   Share Information

Although splitting the time of a quality engineer over multiple projects brings some inefficiency as compared to spending full time on a single project, it does bring one important benefit: information sharing. As has been stressed throughout this chapter, it is especially important for a quality engineer to be knowledgeable in a small-project environment, rather than a box-checker. Quality engineers who participate in multiple projects can share technical information between these projects in a way that someone who is simply checking the boxes never could. This can also help avoid conflicts between products that share requirements or resources. Often the quality engineer can share solutions developed on one project with a different project team that is having similar problems. Being able to recognize that a technical solution that was developed on one project is applicable to another depends upon having highly qualified quality engineers.

12.6.12   Facilitate Process Improvement

Process improvement can be especially difficult in small companies with limited resources. Large companies can afford to assemble teams from within the organization to work on process improvement groups, or even hire outside consultants to assist. Small companies cannot normally afford to do these things, so process improvement efforts must be more practical and efficient. Process tailoring and ad hoc technology solutions created by project teams can be a source of improvement for the whole organization. Even if there are mechanisms in place for propagating these improvements to the rest of the organization, project team members may have such a limited view of the organization that they do not realize the potential benefits their improvements have to other product teams, or they simply may not care about anything outside their own small niche of the organization. The quality engineers can be a conduit for bringing these improvements to the rest of the organization. Their training and experience, coupled with a broad view of the organization by virtue of their working on multiple projects, helps the quality engineer to recognize what project-level innovations can benefit the whole organization.

12.6.13   Institutionalize Processes

In a perfect world there would be no need for quality engineering activities; everyone would be qualified to do their job, they would do it perfectly every time, and everyone would follow the organization's procedures for developing products. The world, unfortunately, is not perfect. Neither is it completely imperfect, where every developer needs a full-time quality engineer sitting next to them watching everything they do. The reality is somewhere in between.

The most effective way to utilize good processes to create outstanding products is to create an environment where the project teams want to follow these processes, rather than do it because they are forced to do so. Thus, process improvement for product development is more effective when it comes from the bottom up, rather than from the top down. The people doing the work suffer the consequences of their own mistakes, and they can identify the ones that could have been avoided through better processes. The most motivated of these people will take it upon themselves to tailor or to extend the organization's processes to meet their needs. The quality engineer is management's representative in the trenches, and can identify process improvements that should be more generally distributed. Some of these improvements will be generally applicable within the organization and should be incorporated as changes to the defined processes.

The organization needs to identify star players who utilize existing processes and work to improve those processes, and those individuals who may not necessarily improve processes, but comply with them. These people should be praised, rewarded, and encouraged to continue process compliance and improvement. They become role models for the other developers, encouraging them to be compliant and innovative as well. Institutionalization occurs when the project team is voluntarily and enthusiastically following the organization's processes, reducing the need for scarce quality engineering resources.

12.7   Objective Evidence for the Auditor/Appraiser

What is objective evidence and how do I get it?

The term "objective evidence" is generally used in connection with independent external audits. These independent audits are often done to achieve an ISO certification or a maturity/capability level evaluation for the Software Engineering Institute's CMMI® objective evidence is required during audits (formal or informal) to determine if a project or organization is performing activities as defined in their process. What is objective evidence and how much extra does it cost? Objective evidence includes standard development work products (e.g., documents, source code, executables, hardware), validation and verification of those work products (e.g., peer reviews, audits, test results, customer reviews), and other process assets. Objective evidence does not have to cost extra if the organization's process is well instrumented, an effective configuration management system exists, and artifacts can be easily linked to the process.

The organization must work together to establish a repository for the objective evidence. The SQA organization may be utilized to interface between the organizational requirements for data and the project team's needs. While performing audits and reviews, the quality engineer can index work products to the process components that they satisfy, and link the audits to the work products. There are appraisal tools that may be utilized to index this data in preparation for internal or external evaluations.

The quality engineers provide artifacts for these external assessments. When quality engineers do their jobs, they are reviewing a project team's compliance with the organization's processes and procedures. The review for each phase of product development should have a written report or a completed audit or review checklist. This report and/or checklist provides an artifact that demonstrates a project team is in compliance with the organization's process as well as an artifact that the quality engineers are performing their defined process for process reviews. Additionally, work product audits that are done using the organization's standards provides an artifact that the project team is utilizing the organization's standards for producing the work product, and the audit report provides an artifact that quality engineer is auditing work products as specified in the organization's process. An important part of the quality engineer's responsibilities is to identify and report on noncompliance issues. The deviation report and the written resolution of the deviation is evidence that shows that noncompliance issues are being identified and followed through to completion. The ability to support process improvement can be identified when one looks at the organization's processes and procedures over time and sees that new procedures are added or existing procedures are modified. This shows that process improvements are being identified and incorporated into the organization's processes.

12.8   Compliance with ISO and CMMI®

How does the material presented in this chapter address ISO and CMMI® concerns?

This section describes at a high-level ISO 9001:2000 and CMMI® areas that are addressed by the activities described and recommended in this chapter. Detailed mappings of ISO 9001:2000 and CMMI® are available from commercial sources [2]. Regardless of the model or assessment methodology being followed, some type of internal evaluation of progress is necessary. For CMMI® these internal evaluations take two forms: (1) quality engineering activities on individual products or projects, and (2) evaluations following SCAMPI^SM methods for internal process improvement purposes. ISO 9001:2000 requires internal audits. Additionally, both CMMI® and ISO 9001:2000 have external audits that establish the audited organization has achieved the capability/maturity level being sought or is compliant with the ISO 9001:2000 standard, respectively.

The ISO 9001:2000 standard defines an audit as a "systematic, independent and documented process for obtaining evidence and evaluating it objectively to determine the extent to which audit criteria are fulfilled." Audit criteria are defined as a "set of policies, procedures or requirements against which collected audit evidence is compared." Audit evidence is defined as "records, verified statements of fact or other information relevant to the audit" [3]. The ISO 9001:2000 audit classification is determined by the purpose or subject of the audit and who performs the audit. The authors believe that these definitions are consistent with the objectives of CMMI® audits.

12.8.1 ISO/CMMI® Internal Audits

The ISO "internal – first party audit" is conducted by members of the organization who are independent of the group being audited. The internal audit may be performed for any of the following reasons: to demonstrate conformance with the systems/models being implemented; to identify strengths and weakness in the current practice for process improvement; to provide management evidence for oversight functions; or to determine the effectiveness of the implemented system in meeting quality objectives. The CMMI® model is more specific in its requirements for internal audits. The Process and Product Quality Assurance (PPQA) process area (see Chapter 11) has two specific goals: (1) Objectively Evaluate Processes and Work Products; and (2) Provide Objective Insight. The PPQA process area is utilized to evaluate all other process areas and allows achievement of compliance with Generic Practice 2.9—Objectively Evaluate Adherence. The Organization Process Focus process area requires an organizational level review of evidence to determine overall organization compliance with the model components being assessed. It also requires establishment of an infrastructure to support process implementation and improvement, both of which are also required by the ISO 9001:2000 standard. SCAMPI^SM B and/or C appraisals may be conducted with internal and/or external lead appraisers to evaluate the quality system for internal improvements or readiness for external evaluations.

12.8.2 ISO/CMMI® External Audits

There are two classifications of ISO audits that are external. One is conducted by a "second party auditor" (customer) to determine the state of the quality system implemented by a potential or current supplier. The other is conducted by a "third party auditor" (registration) and is also conducted to determine the state of the quality system implemented by the organization, but has the additional purposes of seeking registration, keeping discipline among managers, and identifying areas for improvement. To keep a registration active, the organization must have surveillance audits performed (generally a partial audit every 6 months, and a re-registration audit every 3 years). CMMI® also requires a third party auditor to evaluate compliance with the CMMI® model for formal assessment of capability or maturity. Previously a CMMI® evaluation did not formally expire. As of 2006, CMMI® evaluations expire after 3 years.

12.8.3   Document Control

Both ISO 9001:2000 and CMMI® require that documentation be controlled in order to produce records and objective evidence for internal and external audits as well as process improvement. Formal configuration management of both process and project/product assets is necessary to ensure that the quality system operates effectively. Therefore, configuration management processes that exist in a small organization, when followed, will likely result in compliance with the document control requirements for ISO 9001:2000 and configuration management requirements for CMMI®.

12.9   Summary

> What are the key elements to implementing a successful SQA program in a small organization?

The most crucial part of the solution of implementing a successful SQA program is hiring quality engineers who understand the work they are monitoring to the level that they could actually perform that work. Although they are considered to be a member of the project teams for which they perform quality engineering activities, it is important for them to report administratively through a different chain of command. Therefore, a well-qualified quality engineer, who is capable of doing the same type of monitored work, is an extra set of eyes on the project that can "tell it like it is." The quality engineer can provide technical advice when appropriate, bring a dose of reality to a project team when necessary, and may be able to recommend the best people in the organization to provide technical assistance when outside help is needed.

Small organizations and projects may not have the necessary measurement instrumentation to manage them through analysis of data and metrics. Often, the analysis of a projects status must be more qualitative in nature. The quality engineer, using knowledge, experience, and the advantage of being the independent observer, can help assess the true state of a project and bring this information to the project director or senior management, as required.

When a quality engineer must monitor many small projects, this means that each of them must go through some period of time where there is no quality engineering activity. Depending upon how thinly resources are stretched, this project "invisibility" could be for a significant amount of time. The frequency with which a quality engineer interacts with a project team, and the depth of those interactions, should be planned using guiding principles to make wise choices in allocating scarce quality engineering resources. These principles include prioritizing resource allocation based on project risk assessments (which include the project team's history of process violations), use of new technologies, and the project's strategic importance to the organization.

The quality engineers should turn their disadvantage of splitting their time among many projects into an advantage: an opportunity to see many different technical and process solutions, and share the best of them with their other projects that would benefit from them. Any improvements that would benefit the entire organization should be communicated through the organization's process improvement channels.

Overall efficiency of a quality engineer can be improved by using a generic schedule and SQA plan as a starting point for creating the project-specific schedules and plans. A Quality Engineer's Guide, which gives detailed work instructions and is developed incrementally, is a living document and can serve as a training guide.

Quality engineers should always be cognizant that the project team ultimately exists to produce a product, not to respond to the quality engineer, and should be judicious in applying their authority. They should be firm when they believe something needs to be corrected, and take their concerns through the appropriate escalation procedures if warranted. But they should also be willing to listen to the project team when they disagree with a quality engineer's finding, and not be dogmatic in applying the organization's processes. Sometimes a process is wrong for a particular situation and should be waived; sometimes it is wrong for the whole organization and should be amended.

In summary, quality engineering activities should add value to the project team's product development. The quality engineer must value the project team members and take care to minimize the disruption to product development activities. Interviewing team members at their convenience, listening to their concerns, and efficiently interacting with the project team, including participation in project team meetings and critical customer reviews, can go a long way toward fostering a good relationship between the quality engineer and the project team. Efficient and effective SQA, coupled with good processes that make sense and are not unduly burdensome, encourage the project team to work with the quality engineer as a fellow team member, with a common objective of producing a quality product.

References

[1]   Chrissis, M. B., M. Konrad, and S. Shrum, *CMMI®: Guidelines for Process Integration and Product Improvement*, 2nd ed., Boston, MA: Pearson Education, 2007, p. 427.

[2]   Mutafelija, B., and H. Stromberg, *Systematic Process Improvement Using ISO 9001:2000 and CMMI®*, Norwood, MA: Artech House, 2003.

[3]   *International Organization for Standardization, Quality Management Systems— Requirements, ISO 9001:2000*, ISO Publication, December 2000.

## CHAPTER 13

Development Quality Assurance

Joseph Meagher and G. Gordon Schulmeyer

13.1 Introduction

The tools and techniques that have been successfully applied by software quality engineering may also be applicable to assure the fidelity of other development processes. This chapter provides an approach based on using proven software quality assurance (SQA) methodology to evaluate and assure the implementation of systems and hardware development processes. This approach can be characterized by the term development quality assurance (DQA). The DQA implementation to systems is based on experience, whereas the DQA implementation to hardware development is proposed as a workable extension. These processes have been developing over a period of 3 years and actual feedback from the development/design disciplines indicates that a real advantage can be achieved in their application. Because software quality engineering had been more accustomed to looking at, and critiquing, development processes, it followed that software quality would develop the methodology that would be applied to the other disciplines. This was not surprising because in pre-CMMI® days, elements of the CMM® for Software were actually systems engineering functions that in some cases were performed by software engineers, and so software quality engineers were charged with verifying their implementation.

The challenge faced in applying these principles to hardware development quality engineering was greatly complicated by the fact that hardware design encompassed a broad spectrum of design disciplines. Indeed, in the authors' experience, process oversight was required to address hardware development of 40 distinct processes.

In implementing the systems and software quality assurance (SSQA) function, an SQA person is assigned either full time or part time as a quality engineer on the project. While the approach works for systems/software QA functions, the ability to assign a dedicated or even part-time quality engineer on a program basis for all disciplines was not deemed practical. This chapter addresses the systems and software quality assurance as a collaborative function, and then highlights a few main issues particularly relevant only to systems QA. An approach broadly based on software quality may be used but with significant tailoring to accommodate the many hardware design disciplines that may be encountered. The hardware design QA approach is covered later in this chapter.

13.2   Software QA Versus Traditional QA

The traditional role of quality assurance has been to assure that manufactured products conform to drawings and specifications. This is the interpretation as development relates to manufacturing and product acceptance.

Extensive coverage of quality-related standards is provided in Chapter 3; here is a brief summary leading up to DQA. Primarily, it was Mil-Q-9858, *Quality Program Requirements*, from 1963 that provided the requirements for how hardware quality personnel operated in the development/manufacturing environment during that timeframe. It addressed the following subjects:

- Quality program management, dealing primarily with organization, planning, records, and corrective actions;
- Facilities and standards, dealing with drawings, equipment, and production testing;
- Control of purchases, dealing with responsibility and purchasing data;
- Manufacturing control, dealing with materials control, and production fabrication, handling storage and delivery, statistical quality control and analysis, nonconforming material, and inspection status;
- Coordinated government/contractor actions, dealing with government inspection and government property.

Notice that this quality standard did not impose requirements for dealing with hardware development processes—a key element in this chapter.

With the emergence of software quality engineering as a branch of quality engineering through the imposition of MIL-S-52779, *Software Quality Engineering*, in the mid-1970s, quality professionals became involved in assuring the fidelity of the design process associated with development of software. This situation evolved because of the need to have quality oversight in the software development process. What marked the difference between the software quality professional and the hardware quality counterpart was the fact that the manufacturing of the software was basically trivial compared to the very complex manufacturing of the hardware. Indeed, software was easily either written to a tape, burned on a disk, or loaded into a programmable memory device.

MIL-STD-2167A, *Defense System Software Development*, from 1988, provided a documented approach for software development. In conjunction with MIL-STD-2167A, MIL-STD-2168, *Defense System Software Quality Program*, (also from 1988) was developed for verifying the fidelity of software development. In the 1990s, when these standards were no longer imposed, the prepackaged approach to SQA went with them. SQA now had to review the software processes thoroughly and determine at what points they needed to be evaluated to assure faithful implementation. While this is basically what MIL-STD-2168 accomplished relative to MIL-STD-2167A, SQA personnel now had to do it against new requirements/processes that were based on a company's best practices, ISO 9000, and upon the Software Engineering Institute (SEI) Capability Maturity Model® (CMM®) for Software. Because of the nature of the CMMI®, it became apparent that this could also be done for design/development processes other than software.

A key driver in this approach, beyond the obvious desire to improve software development processes, was that it provides an excellent response to elements of the Capability Maturity Model Integration for Development® (CMMI®-DEV). The obvious process area of interest in the CMMI® is Process and Product Quality Assurance (PPQA). This relationship of PPQA to SQA is covered in detail in Chapter 11.

13.3 Development Quality Assurance

DQA is the application of software quality engineering process verification methodology to software engineering, systems engineering, and hardware engineering. DQA is accomplished collaboratively for systems and software QA and independently for hardware design QA. It is collaborative for software and systems because the SQA person has performed very similar activities for software development that apply to systems development and so can perform QA on both functions without any significant retraining. Whereas, for hardware design, the SQA person usually does not have the technical expertise to perform QA of hardware design; hence, this is performed independently until appropriate experience or training is obtained.

Since the DQA approach is based on the software quality model, that approach is reviewed here. This is accomplished through the performance of process and work product evaluations, and through participation in key activities during the development process. The software quality engineer (SQE) ensures the implementation of the development processes and that the developed products meet customer requirements. This process is based on an examination of all tasks specified in the software development process and on identification of the SQA role in assuring that those tasks are implemented. SQE objectively verifies that the project's processes are defined and followed and achieves this verification by performing process evaluations. These evaluations involve comparison of the processes to their related process description for the project. Similarly, work product evaluations are conducted by objective SQEs to ensure that the work product conforms to its template (work product description) and is complete and consistent. Findings of noncompliance are distributed to the person responsible for the evaluated function or work product, to the cognizant manager, and to other appropriate personnel. Other copies are distributed so that all affected persons participating in the software development process are notified. Once the corrective action is formulated, it is evaluated to verify that root causes have been satisfactorily addressed. The proposed actions are tracked to closure, with concomitant verification of the effectiveness of the corrective action.

The participation in key activities during the software development process establishes the collaborative element to the SQE performance. SQEs participate in significant project activities such as: Integrated Product Teams (IPTs); peer reviews of work products; technical reviews of requirements, design, implementation, and test; and Configuration Control Boards (CCBs).

SQEs need to find out which:

- IPTs are on the project and, with the approval of the project manager, the involvement of the SQA personnel on appropriate IPTs;

- Work products are created or revised on the project, and participation in the peer reviews of the appropriate ones;
- Technical reviews are on the project and, with the approval of the project manager, the extent of involvement of SQEs on appropriate technical reviews;
- CCB meetings require involvement from SQEs as a participant on the CCB.

A more detailed description and analyses of these evaluation and participation roles of SQEs are covered in Chapters 1 and 11.

13.4   Systems and Software Quality Assurance: An Integrated Approach

Exactly like the tasks of the SQE, an SSQA engineer ensures the implementation of the systems development processes concurrently with the software development process. These activities, like the software quality activities, are conducted primarily through evaluations. While economies may be achieved if an SQE performs this SSQA function, it is possible that the function may be split and performed independently. Because all practical experience gained to date is based on joint implementation, this section will focus on that approach.

13.4.1   Process Evaluations

The tasks to be performed in assuring both systems and software process implementation are listed in Table 13.1, the SSQA task list. These tasks listed are performed as applicable for the project, meaning that not all of the tasks are performed for all projects. SSQE objectively verifies that the organizational standard software and the systems engineering process are defined and followed. These verifications are accomplished through evaluations and collaborative roles. Findings of noncompliance issues require corrective action and may also bring to light opportunities for process improvement.

The tasks that constitute the SSQE functions in relation to the software and the systems development processes include evaluation activities as well as participatory ones. The evaluation process should create an environment that encourages identifying, reporting, and solving quality issues, while the participation process generates better understanding on the part of SSQE and it solidifies a project team association.

Evaluations involve comparison of work products and processes to their requirements, ensuring appropriate corrective action for the deficiencies found, and tracking them to closure with verification of the corrective action. The scope of the evaluation process includes the following activities:

- Evaluate key processes and work products for compliance with the Project Plan, Software Development Plan (SDP), Systems Engineering Management Plan (SEMP), or an overall Integrated Project Plan, contractual requirements, the tailored standard process, and any other relevant requirements imposed on a project.

Table 13.1   SSQA Implementation Plan

SSQA Task	Area		Description	Frequency	Output
Architectural design process evaluation	SW	SYS	Ensure the architectural design process is per the Program Master Plan/SEMP/SDP	\<monthly\> during the relevant activities	Process Evaluation Report
CM audit participation	SW	SYS	Participate in CM audits such as FCA/PCA and PA/FAI	As scheduled in the CM Plan	Audit minutes
CM evaluation	SW	SYS	Ensure configuration and data management are performed in accordance with the CM Plan; this activity includes participation in CM self-audits when appropriate	\<quarterly\>	Process Evaluation Report
Contract review	SW	SYS	Perform a contract review identifying funding, resources, and skills required for implementing the SSQA process on the program	At contract award and when there are significant contract modifications	a) SSQA Plan b) Product Evaluation Report
Corrective action and configuration change participation	SW	SYS	Attend CCB(s) and review change requests before closure: this activity includes SCCB and CCB as appropriate	Attend CCB meetings when relevant, but at least time per month	CCB minutes; QA engineer sign-off on the change requests
Defect prevention evaluation	SW	SYS	Assure defect prevention is conducted per the SDP and SEMP	\<semiannually\>	Process Evaluation Report
Deliverable system environment certification	SW		Ensure that all deliverable parts of system environment are accounted for and certified prior to delivery	Prior to delivery of system environment	Product Evaluation Report
Detailed design process evaluation	SW	SYS	Ensure the systems and/or software design process is per the SEMP/SDP	\<monthly\> during the relevant activities	Process Evaluation Report
Development library evaluation	SW	SYS	Assure that the development library (systems and software) process is per the SEMP/SDP	\<quarterly\>	Process Evaluation Report
Installation and checkout evaluation	SW		Ensure installation and checkout is conducted according to the Installation and Checkout Plan	\<monthly\>, during the relevant activities	Process Evaluation Report
Integration and testing evaluation	SW		Assure that the integration and testing process is per the SDP and Integration Test Plan/Procedures	\<monthly\> during the relevant activities	Process Evaluation Report
IPT operations evaluation	SW	SYS	Assure that the development IPTs function in accordance with the Program IPT Operations Plan and appropriate procedures	\<semiannually\> for each IPT	Process Evaluation Report
IPT participation	SW	SYS	Participate in the program IPTs that involve design and development and provide real-time feedback	Attend IPT meetings when relevant, but at least one time per month	IPT records reflect attendance
Media verification evaluation	SW		Ensure that the media have been verified by engineering and properly labeled	After media have been verified and labeled	Process Evaluation Report
Nondeliverable software process evaluation	SW		Assure that nondeliverable software is properly selected/created, controlled, and verified to perform per its requirements	\<quarterly\>	Process Evaluation Report

Table 13.1 (continued)

SSQA Task	Area	Description	Frequency	Output
Nondeveloped software evaluation	SW	Ensure that engineering has verified nondeveloped software per incoming inspections process, and they are following the Reuse Plan, if applicable	<quarterly> for all nondeveloped software items and prior to incorporation for specific items	Process Evaluation Report
Nonproduction project close-out evaluation	SW	Ensure that the documentation and software code (as applicable) are consistent	At project close out	Product Evaluation Report
Peer review participation	SW SYS	Participate in the program peer reviews	<n documents>; <n% code>	Peer review minutes reflect participation
Peer review inspection evaluation	SW SYS	Assure the peer review process conforms to SEMP/SDP or peer review directive	<quarterly>	Process Evaluation Report
Project life-cycle model (PLCM) evaluation	SW SYS	Assure that both systems and software development have defined and implemented the PLCM	Upon PLCM definition and <semiannually> thereafter	Process Evaluation Report
Project metrics evaluation	SW SYS	Ensure SSQA program metrics are reported: a) Report evaluation b) Submit performance status	<quarterly>	Process Evaluation Report
QA measures reporting	SW SYS	Ensure SSQA program metrics are reported: a) Report evaluation b) Submit performance status	<monthly>	Evaluation Report to Management
Qualification test environment certification	SW SYS	Ensure that the required environment is in place and functioning	Prior to start of qualification testing and upon each change	Product Evaluation Report
Qualification test process evaluation	SW SYS	Ensure that the qualification testing process is per the qualification test plan and related elements of the Program Master Plan/SEMP/SDP	Prior to the start of qualification testing, during, and at completion	Process Evaluation Report
Quantitative management evaluation	SW	Assure that the program follows Quantitative Management Plan (for software, applies only to programs at CMMI® Level 4 or 5)	<quarterly>	Process Evaluation Report
Release process participation	SW	Participate in the software release process; verify that all included action requests (e.g., SCRs, DCRs, peer reviews) have been fully processed to closure	Whenever there is an applicable release	QA engineer signature on release verification documents
Requirements analysis process evaluation	SW SYS	Ensure that the requirements analysis process is per the SEMP/SDP; all requirements must be complete, correct, consistent, feasible, and testable	<monthly> during the relevant activities	Process Evaluation Report
Requirements management evaluation	SW SYS	Ensure requirements management follows Requirements Management Plan	<monthly> during the requirements analysis activity; <quarterly> thereafter	Process Evaluation Report
Risk management process evaluation	SW SYS	Assure that program has defined and managed risks in accordance with the Risk Management Plan	<quarterly>	Process Evaluation Report

Table 13.1   (continued)

SSQA Task	Area	Description	Frequency	Output
SDP evaluation	SW	Ensure the SDP complies with the criteria documented in the standard process, contract, and SOW	When SDP is created or revised, and when other relevant changes affect it	Product Evaluation Report
SEMP evaluation	SYS	Ensure the SEMP complies with the criteria documented in the standard process, contract, and SOW	When SEMP is created or revised, and when other relevant changes affect it	Product Evaluation Report
Software environment implementation evaluation	SW	Assure that Computer Resources and Facilities Group process is carried out in accordance with the Software Environment Implementation Plan	\<quarterly\>	Product Evaluation Report
Software maintenance process evaluation	SW	Ensure maintenance and operation is accomplished according to the Maintenance Plan	\<monthly\> during the relevant activities	Process Evaluation Report
SSQA cost and schedule control	SW SYS	Ensure SSQA cost and schedule control for the program through status reports and meetings	\<monthly\> or as requested	SSQA Progress Report
SSQA implementation plan maintenance	SW SYS	Maintain the SSQA Plan and update as required	As required	Updated SSQA Plan
SSQA orientation	SW SYS	Affected program personnel are briefed on SSQA activities and interface	After the SSQA task list is completed at program start-up and after major updates	Records recorded in the training database
SSQA records maintenance	SW SYS	Complete SSQA records are maintained throughout and following program per contract and the organization's requirements	Continually, throughout the program	All SSQA program records
SSQA tools certification	SW	SSQA tools certified by ensuring that they meet their requirements	Prior to use of SSQA tool	Product Evaluation Report
Subcontract management evaluation	SW	Ensure program's subcontract management follows Subcontract Management Plan and subcontract SOW	\<semiannually\>	Process Evaluation Report
Subcontract requirements flow down evaluation	SW	Ensure that the subcontract technical and nontechnical requirements are properly flowed down to the supplier	Prior to tendering the subcontract to the supplier; and if the subcontract changes	Product Evaluation Report
Subcontract status review participation	SW	QA engineer participates in status reviews with the subcontractor to ensure that the subcontractor is performing in accordance with their requirements	\<as appropriate for each subcontract\>	Subcontract status review minutes showing QA attendance
Subcontract technical review participation	SW	QA engineer participates in technical reviews with the subcontractor to ensure that the contractual requirements flowed down to the supplier are met and that the coordination of configuration management with the subcontractor is adequate	\<as appropriate for each subcontract\>	Subcontract technical review minutes showing QA Engineer attendance

Table 13.1 (continued)

SSQA Task	Area	Description	Frequency	Output
Subcontracted product acceptance	SW	QA engineer participates in subcontracted product acceptance testing to ensure that testing is conducted in accordance with the subcontractor's test plans and procedures	During acceptance of subcontracted product	"Attendance List;" QA engineer signature on test verification documents (for SW)
Subcontractor QA organization evaluation	SW	Ensure that the subcontractor adheres to the contractual requirements levied on them by performing evaluations of the subcontractor's QA organization	At least one time after award of subcontract and thereafter <as appropriate for each subcontract>	Process Evaluation Report
Subcontractor selection participation	SW	Participate in the subcontractor selection evaluation	During the subcontractor selection process	Minutes from the selection team
System integration testing evaluation	SW SYS	Ensure the system integration testing process is per the System Integration Test Plan/Procedure or equivalent document	<monthly> during the relevant activities	Process Evaluation Report
Technology change management (TCM) evaluation	SW SYS	Assure TCM is conducted per the SDP/SEMP	<annually>	Process Evaluation Report
Technical and management review participation	SW SYS	Participate in technical and management reviews to determine if the contractual requirements are met and to provide QA input	Attend technical reviews per the program schedule when relevant	Minutes of technical reviews reflecting QA attendance
Technical and management review process evaluation	SW SYS	Assure the conduct of technical and management reviews is in accordance with the Program Master Plan/SEMP/SDP	<quarterly>	Process Evaluation Report
Training evaluation	SW SYS	Assure that the program training is compliant with the Program Training Plan	<semiannually>	Process Evaluation Report
Work product evaluations	SW SYS	Evaluate work products (identified in the Program Master Plan/SEMP/SDP) for compliance to the criteria documented in the Program Master Plan/SEMP/SDP, contract, and SOW (other completion criteria, such as peer reviews; complete and correct; standards met; requirements flowed correctly; testing complete and recorded; problems documented and tracked; requirements traced up and down all levels; documentation compared to baseline as applicable)	Upon availability of work product prior to delivery	Product Evaluation Report

- Resolve all noncompliances with project-assigned personnel when possible, but escalate to higher management when necessary. It is advisable to regularly review noncompliances for status and escalate, when necessary, to attain the visibility required for closure.

There are few projects that would invoke all the activities described in the SSQA Implementation Plan; therefore, the elements of the implementation plan are intended to be modified or deleted to match the requirements of the project.

13.4.2   Work Product Evaluations

Work products are evaluated as they become available for delivery or use, including revisions by type and frequency as listed in the SSQA Implementation Plan. Evaluations of work products may be performed using the following criteria:

- Templates;
- Customer supplied data item descriptions;
- Work product specification (if required);
- Standards;
- Procedures;
- Plans;
- Directives;
- Editorial correctness (spelling, grammar).

The SSQE should ensure that the work products undergo a peer review. Each work product to be peer reviewed should be identified as such up front in the detailed list of the project's work products (configuration management identification). One method to implement the work product evaluation is through the SSQE involvement in that work product's peer review. That is assuming there is an effective peer review process as evaluated by the SSQE and the product was peer reviewed; then the product review need cover only the following:

- All peer review actions are closed.
- The version being submitted is correct.
- The product is complete.
- Management approval has been obtained.

When a work product has not been peer reviewed by an effective process, the work product must be reviewed more thoroughly by the SSQE on the project. Chapter 7 provides extensive detail on the peer review process.

13.4.3   Formulating the SSQA Implementation Plan

The SSQA Implementation Plan describes evaluation planning, scheduling, and tracking activities, which are to be considered for application on every systems and software development project. The most important activities are to develop and maintain the SSQA Implementation Plan for software and systems engineering and to perform the specified tasks. Other actions are required to support those activities. As noted previously, it may be advisable to develop separate plans for software and systems. This would not necessarily preclude performing some activities concurrently.

The SSQA review of the contract, SDP, and SEMP are used to identify the resources required to ensure quality of the development process and to write a SSQA Implementation Plan. Individual tasks in the SSQA Implementation Plan may be tailored or removed (delete row) according to project requirements. In particular, the wording of description and frequency entries must be tailored as necessary to meet the requirements of the project. Items in angle brackets in the frequency column are examples and should be considered further in order that they are made consistent with project needs. Consider the available funding versus customer requirements to set limits on the details for implementation (sampling percentage, frequency and schedule of evaluations, and so on). It is the task of the project-assigned SSQE to assure that the plan and schedule are coordinated with project engineering/development. So, the schedule for SSQA evaluations needs to be integrated into the project schedule. It is advisable to create a schedule and status that schedule to assure that key evaluations are being performed in the development life cycle when they will have the greatest benefit. Once a part of the life cycle is completed, the impact of an evaluation performed after the fact is greatly diminished.

The objective evidence required for each activity should be considered and is included as the output column that defines whether it is a process evaluation report, a work product evaluation report, or an attendee list for meetings and/or reviews.

13.4.4 Keeping the SSQA Implementation Plan Current

When changes are made to the SEMP, SDP, or other project planning documents, appropriate changes to the SSQA Implementation Plan must also be made so that it is compatible. The plan is updated if:

- Any project schedule, activities or responsibilities are changed (e.g., SOW, Project Plan, SEMP, SDP, CM plan, and relevant organizational standards);
- Discrepancies are found;
- An approved action request requires a change;
- A revision to the organization's standard process, or more specifically to the systems engineering or software engineering process, requires a change;
- Results of evaluations indicate the frequencies of evaluations should be adjusted (up or down).

If the SSQA Implementation Plan requires monthly evaluations of the project management processes, and those processes for 3 consecutive months have no findings (nonconformance) associated with them, it may be appropriate to extend the evaluations to quarterly. Contrary-wise, if the project management processes appear out of control (many nonconformances), it may be appropriate to increase the frequency of evaluations to bimonthly to identify weaknesses sooner so that they may be eradicated quicker.

13.4.5   SSQA Tools and Techniques

The application of tools and techniques varies from contract to contract, depending on the life-cycle requirements of the project; SSQE personnel must determine which are to be applied on a specific project. Tools that are often used include Microsoft Access, Excel, and Project. Many organizations have devised their own specific evaluation reporting tool based upon a database capability within their own organization. They often have a related tool to track nonconformances to closure with their own tool or use the projects preexisting problem reporting or action item tracking tools to perform this activity.

SSQA techniques and methods include providing orientation, elevating nonconformances to senior management, participating in engineering review activities, and reporting measures, as well as the prime mission of evaluating engineering activities and work products. SSQEs determine from the Project Plan, the SEMP and/or the SDP which:

- IPTs are on the project and the involvement of the SSQE personnel on appropriate IPTs;
- Work products are created or revised on the project;
- Technical reviews are conducted on the project and the extent of involvement of SSQEs on appropriate technical reviews.

The expected extent of SSQE involvement on CCBs (software, project, or other) is based on what is mandated in a CM Plan or a CM CCB program directive.

13.4.6   IPT Participation

Participation in IPTs provides an opportunity for SSQEs to do their job more effectively while contributing to the project. Because these SSQEs have special knowledge of quality concepts, they can monitor and ensure that a product meets quality requirements as it evolves in the IPT. It is important that an SSQE is invited to all meetings of these activities, even though attendance at every one probably is neither required nor possible. Remember that the IPTs are integrated teams that include systems, software, and hardware. Here the emphasis is on systems and software development as done in a collaborative, team environment with participants from multiple disciplines so that all aspects of the subsystem the team is developing has sufficient coverage. The SSQE contributes technical and quality expertise to the IPT by involvement in the following:

- Project training;
- Reviewing directives/processes;
- Up-front IPT decisions;

- Technical reviews;
- Interchanges.

This final bulleted item is elaborated upon here.

The involvement of the SSQE in both system and software activities, as well as a day-to-day interface with the traditional quality professionals, facilitates a "cross-pollination" within a project group. Looking at the development and design process as members of multiple IPTs facilitates connectivity among IPTs that might not otherwise be realized. In addition, the SSQE and their hardware quality counterpart bring to the development teams broad experience and lessons learned throughout the total development/production life cycle that often prevent the recurrence of past mistakes.

13.4.7   Review of Deliverable Products

An SSQE may approach deliverable product reviews through a number of methods. The most frequent is to perform a work product evaluation and write a work product evaluation report concerning the deliverable work product. Next most frequent is the participation in a peer review of the deliverable work product. The details of that method are covered in Section 13.4.2.

Finally, there is participation in an IPT. This method allows the SSQE to provide recommendations to the IPT regarding the production of work products to meet requirements and usually does not function as a developer of the work product except to provide QA-related content. When the deliverable work product is completed, since the SSQE participated in the quality aspects of its production, the only step left for the SSQE to perform is to produce a work product evaluation report of the deliverable work product.

13.4.8   Participative Activities

SSQEs are involved in the day-to-day workings of the project through these participative activities. Having these SSQEs as both participants in and evaluators of an activity does not create a problematic dichotomy because of the following split of tasking. SSQEs provide inputs and perform QA evaluations of the work products and processes within the meeting framework without documenting findings in an evaluation report until the work product is completed. SSQE feedback to the activity helps to improve the process, and the SSQE's involvement permits observation of the actual operation of the activity and the improvements that evolve. Then on a periodic basis, the SSQE uses the participative experience to provide formal feedback on how the process is implemented and documents the state of the process in an evaluation report. This participation evolving into evaluation is a win-win for the project because the knowledge gained while participating enhances the ability to provide evaluations to improve the process. The crucial aspect is to be able to maintain objectivity within a peer review, IPT, CCB, or other activity to which the SSQE contributed. This requires a maturity of judgment probably only the senior SSQEs have obtained. Other more junior SSQEs may be advised by the more senior SSQEs to provide the appropriate balance required to be objective during participative activities.

13.4.9   Results of Evaluations

The results of SSQA evaluations are recorded as an evaluation report (see Figure 13.1) and become the objective evidence that those evaluations have been performed. These evaluation reports contain:

- What was evaluated;
- Date;
- Name of the evaluator;
- Criteria used for the evaluation;
- Evaluation status (conforming or nonconforming);
- Findings (when nonconforming);
- Person(s) required to response;
- Response due date;
- A severity code;
- Updates relative to the acceptance of responses.

Evaluation reports must be entered in a timely manner. When possible, preventive action may be suggested by an SSQE based on this data. At the conclusion of the project or at other appropriate events in the project, the SSQA measurement data may provide the basis for an SSQA lessons learned report.

QA Evaluation Report

Distribution:

Project Evaluated: Date of Evaluation:

Evaluation of Work Product(s):

Evaluation of Process(es):

Evaluation Criteria (Identify standards, project plans, etc.)

Evaluation Results (Conforming or Nonconforming)
              (If nonconforming, describe nonconformances):

Corrective Action Assigned to: _____ Due Date: _____

Duration of Evaluation (Provide hours expended for this evaluation): _____

QA Evaluator: _____

Corrective Action Verified by: _____ on: _____

Figure 13.1   QA evaluation report form.

13.5   Systems Quality Assurance

Systems quality assurance is an element of DQA. Most of the coverage needed for systems QA is discussed in Section 13.4, but there are some key systems activities requiring QA that deserve special mention here. The technical life cycle fits within the overall project life cycle. That technical life cycle bracketed with systems activities is highlighted in Figure 13.2, where blocks 1 and 4 are of interest to this discussion.

The requirements and architectural development phase (block 1 in Figure 13.2) has a number of important activities relevant to systems development, and therefore relevant to DQA. The systems organization is focused on understanding the customer requirements at this phase, especially with interaction with the customers (end users). Also, there is a substantial systems activity to define product requirements derived from the identified customer requirements. Also, there is an effort by systems personnel to produce architectural descriptions/diagrams that lead to a high level design by the developers. Each of these activities described follow a defined process and produce work products that are of interest to the QA person on the project. These process and work product systems evaluations result in appropriate evaluation reports.

The system integration, verification and validation phase (block 4 in Figure 13.2) is similarly relevant to DQA. This phase again brings systems engineering into the forefront of activities in the technical life cycle. After software and hardware developers produce the product, it is up to systems engineering to bring it together, test it as a system, and sell it to the customer. Most often QA becomes involved in the sell-off activities—usually witnessing the acceptance tests for/or with the customer. With this customer (end user) involvement these acceptance tests become the validation of the system. Also, QA often is involved in the "dry runs" of acceptance tests, which are often considered verification of the system.

13.6   Hardware Design Quality Assurance

Hardware quality assurance is an element of DQA. Hardware development/engineering considered in the scope of hardware quality assurance includes such diverse disciplines as:

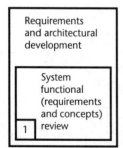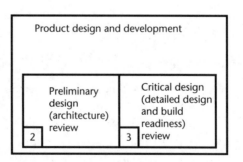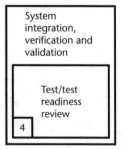

Figure 13.2   Typical overall systems life cycle. (*After:* [1].)

- Electrical engineering;
- Mechanical engineering;
- Digital electronics;
- Analog devices;
- Power supplies;
- Optical engineering.

These are very diverse fields, but they may all be handled by DQA. The traditional QA activities mentioned above primarily had the quality engineer in manufacturing working product issues after the board or whatever device was built. What, then, is the flow for DQA to follow and perform evaluations on? The hardware designer produces design documents, design tool outputs, and/or drawings. They perform reviews with peers, technical experts, and customers. Often for implementation, there is a prototype or first article that receives most of the attention from the hardware designers to remove all functional and interface defects. This step usually results in revision notices (RNs) to the drawings that described how to build the first article. In listing these hardware development steps, one may see that the steps are not that different from systems-software development. Hardware development produces documents (subject to work product evaluations), performs reviews (subject to participation and evaluation), has configuration management (subject to participation and evaluation), and performs various hardware engineering processes (subject to evaluation).

To be more specific, the hardware DQA approach is based on verifying a hardware engineering process to a prescribed model process flow. The assumption is that hardware engineering has defined its processes on a relatively common functional basis—electrical engineering versus mechanical engineering versus optical engineering, and so on—so that the engineers performing the activities have the process flow in front of them to follow. A relatively common process flow over the broad scope of hardware design process is both possible and very desirable. And while processes may vary between engineering disciplines, there are elements or subprocesses that are desirable for all design processes.

For each specific hardware design product or service, a detailed process flow is developed that describes the activities that occur in each applicable phase of the hardware development process. The overall process flow is depicted in Figure 13.3.

Within each phase of the flow are:

- Descriptions of the tasks to be completed for each subtask in the detailed process flow;
- Tools required to complete the applicable phase of the detailed process flow;
- Inputs needed to accomplish the applicable phase of the detailed process flow;
- Outputs that are the results of the activities of the applicable phase of the detailed process flow;
- Exit criteria that indicate completion of the applicable phase of the detailed process flow;
- Related documents and templates.

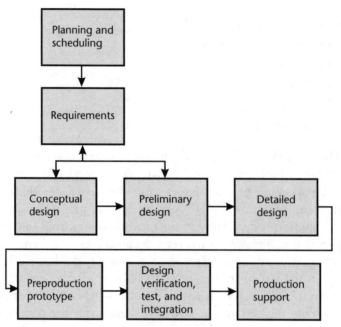

Figure 13.3   Typical overall hardware design process flow.

For each applicable phase in the detailed process flow, a subprocess description may be further defined that breaks down each block to a lower level. Those lower levels include:

- Key design review points, including internal technical review signoffs;
- Checklists and design review point;
- Relationships between process steps;
- Sequential process steps and/or material flow;
- Rework loops;
- Decision points.

Such a common approach facilitates the assignment of design engineers across design departments and facilitates process assurance. The DQA engineer uses this model and lower level submodels to plan evaluations of the design processes and associated interim and final work products. That process flow is one criterion for DQA evaluations of process implementation across the various hardware engineering organizations.

Hardware engineering functions each need to manage those processes described in their process. Each has to provide configuration control to ensure that practitioners have the correct, latest process to work from. They also need to capture appropriate process-related metrics concerning usage and accuracy of implementation by the practitioners to assure that they have a robust process online.

In summary, the functions listed for SSQA are repeated here and basically apply to hardware development QA:

- Process evaluations and audits;
- Evaluation of process work products;
- Formulating an implementation plan;
- Keeping the SSQA Plan current;
- Use of tools and techniques;
- IPT participation;
- Review of deliverable products;
- Participative activities;
- Compiling and distributing the results of evaluations and audits.

The result of this consolidation is a DQA Implementation Plan much like the SSQA Implementation Plan. A DQA Implementation Plan based on the aforementioned is depicted in Table 13.2.

13.7   Overcoming Cultural Resistance

While the concept of quality assurance involvement in software development is well established, it generally has not been sought in either the systems or hardware design world. As was pointed out in the introduction, quality from a hardware design perspective has been to look at it as an "after you design it, let quality makes sure it is built right." There is no recipe that once applied will yield immediate acceptance of QA oversight. However, there are actions that a quality organization can take that will help establish an environment of acceptance of their function in the systems and hardware development arenas.

First, cultural resistance may be reduced by leveraging off of the successes demonstrated by SQA. SQA has played a key part in assuring that a well-defined software development process is implemented. Through the collection of metrics, this effectiveness may be measured with improvements in code generation efficiency, error containment (fixed where introduced), defects per KSLOC, and so on. (See Chapter 16 for further details concerning SQA metrics.) When brought to the attention of management and where SQA's role has clearly be demonstrated as a contributor, SQA will be "invited into the tent."

Next, consider satisfaction of the CMMI® as an integral aspect of reducing the cultural resistance to DQA. What has the impact of the CMMI® been to software and systems development? The CMMI® presents a model of the important aspects (requirements or practices) of development and management of large development projects. Through attention to these practices, organizations using their own methods have produced better products more efficiently, as demonstrated in the many published benefits of the CMMI® [2–5]. In particular, Table 13.3 summarizes the results from many companies. Importantly, the CMMI® is not prescriptive in how to do the practices, but rather insistent on evidence that those practice or sufficient alternative practices are being performed.

The assurance of process integrity is the basis for process improvement. Measurement of a consistently applied process permits its effectiveness to be assessed, deficiencies revealed, and improvement opportunities identified. This in itself

Table 13.2 Sample DQA Plan

DQA Task	Description	Frequency	Output
CM evaluation	Ensure configuration and data management are performed in accordance with the CM Procedures and process documentation; this activity includes participation in CM self-audits when appropriate	\<semiannually\> if no firmware and \<quarterly\> if firmware is developed in area	Process Evaluation Report
Concept design/requirements analysis process evaluation	Ensure that the concept design including requirements analysis process is per the documented process	\<quarterly\> in concept design and requirements analysis phase	Process Evaluation Report
Preliminary design process evaluation	Ensure the preliminary design process is per the process documentation	\<monthly\> during preliminary design	Process Evaluation Report
Detail design process evaluation	Ensure the detail design process is per the process documentation	\<monthly\> during detailed design	Process Evaluation Report
Hardware implementation	Ensure that the process for hardware implementation is being followed	\<monthly\> during the hardware implementation phase	Process Evaluation Report
Test/product validation/verification	Ensure that the design processes associated with test is per the process documentation	\<monthly\> during product validation/verification	Process Evaluation Report
Design management and metrics evaluation	Metrics are collected and maintained in accordance with department direction	\<semiannually\>	Process Evaluation Report
Requirements management evaluation	Ensure requirements management follows Requirements Management Plan	\<quarterly\>	Process Evaluation Report
Internal review process	Assure the conduct and documentation of internal reviews is per the documented process and procedures	\<quarterly\>	Process Evaluation Report
Training evaluation	Assure that the area training needs are documented	\<annually\>	Process Evaluation Report
Technology change management (TCM) evaluation	Assure TCM is conducted per the Hardware Development Plan/SEMP	\<annually\>	Process Evaluation Report
Quantitative management evaluation	Assure that the program follows Quantitative Management Plan (focuses on CMMI® Maturity Levels 4 or 5)	\<quarterly\>	Process Evaluation Report
Integration testing evaluation	Ensure the system integration testing process is per the System Integration Test Plan/Procedure or equivalent document	\<monthly\> during the relevant activities	Process ER; System level test sign-off
Risk management process evaluation	Assure that the area has defined and managed risks	\<quarterly\>	Process Evaluation Report

would be sufficient reason for the consideration of implementing DQA. However, the emergence of CMMI® and its extension to the hardware design discipline, beyond software and systems, provides a powerful incentive for DQA

Table 13.3 Summary of CMMI® Performance Improvements

Improvements	Median	Number of Data Points	Low	High
Cost	20%	21	3%	87%
Schedule	37%	19	2%	90%
Productivity	67%	16	11%	255%
Quality	50%	18	29%	132%
Customer satisfaction	14%	6	–4%	55%
Return on investment	4.8:1	14	2:1	27.7:1

Source: [6].

implementation. The requirement is now there to apply the PPQA process area to hardware development. As companies move to the CMMI®, the need for QA development oversight beyond the traditional SQA role provides a segue for QA into the systems and hardware disciplines.

Once involvement is requested and/or required for hardware and systems development, an orientation describing QA activities and methods can be provided to all engineering personnel. This presentation should include the list of the evaluations to be performed with a schedule, the manner in which the results of the evaluations will be distributed and to whom, and the method for the engineers to respond to nonconforming evaluations. The orientation may be given at a general meeting of the project personnel or to individual IPTs. Attendance should be tracked so that when and if project personnel are changed new engineers are oriented on the QA role in the development cycle.

In assuring adherence to system processes, the software quality engineer may be easily leveraged to perform this task. In the area of hardware design assurance, the duality that is evident with systems-software is not present. This effort, however, may be formulated such that either the SQE or hardware QE could effectively assure hardware development integrity. While the process is straightforward and easily appreciated by the SQA professional, its acceptance by other quality professionals and nonsoftware disciplines may be an issue. These are hopefully mitigated by the points just discussed.

13.8 Conclusion

DQA is not always easy to implement in the overall development environment. However, innovative companies discover ways to accomplish DQA on their projects. They recognize that the quality assurance of software development has paid significant dividends and that the practices in the CMMI®-DEV provide a solid engineering and project management approach (process) to produce products. In fact, some organizations have applied these principles across all of engineering, including the DQA aspect, to assure engineering development excellence.

References

[1]   Berauer, B., "Life Cycle Considerations of the CMMI® Model," *National Defense Industrial Association, CMMI® Technology Conference*, Denver, CO, 2003.

[2]   Gibson, D. L., D. R. Goldenson, and K. Kost, *Performance Results of CMMI®-Based Process Improvement*, CMU/SEI-2006-TR-004, ESC-TR-2006-004, August 2006.

[3]   Hefner, R., "Achieving the Promised Benefits of CMMI®," *CMMI® Technology Conference & User Group*, November 14–17, 2005.

[4]   Reitzig, R. W., et al., "Calculating CMMI®-Based ROI, Why, When, What, and How?" *CMMI® Technology Conference & User Group*, November 14, 2005.

[5]   Goldenson, D. R., D. L. Gibson, and R. W. Ferguson, "Why Make the Switch? Evidence About the Benefits of CMMI®," *SEPG*, Software Engineering Institute, 2004.

[6]   Goldenson, D. R., and D. L. Gibson, "Measuring Performance: Evidence About the Results of CMMI®," *CMMI® Technology Conference & User Group*, November 2005, p. 12.

## CHAPTER 14

Quality Management in IT

Norman Moreau

14.1 Introduction

This chapter examines quality management in information technology (IT). Quality management, which is the coordination of activities to direct and control an organization with regard to quality [1], can be applied to any industry. Many of the principles and concepts of quality management that apply to software development and maintenance activities also apply to IT activities. The principles and concepts that apply to both industries that will be examined in this chapter are:

- Identifying key IT processes, their sequence, and interaction;
- Planning for defect prevention versus detection by applying IT best practices;
- Using and implementing standards to achieve internationally recognized registration or demonstrate appropriate levels of IT governance;
- Resolving the IT equivalent to software bugs, defects, and errors;
- Determining and documenting customer requirements;
- Monitoring and measuring service performance to assure customer requirements are met and continual improvement occurs;
- Assuring procurement quality when outsourcing key IT processes;
- Parallels in the bodies of knowledge between software and IT quality professionals.

To understand the context of this chapter it is important to have a definition of IT. "Information Technology includes any equipment [telecommunication and computer] or interconnected system or subsystem of equipment that is used in the automatic acquisition, storage, manipulation, management, movement, control, display, switching, interchange, transmission, or reception of data or information [may also include voice and video]. The term "information technology" includes [telecommunication equipment and] computers, ancillary equipment, software, firmware and similar procedures, services (including support services), and related resources" [2].

14.2   Key IT Processes

Philip Crosby (see Chapter 2) stated that [3]:

> Quality management is a systematic way of guaranteeing that organized activities happen the way they are planned. It is a management discipline concerned with preventing problems from occurring by creating the attitudes and controls that make prevention possible.

To successfully apply quality management to the "organized activities" performed by an IT organization, it is necessary to be familiar with the key IT processes. This can best be accomplished by examining the key processes associated with IT.

IT services in organizations are provided by an internal department or an outsourced organization known as the IT organization. The IT organization consists of the IT infrastructure. An IT infrastructure describes all the components used in the delivery of the IT services to users, including the computing and telecommunications hardware, software, accommodation, people, documentation, and meta-data [4]. These components and their use must be managed—hence the term IT infrastructure management. Collectively, IT services and the management of the IT infrastructure is referred to as IT service management (ITSM). ITSM is the principles and practices of designing, delivering, and maintaining IT services to an agreed-upon level of quality, all in support of a customer activity [5].

This section describes the key processes found in the typical IT organization. These key processes are analogous to the software engineering processes or functions found in a software life cycle.

14.2.1   ITSM Processes

ITSM is based on implementing key processes that are grouped into two categories of IT service: IT service support and IT service delivery. Within these two broad categories are ITSM processes that assure the agreed-upon levels of quality are achieved. The concept of agreed-upon levels of quality is discussed in Section 14.6. These processes are described next.

14.2.1.1   IT Service Support

IT service support consists of the following processes oriented toward the efficient delivery of IT operational services and includes [6]:

1. *Service desk function:* Provides a strategic central point of contact for customers and support the incident management process by providing an operational single point of contact to manage incidents to resolution.
2. *Incident management:* Responsible for restoring normal state IT service operations as quickly as possible to minimize the adverse impact on business operations.
3. *Problem management:* Minimizes the adverse impacts of incidents and problems on the business caused by errors in the IT infrastructure and initiate actions to prevent recurrence of incidents related to those errors.

4. *Configuration management:* Responsible for identifying, recording, and reporting on configuration items and their relationships to the underpinning IT service.

5. *Change management:* Coordinates and controls all changes to IT services to minimize the adverse impacts of those changes to business operations and the users of IT services.

6. *Release management:* Implements changes to IT services by taking a holistic (people, process, technology, and governance) view that considers all aspects of a change, including planning, designing, building, testing, training, communication, and deployment activities.

14.2.1.2   IT Service Delivery

IT service delivery consists of the following processes that relate to the longer-term planning, control, and managerial aspects of IT services:

1. *Service-level management:* Plans, coordinates, negotiates, reports, and manages the quality of IT services at an acceptable cost.

2. *Availability management:* Responsible for optimizing the capability of the IT infrastructure, services, and supporting organization to deliver a cost-effective and sustained level of service availability that meets business requirements.

3. *Capacity management:* Ensures that current and future capability and performance aspects of the IT infrastructure are provided to meet business requirements at an acceptable cost.

4. *Service continuity management:* Supports business continuity management functions by ensuring that IT services can be recovered in the event of a major business disruption within required timescales.

5. *Financial management for IT services:* Provides budgeting, accounting, and charging services to control, manage, and recover IT costs and expenditures.

6. *Security management:* Responsible for preventing the occurrence of security-related incidents by managing confidentiality, integrity, and availability of IT services and data in line with business requirements at an acceptable cost.

7. *Applications management:* Manages applications from the initial business need, through all stages in the application life cycle, up to and including retirement.

8. *Software asset management:* Provides good corporate governance, namely to manage, control and protect an organization's software assets, including management of the risks arising from the use of those software assets.

14.3   IT Best Practices

14.3.1   ITIL®

In the development and maintenance of software, an organization strives to prevent defects from being introduced into its product versus detecting them after the product has been released. This is accomplished by applying industry best practices (see Chapter 3) such as:

- The Software Engineering Institute's (SEI) Capability Maturity Model Integration® (CMMI®);
- ISO/IEC 12207:1995 Information technology—Software life-cycle processes;
- ISO/IEC 15504:2004 Information technology—Process assessment—Parts 1 to 6 [also know as Software Process Improvement and Capability dEtermination (SPICE)];
- Creation and maintenance of development plans, and performance of software inspections throughout the software life cycle;
- Casual analysis or root cause analysis on all defects that are discovered.

In IT the most recognized example of ITSM best practices is IT Infrastructure Library (ITIL®). ITIL® is a set of books originally published in the late 1980s by the British government that contains guidelines to help IT organizations improve operational efficiency and service quality. In the 1980s, the quality of the IT services provided to the British government was such that the then Central Computer and Telecommunications Agency (CCTA) and now the Office of Government Commerce (OGC) was asked to develop an approach for efficient and cost-effective use of IT resources by British public sector organizations. The aim was to develop an approach independent of any supplier. This resulted in the ITIL® best practices. The ITIL® best practices have grown to become major influencers of IT service management change and process improvement. This effort by the British government closely parallels the initiative funded by the U.S. Department of Defense (DoD) to have the Software Engineering Institute of Carnegie Melon University develop a maturity model for improving the software development and maintenance process (CMM®, and now the CMMI®).

ITIL® is a customer-focused, process-oriented approach to ITSM, and it is similar to the SEI's CMMI®. ITIL® gives a detailed description of a number of important IT practices with comprehensive checklists, tasks, procedures, and responsibilities that can be tailored to any IT organization. Where possible, these practices have been defined as processes covering the major activities of IT service organizations. The broad subject area covered by the ITIL® publications makes it useful to refer to them regularly and to use them to set improvement objectives for the IT organization. Although not organized into a maturity level framework like the CMMI®, an organization can grow and mature with the publications.

ITIL® provides a common-sense framework of processes, functions, and roles in the planning, delivery, and management of IT services in support of business needs. Table 14.1 shows the IT service management structure recommended by ITIL®.

Today, ITIL® is widely adopted by IT organizations in Europe and is increasingly being implemented by IT organizations throughout the world. As more emphasis is being put on the need to adopt best practices, awareness and expectations of ITIL® are rising fast.

ITIL® is now supported by a wide range of quality service providers, accredited training agencies, consultants, and professional qualifications. Users of ITIL® are supported by examination and user group organizations that can support training

Table 14.1   TSM Structure Recommended by ITIL®

IT Service Management				
Service Delivery				
Service Level Management	Financial Management	Capacity Management	Continuity Management	Availability Management
Service Support				
Service Desk	Incident Management	Problem Management	Configuration Management	Change Management	Release Management

and adoption of the ITIL® methodology. One such user group organization is the IT Service Management Forum (itSMF®) [7], which serves as a major focal point and source of information regarding ITIL® processes and best practices and also provides links to related ITIL® publications.

14.3.1.1   Books in the IT Infrastructure Library

The guidance developed by the British Office of Government Commerce (OGC) is documented in a set of books that describe an integrated process of IT service standards and best practices for managing IT services. The following are the eight principal books in the library that guide business users through the planning, delivery, and management of IT services [8].

1. *Service Support.* This book focuses on ensuring that the business has access to appropriate services to support business functions. Issues covered in this book include the Service Desk, Incident Management, Problem Management, Configuration Management, Change Management, and Release Management.

2. *Service Delivery.* This book covers the service the business requires of the provider in order to enable adequate support to the business users. Service Delivery covers all aspects that must be taken into consideration including Service Level Management, Financial Management for IT Services, IT Service Continuity Management, Availability Management, Contingency Planning, and Capacity Management. The purpose of this book is to show the links and the principal relationships between all the Service Management and other Infrastructure Management processes.

3. *Planning to Implement Service Management.* This book answers the question "Where do I start with ITIL®?" It explains the steps necessary to identify how an organization might expect to benefit from ITIL® and how to start reaping results from those benefits. It will help organizations in identifying their strengths and weaknesses, enabling them to develop the former and overcome the latter.

4. *Security Management.* This book looks at security from the service provider standpoint, identifying how Security Management relates to the IT Security Officer and how it provides the level of security necessary for the provision of the total service to the organization. The guide focuses on the process of implementing security requirements identified in the service level agreement (SLA) rather than considering business issues of security policy.

5. *The Business Perspective.* This book is concerned with helping business managers to understand the provisions of IT service. For IT to bring the greatest possible benefits to a business, IT practitioners must develop a deep understanding of their organization's key principles and requirements. Issues covered include Business Continuity Management, Partnerships and Outsourcing, Surviving Change, and Transformation of Business Practices through Change and Innovation.

6. *ICT Infrastructure Management.* Information and Communications Technology (ICT) Infrastructure Management is concerned with the processes, organization, and tools needed to provide a stable IT and communications infrastructure and is the foundation for ITIL® service management processes. The book covers Design and Planning, Deployment, Operations, and Technical Support.

7. *Application Management.* This book provides an outline of the Application Management life cycle and is a guide for business users, developers and service managers of how applications can be managed from a service management perspective. This book positions service management at the heart of the provision of information services to the business. Based on this perspective, applications should be managed throughout their life cycle with the business objectives in mind.

8. *Software Asset Management.* Software is one of the most critical elements of information and communications technologies and most organizations have huge investments in software, whether internally developed or externally procured. However, organizations often do not invest commensurate resources into managing these software assets. This book has been developed to assist with understanding what software asset management is and to explain what is required to perform it effectively and efficiently as identified in industry best practice.

14.3.2 SEI CMMI®-SVC

The United States now recognizes that engineered systems and software are dependent on IT. IT service support and delivery play a critical role in network-centric warfare, a commonly used term for warfare that is dependent on fast and reliable information delivery and sharing. In 2008 the SEI was expected to release the CMMI® for services product suite or CMMI®-SVC. CMMI®-SVC will provide guidance for delivering services within organizations and to external customers. CMMI®-SVC is a minimal and logical extension to CMMI® v1.2 content, allowing current CMMI® users to reuse CMMI® investments to improve service performance. The CMMI®-SVC process areas are similar to the CMMI®-DEV (Development). The proposed process areas for CMMI®-SVC are shown in Table 14.2 [9].

Table 14.2   CMMI®-SVC Proposed Process Areas

Process Management	*Service Establishment and Delivery*
Organizational Innovation and Deployment (OID)	Incident and Request Management (IRM)*
	Service Delivery (SD)*
Organizational Process Definition (OPD)	Service System Development (SSD)*
Organizational Process Focus (OPF)	Service Transition (ST)*
Organizational Process Performance (OPP)	
Organizational Service Management (OSM)*	
Organizational Training (OT)	

Service Support	*Project Management*
Causal Analysis and Resolution (CAR)	Capacity and Availability Management (CAM)*
Configuration Management (CM)	Integrated Project Management (IPM)
Decision Analysis and Resolution (DAR)	Project Monitoring and Control (PMC)
Measurement and Analysis (MA)	Project Planning (PP)
Problem Management (PRM)*	Requirements Management (REQM)
Process and Product Quality Assurance (PPQA)	Risk Management (RSKM)
	Quantitative Project Management (QPM)
	Service Continuity Management (SCON)*
	Supplier Agreement Management (SAM)

*Service addition

14.4   ITSM Standards

14.4.1   ISO 20000

The IT Infrastructure Library is not a standard and thus there exists no auditing criteria for verifying the ITIL® conformance by an organization. For many years, the choice for third party verification was either ISO 9001 or BS 15000-1. ISO 9001 is a quality management standard from the International Organization for Standardization (ISO). Originally developed for manufacturing, about one-third of ISO 9001 users are not manufacturers, but rather service sector companies, including IT organizations.

The British Standards Institute (BSI) created British Standard BS 15000-1 as an audit standard, and while it was not an international standard, it did deliver specifications for managing IT, implementing the ITIL®, and establishing audit criteria and corporate-level certification. Although used primarily in the United Kingdom, BS 15000-1 has had some traction elsewhere in the world. However, following in the path of ISO 9001, the BSI submitted BS 15000-1 to the ISO and in December 2005, the ISO released it as ISO 20000. Now, for the first time, IT has its own dedicated international standard for auditing and certifying conformance to best practice.

ISO 20000 is an international industry standard like ISO 9001, and like ISO 9001, ISO 20000 offers organizational certification. Since ISO 20000 is so closely aligned with ITIL®, IT organizations now have a complete package: the existing ITIL® certifications qualify personnel and ISO 20000 documents organizational conformance and enables auditing.

This natural alignment between the ITIL® and ISO 20000 removes one of the toughest problems IT managers face today: gaining management commitment. ISO

20000 not only provides the means to certify IT organizational quality compliance, but it also will help accelerate ITIL® adoption.

ISO and the International Electrotechnical Commission (IEC) are the international standards bodies responsible for the development and maintenance of ISO 20000. ISO 20000 is really two parts, ISO/IEC 20000-1:2005 and ISO/IEC 20000-2:2005. These are commonly referred to as ISO-20000-1 and 20000-2.

14.4.1.1   ISO/IEC 20000-1: 2005. Information Technology—Service Management Part 1: Specification

ISO 20000-1 is the specification for IT service management. It defines the processes and provides assessment criteria and recommendations for those responsible for IT service management. Organizational certification uses this section. It represents a distillation of the guidance provided in the volumes of the ITIL® to provide the (limited) set of requirements to perform ICT services. It is being revised by the ISO/IEC Committee to better reflect an international (rather than British) approach.

14.4.1.2   ISO/IEC 20000-2: 2005. Information Technology—Service Management Part 2: Code of Practice

This part of ISO 20000, referred to as the Code of Practices, describes the best practices for IT service management processes within the scope of ISO 20000-1. It also provides guidance to auditors and offers assistance to service providers planning service improvements or to be audited against ISO 20000-1.

14.4.2   ISO 20000-1 Content

ISO 20000-1, like ISO 9001, is built upon the continuous improvement Plan-Do-Check-Analyze & Act (P-D-C-A) methodology developed by Dr. Walter A. Shewhart and made popular by Dr. W. Edwards Deming (see Chapter 2). The continuous improvement model in ISO 20000-1 is slightly different than that found in ISO 9001. ISO 9001 is a quality management system standard that can be applied to any industry. ISO 20000-1 applies to a specific industry—that is, it depicts the service management processes of clauses 4 to 10 as inputs/outputs of P-D-C-A. The combined input/output and P-D-C-A models are shown in Figure 14.1 [10].

Similar to the objective of ISO 9001, ISO 20000-1's objective is to promote the adoption of an integrated process approach to effectively deliver managed services that meet business and customer requirements. ISO 20000-1 is comprised of 10 clauses.

1. Scope;
2. Terms-Definitions;
3. The Management System;
4. Planning & Implementing Service Management;
5. Planning & Implementing New or Changed Services;
6. Service Delivery Processes;
7. Relationship Processes;

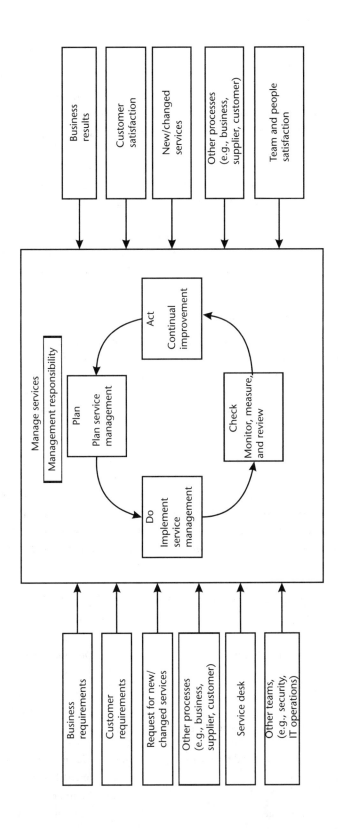

Figure 14.1 Plan-Do-Check-Act model for service management processes. (*From:* [10].© 2005 ISO/IEC 2000-1:2005, Information Technology—Service Management, Part 1: Specification, ISO/IEC 2005. Reprinted with permission.)

8. Resolution Processes;
9. Control Processes;
10. Release Processes.

A closer look at clauses 3 and 4 reveals the similarity of ISO 20000-1 to ISO 9000. These similarities are summarized in Table 14.3.

The clauses that contain requirements are clauses 4 to 10, which closely align to the best practice recommendations of ITIL®. ISO 20000-2 is a "code of practice" and describes the best practices for service management within the scope of ISO 20000-1. It comprises the same sections as Part 1 but excludes the "Requirements for a Management System" as no requirements are imposed by Part 2. ISO 20000-2 follows the approach of ISO 9004:2000 "Quality management system—Guidelines for performance improvements" in that both are tools used for improving the efficiency and effectiveness of the organizations implementing the requirements/specification standard but neither contain additional requirements to the base standard.

14.4.2.1 Resolution Processes

Clause 8 of ISO 2000-1 establishes the requirements for the resolution processes. In IT, bugs, defects, and errors are referred to as incidents (clause 8.2) and problems (clause 8.3). Their resolution, like in software, is handled through education, causal analysis, and corrective and preventive action. The software and IT industry use tools extensively. While software defects are most often tracked with a defect tracking system, IT organizations track incidents and problems using a trouble ticket system.

A common definition of an "incident" is an event that is not a part of the standard operation of a service that causes or may cause disruption to, or a reduction in, the quality of services and customer productivity. A "problem" on the other hand, is the unknown root cause of one or more existing or potential incidents. Like software defects, problems may sometimes be identified because of multiple incidents that exhibit common symptoms. Problems can also be identified from a single significant

Table 14.3 Correspondence Between ISO 2000-1:2005 and ISO 9001:2000

Clause	ISO 20000-1	Clause	ISO 9001
3.1	Management responsibility	5	Management responsibility
3.2	Documentation requirements	4.2	Documentation requirements
3.3	Competence, awareness, and training	6.2.2	Competence, awareness and training
4	Planning and implementing service management	7	Product Realization
4.1	Plan service management	7.1	Planning of product realization
4.2	Implement service management and provide the service	7.5	Product and service provision
4.3	Monitoring, measuring, and reviewing	5.6	Management review
		8.2.2	Internal audit
		8.2.3	Monitoring and measuring processes
4.4	Continual improvement	8.4	Analysis of data
		8.5	Continual improvement

incident, indicative of a single error, for which the cause is unknown. Occasionally problems will be identified well before any related incidents occur.

Other terms that will help one understand how IT handles incidents and problems are "known errors" and "workarounds." A "known error" is a fault in a configuration item (CI) identified by the successful diagnosis of a problem and for which a temporary workaround or permanent solution has been identified. "Workarounds" are methods of avoiding an incident or problem, either by employing a temporary fix or technique that means a customer is not relying on a configuration item that is known to cause failure. In software, workarounds might be referred to as emergency fixes or patches.

One of the key processes for identifying and tracking incidences is the Service Desk. Figure 14.2 shows a simplified flow for reporting and resolving incidences.

Continual improvement in ITSM will ensure that a service delivers the maximum benefit and measures its performance through its life, suggesting improvements along the way. Continual improvement is the "Act" part of the "Plan-Do-Check-Analyze & Act" methodology and is one of the key clauses in ISO

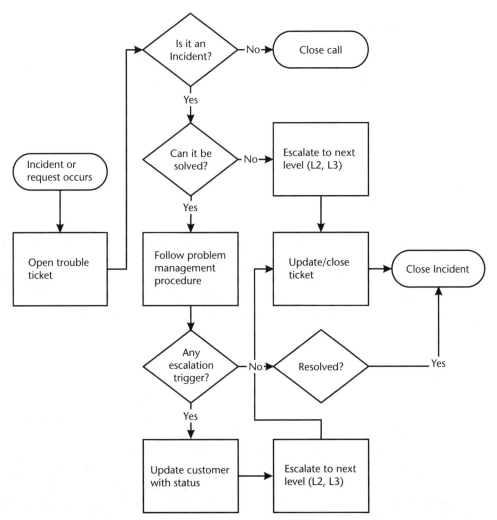

Figure 14.2 High-level service desk incident resolution process continual improvement.

20000. Continual improvement may be monitored via reporting of incident volumes, problem type trends, operator performance, and so on, alongside automated SLA calculations and flexible reports expressed in percentages so that improvements may be measured over time. As found in ISO 9001, continual improvement in ISO 20000-1 includes analysis of data, as well as corrective and preventive action.

14.4.3   CobiT®

Another standard that is gaining broader acceptance because of scandals such as Enron and WorldCom is Control Objectives for Information and Related Technology (CobiT®). CobiT® is an IT-focused governance and control framework created by the IT Governance Institute (ITGI) and Information Systems Audit and Control Association (ISACA). Developed as an open standard, CobiT® is being increasingly adopted globally as the governance and control model for implementing and demonstrating effective IT governance. The first, second, and third editions of CobiT® were published in 1994, 1998, and 2000, respectively. CobiT® is now in its fourth edition (CobiT® 4), published in 2005.

CobiT® is widely accepted as the IT control framework that is used to meet regulatory compliance requirements such as:

- HIPPA (The Health Insurance Portability and Accountability Act of 1996);
- Sarbanes Oxley (The Public Company Accounting Reform and Investor Protection Act of 2002);
- Basel II (International Convergence of Capital Measurement and Capital Standards—A Revised Framework) [11];
- FISMA (Federal Information Security Management Act of 2002), which was meant to bolster computer and network security within the U.S. federal government and affiliated parties (such as government contractors) by mandating yearly audits.

In many organizations software quality professionals have already been asked to support these compliance models by defining and implementing IT processes and auditing IT functions. Although there is no registration scheme for CobiT®, regulatory agencies' recognition of this framework makes it an acceptable method for demonstrating compliance when assessed, using third parties such as certified public accountants (CPA).

14.4.3.1   CobiT® 4

CobiT® 4 [12] is an enhancement of, and fully compatible with, CobiT® 3rd Edition. One of the main thrusts of this enhancement is closer harmonization of CobiT® with ITIL®. CobiT® 4, which is focused on business orientation, does not invalidate any implementation or execution activities based on the CobiT® 3rd Edition. CobiT® 4 consolidates the separate components of CobiT® Third Edition (Executive Summary, Framework, Control Objectives, and Management Guidelines) into a single volume. Its target audience is senior business management, as well as senior IT management and auditors.

The CobiT® 4 volume consists of four sections:

1. Executive overview;
2. Framework;
3. Core content;
4. Appendices.

In more detail, the overall CobiT® framework can be shown graphically as in Figure 14.3, with the CobiT® process model of four domains containing 34 generic IT processes for managing the IT resources to deliver information to the business according to business and governance requirements.

Each of the CobiT® 34 generic processes is covered in four subsections of about one page each. Each subsection describes:

• *A high-level control objective:* Includes a summary of process goals, metrics, and practices; a process description summarizing the process objectives; and a mapping of the process to the process domains, information criteria, and IT resources;

• *Detailed control objectives of the process:* Provides a total of 214 detailed control objectives divided among the 34 high-level processes;

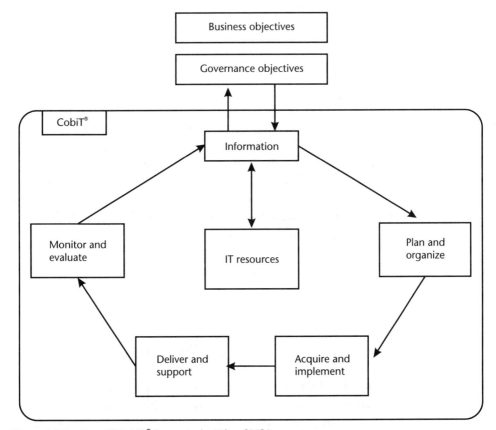

Figure 14.3   Overall CobiT® framework. (*After:* [12].)

- *Management guidelines:* Includes process inputs and outputs, Responsible, Accountable, Consulted, and Informed (RACI) chart, goal, and metrics (RACI charts are discussed next);
- *Maturity model:* Presents a maturity model for the process (derived from SEI CMM®).

A RACI chart is similar to a responsibility matrix and is used to describe the roles and responsibilities of various teams or people in delivering a project. It is especially useful in clarifying roles and responsibilities in cross-functional/ cross-departmental projects and initiatives. The RACI chart splits project tasks down to four participatory responsibility types that are then assigned to different roles in the project. These responsibility types make up the acronym RACI.

- *Responsible:* Those who do work to achieve the task; there can be multiple resources responsible;
- *Accountable:* The resource ultimately accountable for the completion of the task; there must be exactly one "A" specified for each task;
- *Consulted:* Those whose opinions are sought with two-way communication;
- *Informed:* Those who are kept up to date on progress with one-way communication.

Table 14.4 is an example of a RACI chart showing how individual tasks are assigned to different roles for the creation of new user account.

In the example table, the Manager is Responsible and Accountable for completing a new user access form and Informing the System Owner. The System Owner is Responsible and Accountable for reviewing and approving the request after consulting with the Security Department. The System Owner then Informs the Service Desk and Security Department of the result. After the next two tasks are completed, the Service Desk is Responsible for performing the notify requester task by Informing the Manager, and the IT Manager is Accountable for the task being accomplished.

The management guidelines found in CobiT® are generic and action oriented. They are intended to help the organization answer management questions, such as:

- How far should the organization go, and is the cost justified by the benefit?
- What are the indicators of good performance?
- What are the critical success factors?
- What are the risks of not achieving the business' objectives?

Table 14.4   Sample RACI Chart

Task	Service Desk	Security Dept.	IT Manager	Manager	System Owner
Complete new user access form	—	—	—	R, A	I
Review and approve request	I	C, I	—	—	R, A
Create user profile on system	I	R	A	I	I
File supporting documentation	I	R	A	—	I
Notify requester	R	—	A	I	—

- What are others in the business' industry doing and how does the business measure and compare to them?

In combination, the four sections of the core content provide guidance in controlling, managing, and measuring the process:

- Process inputs indicate what the process owner needs from others;
- Process descriptions review what the process owner needs to do;
- Process outputs are what the process owner must deliver;
- Goals and metrics show how the process should be measured;
- The RACI chart defines what must be delegated and to whom;
- The maturity model shows how the process can be improved.

The appendices of CobiT® include various mappings and cross references, additional maturity model information, reference material, a project description, and a glossary of terms.

14.4.3.2 A Unifying Framework

CobiT® is based on established frameworks, such as the Software Engineering Institute's Capability Maturity Model® Integration, ISO 9000, ITIL®, and ISO 27001 ("Information Security Management – Specification with Guidance for Use"). In fact, 13 of the 34 high-level control objectives are derived directly from the ITIL® service support and service delivery areas.

CobiT® is intended to be used at the highest level of IT governance. It provides an overall governance framework based on a high-level process model of a generic nature that makes it applicable to most organizations. Processes and standards that cover specific areas in more detail, such as ITIL® and ISO/IEC 27001:2005 Information technology—Security techniques—Information security management systems—Requirements, can be mapped to the CobiT® framework to create a hierarchy of guidance materials.

CobiT® covers four domains:

- Plan and organize;
- Acquire and implement;
- Deliver and support;
- Monitor and evaluate.

Table 14.5 shows these four domains and the 34 generic processes that establish the high-level control objectives that support what IT produces. The high-level control objectives are discussed further.

14.4.3.3 Plan and Organize

The planning and organization (PO) domain covers the use of technology and how best it can be used in a company to help achieve the company's goals and objectives.

Table 14.5 CobiT® Basics

Plan and Organize		Deliver and Support	
PO 1	Define a Strategic IT Plan	DS 1	Define and Manage Service Levels
PO 2	Define the Information Architecture	DS 2	Manage Third-party Services
PO 3	Determine Technological Direction	DS 3	Manage Performance and Capacity
PO 4	Define the IT Processes, Organization and Relationships	DS 4	Ensure Continuous and Capacity
PO 5	Manage the IT Investment	DS 5	Ensure Systems Security
PO 6	Communicate Management Aims and Direction	DS 6	Identify and Allocate Security
PO 7	Manage IT Human Resources	DS 7	Educate and Train Users
PO 8	Manage Quality	DS 8	Manage Service Desk and Incidents
PO 9	Assess and Manage IT Risks	DS 9	Manage the Configuration
PO 10	Manage Projects	DS 10	Manage Problems
Acquire and Implement		DS 11	Manage Data
AI 1	Identify Automated Solutions	DS 12	Manage the Physical Environment
AI 2	Acquire and Maintain Application Software	DS 13	Manage Operations
AI 3	Acquire and Maintain Technology Infrastructure	*Monitor and Evaluate*	
AI 4	Enable Operation and Use	ME 1	Monitor and Evaluate IT Performance
AI 5	Procure IT Resources	ME 2	Monitor and Evaluate Internal Control
AI 6	Manage Changes	ME 3	Ensure Regulatory Compliance
AI 7	Install and Accredit Solutions and Changes	ME 4	Provide IT Governance

AI = acquire and implement; DS = deliver and support; ME = monitor and evaluate; PO = plan and organize.
Source: [12].

It also highlights the organizational and infrastructural form IT is to take in order to achieve the optimal results and to generate the most benefits from the use of IT.

Referring to Table 14.5, one object calls for the organization to Manage Quality (PO8). To accomplish this objective, a quality management system needs to be developed and maintained; this includes proven development and acquisition processes and standards. This is accomplished by planning, implementing, and maintaining the quality management system by providing clear quality requirements, procedures, and policies. Quality requirements should be stated and communicated in quantifiable and achievable indicators. Continuous improvement is achieved by ongoing monitoring, analyzing, and acting upon deviations, and communicating results to stakeholders. Quality management is essential to ensure that IT is delivering value to the business, continuous improvement, and transparency for stakeholders. The approach is notably similar to ISO 9001.

14.4.3.4 Acquire and Implement

The organization identifies its IT requirements: acquiring the technology and implementing it within the company's current business processes. The Acquisition and Implementation (AI) domain also addresses the development of a maintenance plan that a company should adopt in order to prolong the life of the IT system and its components. These AI objectives align to the goals in the CMMI® for Technical Solution, Supplier Agreement Management, and Configuration Management.

14.4.3.5   Delivery and Support

The Delivery and Support (DS) domain focuses on the delivery aspects of IT. It covers areas such as the execution of the applications within the IT system and its results, as well as the support processes that enable the effective and efficient execution of the IT systems. These support processes include security issues and training. DS objectives align with CMMI® process areas: Supplier Agreement Management, Configuration Management, Project Planning, and Project Monitoring and Control, and the generic practices covering training and resources requirements.

14.4.3.6   Monitor and Evaluate

The Monitoring and Evaluation (ME) domain deals with a company's strategy in assessing the IT needs of the company and whether or not the current IT system still meets the objectives for which it was designed and the controls necessary to comply with regulatory requirements. Monitoring and evaluating also covers the issue of an independent assessment of the effectiveness of IT system in its ability to meet business objectives and the company's control processes by internal and external auditors.

A specific quality-related goal in this domain is ME2, which indicates that an effective internal control program requires a well-defined monitoring process for IT be established. This process includes the monitoring and reporting of control exceptions, results of self-assessments, and third-party reviews. A key benefit of internal control monitoring is to provide assurance regarding effective and efficient IT operations and compliance with applicable laws and regulations. Again, this is very similar to the internal audit and third-party registration process of ISO 9001 and the CMMI® PPQA process area and SCAMPI^SM appraisals.

14.5   Selecting a Process Improvement Model

When implementing an IT Service Management System, the organization has to decide which model or models to select. To select a process improvement model, the organization must be aware of: (1) the organizational scope of the improvement initiative (e.g., whether it covers the IT organization or the entire enterprise); and (2) the ultimate goal, which is operational process improvement or business transformation. This awareness, combined with a solid understanding of the various process improvement models (i.e., their purposes, strengths, weaknesses, philosophical orientations and shared attributes), will make it easier to select and integrate appropriate models and achieve the desired results.

The IT best practices models described in Table 14.6 are extremely relevant to the IT organization and can be powerful tools for improving performance, but the tools themselves will have little meaning to anyone outside the IT organization. The enterprise performance frameworks and quality models in Table 14.6 have achieved high degrees of credibility with business people, so the IT organization that can employ them successfully will earn credibility from its informed management. Deciding which approach to take will depend on a variety of cultural factors, including enterprise tendency for following the "proven path" or charting an

Table 14.6   Process Improvement Models

Process Improvement Models	Description	Audience
IT Best Practices		
ITIL®	IT Infrastructure Library (ITIL®): a set of books published by the British government's Office of Government Commerce (OGC) that contains guidelines to help IT organizations improve operational efficiency and service quality	Organizations can select components from the best practices that will meet their specific needs; good starting point if third-party certification or demonstration of IT governance is not the principle objective
CobiT®	Control Objectives for Information and related Technology (CobiT®): an IT-focused governance and control framework created by the IT Governance Institute (ITGI) and Information Systems Audit and Control Association (ISACA)	This is a commonly used framework for demonstrating IT governance; used by many accounting firms as a model for auditing IT organizations
ISO 20000-1:2005	ISO 20000-1 is the specification for IT service management that defines the processes and provides assessment criteria and recommendations for those responsible for IT service management	Organizations that want or need a third-party registration for their ITSM system; use of other frameworks or models needed to successfully implement
ISO 20000-2:2005	ISO 20000-2 is referred to as the Code of Practices describing the best practices for IT service management processes within the scope of ISO 20000-1	Written to directly support implementation of ISO 20000-1. Similar in purpose to ISO 9004:20000
CMMI®-Service	CMMI®-SVC (scheduled for release in 2008) will provide guidance for delivering IT services within organizations and to external customers	Organizations that are interested in implementing best practices and monitoring their capability and maturity over time; maturity levels are often a condition of contract award
Enterprise Performance Frameworks		
Baldrige National Quality Program (or Award)	The criteria for the Baldrige National Quality Award (BNQA) are now accepted widely as the standard for performance excellence; the criteria are designed to help organizations enhance their competitiveness by focusing on two goals: delivering ever improving value to customers and improving overall organizational performance	Baldrige is a holistic improvement model focusing on all aspects of business operations
Balanced Scorecard	The balanced scorecard (BSC) is a management system that enables organizations to clarify their vision and strategy and translate them into action; it provides feedback around both the internal business processes and external outcomes in order to continuously improve strategic performance and results	The BSC is another holistic model that focuses on all aspects of business operations

independent course; power, influence, and role of the champion; governance maturity; and organizational vision. No "best practice bundle" of approaches will work for every enterprise or IT organization.

Table 14.6 (continued)

Quality Models

ISO 9001:2000	ISO 9001 specifies requirements for a quality management system where the organization has to demonstrate its ability to consistently products or services that meet customer and applicable regulatory requirements with an aim at enhancing customer satisfaction	Organizations that want or need a third-party registration for their QMS. Can be applied to any aspect of ITSM. Use of other frameworks or models can support successfully implementation
Six Sigma	Six Sigma is a disciplined, data-driven approach and methodology for eliminating defects (driving towards six standard deviations between the mean and the nearest specification limit) in any process—from manufacturing to transactional and from product to service	Six Sigma is adopted within the framework of other enterprise models such as Baldrige or ISO 9001, but may also be applied as the process improvement model within any of the best practices frameworks
Lean	Lean production and service is aimed at the elimination of waste in every area of production and service including customer relations, product design and delivery, supplier relations, and management	Lean is adopted within the framework of other enterprise models such as Baldrige or ISO 9001, but may also be applied as the process improvement model within any of the best practices frameworks

14.5.1 IT Service Management Self-Assessment

A starting point for any organization moving toward one of the IT service management models discussed or shown in Table 14.6 is to perform a self-assessment. The itSMF has developed an IT Service Management Self-Assessment based on the ITIL®. This process is one of a number of self-assessments of important processes, enabling an organization to establish the extent to which the organization has adopted the better practice guidance available from the Office of Government Commerce.

The self-assessment scheme is composed of a simple questionnaire that enables the organization to ascertain which areas should be addressed next in order to improve the overall process capability. The assessment is based on a generic framework which recognizes that there are a number of structural elements which need to be in place for process management and for it to satisfy the overall intent and meet the needs of the customer.

To establish where a particular organization stands in relation to the process capability framework, a number of questions should be answered. The questions are weighted and the answers lead to whether an organization has passed or failed a particular area.

The goal of the self-assessment questionnaires is not to test whether there is complete conformance with ITIL® but rather the aim is to give the self-assessing organization an idea of how well it is performing compared to ITIL® best practice. The questionnaire also aims to create an awareness of management and control issues that may be addressed to improve the overall process capability. An outline of the assessment instrument is shown in Table 14.7 and is available for anyone to use at http://www.itsmf.com/bestpractice/selfassessment.asp [13].

Table 14.7   ITSM Self-Assessment Outline

IT Service Management

Service Support

Service Delivery

	Service Level Management	*Financial Management*	*Capacity Management*	*Continuity Management*	*Availability Management*
Assessment Areas	Prerequisites				
	Management Intent				
	Process Capability				
	Internal Integration				
	Products				
	Quality Control				
	Management Information				
	External Integration				
	Customer Interface				
	Service Desk	*Incident Management*	*Problem Management*	*Configuration Management*	*Change Management*	*Release Management*
Assessment Areas	Prerequisites					
	Management Intent					
	Process Capability					
	Internal Integration					
	Products					
	Quality Control					
	Management Information					
	External Integration					
	Customer Interface					

Source: [13].

14.5.2   Implementing an IT Service Management System

Armed with the results of the self-assessment and the selected process model there are few key steps for implementing an ITSM system. Regardless of the model selected, the steps for implementation are similar to the steps in implementing an ISO 9001 quality management system. The exception is where ISO 9001 requires the organization to identify the processes that make up the system for providing its respective product or service, standards such as ISO 20000-1 and CobiT® identify the specific ITSM processes that will be implemented. The key steps to consider are as follows.

Step 1:   Acquire the Standard. Acquire a copy of the standard. In the case of ISO 20000-1, consider purchasing a copy of the Code of Practices as well and become familiar with both.

Step 2:   Conduct a Literature Review. In addition to the standard, there are additional publications available designed to help organizations understand, implement, and bring an ITSM system to registration. The online ITIL® and ITSM community make excellent starting points.

Step 3:   Consider Training. Identify key staff that will be involved in the implementation effort and have them attend standard awareness training. Key staff needs to include a sponsor or champion from top (executive) management. It is vital that top management be involved from the beginning of the process.

Step 4:   Organize an Implementation Team. From the key staff select and organize the implementation team. The implementation team is the principal staff that will prepare a strategy for moving the organization toward registration. The strategy should be converted into an implementation plan that is used to track and measure progress.

Step 5:   Consider the Consultant Option. Depending on the organizations familiarity with the standard and if applicable, the registration process and the availability of internal resources, a consultant may be a resource for aiding in interpreting the standard and implementing of the ITSM system.

Step 6:   Choose a Registrar or Outside Assessment Organization. If registration is desired, select a registrar early. The registrar is the third party who will visit the origination and assess the effectiveness of the organization's ITSM system and issue a certificate if it meets the requirements of the standard. The key is to find the registrar who can best meet the organization's requirements. If an outside assessment organization or third party is used, such as a CPA, the activities suggested apply, but no certificate can be issued.

Step 7:   Develop an IT Service Improvement Policy. Develop and release an IT service improvement policy. This policy is a high-level document that outlines how an organization will improve the effectiveness and efficiency of the service delivery and support provided.

Step 8:   Develop Support Documentation. This is typically policies, plans, procedures, and desktop or work instructions that support each of the key service management processes. These documents outline the roles, responsibilities, and activities involved in managing the components of the ITSM system.

Step 9:   Implement the IT Service Management System. The key to implementation is communication and training. During the implementation phase, documentation is released for use and training on the ITSM system. Work is performed to the released documentation and evidence is collected that demonstrates compliance to the system and to the standard. Periodically check the implementation through audits and management review and revise the ITSM system as needed.

Step 10:   Consider a Preassessment. A preassessment may be of value to the organization. The purpose of the preassessment is to identify areas where the organization may not be in compliance with the standard. This allows corrections to be made before the initial assessment.

a

Step 11:   Gain Registration. Arrange an initial assessment with the registrar. At this point the registrar will review the organization's ITSM system and determine whether a recommendation for registration can be made. If nonconformances are found, they will have to be resolved prior to the issuance of a registration certificate. For a nonregistration approach, a report of compliance should be provided.

Step 12:   Continual Improvement. Once registration or compliance is achieved, celebrate the event and begin advertising as a registered or ITSM compliant provider.

It does not stop here with these 12 steps; the organization then needs to look for ways to continually improve. Whether registered or compliant, the ITSM system will be periodically checked by a third party to ensure that it continues to meet the requirements of the standard, and since continual improvement is now in nearly every standard, improvements must be demonstrated.

14.6   Customer Requirements

14.6.1   Service Level Agreements

At the heart of any product or service are the requirements of the customer. In software those requirements are captured in a requirements document such as a Software Requirements Specification (SRS) and Use Cases. In the IT industry, requirements are almost always communicated through service level agreements (SLA). SLAs ensure quality and codify customer expectations. SLAs for IT systems spell out very specific details about availability, capacity, response time, and support services. The SLA is an effective tool for managing the risks associated with computer applications and describes practices for measuring and monitoring a service provider's performance. Today's IT service providers are required to sign-off on levels of quality for all IT system components.

SLAs are contractually binding clauses documenting the performance standard and service quality agreed to by the business and the service provider [14]. When outsourcing IT, some or all IT system components, the SLA is a key in structuring a successful outsourcing contract. The SLA ensures that the business receives the services it wants at the expected performance standard and price. As such, the SLA is a key in managing the financial and operational risks involving the IT system. It also can be one way to help mitigate risk. By specifying the measurement unit and service range for the selected category, the risk of poor service may be diminished because it becomes an area of focus for the service provider.

The primary purpose of an SLA is to specify and clarify performance expectations, as well as establish respect parties accountability. Therefore, balancing the need for precise measurement standards with sufficient flexibility is important. A common pitfall is excessive oversight or micro-management of the provider responsible for the service, which can also burden the business manager charged with supervising the service provider relationship and monitoring the SLAs.

A well-designed SLA will recognize and reward, or at least acknowledge, good service. It will also provide the measurement structure—or performance metric—to identify substandard service and trigger correction or cancellation provisions as warranted. In today's outsourcing environment, incentives or penalties in the SLA can be an effective tool for managing service. If services received do not measure up to expectations, direct consequences, such as reduced levels of compensation or a credit on future services, should be the result.

14.6.1.1   Structuring and Developing SLAs

Contrary to what is found for software requirements, there are no specific standards or protocols for developing SLAs. However, the typical SLA can be expected to include the following components and can be tailored to fit the nature of the service or application:

- Service category (e.g., system availability or response time);
- Acceptable range of service quality;
- Definition of what is being measured;
- Formula for calculating the measurement;
- Relevant credits/penalties for achieving/failing performance targets;
- Frequency and interval of measurement.

Before an SLA is signed, the service provider and the business should clarify and establish expectations. Unless these expectations are clearly measurable, the service category will be difficult to manage due to the differing goals and perspectives of the businesses and the vendors.

The process for developing a successful SLA requires four basic steps as outlined in Table 14.8:

1. *Determine the objectives:* Review the strategic business needs of the business to include evaluating its day-to-day operating environment, risk factors, and market conditions. Consideration should be given to how the outsourced service fits into the business' overall strategic plan.

2. *Define requirements:* Identifying the operational objectives (e.g., the need to improve operating efficiency, reduce costs, or enhance security) will help the institution to define performance requirements. It will also assist in identifying the levels of service the business needs from the service provider in order to meet its strategic goals and objectives for the outsourced activity.

3. *Set measurements:* Clear and impartial measurements, or metrics, can be developed once the strategic needs and operating objectives have been defined. The metrics are used to measure and confirm that the necessary service levels have been achieved and the objectives and strategic intent have been met.

4. *Establish accountability:* It is useful to develop and adopt a framework that ensures accountability after the measurement units, or the metrics, have been clearly defined. The service provider rarely owns accountability and responsibility for all tasks. Establishing this accountability usually includes a clear statement of the outcome if the level of service is exceeded or if the expected service fails to meet the stated standard.

Table 14.8   Examples of Objectives, Requirements, and Measurements for SLAs

Strategic Objective	Performance Requirement	Measurement
Sensitive system and business/customer data must be protected with strong security	Regular checks for intrusions or other security breaches	Copies of intrusion scan reports to be sent at predetermined frequency
	Periodic security assessments, tests, or reviews	Copies of independent security assessment reports to be provided at predetermined frequency
	Timely reporting of incidents and follow up to business management	Regular incident reports (frequency will depend upon system criticality)
Mission critical systems must be reliable and available	System downtime must be minimal	Specified requirement for system uptime (e.g., 99.9%)
	The system must be able to support certain volumes of activity at a given time	Specified requirement or parameters for capacity (e.g., 10,000 transactions processed per minute)

Representatives from the business (management, legal counsel, and senior IT staff) and the service provider meet to ensure that performance metrics and targets are properly addressed when developing SLAs. The business may also consider interviewing some of the system users to help identify important criteria to incorporate into the SLAs.

Reaching agreement on specific SLAs may involve significant discussion and negotiation between the business and the service provider. The business may wish to consult with peer businesses and trade associations about useful benchmarks for performance standards. This information may be helpful in the contract negotiation process and assist the business in determining if the service levels offered by the provider are reasonable and standard.

14.6.1.2   Drafting the Service Level Agreements

Sufficient time and resources should be devoted to preparing SLAs. The agreement will be the primary document governing the business and service provider that may have a significant impact on the business' performance. The following items are important reminders for businesses drafting SLAs and selecting the metric(s) to be used to measure the service provider's performance:

- *Focus on the most important areas:* Businesses should identify the performance and risk factors that are most crucial to the success of the outsourced function. The business should invest its time drafting strong SLAs for these crucial areas. Areas with minimal effect on the process will be of less importance and, accordingly, should have less prominence in the contracting process.

- *Measure what the business needs:* Make sure that performance metrics measure what the business wants them to measure. Verify that the metrics used to govern the SLA appropriately represent the functions that the business intends to measure.

- *Report metrics for business aggregate of businesses:* The metrics should measure the performance the service provider is giving the business, and not be based on the performance the service provider is delivering in aggregate to all its businesses.
- *Ensure that SLAs are focused on business goals:* Avoid the trap of creating agreements that are focused on the success of the individual process without regard for the how the process addresses a corporate goal. Each measurement should logically support a requirement that is linked to a strategic goal.
- *Be specific:* Ensure that all parties involved in the SLA understand the terms spelled out in the SLA. Terms should be clearly defined to avoid different interpretations. Spending extra time defining terms when creating an SLA can prevent misunderstandings and loss of time and money caused by differing interpretations of the intent of the SLA.

A sample SLA is shown in Figure 14.4. Many samples can be found on the Internet; however, they must be customized to meet the needs of the specific business.

14.6.1.3 Managing SLAs

It is worthwhile for the business to provide for ongoing management of the agreement when a SLA is established. The SLA management process usually goes beyond performance measurement to ensure success. Generally, the measurement process should be kept as simple as possible, emphasizing timely identification of deviations from agreed upon performance metrics. Ongoing communication between the business and the service provider is also important. Industry best practices suggest that an SLA management process follow a four-phase methodology:

1. Measure service activity results against defined service levels.
2. Examine measured results to identify problems and determine causes.
3. Take appropriate action to correct failed activities, functions, and/or processes.
4. Continuously guide service providers through feedback sessions based on objectively measured performance metrics.

Before signing an SLA, the business may find it beneficial to verify that important performance requirements have been addressed, risks have been identified, and each service level is defined. Each measurement should be defined clearly and concisely. This will provide the foundation for effectively managing service levels throughout the four phases of the SLA management process.

SLA management is an ongoing process and is viewed as an integral component of any outsourcing relationship. A suggested practice is to include periodic review and change provisions in the SLA to ensure that service level goals and performance measurements can meet the changing business and technology needs of the business.

Sample Service Level Agreements (SLA)

Purpose
This agreement is between Buyer and Vendor. This document outlines the service level roles, responsibilities, and objectives of Buyer and Vendor in support of the given functional area.

Scope of Services
Vendor will house, manage, and operate all hardware and software necessary to provide Internet applications to Buyer.

Service Category
This SLA addresses application availability.

Acceptable Range of Service Quality
The Internet application shall be available at least 99.5% of each week.

Definition of What Is Being Measured
"Availability" will be measured as the percentage of minutes each day that the business' Internet application will be able to receive and respond to messages from the Internet. The server's ability to receive messages will be ascertained using time-check availability software.

Formula for Calculating the Measurement
System availability shall be measured as the number of minutes per day that the Buyer's Internet application is capable of receiving and responding to messages from the Internet divided by 1,440 (the total number of minutes in a day).

A 30-minute period from 2:00 AM to 2:30 AM shall be excluded from the calculation because Vendor will be performing system maintenance at this time each day.

Relevant Credits/Penalties for Achieving/Failing Performance Targets
If Vendor is unable to provide this service level to Buyer, Vendor will provide priority support to Buyer until performance levels are met. Service below the prescribed level will result in a rebate of 50% of the monthly fee for the month in which the exception takes place.

If Vendor fails to provide the agreed upon service level for more than two consecutive months, Buyer shall have the right to renegotiate the contract and/or terminate this SLA.

Frequency and Interval of Measurement
The system's availability shall be measured daily by Vendor using time-check availability software. Vendor shall submit monitoring reports generated by this program to Buyer on a weekly basis.

Buyer's Responsibilities
Buyer shall review all monitoring reports and advise Vendor of any deviations from this SLA in a timely manner.

(Include any other items that Buyer will need to do so that Vendor may perform its tasks.)

Vendor's Responsibilities
Vendor shall assume responsibility for customer communications at the point that customer messages leave the Internet service provider.

Vendor shall ensure that all messages are processed in a timely fashion. (Be sure to define the specifics of "timely" standards.)

Vendor shall ensure that the system shall be able to accept and respond to 1,200 inquiries per minute.

(Include any other items that Vendor will need to do to provide the prescribed level of service to Buyer.)

Escalation Guidelines
In the event that Vendor is unable to meet the terms of this SLA, the CIO of Buyer and IT Manager of Vendor shall discuss resolution of the situation. If Vendor will be unable to provide service for more than two hours, Vendor's contingency operating plan shall be invoked.

Renegotiations
Authorized representatives of Buyer and Vendor must mutually agree upon changes to this SLA. All changes must be made and agreed to in writing. Either party may request review of this SLA at any time. Each party will review the SLA annually and advise the other party of any desired changes.

Cancellation
Either party may cancel this SLA by written notice by certified mail, stating that the SLA shall be cancelled 90 days after receipt of the notice of cancellation.

Figure 14.4   Sample SLA. (*After:* [14].)

SLAs are tools to measure, monitor, and control the operational and financial risks associated with outsourcing of IT services. Essential to this process is establishing realistic performance metrics and continuous problem tracking and resolution. The business should consider working closely with service providers to identify, verify, and correct problems; perform root-cause analysis; and make process modifications to prevent problems from recurring. As the outsourcing relationship progresses, SLAs should reflect the evolution of services provided. Accordingly, they should be updated to facilitate continued service improvement. Well-constructed SLAs are an effective tool for managing service provider performance and ensuring that the procuring organization receives the quality of service that it needs and expects.

14.6.2   QoS

Another method for defining customer requirements is quality of service (QoS). QoS is a defined level of performance in a data communications system [15]. For example, to ensure that real-time voice and video are delivered without annoying blips, a guarantee of bandwidth is required. The plain old telephone system has delivered the highest quality of service for years because there is a dedicated channel between parties. In the fields of computer networking and packet-switched networks traffic engineering, the term QoS refers to control mechanisms that can provide different priority to different users or data flows, or guarantee a certain level of performance to a data flow in accordance with requests from the application program. QoS guarantees are important if the network capacity is limited, especially for real-time streaming multimedia applications such as Voice over IP (Internet Protocol) and IP-TV. These applications often require fixed bit rate and may be delay sensitive.

QoS is a major concern for enterprises worldwide, especially with the increased use of distributed systems for delivering service when and where it is needed [16]. The challenges posed by enterprise-wide systems transcend traditional localized methods of quality assurance and call for integrated approaches that deliver operational information within a context that provides a basis for action. Managing QoS has many aspects, and among them is the monitoring performance metrics in order to detect instances of anomalous behavior. Traditionally, the monitoring activity periodically samples individual low-level system metrics and raises an alert whenever a sampled value exceeds a predetermined threshold.

The traditional approach to monitoring and measuring performance and raising alerts can be summarized as follows:

- Set a numeric alert threshold for a measured metric. The threshold value is usually metric dependent, but otherwise constant for all systems and time periods.
- Monitor sampled metrics and compare them with alert thresholds.
- Issue critical (or warning) alerts whenever a metric crosses (or approaches) its alert threshold value.

In many organizations the IT group responsible for QoS is the same group that is responsible for the IT service management. There is, however, no practice or process models specifically for QoS. The ITIL® and ISO 20000 requirements for service delivery parallel the types of controls needed to achieve QoS levels. So practices and methodologies described in these and similar best practices and standards can be applied in the QoS environment.

14.7 Monitoring and Measuring ITSM Performance

Basic to any SLA is the requirement to actually measure the level of service that is being delivered. However, there are hundreds, or even thousands of possible variables that could be measured. The challenge lies in determining which ones to measure in order to reflect the appropriate level of service.

Faced with stiffening competition, increasingly demanding customers, high labor costs, and, in some markets, slowing growth, service businesses around the world are trying to boost their productivity [17]. But whereas manufacturing businesses can raise their productivity by monitoring and reducing waste and variances in their relatively homogeneous production and distribution processes, service businesses find that improving performance is trickier: their customers, activities, and deals vary too widely. Moreover, services are highly customizable, and people—the basic unit of productivity in services—bring unpredictable differences in experience, skills, and motivation to the job.

Such seemingly uncontrollable factors cause many organizations to accept a high level of variance and a great deal of waste and inefficiency in service costs. Organizations may be hiring more staff than they need to support the widest degree of variance and also forgoing opportunities to write and price service contracts more effectively and to deliver services more productively and profitably.

As with any task or operation, to improve the productivity of services, lessons of experience must be applied. Consequently, measuring and monitoring service performance (and its variance) is a fundamental prerequisite for identifying efficiencies and best practices and for spreading them throughout the organization. Although some variance in services is inescapable, much of what organizations consider unmanageable can be controlled if they properly account for differences in the size and type of customers they serve and in the SLA they reach with those customers, and then define and collect data uniformly across different service environments. To do so, it is necessary to bear in mind a few essential principles of service measurement.

- Service companies need to compare themselves against their own performance rather than against poorly defined external measures. Using external benchmarks only compounds the difficulties that service companies face in getting comparable measurements from different parts of the organization. This is certainly also true in software, where the definition of such things as lines of code and function points vary from organization to organization.
- Service companies must look deeper than their financial costs in order to discover and monitor the root causes of those expenses.
- Service companies must set up broad cost-measurement systems to report and compare all expenses across the functional silos common to service delivery organizations. The goal is to improve the service companies' grasp of the cross-functional trade-offs that must be made to rein in total costs.

None of these principles are easy to implement. Organizations are likely to face resistance from managers and frontline personnel who insist that services are inherently random and that their service situations are unique. Managers who have grown used to the protection that lax measurement efforts encourage may be reluctant to view their operations through a more powerful lens. But only by adopting these principles and implementing rigorous measurement systems throughout the organization can service organizations begin to identify reducible variances and take the first steps toward bringing down costs and improving the pricing and delivery of services.

14.7.1   Why Variance Is Difficult to Measure

Organizations that launch variance measurement programs in a service business are often surprised at the level of difference they discover among similar sites and groups within their own organization, let alone when they compare one company with another. In general, a company's metrics are not uniform across its business units, so that, for example, one group at a service desk may regard all calls on a given issue as a single incident, while another logs every call separately. Organizations should not be shocked to find that the variance of key metrics among similar sites can range from a factor of 2 to 30. Site managers have explained this vast range by asserting that every site was different—and, according to their metrics, they were right.

14.7.1.1   Service Is Different

To make meaningful comparisons, companies have to identify the sources of difference in their businesses and devise metrics that compare these businesses meaningfully. The considerations that show up frequently include the most obvious differences among jobs and groups, such as regional variations in labor costs, local geographies and difficulties in reaching accounts, the workload mix (e.g., repairs versus installation), and differences in the use of capital (whether equipment is owned or leased by the company or owned by the customer).

The more types of services a business offers the more variability it can expect in its SLA. The metrics for a service desk that provides customer support for 5,000 users in a 9-to-5 office are very different from those for a service desk that supports logistics in a round-the-clock industrial environment. Even when offerings are similar, variance can be introduced locally through the way contracts are interpreted. In one IT outsourcing company, two desktop support accounts with SLAs that specified an 8-hour response time had very different cost metrics. When asked why, the manager of the poorly performing account said that, despite the contract's limits, "If we don't answer within the hour, our client goes ballistic." The written SLA had been trumped by an unwritten one that was costing real money.

14.7.1.2   What Gets Measured?

Underlying all of these problems is an inability to identify what must be measured and how to normalize data across different environments. Even when companies know what to measure, they struggle to achieve accuracy. Data are rarely defined or collected uniformly across an organization's environments. A service call involving the installation of two servers, for example, could be measured as a single installation in one part of a company and as two in another.

Contributing to this ambiguity is the fact that data collection is usually driven by the requirements of financial cost reporting, which often fails to shed light on ways of boosting performance. Accountants for an IT services company may need to know the cost of each server, for instance, but an organization looking to reduce variance would also need to know the number of service incidents by server type and the time spent on each incident. Variance in demand drivers is also important: did the number of calls to a service desk rise because more users bought a product, for example, or because it changed? Financial metrics might fail to detect this important distinction.

14.7.1.3 Cost Tree

A cost tree with detailed metrics is an important tool to help companies define internal benchmarks. A cost tree allows a manager to compare the performance of different accounts against similar metrics and also to calculate which improvements will have the most impact on the top-level figure. Once a team has gathered cost data throughout the tree, for example, it could target opportunities to cut costs and calculate which efforts would have the most impact on the bottom line. Creating cost trees can also help companies write SLAs that exclude unprofitable activities or generate more revenue where service costs warrant it. This tool parallels the lean manufacturing technique of value stream mapping. Value stream mapping, which is gaining in popularity in the software industry, provides a visual method of documenting the material and information flows of a process. A sample cost tree is shown in Figure 14.5 [18].

Consider the case of a cable company that was trying to reduce the resolution times of its service desk and service calls. After setting goals, managers saw resolution times shrink, but total service costs were rising. In this case, service desk representatives, eager to meet their goals, spent less time trying to resolve problems remotely. After asking only a few questions, these employees referred cases to field service reps, who were happy to have a series of fast and easy calls to boost their own metrics. Unfortunately, the number of field service calls, which are far more expensive than service desk calls, rose dramatically.

To resolve this problem, management combined call centers and field services into a single cost tree and monitored the percentage of calls passed from the one to the other, as well as the time spent on each type of call. Managers then encouraged the call center reps to spend more time trying to resolve difficult calls before passing them along to field services, thereby increasing the average call time but helping to reduce total costs. Thus a critical purpose of any cost tree is to yield insights about how better (or worse) performance in one area of the tree might affect another.

14.7.1.4 Goal-Question-Metric in IT

The Goal-Question-Metric (GQM) methodology developed by Victor Basili and his team at the NASA Software Engineering Laboratory (SEL) has been a proven method for monitoring and measuring the performance of software activities. Since then, the approach has been refined and is applicable to other areas that apply a sys-

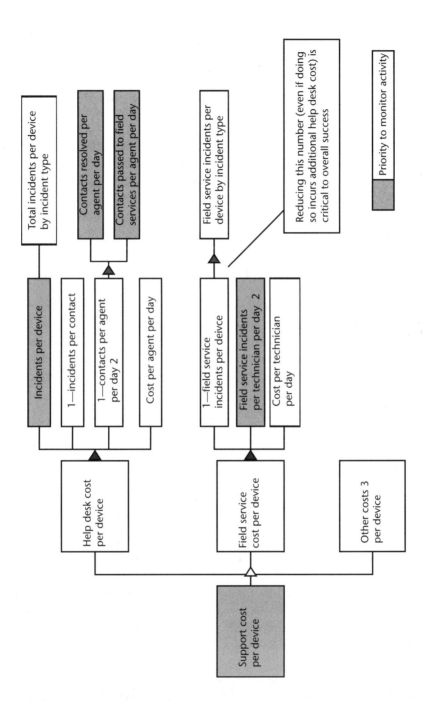

Figure 14.5   Cost tree for support cost per device.

tematic process improvement approach such as SEI's CMMI® model. Recent articles related to IT indicate an interest in applying GQM to the IT industry [19, 20].

The GQM diagram show in Figure 14.6 (adapted from [21]) is an oversimplified example of how GQM can be applied to an IT scenario. It demonstrates the notion of how one gets from a conceptual level goal to the right quantitative data that renders the goal measurable. It also demonstrates the multiple mapping of metrics to questions and questions to goals.

A refined GQM goal statement for Goal 1 in Figure 14.6 might read as follows:

Analyze:	*Change request processing*
For the purpose of:	*Improvement*
With respect to:	*CR processing cycle time*
From the viewpoint of:	*The project team*
In the context of:	*The current project timeframe*

14.8   Procurement Quality—Outstanding

In the 1990s, outsourcing of IT operations was one of the predominant trends in the industry. The Computer Economics Group shows that in every category of IT outsourcing (including software) there are far more organizations increasing their use of outsourcing than decreasing [22]. Outsourcing is a very complex area. It involves taking over all or part of established IT operations. In order to make money, the outsourcing organization is required to use economies of scale and/or automation to reduce costs. Activities commonly outsourced include:

- Well-understood, repetitive and/or monotonous tasks;
- Specialized tasks;
- Expertise transfer;
- Specific support questions;
- Augmentation of geographically or time-dispersed service desks and/or end-user organizations.

The use of an SLA, which was previously discussed, establishes the specific contractual relationship between the outsourcer and service provider. The purchasing process found in generic standards such as ISO 9001 provides a framework for outsourcing an IT function. Of particular value would be the steps for qualifying potential service providers and verifying that the purchased product or service meets the specified purchase requirements (i.e., how service provides are selected and their qualifications and what process will be used to verify that the services are what is expected).

Outsourcing of IT operations parallels well with software. For many years certain aspects of the software life cycle have been outsourced in a similar manner as IT such as: design, testing, and maintenance. The Supplier Agreement Management and Integrated Supplier Management process areas of the CMMI® have similar goals and specific practices as ITIL®, ISO 20000, and CobiT®.

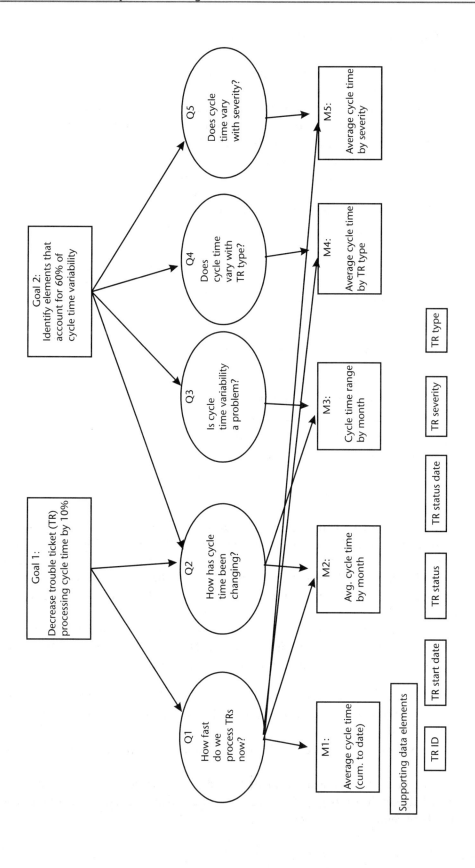

Figure 14.6   IT GQM sample. (*After:* [21].)

14.9   IT Quality Professional

For many years the position of quality in a software organization was related to testing. With the introduction of the CMM® (predecessor to the CMMI®) and such certifications as the American Society for Quality's (ASQ) Certified Software Quality Engineer (CSQE) (see Chapter 10), software organizations recognized the other facet of the software quality professional. IT organizations are in a similar quandary. There are very few requisitions for IT quality professionals. Positions that have quality-related responsibilities are often referred to as data analysts, customer care specialists, customer advocate, or change manager. Since ISO 20000 harmonizes with ISO 9001 and proposed revision to ITIL® is expected to have a service quality management component, it will not be long before an IT quality professional will come into existence.

The knowledge and skills required to become an IT quality professional closely parallel those required for the software quality assurance engineer. A CSQE must understand software quality development and implementation, software inspection, testing, verification and validation; and implements software development and maintenance processes and methods. As detailed in Chapter 10, the CSQE candidate has to have knowledge in seven key areas:

1. General Knowledge;
2. Software Quality Management;
3. Software Engineering Processes;
4. Program and Project Management;
5. Software Metrics, Measurement, and Analytical Methods;
6. Software Verification and Validation;
7. Configuration Management.

IT professionals can begin their professional certifications with a Foundation Certificate in ITIL® Service Management. The ITIL® Service Management Foundation Certificate is intended for people working in the field of IT service management. The ITIL® Service Management Foundation Certificate is a prerequisite for other certificates such as the Practitioner's and Manager's Certificate in IT Service Management [23].

The IT quality professional now has an ITIL® quality-related certificate: the Service Quality Management Foundation (SQMF) Certificate. The SQMF Certificate supplements the ITSM Foundation Certification and covers:

1. An understanding of the importance of quality in IT service management;
2. The quality specifications for IT service management (based on ISO 20000-1);
3. The code of practice for IT service management (based on ISO 20000-2).

The ITIL® Service Management Foundation Certificate candidate has to have knowledge of the following ITIL® 12 processes and an understanding of the relationship between these processes:

1. Incident Management;
2. Problem Management;
3. Change Management;
4. Configuration Management;
5. Release Management;
6. Service Level Management;
7. Availability Management;
8. Capacity Management;
9. IT Service Continuity Management;
10. Financial Management for IT Services;
11. Security Management;
12. Service Desk.

14.9.1   Body of Knowledge

There are 138 basic concepts related to ITIL® in the Service Management Foundation Certificate. When compared to the topics in the ASQ CSQE Body of Knowledge, at least 80 of the 138 basic concepts in the Foundation Certificate are related. Table 14.9 shows how the two certificates relate.

When making the same kind of comparison between the ASQ CSQE Body of Knowledge and the Service Quality Management Foundation Certificate's Glossary of Terms, many of the 290 terms parallel the CSQE Body of Knowledge. So an ASQ CSQE is well suited to make a transition to the IT industry.

14.9.2   IT Quality Analyst

By examining the descriptions of several IT positions that contained quality-related responsibilities for a typical IT quality professional position, the description of an IT Quality Analyst might look like this:

IT Quality Analyst for Contact Center
Analyze and report on day-to-day contact center activities. Observe and score Customer Service and Technical Representatives on all aspects of their jobs. Maintain a customer quality program by monitoring samples of contacts. Identify and communicate performance trends of Service Representatives. Develop call flows and other quality-oriented job aids and tools for Service Representatives and Department Managers. Collaborate with Department Managers to create policies and procedures. Study and standardize procedures to improve efficiency of center. Assist with creating feedback loops and workflow to establish best practices. Implement training program, schedule and curricula for new hires. Maintain knowledge base for the center. Build and administer quality rewards and recognition. Audit prerecorded customer service calls for compliance with standards and policies

Education and Experience Requirements
Bachelor's degree or equivalent experience. At least 2 years experience in IT customer support environment. Experience with quality management and change management systems. Extensive knowledge of MS Office software. Experience in quality assurance, auditing, coaching, and making presentations or leading

Table 14.9   Correspondence Between the CSQE and the Foundation Certificate in Service Management

CSQE	Foundation Certificate in IT Service Management
General Knowledge Quality Philosophies & Principles Standards, Specifications & Models Leadership Tools & Skills Ethics & Professional Development	1. Confidentiality 2. Customer 3. Deming Circle 4. Integrity 5. Management
Software Quality Management Goals & Objectives Methodologies	6. Audit 7. Authorization 8. Escalation 9. Evaluation 10. Functional Escalation 11. Hierarchical Escalation 12. Procedure 13. Process 14. Process Manager 15. Quality Assurance 16. Service Improvements Program (SIP)
Software Engineering Processes	17. Business Process 18. Component Failure Impact Analysis (CFIA) 19. Fault, Failure 20. Fault Tree Analysis (FTA) 21. Modeling 22. Operational Process 23. Operational Level Agreement (OLA) 24. Reliability 25. Request for Change (RFC) 26. Resilience
Program and Project Management	27. Accounting 28. Activity Based Costing 29. Application Sizing 30. Asset Management 31. Budgeting 32. Business Impact Analysis 33. Cost Plus 34. CCTA (Central Computer and Telecommunications Agency) Risk Analysis and Management Method (CRAMM®) 35. Financial Management for IT Services 36. Forward Schedule of Changes (FSC) 37. Notional Charging 38. Performance Management 39. Post Implementation Review (PIR) 40. Priority 41. Proactive Problem Management 42. Problem 43. Problem Control 44. Problem Management 45. Risk Assessment 46. Security 47. Security Awareness 48. Security Incidents

Table 14.9   (continued)

CSQE	Foundation Certificate in IT Service Management
Program and Project Management	49. Security Level
	50. Security Management
Software Metrics, Measurement, and Analytical Methods	51. Maintainability
	52. Mean Time Between Failures (MTBF)
	53. Mean Time To Repair (MTTR)
Software Verification and Validation	54. Known Error
	55. Quality Control
	56. Review
	57. Verification
Configuration Management	58. Change
	59. Change Advisory Board (CAB)
	60. Change Management
	61. Classification
	62. Configuration Baseline
	63. Configuration Item (CI)
	64. CI Level
	65. Configuration Management
	66. Configuration Management Database (CMDB)
	67. Definitive Hardware Store (DHS)
	68. Definitive Software Library (DSL)
	69. Emergency Fix/Release
	70. Error Control
	71. Full Release
	72. Identification of CI
	73. Incident Management
	74. Package Release
	75. Release Management
	76. Release Policy
	77. Release Unit
	78. Rollout
	79. Release
	80. Status

working groups. Demonstrated consistent excellence in all aspects of current role, especially quality aspects. Six-Sigma certification would be helpful.

Key Competencies
A working knowledge and expertise in all aspects of IT service quality management. Strong time management and organizational skills, accompanied by above-average analytical thinking abilities. Ability to apply mathematical operations to such tasks as frequency distribution, determination of test reliability and validity, analysis of variance, correlation techniques, sampling theory, and factor analysis Ability to solve practical problems and deal with a variety of concrete variables in situations where only limited information exists. The ability to lead by example and bring a positive attitude to the customer service environment. Excellent communication skills. The ability to be an innovative and creative problem-solver.

14.10   Conclusion

The IT industry, like the software industry, has not leveraged the value that quality principles and concepts bring to the success of an organization. Only until recently have IT best practices and standards identified quality as a process and recognized the value of a quality management system. As the recognized software industry best practices for quality are adapted by the IT industry, the software quality professional can become an invaluable asset to an IT organization. The Body of Knowledge of an IT quality professional is evolving, and timing for an experienced and motivated software quality professional could not be better. The IT industry appears now ready to welcome their service.

References

[1]   ISO 9000:2005, Quality Management Systems—Fundamentals and Vocabulary.

[2]   36 CFR Part 1194, Electronic and Information Technology Accessibility Standards; Final Rule, December 21, 2006.

[3]   Crosby, P. B., *Quality Is Free,* New York: McGraw-Hill Book, 1979, p. 22.

[4]   Evans, I., *A Dictionary of Service Management Terms, Acronyms and Abbreviations,* Reading, U.K.: itSMF Ltd., 2001, p. 45.

[5]   Evans, I., *A Dictionary of Service Management Terms, Acronyms and Abbreviations,* Reading, U.K.: itSMF Ltd., 2001, p 50.

[6]   "Abbreviations/Glossary," http://www.itilpeople.com/Index.html, December 28, 2006.

[7]   itSMF International, http://www.itsmf.org/, December 29, 2006.

[8]   Publications, http://www.itil.co.uk/publications.htm, December 10, 2006.

[9]   Hollenbach, C. R., and B. Buteau, "CMMI for Services: Introducing the CMMI for Services Constellation," *CMMI Technology/Conference,* Denver, CO, 2006.

[10] ISO/IEC 2000-1:2005, Information Technology—Service Management Part 1: Specification, Switzerland: International Organization for Standardization, 2005.

[11] Basel Committee, "Basel II: International Convergence of Capital Measurement and Capital Standards: A Revised Framework," http://www.bis.org/publ/bcbs107.htm, January 1, 2007.

[12] ITGI, "COBIT 4.0," IT Governance Institute, http://www.itgi.org, December 2005.

[13] ITIL Service Management Self Assessment, http://www.itsmf.com/bestpractice/selfassessment.asp, December 28, 2006.

[14] Federal Deposit Insurance Corporation (FDIC), "Tools to Manage Technology Providers' Performance Risk: Service Level Agreements," http://www.fdic.gov/news/news/financial/2001/fil0150c.html#APPENDIX%202%20–%20Sample%20Service%20Level%20Agreements, December 28, 2006.

[15] QoS, http://www.answers.com/topic/quality-of-service, December 17, 2006.

[16] Tsykin, M., and J. Bouhana, *Beyond Thresholds: New Directions in QoS Monitoring and Alerting,* Sydney: Fujitsu Australia Limited, 2004.

[17] McKinsey & Co, "Measuring Performance in Services," *The McKinsey Quarterly,* http://www.cfo.com/printable/article.cfm/5514575/c_2984284?f=options, January 3, 2007.

[18] McKinsey & Co, "Looking Within: A Cost Tree with Detailed Metrics Is an Important Tool to Help Companies Define Internal Benchmark," *The McKinsey Quarterly,* http://www.cfo.com/chart.cfm/5491176, January 3, 2007.

[19] Marquis, H., "5 Steps To Transparent Metrics," http://www.itsmsolutions.com/newsletters/DITYvol2iss4.htm, December 30, 2006.

[20] Borillo, D., and A. Milotto, "Draft Goals/Questions/Metrics Document," http://proj-pem.web.cern.ch/proj-pem/Progress/Documents/GQM/pem-gqm.pdf, December 30, 2006.

[21] Software Acquisition Gold Practice™ Goal-Question-Metric (GQM) Approach, http://www.goldpractices.com/practices/gqm/index.php, January 1, 2007.

[22] "Growth of IT Outsourcing: No End in Sight," http://www.computereconomics.com/article.cfm?id=1161, January 1, 2007.

[23] Exam ITIL® Foundation, http://www.exin-exams.com/pdfout/200612110609036217771.pdf, December 11, 2006.

## CHAPTER 15

Costs of Software Quality

Daniel Galin

15.1 Introduction

More and more, managements—whether of commercial companies or public organizations—require economic evaluation of their quality assurance systems. Accordingly, it is becoming ever more likely for proposals for development of new quality assurance tools or for investment in improved and expanded operation of existing systems to be examined through an economic microscope. Quality assurance units are thus being forced to demonstrate the potential profitability of any request they may make for the substantial funds required to finance additional system infrastructure or operating costs.

The unique features of costs of software quality (CoSQ) discussed in this chapter reflect the special characteristics of SQA, characteristics that are absent from quality assurance in the manufacturing industry.

The cost of software development has been the subject of many research projects, books, and articles in the past two decades (e.g., [1–5]); publications dedicated to the cost of software quality are nevertheless rare. One indication of the subject's importance is the appearance of publications dedicated to enormous software system failures. These works make it clear that the quality system applied in these projects rested at the heart of the failures [6, 7]. We can assume that a regularly implemented, effective software quality assurance system could have prevented or drastically reduced the immense damages involved in these now "classic" failure cases.

This chapter discusses the classic model of cost of software quality, which applies the general costs of the quality model to the software industry. An additional model, the *extended costs of software quality model*, proposed by the author, is presented in Appendix 15A. The extended model is more comprehensive and includes aspects unique to the software industry. Accordingly, it takes into account additional levels of the organization that have a significant impact on cost of software quality.

15.2   The Concept of Cost of Software Quality

15.2.1   The Concept

The classic cost of quality (CoQ) concept, developed in the early 1950s by Feigenbaum and others [8], provides a methodology for classifying the costs associated with product quality assurance from an economic point of view. This concept was developed to suit the quality situations found in manufacturing organizations, and has since been widely implemented. This concept is applied to the software industry as the CoSQ concept.

According to the CoSQ concept, costs related to software's quality are classified into two general classes: costs of control and costs of failure of control.

Costs of control are assigned to either the prevention or the appraisal costs subclass. Prevention costs include investments in quality infrastructure and quality activities that are general to the organization and not directed to a specific project or system. Appraisal costs include costs of activities performed for a specific project or software system for the purpose of detecting software errors.

Failure of control costs are further classified into internal failure costs and external failure costs.

Internal failure costs include costs of correcting errors that have been detected by design reviews, software tests (carried out by the software developer), and acceptance tests (carried out by the customer) completed before the software is installed at customer sites.

External failure costs include all costs of correcting failures detected by customers or the maintenance team after the software system has been installed.

The classic model that presents the CoSQ concept is presented in Figure 15.1.

Common to costs of control is their being determined and controlled by the organization that establishes the amount of resources to be invested in applying procedures, budget, and other tools. In contrast, costs of failure of control are characterized as consequential and not controlled in nature. Their level, to a great extent, is determined by the level of the costs of control. According to the concept of CoSQ, there is a balance of costs of control and costs of failure of control. Increasing costs of control reduces costs of failure of control and vice versa; decreasing costs of control increases costs of failure of control. Further, according to the CoSQ concept, there is an optimum for the amount of resources to be invested in controlling quality for which the total CoSQ are minimized.

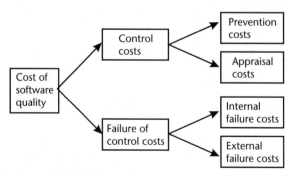

Figure 15.1   The classic model of CoSQ.

It is the aim of management to try and locate this optimum, which determines the optimal level of costs of control. In other words, management is usually interested in minimal total quality costs rather than in control or failure of control cost components. Therefore, managers tend to focus on the optimal quality level and apply this concept when budgeting the annual SQA activity plan as well as when budgeting a project.

Figure 15.2 graphically illustrates the cost of software quality balance concept and the relationship between control and failure of control costs for all the quality levels.

15.2.2   Objectives of Cost of Software Quality Metrics

The main objectives to be achieved by application of CoSQ metrics are managerial. Application of CoSQ metrics enables management to achieve economic control over SQA activities and outcomes. The specific objectives are:

- Control organization-initiated costs to prevent and detect software errors to an optimal level, namely to a level where the total control costs and failure of control costs is minimal;
- Evaluation of the economic damages of software failures as a basis for revising the SQA budget, and bring it to a revised optimal level;
- Evaluation of plans to increase or decrease of SQA activities or to invest in a new or updated SQA infrastructure on the basis of past CoSQ performance.

Managerial control over the cost of software quality is mainly achieved by comparison of actual performance figures with:

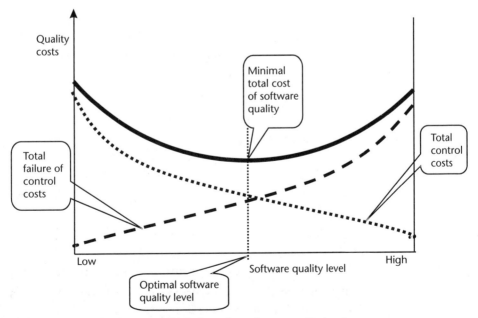

Figure 15.2   Cost of software quality balance by software quality level.

- Control budgeted expenditures (for SQA prevention and appraisal activities);
- Previous year's quality costs (control costs and failure costs);
- Previous project's quality costs (control costs and failure costs);
- Other department's quality costs (control costs and failure costs).

After introducing changes in SQA procedures or SQA infrastructure, a comparison of the following relations may provide better indications of the success of an SQA plan than those just mentioned:

- Percentage of cost of software quality out of total software development costs;
- Percentage of software failure costs out of total software development costs;
- Percentage of cost of software quality out of total software maintenance costs;
- Percentage of cost of software quality out of total sales of software products and software maintenance.

15.3   Costs of Control

This section describes in detail the costs of control, and the next section the details of the costs of failure of control

15.3.1   Prevention Costs

Prevention costs include investments in establishing a software quality infrastructure and updating and improving that infrastructure, as well as performing the regular activities required for its operation. A significant share of the activities performed by the SQA team is preventive in character, as reflected in the SQA budget.

Typical preventive costs include:

1. Investments in development of new or improved SQA infrastructure components or, alternatively, regular updating of those components:
   - Procedures and work instructions;
   - Support devices: templates, checklists, and so on;
   - Software configuration management system;
   - Software quality metrics;

2. Regular implementation of SQA preventive activities:
   - Instruction of new employees in SQA subjects and procedures related to their positions;
   - Instruction of employees in new and updated SQA subjects and procedures;
   - Certification of employees for positions that require certification;
   - Consultations on SQA issues provided to software development team leaders and other team members;

3. Control of the SQA system through performance of:
   - Internal quality reviews;
   - External quality audits by customers and SQA system certification organizations;
   - Management quality reviews.

15.3.2   Appraisal Costs

Appraisal costs are devoted to detection of software errors in specific projects or software systems. Typical appraisal costs cover:

1. Reviews:
   - Formal design reviews (DRs);
   - Peer reviews (inspections and walkthroughs);
   - Expert reviews.

2. Costs of software testing:
   - Unit tests;
   - Integration tests;
   - Software system tests;
   - Acceptance tests (costs involves in participation in tests carried out by the customer).

3. Costs of project progress reporting.
4. Costs of assuring quality of external participants, primarily by means of design reviews and software testing. These activities are applied to the activities performed by:
   - Subcontractors;
   - Suppliers of COTS software systems and reusable software modules;
   - The customer as a participant in performing the project.

15.4   Failure of Control Costs

15.4.1   Internal Failure Costs

Internal failure costs are those incurred when correcting errors that have been detected by design reviews, software tests, and acceptance tests performed before the software has been installed at customer sites. In other words, internal failure costs represent the costs of error correction subsequent to formal examination of the software during its development, prior to the system's installation at the customer's site. It should be noted that corrections and changes resulting from team leader checks or other team-initiated reviews are generally not considered internal failure costs because they are conducted informally.

Typical costs of internal failures include:

- Costs of redesign or design corrections subsequent to design review and test findings;
- Costs of reprogramming or correcting programs in response to test findings;
- Costs of repeated design review and retesting (regression tests); costs of regular design reviews and software tests are considered appraisal costs, any repeated design reviews or software tests directly resulting from poor design and inferior code quality are considered internal failure costs.

15.4.2 External Failure Costs

External failure costs entail costs of correcting failures detected by customers or maintenance teams after the software system has been installed at customer sites. These costs may be further classified into *overt* and *hidden* external failure costs. In most cases, the extent of hidden costs is much greater than that of overt costs. This difference is caused, not least, by the difficulty of estimating hidden external failure costs in comparison to overt external failure costs, which are readily recorded or estimated. In addition, the estimates obtained are frequently disputed among the professionals involved. Hidden external failure cost estimation is rarely undertaken as a result. Therefore, we will use the term *external failure costs* to refer exclusively to overt failure costs.

Typical external failure costs cover:

- Resolution of customer complaints during the warranty period. In most cases, this involves a review of the complaint and transmission of instructions. In most cases, complaints result from failure of the "help" function or the guidelines found in the instruction manual.
- Correction of software bugs detected during regular operation. Those involving correction of code (including tests of the corrected software) followed by installation of the corrected code or replacement of the erroneous version by the correct version are often performed at the customer's site.
- Damages paid to customers in case of a severe software failure detected during regular operation.
- Damages paid to customers in case of a severe late completion of the project.
- Reimbursement of customer's purchase costs, including handling, in case of total dissatisfaction from COTS software packages.
- Insurance premium against customer's claims in case of severe software failure. Insurance premiums are considered as external failure costs as it replaces payments of damages to customers in cases of external failure.
- Damages paid for other projects for delayed completion caused by the overrun schedule of the project (domino effect).

The listed items reflect only overt external failure costs—costs that represent a small part of the full range of external failure costs. These costs are directly incurred by software failures detected and recorded during regular operation of the software. The greater portion of external failure costs—hidden costs—reflect the indirect damages suffered by the software development organization as a result of those same failures.

Typical examples of hidden external failure costs include:

- Damages of reduction of sales to customers suffering from high rates of software failures;
- Losses due to severe reduction of sales motivated by the firm's damaged reputation;
- Increased investment in sales promotion to counter the effects of past software failures;
- Losses due to reduced prospects to win a tender or, alternatively, due to the need to underprice in order to prevent competitors from winning tenders;
- Domino effect damages. These are damages caused to other projects due to delayed completion caused by the overrun schedule of the project. A great part of these losses are not identified or not reported and induce considerable hidden costs.

15.5   Implementation of a Cost of Software Quality System

In order to implement a CoSQ system in an organization, the following is required:

- Definition of cost items for the CoSQ model;
- Definition of the method of data collection;
- Implementation of a CoSQ system.

15.5.1   Definition of Cost Items for the CoSQ Model

At a preliminary stage, an array of cost items is specific for the organization, department, team, or project. Each of the cost items that constitute the model should be related to one of the subclasses of the cost of CoSQ model. The model's cost items are specific to the organization and are relevant to the organization's software development environment. The CoSQ effectiveness is determined, to a great degree, by the efforts the organization will be required to invest to collect the data on the model's cost items.

For example, the SQA unit of the information systems department of a commercial company adopted the classic model as its cost of software quality model. The SQA unit defined about 30 cost items to comprise the model. Some of the quality cost items and their CoSQ subclass are listed in Table 15.1.

The software development and maintenance departments should agree upon the quality cost items to be included in the CoSQ model, and its related cost items should be agreed upon by the department.

Some of the proposed cost items may be unaccepted by the department. It is preferable to omit those items over which agreement is difficult to reach, even at the expense of reducing the variety of quality costs.

Table 15.1   Cost of Quality Items and Their CoSQ Subclasses

Quality Cost Item	CoSQ Subclass
Head of SQA unit (personnel costs)	Prevention and appraisal costs—according to monthly reports
SQA team member reviewing compliance with instructions (personnel costs)	Prevention costs
Other team SQA members (personnel costs)	Prevention and appraisal costs—according to monthly reports
Development and maintenance team participation in internal and external SQA audits (personnel costs)	Prevention costs—recorded time spent on audits
Testing team—first series of tests (personnel costs)	Appraisal costs—recorded time spent
Testing team—regression tests (personnel costs)	Internal failure costs—recorded time spent
Development and maintenance team correction of errors identified by the testing team (personnel costs)	Internal failure costs—recorded time spent
Maintenance team costs for correction of software failures identifies by the customer (personnel costs including traveling expenses to the customer's site)	External failure costs—recorded time spent
Regular visits of unit's SQA consultant (standard monthly fee)	Prevention costs
Unit's SQA consultant's participation in external failure inquiries (special invoices)	External failure costs
SQA journals, seminars, and so forth	Prevention costs

Some software quality cost items may be shared by several departments or other projects. In these cases, the rules determining allocation or costs division should be as simple as possible and agreed to by all the relevant parties, departments, or projects.

Updates and changes of the quality cost items can be expected. These are based on analyses of the cost of software quality reports as well as on changes in the organization's structure and environment.

15.5.2   Definition of the Cost Data Collection Method

The method of cost data collection is a key (although regularly underestimated) factor to the success or failure of the CoSQ system.

Once the list of software quality cost items is finalized, a method for collecting the relevant data must be determined for each cost item. One of the major issues raised at this stage is whether to develop an independent system for collecting data or to rely on the currently operating management information system (MIS). After some adaptations, the MIS it is usually capable of serving the needs of data collection for the chosen cost model. For instance, its human resources costing system can record working hours invested in quality issues. Relatively simple changes in ledger categories enable the accounting system to record the costs of external services and purchases for the SQA system as well as damages paid to customers. In general, use of MIS systems in place is preferable to creating new systems. The reasons for preferring the existing system are:

- Expected savings in costs by running working data collection system already operating instead of creating and running an independent system;
- Disagreements in the interpretation of data typical to cases of independent data collection system. Disagreements of this type reduce the reliability of the software quality cost results.

15.5.3   Implementation of a CoSQ System

Like any other new procedure, implementation of a new cost of software quality system involves:

- Assigning responsibility for reporting and collection of quality cost data.
- Instruction of the team in the logic and procedures of the new system.
- Follow-up:
  - Support for solving implementation problems and providing supplementary information when needed;
  - Review of cost reporting, proper classification, and recording;
  - Review of reports' completeness and accuracy by their comparison with records produced by the general MIS system and previous periods' cost and activity records; this task requires special efforts during the initial implementation period.
- Updating and revising the cost items' definitions together with the reporting and collecting methods, based on feedback.

15.6   The Contribution of a CoSQ System to the Organization

Most of the actions taken in response to the model's findings are the increase or decrease of planned budget for specific sections of control activities. The analysis and subsequent actions taken are rooted in the application of the *cost of software quality balance* concept. According to this concept, an increase in control costs is expected to yield a decrease in failure of control costs and vice versa: a decrease in control costs is expected to lead to an increase in failure of control costs. Moreover, the effect of changes in control costs is expected to vary by the desired software quality level. This relationship is expected to yield a minimal total cost of software quality, a cost that is achievable at a specified quality level—the optimal software quality level.

Examples of typical decisions taken in the wake of CoSQ analysis and their expected results are shown in Table 15.2.

In addition to the direct actions taken by management, other actions can be initiated by the Corrective Action Board, which bases its analysis of the accumulated cost of quality data on factors other than those considered by management.

Table 15.2   CoSQ Analysis: Typical Actions and Expected Results

No.	Actions	Expected Results
1	Improvement of software package's help function	Reduction of external failure costs
2	Increased investment of resources in contract review	Reduction of failure costs
3	Reduction in instruction activities yielding no significant improvement	Reduction of prevention costs with no increase in failure costs
4	Increased investment in training inspection team members and team leaders	Reduction of internal and external failure costs
5	Construction of a list of certified subcontractors allowed to participate in the company's projects	Reduction of failure costs, especially of external failure costs
6	Introduction of automated software tests to replace manual testing with no substantial increase in testing costs	Reduction of internal and external failure costs

15.7   Difficulties in the Implementation

Application of a cost of software quality model is generally accompanied by problems to be overcome, whatever the industry. These problems impinge upon the accuracy and completeness of quality cost data caused by:

- Inaccurate and/or incomplete identification and classification of quality costs;
- Negligent reporting by team members and others;
- Biased reporting of software costs, especially of "censored" internal and external failure costs;
- Biased recording of external failure costs due to indirect if not camouflaged compensation of customers for failures (e.g., discounted future services, delivery of free services) whose implications remain unrecorded as external failure costs;
- Payment of overt (not camouflaged) and formal compensation usually occurs quite some time after the project is completed, and much too late for efficient application of the lessons learned.

The above-mentioned problems also arise within the context of the software industry; special attention should be directed to treat these difficulties and reduce their effect.

15.8   Limitations of the Classic CoSQ Model

The main limitation of the classic CoSQ model is its narrow scope, originally related to the responsibilities to software quality costs. It probably arose because the classic cost of quality model was originated for the environment of the manufacturing industries. Accordingly, the classic model focuses on the operational level and the professional software quality assurance unit. The distribution of responsibility to the various subclasses of the classic CoSQ model is presented in Table 15.3.

Table 15.3   The Classic CoSQ Model: Organizational Units Responsible for Costs

Class of CoSQ	Subclass of CoSQ	Units of the Organization Responsible for Costs
Costs of control	Prevention costs	SQA unit Software development project team
	Appraisal costs	SQA unit Software development project team Software testing unit Software review teams
Costs of failure of control	Internal failure costs	Software development project team
	External failure costs	Software development project team

In the software industry, the management activities and failure of control activities affect substantially the quality costs involved in software development projects. According to Boehm [1], the first two software development risks in the "top 10 software risk items" refer to managerial actions or failure of actions: (1) personnel shortfalls, and (2) unrealistic schedules and budgets. These risks, when realized, are involved in substantial failure costs. Management's failure to recruit sufficient and adequate staff may result from deficient project progress control or unrealistic project team planning at earlier stages of implementation. Unrealistic schedules and budgets are usually products of overly optimistic estimates driven by management's anxiety when compiling a competitive proposal. Results of a similar nature were found in an international study on software project risks carried out in the United States, Finland, and Hong Kong by Schmidt et al. [9] and by Keil et al. [10]. A significant number of risk factors identified in this study relate to project management, staffing, funding, and corporate environment.

The proposed extended cost of software quality model incorporates costs of management's control activities and costs of management's failure of control into a comprehensive model that solves the above-mentioned limitations of the classic CoSQ model. The extended CoSQ model that more effectively represents the circumstances surrounding software development projects is the subject of Appendix 15A.

15.9   Extreme Cases of Costs of Software Quality

Two categories of extreme cases of software development projects are discussed in this section: total failure projects and catastrophic projects.

Total failure cases are projects cancelled during the development process or abandoned after delivery and never used, resulting from the product's total performance failure. The minimal losses incurred in these extreme cases equals the amount invested in the software development project, while in many cases it is doubled or tripled and more, considering the losses to the client being unable to operate its organization as planned. In a large number of these cases, the total failure losses are costs of failure of control. One should not underestimate the number of total failure projects of software development projects. In 2004 surveys reveal that 18% of the projects were found "total failure projects" [11]. The rest of the projects, 82%, were considered "normal" projects, categorized as follows: (1) completed success-fully—29%; or (2) completed and operational but over budget, over the time sched-ule, and/or offering fewer features and functions than originally specified—53%.

The other category of extreme projects refers to catastrophic situation of soft-ware project collapse (usually during its first period of operation). The typical dam-ages in such project catastrophes result from a sizable organization, or substantial group of organizations, being unable to operate during a long period of time. A well-known example of such catastrophic failures of software development projects is the automated baggage handling system of Denver International Airport that caused a 16-month delay in the opening of the airport, $2 billion over budget and hundreds of millions of dollars damages caused to organizations involved in the pro-ject. Flowers [12] and Glass [6] describe and analyze this and other instances of cata-strophic failures. Further illustrations and analyses of such extreme cases can be found in Montealegre and Keil [7]. Common to all these catastrophic collapse pro-jects is management's significant share in creating or not preventing the catastrophic situations characterized by severe budget overruns and very late completion dates. While such failures are very rare in the manufacturing industry, they are real ongoing threats to every large-scale software development project.

Analysis of the sources of the huge losses in these extreme cases reveals that apart from customers contribution to these extreme cases, significant, if not major, losses may be considered costs of external failure, caused mainly by managements' activities or their not-performed activities. (The subject of extreme cases of costs of software quality will not be further discussed in this chapter.)

Problems encountered in collection of data on managerial failure costs, espe-cially schedule failures, include the determination of responsibility for schedule fail-ures. These costs may be assigned to the customer (in which case the customer is required to compensate the contractor), the development team (considered as an external failure cost), or management (considered as a managerial failure cost). Table 15.4 shows examples of typical causes for delays and the associated quality costs.

15.10   Conclusion

The main objective of implementing a cost of software quality system in an organi-zation is to benefit management. Application of CoSQ metrics enables management to achieve control over SQA activities and outcomes based on cost data. It is the aim of management to locate the optimal level of costs of control and determine the SQA activities budget accordingly. This optimum is such that it minimizes the total costs of software quality.

Although attempts to apply the classic model to software development and maintenance have been reported, success has been very limited. One of the reasons for a low success rate is the implementation difficulties mentioned above. Another reason is the partial coverage of actual costs of software quality. Observation of sources of costs of software quality identifies costs originating from manage-ment—that is, caused by management's activities or management's lack of activity. It leads us to widen the scope of software quality costs to include, in addition to

Table 15.4 Causes of Schedule Delays and Related Costs

Cause for Deviation from Schedule	Class of Quality Costs
Changes introduced in the project's specifications during development	Customer responsibility for failure costs
Customer-delayed installation of communication and other hardware, and/or delays in staff recruitment and training	Customer responsibility for failure costs
Poor performance by development team, requiring extensive rework and corrections of software	External failure costs
Project proposal based on unrealistic schedules and budgets	Managerial failure costs
Late or inadequate recruitment of staff or reliance on company professionals whose release from other projects does not meet project needs.	Managerial failure costs

quality costs caused by the software developing level, also those caused by management. This issue reflects the differences between the manufacturing industries and the software industry, as discussed below.

Quality assurance (QA) in the manufacturing industries deals mainly with repetitive production of established products, but software quality assurance (SQA) deals mainly with development of new software products. Accordingly, while in the manufacturing industries the production level departments and the QA unit are responsible for almost all CoQ substance, in the software industry, in addition to the production level (development teams) and SQA units, management is responsible for significant portions of the CoSQ. The management's CoSQ may be classified into three categories: managerial appraisal and control costs, managerial internal failure costs, and managerial external costs. The costs of managerial failures, internal and external, may be defined as those caused by managerial action or inaction in performing managerial appraisal and control tasks.

High evaluation of management's share in the costs of software quality, specifically in software failure costs, is demanded by Glass [6] and Flowers [12]; the title of the latter's book, *Software Failure: Management Failure*, reflects management's share in these costs.

This aspect of management's substantial share of CoSQ is likewise reflected in (1) management's share of software development risks, and (2) its actions and inactions resulting in catastrophic cases of software failure, the latter being a tangible threat for any software project of considerable scale. These aspects that characterize the software industry are included in the extended model for CoSQ presented in Appendix 15A.

References

[1]   Boehm B. W., *Software Engineering Economics*, Upper Saddle River, NJ: Prentice-Hall, 1981.

[2]   Boehm B. W., "Safe and Simple Software Cost Analysis," *IEEE Software*, Vol. 17, No. 5, 2000, pp. 14–17.

[3]   Jones, S., *Estimating Software Costs*, New York: McGraw-Hill, 1998.

[4]   Dobbins, J. H., "The Cost of Software Quality," in G. G. Schulmeyer and J. I. McManus, (eds.), *Handbook of Software Quality Assurance*, 3rd ed., Upper Saddle River, NJ: Prentice-Hall, 1999, pp. 403–443.

[5]   Hale, J., et al., "Enhancing the COCOMO Estimation Models," *IEEE Software*, Vol. 17, No. 6, 2000, pp. 45–49.

[6]   Glass, R. L., *Software Runaways*, Upper Saddle River, NJ: Prentice-Hall, 1998.

[7]   Montealegre, R., and M. Keil, "De-Escalating Information Technology Projects: Lessons from the Denver International Airport," *MIS Quarterly*, Vol. 24, No. 3, 2000, pp. 417–447.

[8]   Feigenbaum, A. V., *Total Quality Control*, 3rd ed., New York: McGraw-Hill, 1991.

[9]   Schmidt, R., et al., "Identifying Software Project Risk: An International Delphi Study," *Journal of Management Information Systems* Vol. 17, No. 4, 2001, pp. 5–36.

[10] Keil, M., et al., "A Framework for Identifying Project Risks," *Communications of the ACM*, Vol. 41, No. 11, 1998, pp. 76–83.

[11] The Standish Group, "The Chaos Demographics," in *2004 Third Quarter Research Report*, http//www.standishgroup/sample_research, 2004.

[12] Flowers, S., *Software Failure: Management Failure*, New York: John Wiley & Sons, 1996.

Selected Bibliography

Crosby P. B., *Quality Is Free*, New York: McGraw-Hill, 1992.

Galin, D., *Software Quality Assurance: From Theory to Implementation*, Reading, MA: Addison-Wesley, 2003, pp. 449–470.

Galin D., "Towards an Inclusive Model for Costs of Software Quality," *Software Quality Professional*, Vol. 6, No. 4, 2004, pp. 25–31.

ISO/IEC (2004), *ISO/IEC 90003-2004, Software Engineering—Guidelines for Application of ISO 9001/2000 to Computer Software Development, Supply, Acquisition, Operation and Maintenance of Computer Software*, Geneva, International Organization for Standardization, 2004.

Juran, J. M., *Quality Control Handbook*, 4th ed., New York: McGraw-Hill, 1988.

Knox, S. T., "Modeling the Cost of Software Quality," *Digital Technical Journal*, Vol. 5, No. 4, 1993, pp. 9–16.

Krasner, H., "Using the Cost of Quality Approach for Software," *Crosstalk*, Vol. XX, No. 11, 1998.

Appendix 15A   An Extended Model for Cost of Software Quality

15A.1   Concept of the Extended CoSQ Model

Analysis of the software quality costs defined by the classic CoSQ model reveals that several costs of substantial magnitude are excluded. These costs are either unique to the software industry or negligible for other industries. For example, typical software quality failure costs include:

- Damages paid to customers as compensation for late completion of the project due to unrealistic scheduling;
- Damages paid to customers in compensation for late completion of the project as a result of failure to recruit sufficient staff.

The element common to these two failures is that they result not from any particular action of the development team or any lack of professionalism; they are actually outcomes of *managerial failure.*

Management can perform several activities to prevent or reduce the costs that result from the types of failure particular to its functions:

- In the software industry, considerable professional work is required to assure that a project proposal is based on sound estimates and comprehensive evaluations of proposed project. There is a significant difference in required resources for performing contract reviews in the software and manufacturing industries that results from the nature of the software development and the manufacturing processes. While a typical contract in the manufacturing industry deals with repeated manufacturing of catalog-listed products, a typical contract in the software industry deals with development of a new, unique software system.

- Intensive progress control of the software project. Here again there is a significant difference. While production control carried out in the manufacturing industry is a repetitive task that can, in most cases, be performed automatically by machines, software development progress control supervises design and coding activities performed for the first time and needs to be intensive and performed by professionals.

The important effect of management on the cost of software quality is reflected by the title of Flowers' book: *Software Failure: Management Failure* (Flowers, 1996). In this book Flowers describes and analyzes several colossal software project failures; he concludes by discussing the critical managerial failures at their root and suggests ways to prevent or reduce them.

The *extended cost of software quality model,* as proposed by the author of this chapter, extends the classic model to include management's "contributions" to the total cost of software quality. According to the extended model, two subclasses are added to complete the model's coverage: (1) managerial appraisal and control costs subclass is added to control costs class, and (2) managerial failure costs subclass is added to failure of control costs class. The extended CoSQ model is shown in Figure 15A.1.

In the following sections, the new cost subclasses are discussed in full.

15A.2   Managerial Appraisal and Control Costs

Managerial appraisal and control costs are associated with activities performed to prevent managerial failures or reduce prospects of their occurrence. Several of these activities have already been discussed in previous chapters related to various SQA frameworks.

Typical managerial appraisal and control costs include managements' important share in the following activities:

- Costs of carrying out contract reviews (proposal draft and contract draft reviews);

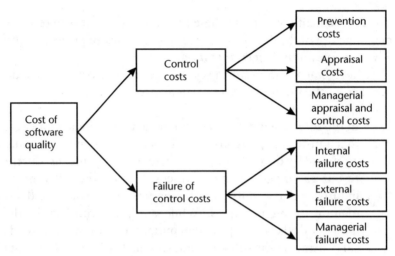

Figure 15A.1 The extended CoSQ model.

- Costs of preparing project plans, including quality plans and their review;
- Costs of periodic updating of project and quality plans;
- Costs of performing regular progress control of internal software development efforts;
- Costs of performing regular progress control of external participants' contributions to the project.

15A.3 Managerial Failure Costs

Managerial failure costs can be incurred throughout the entire course of software development, beginning in the preproject stage. They are most likely to crop up in connection with failed attempts to (1) estimate the appropriate project schedule and budget, and (2) detect in a timely fashion those deviations and problems that demand management intervention. Several of these activities have already been discussed previously and are repeated here for the sake of completeness.

Typical managerial failure costs include:

- Unplanned costs for professional and other resources, resulting from underestimation of the resources upon which the submitted proposals are based;
- Damages paid to customers as compensation for late completion of the project, a result of the unrealistic schedule presented in the company's proposal;
- Damages paid to customers as compensation for late completion of the project, a result of management's failure to recruit sufficient and appropriate team members;
- Damages paid to customers as compensation for late completion of the project, a result of management's failure to perform effective progress control of the project.

15A.4   Difficulties in the Implementation of the Extended CoSQ Model

Implementing the extended CoSQ is involved with all the difficulties that generally characterize implementation of costs of quality models, as well as the difficulties related to the CoSQ model. Implementation of the extended CoSQ model involves additional difficulties related to:

- Collecting of data on managerial appraisal and control costs;
- Determination of responsibility for failure costs;
- Late acquisition of quality cost data and or late agreement of responsibility of costs that reduce or even eliminate implementation of lessons learned.

Typical difficulties in collecting quality costs on managerial appraisal and control costs include the following:

- Contract review and progress control activities are performed in many cases in a "part-time mode." Additionally, they are subdivided into several disconnected activities of short duration. The reporting of time invested in these activities is usually inaccurate and often neglected.
- Many participants in these activities are senior staff members who are not required to report use of their time resources.

Typical difficulties in determination of responsibility for failure costs include the following:

- Difficulties in determining the responsibility for schedule failures. The costs of such failures may be assigned to (1) the customer (in which case the customer is required to compensate the contractor), (2) the development team (classified as external failure costs), or (3) the management (classified as managerial failure costs). Table 15A.1 shows examples of typical causes for schedule delays and the associated quality costs.
- Difficulties in determining the responsibility for budget overruns. The costs of such failures may be assigned to (1) the development team (classified as external failure costs), or (2) the management (classified as managerial failure costs). Table 15A.2 shows examples of typical causes for budget overruns and the associated quality costs.

There are also difficulties in implementing the conclusions in cases of debated responsibilities. The issues of responsibility for failure costs are frequently deliberated for lengthy periods because their direct causes or the specific contributions of each participant to the initial failures are difficult to pinpoint. Agreement often occurs too late in the process for the lessons learned to be applied.

A comprehensive comparison of the classic CoSQ and the extended CoSQ, based on the subclass classification of quality cost items, is presented in Table 15A.3.

Table 15A.1   Causes of Schedule Delays and Related Costs

Cause for Deviation from Schedule	Class of CoSQ
Changes introduced in the project's specifications during development	Customer's responsibility for failure costs
Customer-delayed installation of communication and other hardware, and/or delays in staff recruitment and training	Customer responsibility for failure costs
Poor performance by development team, requiring extensive rework and corrections of software	External failure costs
Project proposal based on unrealistic schedules	Managerial failure costs
Late or inadequate recruitment of staff or reliance on company professionals whose release from other projects does not meet project needs	Managerial failure costs

Table 15A.2   Causes for Budget Overrun and Related Costs

Cause for Budget Overrun	Class of CoSQ
Poor performance by development team, requiring extensive rework and corrections of software	Internal failure costs
Project proposal based on unrealistic budget	Managerial failure costs
Subcontractor that ceased to operate.	Managerial failure costs

Table 15A.3   Comparison of the Classic and Extended CoSQ Models: Summary Table

Typical Quality Cost Items	Classic CoSQ Subclasses *					Extended CoSQ Subclasses *						
	Pr	Ap	IF	EF	NI	Pr	Ap	IF	EF	MAC	MF	NI
Costs of development of new and updates of procedures and work instructions	X	—	—	—	—	X	—	—	—	—	—	—
Costs of development of and updating of support devices: templates, checklists, and so forth.	X	—	—	—	—	X	—	—	—	—	—	—
Costs of development and regular operation of software configuration management system	X	—	—	—	—	X	—	—	—	—	—	—
Costs of development and regular operation of software quality metrics	X	—	—	—	—	X	—	—	—	—	—	—
Costs of instruction of employees in new and updates of SQA subjects and procedures	X	—	—	—	—	X	—	—	—	—	—	—
Costs of instruction of new employees in SQA subjects and procedures	X	—	—	—	—	X	—	—	—	—	—	—
Costs of consultations on SQA issues provided to development team members	X	—	—	—	—	X	—	—	—	—	—	—
Costs of certification of employees for positions that require special certification	X	—	—	—	—	X	—	—	—	—	—	—
Costs of internal and external quality audits	X	—	—	—	—	X	—	—	—	—	—	—

Table 15A.3   (continued)

Typical Quality Cost Items	Classic CoSQ Subclasses *					Extended CoSQ Subclasses *						
	Pr	Ap	IF	EF	NI	Pr	Ap	IF	EF	MAC	MF	NI
Costs of conduct of contract reviews—SQA unit's resources	—	X	—	—	—	—	X	—	—	—	—	—
Costs of conduct of contract reviews—management's resources	—	—	—	—	X	—	—	—	—	X	—	—
Costs for preparation of project and quality plans and their periodic updating	—	X	—	—	—	—	X	—	—	—	—	—
Costs of performance of various reviews	—	X	—	—	—	—	X	—	—	—	—	—
Costs of performance of unit, integration, and software system tests	—	X	—	—	—	—	X	—	—	—	—	—
Costs of participation in acceptance tests	—	X	—	—	—	—	X	—	—	—	—	—
Costs of quality assurance of subcontractors and other external participants	—	X	—	—	—	—	X	—	—	—	—	—
Costs of project progress reporting	—	X	—	—	—	—	X	—	—	—	—	—
Management's costs of project progress control of project parts developed internally	—	—	—	—	X	—	—	—	—	X	—	—
Management's costs of progress control of contributions of subcontractors and other external participants	—	—	—	—	X	—	—	—	—	X	—	—
Costs of redesign or corrections subsequent to design review and test findings	—	—	X	—	—	—	—	X	—	—	—	—
Costs of reprogramming or correcting programs in response to test findings	—	—	X	—	—	—	—	X	—	—	—	—
Costs of repeated design review and retesting (regression tests)	—	—	X	—	—	—	—	X	—	—	—	—
Costs of repeated design review and retesting (regression tests)	—	—	X	—	—	—	—	X	—	—	—	—
Costs of overrun project budget caused by team's professional low capabilities	—	—	X	—	—	—	—	X	—	—	—	—
Costs of overrun development costs resulting from underestimation of resources for submitted proposals	—	—	—	X	—	—	—	—	—	—	X	—
Costs of resolution of customer complaints during the warranty period	—	—	—	X	—	—	—	—	X	—	—	—
Costs of correction of software bugs detected during regular operation	—	—	—	X	—	—	—	—	X	—	—	—

Table 15A.3　(continued)

Typical Quality Cost Items	Classic CoSQ Subclasses *					Extended CoSQ Subclasses *						
	Pr	Ap	IF	EF	NI	Pr	Ap	IF	EF	MAC	MF	NI
Damages paid to customers in case of a severe software failure	—	—	—	X	—	—	—	—	X	—	—	—
Damages paid to customers in case of project late completion resulting from team's low professional capabilities	—	—	—	X	—	—	—	—	X	—	—	—
Damages paid to customers for late project completion resulting from proposal's unrealistic schedule	—	—	—	X	—	—	—	—	—	—	X	—
Damages paid to customers for late project completion resulting from failure to recruit team members	—	—	—	X	—	—	—	—	—	—	X	—
Damages paid to customers for late project completion resulting from failures in managerial progress control	—	—	—	X	—	—	—	—	—	—	X	—
Reimbursement of customer's purchase costs, in case of total dissatisfaction (related to COTS software)	—	—	—	X	—	—	—	—	X	—	—	—
Costs of insurance premium against customer damage claims in case of severe software failure	—	—	—	X	—	—	—	—	X	—	—	—
Management's costs of project progress control of project parts developed internally	—	—	—	—	X	—	—	—	—	X	—	—
Management's costs of progress control of contributions of subcontractors and other external participants	—	—	—	—	X	—	—	—	—	X	—	—
Management's costs of performing periodical management quality reviews	—	—	—	—	X	—	—	—	—	X	—	—
Costs of overrun development costs resulting from underestimation of resources for submitted proposals	—	—	—	X	—	—	—	—	—	—	X	—
Damages paid for other projects' delayed completion caused by the overrun schedule of the project (domino effect failure)—Development team's responsibility for the delayed completion of the original project	—	—	—	X	—	—	—	—	X	—	—	—
Damages paid for other projects delayed completion caused by the overrun schedule of the project (Domino effect failure)—Management's responsibility for the delayed completion of the original project	—	—	—	X	—	—	—	—	—	—	X	—

Table 15A.3   (continued)

Typical Quality Cost Items	Classic CoSQ Subclasses *					Extended CoSQ Subclasses *						
	Pr	Ap	IF	EF	NI	Pr	Ap	IF	EF	MAC	MF	NI
Losses due to reduction of sales as a result of damaged reputation	—	—	—	—	X**	—	—	—	—	—	—	X**
Increased cost of sales promotion due to damaged reputation	—	—	—	—	X**	—	—	—	—	—	—	X**
Losses due to under-pricing of tender bidding to counter the effects of damaged reputation	—	—	—	—	X**	—	—	—	—	—	—	X**
Damages paid for other projects for delayed completion caused by the overrun schedule of the project (Domino effect failure)	—	—	—	—	X**	—	—	—	—	—	—	X**

*CoSQ subclasses: Pr = Prevention, Ap = Appraisal, IF = Internal failure, EF = External failure, MAC = Management's appraisal and control, MF = Management's failure, NI = Not included in the model.

**Hidden failure costs.

## CHAPTER 16

Software Quality Assurance Metrics

G. Gordon Schulmeyer

16.1 Introduction

What is the difference between a measure, a metric, and an indicator? Before delving into the details of software quality metrics, an understanding of these differences is in order. A *measure* (Figure 16.1) is to ascertain or appraise by comparing to a standard. A standard or unit of measurement encompasses: the extent, dimensions, capacity, and so on, of anything, especially as determined by a standard; an act or process of measuring; a result of measurement. Without a trend to follow or an expected value to compare against, a measure gives little or no information. It especially does not provide enough information to make meaningful decisions. A *metric* (Figure 16.2) is a quantitative measure of the degree to which a system, component, or process possesses a given attribute. It is a calculated or composite indicator based upon two or more measures. A metric is a comparison of two or more measures (in Figure 16.2 see body temperature over time) or defects per thousand source lines of code. An *indicator* (Figure 16.3) is a device or variable that can be set to a prescribed state based on the results of a process or the occurrence of a specified condition. An indicator generally compares a metric with a baseline or expected result. This allows the decision makers to make a quick comparison that can provide a perspective as to the "health" of a particular aspect of the project [1].

The purpose of software quality metrics is to assess throughout the development cycle whether the software quality requirements are being met. The use of metrics reduces subjectivity in the assessment of software quality by providing a quantitative basis for making decisions about software quality. The use of metrics, however, does not eliminate the need for human judgment in software evaluations. The use of software quality metrics within an organization or project is expected to have a beneficial effect by making software quality more visible.

One should note that the quality management models and metrics emerged from the practical needs of large-scale development projects and they draw on principles and knowledge in the field of quality engineering (traditionally being practiced in manufacturing and production operations). For software quality engineering to become mature, a systematic body of knowledge should encompass seamless links among the internal structure of design and implementation, the external behavior of the software system, and the logistics and management of the development project [2].

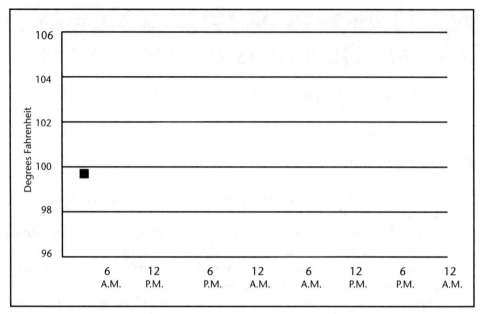

Figure 16.1 Body temperature (measure) sample. (*From:* [1]. © 1995 Bruce Ragland. Reprinted with permission.)

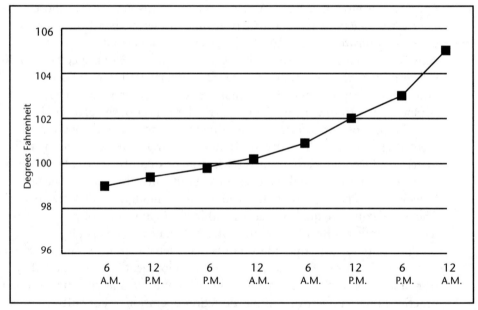

Figure 16.2 Body temperature (metric) sample. (*From:* [1]. © 1995 Bruce Ragland. Reprinted with permission.)

Software quality assurance metrics are intimately connected with software development metrics. So this chapter highlights software quality assurance metrics, but more generally addresses development metrics in order to provide a more complete picture of the interplay among these various metrics.

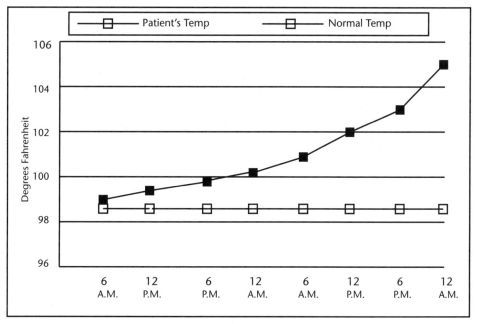

Figure 16.3   Body temperature compared with normal temperature (indicator) sample. (*From:* [1]. © 1995 Bruce Ragland. Reprinted with permission.)

16.2   Software Quality Indicators

Scientific Systems, Inc., under a contract to the Air Force Business Research Management Center, developed a set of software quality indicators (Table 16.1) to improve the management capabilities of personnel responsible for monitoring software development projects. The quality indicators address management concerns, take advantage of data that is already being collected, are independent of the software development methodology being used, are specific to phases in the development cycle, and provide information on the status of a project.

Some recommended quality indicators include:

1. *Progress:* Measures the amount of work accomplished by the developer in each phase. This measure flows through the development life cycle with a number of requirements defined and baselined, then the amount of preliminary and detailed designed completed, then the amount of code completed, and various levels of tests completed.

2. *Stability:* Assesses whether the products of each phase are sufficiently stable to allow the next phase to proceed. This measures the number of changes to requirements, design, and implementation.

3. *Process compliance:* Measures the developer's compliance with the development procedures approved at the beginning of the project. Captures the number of procedures identified for use on the project versus those complied with on the project.

4. *Quality evaluation effort:* Measures the percentage of the developer's effort that is being spent on internal quality evaluation activities. Percent of time

developers are required to deal with quality evaluations and related corrective actions.

5. *Test coverage:* Measures the amount of the software system covered by the developer's testing process. For module testing, this counts the number of basis paths executed/covered, and for system testing it measures the percentage of functions tested.

6. *Defect detection efficiency:* Measures how many of the defects detectable in a phase were actually discovered during that phase. Starts at 100% and is reduced as defects are uncovered at a later development phase.

7. *Defect removal rate:* Measures the number of defects detected and resolved over time. Number of opened and closed system problem reports (SPR) reported through the development phases.

8. *Defect age profile:* Measures the number of defects that have remained unresolved for a long period of time. By month reporting of SPRs remaining open greater than 1 month.

9. *Defect density:* Detects defect-prone components of the system. Provides measure of SPRs/Computer Software Component (CSC) to determine which is the most defect-prone CSC.

10. *Complexity:* Measures the complexity of the code. Collects basis path counts (cyclomatic complexity) of code modules to determine how complex each module is.

These quality indicators have certain characteristics. Quality measures must be oriented toward management goals. One need not have extensive familiarity with technical details of the project. Quality measures should reveal problems as they develop and suggest corrective actions that could be taken. Quality measures must be easy to use. They must not be excessively time consuming, nor depend heavily on extensive software training or experience. Measures that are clearly specified, easy to calculate, and straightforward to interpret are needed. Quality measures must be flexible [3].

16.3   Practical Software and Systems Measurement (PSM)

Practical Software and Systems Measurement (PSM) was developed to meet software and system technical and management challenges. It describes an information-driven measurement process that addresses the unique technical and business goals of an organization. The guidance in PSM represents the best practices used by measurement professionals within the software and system acquisition and engineering communities. PSM is sponsored by the Department of Defense and the U.S. Army. The goal of the PSM project is to provide project managers with the objective information needed to successfully meet cost, schedule, and technical objectives on programs. It is based on actual measurement experience on DoD, government, and industry programs. Measurement professionals from a wide variety of organizations participate in the project. PSM represents the best practices for measurement used within the software and system acquisition and engineering communities. PSM also supports information technology (IT) performance measurement requirements. (See

Table 16.1   Quality Indicators by Development Phase

	Software Requirements Analysis	Preliminary Design	Detailed Design	Code and Unit Testing	CSC Integration and Testing	CSCI Testing
Process Indicators						
Management Concern:						
Progress	Requirements volume	Top level design complete	Detailed design complete	Units completed	Tests accomplished	Tests accomplished
Stability	System requirements stability	Software requirements stability	Top level design stability	Detailed design stability	Software stability	Software stability
Compliance	Process compliance	<————————————————————————————————>				
Quality effort	Quality evaluation effort	<————————————————————————————————>				
Defect detection						
1. Test coverage				Percentage of paths executed	Percentage of paths executed	Percentage of functions executed
2. Defect detection efficiency		Defect detection efficiency	<————————————————————————————>			
Product Indicators						
Completeness	System requirements stability	Software requirements traceability				
1. Defect removal rate	Open and closed problem reports	<————————————————————————————————>				
2. Age profile	Problem report age profile	<————————————————————————————————>				
3. Defect density	Defect density	<————————————————————————————————>				
Complexity	Requirements complexity	Design complexity	Design complexity	Code complexity		

Source: [4].

Chapter 14.) PSM treats measurement as a flexible process, not a predefined list of graphs or reports [5]. The PSM measurement process is defined by a set of nine best practices, called measurement principles [6]:

1. Information needs and objectives drive measurement requirements;
2. Measures based on technical and management processes;
3. Level of detail sufficient to identify and isolate risks and problems;
4. Independent analysis capability implemented;
5. Systematic analysis process to trace measures to decisions;
6. Measurement results in context of other project information;

7. Measurement integrated throughout life cycle;
8. Measurement process as a basis for objective communications;
9. Focus initially on project-level analysis.

An underlying concept of the PSM measurement process is that it should be flexible and able to be tailored based on the unique information needs and characteristics of each project or organization. Measurement must be iterative to support necessary changes that result from changing information needs and improvements in the measurement process itself. The PSM process, shown in Figure 16.4, describes four activities that are part of a successful measurement program:

1. *Plan measurement:* In this activity, measures are defined to provide insight into a project or organization's information needs. This includes identifying what the decision makers need to know, relating these information needs to those entities that can be measured, and then selecting and specifying prospective measures based on project and organizational processes. For example, a comparison of the number of defects written and the number closed addresses the question: "When will the system be ready for user acceptance test?"

2. *Perform measurement:* This activity involves collecting measurement data, performing measurement analysis, and presenting the results so that the information can be used to make decisions. Analysis can include estimation, feasibility analysis of plans, and performance analysis of actual data against plans. The performance analysis of a defect example includes evaluating the trends of written and closed defects, and calculating test readiness.

3. *Evaluate measurement:* In this activity, both the measurement process and the specific measures should be periodically evaluated and improved as necessary. For example, if the defect indicator does not provide enough information to adequately determine readiness for user acceptance testing, additional indicators may be added. The user may add an indicator of defect data by severity (generally all high-priority defects must be closed, but some number of low priority defects may be allowed).

4. *Establish and sustain commitment:* This activity involves establishing the resources, training, and tools to implement a measurement program effectively, and most importantly, ensuring that there is management commitment to use the information that is produced. In the defect example, if the measurement information is not used to develop plans for when user acceptance testing can begin, there is little need for collecting the data.

A measurement process that is flexible and tailored to project and organizational processes ensures that measurement is cost effective. Data should not be collected or reports distributed that are not needed or are not used. In addition, data collection and reporting should be automated whenever possible to provide an automatic by-product of normal project activity.

The process shown in Figure 16.4 provides a foundation for measurement for many disciplines, including software engineering, systems engineering, and process improvement measurement. An important thing to remember is that the same basic

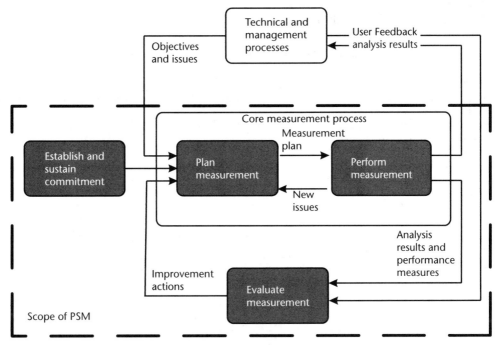

Figure 16.4   PSM measurement process. (*Source:* [7].)

measurement process can support a wide variety of distinct and changing information needs in each of these areas [8].

A highlight of the variety of suggested measures and how they are related is provided in Table 16.2. Drawing on the first example provided in the table, start with the *indicators* of "development milestone schedule" and "milestone progress." They fall under the *measure* of milestone dates. That is in the *measurement category* of "milestone performance." Lastly, it addresses the *common issue area* of "schedule and progress." And so Table 16.2 continues for the PSM suggested measures.

PSM Insight is a free PC-based software tool that automates the PSM process. PSM Insight includes tailoring, data entry, and analysis functions to help develop a project-specific software measurement database and analyses. While PSM Insight provides templates of commonly used issues and measures, it is also completely flexible for you to customize analysis to project-specific needs. Similar to PSM, PSM Insight is sponsored by the Department of Defense and the U.S. Army Software Metrics Office [9].

Inputs to PSM Insight may be manual or may be imported, particularly from Microsoft Excel. However, understanding the metric that one is going to input into PSM Insight is aided immensely by filling in the form shown in Figure 16.5 [10]. Completing the form with responses to proposed questions forces the project to think through aspects of the metric that will clarify why the metric is important for the project to collect and simplify using the PSM Insight tool.

PSM Insight offers a wide variety of outputs, including [11]:

• Trend (line) graphs;
• Snapshot (bar) graphs;

Table 16.2   Index of the Indicator Examples

Indicator	Measure	Measurement Category	Common Issue Area
Development milestone schedule Milestone progress–maintenance activities	Milestone dates	Milestone performance	Schedule and progress
Problem report status Problem report aging—open problem reports Problem report status—open by priority Problem report status—open priority 1 and 2 by configuration item Problem report status—Open priority 1 and 2 by type	Problem report status	Work unit progress	Schedule and progress
Design progress with replan Subsystem acceptance status	Component status	Work unit progress	Schedule and progress
Action item status	Action item status	Work unit progress	Schedule and progress
Incremental content	Incremental content—components	Incremental capability	Schedule and progress
Effort allocation with replan Effort allocation by development activity Staffing level	Effort	Personnel	Resources and cost
Staff experience	Staff experience	Personnel	Resources and cost
Cost and schedule variance	Earned value	Financial performance	Resources and cost
Planned cost profile Cost profile with actual costs	Cost	Financial performance	Resources and cost
Resource utilization—test facilities	Resource utilization	Environment and support resources	Resources and cost
Interface stability	Interfaces	Physical size and stability	Product size and stability
Software size by configuration item Software size—lines of code	Lines of code	Physical size and stability	Product size and stability
Electrical power budget	Physical dimensions	Physical size and stability	Product size and stability
Requirements stability Requirements stability by type of change	Requirements	Functional size and stability	Product size and stability
Multiple indicators for change requests Change requests by priority	Functional change workload	Functional size and stability	Product size and stability
Status of severity 1 defects Defect density Defect density in code inspections Defect classification defects configuration item A Defect density distribution	Defects	Functional correctness	Product quality
System failures and restorations Mean time to repair or fix Mean time to restore system, with threshold	Time to restore	Supportability—maintainability	Product quality

Table 16.2   (continued)

Indicator	Measure	Measurement Category	Common Issue Area
Software complexity—CI A Software complexity—CI A—units with complexity > 10	Cyclomatic complexity	Supportability— maintainability	Product quality
Response time—on-line functions Response time during test—on-line functions	Timing	Efficiency	Product quality
Interface compliance validation	Standards compliance	Portability	Product quality
Problem reports by type of problem data Operator error distribution by reason Device complexity distribution	Operator errors	Usability	Product quality
MTBF ranges based on historical data Reliability growth tracked with mean time to failure	Failures	Dependability— Reliability	Product quality
Reference model level— continuous type Reference model level—staged type	Reference model rating	Process compliance	Process performance
Process audit findings Audit findings by reason code	Process audit findings	Process compliance	Process performance
Software productivity—historical versus proposal Evaluating options using software productivity	Productivity	Process efficiency	Process performance
Requirements defects discovered after requirements phase	Defect containment	Process effectiveness	Process performance
Development effort by activity— compared to total rework effort Rework effort—by activity	Rework	Process effectiveness	Process performance
Critical technology requirements Technology fit—trends	Requirements coverage	Technology suitability	Technology effectiveness
Mean processing time Average cost per picture Estimated yearly maintenance cost	Technology impact	Impact	Technology effectiveness
Technical volatility—cumulative releases Technical volatility—emerging technology Technical volatility—established technology	Baseline changes	Technology volatility	Technology effectiveness
Customer satisfaction survey	Survey results	Customer feedback	Customer satisfaction
Composite performance award scores Performance award category scores	Performance rating	Customer feedback	Customer satisfaction
Total calls per month by priority Mean response time by priority	Requests for support	Customer support	Customer satisfaction

Indicator template
Indicator name/title: _____

Objective: Describe the objective or purpose of the indicator.

Questions: List the question(s) the indicator user is trying to answer. Examples: Is the project on schedule? Is the product ready to ship? Should we invest in moving more software organizations to CMMI® maturity level 3?

Visual display: Provide a graphical view of the indicator (for example).

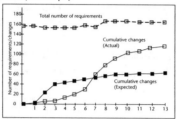

Perspective: Describe the audience (for whom is this display intended) for the visual display.

Inputs

Data elements	Definition
List all the data elements in the production of the indicator.	Precisely define the data element used or point to where the definition can be found.

Data collection
  How: Describe how the data will be collected.
  When/how often: Describe when the data will be collected and how often.
  By whom: Specify who will collect the data (an individual, office, etc.)
  Forms: Reference any standard forms for data collection (if applicable) and provide information about where to obtain them.

Data reporting
  Responsibility for Reporting: Indicate who has responsibility for reporting the data.
  By/to whom: Indicate who will do the reporting and to whom the report is going to. This may be an individual or an organizational entity.
  How often: Specify how often the data will be reported (daily, weekly, monthly, as required, etc.)

Data storage
  Where: Indicate where the data is to be stored.
  How: Indicate the storage media, procedures, and tools for configuration control.
  Security: Specify how access to this data will be controlled.

Algorithm: Specify the algorithm or formula required to combine data elements to create input values for the indicator. It may be very simple, such as Input1/Input2, or it may be much more complex. It should also include how the data is plotted on the graph.

Assumption: Identify any assumptions about the organization, its processes, life cycle models, and so on that are important conditions for collecting and using this indicator.

Analysis: Specify what type of analysis can be done with the information.

Interpretation: Describe what different values of the indicator mean. Make it clear how the indicator answers the "Questions" section above. Provide any important cautions about how the data could be misinterpreted and measures to take to avoid misinterpretation.

Probing questions: List questions that delve into the possible reasons for the value of an indicator, whether performance is meeting expectations or whether appropriate action is being taken.

Evolution: Specify how the indicator can be improved over time, especially as more historical data accumulates, e.g., by comparison of projects using new processes, tools, environments with a baseline; using baseline data to establish control limits around some anticipated value based on project characteristics.

Feedback guidelines: A description of the procedure to use when recommending modification to the indicator template.

X-references: If the values of other defined indicators influence the appropriate interpretation of the current indicator, refer to them here.

Figure 16.5   Metrics Description Form. (*After:* [10].)

- Histogram (bar) graphs;
- Reliability models (SMERFS3 input data file);
- Tables.

One output type from PSM Insight can save valuable time by aggregating hundreds of values in any number of ways, as long as the data items are defined additive. Lines of code may be additive as displayed in Figure 16.6.

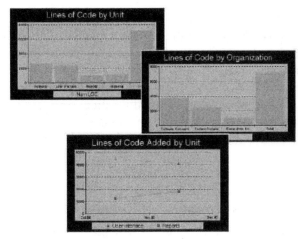

Figure 16.6 Additive lines of code displays from PSM insight. (*Source:* [12].)

Another "output" feature of the PSM Insight tool supports two types of analysis: feasibility analysis and performance analysis. Feasibility analysis determines if project plans are realistic and achievable. It is conducted during the initial planning phase and during all subsequent replanning periods. Performance analysis determines if development is meeting the plans, assumptions, and objectives of the project. It should be conducted regularly throughout the project life cycle, since issues can change at any time [13].

In summary, PSM Insight provides many benefits to the user, including [14]:

- Customization to project-specific needs;
- Templates of commonly-used issues, measures, and indicators from best practices;
- Insight into key software issues;
- Objective data for informed decision making;
- Identification of potential problems and solutions;
- Assistance in meeting cost and schedule objectives;
- Flexible data definitions and analysis tools;
- Presentation-quality graphs and reports;
- Support for risk management of software projects;
- Ease of use in tracking complex projects.

16.4 CMMI® Measurement and Analysis

The CMMI®-DEV, version 1.2 has a process area called Measurement and Analysis. "The purpose of Measurement and Analysis is to develop and sustain a measurement capability that is used to support management information needs" [15]. Within the model, Measurement and Analysis is described as a support process residing at Maturity Level 2. As a support process area, it provides services to other processes. "The Measurement and Analysis process area supports all process areas by providing practices that guide projects and organizations in aligning measurement needs and objectives with a measurement approach that will provide objective results that can be used in making informed decisions, and taking appropriate corrective actions" [15]. It is consistent with the Goal-Question-Metric (GQM) approach (see Section 16.6.7 and Chapter 14) to identify what needs to be measured. Then, the job is to operationally define, collect, and analyze data, and report information back to the "calling" process.

The practices associated with the first goal, Align Measurement and Analysis Activities, include:

- Establish measurement objectives;
- Specify measures;
- Specify data collection and storage procedures;
- Specify analysis procedures.

As can be seen, these practices really establish the plan for measurement and analysis. They address: Why are we measuring? What are we going to measure? How are we going to measure? What will be done with the data once we have it? As with most, if not all, endeavors within organizations (and life), planning is crucial if we want to achieve our goals. The goal and associated practices within the process area explicitly recognize this need and its importance.

The practices associated with the second goal, Provide Measurement Results, include:

- Collect measurement data;
- Analyze measurement data;
- Store data and results;
- Communicate results.

The theme of these practices is to follow through with the plan; just do it. Note, however, that the goal is to get the results of performing measurement and analysis into the hands of those who will take action based on the results. The process area emphasizes the need that results must be communicated to those needing the information. It does no good to the organization to populate a "write-only" database [16].

In "Measurement within the CMMI®" Johnson and Kulpa relate that the Measurement and Analysis process area puts focus on measurement capability that is used to support management information needs [17]. They go on to note that many organizations have learned that measurements need to be [18]:

1. Aligned to the business objectives to provide benefit;
2. Used regularly in order to justify the effort and cost;
3. Well defined in order for people to understand and compare them;
4. Communicated in an unbiased manner.

There is a sample measurement set (Table 16.3) provided by Johnson and Kulpa that cuts across the process areas since it is for a generic practice: GP 2.8 "Monitor

Table 16.3   Sample Measures for GP 2.8

PAs	*Example Measures from GP 2.8 (Monitor and Control the Process)*
REQM	Requirement volatility (percentage of requirement changes)
RD	Cost, schedule, and effort expended for rework
	Defect density of requirement specifications
TS	Cost, schedule, and effort expended for rework
	Percentage of requirements addressed in design
	Size and complexity of product, product-component, interfaces, and documentation
	Defect density of technical solutions work products
PI	Product-component integration profile (e.g., assemblies planned and actual, and number of exceptions found)
	Integration evaluation problem report trends (e.g., number written and number closed)
	Integration evaluation report aging (i.e., how long each problem report has been open)
VAL	Number of activities planned versus actual
	Validation problem report trends
	Validation problem report aging
VER	Verification profile (e.g., number activities planned versus actual, and the defects found)
	Number of defect detected
	Verification problem report trends
	Verification problem report aging

Source: [20].

and control the measurement and analysis process against the plan for performing the process and take appropriate corrective action" [19].

16.5   CMMI® Higher Maturity Measurements

The CMMI® has a natural evolution of measurement that should occur as organizations strive to improve their processes across the levels. People struggle with the apparent paradigm shifts between the levels as they transition from Level 2 to 3, from Level 3 to 4, and from Level 4 to 5.

Measurement concepts are actually consistent and simply evolve through the levels [21]:

- Level 2: Primarily status measures. Planned versus actual size, effort, cost, and schedule; also includes number of changes, number of nonconformances in product and processes.
- Level 3: Adds measures for process improvement and quality measures including defect density and productivity.
- Level 4: Creation and usage of Process Performance Baseline and Process Performance Models. Looks like a drastic change, but Process Performance Baselines and Process Performance Models are based on historical data from lower levels.

- Level 5: Quantitative improvements based on baselines, using Process Performance Baselines to plan and demonstrate improvements.

Johnson and Kulpa tell us that Level 4 is focused on predicting the performance of the processes based on historical and project data and managing accordingly. Continuing with some important Level 4 concepts [22]:

- Event Level Measure: A measure taken at the completion of an event.
- Process Performance Baseline: Documents the historical results from a process. Used as a benchmark against actual project performance.
- Process Performance Model: Describes the relationship among attributes of a process and its work products. Process Performance Models are based on Process Performance Baselines and calibrated to the project. Process Performance Models are used to estimate or predict a critical project value that cannot be measured until later in the project's life (e.g., number of delivered defects or total effort).

To illustrate their description above, Table 16.4 contains example measures leading to Maturity Level 4 of the CMMI®.

Johnson and Kulpa then elaborate that Level 5 is focused on quantitative improvement based on quantitative understanding of the common causes of variation inherent in the processes. Continuing with some important Level 5 concepts [24]:

- Incremental Improvements: Stepwise improvement accomplished by making the current processes and tools a little better.
- Innovative Improvements: Major performance leaps accomplished by bringing in a significantly different process or technology.
- Target Improvements: Specific areas that have been identified as problematic, often by senior management (e.g., 20% decrease in complaints).

Table 16.4 Measures Leading to Maturity Level 4

Status Measures	Event Level Measures	Process Performance Baselines	Process Performance Models
Size	Hours per event—	Review Baseline	Effort (estimation and prediction)
Effort	Productivity	Defects per page and per hour	
Cost	Requirement (defined)		New development
Schedule	Requirement (designed)	Productivity Baseline	Maintenance
	Object implemented	Hours per requirement by phase	Defect Insertion and Removal
	Test executed		New development
	Defects, Size, Hours per Event-Quality	Effort Distribution	Maintenance
	Design review	Percentage of effort by phase	
	Inspection		↓
	Test executed		Result in real project decisions
	Days late or early		
	Task completed		

Source: [23].

• Common Causes of Variation: Variation caused by normal and expected interactions among components of the process.

To illustrate their description above, Table 16.5 contains example measures leading to Maturity Level 5 of the CMMI®.

Successful organizations focus on a small number of Process Performance Baselines and Process Performance Models that are used to make real decisions; for example, (1) Review Process Performance Baseline, Effort Distribution Process Performance Baseline, and Productivity Process Performance Baseline; and (2) Estimation/Prediction Process Performance Model for effort and duration and a Defect Insertion and Removal Model [26].

16.6 Practical Implementations

16.6.1 Hewlett Packard

Hewlett Packard (H-P) was an early leader in software quality metrics. Their improvement efforts have been reported at various conferences. The following is a list of those early H-P company-wide efforts:

• Management awareness training for every general manager and above;
• Developed Functionality, Usability, Reliability, Performance, and Supportability (FURPS) to describe software quality attributes, which was later revised to FURPS+ to include localization, predictability, and portability;
• Created the function of productivity manager in each research and development division;
• Formed a metrics council of interested engineers and managers and explored/collected many metrics from divisions, highlighted in the 1986 book, *Software Metrics: Establishing a Company-wide Program* [27]; H-P has for years kept very detailed records of software defect data after product release, and they have also had some divisions analyze the causes of defects found prior to release [28];

Table 16.5 Measures Leading to Maturity Level 5

Process Performance Baselines	*Process Performance Models*	*Quantitative Improvements*
Review Baseline	Effort (estimation and	Identify including Incremental,
Defects per page and per hour	prediction)	Innovative, and Targeted
Productivity Baseline	New development	Analyze expected effect on
Hours per requirement by	Maintenance	Process Performance Baselines
phase	Defect Insertion and Removal	Define and pilot improvements
Effort Distribution	New development	Measure improvements and
Percentage of effort by phase	Maintenance	recalculate process performance baselines

Source: [25].

- Set up the Software Engineering Laboratory in corporate engineering for tools and methods;
- A high management level software 10X task force reaffirmed the magnitude of the issues, and the need for focus on software;
- The Break Even Time (BET) metric was introduced; this focuses on getting the right product to market in a timely manner with a goal of halving it in 5 years.

Company-wide measures at H-P are very few and very focused, and they serve as drivers for division efforts and programs, which have resulted in a set of best practices at the divisions [29]. A list of some of these measures from HP include [30]:

- *Defects found by customers:* Defects normalized by KLOC uncovered by the customer after a customer release of the system;
- *Percent of code tested:* Percent of code tested (count of LOC tested versus total LOC) by project;
- *Defect analysis by code module:* Defects per KLOC versus cyclomatic complexity of a module and post release defect density of the module;
- *Source of defects by category:* Provide percentage of defects by phase for identified categories of defects for that phase, as shown in Table 16.6;

Table 16.6   Source of Defects by Category

Phase	Categories
Requirements/specifications	Requirements
	Specifications
	Functionality
	Hardware interface
	Software interface
	User interface
	Functional description
Design	Functionality
	Hardware interface
	Software interface
	User interface
	Functional description
	Procedural communications
	Data definition
	Module design
	Logic description
	Error checking
	Standards
Code	Logic
	Computation
	Data handling
	Module interface/implementation
	Standards
Test environment	Test software
	Test hardware
	Development tools
	Integration software

- *Inspection effectiveness:* Number of defects found by inspection in the same phase as created, and number of defects found by inspection in later phase than created versus phase inspection conducted in this later phase;
- *Defects released to a customer:* Number of defects uncovered by the customer for each external release to the customer.

16.6.2   Quantitative SQA

Basili and Rombach suggest a model for quantitative SQA that consists of three phases:

1. Define quality requirements in quantitative terms. Select the quality characteristics of interest, define priorities among and relations between those quality characteristics, define each characteristic by one or more direct measures, and define the quality requirements quantitatively by assigning an expected value.
2. Plan quality control through adequate actions to assure fulfillment of the defined quality requirements, control the proper execution of these actions, and evaluate the results.
3. Perform quality control, which consists of: (1) measurement, in which the methods and techniques specified during the planning phase are applied to gather actual values for all defined measures; and (2) evaluation, in which the direct measurements are compared to the quality requirements and indirect measurements are interpreted to explain or predict the values of direct measures. Evaluation also involves deciding if the requirements were met for each quality characteristic and for the entire set of project requirements.

The quantitative SQA model considers the importance of the process, not just the product. One reason quality and productivity are perceived as conflicting is that process quality is often neglected, at least until ISO. It is believed that productivity increases if a high-quality development process is employed.

The quantitative SQA model also accounts for the equal importance of analytic and constructive SQA activities. The term "assurance" (as opposed to analysis) indicates that the objective is both to determine if quality requirements are met (the analytic aspect) and, when they are not met, to suggest corrective action (the constructive aspect). The quantitative SQA model covers all phases of software development so that effective software quality corrective action may be suggested.

Finally, the model stresses the importance of separating responsibilities for development and SQA. It is not important *who* performs the measurement part of quality control as long as it is planned for and evaluated by development-independent personnel [31].

16.6.3   Pragmatic Quality Metrics

Walker Royce at TRW Space and Defense has calculated metrics on real-time Ada projects. Simplicity is achieved by keeping the number of statistics to be maintained in a Software Change Order (SCO) database to five (type, estimate of damage in hours and SLOC, actual hours, and actual SLOC to resolve) along with the other required parameters of an SCO. (An SCO constitutes a direction to proceed when changing a configured software component.) Furthermore, metrics for configured source lines of code ($SLOC_C$) and total source lines of code ($SLOC_T$) need to be accurately maintained.

The metrics described here were easy to use by personnel familiar with the project context. Furthermore, they provide an objective basis for discussing current trends and future plans with outside authorities. Table 16.7 provides raw data definitions for source lines, errors, improvements, and rework. Table 16.8 shows the in-progress indicator definitions of rework ratio, backlog, and stability. Table 16.9 defines the end-product quality metrics of rework proportions, modularity, changeability, and maintainability, as well as some values determined from real projects [32].

16.6.4 Effectiveness Measure

Measuring the effectiveness of individual quality assurance procedures and of the entire program is an important component of quality control. Robert Dunn's simple effectiveness measure for individual activities is [36]:

$$E = \frac{N}{N + S}$$

where E = effectiveness of activity, N = number of faults (defects) found by activity, and S = number of faults (defects) found by subsequent activities.

This measure can be tuned by selecting only those faults (defects) present at the time of the activity and susceptible to detection by the activity [36]. Testing

Table 16.7   Raw Data Definitions

Statistic	Definition	Insight
Total source lines	$SLOC_T$ = Total Product SLOC	Total effort
Configured Source lines	$SLOC_C$ = Standalone Tested SLOC	Demonstrable progress
Errors	SCO_1 = No. of Open Type 1	Test effectiveness
	SCO_1 = No. of Closed Type 1	Test progress
	SCO_1 = No. of Type 1 SCOs	Reliability
Improvements	SCO_2 = No. of Open Type 2 SCOs	Value engineering
	SCO_2 = No. of Closed Type 2 SCOs	Design progress
	SCO_2 = No. of Type 2 SCOs	
Open rework	B_1 = Damaged SLOC Due to SCO_1	Fragility
	B_2 = Damaged SLOC Due to SCO_2	Schedule risk
Closed rework	F_1 = SLOC Repaired after SCO_1	Maturity
	F_2 = SLOC Repaired After SCO_2	Changeability
Total rework	$R_1 = F_1 + B_1$	Design quality
	$R_2 = F_2 + B_2$	Maintainability

Source: [33].

Table 16.8   In-Progress Indicator Definitions

Indicator	Definition	Insight
Rework ratio	$RR = \dfrac{R_1 + R_2}{SLOC_C}$	Future rework
Rework backlog	$BB = \dfrac{B_1 + B_2}{SLOC_C}$	Open rework
Rework stability	$SS = (R_1 + R_2) - (F_1 + F_2)$	Rework trends

Source: [34].

Table 16.9   End-Product Quality Metrics Definitions

Metric	Definition	Insight	Value
Rework	$R_E = \dfrac{Effort_{SCO} + Effort_{SCO}}{Effort_{Total}}$	Productivity rework	6.7%
Proportions	$R_S = \dfrac{(R_1 + R_2)_{Total}}{SLOC_{Total}}$	Project efficiency	13.5%
Modularity	$Q_{mod} = \dfrac{R_1 + R_2}{SCO_1 + SCO_2}$	Rework localization	54 SLOC/SCO
Changeability	$Q_C = \dfrac{Effort_{SCO} + Effort_{SCO}}{SCO_1 + SCO_2}$	Risk of modification	15.7 Hours/SCO
Maintainability	$Q_M = \dfrac{R_E}{R_S}$	Change productivity	0.49

Source: [35].

effectiveness (the percentage of all errors found in testing that were found in system testing) is one such important measure. The development manager needs to know how the testers are doing, as well as how the programmers are doing. Like error rate, testing effectiveness can be analyzed with a control chart. Establishing a chain of effectiveness measures spanning the life cycle also supports process improvement goals.

The percentage of effort spent in rework provides the best measure of the overall effectiveness of a quality assurance program. Estimates of rework in software development range from 30% to 50% (i.e., 30% to 50% of the total effort is spent on corrective problems). More errors mean more rework. More rework means lower productivity. An effective quality assurance program will decrease rework effort over time. Unfortunately, most software enterprises are very sensitive about measuring rework effort because it tends to be a measure of "failure" rather than of "success" [37].

16.6.5   Team Software Process (TSP®) and Personal Software Process (PSP®)

A principal TSP® and PSP® objective is to apply proven quality principles to the work of individual and teams of software engineers. The expectation is that this will give software work more of an engineering flavor and make it more manageable. (See Chapter 2.) A basic principle of quality management is that "If you don't demand quality work, you are not likely to get it." With TSP® and PSP® quality management, engineers and development teams track their own defects, find their defect removal yields, and calculate cost of quality measures. Pareto defect analysis (see Chapter 6) is used to derive personal design and code review checklists, which the engineers update with defect data from each new project [38]. The following is a list of measures that are usually collected as part of the PSP®, as well as of the TSP® [39]:

- *Regression calculation—size:* Estimated versus actual new and changed lines of code;
- *Test defects versus appraisal to failure cost ratio—class:* Test defects per thousand lines of code versus appraisal to failure cost ratio;
- *Review yield:* Percent of defects that were in the product at review time found in the review [100 * (defects found)/(defects found and not found)];
- *Compile versus development test and postdevelopment defects:* Compile defects versus development test defects;
- *Size estimating error:* Size estimating error percent by projects;
- *Time estimating error:* Time estimating error percent by projects;
- *Compile time range:* Percent of total time by projects;
- *Defects found in compile:* Compilation defects per thousand lines of code by projects;
- *Test time range:* Percent of total time by projects;
- *Defects found in test:* Test defects per thousand lines of code by projects;
- *Productivity by project size:* Lines of code / hour versus project size (number of lines of code).

The value of PSP® and TSP® is better understood by reviewing the results of TSP® and PSP® measures which show the benefits gained from their use, as shown in Table 16.10.

16.6.6　Software Quality Fault Prediction

Software quality metrics dealing with fault predictions permit the evaluation of trends and the quantifiable analysis of quality, starting with system test. The measurements quantify:

Table 16.10　TSP® Measures Results

Measure	Pre-TSP®	Post-TSP®
Deviation from schedule	27% to 112% late	8% early to 5% late
System test duration	1 to 5 days/KLOC	0.1 to 1 day/KLOC
Acceptance test defects/KLOC	0.1 to 0.7 defect/KLOC	0.02 to 0.1 defect/KLOC
Postrelease defects/KLOC	0.1 to 1 defect/KLOC	0.0 to 0.1 defect/KLOC

Source: [40].

- The number of faults in generic software, normalized by software size;
- The responsiveness of development and customer support organizations in resolving customers' problems;
- The impact of software field fixes on customers.

Descriptions of these measurements follow [41]:

- *Cumulative fault density found internally:* Faults found internally depict the faults found by the development organization normalized by the total software size in the system test phase.
- *Cumulative fault density found by customers:* Faults found by customers depict the faults found by customers in the normal operation of released software, normalized by the total size of the released software.
- *Total serious faults found:* Provides the number of serious faults found and the status of those faults—open (uncorrected) or closed (corrected)—as of the report date.
- *Mean time to close serious faults:* Provides a measure of the responsiveness of the development and customer support organizations by showing the average time that the serious faults remain open.
- *Mean time still open for serious faults:* Provides a value for each month of the mean length of time that the serious faults, open at the end of the current month, have been open.
- *Total field fixes:* Provides a measure of the impact of software field fixes on customers.

A general model utilized by Bellcore is concerned with a number of customer releases of a certain software product and the underlying trend of software quality. In order to give a numerical illustration of the application of the methodology, consider a problem involving R = 3 releases of a software product. The number of lines of code in the three releases are:

- $L_1 = 160,000$;
- $L_2 = 150,000$;
- $L_3 = 155,000$.

Initially, the variances of predicted faults versus actual faults detected by the customer for the three releases based upon exponentially distributed fault discovery times were calculated as follows:

Release	Variance
# 1	0.04
# 2	0.03
# 3	0.02

But, the use of a formulation for tracking the quality of manufactured hardware which is used to predict the faults detected by customers for each release proved to be a better predictor for software released faults than the assumption of exponentially distributed fault discovery times as shown by the smaller variances between predicted and actual fault detected by the customer, as follows [42]:

Release	Variance
# 1	0.003
# 2	0.012
# 3	0.093

16.6.7 Measuring Process Improvement Using Stoplight Charts

Using the Goal-Question-Metric (GQM) paradigm is a useful way to determine what the appropriate measures for process improvement status in an organization are. The goals are conceptual:

1. Business goals;
2. Initiative objectives;
3. Strategy or conceptual idea;

then the questions are operational:

1. How do we achieve goals?
2. What is the plan?
3. How do we execute or implement?

and finally the metrics are quantitative:

1. Data;
2. Measures and metrics;
3. Subjective and objective metrics.

Typical goals for a CMMI® program include: (1) better control on IT/software development budget; (2) high quality software delivery; (3) better control over project management; (4) obtain institutionalization of processes; and (5) achieve target maturity level. Of these five typical goals, the usual goal of interest for measuring process improvement is goal 5, achieve target maturity level. What follows are the suggested questions and associated metrics flowing from goal 5, achieve target maturity level [43]:

- Question 1: What is the CMMI® program plan for targeted maturity level?
- Measure 1: Track the percent of schedule variance predicated on the CMMI® program plan.
- Question 2: Is the performance of the process improvement initiative on track?
- Measure 2: Track actuals versus planned program staffing for the CMMI® process improvement initiative.
- Question 3: What is the status of implementation for all process areas within the CMMI®?
- Measure 3: Process area compliance score in the CMMI®.

A very convenient process area compliance score in the CMMI® measure is the "stoplight" chart. The stoplight chart is a roll-up measure of the status of each practice within a process area to a color code, hence the name stoplight chart. The measure is green if all practices in the process area are satisfactory, yellow if most of the practices are satisfactory, and red if many practices are unsatisfactory. That chart (Figure 16.7) provides a quick visibility into both projects and organization status of CMMI® implementation. It also provides some objective evidence for all process areas in the CMMI® for Generic Practice 2.8 (monitor and control "every" process area). Management can easily see the progress achieved in each process area by analyzing the prior reporting period data, as shown.

16.6.8   Six Sigma

An approach that aids in achieving higher maturity levels includes the use of Six Sigma in an organization. Initially, the focus of Six Sigma was to improve manufacturing processes. As it has matured and become more widely used, organizations have been applying this data-driven improvement initiative to the rest of their business life cycles and supply chains. Applications in service or transactional organizations are sometimes termed the "second wave" of Six Sigma implementation. Applications in engineering, including those in software and systems, are sometimes termed the "third wave" of Six Sigma implementation. The paradigm of statistical thinking is embodied in Six Sigma's methodologies, which are used as a basis for executing improvement projects. The framework of Define, Measure, Analyze, Improve, Control (DMAIC) currently prevails. DMAIC is used to improve and optimize existing processes and products. An example DMAIC roadmap is shown in Figure 16.8 [44].

From a process definition standpoint, there is natural synergy between the high maturity process areas and the tenets of Six Sigma's DMAIC framework. As such, the tactics of Six Sigma can be used to directly enrich the defined processes that address the high maturity process areas. For instance, the processes related to the Quantitative Process Management and Causal Analysis and Resolution process areas would reflect both the specific practices of those process areas and the roadmap steps, substeps, and tools of DMAIC [46].

16.6.9   Project Managers Control Panel

The Project Control Panel (Figure 16.9) is a concept and a tool that enables project managers to quickly and clearly monitor project status. Crucial metrics data is displayed on easy-to-read gauges that provide a means of predicting future project health and facilitating timely corrective actions, if required. Besides the typical project management metrics, the Control Panel highlights some specific quality-related metrics, as described.

This Month graph shows the completion status of tasks during the current reporting period. A quality gate is a predefined completion criterion for a task. The criterion must be an objective yes/no indicator that shows a task has been completed. The indicators are as follows:

Software Quality Assurance Metrics

Review date	Project planning	Project monitoring and control	Requirements management	Configuration management	Measurement and analysis	Product and process QA	Supplier agreement management
1/15/2006	NS	NS	NS	NS	NS		
2/1/2006	NS	NS	NS	NS	NS		
2/15/2006	G	G	G	G	G		
3/1/2006	G	G	G<Y	G	Y		
3/15/2006	G	Y	Y	G	G		
4/1/2006	Y	Y	Y>R	G	G<Y		
4/15/2006	G<Y	G	R	G	Y		
5/1/2006							
5/15/2006							
6/1/2006							

Organization status

LEGEND:
Please insert the letters and symbols to accommodate gray scale printouts

NS	Not started
	Not applicable
G	Good shape
G<Y	Between Green and Yellow
Y	In between Green and Red
Y>R	Between Yellow and Red
R	Bad shape

(a)

Figure 16.7 (a) Process area organization status report. (b) Process area projects status report.

Project name	Project planning 1/15	Project planning 2/11	Project monitoring and control 1/15	Project monitoring and control 2/11	Requirements management 1/15	Requirements management 2/11	Configuration management 1/15	Configuration management 2/11	Measurement and analysis 1/15	Measurement and analysis 2/11	Product and process QA 1/15	Product and process QA 2/11	Supplier agreement management
Project 1	G	G	Y>R	Y>R	G	G	G	G	G<Y	G<Y	G	G	
Project 2	G<Y	G<Y	NS	NS	NS	NS	NS	NS	NS	NS	NS	NS	
Project 3	G<Y	G<Y	G<Y	G<Y	Y	Y	G	G	G	G	Y	Y	
Project 4	G<Y	G<Y	NS	NS	NS	NS	NS	NS	NS	NS	Y	Y	
Project 5	NS	NS	NS	NS	NS	NS	NS	NS	NS	NS	NS	NS	
Project 6	R	R	R	R	R	R	R	R	R	R	R	R	
Project 7	R	R	R	R	R	R	R	R	R	R	Y>R	Y>R	
Project 8	G	G	Y>R	Y>R	Y>R	Y	Y	Y	R	R	G	G	
Project 9	Y	Y	R	R	Y>R	Y>R	Y	Y	G<Y	G<Y	G	G	

LEGEND:

Please insert the letters and symbols to accommodate gray scale printouts

NS	Not started
	Not applicable
G	Good shape
G<Y	Between green and yellow
Y	In between green and red
Y>R	Between yellow and red
R	Bad shape

(b)

Figure 16.7 (continued)

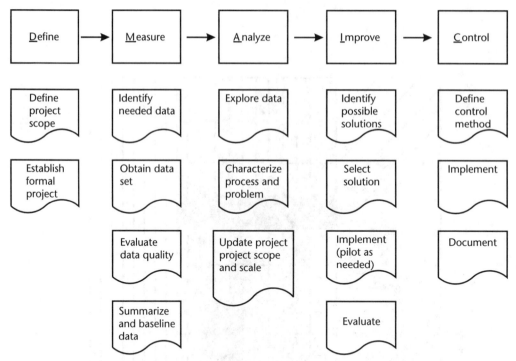

Figure 16.8   DMAIC road map. (*From:* [45]. © 2005 Software Engineering Institute. Reprinted with permission.)

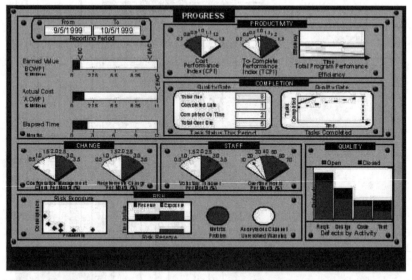

Figure 16.9   Project Manager's Control Panel. (*From:* [47]. © 2000 Integrated Computer Engineering, Inc. Reprinted with permission.)

- *Total Due* is the total number of tasks scheduled for completion during this reporting period plus any overdue tasks from previous periods. This indicates the total quantity of work required for the project to keep pace with the schedule.

- *Completed On Time* is the number of tasks originally scheduled for completion during this reporting period that were completed by their original scheduled due date. This number indicates how well the project is keeping up with scheduled work.

- *Completed Late* is the number of tasks completed late during this reporting period. This number includes those tasks scheduled for this period that were completed late, as well as any overdue tasks from previous periods that were completed in this period. The Completed Late number indicates how well the project is completing work, even if it is late according to the original schedule.

- *Total Overdue* is the total number of tasks for all previous reporting periods that are overdue by the end of the current reporting period. This is an indicator of the quantity of work needed to get the project back on schedule.

Note that the total number of tasks completed in this reporting period is the sum of Completed On Time and Completed Late. Total Overdue then is equal to Total Due minus Completed On Time and Completed Late.

The *Quality Gate Tasks Completed* graph shows the cumulative number of tasks completed by the end of each reporting period to date plotted with the cumulative number of tasks scheduled for completion.

Note that if the number of tasks completed falls below the number planned, then the horizontal distance on the time axis gives an idea of the current schedule slip to date.

Defects by Activity graph displays the number of detected defects open (i.e., yet to be fixed) and the number of defects closed in each phase of the project. Defects are problems that, if not removed, could cause a program to fail or to produce incorrect results. Defects are generally prioritized by severity level, with those labeled 1 being the most serious.

Note that the quality indicators on this chart help answer the question, "What is the quality of the product right now?" [48].

16.6.10   Predicting Software Quality

Basic models for predicting software quality from various contributors include:

- Akiyama: $D = 4.86 + 0.018 \, L$.
- Gaffney: $D = 4.2 + 0.0015 \, L^{3/4}$ where D is defects and L is lines of code (optimum module size 877 LOC).
- Compton and Withrow: $D = 0.069 + 0.00516 \, L + 0.00000047 \, L^2$ (optimum module size 83 Ada LOC).

The problems with models such as these are that:

- Defects are not solely caused by design complexity or size.
- Models ignore complexity of problem.
- If you do not test, then you do not find defects.

- Component people produce "better" designs.
- We cannot trust defect density figures.

The solution involves a need to better reflect "difficulties" of quality management. Synthesize partial quality models to (1) include elements from each approach, (2) explain existing empirical results, and (3) be consistent with good sense. There is a need to cope with uncertainty and subjectivity. These solutions are addressed by the Bayesian Belief Networks (BBNs). BBNs consist of three major components: (1) graphical models, (2) conditional probability tables which model prior probabilities and likelihoods, and (3) Bayes' theorem applied recursively to propagate data through the network. The graph topology models the cause-effect reasoning structures. A BBN is a graphical network that represents probabilistic relationships among variables. BBNs enable reasoning under uncertainty and combine the advantages of an intuitive visual representation with sound mathematical basis in Bayesian probability. With BBNs, it is possible to articulate expert beliefs about the dependencies between different variables and to propagate consistently the impact of evidence on the probabilities of uncertain outcomes, such as "future system reliability." BBNs allow an injection of scientific rigor when the probability distributions associated with individual nodes are simply "expert opinions." A BBN will derive all the implications of the beliefs that are input to it; some of these will be facts that can be checked against the project observations, or simply against the experience of the decision makers themselves. There are many advantages of using BBNs, the most important being the ability to represent and manipulate complex models that might never be implemented using conventional methods.

At a general level we can see how the use of BBNs and the defect density model provide a significant new approach to modeling software engineering processes and artifacts. The dynamic nature of this model provides a way of simulating different events and identifying optimum courses of action based on uncertain knowledge. These benefits are reinforced when we examine how the model explains known results, in particular is the "is bigger better?" dilemma. The new approach shows how we can build complex webs of interconnection between process, product, and resource factors in a way hitherto unachievable. It may also be seen how we can integrate uncertainty and subjective criteria into the model without sacrificing rigor and illustrate how decision making throughout the development process influences the quality achieved.

The benefits of this new approach are as follows [49]:

- It is more useful for project management than other analysis and classical statistics.
- It incorporates current research ideas and experience.
- It can be used to train managers and enable comparison of different decisions by simulation and what-if analyses.
- It integrates a form of cost and quality forecasting.

16.7 Conclusion

Traditionally, most of our business measurement processes have been financially based—produced by accountants, designed for accountants (or regulators), and not by or for managers. Measures come in the form of balance sheets, monthly profit and loss statements, and ROIs. They are often damage reports, telling nothing about what is being done do today or tomorrow. We can extrapolate from them, but we know how dangerous that is. Nor do most of our measurement processes tell us about those other objectives that a reengineer wants to constantly scrutinize, such as cycle time and quality, or if they do, reports come too late for us to take action. On the whole, today's measurement processes do not really help us manage [50].

Although the idea of measuring quality by surveying users is novel in software engineering, it is not at all unusual in reviewing other products. Reviews are by experts, who rely for their credibility primarily on the reputation of the organization, not on their personal qualifications. Such reviews are published for many kinds of products: audio equipment, cameras, automobiles, and PC software, to name a few.

We have argued that measuring quality is not just for quality assurance. We have suggested that it is wise to break free from narrow notions of what constitutes quality. From a user's perspective, we have indicated the importance of software multiple releases. We have asserted that subjective assessment of quality can be useful, and that objective measures should be used to support subjective assessment [51].

There are many software quality assurance metrics to choose from and many are being used rather successfully by various companies. Personal experience has shown that any metrics program is very time consuming to implement and difficult to define. I have chaired a software metrics working group for more than 2 years. The progress shown by the working group has been slow, and seemingly every software metric needs to be redone for a myriad of reasons.

While collecting and analyzing metrics remain difficult, that difficulty is diminishing as software tools make the task more manageable. Remember: You cannot control what you cannot measure [52].

Finally, listen to Andy Grove, former CEO of Intel: "What gets measured, gets done" [53].

References

[1] Ragland, B., "Measure, Metric, or Indicator: What's the Difference?" *CrossTalk*, Vol. 8, No. 3, March 1995, p. 29.

[2] Kan, S. H., *Metrics and Models in Software Quality Engineering*, Upper Saddle River, NJ: Pearson Education, Inc., 1995, p. 336.

[3] MacMillan, J., and J. R. Vosburgh, *Software Quality Indicators*, Scientific Systems, 500 West Cummings Park, Suite 3000, Woburn, MA 01801, (781)933-5355, 1986, pp. 1, 2, 7.

[4] MacMillan, J., and J. R. Vosburgh, *Software Quality Indicators*, Scientific Systems, Inc., 500 West Cummings Park, Suite 3000, Woburn, MA 01801, (781)933-5355, 1986, p. 25.

[5] About PSM, http://www.psmsc.com/AboutPSM.asp, December 2006.

[6]   Jones, C., "Using PSM to Implement Measurement in a CMMI® Process Improvement Environment," *Software Technology Conference*, April 2003, p. 29.

[7]   Jones, C., "Using PSM to Implement Measurement in a CMMI® Process Improvement Environment," *Software Technology Conference*, April 2003, p. 25.

[8]   Jones, C., "Making Measurement Work," *CrossTalk*, Vol. 16, No. 1, January 2003, pp. 16, 17.

[9]   PSM Insight, http://www.psmsc.com/PSMI.asp, December 2006.

[10] Goethert, W., and J. Siviy, "Applications of the Indicator Template for Measurement and Analysis," Technical Note CMU/SEI-2004-TN-024, Pittsburgh: Software Engineering Institute, © copyright 2004 Carnegie Mellon University, September 2004, pp. 17–19. Special permission to reproduce is granted by the Software Engineering Institute.

[11] Jones, C., *PSM Insight User's Manual*, February 2002, p. 60.

[12] Jones, C., *PSM Insight User's Manual*, February 2002, p. 73.

[13] Jones, C., *PSM Insight User's Manual*, February 2002, pp. 74, 75.

[14] Highlights and Benefits, http://www.psmsc.com/PSMIHighlights.htm, December 2006.

[15] *CMMI®—Development*, version 1.2 (CMMI®—DEV, v1.2), CMU/SEI-2006-TR-008, Pittsburgh: Software Engineering Institute, August 2006, p. 178. © 2006 Carnegie Mellon University. Special permission to use portions is gratned by the Software Engineering Institute.

[16] Zubrow, D., "The Measurement and Analysis Process Area in CMMI®," http://www.sei.cmu.edu/cmmi/publications/meas-anal-cmmi.pdf, December 2006, © 2006 Carnegie Mellon University. Special permission to use portions is granted by the Software Engineering Institute.

[17] Johnson, K., and M. Kulpa, "Measurement Within the CMMI®," Software Engineering Process Group (SEPG) Conference, March 2004, p. 5. Certain definitions were derived from the book *Interpreting the CMMI: A Process Improvement Approach,* M. Kulpa and K. Johnson, Boca Raton, FL: Auerbach Publications, 2003.

[18] Johnson, K., and M. Kulpa, "Measurement Within the CMMI®," Software Engineering Process Group (SEPG) Conference, March 2004, p. 4. Certain definitions were derived from the book *Interpreting the CMMI: A Process Improvement Approach,* M. Kulpa and K. Johnson, Boca Raton, FL: Auerbach Publications, 2003.

[19] *CMMI® – Development*, version 1.2 (CMMI®—DEV, v1.2), CMU/SEI-2006-TR-008, Pittsburgh: Software Engineering Institute, August 2006, p. 195.

[20] Johnson, K., and M. Kulpa, "Measurement Within the CMMI®," Software Engineering Process Group (SEPG) Conference, March 2004, p. 10.

[21] Johnson, K., and M. Kulpa, "Measurement Within the CMMI®," Software Engineering Process Group (SEPG) Conference, March 2004, pp. 18–21.

[22] Johnson, K., and M. Kulpa, "Measurement Within the CMMI®," Software Engineering Process Group (SEPG) Conference, March 2004, p. 13.

[23] Johnson, K., and M. Kulpa, "Measurement Within the CMMI®," Software Engineering Process Group (SEPG) Conference, March 2004, p. 14.

[24] Johnson, K., and M. Kulpa, "Measurement within the CMMI®," Software Engineering Process Group (SEPG) Conference, March 2004, p. 15.

[25] Johnson, K., and M. Kulpa, "Measurement Within the CMMI®," Software Engineering Process Group (SEPG) Conference, March 2004, p. 16.

[26] Johnson, K., and M. Kulpa, "Measurement Within the CMMI®," Software Engineering Process Group (SEPG) Conference, March 2004, p. 17.

[27] Grady, R. B., and D. L. Caswell, *Software Metrics: Establishing a Company-Wide Program*, Upper Saddle River, NJ: Pearson Education, Inc., 1987.

[28] Grady, R. B., and D. L. Caswell, *Software Metrics: Establishing a Company-Wide Program*, Upper Saddle River, NJ: Pearson Education, Inc., p. 22.

[29] Ward, T. M., "Software Measures and Goals at Hewlett Packard," *Juran Institute Conference Proceedings*, Atlanta, GA, 1989, pp. 8B-41–8B-42.

[30] Grady, R., "Practical Results from Measuring Software Quality," *Communications of the ACM*, Vol. 36. No. 11, November 1993, pp. 62–68, © 1993 ACM, Inc., included by permission.

[31] Basili, V. R., and H. D. Rombach, "Implementing Quantitative SQA: A Practical Model," *IEEE Software,* March 1990, p. 8, © 1990 IEEE.

[32] Royce, W., "Pragmatic Quality Metrics for Evolutionary Software Development Models," Private paper, May 1990, pp. 5, 17, 18, © 1990 ACM, Inc., included by permission.

[33] Royce, W., "Pragmatic Quality Metrics for Evolutionary Software Development Models," Private paper, May 1990, p. 8, © 1990 ACM, Inc., included by permission.

[34] Royce, W., "Pragmatic Quality Metrics for Evolutionary Software Development Models," Private paper, May 1990, p. 9.

[35] Royce, W., "Pragmatic Quality Metrics for Evolutionary Software Development Models," Private paper, May 1990, pp. 11, 14.

[36] Dunn, R. H., "The Quest for Software Reliability," in *Handbook of Software Quality Assurance*, G. Gordon Schulmeyer and J. I. McManus, (eds.), Upper Saddle River, NJ: Pearson Education, Inc., 1987, pp. 137–177.

[37] Card, D. N., and R. L. Glass, *Measuring Software Design Quality*, Upper Saddle River, NJ: Pearson Education, Inc., 1990, pp. 88, 89.

[38] Humphrey, W. S., "Making Software Manageable," *CrossTalk*, Vol. 9, No. 12, December 1996, pp. 3–6.

[39] Humphrey, W., "Personal Software Process Tutorial," *SEPG Conference Proceedings*, Software Engineering Institute, Pittsburgh, PA, March 1997, pp. 7–53.

[40] Goodenough, J., "Team Software Process Reliability Results," originally printed in the DoD DACS *Software Tech News*, Vol. 3, No. 4, June 2000, pp. 15–16. Requests for copies of the referenced newsletter may be submitted to the following address: DoD Data & Analysis Center for Software, Attn: Lon R. Dean, Editor, PO Box 1400, Rome, NY 13442-1400, (800) 214-7921; Fax (315) 334-4964, news-editor@dacs.dtic.mil.

[41] Inglis, J., "Standard Software Quality Metrics," *AT&T Technical Journal*, Vol. 65, Issue 2, March/April 1986, pp. 113–118, © 1986 Lucent Technologies, Inc., reprinted with permission of John Wiley & Sons, Inc.

[42] Weerahandi, S., and R. E. Hausman, "Software Quality Measurement Based on Fault-Detection Data," *IEEE Transactions on Software Engineering*, 1994, pp. 665–676, © 1994 IEEE.

[43] Prasad, R..T., "Measuring and Managing the CMMI® Journey Using GQM," *Software Engineering Process Group Conference*, March 2006, pp. 5, 6, 11.

[44] Siviy, J., M. L. Penn, and E. Harper, *Relationships Between CMMI® and Six Sigma*, Technical Note CMU/SEI-2005-TN-005, Pittsburgh, PA: Software Engineering Institute, December 2005, pp. 7, 8, © 2005 Carnegie Mellon University. Special permission to use portions is granted by the Software Engineering Institute.

[45] Siviy, J., M. L. Penn, and E. Harper, *Relationships Between CMMI® and Six Sigma*, Technical Note CMU/SEI-2005-TN-005, Pittsburgh, PA: Software Engineering Institute, December 2005, p. 9, © 2005 Carnegie Mellon University. Special permission to use portions is granted by the Software Engineering Institute.

[46] Siviy, J., M. L. Penn, and E. Harper, *Relationships Between CMMI® and Six Sigma*, Technical Note CMU/SEI-2005-TN-005, Pittsburgh, PA: Software Engineering Institute, December 2005, p. 11, © 2005 Carnegie Mellon University. Special permission to use portions is granted by the Software Engineering Institute.

[47] Integrated Computer Engineering, Inc., *Project Control Panel Users Guide* (Version 2.0 for Excel), http://www.iceincusa.com/supportlibrary.aspx?p=supportlibrary_controlpanel, December 2006.

[48] American Systems, *Project Control Panel Users Guide* (Version 2.0 for Excel), Copyright © 1996–2007 American Systems, All rights reserved, pp. 22, 23, 25, http://www.americansystems.com, keyword: Project Control Panel.

[49]   Martin, N., and N. Fenton, "Predicting Software Quality Using Bayesian Belief Networks," *Software Engineering Workshop Proceedings*, December 1996, pp. 219, 223.

[50]   Champy, J., *Reengineering Management: The Mandate for New Leadership*, New York: Harper Collins, 1995, p. 122, © 1995 James Champy.

[51]   Gentleman, W. M., "If Software Quality Is a Perception, How Do We Measure It?" Ottawa: Institute for Information Technology, National Research Council of Canada, 1996, p. 9.

[52]   Mills, H. D., and P. B. Dyson, "Using Metrics to Quantify Development," *IEEE Software*, March 1990, p. 16, © 1990 IEEE.

[53]   Grove, A., *Only the Paranoid Survive*, New York: Random House, 1999.

More Reliable Software Faster and Cheaper: An Overview of Software Reliability Engineering

John D. Musa

17.1   Introduction

Arguably the most important software development problem is building software to meet customer demands that it be more reliable, built faster, and built cheaper (in general order of importance). Your success in meeting these demands affects the market share and profitability of a product for your company, and hence your career. These are conflicting demands, causing risk and overwhelming pressure, and hence, they call for a practice that can help you with them.

Software reliability engineering (SRE) is such a practice, one that is a standard, proven, widespread best practice that is widely applicable. It is low in cost, and its implementation has virtually no schedule impact. We will show what it is, and how it works.

We will then outline the SRE process to give you a feel for the practice, using a single consistent example throughout. Finally, we will list some resources that will help you learn more about it.

17.2   Software Reliability Engineering

SRE differs from other approaches by being primarily quantitative. In applying SRE, you add and integrate it with other good processes and practices; you do not replace them. With SRE you control the development process, it does not control you. The development process is not externally imposed. You use quantitative information to choose the most cost-effective software reliability strategies for your situation.

17.2.1   What it Is and Why it Works

Let us now look with a little more depth at just what SRE *is*. SRE is a practice for *quantitatively* planning and guiding software development and test, with emphasis on reliability and availability. It is a practice that is backed with science and technology [1], but we will describe how it works in business-oriented terms.

SRE works by quantitatively characterizing and applying two things about the product: the expected relative use of its functions and its required major quality characteristics. The major quality characteristics are reliability, availability, delivery date, and life-cycle cost. In applying SRE, you can vary the relative emphasis you place on these factors.

When you have characterized use, you can substantially increase development efficiency by focusing resources on functions in proportion to use and criticality. You also maximize test effectiveness by making test highly representative of use in the field. Increased efficiency increases the effective resource pool available to add customer value, as shown in Figure 17.1. For a detailed discussion of ways in which use data can increase development efficiency, see [2].

When you have determined the precise balance of major quality characteristics that meets user needs, you can spend your increased resource pool to carefully match them. You choose software reliability strategies to meet the objectives, based on data collected from previous projects. You also track reliability in system test against its objective to adjust your test process and to determine when test may be terminated. The result is greater efficiency in converting resources to customer value, as shown in Figure 17.2.

We have set delivery times and budgeted software costs for software-based systems for some time. It is only relatively recently that SRE, the technology for setting and tracking reliability and availability objectives for software, has developed [1].

17.2.2 A Proven, Standard, Widespread Best Practice

Software reliability engineering is a proven, standard, widespread best practice. As one example of the proven benefit of SRE, AT&T applied SRE to two different releases of a switching system, International Definity PBX. Customer-reported problems decreased by a factor of 10, the system test interval decreased by a factor of 2, and total development time decreased 30%. No serious service outages occurred in 2 years of deployment of thousands of systems in the field [3].

SRE has been an AT&T Best Current Practice since May 1991 [3]. To become a Best Current Practice, a practice must have substantial application (usually at least 8 to 10 projects) and this application must show a strong, documented benefit-to-cost ratio. For SRE, this ratio was 12 or higher for all projects. The practice undergoes a probing review by two boards, at third and fourth levels of management. More than

Figure 17.1   Increased resource pool resulting from increased development efficiency.

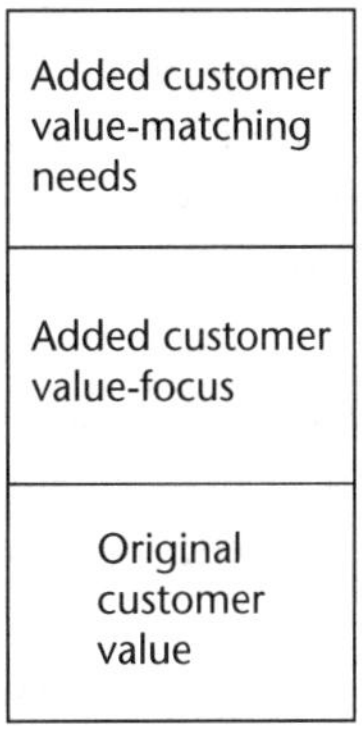

Figure 17.2   Increased customer value resulting from increased resource pool and better match to major quality characteristics needed by users.

70 project managers or their representatives reviewed the SRE proposal. There were more than 100 questions and issues requiring resolution, a process that took several months. In 1991, SRE was one of five practices that were approved, out of 30 that were proposed.

SRE is also a standard practice. McGraw-Hill published an SRE handbook in 1996 [3]. SRE has been a standard of the American Institute of Aeronautics and Astronautics since 1993, and IEEE standards are currently under development.

SRE is a widespread practice. There have been more than 65 published articles by *users* of SRE, and the number continues to grow [2]. Since practitioners do not generally publish very frequently, the actual number of users is probably many times the above number.

Users include Alcatel, AT&T, Bellcore, CNES (France), ENEA (Italy), Ericsson Telecom, Hewlett Packard, Hitachi, IBM, NASA's Jet Propulsion Laboratory, Lockheed-Martin, Lucent Technologies, Microsoft, Mitre, Nortel, Saab Military Aircraft, Tandem Computers, the U.S. Air Force, and the U.S. Marine Corps.

Tierney [4] reported the results of a 1997 survey that showed that Microsoft had applied software reliability engineering in 50% of its software development groups, including projects such as Windows and Word. The benefits they observed were increased test coverage, improved estimates of amount of test required, useful metrics that helped them establish ship criteria, and improved specification reviews.

SRE is widely applicable. From a technical viewpoint, you can apply SRE to any software-based product, starting at the beginning of any release cycle. From an economic viewpoint, you can apply SRE to any software-based product also, except for very small components—perhaps those involving a total effort of less than 2 staff months. However, if a small component such as this is used for several projects, then it probably will be feasible to use SRE. If not, it still may be worthwhile to implement SRE in abbreviated form.

SRE is independent of development technology and platform. It requires no changes in architecture, design, or code, but it may *suggest* changes that would be useful. It can be deployed in one step or in stages.

SRE is very customer-oriented: it involves frequent direct close interaction with customers. This enhances a supplier's image and improves customer satisfaction, greatly reducing the risk of angry customers. Developers who have applied SRE have described it with adjectives such as "unique, powerful, thorough, methodical, and focused." It is highly correlated with attaining Levels 3, 4, and 5 of the Software Engineering Institute Capability Maturity Model®.

Despite the word "software," software reliability engineering deals with the entire product, although it focuses on the software part. It takes a full life cycle, proactive view, as it is dependent on activities throughout the life cycle. It involves system engineers, system architects, developers, users (or their representatives, such as field support engineers and marketing personnel), and managers in a collaborative relationship.

The cost of implementing SRE is small. There is an investment cost of not more than 3 equivalent staff days per person in an organization, which includes a 2-day course for everyone and planning with a much smaller number. The operating cost over the project life cycle typically varies from 0.1% to 3% of total project cost, as shown in Table 17.1. The largest cost component is the cost of developing the operational profile.

The schedule impact of SRE is minimal. Most SRE activities involve only a small effort that can parallel other software development work. The only significant critical path activity is 2 days of training.

17.3   SRE Process and Fone Follower Example

Let us now take a look at the SRE process. There are six principal activities, as shown in Figure 17.3. We show the software development process below and in parallel with the SRE process, so you can relate the activities of one to those of the other. Both processes follow spiral models, but we do not show the feedback paths for simplicity. In the field, we collect certain data and use it to improve the SRE process for succeeding releases.

The Define the Product, Implement Operational Profiles, Define "Just Right" Reliability, and Prepare for Test activities all start during the Requirements and Architecture phases of the software development process. They all extend to varying degrees into the Design and Implementation phase, as they can be affected by it. The Execute Test and Guide Test activities coincide with the Test phase.

Before we proceed further, let us define some of the terms we will be using. *Reliability* is the probability that a system or a capability of a system functions without failure for a specified period in a specified environment. The period may be specified in natural or time units.

Table 17.1   Operating Cost of SRE

Project Size (Staff Years)	Percent of Project Costs
5	3
10	2
20	1.5
100	0.4
500	0.1

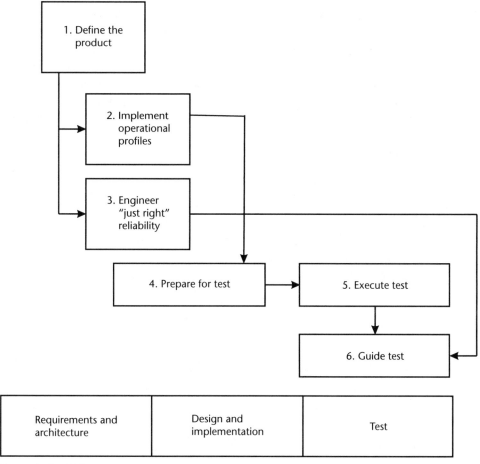

Figure 17.3   SRE process.

The concept of natural units is relatively new to reliability, and it appears to have originated in the software sphere. A *natural unit* is a unit other than time that is related to the amount of processing performed by a software-based product, such as pages of output, transactions, telephone calls, jobs, semiconductor wafers, queries, or application program interface calls. *Availability* is the average (over time) probability that a system or a capability of a system is currently functional in a specified environment. If you are given an average down time per failure, availability implies a certain reliability. *Failure intensity,* used particularly in the field of software reliability engineering, is simply the number of failures per natural or time unit. It is an alternative way of expressing reliability.

Some people speak of software products, but this is really incorrect, because pure software cannot function. You really have "software-based products." In discussing SRE, we should always be thinking of total systems that also contain hardware and often human components.

Note that we deliberately define software reliability in the same way as hardware reliability. This is so that we can determine system reliability from hardware and software component reliabilities, even though the mechanisms of failure are different [1].

We will illustrate the SRE process with Fone Follower, an example adapted from an actual project at AT&T. We have changed the name and certain details to keep the explanation simple and protect proprietary data. Subscribers to Fone Follower call and enter, as a function of time, the phone numbers to which they want to forward their calls. Fone Follower forwards a subscriber's incoming calls (voice or fax) from the network according to the program the subscriber entered. Incomplete voice calls go to the subscriber's pager (if the subscriber has one) and then, if unanswered, to voice mail. If the subscriber does not have a pager, incomplete voice calls go directly to voice mail.

17.3.1   Define the Product

The first activity is to define the product. You must establish who the supplier is and who the customers and users are, which can be a nontrivial enterprise in these days of outsourcing and complex inter- and intracompany relationships. Then you list all the systems associated with the product that for various reasons must be tested independently. These are generally of two types:

1. Base product and variations;
2. Supersystems.

Variations are versions of the base product that you design for different environments. For example, you may design a product for both Windows and Macintosh platforms. Supersystems are combinations of the base product or variations with other systems, where customers view the reliability or availability of the base product or variation as that of the combination.

17.3.2   Implement Operational Profiles

This section deals with quantifying how software is used. To fully understand it, we need to first consider what operations and operational profiles are.

An *operation* is a major system logical task, which returns control to the system when complete. Some illustrations from Fone Follower are Phone number entry, Process fax call, and Audit a section of the phone number data base. An *operational profile* is a complete set of operations with their probabilities of occurrence. Table 17.2 shows an illustration of an operational profile from Fone Follower.

There are five principal steps in developing an operational profile:

1. Identify the operation initiators.
2. List the operations invoked by each initiator.
3. Review the operations list to ensure that the operations have certain desirable characteristics and form a set that is complete with high probability.
4. Determine the occurrence rates.
5. Determine the occurrence probabilities by dividing the occurrence rates by the total occurrence rate.

Table 17.2 Fone Follower Operational Profile

Operation	Occurrence Probability
Proc. voice call, no pager, ans.	0.21
Proc. voice call, pager, ans.	0.19
Proc. fax call	0.17
Proc. voice call, pager, ans. on page	0.13
Proc. voice call, no pager, no ans.	0.10
Proc. voice call, pager, no ans. on page	0.10
Enter forwardees	0.09
Audit sect.—phone number data base	0.009
Add subscriber	0.0005
Delete subscriber	0.0005
Recover from hardware failure	0.000001
Total	1

There are three principal kinds of initiators: user types, external systems, and the system itself. You can determine user types by considering customer types. For Fone Follower, one of the user types is subscribers and the principal external system is the telephone network. Among other operations, subscribers initiate Phone number entry and the telephone network initiates Process fax call. Fone Follower itself initiates Audit, a section of the phone number database.

When implementing SRE for the first time, some software practitioners are initially concerned about possible difficulties in determining occurrence rates. Experience indicates that this is usually not a difficult problem. Software practitioners are often not aware of all the use data that exists, as it is typically in the business side of the house. Occurrence rate data is often available or can be derived from a previous release or similar system. New products are not usually approved for development unless a business case study has been made, and this must typically estimate occurrence rates for the use of various functions to demonstrate profitability. One can collect data from the field, and if all else fails, one can usually make reasonable estimates of expected occurrence rates. In any case, even if there are errors in estimating occurrence rates, the advantage of having an operational profile far outweighs not having one at all.

Once you have developed the operational profile, you can employ it, along with criticality information, to:

1. Review the functionality to be implemented for operations that are not likely to be worth their cost and remove them or handle them in other ways (Reduced Operation Software, or ROS).
2. Suggest operations where looking for opportunities for reuse will be most cost-effective.
3. Plan a more competitive release strategy using operational development. With operational development, development proceeds operation by operation, ordered by the operational profile. This makes it possible to deliver the most used, most critical capabilities to customers earlier than scheduled because the less used, less critical capabilities are delivered later.

4. Allocate development resources among operations for system engineering, architectural design, requirements reviews, and design to cut schedules and costs.

5. Allocate development resources among modules for code, code reviews, and unit test to cut schedules and costs.

6. Distribute the new test cases of a release among the new operations of the base product and its variations.

7. Invoke test and in effect distribute test time among all operations.

17.3.3   Define "Just Right" Reliability

To define the "just right" level of reliability for a product, you must first define what "failure" means for the product. We will define a *failure* as any departure of system behavior in execution from user needs. You have to interpret exactly what this means for your product. The definition must be consistent over the life of the product, and you should clarify it with examples. A failure is not the same thing as a fault; a *fault* is a defect in system implementation that causes the failure when executed. Beware, as there are many situations where the two have been confused in the literature.

The second step in defining the "just right" level of reliability is to choose a common measure for all failure intensities, either failures per some natural unit or failures per hour.

Then you set the total system failure intensity objective (FIO) for each associated system. To determine an objective, you should analyze the needs and expectations of users.

For each system you are developing, you must compute a developed software FIO. You do this by subtracting the total of the expected failure intensities of all hardware and acquired software components from the system FIOs. You will use the developed software FIOs to track the reliability growth during system test of all the systems you are developing with the failure intensity to failure intensity objective (FI/FIO) ratios.

You will also apply the developed software FIOs in choosing the mix of software reliability strategies that meet these and the schedule and product cost objectives with the lowest development cost. These include strategies that are simply selected or not (requirements reviews, design reviews, and code reviews) and strategies that are selected and controlled (amount of system test, amount of fault tolerance). SRE provides guidelines and some quantitative information for the determination of this mix. However, projects can improve the process by collecting information that is particular to their environment.

17.3.4   Prepare for Test

The Prepare for Test activity uses the operational profiles you have developed to prepare test cases and test procedures. You allocate test cases in accordance with the operational profile. For example, for the Fone Follower base product there were 500 test cases to allocate. The Process fax call operation received 17% of them, or a total of 85.

After you assign test cases to operations, you specify the test cases within the operations by selecting from all the possible intraoperation choices with equal probability. The selections are usually among different sets of values of input variables associated with the operations, sets that cause different processing to occur. These sets are called *equivalence classes*. For example, one of the input variables for the Process fax call operation was the Forwardee (number to which the call was forwarded) and one of the equivalence classes of this input variable was Local calling area. You then select a specific value within the equivalence class so that you define a specific test case.

The test procedure is the controller that invokes test cases during execution. It uses the operational profile, modified to account for critical operations and for reused operations from previous releases.

17.3.5 Execute Test

In the Execute Test activity, you will first allocate test time among the associated systems and types of test (feature, load, and regression).

Invoke feature tests first. *Feature tests* execute all the new test cases of a release independently of each other, with interactions and effects of the field environment minimized (sometimes by reinitializing the system). Follow these by *load tests*, which execute test cases simultaneously, with full interactions and all the effects of the field environment. Here you invoke the test cases at random times, choosing operations randomly in accord with the operational profile. Invoke a regression test after each build involving significant change. A *regression test* executes some or all feature tests; it is designed to reveal failures caused by faults introduced by program changes.

Identify failures, along with when they occur. The "when" can be with respect to natural units or time. This information will be used in Guide Test.

17.3.6 Guide Test

The last activity involves guiding the product's system test phase and release. For software that you develop, track reliability growth as you attempt to remove faults. Then we certify the supersystems, which simply involves accepting or rejecting the software in question. We also use certification test for any software that we expect customers will acceptance test.

To track reliability growth, input failure data that you collect in Execute Test to a reliability estimation program such as CASRE (available through *Software Reliability Engineering* Web site; see Section 17.5). Normalize the data by multiplying by the failure intensity objective in the same units. Execute this program periodically and plot the FI/FIO ratio as shown in Figure 17.4 for Fone Follower. If you observe a significant upward trend in this ratio, you should determine and correct the causes. The most common causes are system evolution, which may indicate poor change control, and changes in test selection probability with time, which may indicate a poor test process.

If you find that you are close to your scheduled test completion date but have an FI/FIO ratio substantially greater than 0.5, you have three feasible options: (1) defer

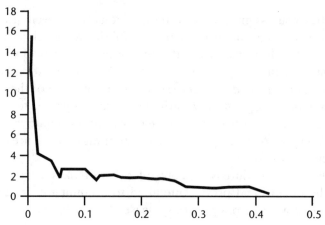

Figure 17.4 Plot of FI/FIO ratio for Fone Follower.

some features or operations, (2) rebalance your major quality characteristic objectives, or (3) increase work hours for your organization. When the FI/FIO ratio reaches 0.5, you should consider release as long as essential documentation is complete and you have resolved outstanding high severity failures (you have removed the faults causing them).

For certification test you first normalize failure data by multiplying by the failure intensity objective. The unit "Mcalls" is millions of calls. Plot each new failure as it occurs on a reliability demonstration chart as shown in Figure 17.5. Note that the first two failures fall in the Continue region. This means that there is not enough data to reach an accept or reject decision. The third failure falls in the Accept region, which indicates that you can accept the software, subject to the levels of risk associated with the chart you are using. If these levels of risk are unacceptable, you construct another chart with the levels you desire [2] and replot the data.

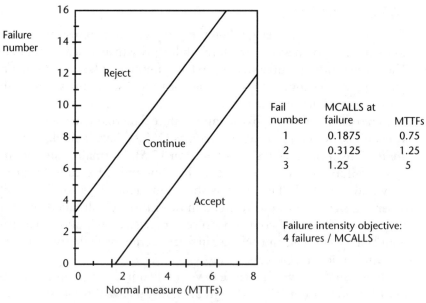

Figure 17.5 Reliability demonstration chart applied to Fone Follower.

Developers sometimes worry that systems with ultrareliable FIOs might require impractically long hours of test to certify the FIOs specified. But there are many ameliorating circumstances that make the problem more tractable than that for ultrareliable hardware [2]. First, in most cases only a few critical operations, not the entire system, must be ultrareliable. Second, software reliability relates to the execution time of the software, not the clock time for which the system is operating, as does hardware. Since the critical operations often occur only rarely, the execution time of the critical operations is frequently a small fraction of the clock time. Thus the FIO for the entire system need not be ultrareliable. Finally, since processing capacity is cheap and rapidly becoming cheaper, it is quite feasible to test at a rate that is hundreds of times real time by using parallel processors. Thus testing of ultrareliable software can be manageable.

17.3.7 Collect Field Data

The SRE process is not complete when you ship a product. We collect certain field data to use in succeeding releases and in other products. In many cases, we can collect the data easily and inexpensively by building recording and reporting routines into the product. In this situation, we collect data from all field sites. For data that requires manual collection, take a small random sample of field sites.

We collect data on failure intensity and on customer satisfaction with the major quality characteristics and use this information in setting the failure intensity objective for the next release. We also measure operational profiles in the field and use this information to correct the operational profiles we estimated. Finally, we collect information that will let us refine the process of choosing reliability strategies in future projects.

17.4 Conclusion

If you apply SRE in all the software-based products you develop, you will be controlling the process rather than it controlling you. You will find that you can be confident of the reliability and availability of the products. At the same time, you will deliver them in minimum time and cost for those levels of reliability and availability. You will have maximized your efficiency in satisfying your customers' needs. This is a vital skill to possess if you are to be competitive in today's marketplace.

17.5 To Explore Further

Books

Musa, J. D., *Software Reliability Engineering: More Reliable Software Faster and Cheaper*, Second Edition, 2004. Detailed, extensive treatment of practice. Browse and order at http://members.aol.com/JohnDMusa.

Musa, J. D., A. Iannino, and K. Okumoto, *Software Reliability: Measurement, Prediction, Application,* New York: McGraw-Hill, 1987. Very thorough treatment of software reliability theory.

SRE Web Site

This is the essential guide to software reliability: http://members.aol.com/JohnDMusa/.

SRE Orientation (overviews of different lengths)

Courses (classroom and distance learning)

Consulting information

Practitioners' Corner (extensive user experiences with SRE and important application examples, advice on deploying SRE, comprehensive standards information)

Resources for Everyone (download free failure intensity estimation program CASRE, join free SRE professional organization, access SRE Network, view conference information, learn from Question of the Month, use glossary)

Researchers' Corner (access to failure interval data and enormous debugging history archive, access to comprehensive lists of open source projects likely to have free access to all kinds of data)

Professors' Corner (how to teach SRE, slides and material for SRE courses, network to other professors teaching SRE)

Courses

John D. Musa conducts 2-day on-site and public, and also distance learning courses for practitioners; see SRE Web site.

University of Maryland has a doctoral program; contact Professor Carol Smidts

Conference

International Symposium on Software Reliability Engineering (ISSRE)

Professional Organizations

IEEE Computer Society Technical Committee on Software Reliability Engineering. Publishes newsletter, sponsors ISSRE annual international conference. Join through SRE Web site.

SRE Network

Communicate by e-mail with hundreds of people interested in field. See SRE Web site.

Journals Publishing in the Field

IEEE Software

IEEE Transactions on Software Engineering

IEEE Transactions on Reliability

References

[1]   Musa, J. D., A. Iannino, and K. Okumoto, *Software Reliability: Measurement, Prediction, Application,* New York: McGraw-Hill, 1987.

[2]   Musa, J. D., *Software Reliability Engineering: More Reliable Software Faster and Cheaper,* 2nd ed., New York: McGraw-Hill, 2004.

[3]   Lyu, M., (ed.), *Handbook of Software Reliability Engineering*, New York: McGraw-Hill, 1996.

[4]   Tierney, J., "SRE at Microsoft," *Keynote speech at 8th International Symposium on Software Reliability Engineering*, Albuquerque, NM, November 1977.

List of Acronyms

4Ms	manpower, machines, methods, and materials
ABEND	abnormal ending
ACM	Association for Computing
ADP	automated data processing
AI	acquire and implement
AIAA	American Institute of Aeronautics and Astronautics
AIDS	Acquired immune deficiency syndrome
AIEE	American Institute of Electrical Engineers
ALARP	as low as reasonably practical
AMA	American Management Association
ANSI	American National Standards Institute
AP	appraisal
ASME	American Society of Mechanical Engineers
ASQ	American Society for Quality
ASQC	American Society for Quality Control
BBN	Bayesian belief networks
BNQA	Baldrige National Quality Award
BOK	body of knowledge
BSA	Business Software Alliance
BSI	British Standards Institute
CAB	Change Advisory Board
CAR	causal analysis and resolution
CAM	capacity and availability management
CBA	Certified biomedical auditor
CBA-IPI	CMM®-based appraisal for internal process improvement
CCB	Configuration Control Board
CCT	certified calibration technician
CCTA	Central Computer and Telecommunications Agency (United Kingdom)
CDP	certificate in data processing
CEO	chief executive officer
CFO	chief financial officer
CHA	certified HAACP auditor

CI	configuration item
CISA	Certified Information Systems Auditor
CM	configuration management
CMDB	configuration management database
CMM®	Capability Maturity Model®
CMMI®	Capability Maturity Model Integration®
CMMI®-DEV	CMMI® for Development
CMQ/OE	certified manager of quality/organizational excellence
CMU	Carnegie Mellon University
CNS/ATM	communications, navigation, surveillance, and air-traffic management
CNSS	Center for National Software Studies
CobiT®	Control Objectives for Information and related Technology
COQ	cost of quality
CoSQ	costs of software quality
CPA	certified Public Accountant
CPAS	continuous process auditing system
CPM	critical path method
CPU	central processing unit
CQA	Certified quality auditor
CQE	certified quality engineer
CQI	certified quality inspector
CQIA	certified quality improvement associate
CQPA	certified quality process analyst
CQT	certified quality technician
CRAMM	CCTA risk analysis and management method
CRE	certified reliability engineer
CRM	computer resource management
C/SCSC	cost/schedule control systems criteria
CSC	computer software component
CSCI	Computer Software Configuration Item
CSQE	certified software quality engineer
CSSBB	Certified Six Sigma Black Belt
CSSGB	Certified Six Sigma Green Belt
DAR	decision analysis and resolution
DCMA	Defense Contract Management Agency (DoD)
DCR	document change request
DEV	development
DFD	data flow diagram
DHS	definitive hardware store
DoD	Department of Defense

DM	data management
DMAIC	Define, Measure, Analyze, Improve, Control
DQA	development quality assurance
DR	design review
DS	deliver and support
DSL	definitive software library
DSP	Defense Standardization Program
DTI	Department of Trade and Industry (United Kingdom)
EF	external failure
EIA	Electronics Industries Alliance
ELSYS	Electronic Systems Laboratory
EPG	Engineering Process Group
ER	Evaluation report
ERD	entity relationship diagram
EVMS	earned value management systems
FAI	first article inspection
FCA	Functional Configuration Audit
FDA	Food and Drug Administration
FEMA	failure modes and effects analysis
FI	failure intensity
FIO	failure intensity objective
FISMA	Federal Information Security Management Act
FSC	forward schedule of changes
FURPS	functionality, usability, reliability, performance and supportability
GEIA	Government Electronics & Information Technology Association (EIA)
GG	generic goal
GP	generic practice
GPS	global positioning satellite
GQM	goal, question, metric
GTRI	Georgia Tech Research Institute
HACCP	hazard analysis and critical control point
HIPPA	Health Insurance Portability and Accountability Act
H-P	Hewlett Packard
I/O	input/output
IBM	International Business Machines
ICT	information and communications technology
IDEAL	Initiating, diagnosing, establishing, acting, and leveraging
IEC	International Electrotechnical Commission
IEEE	Institute of Electrical and Electronics Engineers

IF	internal failure
IMS	information management systems
IP	Internet Protocol
IPM	integrated project management
IPPD	integrated process and product development
IPT	integrated product team
IRCA	International Register of Certified Auditors
IRE	Institute of Radio Engineers
IRM	incident and request management
ISACA	Information Systems Audit and Control Association
ISBN	International Standard Book Number
ISO	International Organization for Standardization
IT	information technology
ITGI	IT Governance Institute
ITIL®	IT Infrastructure Library
ITSM	IT service management
itSMF	IT Service Management Forum
ITT	International Telephone and Telegraph
JAD	joint application development
JCG	Joint Coordinating Group
JCL	Job Control Language
JTC	joint technical committee
JUSE	Union of Japanese Scientists and Engineers
KLOC	thousand lines of code
KSLOC	thousands of source lines of code
LOC	lines of code
MA	Measurement and analysis
MAC	management's appraisal and control
ME	monitor and evaluate
MF	management's failure
MIL	military
MIS	Management Information System
MTBF	mean time between failures
MTTR	mean time to repair
NCLOC	noncommented lines of code
NDIA	National Defense Industrial Association
NGS	Nongovernment standard
NGT	Nominal group technique
NI	not included in the model
NSC	National Software Council
NSIA	National Security Industrial Association

OGC	Office of Government Commerce (United Kingdom)
OID	organizational innovation and deployment
OMB	Office of Management and Budget
OOAD	object-oriented analysis and design
OPD	organizational process definition
OPF	organizational process focus
OPP	organizational process performance
OS/2	Operating System 2
OS/360	Operating system for IBM 360
OT	organizational training
PA	Performance audit
PA	Process area
PBX	Private Branch eXchange
PC	personal computer
PCA	Physical Configuration Audit
PDA	Parental Drug Association
P-D-C-A	Plan-Do-Check-Analyze and Act
PDPC	Process decision program chart
PEPG	Project Engineering Process Group
PERT	Program Evaluation and Review Technique
PHA	preliminary hazard analysis
PI	product integration
PIR	postimplementation review
PLCM	project life-cycle model
PM	program/project manager
PMC	project monitoring and control
PMP	Project Management Professional
PMSC	Program Management Systems Committee (NDIA)
PO	plan and organize
PP	project planning
PPQA	Process and Product Quality Assurance
PQA	project quality assurance
PQEP	Product Quality Evaluation Plan
PQM	project quality manager
PR	prevention
PSP	personal software process
PSQT	Practical Software Quality & Testing
PSM	Practical Software and Systems Measurement
QA	quality assurance
QC	quality circle
QE	quality engineer

QE	quality evaluation
QFD	quality function deployment
QM	quality manager
QMF	quality management framework
QMS	quality management system
QoS	quality of service
QP	quality program
QPM	quantitative project management
RACI	responsible, accountable, consulted, and informed
RAD	rapid application development
RD	requirements development
RN	revision notice
ROI	return on investment
ROS	reduced operation software
RSQM	risk management
RTCA	Radio Technical Commission for Aeronautics
S2ESC	Software and Systems Engineering Standards Committee
SA-CMM®	Software Acquisition Capability Maturity Model®
SAD	structured analysis and design
SAM	supplier agreement management
SCAMPI^{SM}	Standard CMMI® appraisal methodology for process improvement
SCE	software capability evaluation
SCM	software configuration management
SCO	software change order
SCON	service continuity management
SCR	software change request
SD	service delivery
SDP	software development plan
SEI	Software Engineering Institute
SEL	software engineering lab
SEMP	systems engineering management plan
SEPG	Software Engineering Process Group
SESC	Software Engineering Standards Committee
SG	specific goal
SIIA	Software & Information Association
SLA	service level agreement
SLOC	source lines of code
SMERFS3	Statistical Modeling and Estimation of Reliability Functions for Systems: (Software, Hardware, and Systems)
SP	specific practice

SPC	statistical process control
SPICE	Software Process Improvement and Capability dEtermination
SPIN	software process improvement network
SPR	System Problem Report
SQA	Software Quality Assurance
SQC	Statistical Quality Control
SQEP	Software Quality Evaluation Plan
SQM	software quality management
Squale	security, safety, and quality evaluation for dependable systems
SquaRE	software engineering—software product quality requirements and evaluation
SRE	software reliability engineering
SRS	Software Requirements Specification
SSD	service system development
SSQA	systems and software quality assurance
ST	service transition
STD	standard
SVC	services
SW	software
SW-CMM®	CMM® for Software
SYS	systems
TC	technical committee
TCM	Technology Change Management
TickIT	√ information technology
TQM	Total Quality Management
TR	technical report
TS	technical solution
TSO	The Stationery Office (United Kingdom)
TSP	team software process
UL	underwriters laboratory
UML	unified modeling language
VAL	validation
VER	verification
WBS	work breakdown structure
WG	working group
WWMCCS	World Wide Military Command and Control System

About the Authors

Emanuel R. Baker (Chapters 1 and 5) is the president of Software Engineering Consultants, Inc. (SECI), a consulting firm based in Los Angeles, California, specializing in software engineering and training services, and a principal owner of Process Strategies, Inc., an internationally recognized software engineering process consulting firm based in Los Angeles, California, and Walpole, Maine. He has been a consultant in software engineering and software acquisition management since 1984. He has over 30 years of technical and managerial experience in the field of software development with specific emphasis on proposal development, software process assessments, software systems engineering, software configuration management, software quality assurance, software test, software standards development, acquisition management, as well as training in these disciplines. Prior to that, he was manager of the Product Assurance Department of Logicon's Strategic and Information Systems Division (now part of Northrop Grumman). In that capacity, along with his duties of managing the department, he also had responsibility for the contract to develop the Department of Defense software quality standard, DoD-STD-2168.

Dr. Baker has authored and coauthored a number of papers and articles on software quality, configuration management, and software process assessments. He is the coauthor of the book *Software Process Quality: Management and Control* (Marcel Dekker, 1999). He has conducted seminars in the United States, Canada, Mexico, Australia, New Zealand, Israel, England, Italy, Sweden, Germany, and Spain on the topics of product quality management, total quality management for product, and product process assessments. In addition, he has appeared as a panelist at a number of conferences and workshops, speaking on the topic of software quality and process improvement.

Dr. Baker is authorized by the SEI as a SCAMPI[SM] lead appraiser and as an instructor in the Introduction to the CMMI[®] course. He has performed appraisals for organizations in the commercial and defense sectors, as well as government agencies. He has a B.S.M.E. from New York University and an M.S.M.E. from the University of Southern California. In addition, he holds an M.S. and a Ph.D. in education from the University of Southern California.

Jeanne Balsam (Chapter 12) is a senior research scientist with the Georgia Tech Research Institute's (GTRI) Electronic Systems Laboratory (ELSYS) at the Georgia Institute of Technology. She has over 20 years of experience in computer software systems with 13 years of that experience at GTRI in the fields of real-time computer systems, database design, software engineering, and quality assurance.

Ms. Balsam is a quality engineer with ELSYS and a member of the ELSYS Engineering Process Group. She was instrumental in the ELSYS laboratory achieving the

Software Engineering Institute's Software-CMM® Level 3 rating in June 2003. As a software engineer, she was involved in all phases of system and software development. In her role of quality engineer, she is responsible for institutionalizing best in class practices on a wide variety of projects conducted within ELSYS.

Ms. Balsam has published and presented numerous papers at national conferences on software development, testing, and systems engineering, including the Software Engineering Process Group (SEPG) Conference, the National Defense Industrial Association (NDIA) Systems Engineering Conference, the NDIA CMMI® Technology Conference and User Group, the STARWEST Conference, the Better Software Conference, and the Practical Software Quality & Testing (PSQT) Conference. The topics include quality assurance on small projects, configuration management, and implementing an effective peer review process. She coauthored the paper "Let's Do It All Over Again! Ruin Your Reputation Through Configuration Mismanagement," which earned the 2005 Better Software Conference Best Paper Award.

Ms. Balsam has both B.S. and M.S. degrees in information and computer science from the Georgia Institute of Technology.

Matthew J. Fisher (Chapters 1 and 5) is currently a visiting scientist with the Software Engineering Institute (SEI) as a member of Software Engineering Process Management initiative. He is responsible for planning and coordinating work products for the SEI's Software Engineering Process Management Initiative, including the Software Acquisition Capability Maturity Model (SA-CMM®) and the Software Acquisition Improvement Framework (SAIF). Other work involves acquisition aspects of architectures, product lines, and, measurements.

A civilian employee with the federal government for 30 years, Dr. Fisher has worked as a research engineer in computer technology and software, navigation systems, and product assurance. During this tenure, he was Deputy Director of a Software Engineering Center for IEW systems. Dr. Fisher was the U.S. Army's representative to the Joint Logistics Commanders subgroup for Computer Resource Management, which was responsible for efforts to standardize computer resource policies and military standards within DoD. He is coeditor, with John D. Cooper, of *Software Quality Management* (Petrocelli Books, 1979). The author of more than 25 published technical papers on software and quality, Dr. Fisher has lectured at numerous seminars.

Dr. Fisher is authorized by the SEI as a SCAMPI^SM lead appraiser and as an instructor for the Introduction to the CMMI® course. He has performed assessments for organizations in the commercial and defense sectors, as well as government agencies. He has an M.S.E.E. from the University of Pennsylvania and a Ph.D. from Drexel University. He is a member of the Tau Beta Pi, Eta Kappa Nu, and Phi Kappa Phi honor societies.

Daniel Galin (Chapter 15) is the head of the Information Systems Studies at the Ruppin Academic Center, Israel, and an Adjunct Senior Teaching Fellow at the Faculty of Computer Science, the Technion, Haifa, Israel. Dr. Galin has a bachelor's degree in industrial and management engineering, and master's and doctorate in operations research from the Faculty of Industrial and Management Engineering of the Technion, Israel Institute of Technology, Haifa, Israel.

Dr. Galin has been a visiting research scientist at the Australian Road Research Board, Melbourne, Australia; senior chief research officer at the National Institute for Transport and Road Research – CSIR, South Africa; and visiting scholar at the University of California, Berkeley, School of Business Administration. His professional experience includes numerous consulting projects in the areas of software quality assurance, analysis and design of information systems and industrial engineering. He is a member of the IEEE Computer Society (the Israeli Chapter, ILA), the Information Technology Association of Israel, and the Israel Society for Quality (ISQ).

Dr. Galin's main research interests include software quality assurance and analysis and design of information systems. His publications include many papers that appeared in professional journals and in conference proceedings. He is also the author of several books in software quality assurance and in analysis and design of information systems. He is the author of the book *Software Quality Assurance: From Theory to Implementation* (Addison-Wesley, 2004). He can be contacted at dgalin@bezeqint.net.

Lewis Gray (Chapter 3) has more than 25 years of technical and management experience in software development and acquisition. Since 1989, he has been a consultant for Abelia Corporation (http://www.abelia.com), which provides training, assessment, and other support for software acquisition and software development, and for systems and software process improvement. During that period, he was also manager of engineering process improvement at Northrop Grumman IT (formerly Logicon Information Solutions & Services), and a visiting scientist at the Software Engineering Institute (SEI). Previously, he was a senior staff engineer at TRW Federal Systems Group, and assistant technology director of the Army WWMCCS Information System (AWIS) program (Phase 1).

Dr. Gray is the author of the *Guidebook to IEEE/EIA 12207 Software Life Cycle Processes* (Abelia Corporation, 2002). He has been a frequent speaker at the annual Systems and Software Technology Conference by the U.S. Department of Defense. He is a past speaker at Software Engineering Process Group (SEPG) national conferences and at the SEI's Software Engineering Symposium, and a past speaker at Association for Computing Machinery (ACM) Special Interest Group on Ada (SIGAda) national conferences. He is former Chairman of the ACM SIGAda Software Development Standards and Ada Working Group, and a former national lecturer for ACM. His articles on software life-cycle standards have appeared in *CrossTalk* magazine, and *IEEE Computer* magazine.

He participated in the San Antonio I conference that set the direction for improvements to DOD-STD-2167A. He was a member of the technical leadership teams that guided the development of MIL-STD-498, J-STD-016, and IEEE/EIA 12207.

Dr. Gray is a member of the Project Management Institute, the IEEE, the Association for Computing Machinery, and the American Society for Quality. He holds a Project Management Professional (PMP) certification by the Project Management

Institute. He holds multiple degrees, including a B.A. in mathematics and a Ph.D. in the philosophy of science from Indiana University, Bloomington.

Katharine B. Harris (Chapter 10) is currently a senior program manager at Intel Corporation in Hillsboro, Oregon, where she works in the Intel Software Quality organization. She is currently responsible for developing and deploying an internal maturity assessment model and administers the Intel Software Quality award, given annually to selected software organizations within the corporation. Ms Harris is an active member of the steering committee for Intel's internal Software Process Improvement Network (SPIN). She has worked at Intel for 12 years in several organizations and positions, contributing to Product Life Cycle and software qualification initiatives that have been deployed throughout the corporation. Her career in software development and software quality spans more than 20 years.

Prior to joining Intel, Ms. Harris worked for Mentor Graphics, becoming an employee through the acquisition of Silicon Compiler Systems. While employed by these companies, she held a number of positions including program manager, software quality manager, build and release administrator, product trainer, and author of end-user documentation. At Mentor Graphics, she was trained as an ISO9000 internal auditor.

She is a senior member of American Society for Quality (ASQ) and holds the Certified Quality Improvement Associate (CQIA) and Certified Software Quality Engineer (CSQE) certifications. Ms. Harris has been involved in the development of the CSQE exam for several years and has participated in job analysis, test specification, item writing, exam review, and item pool maintenance workshops. She is currently serving as chair for the CSQE exam.

Ms. Harris holds a B.A. from Brigham Young University in vocal pedagogy and an A.S. from Utah Valley State College in electronics technology. She is a member of ASQ and the steering committee for the Rose City SPIN. She can be reached at kathi.harris@intel.com.

Tim Kasse (Chapter 11) serves as the CEO and principal consultant of Kasse Initiatives LLC. Mr. Kasse spent 4 years at the Software Engineering Institute and was a major contributor to the development of the Capability Maturity Model® for Software. He is recognized as the individual most responsible for the evolution of the SEI's assessment method that was commercialized in October 1990. He also led the development of the SEI's Intermediate CMMI® Workshop for Lead Assessors. Mr. Kasse has been authorized by the SEI to conduct SCAMPI^{SM} assessments. He has participated in over 100 Process Assessments and Consulting engagements in 25 countries throughout North America, South America, Europe, Asia, and the Middle East.

Mr. Kasse is the architect of the Action Focused Assessment that has been applied in major organizations throughout the world. He is the author of the books, *Action Focused Assessment for Software Process Improvement* (Artech House, 2002) and *Practical Insight into CMMI®* (Artech House, 2004). He is the primary developer of many Kasse Initiatives workshops including: Supplier Management, Software/Systems Quality Engineering, Software/Systems Configuration Management, Risk Management, Systems Engineering, and Change Management Tool Kit.

Mr. Kasse is a recognized speaker at major process improvement and quality management conferences around the world.

Mr. Kasse serves the SEI as a visiting scientist supporting the CMMI® through training and presentations worldwide. He holds the position of visiting fellow at the Institute of Systems Science/National University of Singapore. He holds an M.S. in computer science and a B.S. in systems engineering with more than 35 years of systems/software related experience. His focus is on helping companies balance the achievement of business objectives with planned process improvement. He can be contacted at kassetc@aol.com or at http://www.kasseinitiatives.com.

Thomas J. McCabe (Chapter 6) is the president and CEO for McCabe & Associates, Inc. He is widely known as a consultant and authority in software development, testing, and quality control. The company is a major supplier of software testing and re-engineering tools.

He has held a variety of high-level positions within the Department of Defense, accumulating extensive hands-on experience in the following areas: software specification, design, testing, and maintenance, software quality assurance, compiler construction, optimization, operating systems, software acquisition, and project management.

Mr. McCabe is best known for his research and publication on software complexity (*IEEE Software Engineering Transactions*, December 1976) and by the complexity measure that bears his name. (This measure allows the quantification of the paths within a module, leading to an understanding of its complexity). He has personally developed and published a structured testing methodology now being adopted extensively throughout the United States and internationally. He has developed advanced state-of-the-art courses in software quality assurance, structured testing, software specification and design, and software engineering, which he and his company present monthly throughout the United States, Canada, and Europe.

Mr. McCabe holds both a B.S. from Providence College and an M.S. from the University of Connecticut, both in mathematics.

Joseph Meagher (Chapter 13) is the manager of process effectiveness in the Missions Assurance Department of Northrop Grumman Corporation, Electronic Systems Sector. He has more than 40 years of experience in testing and quality disciplines. Mr. Meagher manages a staff of 21 professionals engaged in assuring the successful implementation of systems, software, and hardware design engineering processes.

Mr. Meagher has worked in the field of environmental testing with specific emphases on electromagnetic compatibility. Prior to entering management he was responsible for electromagnetic compatibility on the E-3A AWACS radar and later had supervisory responsibility for electromagnetic compatibility at the former Westinghouse Electronic Systems Group.

In 1982 Mr. Meagher joined the Quality Systems and Engineering Department and until 1995 was the engineering manager for all of Hardware Quality Engineering responsible for the support of all programs at the Westinghouse Electronic Systems Group (later part of Northrop Grumman).

Mr. Meagher was subsequently assigned responsibility for Software Quality Engineering and that responsibility grew to include both Hardware Design and Systems Engineering Quality Assurance. In that capacity he participated in CMM® CBA-IPIs and SCAMPIs^{SM}, the last of which resulted in Electronic Systems BWI Campus being awarded CMMI® Maturity Level 5 in systems, software and hardware design.

Mr. Meagher has been president and national director of the Chesapeake Chapter of the Institute of Environmental Sciences, Chairman of Aerospace Industries Association Working Subcommittee #2, New Technologies Sub Committee for Quality, and is an American Society for Quality Certified Quality Auditor and has taught auditor certification classes at several Baltimore area Community Colleges.

He has a B.S. degree from the New York Institute of Technology.

Kenneth S. Mendis (Chapters 4 and 9) is the director of IT quality assurance at Novartis Consumer Health. He has over 25 years experience in design-proving activities involving a full range of system integration, quality assurance, validation, information and data security services for integrated computer systems.

Mr. Mendis has been responsible for developing and instituting Computer Quality Assurance and Validation programs for real-time Command and Control and Distributed Computer Systems both military and in the pharmaceutical and biopharmaceutical industries. Mr. Mendis' computer quality assurance and validation experience have been successfully applied to such programs as the Patriot and Cruise missile programs, command, control and communication systems for nuclear submarines and surface ships, weather radar control systems and air traffic control systems. More recently Mr. Mendis has applied this expertise to pharmaceutical and vitamin distributed control systems, manufacturing execution systems both in the United States, South America, Europe, Asia, and Australia

Mr. Mendis holds a B.S. in engineering from Capitol College and an M.B.A. in management from Bryant College. He is a graduate of the advanced manufacturing management program of Boston University School of Management. From 1981 to 1987 Mr. Mendis served as the founding chairman of the Software Quality Assurance Subcommittee of the National Security Industrial Association, a committee that today represents over 100 major defense contractors. Mr. Mendis has spoken before several professional organizations; among them the American Society for Quality (ASQ), the Institute of Electrical and Electronics Engineers (IEEE), and the American Institute of Aeronautics and Astronautics (AIAA), Parental Drug Association (PDA) and the International Association for Pharmaceutical Technology. Mr. Mendis is also the published author of several technical articles on software quality assurance and management.

Norman Moreau (Chapter 14) has over 30 years of experience in quality and process improvement, project management, engineering, and organizational administration. Mr. Moreau is the President of Theseus Professional Services, LLC and has coached, mentored, assisted, and trained organizations in their quest for process improvement, implementing quality systems, and achieving performance excellence. He has been a quality professional for over 20 years and has supported a wide range of organizations including software and hardware developers, manufacturers including medical devices manufacturers; government agencies and government contractors, telecommunications firms, and nuclear power industry and managers of nuclear waste. Mr. Moreau has successfully established and implemented ISO/TL 9000, SEI-CMMI® and ITIL® (including ISO 20000) programs for software development, systems engineering, and information technology organizations.

Mr. Moreau has published and presented numerous papers on the subject of quality and process improvement. Mr. Moreau has been a member of the American Society of Mechanical Engineers (ASME) since 1982. His significant contributions have been in the areas quality assurance for computer software and records management. He has been on Main Committee since 2002 and since 2004 he has served as the vice chair, Subcommittee on Engineering and Procurement Processes. Mr. Moreau is a senior member of the American Society for Quality.

Mr. Moreau received a B.S. in mechanical engineering from Colorado State University and an M.S.A. in software engineering administration from Central Michigan University.

John D. Musa (Chapter 17) is an independent senior consultant in software reliability engineering. He has more than 35 years of experience as software practitioner and manager in a wide variety of development projects. He is one of the creators of the field of software reliability engineering and is widely recognized as the leader in reducing it to practice. He was formerly Technical Manager of Software Reliability Engineering (SRE) at AT&T Bell Laboratories, Murray Hill, New Jersey.

Dr. Musa has been involved in SRE since 1973. His many contributions include the two most widely used models (one with K. Okumoto), the concept, practice, and application of the operational profile, and the integration of SRE into all phases of the software development cycle. Dr. Musa has published some 100 articles and papers, given more than 200 major presentations, and made a number of videos. He is the principal author of the widely-acclaimed pioneering book *Software Reliability: Measurement, Prediction, Application* (McGraw-Hill, 1987) and the author of the eminently practical books *Software Reliability Engineering: More Reliable Software, Faster Development and Testing* (McGraw-Hill, 1999), and *Software Reliability Engineering: More Reliable Software, Faster and Cheaper* (McGraw-Hill, 2004).

Dr. Musa organized and led the transfer of SRE into practice within AT&T, spearheading the effort that defined it as a "best current practice." He was actively involved in research to advance the theory and practice of the field. Musa has been an international leader in its dissemination.

His leadership has been recognized by every edition of *Who's Who in America* and *American Men and Women of Science* since 1990. Dr. Musa is an international leader in software engineering and a Fellow of the IEEE, cited for "contributions to software engineering, particularly software reliability." He was recognized in 1992 as the individual that year who had contributed the most to testing technology. He was the cofounder of the IEEE Committee on SRE. He has very extensive international experience as a lecturer and teacher. In 2004 the IEEE Reliability Society named him "Engineer of the Year."

Don O'Neill (Chapter 7) is a seasoned software engineering manager and technologist currently serving as an independent consultant. Following his 27-year career with IBM's Federal Systems Division, Mr. O'Neill completed a 3-year residency at Carnegie Mellon University's Software Engineering Institute (SEI) under IBM's technical academic career program and currently serves as an SEI visiting scientist.

As an independent consultant, Mr. O'Neill conducts defined programs for managing strategic software improvement. These include implementing an organizational Software Inspections Process, directing the National Software Quality Experiment, implementing software risk management on the project, conducting the project suite key process area defined program, and conducting global software competitiveness assessments. Each of these programs includes the necessary practitioner and management training. As an expert witness, he provides testimony on the state of the practice in developing and fielding large-scale industrial software and the complex factors that govern their outcome.

In his IBM career, Mr. O'Neill completed assignments in management, technical performance, and marketing in a broad range of applications including space systems, submarine systems, military command and control systems, communications systems, and management decision support systems. He was awarded IBM's outstanding contribution award three times.

Mr. O'Neill served on the executive board of the IEEE Software Engineering Technical Committee and as a Distinguished Visitor of the IEEE. He is a founding member of the Washington, D.C. Software Process Improvement Network (SPIN) and the National Software Council (NSC) and served as the president of the Center for National Software Studies (CNSS) in 2006. He was a contributing author of "Software 2015: A National Software Strategy to Ensure U.S. Security and Competitiveness," a report on the Second National Software Summit. He has two patents pending. He is an active speaker on software engineering topics and has numerous publications to his credit. Mr. O'Neill has a B.S. in mathematics from Dickinson College in Carlisle, Pennsylvania. He can be reached at ONeillDon@aol.com.

Mark Pellegrini (Chapter 12) is a research engineer with the Georgia Tech Research Institute's (GTRI) Electronic Systems Laboratory (ELSYS) at the Georgia Institute of Technology. He has more than 25 years of experience in a diverse range of assignments that include: material handling, operations research, digital electronic design, software engineering, configuration management, process development, and quality engineering. Mr. Pellegrini is currently a Quality Engineer and an Engineering Process Group member for ELSYS. He was instrumental in ELSYS achieving the Software Engineering Institute's Software-Capability Maturity Model (CMM®) Level 3 rating in June 2003. Mark has been the lead in developing and improving configuration management practices within ELSYS.

Mr. Pellegrini has published papers and presented at several annual national conferences on software development, testing, and systems engineering, including the National Defense Industrial Association (NDIA) Systems Engineering Conference, STARWEST, Practical Software Quality & Testing (PSQT) Conference, and the Better Software Conference. The topics include quality assurance on small projects, configuration management, and implementing an effective peer review process. He coauthored the paper "Let's Do It All Over Again! Ruin Your Reputation

Through Configuration Mismanagement," which was presented at the 2005 Better Software Conference and earned the conference's Best Paper Award. He also is a coinventor on a U.S. patent for delivering digital video and data over a communications channel. He holds a B.S. and an M.S. in electrical engineering from the Georgia Institute of Technology.

G. Gordon Schulmeyer (Chapters 2, 6, 8, 13, and 16) has 36 years experience in management and information processing technology. He is president of PYXIS Systems International, Inc. [(410) 741–9404], which specializes in software process improvement and software quality and management. He was manager of software engineering at Westinghouse Electronic Systems Group, and was previously manager of software quality assurance, also at Westinghouse.

Mr. Schulmeyer is the author/editor of *Total Quality Management for Software* (Van Nostrand Reinhold, 1992), *Handbook of Software Quality Assurance* (Van Nostrand Reinhold, 1987 and 1992), *Zero Defect Software* (McGraw-Hill Book Co., 1990), and *Computer Concepts for Managers* (Van Nostrand Reinhold, 1985); and *Verification and Validation of Modern Software-Intensive Systems* (Prentice-Hall, 2000). He has published numerous other papers and lectured on software and software-quality subjects. He was a panelist on DOD-STD-2168 (Software Quality Evaluation) at the October 1985 IEEE COMPSAC Conference. He has taken two long-term foreign assignments to provide information processing technology abroad.

Since 1968, Mr. Schulmeyer has been a holder of the CDP issued by the Institute for the Certification of Computing Professionals (ICCP). He is a member of the Association for Computing Machinery and the IEEE Computer Society. Mr. Schulmeyer is the 1992 recipient of the prestigious Shingo Prize, the First Prize for Professional Research, administered by the Utah State University College of Business. Mr. Schulmeyer received this award in May 1992 for his work in zero defect software—a first in the business sector.

He holds the following degrees: a B.S. in mathematics from Loyola College; a J.D. in law from the University of Baltimore; and an M.B.A. in management from Loyola College.

Jean Swank (Chapter 12) is the director of process and quality for Georgia Tech Research Institute (GTRI). She is also the process improvement and quality assurance manager for the GTRI's Electronic Systems Laboratory (ELSYS) at the Georgia Institute of Technology. Ms. Swank has over 25 years of experience in all phases of system and software development as a software engineer and project manager. She has led the process improvement program in ELSYS for the past 8 years, including the initiative that resulted in the laboratory achieving the Software Engineering Institute's Software-Capability Maturity Model® (CMM®) Level 3 rating in June 2003. In addition to her experience with Software-CMM®, she has been trained in the Capability Maturity Model Integration® (CMMI®) model and as an ISO 9001:2000 Lead Auditor. She is a former chairperson for the Atlanta Software Process Improvement Network (SPIN). Ms. Swank has developed and implemented the quality assurance program in ELSYS. She and her team continue to improve this program based on insight gained in the implementation of this ELSYS processes. In her roles as the director of process and quality and process improvement and quality assurance manager, she is responsible for managing process improvement and effective quality assurance in a diverse development environment.

Ms. Swank has published papers and presented at several annual national conferences on process development, software development, testing, and systems engineering. These conferences include the Software Engineering Process Group (SEPG) Conference, the NDIA CMMI® Technology Conference, the National Defense Industrial Association (NDIA) Systems Engineering Conference, STARWEST, Practical Software Quality & Testing (PSQT) Conference, and the Better Software Conference. The topics include implementing quality assurance on small projects, configuration management, developing systems engineering processes, and implementing an effective peer review process. She coauthored the paper "Let's Do It All Over Again! Ruin Your Reputation Through Configuration Mismanagement," which was presented at the 2005 Better Software Conference and earned the conference's Best Paper Award. Ms. Swank has a B.S. in information and computer science and an M.S. in management of technology, both from Georgia Tech.

Index

Recent Related Artech House Titles

Achieving Software Quality Through Teamwork, Isabel Evans

Agile Software Development, Evaluating the Methods for Your Organization, Alan S. Koch

Agile Systems with Reusable Patterns of Business Knowledge: A Component-Based Approach, Amit Mitra and Amar Gupta

Discovering Real Business Requirements for Software Project Success, Robin F. Goldsmith

Engineering Wireless-Based Software Systems and Applications, Jerry Zeyu Gao, Simon Shim, Xiao Su, and Hsin Mei

Enterprise Architecture for Integration: Rapid Delivery Methods and Technologies, Clive Finkelstein

Implementing the ISO/IEC 27001 Information Security Management Standard, Edward Humphreys

Open Systems and Standards for Software Product Development, P. A. Dargan

Practical Insight into CMMI®, Tim Kasse

A Practitioner's Guide to Software Test Design, Lee Copeland

Role-Based Access Control, Second Edition, David F. Ferraiolo, D. Richard Kuhn, and Ramaswamy Chandramouli

Software Configuration Management, Second Edition, Alexis Leon

Systematic Software Testing, Rick D. Craig and Stefan P. Jaskiel

Utility Computing Technologies, Standards, and Strategies, Alfredo Mendoza

Workflow Modeling: Tools for Process Improvement and Application Development, Alec Sharp and Patrick McDermott

For further information on these and other Artech House titles, including previously considered out-of-print books now available through our In-Print-Forever® (IPF®) program, contact:

Artech House
685 Canton Street
Norwood, MA 02062
Phone: 781-769-9750
Fax: 781-769-6334
e-mail: artech@artechhouse.com

Artech House
46 Gillingham Street
London SW1V 1AH UK
Phone: +44 (0)20 7596-8750
Fax: +44 (0)20 7630 0166
e-mail: artech-uk@artechhouse.com

Find us on the World Wide Web at: www.artechhouse.com